WITHDRAWN

MORI ARINORI

Harvard East Asian Series 68

The East Asian Research Center at Harvard University administers research projects designed to further scholarly understanding of China, Japan, Korea, Vietnam, and adjacent areas.

Mori Arinori in 1872

MORI ARINORI

Ivan Parker Hall

Harvard University Press
Cambridge, Massachusetts
1973

952.031092
M854h
1973

© Copyright 1973 by the President and Fellows of Harvard College
All rights reserved
Preparation of this volume has been aided by a grant from the Ford Foundation
Library of Congress Catalog Card Number 78-188348
SBN 674-58730
Printed in the United States of America

*For My Parents
Bill and Lucy Hall*

ACKNOWLEDGMENTS

My very special thanks go to Professor Albert M. Craig of Harvard University for his encouragement and thoughtful supervision of this study from its beginnings as a seminar paper to its final dissertation form, and to Professors Edwin O. Reischauer and Donald H. Shively of Harvard, who also read the manuscript in its entirety and made many valuable suggestions.

Significant new material on Mori Arinori has been discovered by Professor Hayashi Takeji of Tōhoku University and freshly assembled by Professor (Emeritus) Ōkubo Toshiaki of Rikkyō University in preparation for the forthcoming publication of the *Mori Arinori Zenshū* (Collected works of Mori Arinori). I should like to express my thanks to both Professors Hayashi and Ōkubo for making available to me materials in their personal possession, as well as to the publisher of the *Zenshū,* Mr. Nishimura Nobuo, of the Senbundō Shoten, for permitting me to make use of proof copies of the projected three-volume work. I am particularly indebted to Professor Hayashi not only for materials and for many personal kindnesses but also for much substantive discussion and advice, without which this book could not have been written. Professor Hayashi's own forthcoming study of Mori is awaited with great anticipation.

I should like to express my deep gratitude to Professor Allan B. Cole, of the Fletcher School of Law and Diplomacy, for first stimulating my interest in Japan, and to Professor Herbert Passin, of

Columbia University, for early and strategic assistance in this study.

I am indebted also to Professors Mori Arimasa, of the École Nationale des Langues Orientales de Paris, Haraguchi Torao, of Kagoshima University, W. H. G. Armytage, of Sheffield University, and Kaigo Tokiomi, of Tokyo University, for their ample assistance and advice; to Mr. Inoue Isao, of the graduate school (History) of Tokyo University, for precious help in reading some of the more difficult Mori documents; and to the Foreign Area Fellowship Program and Harvard University for financial support during the preparation of the doctoral thesis on which this study was based.

To my excellent Japanese typists, Mrs. Nakamura Sachiko and Mrs. Katō Yuriko, go renewed thanks. My gratitude is extended also to the staffs of the following libraries and institutions who assisted my search for new material on Mori: the Harvard University Library, Cambridge; the Columbia University Library, New York City; the Wagner State College Library, New York City; the Yale University Library, New Haven; the Library of Congress, Manuscripts Division, Washington, D.C.; the National Archives, Washington, D.C.; the British Museum, London; the Public Record Office, London; the Controller of H.M. Stationery Office for permission to quote from Crown-copyright records in the Public Record Office; the National Register of Archives, London; the Lyon Playfair Library, Imperial College, University of London; the Library of University College, University of London; the British Library of Political and Economic Science, London School of Economics and Political Science, University of London; the Athenaeum, London; the Royal Asiatic Society, London; the Royal Archives, Windsor; the University Library, Cambridge; the Library of the University of Sheffield; the Hampshire Record Office, Winchester; the Broadlands Archives Trust, for permission to quote from the correspondence between the Oliphants and the Cowper Temples, now held by the Hampshire Record Office; the National Diet Library, Toyko; the Library of the Faculty of Education, Tokyo University; and the Kagoshima Prefectural Library.

For all statements and conclusions in this study and for all errors of fact, judgment, or translation, I assume the sole responsibility.

This volume, finally, is dedicated with filial affection to my parents: to Dr. William Webster Hall, who made helpful comments on several portions of the manuscript, and to Lucy Street Hall, who painstakingly proofread the original copy.

CONTENTS

Introduction	THE IMAGES TABLED	1
One	SATSUMA ORIGINS (1847–1865)	19
Two	AWAKENING TO THE WEST (1865–1866)	59
Three	THE STUDENT TURNED PILGRIM (1866–1868)	95
Four	IN AND OUT OF THE NEW GOVERNMENT (1868–1870)	129
Five	REPRESENTING JAPAN AT WASHINGTON (1871–1873)	155
Six	THE EXTRACURRICULAR HARVEST OF AMERICA (1871–1873)	188

Seven	APOSTLE OF ENLIGHTENMENT (1873–1876)	231
Eight	THE DIPLOMAT AS KIBITZER ON POLITICS (1877–1884)	279
Nine	THE MAKING OF AN EDUCATION MINISTER (1879–1884)	324
Ten	MORI AT THE MONBUSHŌ (1884–1889)	390
Conclusion	THE IMAGE REVISED	467
Appendix		489
Bibliography		494
Glossary		509
Index		519

ILLUSTRATIONS

Frontispiece Mori Arinori in 1872

Pages 229–230 Laurence Oliphant *courtesy of Herbert W. Schneider*
Thomas Lake Harris *courtesy of Herbert W. Schneider*
The Satsuma Students in 1865 *courtesy of Haraguchi Torao*

MORI ARINORI

ABBREVIATIONS USED IN NOTES AND BIBLIOGRAPHY

ED	Great Britain, Public Record Office, Ministry of Education MSS
FO	Great Britain, Public Record Office, Foreign Office MSS
HOP	Columbia University Library. Special Collections, Harris and Oliphant Papers
JWM	*The Japan Weekly Mail*
KKM	Kimura Kyō, *Mori sensei den*
KSM	Kaimon Sanjin, *Mori Arinori*
LCM	Library of Congress, Manuscripts Division
LCT	*The London and China Telegraph*
MBZ	*Meiji bunka zenshū*, 1928 edition. Volumes used in this study:
	MBZ, IV: *Kenseihen* (Constitutional government)
	MBZ, VI: *Gaikōhen* (Diplomacy)
	MBZ, X: *Kyōikuhen* (Education)
	MBZ, XI: *Shūkyōhen* (Religion)
	MBZ, XVIII: *Zasshihen* (Periodicals)
MRZ	*Meiroku zasshi*
NAW	National Archives, Washington, D.C.
OTM	Ōkubo Toshiaki, *Mori Arinori*
PRO	Great Britain, Public Record Office
SPM	Speeches of Mori as Education Minister
Zenshū	*Mori Arinori zenshū*

Introduction

THE IMAGES TABLED

On 11 February 1889, as all Tokyo prepared to celebrate the promulgation of the Meiji Constitution, an assassin's blade brought to an untimely end the life of Mori Arinori, Japanese minister of education. It failed, however, to lay low the hydra of Mori's already ambivalent reputation, which immediately sprang two heads and, within a short time, four. For twenty years Mori had been a symbol to Japanese and Westerners alike of his country's rapid, yet often painful, strides toward modernization. As first diplomatic envoy to America, as founder of Japan's first modern philosophical society and her first commercial college, as the first to marry in the Western fashion, as the first to advocate the discarding of samurai swords, as the first and last and only to recommend the abolition also of the Japanese language, and, finally, as the first education minister under the new cabinet system, Mori had managed variously to amaze, to amuse, or to horrify—depending on the viewer. The man had been a maverick among the modernizing leaders of Meiji Japan.

Nihon no unda seiyōjin—"a Westerner born of Japan" was the way Mori's own prime minister and lifelong friend, Itō Hirobumi, would one day characterize him.[1] But if Mori was indeed Japan's "Western offspring" did that make him a paragon of progress or

1. Hayashi Takeji, "Kindai kyōiku kōsō to Mori Arinori," in *Chūō Kōron*, August 1962, p. 208.

something close to a traitor? That was how the argument stood in the months following the assassination.

During the following decade a careful look at Mori's work as education minister revealed an intense effort on his part to enhance the power of Japan through modern education. In the world's heyday of imperialism that fact effectively reestablished him as a good nationalist, after all. In the ashes of defeat a half century later, however, it made Mori look to many Japanese like one of the major architects of ultranationalism, totalitarianism, and military disaster. Was Mori to be praised as a pioneer of enlightenment or reviled as an apostate from tradition? Was he to be appreciated as a nation-builder or condemned for his faulty design? For a man of Mori's public stature the historical record was unusually fragmentary and obscure, and these four facets of Mori's reputation rapidly hardened into images with a tenacious vitality of their own—images which, for convenience's sake, might be labeled as those of the Westernizer Commendable, the Westernizer Reprehensible, the Nationalist Commendable, and the Nationalist Reprehensible.

What people later made of Mori, that is to say the development of these four images, is perhaps even more interesting and significant as a problem in intellectual history than the life of Mori himself. Much mischief has been created, however, by confusing the images with the actuality. For many of his contemporaries Mori was an epitome of the cultural dislocations in which they found themselves caught. For his posterity he has been something of a touchstone for the political wisdom, or imprudence, of the Meiji leadership. Then as now, however, Mori's several images have lent themselves all too readily to people with political, cultural, or ideological axes to grind and have served rather to restrict than to enhance meaningful discussion of the man. Who was the real Mori? Was he indeed a westernizer? If so, how much of one—and why? A nationalist? How much of one? Why? These are the questions that need answering.

Here was a man who shared not only political responsibility for Japan's plunge into the modern world but intellectual and moral responsibility as well. Philosophically inclined, and thoroughly familiar with the West, Mori willed and welcomed his country's cultural transformation with a degree of personal conviction and commitment unique among the top echelons of the Meiji government. His career, indeed, in many ways exemplified the peculiar energy, flexibility, and vision which permitted the Japanese to modernize quickly, and on their own terms, sparing themselves both the colonial subjugation of India and the revolutionary paroxysm of China.

This study aims to reconstruct only that career which ended so prematurely in 1889, working as free as possible from Mori's reputation as it developed following the assassination. It will conclude necessarily with a revised image of its own, imperfect in its own way, no doubt, but providing at the very least something of an obstacle course for pursuers of the instant image.

The absence of a biography in any Western language on a historical figure of Mori's proportions would in itself justify an account of his life, even one that did not venture beyond the three standard Japanese biographies: Kaimon Sanjin's *Mori Arinori,* of 1897; Kimura Kyō's *Mori sensei den* (Life of Mori), of 1899; and Ōkubo Toshiaki's *Mori Arinori,* of 1944. A second motive arises from the recent availability of new material on Mori, much of it of Western origin, which hopefully would make a fresh study of interest even to Japanese readers already familiar with the man. The third, and perhaps soundest, reason for a reconsideration of Mori is the need to get behind the images to as faithful an account as possible of a man often referred to, but seldom understood, in the increasingly lively discourse on the nature and significance of Japan's modernization.

The images which sprang to life with Mori's own death have tended to become answers, when they should be questions. As questions rather than answers, as problems rather than solutions, they are more appropriately tabled here at the beginning than at the end of the account.

THE ASSASSINATION

Viscount Mori had been a good deal less than popular with the students of Tokyo Imperial University. Not only had he recently decreed a gradual increase in tuition fees over their strenuous protest but he had also succeeded in turning their anger into rage by declaring that they themselves had been responsible for a dormitory fire on 25 January 1889, and for the death therein of one of their own number. Carelessness in the use of oil had brought down the old wooden structure, in the ruins of which were discovered the charred remains of a second-year medical student noted for shortness of sight. He apparently had rushed back into the burning building to retrieve his notebooks.[2]

On 6 February the students had massed, in falling snow, outside the engineering college of the university in hopes of questioning the minister of education regarding the increase of fees. When Mori finally appeared, a full forty minutes late, there were loud cries of

2. JWM, 2 Feb. and 22 June 1889.

"Behind time! Behind time!" Mounting a veranda, the viscount expressed his dissatisfaction with the university on many points, compared the present attitude of the students unfavorably with that of the young scholars of the Restoration, upbraided them for the outbreak of the fire, and concluded by asking them whether this recent tragedy lay lightly on their consciences. To continued cries of "No! No!," Mori abruptly left the premises without entertaining a single question.[3]

It was natural enough, therefore, for Mori's personal guard, Zada Shigehide, not to have sensed anything amiss when a man of about twenty-five presented himself at the entrance of Mori's ministerial residence in Nagata-chō, Kōjimachi, at about eight o'clock on the morning of 11 February, mumbling something about a plot by students to assassinate the education minister during the evening's torchlight procession.[4] The young visitor—a short, weakly built, thin-faced fellow in Japanese dress, with a wild shock of disheveled hair—gave his name as Nishino Buntarō and insisted on reporting the particulars to the viscount in person. Zada (although sending, on instinct, for his sword cane) saw fit to wave him on through to the front parlor. Here Okamoto Seien, a family steward, showed the man to a seat and carried his message to Mori, who was dressing on the second floor.

Mori treated the news with some disdain and instructed the steward to question the visitor further. Okamoto was explaining the impossibility of seeing the minister, who was about to depart for the promulgation of the constitution at the Imperial Palace, and Nishino himself was on the point of leaving, when the minister, unmindful of the two voices in the parlor, came down the stairs to the vestibule and took up his customary stance with both hands in his trousers pockets, to await the arrival of his carriage.

On that morning Mori was not only resplendent in formal uniform for attendance at court but also, at forty-one, in the very prime of life. He probably stood no taller than the somewhat pathetic figure who had risen to accost him, but he was contrastingly endowed (to judge by photographs) with a robust, stocky frame, a rather thickish neck, and a clean and forceful countenance positively brimming with determination and self-possession. The two lines of closely clipped side whiskers converging on a Van Dyke beard had shaped the roundish features of a still young and unlined face into an oval, enhancing if anything its air of prim austerity.

Approaching Mori and feigning to start a conversation, the young

3. LCT, 25 March 1889; KSM, p. 96.
4. Erwin Baelz, *Awakening Japan: The Diary of a German Doctor*, tr. Eden and Cedar Paul (New York, 1932), p. 83.

stranger suddenly flew at him with a well-honed, flat, triangular kitchen knife he had been hiding in the sleeve of his kimono. Holding Mori by the waist with his left hand, Nishino plunged the weapon deep into his victim's abdomen. Okamoto grabbed Nishino's shoulder with a call for help, which brought Zada running. A light stroke across Nishino's back with Zada's sword failed to dislodge the assassin, who only clung the tighter to his victim; but in the next instant Okamoto somehow managed to pry Nishino loose. Whirling around with a scream and raising his knife to threaten the steward, Nishino exposed himself full length to Zada, who killed him instantly with three powerful slashes of his sword.[5]

On the assassin's person was found a manifesto declaring his intention of avenging a sacrilege perpetrated by the viscount at the Grand Shrine of Ise on 28 December 1887. The manifesto proclaimed that: "Education Minister Mori Arinori while visiting the shrine mounted the steps of the sanctuary without removing his shoes, in defiance of the Imperial prohibition, lifted the sacred veil with his walking stick to peer inside, and retired without performing the customary obeisance."[6] Some accounts have it that after the attack Mori lapsed almost immediately into unconsciousness; others, that his last words were to reprove Zada for felling the assassin; still others, that he was able to hear from the lips of Prime Minister Kuroda hours later that the constitution had been warmly received by the people, and had managed to muster up a faint smile and nod of approval. In any case, Mori lived on until five o'clock the following morning. That by itself was evidence of a sturdy physique, and perhaps he would have survived altogether if professional help had not been a full three hours in getting to him. By the time Tokyo's best doctors arrived, Mori's heavy loss of blood had already precluded recovery. And where had the surgeons been? Invited to the court. That made Mori, in a manner of speaking, the first "victim" of the Meiji Constitution.

On 13 February the emperor, empress, and empress dowager

---

5. The accounts of the assassination given in KSM, p. 87, KKM, p. 240, and OTM, pp. 147–148, do not agree in every detail. This reconstruction of the event has relied chiefly on contemporary newspaper reports, which have been most conveniently assembled in Sakai Kunio, *Meiji ansatsushi* (Tokyo, 1933), pp. 172–200. Among these newspaper accounts (which again do not all agree), greatest reliance has been placed on the judgment of acquittal rendered by the court of law which tried Zada Shigehide on a charge of murder. After a minute examination of the circumstances of the assassination, the court acquitted Zada on 23 February 1889. Its judgment was carried in the *Jiji shinpō* three days later (Available in Sakai, *Ansatsushi*, pp. 197–200. Much of Sakai's material will reappear in *Zenshū* II).

6. Sakai, *Ansatsushi*, p. 182, quoting Nishino Buntarō's manifesto.

all dispatched separate emissaries to Mori's widow and three young sons, and on the fourteenth the emperor further showed his appreciation of Mori's official services by promoting him posthumously to the Senior Second Rank and by bestowing on Viscountess Mori a condolence gift of 5,000 yen. On the sixteenth Mori was laid to rest in a state funeral conducted according to traditional Shinto rites. University students, together with schoolboys and schoolgirls from all over Tokyo, were conspicuous in the dense crowd of mourners which slowed the progress of the cortege as it left Nagata-chō. Accompanying the immense procession on its way to Aoyama Cemetery were a squadron of cavalry, a battalion of infantry, and a battery of field pieces. And as the dignitaries of the Meiji government and the diplomatic corps watched the white-robed priests go through their gestures immemorial before Mori's bier, some of the sincerest of mourners may well have been found among the Foreign Representatives and other Westerners in attendance; for certainly they had been among those most shocked and horrified by the event.

The encomiums bestowed upon Mori by the Western community provide us with his first image in its purest form. The second image, a bitter travesty of the first, lay concealed (we may imagine) in the hearts of the officiating priests; but it would soon find public expression as the fickle crowds deserted Mori's grave for that of his assassin. Prominent Japanese friends of Mori, alarmed by this second image, would go on to create a third, mainly by way of emending the first image. The fourth image, a bitter incrimination in turn of the third, was destined eventually to be held widely by the grandchildren of the men and women, both Japanese and Western, who attended Mori's funeral. Its spirit, however, had already been anticipated in the animosity harbored by the university students toward their minister of education.

AFTERMATH: DEVELOPMENT OF THE IMAGES

The basic image is that of Mori as Westernizer Commendable. The expression "Westernizer" serves here to suggest a rather flexible compass of Western institutions (including at its broadest both Christianity and political liberalism), the benefits of which Mori presumably had done his utmost to secure for Japan. The precise content is less important than the two basic assumptions: that Mori was primarily Western-oriented, and that this was a good thing. The second image accepts the same reading of the facts but responds negatively, reading black where the positive showed white. It also throws the focus less on what Mori was attempting to create than on what he surely would destroy, depicting him as a reckless renegade from Japanese tradition: he was infatuated with the West all right; but that very fact made him reprehensible.

The third image attempts to reestablish Mori as commendable by arguing, from a fresh interpretation of the facts, that he was not really that much of a westernizer after all. It was neither feasible nor necessarily desirable to argue away all of Mori's Westernism, but it was possible by shifting emphases here and there, by proclaiming seeming ends to have been no more than means, and by standing alleged priorities and preferences on their head, to conclude that Mori's fundamental orientation was rather that of a nationalist, and that this, of course, was a good thing. The expression "nationalist" as used here is again a fluid one. There is some attempt in the third image to argue defensively that Mori had never at heart been a Christian and certainly not a dangerous political radical; but the main effort is to describe him in positive terms as a patriot, loyal to his emperor, possessed of the traditional virtues, and deeply concerned to promote the power and prosperity of the Japanese state. The fourth image likewise accepts Mori as a nationalist but redefines the characterization as reprehensible. All the praiseworthy features of the third image now receive a negative valuation. Mori's nationalism becomes in its international dimension a militaristic ultranationalism and in its domestic aspect an oppressive statism.

With the achievement of some historical perspective, many found it possible to interpret Mori as having been both westernizer and nationalist, but in temporal sequence. This gives rise to four additional, dual-image, combinations. If Mori's evolution is considered to have been from Westernizer Commendable to Nationalist Commendable (that is, from the first to the third image), we get the "sensible realist" judgment that many Westerners were willing to pass prior to the Pacific War. If the progression is from Westernizer Reprehensible to Nationalist Commendable (second to third image) we get the alibi of "youthful foolishness," which was used to rehabilitate Mori in the eyes of prewar Japanese orthodoxy. If it is from Westernizer Commendable to Nationalist Reprehensible (first to fourth image), we get a classic instance of *tenkō,* or intellectual recantation. This interpretation, particularly popular since World War II, has stimulated students of intellectual history to search for causes in everything from inborn Confucian rigidities to a misplaced admiration of Germany to a historical inevitability in straightforwardly Marxist terms. The progression from Westerner Reprehensible to Nationalist Reprehensible (second to fourth image) is not, finally, entirely without representation, although this double pejorative would seem to exist only in what might be called the xenophobically Marxist mind.

Finally, if one argues that Mori was both westernizer and nationalist, not successively but simultaneously and throughout his life, two more dual-image combinations emerge. The choice between the two depends on the viewer's own attitude toward nationalism. If the latter is assumed to be compatible with westernism, we get a felicitous congruence or identity of the first and third images. However, if nationalism is seen as reprehensible, and therefore unbecoming for a westernizer, we get an agonizing tension between the first and fourth images, with Mori emerging as something of a split personality.

Captain F. Brinkley's *Japan Weekly Mail* (Yokohama) described Mori during the weeks following the assassination as "one of the ablest statesmen and most brilliant scholars in Japan"; as a man who "had served his country so faithfully and played such a conspicuous part in the most momentous episodes of her history"; and as "one of Japan's most talented and cultured statesmen."[7] Mori's obituary in the *London and China Telegraph* (London) remarked on the "many friends who have a very kindly recollection of His Excellency during the period he was accredited to the Court of St. James,"[8] while Secretary of State James G. Blaine in Washington issued instructions to the American envoy in Tokyo, Richard B. Hubbard, to convey to the foreign ministry "a suitable expression of this Government's condolence at the death of so eminent a statesman whose services as the diplomatic representative at this capital from 1871 to 1873 are recalled with gratification."[9] Hubbard had written the department that Mori had "served his country in many honorable capacities," and that "under his administration of the Department of Education, Japan has made wonderful strides in educational development."[10]

Foreign residents in Japan contributed generously to an educa-

7. JWM, 16 and 23 Feb. and 2 March 1889. Some of the Japanese newspaper accounts of the assassination and its aftermath appear in abbreviated translation or paraphrase in these issues of JWM.
8. LCT, 18 Feb. 1889.
9. NAW, dispatch from James G. Blaine to Richard B. Hubbard, 13 March 1889, in *Papers Relating to the Foreign Relations of the United States,* no. 288.
10. Dispatch from R. B. Hubbard to T. F. Bayard, 14 Feb. 1889, ibid., no. 548.

tion endowment fund established in Mori's memory,[11] and the later recollections of personal friends abroad testify amply to the affection and esteem in which the Western world generally had held him. Professor David Murray of Rutgers University wrote in 1894 that: "Viscount Mori Arinori fell a victim to the fanatical hatred of those who looked with distrust upon the progress which his country was making. No one could look, or did look, on this progress with more interest than Mori. He had so long and so earnestly advocated a liberal and tolerant policy in the councils of his country, and had been a leader in all that was high and noble, that we cannot regard, except with profound regret, his untimely death."[12] William Elliot Griffis, another Rutgers teacher who had seen service in Japan, would write very similarly in 1927: "Arinori Mori, a sincere and zealous servant of his country and of the Tennō, was ever sincerely unselfish, patriotic, and a lover of mankind and of freedom of conscience. He may have been sometimes too eager for Japan's adoption of the Occidental civilization. But he was a sincere patriot and deserves immortal renown, because of his services in promoting the good name and prosperity of Japan."[13]

Griffis certainly assumed that a westernizer could also be patriotic, and this view received support (and Mori's negative second image a notable rebuttal) from Fukuzawa Yukichi, who wrote an editorial in the *Jiji shinpō* on the day of Mori's funeral, excoriating the assassin:

> I mourn not alone the passing of a Minister of State, but also the loss of one of the most capable and active young statesmen who ever worked for the enlightenment of Japan . . . Having been brought up from his youth in Western-style education, and having been regarded as one of the pioneers of modern reform, it was only natural that . . . his customary language should have been that of the Western School. Considering also the fact that he was straightforward and indomitable by nature, and not inclined to cower before others, it is only natural that his speech and action should have caused some displeasure in conservative circles . . . If this Nishino had only taken the trouble to visit Mori at his home on some suitable pretext, to

11. JWM, 15 Feb. 1890.
12. David Murray, *Japan* (New York, 1894), p. 396.
13. Personal inscription by William Elliot Griffis on the back of the title page of Arinori Mori, *Religious Freedom in Japan: A Memorial and Draft of Charter* (privately printed in the United States, 1872), in MBZ, XI, 547.

listen carefully to what he had to say and to observe his conduct, a mutual understanding would have been achieved after a few weeks of friendly discussion; and Nishino certainly would have dismissed any idea of assassination.[14]

Fukuzawa had gone on to argue that earlier advocates and opponents of westernization, although the deadliest of enemies in the pre-Restoration decades, were now on the friendliest of terms because they gradually had come to appreciate the importance of discussing and trying to understand each others' viewpoint. Since progress depended on such rational and tolerant dialogue, Fukuzawa prayed in conclusion that "the land be swept clean of this thirst after blood." The anti-Mori sentiment, however, was implacable. Nishino's manifesto was taken at face value, and the wave of anti-foreign feeling which was just reaching its crest at the end of the decade lifted the young Chōshū fanatic up overnight into the role of national hero and martyr. His remains, buried without ceremony or coffin by police agents at Aoyama, were soon disinterred by friends and given a proper Shinto funeral at Tanaka Cemetery. His grave, never to be wanting for flowers or burning incense for years to come, attracted huge and steady crowds throughout the months following the assassination.[15] Mori's bodyguard, Zada, though acquitted, was forced to stand trial for murder, and it seems that even officials as highly placed as former Foreign Minister Inoue Kaoru and Justice Minister Yamada Akiyoshi (both from Chōshū) had contributed (or had been pressured into contributing) anonymously to the fund subscribed to defray Nishino's funeral expenses.[16] The press with few exceptions soon began to eulogize Nishino, and by mid-March three provincial and three Tokyo newspapers (including the reputedly liberal *Chōya shinbun*) were under suspension for applauding and encouraging such assassinations.[17] So feverish was the mood that eventually the government moved to interdict public pilgrimages to Nishino's grave.

Nishino, eldest son of an ex-samurai family, had left his Chōshū home in 1886 for Tokyo, where he had taken a minor post in the ministry of interior. He was not, as Fukuzawa pointed out, the

---

14. KKM, pp. 243–244, quoting editorial in *Jiji shinpō*, 16 Feb. 1889.
15. James Murdoch, *History of Japan* (London, 1926), III, 404; Karl Rathgen, *Staat und Kultur der Japaner* (Leipzig, 1907), p. 15.
16. KKM, p. 242; JWM, 2 March 1889. Kimura implies that there was substance to the rumor denied by the *Japan Weekly Mail*.
17. JWM, 16 March 1889.

lunatic who figured in the initial press accounts. Highly educated and intelligent, but possessed also of a passionate reverence for the imperial house, he had been carried away by the popular excitement which greeted the report of Mori's alleged behavior at Ise. In a letter to his father three days before the assassination, Nishino revealed that he had visited Ise during 1888, had checked out the rumor and found it to be true, and had then given much careful thought to his course of action. "Come what may," he had further confided to a friend, "I shall have done something to protect our sacred land and its people from this spirit of degeneracy."[18]

The true facts of the Ise incident remain a mystery. The *Ise shinbun* for 19 February reported after a careful investigation that it had found the rumor, although not false as such, to have been greatly embellished and exaggerated. Mori had indeed lifted the white muslin drapes; but he had immediately released them upon being informed that only members of the imperial family might proceed beyond and, performing an obeisance, had returned forthwith to his inn.[19] Koba Sadanaga, however, who was with the party at the time as Mori's private secretary, saw clear evidence of a deliberate trap.

The site of the incident was the thatch-roofed, curtained gateway set in the second wooden palisade at the south entrance of the Gekū, or outer shrine, of Ise. Koba claims that Mori had been walking second, and he himself third, at the head of a sizeable procession of prefectural officials, with one of the shrine priests in the lead. The priest, as Koba has it, walked briskly without slackening his pace, and with Mori hard on his heels, up the four flagstone steps across the nine-foot flagstone terrace to the curtained gateway. Here he suddenly ducked to the side, letting Mori jog right on into the curtain out of sheer momentum. The priest then seemed to make some remark at which Mori immediately backed up a few steps, bowed deeply, and quit the outer shrine at once, without waiting for the priest's further instructions. Koba had watched the incident from the bottom of the steps.[20] The fact that Mori returned directly to his lodgings at Futamigaura, cancelling

18. Sakai, *Ansatsushi*, p. 190, quoting a letter from Nishino Buntarō to an unidentified friend, 9 Feb. 1889. Sakai, pp. 190–191, has a letter from Nishino to his own father, dated 8 Feb. 1889. Biographical material on Nishino is available in Sakai, pp. 186–187, and in JWM, 23 Feb. 1889.
19. Sakai, *Ansatsushi*, pp. 185–186, has the article from the *Ise shinbun*, 19 Feb. 1889.
20. OTM, pp. 150–151.

a scheduled visit to the inner shrine, suggests that he too seems to have suspected foul play.

Nishino's manifesto is politico-religious, emphasizing the slight not so much to the ancient gods as to the living imperial house, the spirit of reverence for which was to him "the great principle on which our state is founded."[21] Ōkubo Toshiaki has suggested that the Ise priests may have credited rumors that Mori intended to make Christianity the national faith: Motoda Eifu, the emperor's tutor, was convinced, after all, that Mori was secretly a Christian; and as minister of education, Mori had certainly made no effort to promote Shinto in the schools. The priests may also have harbored a more tangible grudge: Mori's transfer of the official calendar-making prerogative to Tokyo University had deprived them of a lucrative side-business.[22] The Western calendar, Christianity, and *lèse majesté* against the imperial house respectively symbolized three facets—cultural, religious, and political—of Mori's second image.

Kimura Kyō, a ministry of education official, had been appalled at the dispatch with which Mori's friends deserted his memory. Attending the hundredth-day vigil (held a mere two weeks after burial, in order to expedite the vacating of the official residence), he was sufficiently struck by their coolness to determine upon writing the biography which finally appeared a decade later.[23] Mori's rehabilitation, along the lines of our third image, began almost immediately, however. This image owes its initial and greatest impetus to Mori's close confidant and eventual successor as education minister (1893–1894), Inoue Kowashi.

In a lecture before the Kōten Kōkyūjo (Research Institute for Japanese Classics) on 9 March 1889, Inoue made public a draft cabinet proposal (*kakugian*) which he claimed he had drawn up according to Mori's instructions. This draft, Inoue announced,[24] reflected the true import of Mori's educational policy, which he had not lived to carry out and which the public had grossly failed to appreciate. Inoue characterized that basic policy as *kokutai no kyōiku shugi,* or "a philosophy of education based on the national polity." The first of Mori's two great educational tenets, Inoue averred, was the national polity or *kokutai* itself: this provided the

21. Sakai, *Ansatsushi*, p. 182. From Nishino's manifesto.
22. OTM, pp. 151–152.
23. KKM, p. 251.
24. OTM, pp. 1–6, gives the speech of Inoue Kowashi before the Kōten Kōkyūjo (Research Institute for Japanese Classics), 9 March 1889, in its entirety.

unifying principle for all educational problems, as well as a focus (in the unbroken imperial line) for the spiritual needs of the Japanese people. Mori's second great tenet was *taiiku,* or "physical education." Its purpose was to strengthen not only the body but the will and spirit of the nation as well, and much of it according to Mori's scheme was to be carried out in paramilitary fashion. Finally, to illustrate how good a nationalist Mori really had been, Inoue related that Mori had once confided to him: "Sometimes when walking down the street, or riding say in a rickshaw, I wonder to myself, 'does this rickshaw puller have any notion in his head of what we call Japan?' and at such moments I am beset with feelings of helplessness."

This statist philosophy of education was taken to absolve Mori of his earlier, unpatriotic westernizing proclivities, if one could not indeed read basically nationalistic motivations back even into those earlier foibles. In very broad terms of emphasis, the Kaimon and Kimura biographies lean toward the "youthful foolishness" interpretation, i.e., toward a sequence of the second and third images. Ōkubo by contrast sticks closer to a pure third image, carrying Mori's nationalism all the way back to his childhood and youth and developing what might be called the "patriot-from-the-very-beginning" argument. A good example, finally, of a Western work which, while crediting Mori with general progressivism, sees nothing wrong with a sensibly realistic statist educational system, is Keenleyside and Thomas' *History of Japanese Education and Present Educational System,* 1937, the standard prewar English-language authority on the subject.[25]

The pure fourth image, which would have to describe Mori as having been an "autocrat-from-the-very-beginning," is something of a rarity. Nagai Michio, like Ōkubo, has traced Mori's concern with national power back to an early date, emphasizing in his case Mori's unwavering awareness of the scientific, technological, and industrial components of that power. But Nagai does credit Mori with progressive political and social thinking, which he gradually came to shed in the latter half of his life.[26] The fourth image indeed is almost always linked with the first. The originator of Mori as Jekyll and Hyde was Tokutomi Sohō, who thereby introduced the *tenkō* concept (in effect, if not in so many words) as an analytical device of Japanese intellectual history. In the February

25. Hugh L. Keenleyside and A. F. Thomas, *History of Japanese Education and Present Educational System* (Tokyo, 1937).

26. Nagai Michio, "Mori Arinori: Meiji kyōiku no kensetsusha," ed. *Asahi Jānaru,* in *Nihon no shisōka* (Tokyo, 1962), I, 144–146.

1889 issue of *Kokumin no tomo* Tokutomi wrote of Mori: "In the former half of his life he was influenced by America, in the latter half by Europe; in the former half he had proclaimed an individualistic doctrine, in the latter half a nationalistic one; in the former half of his life he was, in the extreme, a radical, in the latter half in the extreme a conservative; in the former half, he was a valiant battler for freedom of speech, in the latter half a defender of despotism."[27]

Tokutomi by juxtaposing America and Europe had in passing also suggested the nature of the potion which had transmogrified the innocent Dr. Jekyll; for by "Europe" Tokutomi meant Germany. Critics of Mori, favorable and unfavorable alike, tend to assume that a general conversion to German statism took place, and that the example of Prussian schooling in particular was highly formative of Mori's own educational philosophy and heavily influenced his own administration. This view, first advanced in Kaimon's biography and more fully developed by Ōkubo, has been most succinctly expressed for the Western reader in Chitoshi Yanaga's *Japan since Perry,* where Mori is described as having been an unmitigated exponent of Westernism until 1879: "In that year he toured Europe and came in contact with the intense nationalism which was rampant on the continent. As a result his attitude underwent considerable change. Reacting against the doctrine of freedom and popular rights, he became converted to nationalism and assumed the view that it was proper to sacrifice the individual for the State. If he still believed in Westernism, he had certainly veered to the right to the extent of upholding absolutism."[28] This alleged conversion to statism could also be viewed, however, as a reversion to something traditional, and ascribed rather to the strength of native values than to the impact of imported ideas. Kaigo Tokiomi, for example, concludes that the study of Mori presents not only "a radical, enlightened aspect common to many contemporary intellectuals in government service," but also "a traditional aspect exemplified by his *kokutai*-centered philosophy of education."[29]

Among Western scholars, George Sansom has stated a similar view: "The underlying theory that learning must subserve the purposes of the state . . . was not essentially Western but a rever-

27. Tokutomi Sohō, "Mori Arinori kun," in *Kokumin no tomo,* no. 42 (February 1889).
28. Chitoshi Yanaga, *Japan since Perry* (New York, 1949), p. 109.
29. Kaigo Tokiomi et al., "Mori Arinori no shisō to kyōiku seisaku," *Bulletin of the Faculty of Education, University of Tokyo,* 8:2 (1965).

sion to the outlook that had inspired feudal rulers to treat one doctrine as orthodox and all others as heretical . . . His emphasis on the supremacy of the state in the scheme of education brought him nearer to the stand of the conservative "National Scholars" and to Confucianists like Motoda than he would have cared to admit."[30] Pointing to the traditional element not only in Mori's educational administration but also in his thought as a whole, Motoyama Yukihiko has described Mori as a "typical bureaucrat" and characterized his ideology as "*bushidō* [the samurai ethical code], modern-edition."[31] This coexistence of traditional and modern attitudes suggests something more complex, psychologically, than the simple shift from American democracy to German absolutism implied in Tokutomi's analysis. This has led to descriptions, such as the following, of a Mori beset with unresolved inner tensions: "Two opposing factors, in short, were to be found in Mori from the very start: East and West, Japan and America, conservatism and liberalism. The dual structure of his spirit, in anguish over the conflict, closely resembles that of present-day Japanese-Americans who have returned to America after spending their childhood in Japan."[32]

In a similar but more sophisticated vein, Takeda Kiyoko has argued, as against Tokutomi, that Mori's two sides run parallel through time, rather than succeeding each other; and that this illustrates the difficulty of establishing a modern individualistic sense of self against the powerful psychological and philosophical pull of traditional culture: "What was, then, the main stream of his thought? May we not say that two conflicting principles—a modern view of man, and a statist view of man—existed side by side for him, without his sensing any contradiction between the two? And may we not conclude that Mori, who sought liberation as a modern man in terms symbolized by Western culture, had in fact failed to establish clearly the autonomy of his own self, being able to conceive of that self only as a part—or at the most a semi-detached part—of the Japanese nation?"[33]

The Marxist historian on the other hand wonders, in effect, why the others should be so disappointed or surprised: for the forces

30. George B. Sansom, *The Western World and Japan* (New York, 1950), p. 460.
31. Motoyama Yukihiko, "Mori Arinori no kokka shugi to sono kyōiku shisō," *Jinbun gakuhō*, 8:106–108 (1958).
32. Ōmura Kakichi, "Mori Arinori: eigaku o sasaeta hitobito: dai roku," *Eigo seinen*, July 1965, p. 27.
33. Takeda Kiyoko, *Ningenkan no sōkoku* (Tokyo, 1959), pp. 219–220.

restraining Mori are not simply cultural and ideological but social as well; and these social forces proceed at their own predetermined historical pace. Tōyama Shigeki has relegated Mori to the limbo of enlightened despots;[34] while Suzuki Tadashi, who has credited Mori with a genuine earlier liberalism, makes him a typical "bourgeois" liberal who is bound, "as Lenin explained," to make his peace sooner or later with feudal reaction.[35] Tsuchiya Tadao, finally, is even harsher in his judgment: "In the development of this anti-traditional thought of his one perceives not so much a true leadership of the times, as the foolish frivolity of a man jumping to catch the bandwagon."[36] This statement ostensibly recaptures something of the spirit of the suspended *Chōya shinbun,* which, although as a general rule opposed to the government from a liberal standpoint, had found little difficulty in taking the side of Nishino Buntarō.

METHOD OF APPROACH

Thus from one single set of facts on Mori have been drawn two reciprocal readings of those facts, one emphasizing his role as westernizer, the other his role as nationalist. Positive and negative reactions to each of these two roles have produced our four fundamental Mori images. The perpetuation of such widely divergent images has been greatly abetted by an unusual number of gaps and ambiguities in the historical record. The Kaimon, Kimura, and Ōkubo biographies, for instance, touch only briefly on Mori's religious views and do not discuss his constitutional thinking at all. Data relating to Mori's personal life is particularly thin and disappointing. He left us neither a proper diary nor an extensive collection of personal correspondence, and there are entire years (even in adulthood) for which we have only the skimpiest of facts. The register of his essays, memorials, letters, speeches, and interviews is similarly uneven. There are lengthy silences, sudden shifts of focus, and seemingly enigmatical passages which combine to puzzle the reader as to the actual development in time of any given component of Mori's thought, or the mutual articulation of the several components of his thought at any given instant, or the relationship of his thought as a whole to his personal life and professional career.

34. Tōyama Shigeki, *Meiji ishin* (Tokyo, 1951), p. 303.
35. Suzuki Tadashi, "Meiji kanryō to kindai shisō: Mori Arinori o meguru kōsatsu," *Rekishi hyōron,* 90:7 (November 1957).
36. Tsuchiya Tadao, "Mori Arinori no kyōiku seisaku," in *Ishiyama Shuhei* et al., *Kyōiku no shiteki tenkai* (Tokyo, 1952), p. 446.

An interpretation of Mori based on ample, incontestable, and widely familiar facts could be accomplished in half the space of a study in which new material must be introduced, old information sufficiently sifted, and in some instances where direct data fails us an entire milieu recreated, *faute de mieux,* by way of indirect evidence.

A chronological approach recommends itself for a man of action like Mori. It should also help us to lay bare step by step the evolution of his thought. The topical approach, particularly to an individual's thought, almost invariably imposes a spurious coherence on its material. This is not to say that the chronological segments do not individually retain a certain topical orientation. Chapter breaks generally correspond to intercontinental shifts of locale and necessarily entail some shift of focus as well. In addition, each of the ten chapters tackles its share of the problems posed by the Mori images: (1) If Mori was indeed a "renegade from tradition," was there anything in the tradition that had helped produce the renegade? (2) If Mori was indeed "infatuated with the West," what initially prompted him to become so? (3) If Mori was indeed "at heart a Christian," what sort of Christianity had he laid to heart and why? (4) Can Mori's early political position really be described as "liberal" or "radical"? (5) If Mori was a "westernizer," how did he learn from the West? (6) And what was it he learned from the West? (7) And how did he try to apply it to Japan? (8) Can his later political position really be described as "authoritarian" or "reactionary"? (9) Was his educational thinking indeed significantly swayed by German example? (10) And does his educational administration really live up to (or can it live down?) its historical reputation?

The unevenness of the reliable record has necessitated somewhat differing methods of exposition. Where the record has been the most adequate, as in Chapters Four, Seven, and Ten, it has been possible to draw copiously on the three Japanese biographies, adding occasional fresh interpretation in passing. These three chapters deal with most of Mori's writings in the Japanese language and with his adult career in Japan. In Chapter Ten, indeed, it has been necessary to distill the bare essence from an ocean of available materials, bearing in mind that it is a biography and not a history of Mori's educational administration which is being written here. In Chapters Two, Five, Six, and Eight, by contrast, it was necessary to reconstruct Mori's overseas career from very spotty biographical data and to discuss at some length his English-language writings which, although ample, have been given very little attention to date. Where we have very little in the way of either biographical data or authored works as in Chapters One, Three, and Nine, an attempt has been made to get at the life and thought of Mori by reconstructing the known environments, respectively, of mid-nineteenth-century Satsuma, of the Brotherhood of the New Life at Brocton, New York, and of European education in the early 1880's.

The first and most significant of these environments was virtually taken for granted by Mori's three Japanese biographers, who assumed that the Japanese reader would already know what it meant to be brought up in Bakumatsu Japan, or even in the castle town of Kagoshima in the forties, fifties and sixties. They have left us but the briefest of accounts of Mori's childhood and adolescence, and that all very much in the traditional panegyric mode.

One 1847–1865

SATSUMA ORIGINS

Had the likes of Huckleberry Finn been kidnaped off his Mississippi River bluff and sent around the world to pay his respects to the sultan, the pope, and the empress of China in his late teens, his biographers no doubt would have dwelt on the youthful precocity of the world traveler of *"only* eighteen." Had his luck taken him only as far as St. Louis or Chicago, however, it is not hard to imagine how the sophisticates of those cities would have wagged their heads and wondered openly how someone *"all of* eighteen" could have grown to manhood without having picked up at least a few of the manners of polite society. Contradictory as these two appraisals would seem to be, they nevertheless would have applied to one and the same person: prior, of course, to the commencement of that extraordinary journey which was to make all the difference.

Mori arrived in England, on the first of his three extended journeys to the West, within a few days of his eighteenth birthday. Much has been made, and rightly so, of the early age at which the impressions of a strange culture and the burdens of high office were thrust upon him. Less attention has been given to the fact that up through his seventeenth year Mori had not set foot outside his own native Satsuma han, indeed had not even visited nearby Nagasaki, and had received an education and an upbringing the extraordinariness of which had consisted, if anything, in being more than ordinarily Japanese.

What does it mean to turn eighteen years of age, in terms of the growth process of the human individual? From the standpoint of professional and intellectual development a young man stands on the bare threshhold of maturity. In terms of personality and psychological "set," however, the story it seems has for the most part already been told. According to the classic Freudian view, basic patterns on this level are determined in early childhood by the primary formative influence of infantile sexuality; while Erikson, who argues for a considerably lengthier process of development and takes a more optimistic view of the leeway for later change, still places his pivotal identity crisis in late adolescence or very early adulthood.[1]

An evaluation of the years of childhood and adolescence is particularly germane to a study of Mori for two reasons. First, it is appropriate to ask of an educator precisely what his own education may have been. Secondly, Mori's somewhat unusual personality, as a factor of interpretation, plays a pivotal role throughout the story of his life. Influences formative of Mori's personality and thought group themselves naturally enough, for this period, into those of the home, the school, and the han at large. The very scarcity of facts available on Mori's Kagoshima upbringing requires that we elucidate them by such background statements as safely may be ventured with regard to family life, educational institutions, and ideological trends in Satsuma during the immediate pre-Restoration period.

FAMILY: LIKE MOTHER LIKE SON

The former Jōgatani district[2] of Kagoshima city, like its modern counterpart, Nagata-chō, formed one of the northernmost reaches

1. See Sigmund Freud, *Three Contributions to the Theory of Sexuality*, tr. James Strachey (New York, 1963); and Erik H. Erikson, *Young Man Luther: A Study in Psychoanalysis and History* (New York, 1958).

2. The geographical information which follows has been based for the most part on a gigantic city map (with an estimated date of 1848 or soon thereafter) in the Kagoshima Prefectural Library. On this map Mori's father's name appears on the uppermost property in the Jōgatani valley. Another map, at the Shūseikan in Iso, and dated "around 1843," shows a Sakamoto Hirazaemon on this same plot, while the name "Mori" appears on a tiny piece of land next to the Kasuga Shrine, where Mori's official birthplace marker now stands. For some reason, therefore, Mori's father moved the family from Kasuga to Jōgatani within a very few years of his youngest son's birth. The Kasuga location was right by the main road to Iso and therefore may have represented a valuable, if very small piece of land. By contrast, 418 *tsubo* of gravelly hillside may not have been worth much: except of course for the elbow room it provided this family with five energetic growing boys.

of habitation in the old Shimazu castle town. Its dozen-and-a-half samurai households straggled single file up the bottom of a steep, lonely ravine on the back side of Mt. Shiroyama. The family living furthest up at the head of the ravine held a plot of land 418 *tsubo* (over 1,500 square yards) in area, on several terraced levels. The converging hillsides, with their lush cover of camphor trees and bamboo, were so close here as to block out all but a few hours' daily sunshine. Immediately above this plot of land, a small stream led through a deep, chilly, canyon-like defile to the broad upper slopes of the mountain.

At its lower, or eastern, extremity the Jōgatani valley joined the seaside plain about half a mile from the water's edge, and about one mile north of the Kakumaru, as the daimyo's castle was called. In the immediate shadow of the Kakumaru were to be found the residences of the highest-ranking Shimazu retainers. Along the slopes and valleys of Mt. Shiroyama behind the castle, and throughout the northern half of the city as a whole, lay the homes of samurai of the middle rank. Along the widening plain to the south of the Kakumaru, crowded into a rabbit warren of tiny household plots, lived the lower-ranking samurai. Here in the real center of the city, a good two miles south of Jōgatani, lay the Kajiya district, whose household registers would someday read like a veritable hall of fame for Meiji Japan: Saigō Takamori, Ōkubo Toshimichi, Ōyama Iwao, Tōgō Heihachirō. And from the immediately adjacent districts would come others like Kuroda Kiyotaka and Matsukata Masayoshi.

Turning north, rather than south, from the foot of the Jōgatani valley, a mile's walk led to the Kasuga district and the Kasuga Shrine, on the near side of the Inari River. Crossing the Inari (the northern limit of the city), it was only another mile's walk northward along the picturesque cliff-hung beaches to the small coastal village of Iso. Here, from the mid-1850's, were to stand a steamship construction yard and the Shūseikan (Experimental Hall) with its reverberatory furnace, smeltery, and assorted scientific laboratories.

As of 1847, however, Iso could boast of little other than its fish. The promoter of its new industries, Shimazu Nariakira, would wait four years yet for the retirement of his father, the incumbent daimyo, Shimazu Narioki. In the Western world, American troops were overrunning Mexico; the Chartist agitation in England was approaching its fever pitch; and the continent stood poised on the brink of the momentous events of 1848. In Japan as a whole, by contrast, politics were temporarily in a state of suspended animation. The Tempō reforms of the 1830's and early 1840's had run their course; the controversial Mizuno Tadakuni had been out of office for four years; and a full six years' grace was to be granted before the arrival of Commodore Matthew Perry.

It was on 23 August 1847 (13 VII Kōka 4 in the traditional calendar)[3] in a humble samurai dwelling just south of the Inari, next to the Kasuga Shrine, that the youngest child in a family of five sons was born to Mori Kiuemon Yūjo, age 39, and his wife Osato, née Kumasaki, age 36.[4] The boy's full name was Mori Kinnojō Arinori. During infancy he was called Sukegorō, denoting his position as fifth son, and from his eighteenth through twenty-first years he would go also by the alias of Sawai Tetsuma. In family circles he was known as Kinnojō, the name he continued

3. Dates referring to events occurring in Japan prior to the adoption of the Western calendar as of 1 January 1873 will be rendered in the text according to the modern solar and the old Japanese lunar calendars, in that order. The latter will appear in parentheses, with the lunar month expressed in Roman numerals and the year placed after its era name (*nengō*). For instance, in the case of Mori's birthday (13 VII Kōka 4) indicates the thirteenth day of the seventh lunar month of the fourth year of the Kōka era. In justification of this seemingly cumbersome device, it should be pointed out that the Japanese sources almost invariably give lunar dates and that Japanese scholars continue to use the old system of reckoning for events in Japanese history prior to 1873. Lunar dates for events prior to 1873 which occurred in the Occident will be entered only when specifically mentioned in the Japanese sources. No lunar date will be given without its solar equivalent; therefore any date appearing singly refers to the Gregorian calendar. Arbitrarily, *nengō* will be given only in connection with lunar dates and years of the Christian Era in connection with all solar calculations of month and day of month.

4. Age wherever possible will be given according to the Western scheme of computation. Occasionally, however, as in the case of Mori's parents, the only information available is a figure computed according to the traditional Japanese method of counting years of age (*kazoedoshi*). In such instances, the figure given in the text will have been arrived at arbitrarily by subtracting one year from the Japanese figure. Often as not a subtraction of two years might be equally appropriate. A Japanese child was reckoned one year of age at birth, with an additional year added at every succeeding New Year's Day. Hence a child born on the last day of the year would be reckoned age two as of the following day. Accordingly, a traditional Japanese reckoning of age for a person born in January tends to exceed its Western equivalent by one year; for a person born in July by a year and a half; and for a person born in December by two years. The Japanese sources tell us of Mori's father only that he was "forty" at the time of Mori's birth; actually he may have been only thirty-eight by Western-style calculation. Mori's own age at death has been given in his biographies as forty-three. By Western reckoning, however, he was on 11 February 1889 still forty-one, a full six months short of his forty-second birthday, which would have fallen on 23 August of that year.

to use officially until his twenty-fourth year, when he shifted exclusively to Arinori, by which he has chiefly been remembered in the West. Posterity in Japan recalls him also as Yūrei, the Sino-Japanese rendering of Arinori. Here from the very start, however, we shall take the liberty of calling him, quite simply, Mori.[5]

Mori was descended, by hoary legend, from a scion of the Seiwa Genji of the Junior Fifth Rank, Mori Yoshitaka Mutsu no Rokurō, who had perished on the flight from Kyoto in the company of Minamoto Yoshitomo in early 1160, and from Yoshitaka's grandchildren, who in turn had fled Kamakura in the company of Miura Iemura in 1247, taking refuge under the Shimazu in southern Kyushu. With a bit more plausibility he traced his lineage back to a Mori Jusae who lived around 1600 and was reputed to have been the progenitor of all the Moris of samurai status in Kagoshima. The family tree, however, is established with complete reliability only from the seventh generation ascendant, with the appearance of Mori Kiuemon Arinaga (d. 1693), who had served as personal attendant (*soba yaku*) to the daimyo, studied Zen in Edo, and retired while still short of forty into his own private hermitage within the precincts of the Jōkōmyō temple at Kagoshima. For the next five forebears we have nothing but a string of names, and distressingly little has been transmitted regarding even Mori's own father, Yūjo. Kimura Kyō, calling attention to a Mori Jirōsaburō Yukishige who served the Shimazu both as elder (*karō*) and as vice constable (*shugodai*) at some unspecified point between the thirteenth and seventeenth centuries, is willing to call the Satsuma Moris a "distinguished han family."[6] But there had been in any case a rapid proliferation of family branches after

---

5. KKM, p. 2, and OTM, p. 9, give Sukegorō as Mori's *yōmyō* or "infant name," Kinnojō as his *tsūshō* or "common name," and Arinori as the name which he assumed at a later age in place of Kinnojō. Ōkubo dates the changeover from the time of Mori's appointment to Washington in 1870, when he first began to sign his letters (in Roman letters, surname last) as "Arinori Mori." As late as the previous year he was still signing himself "Kinnojō" in letters to Ōkubo Toshimichi (OTM, p. 37). His father's farewell poem (see below) of 1865, on the other hand, is addressed to "my child Arinori." It would be more correct perhaps to assume that like his father, Kiuemon Yūjo, Mori bore the two given names Kinnojō and Arinori simultaneously, and not in succession, with general currency shifting at some point from the former to the latter. The suicide of the fourth son in August 1870 left Mori sole heir to the family name, and conceivably may have involved a decision to emphasize "Arinori," the first character of which (*ari*, read also as *yū*) had consistently graced the given names of the heads of the Mori household for seven generations.

6. KKM, p. 2.

1600, and Mori's biographers tell us nothing about his social status or his father's samurai rank.[7]

Of Yūjo's professional dimensions we know only that he was by vocation a minor han official, by avocation a student of *kokugaku* (national learning) with inclinations toward the poetical rather than the political side of that tradition,[8] and financially in straits so narrow "as normally would have required him to put his children to work as copyists."[9] This, we gather, he refused to do, keeping all five of his sons at their books, and the family as a whole in a state of genteel poverty. Socially, he would have ranked in one of the following eleven grades into which the Satsuma samurai in the Bakumatsu period were divided:

1. *GOICHIMONKE* (4 households). Accorded the same treatment as relatives of the daimyo. Held rear vassals.

2. *ISSHŌMOCHI* (17 households). Possessed of one of the *tojō*, or outlying military districts, into which the han was divided.

3. *ISSHŌMOCHIKAKU* (41 households). Not in charge of a *tojō*, but possessed of territory and retainers equal to those of the *isshōmochi*.

4. *YORIAI* (45 households).

5. *YORIAINAMI* (10 households).

6. *MUKAKU* (2 households). "Ungraded"; referred to branch families of the Shimazu who had resigned rights to the succession.

7. Genealogical tradition, given in KKM, pp. 1–2, may be of some relevance to the extent that it informed young Mori's imagination and contributed to his sense of identity. Yoshitaka, the accounts have it, was felled by an enemy arrow while attempting to cross Mt. Hiei. Yoshitomo deposited his severed head, as a token of respect, in the waters of Lake Biwa. Yoshitaka's son Yoritaka Mori Kanja swore allegiance to Minamoto Yoritomo in Shimōsa, married Miura Yoshimura's daughter, and in 1247 at the age of ninety committed suicide at the side of Yasumura and 500 other Miura warriors in the Hokkedō temple in Kamakura as it fell before the onslaught of besieging Hōjō forces. Shimazu records are clear on the point that Miura Iemura, with wife and three children, fled to Satsuma and took service with the family there at that time. The Satsuma Moris traditionally maintained, with no recorded proof, however, that all five of Yoritaka's children got out of Kamakura alive, and were taken to Kagoshima by Iemura. From 1247 to the time of Jūsae (ca. 1600) the family record is blank except for the sole figure of Jirōsaburō Yukishige, and the links between the Kantō Moris of the Kamakura period and their namesakes in Kagoshima in the Tokugawa period seem, on the face of it, somewhat tenuous.

8. Interview with Mori Arimasa, grandson of Mori Arinori, at Ivry-sur-Seine, June 1965.

9. KKM, p. 3.

7. *KOBAN* (760 households). Equivalent of the class known as *umamawari* in the Bakufu and other han. Guards assigned to march at the side of the daimyo when the latter was mounted on horseback. Held important administrative posts.
8. *SHINBAN* (24 households). A newly established grade.
9. *KOSHŌGUMI* (3,094 households). Footsoldiers, also called *ōban*.
10. *GŌSHI*. The farmer-samurai settled in the outlying *tojō*.
11. *YORIKI*, also called *zatsukishi*. Attached as specialists with subordinate staff functions in various government offices.

Below these in status, and living in the *tojō*, were the rear vassals (*kachū* or *matazamurai*) attached to the first three grades, who, although still classified as samurai (*shi*), were very much looked down upon by the others; and two grades of warriors, the *tojō no zatsukishi* and the *ashigaru*, who did not qualify as samurai at all.[10]

Despite his alleged poverty, there are good reasons for surmising that Yūjo's family ranked among the 912 households constituting the eight uppermost grades, rather than among the 3,094 *koshōgumi* from which both Saigō and Ōkubo hailed, or among the 5,000 *yoriki* at the bottom of the social scale. To begin with, there was not only the ample size but more importantly the location of the plot on which the family residence stood. The northern half of the city, including jōgatani, was known as Kanmachi (Upper City), a term with many of the same connotations of wealth, sophistication, and social prestige as were (and still are) conveyed by Yamanote or Yamate (Upland) in the case of uptown Tokyo. Well on into the Meiji and Taishō periods the descendants of the upper- and middle-class samurai who had lived in Kanmachi still bore themselves with a certain dignity, a certain intellectual broadmindedness, and a certain condescension toward the rougher, countrified, headstrong types from the southern, or "downtown," section. And Jōgatani specifically has been remembered by one of its oldest living residents as the former home of "rather eminent" persons.[11]

10. Haraguchi Torao, *Bakumatsu no Satsuma* (Tokyo, 1966), pp. 12–14.
11. The recollection is that of Mrs. Matsuda Kuni. (Interview at Kagoshima, October 1967). For the description of the Kanmachi "type," and for the several enumerated clues to Mori's social standing I am indebted to Professor Haraguchi Torao of Kagoshima University. For more detailed information on Jōgatani I am indebted to Mr. and Mrs. Ōshiro Baiichirō, who owns a portion of the old Mori property, including a small bungalow estimated to be at least 100 years old, which may have been the old Mori home,

Secondly, the ability to send all five sons to the Zōshikan, as the han-operated samurai school was known, to some extent belies the alleged poverty, which may well have been exaggerated in line with the standard eulogistic biographical practice. The impression, thirdly and finally, that this was a family with a long tradition of scholarship (and by implication, at least some degree of affluence) is reinforced by the fact that the heads of the family from Arinaga on down all assumed by-names in later life, a practice suggestive of an early retirement and taking of the tonsure. Assuming that the Moris belonged neither to the upper-crust *yoriai* or *yoriainami*, nor to the special category of *shinban*, we are left with the *koban*, or seventh grade.

As to character, Yūjo has been described as "gentle and sincere," a man of "rugged honesty" who encouraged in his own sons a spirited and forthright approach to life.[12] Of a "philosophic turn of mind," "generously lenient" and "inclined to laissez faire" with his own children,[13] he left disciplinary matters to his wife, Osato, who seems to have been eminently up to the task. Mori's mother was a martinet, an ardent soul with a rigorous and solemn sense of purpose, a resolute will, and an "exceedingly masculine disposition."[14] She was clearly the chief influence in moulding the ideals and supervising the early training of her children. One can imagine that her imprint must have been particularly strong in the case of her youngest son.

Both parents had an "eccentric streak" in them according to Kaimon, who takes pains to gloss the Japanese expression *"henpeki"* with a *furigana* transcription of the English term, "eccentricity." Yet it was not uncommon then, nor for that matter in modern Japan today,[15] for fathers to assume a benign, aloof posture, maintaining the charisma of their formal authority by a judicious non-exercise of the same, while surrendering to mothers both the emotional satisfactions and the daily disciplinary chores deriving from intimate and virtually uninterrupted contact with the children. Nor were virtues of a masculine stamp unknown to girls of a samurai family, whose training often as not had included

---

or perhaps an annex to the home in which Mori was raised. Mr. Ōshiro has heard it said that Mori used the bungalow as a "hunting lodge" while he was minister of education.
12. KKM, pp. 2–3.
13. OTM, p. 9.
14. KSM, p. 4.
15. Ezra Vogel, *Japan's New Middle Class* (Berkeley, 1964), pp. 212–216, 241–243.

familiarity with the art of fencing and the use of the halberd.[16] Mori's parents were "eccentric" perhaps in the sense of being extreme, representing, that is to say, not a negation but rather an exaggeration, of a typical pattern. And here we have the first instance of a phenomenon which will hold true of much of Mori's early life.

Yūjo's "laissez-faire" expressed itself most significantly in his ready accession to Mori's request to study English at a time when it was still politically dangerous to do so, in his willingness to see his son embark on the study of *yōgaku,* or Western learning, a pursuit so very alien to his own devotion to *kokugaku,* and in his unstinted moral support at the time of Mori's departure for England. His two brief farewell poems of May 1865 proclaim an intellectual breadth and flexibility which was to be perhaps his chief legacy to his son:

> My child rides the unfathomable deep
> In pursuit of noble ambition;
> Far must he sail—ten thousand leagues—
> Outpacing the breezes of spring.
> Some say that East and West
> Have naught in common;
> But I say the same heaven
> Overarches both.
> His own life he risks, on command of his han,
> Braving great danger to learn from far places;
> For family's sake, he spares no effort,
> Seeking for wisdom in face of great hardship.
> He travels far beyond
> The fabled rivers of China;
> His scholarly labors shall someday
> Bear fruit in splendid achievement.

and:

> My own child, at seventeen,
> Takes leave of Kagoshima;
> By stroke of good fortune
> Great blessing lies in his grasp;
> Profoundly does he understand the

[16]. Frank A. Lombard, *Pre-Meiji Education in Japan: a Study of Japanese Education Previous to the Restoration of 1868* (Tokyo, 1913), p. 196.

True spirit of our Imperial Land.
The stars of the spacious firmament
Bind all five continents together.[17]

These poems evince, in addition to the entirely predictable samurai-bureaucrat's homage to scholarly labors, two fresh, dynamic elements: first, in the reference to East and West, a disposition to confront dispassionately the challenge of a new and unfamiliar world; and secondly, in the reference to the "true spirit" (*seiki*) of the "Imperial Land" (*kōkoku*), a clearcut advocacy of imperial rule, a cause which must have lain close to the heart of a lifelong devotee of *kokugaku*.

If father served to liberate the boy's mind, mother certainly lent strength (or rigidity) to his personality and character. The single surviving photograph of Osato, taken in old age, reveals a massive, heavy-set, squarish head with very small eyes which transfix the viewer in their beam of unimpeachable authority. As a strict disciplinarian and as chief transmitter of the traditional value system to her offspring Osato was, however, merely conforming to a widespread pattern. The very same qualities have also been ascribed, for instance, to the Kagoshima mothers of Saigō Takamori, Tōgō Heihachirō, Yamamoto Gonnohyōe, and Matsukata Masayoshi.[18] Mishima Michiharu, son of Mishima Michitsune (later governor of Fukushima prefecture), would one day write of his own Satsuma upbringing: "The ethics and morals courses at school merely put me to sleep; I have no recollection of what it was that I learned there. Such ethical feelings as I possess were imparted to me by my mother and my grandmother in an atmosphere of maternal love. My grandmother, who came from a Satsuma family, was particularly exacting."[19]

It is important to note that in Osato's case, too, strictness and authority were by no means remote or impersonal, but went hand in hand with an overpowering affection: a combination which, theoretically at least, tends to hone the superego to a fine point, expanding both the capacity for feeling guilt and the potentiality for achievement which may be mobilized to counteract such feel-

---

17. Cited in KKM, pp. 9–10.
18. For the mothers of Saigō, Tōgō, and Yamamoto see Sera Kōichi, ed., *Sappan katei kyōiku no kenkyū* (Kagoshima, 1937), pp. 96–104; for the mother of Matsukata see Matsumoto Hikosaburō, *Gōjū kyōiku no kenkyū* (Tokyo, 1932), p. 308.
19. Cited in Matsumoto, *Gōjū*, p. 353.

ings. Edward Norbeck and George A. DeVos have noted the existence in Japanese culture of guilt deriving not from supernatural sanctions but from interpersonal relationships within the family itself, particularly from the intensity of the bond between mother and child.[20] If one may indeed define guilt as the remorse that comes from having injured a loved person, then we may very well have in the case of Mori and Osato a classic instance of drives to achievement harnessed not by the setting of strict and lofty standards alone but also by the collateral of affection which has been staked on their fulfilment.

Only one specific episode involving Osato has been recorded. Mori reported his selection for study overseas in 1865 first of all to his mother. Ōkubo Toshiaki tells us that: "She was overjoyed at the news and waited breathlessly with suspense while Mori reported the matter to his father, wondering whether or not he would grant his approval. When she heard that consent had been given her joy knew no bounds. It would have required unusual qualities even in a man to have gone into quite such transports at the prospect of seeing one's favorite child off for study in a strange and distant land. Like mother like son, Mori owed to her in great measure his firmness of character."[21]

Mori's brothers, if they were indeed "all outstanding,"[22] may well have provided an attractive embodiment of many of the ideals enjoined upon him by his parents. His relationship to each of his four elder brothers very probably paralleled, and buttressed, the pattern established vis-à-vis his mother. Although one might smile at the biographer's insistence that the older boys all stood in some awe of their juniormost member as the one with the greatest promise,[23] it is not difficult to imagine the cumulative force of both authority and affection which converged upon the youngest member of this all-male sibling group.[24] The solidarity of the four surviving brothers[25] was symbolized by the single receptacle in which

20. Edward Norbeck and George A. DeVos, "Japan," in L. K. Hsu, ed., *Psychological Anthropological Approaches to Culture and Personality* (Homewood, Ill., 1961), p. 27.
21. OTM, p. 14.
22. Ibid., p. 8.
23. KKM, p. 3.
24. Osato was Yūjo's second wife and mother of his five sons. His first wife died very soon after marriage leaving a daughter who apparently married very early, since no further record of her exists beyond simple mention in KSM, p. 3. This half-sister is included in the family tree to be published in *Zenshū* II.
25. OTM, p. 10. The third son died at the age of eleven.

they all kept their chopsticks, their *shiketsubako,* or "Four Worthies Box," as they chose to dub it.

Mori's eldest brother, Kitōta, who first taught him his Chinese classics, was nine years his senior. He is described as a young man of promise, respected by his neighborhood peers, but like all of Mori's brothers he was destined for an early death, in his case at the age of twenty-six, when Mori was only seventeen. Second in line, and a year younger than Kitōta, was Kihachirō, who changed his name to Aoyama Yoshiaki upon adoption by his wife's family. Possessed of a strong flair for traditional scholarship, he had studied at the Confucian Academy (Shōheikō) in Edo. Upon returning to Kagoshima he endured a long illness, and had just recovered and begun teaching at the Zōshikan when a sudden relapse removed him from the family scene at the age of twenty-five, in the very same year as Kitōta (ca. 1864). It was Mori who had nursed, cooked, and kept house for him at a hot-spring resort during the long months of illness, in return for which Kihachirō regaled his youngest brother with tales of the magnificent exploits of one George Washington.[26] The third son, Mikuma, had died at the age of eleven, when Mori was only five.

Mori was closest to the fourth son, four years his senior. This brother, Genshirō, established his own niche in history with a protest suicide in Tokyo in 1870 in remonstrance against extravagance and corruption in ruling circles and the government's bellicose stand on Korea. Better known as Yokoyama Shōtarō Yasutake, the name he assumed upon adoption as heir by Yokoyama Yasukata, Genshirō possessed great personal courage, a passion for individual probity and social justice, and a generous capacity for righteous indignation. Saigō Takamori, in writing his epitaph, would one day affirm: "Faithful he was, and overflowing with love for all. In serving his parents, he supported them with a glad and pleasing countenance. In the service of his lord, he was not fearful of betraying his feelings, and said what others did not dare to say. All these qualities proceeded from a loyal and devoted heart."[27] There were tales of his slipping out late at night to give money secretly to the poor, and of remonstrating with the Satsuma daimyo for two days running, after ritual purifications taken to underline the implicit threat of suicide. The new imperial government was not to escape his exacting regard either.

The moral hold which Genshirō apparently exercised over Mori

26. KSM, pp. 10–11. For Mori's four elder brothers see also KKM, p. 2.
27. Cited in KSM, p. 103.

is suggested by an early childhood incident in which the latter, having lost a letter of Genshirō's on the road, reported the mishap to his mother and begged her to apologize for him to his brother. Genshirō scolded his younger brother roundly for his cowardice in not coming forward directly with an apology of his own. It was a reprimand which Mori was not to forget even in his later years.[28]

It was natural enough for Genshirō to have appointed himself guardian-in-chief of his younger brother's deportment, and it was to this brother, rather than to his parents, that Mori would address his highly revealing and semi-confessional letters from Britain. Genshirō very possibly deserves to be ranked second, after Osato, as chief shaper of Mori's personality and character. In determining the thrust of Mori's public behavior, however, Genshirō's influence no doubt ranks first, going well beyond the mother's vague though vibrant expectations of success. For his was a specific and highly critical vision of society and politics, backed up by a restlessness verging on the desperate to have his ideals fully realized.[29]

Mori lost his third brother when he himself was five; his first and second brothers when he was seventeen; while Genshirō's suicide occurred the day before Mori's own twenty-third birthday, leaving him from that time forward sole surviving son and heir to the family name. Although both father and mother were to live on into their seventies, and although the loss of children in those days was perhaps too common to have evoked any acute sentiment of the tragic, the total loss of elder siblings must have left some mark. Perhaps, however, in a culture in which the moral authority of a person was often enhanced by his own death,[30] Mori's brothers by dying may simply have made their presence more felt than ever as models, as mentors, and as monitors of his conduct.

Three friends of the family, resident in the same neighborhood, instructed and befriended the several Mori children at one time or another. Genshirō's father-in-law, Yokoyama Yasukata, an advisor to Shimazu Hisamitsu, was well known throughout the han as an accomplished poet and Confucian scholar. It was a "blessing in disguise," according to Kaimon, however, that he should have died while Mori was only nine, for he surely would have made a zealous

28. KKM, p. 4. The account presented by Kaimon in KSM, p. 7, gives Mori's age at the time as six, the brother involved as Kitōta rather than Genshirō, and the reprimand as a rather mild one. Here we have followed Ōkubo, who follows Kimura's version of the incident.
29. For the suicide of Mori's fourth brother, see Chapter Four.
30. John W. Hall and Richard K. Beasley, *Twelve Doors to Japan* (New York, 1965), pp. 368, 373.

Confucianist out of his young charge if he had lived any longer.[31] Of greater significance were the Godai brothers. Godai Kyōta had familiarized himself with Western texts through Chinese translations. Godai Tomoatsu (1836–1885), who had taken up *rangaku,* or Dutch studies, in Nagasaki in 1857, made a secret voyage to Shanghai on han orders in 1859, and was to accompany Mori to England in 1865. He was one of the most outspoken advocates of opening the country and learning from the West.

Ambition, self-reliance, a sense of personal and intellectual independence—all these seem to have had their roots in the human relationships of Mori's home. His formal schooling likewise had its beginnings under the parental roof, and we are told that parents and brothers wasted no time in setting the young child to work on his Chinese classics. By his fifth birthday, however, he found himself thrown into a second, and progressively more demanding, crucible of socialization. It was the custom of each Kagoshima samurai lad on the tenth day of the eleventh lunar month of his fifth year of age to don for the first time a crested kimono (or if very poor only a *hakama*), and to gird himself with the long and short swords which were then presented to him for life. Thus attired he would accompany his father in making the rounds of the local clan shrine and the ancestors' graves. The swords were usually a family treasure, but with new handles and sword-knots attached for the occasion. The short sword might then be worn regularly up to the age of ten, and both swords worn thereafter. This ceremony was known as *kamishimo kihajime,*[32] or "first donning of ceremonial dress," and marked also the boy's entry into Satsuma's "unique" pedagogical device, the Gōjū or "village fraternity."

GŌJŪ: EDUCATION FOR THE SUPER-SAMURAI

Was the Gōjū really unique to Satsuma or merely more unusual than what was to be found elsewhere in Japan at that time? Here again, as with the "eccentricity" of Mori's parents, the question of typicality must be posed. The leading prewar authority on the Gōjū likened it enthusiastically in the same breath to both the Boy Scouts and the Hitler Youth.[33] He might better have compared it to the *wakashūgumi,* or young men's confraternities found in one

31. KSM, pp. 5–6.
32. Matsumoto, *Gōjū*, pp. 290–291.
33. Ibid., p. 16.

form or another throughout Tokujawa Japan, of which the Satsuma Gōjū was perhaps the most highly developed example. Unlike the scouting movement or the twentieth century fascist or communist youth auxiliaries, however, the Gōjū provided not only physical training, moral guidance, and political indoctrination but also, in an era before the establishment of a modern educational system, the only formal schooling available to most Kagoshima children of primary- and secondary-school age. Book learning was one of its most central and regular activities. On the other hand, unlike confraternities which existed elsewhere in Japan chiefly to assist with local festival preparations or to teach the customary military arts, the Gōjū seems to have made all but total demands upon the time, the energies, and the loyalties of its members. Writers on Satsuma agree that the Gōjū was peculiar to the han, and that it was an indispensable ingredient in the production of the Restoration leadership from that part of Japan.[34] Yet in many respects the Gōjū was simply a matter of out-Japanizing the Japanese and owed its origin to Satsuma's decision to take quite literally the familiar watchword accorded lip service the length and breadth of Japan: "Hito wa shiro, hito wa ishigaki, hito wa hori" ("Men are our castles; men our ramparts; men our moats").[35]

Satsuma's unique *tojō seido,* or outer castle system, as it may literally be translated, was the strategical adjunct of its so-called *gōshi seido,*[36] or farmer-samurai system, which had been contrived following the excision by Hideyoshi in 1586 of the extensive conquests of the Shimazu in central and northern Kyushu and the reduction of the han to the three "home" provinces of Kagoshima, Ōsumi and Hyūga. Like other losers to Ieyasu at Sekigahara,[37] but nearly two decades ahead of them, Satsuma faced the problem of accommodating the samurai from the lost territories who came crowding into Kagoshima. Instead of following the typical Edo

34. Ibid., pp. 15, 350; Haraguchi, *Satsuma,* p. 28; KKM, p. 11; and OTM, p. 9.
35. Matsumoto, *Gōjū,* p. 349.
36. The *tojō* and *gōshi* systems have been well described in the English language by Robert K. Sakai in "Feudal Society and Modern Leadership in Satsuma Han," *Journal of Asian Studies,* 16.3:366–373 (May 1957).
37. The Shimazu, although on the losing side in 1600, managed to retain their former holdings intact in the peace settlement concluded with the Tokugawa in 1602. This is in marked contrast to the Mōri (Chōshū) and Uesugi (Yonezawa), the dominant pre-Sekigahara powers in western and northern Honshu respectively, who forfeited all but a fraction of their territory. Satsuma received her trimming-down at the hands of Toyotomi Hideyoshi, not Tokugawa Ieyasu, and in that sense had a head start in developing a new political and social structure.

period pattern of resettling them in the daimyo's castle town, however, the han chose to rusticate its overflow of warriors in the outlying towns and villages. By so doing, it achieved at one stroke three important objectives. First, the great majority of samurai, as soldier-farmers, became economically self-supporting, thus forestalling the emergence of that parasitic town-dwelling warrior class which was to burden other han with major problems of finance and of maintenance of morale. Secondly, direct surveillance and control of the general population by locally resident samurai so eased the management of internal security that the han survived the entire Edo period without a single peasant uprising.[38] Thirdly, with the strategic dispersal of the warrior class throughout the han, and their integration into the military command structure of the *tojō* system, Satsuma presented a sobering prospect to any would-be invader. Here was a countryside saturated with militia. Here were soldiers close both to the soil and to the simpler virtues of the "heroic," and bloody, sixteenth century.[39] If there was at any time in Japanese history an analog to ancient Sparta, this was it.

Under the rubric of "One Han, One Castle," the Bakufu in 1615 had ordered the han to raze all forts with the exception of the daimyo's own seat of residence, had forbidden new construction, and had placed heavy restrictions on repairs.[40] Satsuma's *tojō* system, therefore, has been hailed as a clever circumvention of the Bakufu ordinances. The rendition of the term as "outer castle system," however, misleadingly suggests an audacious program of fortified construction which in fact was never undertaken.

38. Tōyama Shigeki, in *Meiji ishin*, p. 36, refers to a "total absence" of peasant uprisings in Satsuma during this period. According to the *Kagoshima ken kyōkushi* peasant discontent never managed to produce a "positive" uprising. Such resistance as there was occurred outside the purview of the *gōshi* system (for instance in the Ryukyu Islands, or under lower samurai leadership, never reaching the proportions of a true *ikki* [insurrection]), and petered out in the mere absconding of disaffected peasants into neighboring territory. See Toyoda Takeshi and Kagoshima Ken Kyōiku Iinkai (Kagoshima Prefectural Board of Education), comps., *Kagoshima ken kyōikushi* (Kagoshima, 1960), I, 7.

39. Unlike most other han, where a rigid separation of samurai and farmer classes (*heinō bunri*) gradually came into force, Satsuma was able to retain right up to the modern era the pattern of samurai-farmer fusion (*heinō itchi*) which had characterized the class structure throughout most of Japan during the Kamakura period. Thirteenth-century society was held up as a positive ideal by the han rulers. As the daimyo Yoshihiro (1535–1619) put it, speaking of his warriors, "Rustics they are, so rustic let them be." See Toyoda, *Kyōikushi*, I, 33.

40. Inoue Mitsusada, *Nihonshi*, 3d rev. ed. (Tokyo, 1961), p. 198.

It was the spirit rather than the letter of the edicts which Satsuma had violated by relocating its soldiery to its own strategic advantage. *Tojō* referred actually not to castles but to the 113 administrative subdivisions of the han and might more properly be rendered as "outlying military district" or "march" (as the term applied, for instance, to England's Welsh and Scottish borderlands, or to medieval Germany's Slavic frontier).

Ninety-two of the *tojō* were governed by *jitō* (prefects) dispatched directly on rotating assignment from Kagoshima, while twenty-one of them were held in permanent fief by prominent vassals of the daimyo. Altogether they accounted for nearly ninety percent of the han's total samurai population.[41] *Gōshi* residing in the *fumoto,* or headquarters town, of each *tojō,* assisted with the administration of the local district, while those in the smaller hamlets devoted themselves primarily to farming. They all, however, kept their swords within easy reach of their "plowshares" and remained organized in their traditional military formations, which could be mobilized instantly on command from the *jitō*. The concentration of *gōshi* was particularly strong at strategic points, such as Izumi and Takaoka and Shibushi along the landward frontier.[42]

The *tojō* system, in short, was a matter not of architecture but of men. Satsuma had outflanked the Bakufu edicts not with castles but with a militia. The han's strategic posture suffices to suggest the general character of its educational response: physical fitness, skill in the military arts, a spirit of loyalty, and habits of obedience would all be at a premium. But the particular institutional form which that response was to assume in the Gōjū was dictated by historical pressures and precedents peculiar to Satsuma.

The Gōjū of Mori's day developed directly out of the Hanashiaijū (literally "caucus," but in essence a "fraternity") established by the caretaker government for the adolescent boys of Kagoshima during the Korean campaigns of Hideyoshi. The elderly Niiro Tadamoto, left in charge of a population topheavy with women, children, and the aged, became alarmed at the slackening of discipline among the teen-age samurai in the absence of

---

41. The respective figures for 1826, for instance, show 8,791 samurai households in Kagoshima city, as opposed to 83,567 in the *tojō* (Toyoda, *Kyōikushi,* I, 120).

42. See Kagoshima Ken, comp., *Kagoshima Ken shi* (Kagoshima, 1939–43), II, 157–160; Haraguchi, *Satsuma,* pp. 14–23; Toyoda, *Kyōikushi,* I, 119–121; and Tsukada Akio, comp., *Kagoshima: kyōdo no rekishi to monogatari* (Kagoshima, 1964), pp. 109–113.

their fathers. With 10,000 men overseas, and most of them gone for a matter of several years, mothers were beginning to spoil their sons, manly simplicity was giving way to dandyism, and young men who could read were associating altogether too freely with illiterate matrons, if only on the pretext of deciphering their husbands' letters for them. Niiro, recalling that the daimyo Yoshihiro had in the mid-sixteenth century regularly invited young samurai to the castle for the study of Chinese classics and the discussion of appropriate ethical themes, revived and institutionalized the practice, promulgating in 1596 the "Nise banashi kakushiki jōmoku" (A code of conduct for young samurai of the fraternity), which was to define for nearly 300 years the spirit of the Hanashiaijū, or Gōjū, as it came to be called after the mid-eighteenth century.[43] This code, in full, ran as follows:

1. Cultivate first of all the military arts.
2. At the same time achieve a thorough understanding of the samurai's code.
3. If you must deal with persons outside the fraternity do not tarry long with them but return immediately after concluding your business.
4. Whatever you choose to discuss in the fraternity, discuss it in a serious manner.
5. When speaking to your fellow members remember that overfamiliarity is a discourtesy, and strive to maintain the traditional etiquette on this point.
6. Whenever a member must absent himself from the fraternity, and has difficulty in freeing himself from an outside engagement, the fraternity will see to it that no violation of the code has been incurred.
7. The injunctions against lying are the very heart of the samurai code and are to be observed absolutely.
8. Cultivate the virtues of loyalty and filial piety without ostentation. When the occasion arises, however, the true samurai takes pains not to come out the loser.
9. Become expert at negotiating mountainous terrain.
10. It is not the shaving of his head which qualifies the young samurai. What makes him worthy of the name, rather, is his mastery of military skills and his profound devotion to the principles of loyalty and filial piety. People outside the fraternity simply cannot grasp this point.

43. Matsumoto, *Gōjū*, p. 62; Toyoda, *Kyōikushi*, I, 72.

11. The foregoing articles are to be strictly observed. Anyone failing to do so is not fit to be called a young samurai, and the gods of war, Marishiten and Daibosatsu, will surely withdraw their favor from him in time of battle.[44]

The emphasis on group solidarity (articles 3 and 6) no doubt reflected Niiro's attempt to rein in the wayward through a system of mutual surveillance. The Hanashiaijū for a long time, however, remained a loosely organized, geographically undifferentiated fellowship (or "pow-wow," as the term implies), of Kagoshima youths who met irregularly to talk things over and to encourage each other in the pursuit of the lofty ideals established for them by Niiro. The appearance in 1753 of the term *Gōjū,* which contains the character *gō* meaning "village," bespoke the gradual proliferation of the Hanashiaijū into a number of exclusive and fiercely competitive neighborhood fraternities, one for each of the thirty-three (in Mori's day) *hōgiri,* or wards, into which the city was divided. The Gōjū in its internal structure was inevitably influenced also by the example of the *kumi* (brigades) into which the youngsters' fathers had long been organized. All adult samurai in Kagoshima from the seventh rank down had, since 1642, been grouped into six *kumi,* further divided into sixty *kogumi* (subbrigades) which served not only as a structure of military command but also as an instrument for political and ideological control. *Kumi* discipline required, for instance, that not only Christian and Jōdo Shinshū sectarians but also the lazy and the quarrelsome as well be ferreted out of the ranks and reported at once to the han authorities. Younger boys were brought within the purview of the Gōjū in 1754 by the "Osachigo aijū okite" (Fraternity regulations for older children) and "Kochigo aijū okite" (Fraternity regulations for younger children) issued that year, and the institution reached maturity in the 1770's under the daimyo Shigehide, whose educational innovations also included the establishment in 1773 of the Zōshikan, which complemented the Gōjū as a seat of more advanced, academic, learning.

The institution which largely defined Mori's social horizons from the age of five to the age of eighteen was far from moribund. If anything, the Gōjū was undergoing a rejuvenation at the hands of the daimyo Nariakira, who, in the very year of Mori's probable admission (1852), had announced a drastic return to the original standards of the fraternities, called for strict enforcement of pun-

---

44. Toyoda, *Kyōikushi,* I, 73, cites the code of conduct in full.

ishments, and had extracted (for the first time in the history of the institution) written pledges of good conduct.[45]

Gōjū[46] members were divided by age into three ranks, which observed strict leader-follower relationships: the *kochigo* (younger children), ages roughly five to ten; the *osachigo* (older children), ages approximately eleven through fourteen; and the *nise* (young samurai, or youth), who ranged from fourteen or fifteen to twenty-four or twenty-five years of age. Fathers and elder brothers who had "graduated" from the Gōjū in their mid-twenties to marry and take full-time employment were known as *chōrō* (elders), and boys on occasion consulted them when self-government failed. The Gōjū was, however, to all intents and purposes an autonomous fraternity. A *chigogashira* (Head Child) was appointed from the *osachigo* to supervise the two junior ranks, while a *nisegashira* (Head Boy) was chosen (as Saigō Takamori had in his youth been chosen) from the *nise* to lead not only his peers of the top rank but the Gōjū as a whole.[47]

Matriculation was a simple affair. The samurai father took his five- or six-year old son to the local Gōjū during one of its sessions and left him there with no more than an "if you please." Promotion to the *osachigo* was, for the lad involved, a bit more painful. His *kochigo* peers rolled him around inside a wooden box and in other ways thoroughly hazed him before he joined the next higher rank and became entitled to their respectful obedience. Initiation to the *nise*, finally, was a solemn and impressive affair in which the neophyte recited his pledges in a resounding voice before the assembled *nise* and *chōrō*. It usually coincided with the coming-of-age ceremony, in which the youth of fourteen or fifteen received official recognition as an adult samurai, together with gainful employment if he wanted it. Few indeed were the moments which might be spent at home. The center of a boy's activity shifted from his family to his fraternity, and his sense of identity very rapidly expanded beyond that of being merely *ie no ko,* or "child of the family," to an awareness of broader loyalties and responsibilities.

The two ranks of *chigo* upon awakening around 6:00 A.M. would hurry to the home of some scholar in the neighborhood who would help them through a first reading of the texts for that day.

45. Ibid., I, 71–76; Matsumoto, *Gōjū,* pp. 56, 66, 75–82.
46. The following description of the Gōjū is based on Matsumoto, *Gōjū,* pp. 349–370, and Toyoda, *Kyōikushi,* I, 70–110.
47. Toyoda, *Kyōikushi,* I, 80, stresses the self-governing nature of the fraternity.

Yokoyama Yasukata, the Godais, or even Mori's own elder brothers may have served as *sensei,* or "teacher," to the Jōgatani Gōjū during Mori's *chigo* days. The immediate objective of the day's assignment was *anshō,* the ability to recite from memory, and the chief device a rote reading aloud, without particular attention to meaning, known as *sodoku.* Kimura tells us of Mori: "He would burst into a flood of tears whenever his memory reached the breaking point in assimilating the Chinese classics. However he would not leave his seat until he had memorized his material completely. As a result texts once studied were never forgotten."[48]

The boys would then return home, working on their assignments until breakfast and helping with household chores until 8:00, when they rejoined their Gōjū comrades for two hours of outside games such as *taishōdori* (King-of-the-mountain) under the direction of their *chigogashira.* On rainy days they played edifying indoor games, such as *daimyō karuta* (daimyo pinochle) in which the names of the daimyo, with their respective han and *kokudaka* (annual crop yield) were inscribed on the playing cards. *Fukushū zamoto* (review session, or study hall) was held from 10:00 A.M. to noon and from 2:00 to 4:00 P.M. Here the *osachigo* first drilled the *kochigo,* and then each other, on the assigned texts, working together in pairs. Guidance of the younger by the older often included such questions as, "Have you been obeying your mother?," or "Do you have any special problems today?" No special school buildings were constructed for *zamoto* purposes. The sessions were rotated among the several families represented in the Gōjū. It was considered an honor to play host, and the initial session in any home was likely to be a festive affair, with the mother putting out her best pastries and sweets.

From 4:00 to 6:00 P.M. Gōjū members practiced fencing and other martial skills on the local training ground under the instruction of the *nise.* The *kochigo* would remain at home after supper, but the day was not yet over for the *osachigo,* who were privileged to attend the first hour or so of the *yobanashi zamoto* (evening conclave) of the *nise.*

The *nise* during the morning hours were either busy at menial tasks or, if they were somewhat scholarly and could afford it, attending lectures in the Zōshikan, which ran from 10:00 A.M. to 2:00 P.M. Their Gōjū activities commenced around 4:00 P.M. at the exercise ground, where they drilled the *chigo* (and engaged each other) in two strenuous hours of fencing. Mori, who attended

48. KKM, p. 6.

the Zōshikan from the age of eleven until he was nearly eighteen, was one of the privileged few who spent the first half of the day at their studies.

The high point of the day for the *nise* was their *yobanashi zamoto,* which seems to have mixed fellowship and good fun with more serious fare. During the first hour of the conclave the *osachigo* were assisted with their homework or permitted to look on as the *nise* grilled each other in a cross-questioning procedure known as *sengi.* At about 8:00 the *nise* escorted the *osachigo* home individually and then returned for another hour or two to continue *sengi,* to read military histories aloud by turns, take long walks together, or possibly even stage war games out of doors under cover of night.

The scholastic emphasis in the Gōjū lay in the memorization and recitation of texts. Several *zamoto* sessions each month were devoted to group reading, with a particular classic scheduled for a fixed day of the month. Instruction in calligraphy, composition, or the *biwa* lute was available at the Zōshikan, but boys often used the *fukushū zamoto* in the Gōjū to prepare their Zōshikan lessons.

The *chigo* were first brought up on three Satsuma classics with a pronounced local flavor: the *Iroha uta* (Alphabet poem), a ballad of forty-seven ethico-politico-military maxims, each commencing with a different syllable according to the traditional *i-ro-ha* sequence, and originally composed by Shimazu Tadayoshi around 1547; the *Toragari monogatari* (Tale of the tiger hunt), relating the feats of Shimazu Yoshihiro during the Korean campaign; and the *Rekidai uta* (Chronicle poem), a catalog of appropriate information regarding the successive rulers of Satsuma han. The *nise* would go on to the Four Books, the Five Classics and related staples of the Chinese literary canon, to the *Sankokushi* (History of the three kingdoms) and the *Taiheiki* (Record of the great peace) and other military annals of China and Japan, and to native Japanese sagas such as the *Soga Monogatari* (Tale of the Soga) and stories of the forty-seven loyal samurai.

The Gōjū was a school without a teacher. Instruction proceeded on an "Each One Teach One" basis, with the older boys instructing the younger, and with members of the same rank drilling, prodding, and assisting each other mutually. The neighborhood scholar who passed out the morning's assignment was available during the day for further assistance, but the initiative and authority and responsibility of the schoolmaster rested entirely with the *nise.*

The *sengi* (cross-examination) of the evening conclave better served the purposes of moral edification than of substantive learning. The questions often probed the proper response of the young samurai in a variety of situations, most of them as hair-raising as they were hypothetical. For example:

> QUESTION: Suppose that, after hunting for your father's murderer all over Japan, you should at last come across him on the open sea—your own boat in shipwreck and about to go under, and his the only vessel that can save you—what would you do?
> ANSWER: After permitting myself to be rescued I should thank him cordially; but then announcing, "Prepare for death, for thou art my father's slayer!" I should accomplish my revenge.[49]

Boys took turns, by lot, in submitting to such interrogation in front of their assembled peers. Answers were to be delivered promptly, and the same question was hammered at until a satisfactory response was forthcoming. The procedure put the examinee under considerable nervous strain and was an awesome experience for the beginner. The *sengi* was Socratic neither in its method nor in its concept of the truth, but it did at least teach the boys to muster their poise in a public forum.

The line between military drill and purely athletic activity was virtually nonexistent. Gōjū members climbed mountains, swam rivers, and vaulted ditches with imaginary invaders in mind. On the other hand many of the military skills, though warlike, were perhaps not all that different from football or rugby in their physical-fitness and character-training functions. Boys began fencing at the *chigo* stage, and as *nise* received further training in archery, pole-fighting, spear-throwing, horseback riding, judo and (by Mori's day) in the firing of cannon and small arms as well. The two qualities especially striven for were aggressiveness and endurance, which found their clearest expression in fencing and mountain-climbing, respectively. The former, by far the most assiduously practiced of the military arts, was executed with mock swords of oak wood according to Satsuma's indigenous *jigenryū* style, in which all was staked on a single daring offensive lunge. The aim was to kill with the first blow or be killed. The forward stroke was simply to be dealt with maximum head-on violence, without any subtlety of timing or maneuver, while defensive tactics were not taught at all. *Jingenryū* was indeed an "exercise in courage,"[50] if not in audacity. The importance of mountain-climbing

49. Toyoda, *Kyōikushi,* I, 91.
50. Ibid., I, 101.

(in the sense of hiking rather than mountaineering) is suggested by its specific mention in both the "Kochigo okite" and the "Nise jōmoku." The steep, gravelly hills of the northern frontier apparently were to be raced up and down without pause for breath, preferably in the humid days of summer, as a test of will and stamina.

Finally, if anything else was needed to round out the education of a super-samurai, it surely was supplied by another Satsuma specialty, the *hiemondori:* literally, the "snatching of the cold thing." This was a free-for-all staged by the Kagoshima *nise* on the public execution ground, in which they rushed upon the corpse, the first one in tearing off an ear or a finger and holding it up to the crowd, thereby establishing his right to flesh his sword first on the criminal's body. This was considered to be an honor without equal and was won, among others, by the future Admiral Yamamoto Gonnohyōe in his *nise* days.

There is no reason to suppose that Mori during his eleven or twelve years in the Gōjū would have missed the *hiemondori* or any of the other activities. He also must have been thoroughly familiar with the Western-style parade drill introduced into the Gōjū by the daimyo Nariakira.[51] Appropriating for their purposes the gardens of the larger Gōjū homes, the boys would almost daily devote some of their late afternoon exercise time to marching in formation to the accompaniment of drums, the *nise* shouldering real rifles and the *chigo* wooden replicas. On special occasions they would assemble on the castle grounds with boys from other Gōjū throughout the city, and stage a command performance in the presence of Nariakira. In the long run, however, the Gōjū was probably less significant for its book-learning and body-training than for the social habits and moral attitudes it sought to instill.

There was an absolute quality to the demands made by the Gōjū upon its members. Family life was well integrated with, if not subordinated to, that of the Gōjū. Mothers worked hard to raise their boys fast and have them join at an early age. It brought ridicule to have a son who could not attend, and boys who for one reason or another had to be kept at home were handicapped socially for the rest of their lives. Fathers and elder brothers, as members *emeriti,* were answerable to the Gōjū for the behavior of the *chigo* and *nise* in their own family and stood themselves under the threat of expulsion if they failed to exercise proper guidance of the latter. Standards were spelled out in well-known codes

51. Ibid., I, 78.

which were rehearsed, reviewed, and recommitted to memory at regular intervals on the Gōjū calendar. Sanctions were usually applied through a special session of the *sengi* in which members were encouraged to bring forth mutual criticism and complaints against each other, with the *nise* then taking counsel together as to proper punishment. Penalties ranged all the way from the memorization of additional texts while sitting dunce-like in a dark corner, through several gradations of corporal punishment, to *gōjūbanashi* (expulsion), which in the context of the times was "an ordeal worse than death."[52]

Personal relationships within the fraternity were intimate and demanding. Gōjū members were "closer than brothers."[53] What bound them together, however, was not the "fraternal" fellowship of peers, but rather the very strictest observance of hierarchy between young and old. Not that there was anything impersonal about this formally authoritarian pattern. As has been noted elsewhere with respect to similar vertically structured groups in Japan,[54] the Gōjū exhibited considerable warmth and emotionality along its vertical axes of patronage and dependence, while presenting to the outside world an implacably hostile and exclusive front. Within the fraternity, the *nise* assumed pedagogical responsibilities for the *chigo* which were worthy of an adult; their dealings with *nise* of neighboring Gōjū, however, were more likely to be characterized by bloody noses. The nasty rivalries among the thirty-three Kagoshima Gōjū were first moderated by the joint parade drills imposed on them by Nariakira, and one writer has seen this as the beginning of a process whereby the intense feelings nurtured within the fraternity were gradually transferred outward: the loyalties from the Gōjū to the han and finally to the nation; and the hostilities from the adjacent Gōjū to the Bakufu, and finally to the enemies of Japan;[55] the fraternity having already shaken the growing boy out of any comfortable emotional dependence on the home.

The three basic codes of the fraternity, the "Nise jōmoku" and the two "Chigo okite," devote nearly a third of their precepts to enjoining minimal association with outsiders, whether the foppish young swells known as *yoshiya* or simply members of rival Gōjū. The posture to be assumed when such contacts were unavoidable

52. Haraguchi, *Satsuma*, p. 28.
53. Matsumoto, *Gōjū*, p. 363.
54. Nakane Chie, *Tate shakai no ningen kankei* (Tokyo, 1967), pp. 49–64.
55. Matsumoto, *Gōjū*, pp. 365, 370.

was suggested by the injunction ("Nise jōmoku," article 8) against coming out a loser. Parents were indulgent with torn sleeves, muddied kimonos, even with broken bones. Rough, even violent, behavior was to be borne with, but cowardly conduct was unpardonable. A boy returning home defeated in a neighborhood brawl was likely to be scolded, turned around, and sent right back out with instructions to win. Relative emphases in the Gōjū are indeed suggested by the fact that the codes contain several exhortations pertaining to the martial, but none to the literary, arts: both of which were commonly esteemed throughout the samurai class of Tokugawa Japan.

Positive ethical injunctions in the codes emphasized loyalty and filial piety, truthfulness, and adherence to the standards of conduct established for adult samurai, while the articles governing daily comportment stressed courteousness and sobriety. The *nise* were warned against being overly familiar, the *osachigo* against too much joking, the *kochigo* against laughing and singing in public. Economic and sexual morality were apparently so deeply imbedded in the culture as to require no mention in the codes. Shirao Kunihashira, describing Satsuma youth around 1812, related that: "any fellow trying to turn a fast penny, or currying favor with powerful families, or offering his opinion on women, or making a fuss about food or clothing, would forthwith be ostracized and expelled from the Gōjū."[56] It was a natural result of their training, Shiraoka continued, "that they should come to detest women, loathing them as one loathes snakes, and making wide detours around pretty girls on the street as if threatened by some physical pollution." Public encounter between the sexes, even a roadside chat between siblings outside the home, was strictly prohibited. On Girls' Day in early spring, the one occasion of the year when maidens were out in force, the boys took off, literally, to the hills.[57]

How deeply Mori, at least, had internalized the formal ideals of frugality and sexual purity is suggested by the sole scrap of writing from his early Satsuma days. It is a catalog of proper intentions, recalling both the spirit and the format of the Gōjū codes, yet also reflecting Mori's own particular preoccupations at the age of seventeen. Entitled "Shi tashinamu beki jōjō" (Points to be cultivated by the samurai), and dated 5 December 1864 (7 XI Genji 1), it read:

56. Haraguchi, *Satsuma*, p. 26, quoting Shirao Kunihashira, *Shizu no Odamaki* (Winding spool).
57. Ibid., p. 26; Matsumoto, *Gōjū*, p. 295.

1. Hold fast to right conduct.
2. Maintain composure.
3. In all matters, think twice.
4. Be patient in everything.
5. Root out desire.
6. Root out the sexual passion.
7. In speaking, come quickly to the point and go no further.
8. In confrontations and disputes, give way on nonessentials.
9. Eat and drink only to satisfy hunger and thirst; except, that is, for energy-giving fare, which may be consumed in abundance.
10. He who fails to observe even one of the foregoing is to be numbered not with the samurai but with the dumb beasts.[58]

If family relationships furnish the most important clues to Mori's psychic structure, it was family and Gōjū together which had molded his ethical attitudes and social responses—in short, his character—as of age eighteen. Here the role of the Gōjū was perhaps the weightier of the two. It intruded early and massively upon the life of the growing child, putting an extra existential edge, so to speak, on the value system nominally endorsed by the Tokugawa warrior class as a whole: an edge historically traceable, it would seem, to Satsuma's traditional strategic stance "at the ready."

The puritanistic self-restraints imposed in certain areas such as money, sex, and general social comportment were balanced by an exuberant, aggressive, competitive self-expression in other parameters, notably in the athletic. From the tears shed over *anshō*, however, and from the list of resolves just quoted, one would gather that Mori was disposed to assault not only his fencing partners but also his books, and the summits of virtue as well, in pure *jigenryū* style.

There were bound to be differences in quality and in atmosphere among the thirty-three Kagoshima Gōjū, but unfortunately nothing remains but a list of their locations and a roster of famous graduates.[59] Three generalizations, however, may safely be made

58. Mori Arinori, "Shi tashinamu beki jōjō" memorandum, 5 Dec. 1864 (7 I Genji 1), quoted in KKM, p. 7. To appear in *Zenshū* II.
59. Locations of the several Gōjū, together with the names of their most illustrious graduates, are given in Kagoshima Shidan Kai (Kagoshima Historical Association), comp., "Gakusha to Gōjū narabi shusshin meishi," mimeographed brochure in the Kagoshima Prefectural Library. Saigō, Ōkubo, Ōyama, Tōgō (as well as Saigō Tsugumichi, Kuroki Tamesada, and Makino Nobuaki) were all at one time, for instance, in the Lower Kajiya Gōjū.

about the Jōgatani Gōjū, judging from this list and from contemporary maps[60] of the area: (1) that it was not very large in membership; (2) that its members came from a reasonably well-to-do, and probably middle-ranking, stratum of the warrior society; and (3) that it was evidently dominated by families with strong literary and scholarly interest, such as the Godais, the Yokoyamas, and the Moris themselves. Scholastic effort, in other words, would have received strong encouragement from parents, neighbors, and peers alike, with less value placed here than elsewhere on brute physical prowess. The isolation of the valley geographically would, if anything, have strengthened such an ethos in Mori's own Gōjū. He would have met the youngsters from the Kajiya district during joint military drills or other exercises on the larger downtown exercise grounds, but assuming the major Gōjū activities took place in Jōgatani, Mori may have joined less frequently in the physical rough-and-tumble which must have occurred regularly among the cluster of Gōjū south of the Kakumaru.

The somewhat unusual character of the Jōgatani Gōjū may have encouraged a certain capacity for intellectual detachment, perhaps even a certain assumption of intellectual superiority. It would not, however, have explained the specific direction of Mori's early intellectual interests, nor the enthusiasm with which he was to embrace Western culture and thought from his late teens.

ZŌSHIKAN AND KAISEIJO: FALLOW BUT FERTILE GROUND

Did the West come crashing in upon a *tabula rasa,* or was there something in young Mori's academic training which provided a springboard to the Occident? The answer must be sought for in the institution of "higher" learning which he attended in Kagoshima, in the broader currents of thought in Satsuma han, and in stimuli in his own immediate environment apart from those of the family and Gōjū.

Mori entered the Zōshikan, or han Samurai School, at the age of eleven or twelve, rising eventually to the rank of assistant instructor in reading (*kutōshijo*) and remaining affiliated with it until the age of seventeen, when he enrolled in the Kaiseijo, or School for Western Studies, shortly before his departure for Eng-

---

60. See note 2 above. There were twenty-five household plots located single file along the small brook downstream from the Moris. The smallest of these comprised 150 *tsubo;* most of them had 200 to 300 *tsubo*.

land.[61] At the age of thirteen, however, a reading of Hayashi Shihei's *Kaikoku heidan* (On the defense of a maritime country) had inspired him to pursue the study of English secretly under the tutorship of Ueno Keihan. His beginner's command of that language assured him both admission to the new school in 1864 and selection for study overseas. Before asking how great a leap it was mentally for Mori from Kagoshima to London, we must consider: first, whether there was anything about the Zōshikan and its intellectual tradition which might have encouraged Mori's already considerable jump into the study of English; second, what the motivational impact of the Hayashi treatise may have been; and third, the orientation and equipment with which Mori finally emerged from the Kaiseijo headed West.

The Zōshikan,[62] established by Shigehide in 1773, occupied a spacious quadrilateral enclosure not far from the Kakumaru, in layout a smaller copy of the Shōheikō in Edo. In the northwest quarter stood an imposing temple to Confucius where the entire Shimazu household led the semiannual *sekiten* festivals in honor of the Chinese sage and his disciples. Dormitories housing several dozen boarders occupied the northeastern, and a rambling complex of lecture halls the southeastern, quadrant. A principal, fifteen senior professors, and a junior staff of sixty taught a group of 400 to 800 pupils, ages eight to twenty-two. Most of the boys were day students like Mori and were marched to school at appropriate hours by the *nise* of their Gōjū. All of them were on free tuition, including children of the non-samurai classes, who were admitted but segregated into a separate hall or onto the ends of benches.

The same Chinese classics used in the Gōjū were studied here in greater depth, and from the time of Nariakira *kokugaku* and *yōgaku* were also represented in the curriculum. The Gōjū and the Zōshikan stood in a parallel, rather than a sequential, relationship to each other. A *chigo* if sufficiently talented might start attending lectures at an early age and upon becoming a *nise* would continue to do so if his parents could afford it, as was the case with Mori in both instances. He would still participate in all the activities of the Gōjū and use the *fukushū zamoto* to prepare his Zōshikan lessons; but the latter would offer him lectures on his texts by the leading han authorities, together with scholarly discussion and analysis. In a typical classroom procedure the lecturer might read a page or so, expound it (this being known as

61. OTM, p. 10.
62. The following description of Zōshikan activity is based on Toyoda, *Kyōikushi*, I, 45–53, 66–67.

kōdoku), then read a second page and this time ask the students to comment on it (*kaidoku*). Unimaginative regurgitation of the text was frowned upon. Books were closed and laid upon the table. An exchange between one student attempting a paraphrase and a second student challenging him, might proceed as follows:

> A: Young men should conceive a noble aim and devote their lives to realizing it.
> B: Well, what do you mean by "noble aim"?
> A: Diligence in service to one's country.
> B: And what do you mean by "diligence"?
> A: The cultivation of my own mind.[63]

Two hours' drill was devoted to *sodoku,* which continued to serve as the central pedagogical device. Calligraphy was taught as an adjunct to it, and suitable passages were practiced with the brush as soon as they had been memorized. Neatly written specimens were to be submitted to the instructor for appraisal twice a month. There were exercises and competitions in poetry and prose composition and, finally, expert instruction in the military arts at the Enbukan, or Military Exercise Hall, which abutted the Zōshikan on the north.

The Zōshikan at the time Mori attended it offered an education that was more organized and in many ways more sophisticated than what was available on the secondary level in the frontier areas of America around 1860 and certainly more than was offered to the offspring of Britain's teeming industrial proletariat. Much of what it taught, of course, bore little relevance to the challenge which confronted Japan. The comprehensive political and moral philosophy which the Zōshikan presented, however, must at least have trained Mori to think systematically about these two areas of life. And the samurai school must have communicated to Mori in abundance that respect for learning and that joy in the life of the intellect which were to be among the most precious legacies from traditional to modern Japan.

Finally, and very simply the Zōshikan had trained Mori to read, to think, and to express himself in writing. His later career as social critic and man of letters is unthinkable without that basic foundation. In our highly practical Western culture some schools still require study of the Greek and Latin classics in the original, not only for their philosophical insights but also as a disciplining

---

63. Ibid., I, 68.

of the mind; and Confucius and Mencius performed a very similar function for Mori.

How did Mori manage to become so ungrateful a disciple? The Zōshikan had since its inception become the focal point of such ideological controversy as was to be found in Satsuma han.[64] Had there been any weakening of orthodox positions, or any infusion of new ideas which might have spurred that ingratitude? In still another "first" among the Japanese han, Satsuma had not only received the Chu Hsi tradition but also established its orthodoxy in advance of the rest of the country. Kagoshima samurai down through the fifteenth century had turned chiefly to Zen Buddhism for spiritual sustenance, and several leading scholars had journeyed to northern Kantō to study at the Ashikaga Gakkō (Ashikaga School). Practical behavior had been regulated quite simply by the Shimazu house codes. What was lacking was a broad political ethic with a firm philosophical underpinning. It was with the same enthusiasm therefore as the Tokugawa several decades later that Shimazu Tadayoshi (1533–1611) perceived the political uses of the Sung philosophy. Chu Hsi had placed particular emphasis on the strict maintenance of the traditional Confucian social relationships in which sons were subordinate to fathers, wives to husbands, younger brothers to their elder brothers, and subjects to their sovereign, and had among these several relationships stressed above all the loyalty of the vassal to his lord. These concepts were popularized in that staple of the Gōjū, Tadayoshi's *Iroha uta* (ca. 1547).

Tadayoshi had learned about the Chu Hsi philosophy from Shunden, a first-generation disciple of the Zen monk Keian (1427–1508) who had first brought the teachings of the Sung school to Japan after studying in China from 1467 to 1473. Entering Satsuma in 1478 as tutor to the daimyo Tadamasa, Keian had remained there until his death thirty years later. His publication in Kagoshima shortly after his arrival of the *Daigaku shōku* (Chu Hsi's new annotation of the *Great Learning*) was not only the first Sung text to be reproduced in Japan but also the oldest book published in Satsuma. Keian and the succeeding line of his disciples were all Zen priests in name but Confucian scholars in practice, attracting to their lectures not only the Buddhist clergy but also the leading lay statesmen of the day. The so-called Satsunan (Satsuma-Southern) school of Chu Hsi learning which they established readily found patronage among Tadamasa and his succes-

64. The following description of the history of the Zōshikan is based on Ibid., I, pp. 2–10, 25–31, 54–57, 202–206, 212.

sors and became the orthodox philosophy of the Zōshikan in 1773. The regulations of the Samurai School stipulated, in addition to exhortations on diligence, economy and good behavior, that:

> 1. Regarding the exposition of texts, the Four Books, the Five Classics, the *Lesser Learning* and the *Kinshiroku* shall be used, and interpretation made according to the teachings of the Sung School. Divergent doctrines are not to be interpolated without permission . . .
> 3. Students may consult with one another on points of uncertainty, but should yield to recognized authority, relinquishing their own personal views entirely.
> 4. Discussion of the ancient sages and their moral teaching shall not be used to criticise present conditions.[65]

This was a rather precise definition of orthodoxy. The *Kinshiroku* was the *Chin-ssu lu* (Reflections on things at hand) of Chu Hsi and Lü Tsu-ch'ien. Satsuma, in other words, had issued its own ban against heterodox thought seventeen years ahead of the Bakufu's edict of 1790.

The orthodox faculty clique which revolved around the first principal of the Zōshikan, Yamamoto Denzō, and his successors was, however, repeatedly put on the defensive. The school had no sooner opened than a faction of the staff sympathetic to the teachings of Ogyū Sorai found courage to attack not only Yamamoto but han government policies as well. The faction leader, Kawakami Kazen, and one of the han elders were severely punished in what came to be known as the *kogaku kuzure,* or "Ancient Learning Purge," the first of three major purges to shake the institution. In 1774, Yamamoto issued an almost frantic injunction against heterodoxy, urging his faculty and students to ferret out nonconformists in their midst and warning that lip service to Chu Hsi often hid a dissident and unrepentant heart—all of which suggests that the purge had been far from thoroughgoing.

The orthodox Chu Hsi party found itself threatened on two fronts. On the theoretical level it was attacked for overemphasizing purely literary skills and for preoccupation with arid textual criticism at the expense of more useful learning. On the level of practical politics, the Zōshikan inevitably was drawn into the factional struggles of the han government itself, and the true followers of Keian suffered serious reverses whenever a rival faculty

65. Ibid., I, 48–49, quoting "Gakki" (school regulations) of the Zōshikan, 1773.

clique managed to gain favor with the han authorities, as happened before the second great shakedown, the so-called *Kinshiroku kuzure* of 1808.

With the retirement of Shigehide in 1807, the han elders Chichibu Tarō and Kabayama Hisanobu had introduced a program of drastic economic retrenchment, throwing a number of high officials out of office in the process. Ideologically the two new *karō* were aligned with the *Kinshiroku* faction in the Zōshikan. This party had formed around Kitō Takekiyo, a scholar of the Yamazaki Ansai school who had raised the standard for *jitsugaku* (practical learning), placing particular stress on the *Kinshiroku*. "We learn," Kitō insisted, "in order to perfect ourselves and to govern others: these purposes do not necessarily require a catholic erudition or a tenacious memory."[66] Character training was to Kitō the central aim of education and, like Ansai,[67] he discouraged the attempt to devour the entire Chinese literary canon, preferring to single out those few texts which best suited the function of learning as he chose to define it.

Kitō himself was shaky on the earlier Confucian classics and on poetry in general, as the Yamamoto faction was quick to point out. His own adherents counterattacked by charging the latter with slavish adherence to the tradition of Keian and with excessive partiality for *belles lettres*. This academic confrontation was already under way when Chichibu and Kabayama came into office. Under the protection of the new *karō*, the *Kinshiroku* clique engineered the dismissal of Principal Yamamoto, after thirty years of service, and suspended the semiannual festivals to Confucius. The reform party, however, had overplayed its hand, incurring the wrath of the retired Shigehide and bringing about its own liquidation. Chichibu, Kabayama, and eleven others were forced to commit suicide; another ninety were driven into exile, retirement, or house arrest; *Kinshiroku* scholars lost their posts, and the Zōshikan slipped back into its exegetical doldrums.

The third major crisis, the "Takasaki Purge" of 1849, saw the Zōshikan drawn into what was again primarily a political power struggle. Overlaying a succession contest between Shimazu Nariakira (the legitimate heir of Narioki) and his half-brother, Hisamitsu, were important policy cleavages between the supporters and opponents of the *karō* Zusho Hirosato, a protégé of Hisamitsu and the architect of Satsuma's controversial, belt-tightening Tempō

66. Cited in Ibid., I, 205.
67. See David M. Earl, *Emperor and Nation in Japan: Political Thinkers of the Tokugawa Period* (Seattle, 1964), p. 53.

reforms. The supporters of Hisamitsu then in charge of the government managed in 1849 to purge the pro-Nariakira party, which had emerged under the leadership of Takasaki Gorōemon. Among the Takasaki group were a number of scholars of the *kokugaku* and Ōyōmei (Wang Yang-ming) schools who, like the "outs" of 1808, had chafed under the officially sponsored Chu Hsi orthodoxy. The academic debate in 1808, however, had been over two different approaches to Chu Hsi: the "literary" versus the "practical." By 1849 the spectrum of philosophical dissent was much wider.

One gets the impression that Satsuma, despite an initial enthusiasm for Chu Hsi, was not far behind other han in absorbing other strains of Tokugawa thought and that new ideas never presented quite the same political threat to the han government as they did to the Bakufu. Academic cliques were purged from the Zōshikan whenever they chose a loser in the shifting game of han politics, but not for their doctrinal positions as such. It is a truism of Japanese history that the outlying han of the Tokugawa period provided a refuge for scholars and schools of thought unpopular in Edo, contributing significantly to the ideological elasticity which set early modern Japan apart from her more rigid Chinese neighbor. Two possible explanations of Satsuma's relative hospitality come to mind.

First, in the small world of the han, academicians were perhaps a bit more manageable than in Edo. Visiting scholars were particularly beholden to the continued patronage of the Shimazu. Academic controversy in the Zōshikan, therefore, never really exceeded the bounds of a family tiff. Secondly, and more importantly, the question of political legitimacy (i.e., of the emperor-Shogun relationship), which many of the heterodox schools had raised,[68] and which more than anything else had placed the Bakufu on its guard against new thought, presented no threat to the claim of the Shimazu on their own han. Here they had ruled uninterruptedly since the thirteenth century. When heterodox belief did harbor a real threat to political authority or to the established social structure in the Shimazu domains, repression was savage and thoroughgoing. Christianity and Jōdo Shinshū, which had proved alarmingly popular with the peasantry, remained under proscription in Satsuma throughout the Tokugawa period.

In seeking to account for Satsuma's receptivity to ideas of foreign import, one could also point to Kyushu's longstanding role

68. Ibid., pp. 15–17, and pp. 18–81 *passim*.

as the portal for both Chinese and Western civilization: to its quick response to Sung thought, to the illicit trade of its Ashikaga daimyo with the Ming ports, to the Portuguese arquebuses which excited the inhabitants of Tanegashima in 1542, to Christianity, which first touched Japanese soil at Kagoshima in 1549 in the person of St. Francis Xavier, who stayed on for nearly a year in the city preaching at will among an intrigued and friendly populace;[69] and finally to nearby Nagasaki, where one could inquire after exotic things as the young Shigehide did during an excursion to that city in 1771.

For valid influences in Mori's case, however, one probably need look no further back than Shimazu Nariakira,[70] who was daimyo of Satsuma from 1851 to 1858. The conservative party which succeeded him put a temporary halt to many of his new industrial enterprises, but he did lay a solid foundation in terms both of institutions, and of a rationale, to which the han could turn in 1863 after its decision to learn from the West.

The list of Nariakira's excursions into modern industrial and military production and into modern scientific research is impressive. At the Shūseikan, 1,200 technicians were producing cannon from the blast furnace, smeltery, and gunbarrel bore installed there in 1853; manufacturing glassware, bread, salt, and rock candy according to the latest Western processes; and conducting experiments in such diverse areas as vaccination, photography, the telegraph, torpedoes, land mines, and gas lighting. Five large ocean-going sailing vessels, modeled after Western men-of-war, were constructed by Satsuma during Nariakira's incumbency, and the first attempt in Japan to construct a steam-powered vessel took place on the Iso shore in 1854.[71]

Even more significant were the attitudes which underlay all this activity, attitudes which were articulated in Nariakira's educational policies regarding the Zōshikan. "We are not spending money on Western-style culture," the daimyo insisted, "out of mere curiosity; this is an investment on behalf of the wealth and military strength of our realm."[72] Within this thoroughly traditional motive of *fukoku kyōhei* (rich country, strong soldiery), however, what

69. Toyoda, *Kyōikushi*, I, 5.
70. The following account of Shimazu Nariakira's educational activities is based on ibid., I, 57–66, 199–201, 207–211.
71. Ibid., I, 199–200; Kagoshima Ken Kyōiku Kai (Kagoshima Prefecture Educational Association) comp., *Sappan no bunka* (Kagoshima, 1935), pp. 238–246.
72. Cited in Haraguchi, *Satsuma*, p. 162.

new light if any may have glimmered on the intellectual horizon?

Nariakira's impact on the educational ethos of the han was both broadening, in that he encouraged new strains of thought, and deepening in the sense that he tried, as Kitō had tried, to reorient the Zōshikan back toward character training and preparation for public service, in other words back toward the goal of "samurai-building," which its name literally implied. A formal statement of his philosophy was contained in his very brief "Gakumon no taihon" (Cardinal principles of learning) posted at the Zōshikan in 1854, and in the much longer "Jukkajō no kunyu" (Tenfold exhortation) of 1857, which was recited at the annual opening of the Samurai School and repeated in every household.

The "Cardinal Principles" asserted: "Learning which cannot tear itself loose from literary exegesis and enlighten men on ethics and other practical matters, is as good as no learning at all. We insist that the essence of education lies in the fulfilment of our most urgent task, which is to serve the sovereign and our parents in a spirit of loyalty and filial piety, and to keep ourselves above reproach. To this end we must clarify our sense of duty, and bring our moral dispositions into alignment, so that by learning to govern ourselves we may achieve the capacity for governing others."[73]

Education, in short, was to be rooted in ethics, and oriented toward politics, in the broadest sense of the term, as the "Exhortation" went to considerable lengths to explain:

> 2. Learning should have as its aim the study of those principles by which we order our own lives, manage our households, govern our country and maintain the tranquillity of our domain; it should seek to establish the proper relationship between these activities; and it should enable us to devote ourselves to the faithful fulfilment of our political duties in today's world . . .
> 4. We deem that learning true which trains the student to bring his personal conduct into line with the teaching of the sages of antiquity and, by applying those lessons to the present, to administer the affairs of State in accordance with the needs of the times . . . We must impress upon our teachers and junior staff the urgency of bringing forth in increasing numbers a new generation of outstanding retainers . . .
> 5. Officially appointed scholars in particular, and all others however inadequate their literary skills may be, should aim to

---

73. Cited in Toyoda, *Kyōikushi*, I, 57.

be of some help in the political business of the day, and should train themselves to that end. This is of vital importance. Today's scholars, so-called, are far removed from the mundane affairs of the moment; they are disregardful of matters economic and live in a world apart, quite like the Buddhist clergy.[74]

Nariakira established for his own further schooling the Bunbu Kōshūjo (Literary and Military Training Center) in the castle grounds, sent his own sons to the Zōshikan, and took a personal interest in that institution. Every now and then he would pay it a surprise visit: inspecting the facilities, commanding the instructors to lecture and the pupils to answer questions in his presence, and occasionally handing out prizes and scholarships (or even offers of employment at the castle) to the ablest performers.

If the purpose of education was to create men of character, with new political awareness and new capacity for political involvement, then its content required a drastic broadening in the direction both of native Japanese studies and of Western Learning. In his instructions to the scholars who helped him prepare the final draft of the "Exhortation" Nariakira asserted:

> In coping with the actual conditions of our contemporary world, we can no longer rely as in the past on the sole guidance of our official Confucian scholars. It has become impossible to rule the realm properly without opening our eyes widely to the world around us. The time has come to permit communication with foreign countries and to enter broadly upon intercourse with the entire globe. It is of the foremost importance that we exhibit our national power by embarking upon relations with the outside world. To this end we must firmly establish the national polity, make good our weak points by learning from others where they are strong, undertake vigorous military preparations, and promote our shipping capacity. If we follow this policy, the prestige of our Imperial realm will shine throughout the world. It is with this aim in mind that I wish to establish our academic instruction upon a broadened base of scholarship.[75]

Here was enunciated the overriding national purpose which Japanese and Western studies, both urgently recommended in the

74. Cited in ibid., I, 59–61.
75. Ibid., I, 58.

"Exhortation," were to serve each in its own way. Nariakira had plans to establish separate institutions for both traditions. Instructing a scholarly committee to lay the groundwork for a Kokugakukan (Institute of National Learning), he complained:

> The academic tradition of the Zōshikan has adhered to the teachings of Chu Hsi exclusively, neglecting the historical annals of our own native land. Some, I have heard it said, go so far as to despise Japan in their adulation of China and try to do everything in the Chinese fashion. That is a frightful mistake . . . We ought to establish an Institute of National Learning in which the ways of our native land may be studied, supplemented by Chinese- and Western-type subjects, with a set of school regulations defining relative priorities in the curriculum.[76]

The Kokugakukan remained on the drafting board, but the study of national learning within the Zōshikan was effectively promoted with the appointment of Godaiin Mihashira, a disciple of Hirata Atsutane.

Nariakira's plans for a Yōgakukan (Institute for Western Learning) likewise went unrealized during his own lifetime, but he sponsored a number of projects which prepared the ground for the Kaiseijo of 1864, which has been characterized as having "brought to fruition his dying wish."[77] In 1855 he set up in the official residence of the court astronomer his Rangaku Kōshūjo (Dutch Learning Institute), a government office properly speaking rather than a school, which was to perform the same function as the Bakufu's Bansho Shirabedokoro (Office for the Investigation of Barbarian Books). Here the *yōgaku* scholar Ishikawa Kakutarō, invited down from Nara, was commissioned to investigate the Dutch educational system and to explore the "sentiments and actual conditions" of the Occident.[78] Meanwhile, similar exertions were pressed upon the Zōshikan:

> Since defense against the foreign threat is the most vital business of the day, we must go beyond our Japanese and Chinese texts to achieve a true understanding of the world of the barbarians, and adopt those things in which we are weak and they strong. Government and people in perfect harmony should

76. Cited in ibid., I, 210.
77. Ibid., I, 211.
78. Ibid., I, 210.

expand the Imperial might to check these barbarians of the West. This is the urgent duty of the valiant men of today. Remaining strength should be devoted to the diligent study of Western texts in Japanese translation, so that we may be able to discriminate the worthwhile from the worthless among the customs and artifacts of the West, and make use of them in displaying the Imperial authority towards all nations.[79]

Under Nariakira's aegis the han in 1854 published two Western texts in translation, the *Ensei kiki jutsu* (An account of the strange artifacts of the distant West), a transcription of Kawamoto Miyuki's lectures on the works of J. K. van den Broek, and the *Sange kogoto* (In dispraise of heroic death), a translation of van Meerdervoort's text on vaccination. Nariakira also ordered the Edo printer Kimura Kahei to develop modern Roman type, a project which after nearly a decade of clandestine research finally bore fruit in 1864. Even more significant perhaps was his invitation to Satsuma of *yōgaku* scholars like Ishikawa, and his establishment in 1856 of a scholarship system for the pursuit of Western learning at Edo, Nagasaki, and elsewhere outside the han.

When Mori came across the *Kaikoku heidan* in 1860, in his second or third year at the Zōshikan, Nariakira's educational projects and policies were in abeyance and popular sentiment was running toward a xenophobia which would crest with the bombardment of Kagoshima by the British fleet in 1863. The swift reversal of the tide thereafter, however, proved the strength of the countercurrent which Nariakira had set in motion. It is difficult to believe that Nariakira, hero both to Saigō Takamori and to Ōkubo Toshimichi, was not also an attractive and familiar figure to Mori. The "Exhortation" would have been read aloud in Mori's home, perhaps by his elder brothers then attending the Zōshikan; within Mori's own immediate circle, Nariakira's emphases on *yōgaku* and *kokugaku* were represented by Godai Tomoatsu and his own father respectively; while it is very probable that even at the Zōshikan a discreet interest in things barbarian had not entirely died out.

The history of that institution, and with it of Satsuma thought in general, suggests that diverse eddies of thought were permitted to murmur along peacefully as long as they stayed clear of the menacing boulders of han politics. In that sense, orthodoxy as such was never very strong to begin with. Add to this Nariakira's

79. Ibid., I, 63–64, from Nariakira's "Exhortation," Article 9.

positive interest in the West, extending to "sentiments" and "customs," be it only for the purpose of knowing one's enemy, and our clandestine young student of English comes into focus as very much the product of one of Satsuma's several intellectual "traditions."

It was the *Kaikoku heidan,* however, which jolted Mori into the active pursuit of *yōgaku.* Mukai Shinbei, a relative of his brother Yokoyama's wife, had brought a copy down from Edo, and within a year of reading it Mori had resolved to learn English, traveling in 1861 all the way to Miyakonojō to seek permission for this hazardous project from his father, temporarily posted in Hyūga. Since his tutor, Ueno Keihan, was absent in Nagasaki most of the time, lessons must have been few and far between. The zeal with which Mori applied himself to English, however, is suggested by the thick bamboo pipe which he apparently used as a pillow at the time to prevent wasteful oversleeping.[80]

The *Kaikoku heidan,* written in 1786, opens as follows: "The defense line of a maritime power lies along its coast; coastal defense is a matter of naval strategy; and the essence of naval strategy is heavy armament. This is the natural military policy of an island country."[81] Japan had for centuries thought strategically in terms of land defenses against domestic troublemakers. Hayashi's treatise by contrast argues for the absolute priority of seapower in meeting the new waterborne foreign threat. From Nihonbashi in Edo all the way to China and far-away Holland, he warns, run the sea lanes without obstruction. Why are the approaches at Awa and Sagami not protected? The entire coast north, south, east, and west, should be fortified like Nagasaki. After the fifty years which he estimates his plan will require, he hopes to see "the great ocean reduced to a pond, our shoreline a rampart of stone, and Japan built up a mighty fortress five thousand *ri* in circumference."[82]

Following a lengthy introductory chapter on naval tactics and naval construction, Hayashi writes another fourteen on land warfare, drawing copiously on his knowledge of Western armament and strategy and often illustrating the text with sketches in his own hand. The sixteenth and final chapter delves into the political, economic, educational, and moral foundations of a viable defensive posture, and it was this chapter, together with the thoroughly

80. KSM, p. 10.
81. Hayashi Shihei, *Kaikoku heidan,* Iwanami Shoten edition (Tokyo, 1930), p. 17.
82. Ibid., p. 18.

alarmist tone of the work as a whole, which probably accounted for his jailing and the confiscation of his text in 1792.

Since the threat which Hayashi describes had by Mori's time become infinitely more apparent, one can imagine the excitement with which certain intelligent young samurai must have read it. Beyond an arousal of patriotic sentiment, and a new awareness of the importance of naval preparedness, we can only speculate as to the detailed impact of the text on Mori's young imagination. Hayashi predated Nariakira by half a century, and his treatise betrays no inkling of a need to scratch below the surface of Western military might. His attitude toward Western people indeed was clearly one of contempt: physically they were largely built, but in matters of the spirit they were dull; they won their battles with the aid of ingenious and terrifying devices, but they preferred to avoid honest, bloody conflict, hiding behind shields, and coating their swords with poison.[83] Since Hayashi had been prompted to write his book by the specious warning against Tzarist designs delivered by the Polish exile Moritz von Benyowsky in 1771,[84] it is not surprising that the barbarians he is most concerned with are those from the north. Russia looms as the major peril to Japan.

Among the nine points he lists as fundamentals of national strength, wealth (especially the production of foodstuffs) and education receive heavy attention. "Learning," his last chapter opens, "is the foundation of military power," and in it he goes on to detail his plans for a Bunbu Gakkō (Literary and Military Academy) where samurai are to be trained both in the old civil and in the new military arts. The remaining seven points include: the maintenance of proper etiquette as the basis of ethics, military preparedness, legal regulations properly established and enforced, fulfilment by all of their respective social functions, the advancement of talent in the bureaucracy, the maximum productive use of land, and dressing in accordance with one's social status. There is also a lengthy and wistful description of the *gun-ken* (county-prefecture) organization of the pre-Kamakura period.[85] If, however, Mori had been impressed by Hayashi's main point—the need to study naval warfare, to build warships, and train the men to operate them—the chance was his in 1864.

83. Ibid., pp. 45, 100, 128.
84. George B. Sansom, *The Western World and Japan* (New York, 1950), p. 213.
85. For Hayashi's nine points see *Kaikoku heidan,* p. 256; for the Bunbu Gakkō, p. 230; for the *gunken* system, p. 252.

The Kaiseijo (School for Western Studies), established in response to the débacle in Kagoshima Bay, was located at the bureau of shipbuilding and offered instruction in fourteen subjects divided into five departments, all of them of a military or military-related nature: (1) naval and land artillery, military drill, tactics, fortifications; (2) astronomy, geography, mathematics, surveying, navigation; (3) engineering, shipbuilding; (4) physics, assaying; and (5) medicine.[86] These were taught by a staff of ten senior professors, ten junior professors, and fourteen instructors. Mori was one of a mere eight or nine students who worked in English, as opposed to sixty or seventy who received instruction in Dutch.[87] This may well reflect the success of Ishikawa Kakutarō of the Rangaku Kōshūjo in training a sizeable number of Dutch linguists. Why Mori should have picked English in the first place is nowhere explained. Hayashi's references to Europeans other than the Russians are primarily to the Dutch. Perhaps even before the Kagoshima Bay encounter, Mori may have known enough about Uraga and Canton to realize that in his day the waterborne peril was in great measure Anglo-American. In addition to English the only subject that he is officially listed as having studied during his brief sojourn at the Kaiseijo is naval surveying.[88]

Students at the Kaiseijo were all on stipend, and promising scholars were encouraged to proceed to other schools throughout Japan offering more advanced instruction. Satsuma scholars at work in other han during this period included Godai Tomoatsu at the Bakufu's naval academy in Nagasaki; Terajima Munenori (known as Matsuki Kōan before the Restoration) at the Bansho Shirabedokoro in Edo, for medicine; Kuroda Kiyotaka at the Edogawa Juku in Edo, for artillery; Tōgō Heihachirō studying English military tactics under Akamatsu Tomohiru in Kyoto; and Samejima Naonobu at Nagasaki for Western medicine.[89]

Nor was the idea of sending students abroad to Europe entirely without precedent. Nariakira shortly before his death had dispatched his retainer Ichiki Hirotsuwa to the Ryukyu Islands to discuss with the Frenchmen resident there the possibility of buying ships and guns from France and of sending Satsuma and Ryukyu students on *ryūgaku* (study abroad) to England or

86. Toyoda, *Kyōikushi,* I, 211.
87. KSM, p. 14.
88. Toyoda, *Kyōikushi,* I, 217. The Kaiseijo is described in ibid., p. 211. The only date we have for the opening of this institution is the year 1864. It seems unlikely therefore that Mori spent more than a few months in it.
89. Ibid., I, 215.

France.[90] That project died with the daimyo, but the idea of dispatching young men to Europe was revived by Godai Tomoatsu and by Terajima Munenori, who had been taken prisoner on a British warship prior to the battle of Kagoshima Bay and, walking into the jaws of the lion, had emerged thoroughly impressed with the sharpness of his teeth.[91] Godai's memorial[92] of late spring 1864 also called for the purchase of warships, cannon, rifles, and sugar-processing machinery, all to be financed by a lively Satsuma-China trade—avoiding the middlemen at Osaka and shipping the sugar produce of the Ryukyus and the surplus grains of the Japan Sea side of Honshu direct to Shanghai in Satsuma bottoms.

Godai's arguments carried the day, and on 13 February 1865 (18 I Keiō 1) fourteen young men, ten of them from the Kaiseijo, were selected for study in England and France. Two days later, on 15 February 1865, after securing his parents' permission, Mori found himself traveling under an assumed name to Hashima, a small fishing village on Satsuma's East China Sea coast, where his party was to go into hiding for two months while awaiting rendezvous with a British steamer out of Nagasaki. Travel outside Japan was still forbidden under penalty of death, and the students had all agreed to plead, in the event of capture, that they were simply contemplating *dappan* (flight from the han), in itself a serious offense. Leaving behind the rumor that they were bound for the offshore islands on government business, they took cover in the home of Fujisaki Ryūsuke, where both Yūjo and Genshirō joined the farewell festivities.

Godai meanwhile had gone to Nagasaki to arrange with Thomas Glover & Co. for appropriate transportation. On 15 April 1865 (20 III Keiō 1) Godai and Terajima boarded the S. S. *Australian* at Nagasaki together with their interpreter, Hori Takayuki, and Ryle Holme of Glover & Co., who had been assigned to chaperone the group all the way to London. On the morning of the eighteenth the *Australian,* diverted from its scheduled course, put in at Hashima, took on the remainder of the party, and set its course for Hong Kong.[93]

Mori left with the blessing of his parents, and the rigors of his Gōjū upbringing gave additional assurance that he would be equal

90. Ibid., I, 216.
91. *Sappan kaigunshi,* comp. Kōshaku Shimazuke Henshūjo, 3 vols. (Kagoshima, 1928), II, 936–939.
92. Ibid., II, 876–886, cites Godai Tomoatsu, "Joshinsho" (Memorial), May or June 1864.
93. OTM, pp. 14–15.

to any of the "many dangers" alluded to by his poetic father. Much of Mori's intellectual and spiritual preparation, indeed, was not different from, but simply better than, that of the average young samurai of his day—better, that is, in terms of the traditional pattern itself. For instance, the exceptionally high standards of performance and of ethical conduct which Mori set for himself, and for others, were largely derived from a typically exacting Satsuma mother, four typically solicitous elder brothers, and a neighborhood fraternity which traced its inspiration to the "heroic," pre-Edo, "Warring States" period. The respect for education which permeated the Zōshikan and which was reinforced by the presence of scholars in the family and among the closest neighbors was entirely within the scope of Confucian tradition, as was also Nariakira's call for scholarship that was politically aware and public-service minded. Yūjo's imperial sentiments and Hayashi Shihei's strident warnings, finally, must have combined to create (within entirely traditional intellectual terms) some political and strategic awareness of Japan as a national entity, set against other national entities and beset by internal dissensions it could ill afford.

If there was an exceptional factor in Mori's early background, it might best be described as a capacity for independence, or nonconformity, all the more remarkable for the highly conformist soil in which it had grown. Mori's pluck and initiative in undertaking the secret study of English provided the first evidence of this trait. Temperamentally, Mori's nonconformity was something he owed his parents, themselves remembered as "eccentrics." In intellectual terms, he owed it to the tolerant attitude of his father, to the somewhat isolated and intellectually oriented nature (very probably) of the Jōgatani Gōjū, and to the propinquity only five houses down the road of Satsuma's indefatigable advocate of *kaikoku,* or "opening the country," Godai Tomoatsu.

What could not have been predicted from Mori's Satsuma upbringing was the extent to which he eventually would go in seeing the West in, and accepting the West on, its own terms. Hayashi, Nariakira, and Godai—Mori's chief points of reference in matters barbarian—represented, it is true, a hopeful progression from contemptuous hostility, through a respectful admiration of technology to an insistent call for study of Western civilization in general. All three viewpoints, however, remained variations on the same basic theme of *fukoku kyōhei.* Would Mori ever go beyond this to a more disinterested, a less instrumental, appreciation of the West? Only time would tell. The smell of ship's tar and gunpowder must have hung rather heavily over the Kaiseijo where Mori had spent his pre-departure months. As an intellectual, much less a personal experience, Western culture was a seed yet to be planted. The ground lay fertile perhaps, but certainly fallow. The real education of Mori Arinori had just begun.

Two   1865–1866

AWAKENING
TO THE WEST

Nihon no unda seiyōjin—"a Westerner born of Japan," or "Japan's Western offspring"—was the way an intimate friend, Itō Hirobumi, would remember Mori. Hayashi Takeji, too, has described Mori as being "more profoundly Western than any other leading figure of his time," as "very un-Japanese in the structure of his spirit and character," and as "a man who, though a product of his own age, lived from start to finish as an anomaly to his own society and times."[1] There is little doubt that most Japanese at the time would have endorsed Itō's characterization, though the majority of them, again, probably would have intended it as an epithet of scorn rather than as a friendly compliment. In whatever he did, Mori managed to impress himself upon the popular mind of his age as one of the most outstanding (or outrageous) examples of a new breed of Western-educated and Western-oriented Japanese.

Of the forty-one years of his life, Mori would spend nearly a decade resident in the West, in three periods: 1865–68, 1871–73, and 1880–84. His "birth" as a "Westerner," to continue the Itō metaphor, dates from the first of these periods, and it is here that we must seek for the roots of his distinctive brand of westernism.

1. Hayashi Takeji, "Kindai kyōiku kōsō to Mori Arinori" in *Chūō kōron*, August 1962, p. 208; Hayashi Takeji, "Bakumatsu no kaigai ryūgakusei" (Overseas students in the Bakumatsu period), part I, *Nichibei fōramu*, January 1964, p. 40.

Although the second and third periods represent a significant new intake of ideology and program, the mode in which Mori perceived and approached the West, the unusual spiritual structure of which Hayashi speaks, the psychology in short of Mori-as-Westerner, takes its set from the three years 1865–68.

Mori turned eighteen two months after arrival in London and returned to Japan just short of his twenty-first birthday. Leaving aside two members of the party who were still to all intents and purposes children, Mori was the youngest of the group of Satsuma students, whose median age at the time of departure was twenty-two. The West made its initial impact upon him during those transitional years of late adolescence when the rational, critical faculties of the adult are for the most part in place, without having yet entirely dislodged the impressionability of the child. Had Mori undertaken this voyage a few years later, he might no longer have possessed the flexibility to be deeply moved by new things; had he traveled but two years sooner, it is questionable whether he would have been able to make any of his impressions stick at all. As it was, he proved capable both of an immediate, emotional response to his new environment and of the reflection required to give those responses coherent intellectual shape.

These would be the "college years" by today's reckoning. There was very little, however, of the "collegiate" that we would recognize in them. In terms of contemporary Satsuma upbringing, Mori already had left adolescence behind, and at least some of the seriousness of purpose which he and his colleagues displayed must be attributed simply to a self-awareness as adults rather than to a more specific sense of political trust and mission. Their streak of youthfulness derives less from their ages than from the fact that, unlike later generations of Japanese students abroad, they were little prepared for what awaited them. Delightfully unfeigned both in their enthusiasms and in their aversions, they were all but totally untutored in their responses to the West.

The summers of 1866 and 1867 were watersheds which divided Mori's first voyage abroad into three distinct phases of approximately one year's length. From arrival in London in June 1865 through the excursion to Russia in August–September 1866 we have a year of regulated scholarly enterprise, highlighted by a good deal of sightseeing and characterized by an eager receptivity to the West. We also have much reflection, generally adverse, upon the current condition of Japan. The series of ten intimate letters written home between 7 August 1865 and 26 July 1866 to his brother Yokoyama Yasutake (formerly Genshirō), and the

"Kōro kikō" (Journal of a voyage to Russia), kept from 1 August through 10 September 1866, provide us with the lengthiest and most intimate swatch of autobiographical material to be encountered anywhere in Mori's entire career. A puzzling silence then ensues for the second year in London, although the students' remarkable memorial of 10 July 1867, with its virulent denunciations of the West, helps us guess what had gone on in the interim, and why. For the third year, August 1867–June 1868, there is a shift of scene to America and with it a transfer of focus from secular and public issues to concerns of a more specifically religious and personal nature. Unfortunately, for what was possibly in spiritual terms the most critical year of Mori's life, we are forced to rely, save for his farewell letter of 17 June 1868, on the disappointingly general observations of Laurence Oliphant in letters to William Francis Cowper and on a reconstruction of Mori's probable environment from a variety of Western sources.

BRITAIN AND RUSSIA: THE WEST OBSERVED

Heading the Satsuma mission to Europe were four han officials who, like their fourteen student charges, were young, were camouflaged by aliases the duration of their journey, and were in terms of future career a curious company of the well known and the totally forgotten. Niiro Keibu (alias Ishigaki Einosuke), 33, who ranked as an *ōmetsuke* (chief inspector) and led the group as a whole, ended his days an obscure provincial judge in Kagoshima. And few save art historians recall the name of his deputy, Machida Hisanari (Ueno Ryōtarō), 27, who left the principalship of the Kagoshima Kaiseijo to supervise the accompanying students, and later became the first curator of the Imperial Museum at Ueno. By contrast Godai Tomoatsu (Seki Kenzō), 29, and Terajima Munenori (Izumi Senzō), 33, both loom large in the industrial and diplomatic annals of Meiji Japan. Godai, in 1865 an officer in the Satsuma navy, had joined the mission in order to investigate manufacturing and commerce in Western Europe, and one day would found both the Osaka Chamber of Commerce and the Osaka Higher Commercial School. Terajima, commonly known before the Restoration as Matsuki Kōan, had been a teacher of medicine at the Edo Kaiseijo. In charge of the mission's diplomatic negotiations with the British, he was destined to distinguish himself in later years as foreign minister of Japan and as envoy to Washington and London.

The students who eventually made the pages of history were those five who became Mori's most intimate companions and who crossed to America with him in the summer of 1867. Yoshida Kiyonari (alias Nagai Iosuke), 20, who was trained in Dutch at the Kagoshima Kaiseijo and joined Mori in the study of naval surveying, later became envoy to Washington, vice foreign minister and vice minister of agriculture and commerce. Matsumura Junzō, 23, who dropped his original name of Ichiki Kanjurō in favor of his alias, had a similar background and assignment, and would serve as vice admiral and commander of the imperial fleet off Kagoshima during the Satsuma Rebellion. Samejima Naonobu (Noda Chūbei), 20, had, like Mori, been trained in English at the Kaiseijo but was assigned to literature and would serve later as Japanese minister at London, Berlin, and Paris. Hatakeyama Yoshinari (Sugiura Kōzō), 22, is remembered as the principal of the Daigaku Nankō, the successor of the Edo Kaiseijo, which in 1877 became part of the new Tokyo University. At this time, however, his mind was on land warfare, and he had recently been a *koshōgumi bangashira,* or head of one of the Kagoshima guard brigades. Nagasawa Kanaye, 12, was destined to live out his life in the United States as a member of the Thomas Lake Harris religious community at Santa Rosa, California. Born Isonaga Hikosuke, he also retained his alias, and as the youngest of the group was without specific assignment.

The eight remaining students have to all intents and purposes been lost to posterity. Two of them with medical training, Nakamura Sōken, 24, and Tanaka Seisu, 22, left the group at London to pursue their studies in French schools. Of the six who studied in London and returned to Japan directly in the summer of 1867, three had been trained in Dutch and were assigned to naval studies: Takami Yaichi, 30, Tōgō Ainoshin, 22, and Machida Shinjirō, 18. Murahashi Naoe, 22, and Nagoshi Heima, 20, had been *koshōgumi bangashira* and were, like Hatakeyama, set to study land warfare, while young Machida Kiyozō, 14, remained unassigned.[2] A Japanese interpreter, Hori Takayuki, and an English guide and assistant by name of Ryle Holme rounded out the party of twenty.

Matsumura Junzō's "Yōkō nikki" (Diary of a voyage to the West),[3] which covers the sea voyage via Hongkong, Singapore, Penang, Bombay, Aden, Suez, Cairo, Alexandria, Malta, and

2. *Sappan kaigunshi,* comp. Kōshaku Shimazuke Henshūjo (Kagoshima, 1928), II, 896–898.
3. Ibid., II, 918–933, has the complete text of Matsumura Junzō, "Yōkō nikki" (Diary of a voyage to the West).

Gibraltar to Southhampton, serves to remind us just how unprepared these Kagoshima youths were even for the most commonplace accoutrements of Western living, which might not quite have so startled residents of the Nagasaki or Edo areas.

Swords were packed away in boxes as soon as the party had boarded ship. On the fourth day out, after recovery from a universal bout of seasickness, those whose hair had grown long at Hashima had it shorn to a respectable length, "all for the sake of country"; and debarkation in Hongkong was delayed three days while tailors cut and stitched a wardrobe befitting the well-dressed mid-Victorian gentleman. Of great interest here were the street lamps, which made "the night as bright as day" and which, viewed from the ship's deck, reminded Matsumura of the "fireflies of summer." A visit to a shipyard, however, presented no novelty: "small enough, and very similar to what we have at the Shūseikan." The effusive hugging and kissing that marked the farewells between husbands and wives and parents and children at the Singapore docks left the young Japanese dumbfounded and may well have given them their first inkling of a radically different set of intrafamily relations from those to which they had been accustomed: "Leave-taking among Westerners is an extremely ardent affair . . . They seem scarcely able to endure their intense feeling at being separated from one another. As the moment of parting approaches, the husband takes leave of his wife by sipping at her mouth. It looks ever so much more poignant than our manner of leave-taking . . . and parents take leave of their children in precisely the same fashion. We were struck with wonder at this procedure, which we had never witnessed before.[4]

Matsumura's log deals mostly, however, with Asia and Asians; for the long, leisurely swing along the classical World Tour route had left the Japanese with images, however fleeting, of at least four great non-Occidental cultures (the Chinese, the Southeast Asian, the Indian, and the Islamic) before bringing them their first impressions of Europe. The account is a catalog of exotica, from pineapples and camels to the strange *furoshiki* with which the Moslem women veil their faces: all without a shred of identification with, or Asiatic fellow-feeling for, the "natives," on whom Matsumura is more often than not looking down, quite literally, from the deck of a steamer or from his sightseeing carriage. The Chinese are the "barbarians' menials," busily rowing boats or rushing around the streets on their masters' errands. The Malays

4. *Kaigunshi*, II, 923.

are a black, naked people who dive for coins at ship's side, and the blackness and the nakedness become increasingly marked, along with the very uncomfortable heat, as one progresses westward across the Indian Ocean. The boatmen who ferry them ashore in a dugout canoe at Galle, Ceylon, either have their "heads shaven like bonzes, or wear their hair wildly dishevelled like a runaway from home; they are born black and are exceedingly mean in appearance." By Aden, Matsumura was thoroughly homesick, but excitement picked up again with the train which whisked the party at 35 m.p.h., "fast as the wind," from Suez to Cairo, and the telegraph which relayed luncheon orders ahead to the halfway station en route to Alexandria.

Fortifications at all points along the route were noted with interest and often admiration, and nowhere more so than at Malta, where the Japanese first touched European soil. Godai would recall in a letter to the home government half a year later: "More than half of our number had been leading instigators of antiforeign sentiment, but when they went ashore at Malta in the Mediterranean and saw for the first time the enlightened progress and mighty power of Europe, they awoke at once to their own benightedness and were overcome with shame and regret at the foolish prejudices they had held up to that time."[5] Upon arrival in London on 21 June 1865, sixty-six days out of Hashima, they went into the Langham at a pound per person per day.[6] The following morning the party save for Niiro and interpreter Hori moved to an apartment house in Bayswater, hired a maid, and rented the entire sixth floor. Holme had suggested that they live together and invite in tutors to instruct the group as a whole.[7] When this proved too expensive, the students were relocated, by pairs, in the private homes of various professors of the University of London to receive individual tutorial, and especially training in the English language, in preparation for matriculation in University College, Gower Street, at the coming Michaelmas term. Mori and Takami were placed with a Dr. Green of the chemistry department; Matsumura and Nagoshi with a Dr. Davis of mathematics; Tōgō and Machida Shinjirō with a professor of French; Yoshida and Hatakeyama with a gentleman in literature; Machida Kiyozō and Samejima with someone in chemistry; and Murahashi with an unspecified party. Tanaka and Nakamura proceeded to

5. Ibid., II, 946, quoting letter from Godai Tomoatsu to Katsura Uemon, 29 Nov. 1865 (12 X Keiō 1).
6. Ibid., II, 933.
7. KSM, p. 16.

Paris, while Nagasawa, too young for college, was sent to the Thomas Glover home at Aberdeen. Machida Hisanari, in direct charge of the students, and Terajima, who remained in close touch with them, stayed on in hotels, as did the more peripatetic Godai, Niiro, and Hori.[8]

In overall charge of arrangements for housing and tutorial was Professor Alexander H. Williamson of the chemistry department, president of the Royal Chemical Society and dean of British chemistry, who had similarly assisted Itō Hirobumi and Inoue Kaoru of Chōshū in 1863. Glover had been able to enlist the services of Williamson through a mutual friend, Laurence Oliphant, who had served briefly as first secretary under Rutherford Alcock at the Edo legation during 1861 and had just that July been elected Member of Parliament for Stirling burghs.

The training of the students was one of three central functions of the Satsuma expedition: academic, economic, and diplomatic. The latter two, although the special assignment of Godai and Terajima respectively and a considerable story in themselves, deserve brief mention, inasmuch as they helped round out the motivational horizons of the group as a whole. Godai Tomoatsu, in keeping with his original memorial, undertook between September and December 1865 an extensive tour of the manufacturing districts of Britain, Belgium, Holland, Germany, and France in the company of Niiro, Hori, and Holme. The students as a group went along on some of his observation tours in southern England. They inspected factories, tested and priced machinery, and placed orders.[9] The negotiations in Brussels with the Belgian entrepreneur

8. *Kaigunshi,* II, 900.

9. The visits of the "three senior members of the party" and Holme to the Brocklehurst silkspinning plant at Macclesfield on 19 August 1865 and to the copper mines at Alderley on 9 September 1865 were covered in detail in the 25 August 1865 and 16 September 1865 issues, respectively, of the *London and China Telegraph.* At the former, the largest plant of its type in the world, "they were greatly surprised at the ingenuity and talent evinced in the waste spinning department . . . and on entering a large power-loom shed, containing upwards of five hundred steam looms at full work, their astonishment was undisguised, and their exclamations of gratification frequent. Throughout the day the interest of the party never had time to flag for an instant." At Alderley they "made a minute inspection of the works above ground," and then proceeded into the galleries which had been "illuminated *al giorno*" for them. A half-mile down, "at this the culminating point of interest, the Japanese could be seen gliding with alacrity into the different lodes or subsidiary galleries from which the copper stone is daily being extracted in large quantities." At the "sumptuous repast" which followed, the Japanese "handled their knives and forks and ate and drank like men who had never in their lives done otherwise."

Count Descantons de Montblanc, Baron of Ingelmuenster, for the establishment of a joint trading company proved in the end abortive, but did provide an index to Godai's ambitious program for Satsuma and, by extension, for Japan. His plans included the direct importation, or local construction with foreign technical assistance, of steamships and ironclads, railways and telegraph, mines and arsenals, and plants for the manufacture of silk thread, cotton cloth, tea, wax, and tobacco.[10]

Godai characterizes himself in his own correspondence as an exponent of *fukoku kyōhei*. He is unmistakably concerned with national power. In one sentence he warns of steady Western encirclement: "We shall end up having to lick their boots"; while in the next he predicts that if his recommendations are followed Japan in less than a decade will be able to "bestride Asia." The indispensable prerequisites for national power, however, are the "dispelling of ignorance" and the "opening of the country."[11] *Fukoku kyōhei*, Godai notes, is the central policy of all the nations of Europe, and they achieve it by balancing their budgets carefully; by extending political justice to all without respect to social class; by listening to good advice; by promoting talent regardless of personal feelings and appointing people to positions for which they are best equipped; and by maximizing human resources through the establishment of hospitals, orphanages, institutes for the deaf and blind and insane, and schools to cover every field of human endeavor. France he praised for her superb educational system; England for the fairest laws and the most benevolent political system in the world; while the foundations of wealth and military power, he insists, are "commerce" and "industry."[12]

There are echoes of these viewpoints in Mori's letters home, and even though many of the group may have been arriving at similar conclusions simultaneously, it seems highly probable that Godai, the old family friend and neighbor, would continue to have had considerable influence on Mori during the first half year in London. The great gulf between Godai's philosophy and a narrower concept of national power originally held by Yoshida Kiyonari, became clear during the former's successful efforts in "converting" the latter: "When Yoshida Kiyonari left Japan he was

10. Japan's first cotton-carding plant, purchased by Godai at Manchester, was subsequently set up at the Shūseikan.
11. *Kaigunshi*, II, 945 quoting letter from Godai Tomoatsu to Katsura Uemon, 29 Nov. 1865 (12 X Keiō 1).
12. Ibid., II, quoting on p. 945 a letter from Godai Tomoatsu to Katsura Uemon, 29 Nov. 1865 (12 X Keiō 1), and on p. 949 a letter from Godai Tomoatsu to Nomura Sōshichi, 28 Dec. 1865 (11 XI Keiō 1).

one of the most outspoken of the group that was all for expelling and subduing the barbarians. That was what he hoped to accomplish by procuring a lot of ships and cannon and cramming down his naval science, all in great haste. A short time after arrival in England, however, he switched completely around to the 'national wealth' (*fukoku*) viewpoint. He came to realize that wealth could not be created without machines (*kikai*) of all types, and suggested that he study mechanical engineering. To this I agreed."[13] The distinction between (mere) cannon and "machines of all types," ostensibly a quibble over means, actually involved, for some of the party at least, a reorientation so drastic as to remind one that, beyond a certain point, means do tend to define, or redefine, their own ends.

Unlike later generations of Japanese students abroad, however, the Satsuma youngsters conceived of themselves less as technologists, or specialists, than as generalists preparing for service which would probably be, in the broadest sense of the term, political.[14] They followed events in Japan with keen interest, often through the pages of the *London and China Telegraph*,[15] as Terajima Munenori worked quietly and effectively over a period of nine months to nudge the foreign office into active support of Satsuma and the imperial party. Both the arguments communicated to, and the hopes placed upon, the British government probably were a common topic of discussion among the students, with whom Terajima maintained regular contact while in London.[16]

On 28 July 1865, a bare month after arrival in England, Terajima had been able, through the good offices of Laurence Oliphant, to present his case to Sir Austen Henry Layard, under secretary of state for foreign affairs. The British memorandum of the discussion noted that Terajima's party had come "for the purpose of seeing the institutions, habits and manufactures of England"; that they had expressed the hope that by training the students "their country may in time become like England"; that they were "anxious to establish a direct trade by opening a port in the Loochew Islands," but that their daimyo was "unable to act himself lest he should involve himself in trouble with the Tycoon's government";

---

13. Ibid., II, 952, quoting letter from Godai Tomoatsu to Nomura Sōshichi, 25 Dec. 1865 (8 XI Keiō 1).
14. Hayashi, "Ryūgakusei," part IV, *Nichibei fōramu*, June 1964, p. 73.
15. HOP, letter from Laurence Oliphant to William F. Cowper, 29 Dec. 1867.
16. *Kaigunshi*, II, 940, quoting Terajima Munenori, "Rirekisho" (A summary of my career).

that they accordingly hoped that Her Majesty's Government would "be enabled ere long to move in the matter"; and that they had presented a cup, this being "by Japanese custom a token of restitution of good feelings after having been on unfriendly terms."[17]

Prime Minister Palmerston was disinclined toward new adventures in the Far East. The shogunal mission under Shibata Masanaka which visited England in December 1865 received full diplomatic honors, and at their request the British government turned down the applications of Matsumura and several of his colleagues (probably including Mori) for admission to the Royal Naval College at Greenwich.[18] Palmerston, however, died in October 1865 and was succeeded by Russell, who was Laurence Oliphant's political patron and in Godai's own estimate a man "of active disposition."[19] Russell was himself replaced at the Foreign Office by Clarendon. Sometime in mid-March 1866 Terajima found occasion to press upon Oliphant the following four points: (1) that the various han were attempting to restore the treaty-making power to the emperor; (2) that attacks upon foreigners though deplorable in themselves were part of a deliberate attempt to disrupt, and thereby display the ineffectiveness of, Bakufu diplomacy, and should be viewed primarily as acts of rebellion against the Bakufu; (3) that the various han were eager for foreign trade but that the Bakufu prevented them from engaging in it; (4) and that if Britain were to assist in restoring full sovereignty, including the treaty-making function, to the imperial house, it would redound to the profit of both countries. Oliphant, in enthusiastic agreement, offered to escort Terajima personally to the Foreign Office and to do

17. PRO. Japan/General Correspondence, FO-46-61, Foreign Office Memorandum, 28 July 1865, entitled "Interview with Prince of Satsuma's Officers." As Hayashi Takeji has pointed out in "Ryūgakusei," part IV, pp. 66–67, this very early meeting in July 1865 between the British and Satsuma officials, unlike their meetings in March and April 1866, is not mentioned in the authoritative diplomatic history texts for the period. There is in the British Museum, Manuscripts Division, Layard Papers, a letter from Oliphant to Layard also dated 28 July 1865, introducing the Satsuma representatives as gentlemen "most intelligent and worthy of attention." Oliphant argues that "as long as the treaty ports are confined to Imperial territory there will be dissatisfaction among the Daimios who are now becoming anxious to derive some share of the advantage which they see is accruing to the government of the Tycoon," and asks whether the latter might not "be given to understand through Parkes that it would be for his interest to allow some Ports to be opened in Daimios' territory."
18. *Kaigunshi*, II, 904.
19. Ibid., II, 949, quoting letter from Godai Tomoatsu to Nomura Sōshichi, 28 Dec. 1865 (11 XI Keiō 1).

the talking himself. An interview with Clarendon was arranged for the following day, and was followed by a second session in April. Oliphant in the interim brought the issue wide attention through two speeches in Parliament, and on 26 April 1866 confidential instructions went out to Parkes in Japan to explore the possibility of an active alignment with the anti-Bakufu forces.[20] Terajima, his own mission accomplished, left London for Japan on 7 May. Godai and Niiro had already started for home that January.[21]

A perceptive characterization of the students left behind with Machida Hisanari in London comes from the pen of F. V. Dickins, the biographer of Sir Harry Parkes, writing to Ernest Satow in reminiscence in 1905: "When I was home in '66 and '67, I came into contact with the Satsuma and Chōshū students then in London. They came constantly to my lodgings in Wimbledon, and with some of them I read a great deal. For instance I went right through Hawley's book and some epitome of Jomini. None of the men (some rose to high office later) showed any particular capacity, but most of them displayed great qualities of character, indomitable perseverance and application and a curious intensity of desire to acquire accurate knowledge with a practical view."[22]

20. Terajima gives his own account of the negotiations in his "Rirekisho" (A summary of my career) in *Kaigunshi*, II, 940–941. Ishii Takashi in *Meiji ishin no kokusaiteki kankyō* (Tokyo, 1960), chapter IV, dates the first meeting between Terajima and Clarendon a few days before 25 March 1866, the second meeting sometime before the dispatch of Parkes' orders. Parkes on 29 May 1866 had sent the foreign office a memorandum commenting on a letter written by Oliphant to Clarendon on 25 March 1866 in promotion of the Satsuma viewpoint. (PRO, Japan/General Correspondence, FO-46-68, memorandum of Harry Parkes to foreign office). Parkes referred to the mutual jealousies of the daimyos, questioned how far Terajima represented their views or even those of his own chief, pointed out that he for his part was still treating exclusively with the Bakufu, expressed little hope for the establishment of a daimyo council on Bakufu initiative (this having been one of Oliphant's pet proposals), warned that Satsuma had its own motives in supporting the emperor and that any British initiative in the imperial question would poison relations with Edo, and insisted that the daimyos be held to the letter of treaties already concluded, particularly to the agreement for the opening of new ports. Orders overriding Parkes' scruples, however, were already in the mail (British Museum, Manuscripts Division, Layard Papers, Letter from Foreign Office to Harry Parkes, 26 April 1866). The persistent initiative of Terajima and the favorable intervention of Oliphant at this juncture were critical in determining the future course of Anglo-Japanese relations, and of the Restoration itself.

21. *Kaigunshi*, II, 942.

22. PRO, Satow Papers, PRO-30-33-11-4, letter from F. V. Dickins to Ernest Satow, 28 March 1905.

Antoine Henri Baron Jomini (1779–1869) was one of the foremost military theorists of the day and an authority on the Napoleonic and Crimean wars who had been read very closely on tactics by the Civil War generals in the United States. The "epitome" referred to may well have been some English translation of his most popular work, *Un précis de l'art de la guerre* (A summary of the art of war; 1836). The most likely candidate for "Hawley's book" would seem to be John Hugh Hawley's *A First Course of English Composition* (1865).[23] And here we have in a nutshell the ethos of the group in its first London year: patriotic in motivation, practical in orientation, and in terms academic mere beginners.

The curriculum originally assigned by the Satsuma government had an unmistakable military bias: naval surveying for Mori, Matsumura, Yoshida, and Takami; naval engineering for Tōgō and Machida Shinjirō; land warfare for Hatakeyama, Murahashi, and Nagoshi; and chemistry, medicine, and literature for Nakamura, Tanaka, and Samejima respectively. Mori concentrated on mathematics, for which he had a marked flair, covering the ground from simple arithmetic to spherical trigonometry in two years. The students, however, fired by a curiosity about Western culture in general, were quick to break the confines of their original study objectives in favor of a more general education. Mori went on to physics, chemistry, and history,[24] and the only student to see his original program through to completion was the future vice admiral, Matsumura.[25]

Much, perhaps the most significant part, of their education falls properly under the heading of sightseeing. This they went at avidly, taking in churches, hospitals, schools, soup kitchens, mines, spinning mills, ordnance factories. Hatakeyama sought out the neighborhood gunsmith; Matsumura was overawed by the company of so many famous men—though all in wax—at Madame Tussaud's; Yoshida attended Parliament frequently and became a lifetime admirer of Gladstone; and several of them went down together to Dover for the Grand Maneuvers.[26] There were visits to the naval

23. The British Museum Catalogue shows two other possible but far less probable entries: Frederick Hawley, *The Royal Family of England* (London, 1851) and Richard M. Hawley, *Genuine Christianity Contrasted with Its Corruptions, with Its Idolatry, and with the Religion of Mahomet* (Edinburgh, 1839).
24. KSM, p. 16.
25. *Kaigunshi*, II, 943.
26. These are the recollections of Nakai Hiroshi in his *Kōkai Shinsetsu* (New light from across the seas), quoted in Hayashi, "Ryūgakusei," part IV, p. 69. Nakai, a young protégé of Gotō Shōjirō, saw a good deal of the

"Dock and Victualling Yards" at Portsmouth,[27] and (with permission to make sketches) to the small arms factory at Enfield and the Arsenal at Woolwich.[28] The bent for the practical alluded to by Dickins was amply demonstrated during a visit to the Britannia Iron Works at Bedford: "The Japanese, whose remarkable physique caused considerable interest, the Mongolian type being very striking, took great interest in the machinery and various processes in operation at these important works, and seemed astonishingly quick in comprehending the various details. They appeared unwilling to leave the works, but steam having been got up in one of the new steam-ploughing engines, about 15 of the Japanese crowded on to it wherever they could get a footing, and it was highly amusing to see with what delight they travelled in all directions over the extensive quadrangle of the works ... A reaping machine which was at work was quickly handled, and cleverly managed by them."[29]

Of the daily routine, very little is conveyed in Mori's letters to his brother, except to assure Yokoyama that he has resumed a physical-fitness regimen, evidently neglected during the voyage and the early months of adjustment. He wrote on 19 September 1865: "I too have been giving thought recently to the matter of self-discipline and have been paying particular attention to bodily hygiene. Upon awaking each morning I immediately take a cold bath, cleansing my entire frame. I am building up my robustness by means of nutritious food, of course, and also by setting apart a full hour at a fixed time each day for various kinds of physical exercise, including rope climbing and long walks. Any interruption of this routine even for one day sets me ill at ease."[30]

Our greatest fund of diurnal detail on Mori is to be found rather in the "Kōro kikō."[31] In accordance with the practice of British university students, Mori explains in his prolog, he and

---

Satsuma students while they were in London in 1866–1867. For Yoshida's interest in Parliament see also Charles Lanman, *Japan: Its Leading Men* (Boston, 1886), p. 246.

27. PRO, Japan/General Correspondence, FO-46-74, note from admiralty to foreign office, 29 March 1866, granting permission for the visit.

28. Ibid., FO-46-74, letter from A. H. Layard to W. Hammond, 11 April 1866, forwarding admission cards and permission to make sketches.

29. *The Times* (London), 2 Aug. 1865.

30. KKM, p. 14.

31. Pending the publication of volume 2 of the *Mori Arinori Zenshū*, the most legible reprint of the "Kōro kikō" is to be found in Ōkubo Toshiaki, ed., *Meiji keimō shisō shū* (Tokyo, 1967), volume 3 of Chikuma Shobō, compilers, *Meiji bungaku zenshū*. In the discussion which follows entries will be referred to by date rather than by page number.

Matsumura determined to undertake a trip during the summer recess of 1866 which would serve both as a break from, and as a supplement to, their formal studies. A bit more conscience-stricken than the others about their relative neglect of naval science, they concluded that Russia was sufficiently distant for a long sea voyage and were also eager to meet (and proselytize for the imperial cause) the Bakufu students who had recently been sent to the Russian capital. They accordingly apprenticed themselves as deck hands on the *George & Emily* (350 Registered Tons), a three-masted sailing barque carrying coal from Newcastle to Kronstadt.

Making the coastal run from London to Newcastle on 1–2 August 1866, Mori and Matsumura spent six impatient days sightseeing in the Newcastle-Tynemouth area while their vessel loaded. Departure etiquette, so puzzling in Singapore, was apparently still something of a novelty when anchor finally was weighed on the eighth: "We took our leave from the ship's owner and dozens of the captain's friends who had come to see us off. As a distance of approximately one *chō* [119 yards] was opened between us, the captain and all hands lined up on deck and raised a 'hurrah'—an English expression of congratulations—towards the farewell party. Then they too lined up and shouted back the same. This exchange was repeated three times, as they slipped out of sight in the west. The customs of foreign countries have their delightful points too."

That Mori had lost his sea legs, yet not his genuine feeling for the sea, is clear from the passage which immediately follows:

> No sooner had we turned our prow towards the east than a stiff breeze came up out of the southwest. Our vessel shot along exultantly, like an arrow, thirty miles, forty miles out onto the deep. Now the wind came on full strength, and as far as the eye could wander over the boundless ocean, stretched a wide silvery world of whitecaps thrusting after the firmament. No doubt because I had not been at sea for over a year, my heart gradually began to flutter and my stomach and head started to turn 'round and 'round together. My legs lost their firm footing. I started to totter and fall, until at last cowardice got the better of me and I found myself heading for the cabin where I tumbled down on my berth and fell into a deep sleep, oblivious to the passing of night and day, beholding nothing but my dreams. 9 August: Slept out the entire day without once awaking.

By 12 August they were in the Kattegat, and, spirits restored, the two Japanese settled down to their sailors' training. "We did not, however," Mori confesses, "even know the name of the mast, so we had to start by learning the proper terms for everything. Luckily for us the captain and crew were most helpful and polite."

Mori had yet to master the basic rudiments of navigation, as shown by his fascinated introduction to the art of tacking against their first head wind, which came up in the Gulf of Finland on the eighteenth: "No matter how contrary or strong the wind, at least two to three *ri* [4 to 6 miles] per hour can be made by altering course freely, throwing the sails out first to starboard and then to port, proceeding at an angle to the wind and employing a whole bag of other tricks. What a perilous procedure this would be with one of our native vessels!" That the whole world indeed was still an object of exciting new discovery shows in Mori's entry for 19 August: "Shortly after noon I searched for land in all four directions, but could find none. Then by chance I climbed up one of the masts, and was amazed to make out the coast of Finland—a mere hair's breadth of green above the watery horizon—at a distance of about eighteen miles. I shouted out to Matsumura: 'Come here! Come here! Here's our first proof that the earth is round: while I was standing down there on deck I couldn't see a thing; but land is distinctly visible from up here. This is proof that the surface of the sea is curved; and if that's curved, why then so is the whole earth!' Matsumura came right on up and exclaimed: 'It's fantastic—it's just the way you say—our first real proof!' "

Upon arrival at Kronstadt on the twenty-third, Mori delivered himself of an elaborate report on the habor fortifications worthy of a naval attaché. In the "Kōro kikō" Mori reveals a meticulous eye for detail, jotting down fact after fact—dimensions, materials used, construction time, costs converted to Japanese monetary units—concerning such diverse items as the High Level Bridge at Newcastle, the breakwaters at Tynemouth, and the churches, palaces, parks, and museums of St. Petersburg. Even the peculiar wooden and metal street pavements of the Russian capital are exhaustively described, with sketches attached. From their arrival in the capital on the twenty-fourth until their departure for England on 3 September, the two Japanese stayed at the Hotel de France. Oliphant had given them a letter of introduction to the British ambassador,[32] but their chief custodian and guide seems to have been a wealthy resident English merchant by name of Morgan.

That very first evening they sought out the six Bakufu students (Yamanouchi Sakuzaemon, Ogata Jōjirō, Ozawa Seijirō, Ichikawa

---

32. *Kaigunshi,* II, 905.

Bunkichi, Ōtsuki Hikogorō, and Tanaka Jirō), and dropped in unannounced. The Bakufu six were overjoyed to see the Satsuma two, eager to discuss national affairs, and unexpectedly sympathetic in political view. "Fortunately," Mori wrote, "they lacked the Kantō spirit," and he struck up an immediate and ebullient friendship with Yamanouchi, who turned out to be a thoroughgoing loyalist and extremely well versed in the writings of Motoori Norinaga. The six were most unhappy with their situation: no one, they complained, ever came to Russia to learn anything (whatever the Russians had that was worth learning about having been borrowed elsewhere); the language was monstrously difficult and of no utility outside Russia itself, and the climate was all but unbearable. They attached themselves gladly to the two, calling in a group that same evening on Tachibana Kōsai, a former retainer of Tōtōmi han who had persuaded Admiral Putiatin to take him on board at Izu in 1854 and now worked as a translator in the foreign ministry. The following evening they treated their visitors to a Japanese dinner and were with them on and off throughout their stay.

On the twenty-eighth Mori and Matsumura viewed the American "turret ship," the "most powerful warship in the world" (the *Monitor?*), then on visit to Russia: "in truth, a floating fortress!" The twenty-ninth, thirtieth, and first were also devoted to sightseeing, often under the guidance of Tachibana; the other days to interviews and dinners arranged in their honor. On the twenty-sixth Morgan escorted them to the summer villa of the British ambassador, who entertained them in very generous style. On the twenty-seventh they called on the former Hakodate consul Iosif A. Goshkevitch and his son, both of whom were well versed in the Japanese language and had some knowledge of Chinese and Manchu as well. When asked whether Japanese was not impossibly difficult, father and son replied: "No, not at all. Pure Japanese is extremely easy to learn, and a very beautiful language too. However, the admixture of Chinese which you now have is exceedingly regrettable; this defect gets worse as the years go by, so that over half of your language is now Chinese. It's a great pity, really."

During the morning of the thirty-first they paid their respects to Petr Stremoukhov, who was in charge of the Asia desk at the foreign ministry, engaging in a frank and cordial discussion and exchanging photographs; and in the afternoon they met Admiral and Mme. Putiatin at a garden party in their honor at Morgan's country retreat. "We were overawed," Mori reported, "by his knowledgeable discussion of the backward customs of our land."

The Bakufu students, Tachibana, and the younger Goshkevitch attended a farewell dinner on 2 September, where Mori and Yamanouchi exchanged lengthy farewell poems. Boarding a regular mail packet on the third, Mori reached England on the tenth: "Arrived at Hull, Britain's third port city, at 3:30 P.M. with the sensation of having come home to my own country. Rail to London. Arrived Kings Cross Station 10:00 P.M. A splendid journey in every respect." But what was it that had made England, after only a year, seem so much like home—particularly in contrast to Russia?

LETTERS TO YOKOYAMA: OBSERVATIONS ON THE WEST

Mori wrote his brother as early as 1 September 1865: "No one who has not seen the wide world for himself will be equal to the great task that awaits him. Although everything is not yet clear to me, I have experienced a profound change in spirit since coming abroad, to an extent which surprises even me. I have hit on the idea that the proper object of my education is the study of humanity itself, and I am making strenuous efforts to abandon my backward ways of thought and behaviour."[33] This one paragraph epitomizes the major concerns of the ten letters which Mori wrote to Yokoyama during his first year in Britain.[34] First, there are

---

33. Mori here uses the curious expression, *okon o sentaku suru,* literally "to wash my dirty spirit," which I have rendered as "to abandon my backward ways of thought and behavior." Mori is under no Christian influence as yet, and the expression should be understood entirely in terms of the traditional Japanese imagery conveyed by the characters *o* (impurity, iniquity) and *kon* (soul, spirit). His discontent with himself extends to the realms both of moral conduct and of ideas. The modern Japanese idiom *tamashii o irekaeru* (reform oneself, mend one's ways) subsumes both thought and conduct and comes close to the sentiment probably intended by Mori, except that *okon o sentaku suru* is more explicit in its disgust with the old dispensation. Hayashi Takeji has suggested that the specific, if unstated, object of Mori's attack is the Confucian view of man and of human relations. See "Bakumatsu kaigai ryūgakusei no jiseki (The achievements of the overseas students in the Bakumatsu period), in *Yamagata kōkō toshokan,* no. 3 (undated), p. 12.

34. The ten letters are given, with some abbreviation, in KKM, pp. 11–26, and will appear in *Zenshū,* II. Hayashi Takeji, in "Ryūgakusei," part IV, p. 75, has argued convincingly for the rearrangement of the letters listed by Kimura as first (undated), second (7 August 1865), third (19 September 1865), and fourth (1 September 1865) in the following sequence: fourth, first, third, and second. I further would reserve the order of the letters listed as fifth (3 December 1865) and sixth (undated) by Kimura. The latter letter

problems to be solved; second, a search for appropriate solutions; and third, an awareness of the personal implications of those solutions. Mori's "great task" is the political one which occupies all of his first letter (7 August 1865); "seeing the wide world for oneself," an exercise of the intellect and understanding, indicates that Mori has already by the second letter (1 September 1865) perceived the educational nature of his responses, while the intention to reform his own thought and conduct expresses the heavy weight with which public matters rested upon his private conscience. This tripartite analytical framework, although ours rather than Mori's, does manage to subsume all but the most random items in the letters and is at least implicit in the correspondence when viewed retrospectively and as a whole.

Mori's communications generally open with reflections upon recent events in Japan and requests for additional information and then go on to describe and recommend to the elder brother the younger brother's own self-educational program, stressing at all times their joint responsibility for the future of Japan.

The first letter begins with an inquiry after the policies of the Satsuma daimyo: "How fares His Lordship? Is he making solid progress in his study of civil and military affairs? What policy, may I with due respect ask, has he determined to adopt with regard to the future of Japan?" Mori continues, giving vent to a growing doubt:

> The sword and the pen have been the appointed calling of the samurai, but do they suffice, I wonder, for a profound understanding of the situation today? Even among the military arts, much depends on the weapon in question; and are not the skills attaching to the sword and halberd of a rather petty order? The sword, really, is just one man's protection against an individual enemy. I reckon His Lordship has a far-sighted policy. How very difficult will the task of young men like ourselves be if he fails to achieve the extraordinary vision required by these extraordinary times!

---

mentions the arrival of the Shibata mission in France, from whence it proceeded to England. According to the *London and China Telegraph* for 4 January 1866, the mission had left England on that date "after a stay of barely three weeks." It would seem likely, since the visit was well covered in the press, that the undated letter, if written in December, would have mentioned the mission as already in, or about to proceed to, England. It is also to be judged from the content of the letters that the dates given by Kimura refer to the Western calendar.

Mori already realizes, as Godai had taken pains to argue with Yoshida, that mere weaponry will not do.

The second letter spells out the "problem" dramatically:

> The purpose of the Bakufu mission now touring France is not at all clear to me. Ostensibly they have come to purchase machinery and the like, but their real purpose is to line up French support for their next political move. They naturally imagine that Satsuma, which already has sent students to England, will be giving them a great deal of trouble in the future. And that, I have been told, is one reason why they have come over. If such be the case, then we can only laugh at them. Is there a single person born in Japan who does not deplore its present condition? Truly, the age-long evils beggar description. In the West as well, the name of the Bakufu is held in extremely low esteem. The present plight of our Empire, and the criticism we have to take from foreign officials, are humiliations which arouse me to an extreme sense of indignation. One day, mark my word, there must come a reversal of the Will of Heaven.

"For Mori," as Ōkubo Toshiaki puts it, "the Bakufu no longer really existed";[35] *Baka-fu,* or "Government of Fools," Mori derisively would call it in his last letter. In the fifth letter (undated, but probably November 1865) Mori while checking out rumored moves for a Satsuma-Chōshū coalition and for a second Bakufu expedition against it laments: "It is exceedingly regrettable that the foregoing conditions should prevail in Japan precisely at a time when the entire Western world lies tranquil and preaches peace. What do you make of this state of affairs? It keeps me on edge day and night. This is indeed the time for every valiant young man to repay in some small measure his obligations in this world [*on*] by serving loyally, and by applying himself diligently to his vocation."

In the sixth letter (3 December 1865), Mori emerges even more strongly as an ardent Loyalist, anxious to see Japan united under the emperor's standard and close to panic over the encroachment of the Western powers: "This minor scruple [whether it is appropriate for a younger brother to speak out so rashly on the subject] fades before the momentous fact that Japan is about to pass into the foreigners' maw. I am convinced that it is altogether a matter of life and death for us, and that every loyal subject must do his utmost, as occasion provides, to put an end once and for all to the

---

35. OTM, p. 18.

unseemly commotions, to extend the national writ throughout the land, and to secure the prestige of our Imperial House among the nations of the West." Mori continues, "In any case we shall need strength for our task. And where will that strength come from?" Mori suggests in his second letter that it would come from seeing the world for oneself and from an inner renovation of the individual young Japanese. In the third letter (19 September 1865), devoted entirely to the matter of cold baths and physical exercise, he indicates how deliberately he is going about the task on at least one front. In the fourth letter (undated, but probably October 1865), Mori reassures his brother that he is keeping up with his books as well, and takes the "quite unexpected" closing of the Zōshikan as an occasion to inquire at length after his former professors and colleagues. It was in the sixth letter, however, that he was most explicit about his own projects: "I believe that the most important thing for me is to travel widely around the world, observing not only various political systems but, more importantly, the people and their customs. Beyond that, I must master two or three scholarly disciplines; walk faithfully in the path where my parents have gone before; carry out the intentions of my two elder brothers departed this world; and take heed not to leave upon the record of history any mark which would disgrace my good name." This was as of 3 December 1865. Except for a brief message on 16 March 1866 expressing hope for the peaceful opening of new ports, there follows nearly half a year's hiatus until the unusually lengthy eighth and tenth letters of 3 June and 26 July in which Mori gives his brother a voluminous account of "matters that have in due time come to my attention" as a result of his promised study of humanity at large. Since what Mori offers is, for the most part, a sequence of highly contrasting appraisals of Russia and America and Britain, the brief ninth letter (dated 3 June 1866 and perhaps an attachment to the eighth) serves as a useful reminder of what his underlying animus towards the Western powers *en bloc* must have been:

> I have been rejoicing, from afar, at reports carried in papers recently received by express mail from China, that the Japanese have made a fine start with their Western-style artillery drills in Yokohama, evoking not only the surprise but also the anxiety of all Westerners with the precision of their formations. The Chinese repeatedly have suffered humiliation at the hands of the English and the French, yet they have failed to bestir themselves, and the Westerner has already come to regard the

Chinaman as little better than a menial. Although the situation in Japan of course bears no resemblance to that of China, we have not yet embarked fully upon the road of progress, and are subjected to our own share of humiliation. Nevertheless, events such as these do portend a gradual improvement of our reputation with the rest of the world. It should be a source of gratification to us both that it is our own beloved Japan alone which, though a small island country, stands majestically above the waning fortunes of all other Asian nations.

The eighth letter describes and evaluates first Russia and then America from the standpoint of political system, national power, and international behavior; and the tenth letter, in the course of lengthy recommendations for Yokoyama's own education, reveals Mori's profound respect for the polity of England. Mori first explains: "The government of Russia rests not on public opinion but depends entirely on the monarch. This is the source of much injustice. If the monarch is wise, they enjoy good government. If he is foolish, the country falls into confusion. They treat their Emperor as a god. Could anything be so unrighteous or silly?" This last remark about the Tzar is particularly interesting coming from a Japanese whose sympathies lay with his country's own imperial cause. Mori takes a very clear stand against autocracy, and it would seem that the intense devotion which he felt for the Japanese emperor was of a purely political nature, devoid of any sentiment that properly could be called religious.

Mori takes pains to disabuse his brother of the impression, generally held by Japanese at the time, that Russia was both a power to be reckoned with and one that could be trusted. "They boast of their strength and look down on other countries," he writes, "but past events prove that they are in fact just a cold country, not a powerful one"—a land where foreigners unaccustomed to that cold stand a good chance of damaging their noses. He cites as evidence of Russian weakness the Crimean fiasco and the near-defeat of her huge armies by Napoleon.

"Many of our countrymen," he further warns, "take Russia for a principled power. But what a sordid record she has!" Her designs on Turkey, the recent annexation of a part of Poland, and the attempt in 1861 to establish a secret naval base on Tsushima are proof to Mori that the tzarist empire continues to press its expansionary ambitions. Frustrated in the Mediterranean and along the Indian frontier, she is now turning her attention increasingly toward Japan:

> It is a port like Hong Kong that Russia is after. If we were to enter into friendly relations with her now, it would not be long before she certainly would say: "Britain, France, America and the others are intent on swallowing up Japan; therefore let us add our strength to yours in order to prevent this." Dangling this bait in front of us she then probably would request permission to set up a fortress in a strategic point in one of our harbors; then she would ask permission to station her warships there and, if that succeeded—her troops. If this were ever to come about, it takes no great eloquence to explain that Japan already would be safely inside the Russian belly.

Mori then paints a picture of democratic, puissant, and thoroughly reliable America, the virtual opposite of Russia on nearly every count:

> Although barely two hundred years have passed since the opening of their country, the government of the Americans, in matters both great and small, proceeds in consultation with all of the people. Their political life is based on justice and impartiality. The Japanese are not yet aware of the sudden emergence of the United States upon the stage of world affairs. But Europeans all describe it as the rising power of the future. The English, even though they harbor an aversion to Americans, are very much agreed on this point . . . Secretly, I have come to the conclusion that America is the country with which the greatest mutual advantage is to be secured by establishing friendly relations.

Mori's alarms on the subject of Russia, which would have warmed the heart of the most rabid Russophobe in Britain, led Ōkubo Toshiaki to comment, "Mori's keen eye espied at a very early date the perils which lay athwart the future course of Russo-Japanese relations."[36] These precocious pronouncements on two countries he had yet to see for himself are in fact proof less of Mori's unaided political perspicacity than of the paramount influence wielded over the intellectual development of the Satsuma students during their two years in London by one particular Englishman: Laurence Oliphant (1829–88). At this juncture, where that influence becomes incontestable, it seems appropriate to interrupt the exposition of Mori's ideas to consider a source decidedly more significant even than Godai.

36. OTM, p. 19.

It was Oliphant who, during his brief tour in Edo, had discovered a clandestine Russian naval station abuilding on Tsushima and had lodged the diplomatic representations which led to its immediate evacuation. This no doubt more than anything else credited Oliphant's standing in the eyes of the students as a true friend of their country.[37] That friendship had been severely tested on the night of 5 July 1861, when a band of ruffians attacked the British Legation. Oliphant, defending himself with nothing more than a riding crop, had sustained a severe shoulder wound which partially paralyzed his left arm for life and necessitated his prompt return to England. His affection for the Japanese, however, came through unscathed, an attachment which dated back to his first visit to Japan in 1858 with the Earl of Elgin. In his *Narrative* of that earlier mission, he had recalled that "each day gave us fresh proofs of the amiable and generous character of the people among whom we were . . . the beauty and elegance of all we saw delighted and astonished us"; and again, in a letter home: "The commissioners were capital fellows and so different from the Chinese, so full of animation and life and very go ahead. They are the most good-tempered people I ever met."[38]

Oliphant was amateur politician, professional adventurer, best-selling author, and distinguished London socialite all rolled up in one. He had hunted tiger in Nepal, superintended Indian affairs in Canada, covered the Crimean War as a correspondent for the *Times,* sailed to Nicaragua as secret agent, and traveled in official diplomatic capacity to Prussia, Poland, China, and Japan. And all along he had entertained the reading public with colorful accounts of his adventures. With his recent election to Parliament he now stood at the pinnacle of his career, and the Satsuma students were fortunate in having as their most general preceptor not only a man knowledgeable and sympathetic with respect to Japanese affairs but a sophisticated, well-informed, well-connected and widely traveled observer of the West as well.[39]

Since Oliphant had made the initial arrangements with Professor

37. *Kaigunshi,* II, 907.

38. Philip Henderson, *The Life of Laurence Oliphant: Traveller, Diplomat and Mystic* (London, 1956), p. 77, quoting Laurence Oliphant, *Narrative of the Earl of Elgin's Mission to China and Japan,* II, and letter from Laurence Oliphant to Lady Mary Oliphant, 1 Sept. 1858.

39. For further material on Oliphant the reader is referred to the following three biographical studies: Henderson, *Life of Oliphant;* Margaret W. Oliphant, *Memoir of the Life of Laurence Oliphant and Alice Oliphant, His Wife* (London, 1891); and Herbert W. Schneider and George Lawton, *A Prophet and a Pilgrim* (New York, 1942)

Williamson, it is reasonable to suppose that he was in touch with the students from the moment of their arrival. Matsumura describes him as their "helpful guide in all things," by whom they were "tutored exhaustively on conditions in England and every other country," and remembers him as having criticized Russia in extremely harsh terms.[40] Oliphant was by contrast a sympathetic observer of the American scene, who once went so far as to describe that country as the hope of the world.[41] Mori's views on Russia and America in the eighth letter are pure Oliphant, although the lack of acknowledgment suggests that Mori already had adopted them as his own. This is not to imply that he was incapable of forming his own opinion according to his own point of view where observation was at first hand, as in the case of remarks on England and Japan. But the students depended heavily and not unnaturally for their images of distant countries, and of the diplomatic game itself, on Terajima's closest English confidant.

As the months pass, Mori gains confidence in the rightness of his educational views, and by the tenth letter he is prepared to recommend specific projects to his own elder brother:

> Chinese learning, my dear brother, you have already mastered; its essence goes no further than the Four Books and Five Classics. If you seek a profound understanding of ancient and modern history, you must venture beyond the obscurantist old Chinese tradition. Would it not profit you double, nay quadruple, to learn the history of Asia, Europe, Africa and the Indies as well? I have given a great deal of thought to the matter since receiving your last letter, and would like to suggest the following: Why not drop the purely technical disciplines and study that which constitutes the very foundation of a nation, namely "the law"—that which in Japan today is the professional concern of the *ōmetsuke* [chief inspectors]? For, as you know, law is the cornerstone of the nation. Where it is obscure, the business of government proceeds with great difficulty ... The Japanese today are beginning to discover the out-

---

40. *Kaigunshi*, II, 903, 905, 907.

41. In an undated letter to his publisher, John Blackwood, Oliphant wrote of the United States that "I believe the highest hopes of humanity are bound up with its future ... and with that of Japan, widely dissimilar though they be ... The revolution here is not political but moral." Quoted in Margaret Oliphant, *Memoir*, p. 63. Professor Hayashi Takeji, who kindly called this letter to my attention, suggests a date of 1869 or perhaps 1870. Letter from Hayashi Takeji to the author, 15 January 1969.

side world and quite a few of them have turned to Western studies. But they all haste after the technological disciplines at the periphery, without giving any heed to the base. If you agree with me up to this point, then perhaps the following suggestions may be of help to you: (1) Begin at once the study of English. (2) Make a thorough study of your own native [legal] system; why not have a look at documents of the *ōmetsuke* and at government edicts? (3) Begin the study of mathematics, too, in accordance with Western principles. These three subjects are the most essential.

In what may be viewed as the germ of a philosophy of education, Mori thus outlines his concept of what he calls *moto no gakumon* as opposed to *sue no gakumon,* of "fundamental learning" as opposed to "peripheral learning" or mere technology. He expresses a profound dissatisfaction with the state of the schools in Satsuma and advances one more important *desideratum:* "If the fundamental purpose of both institutions," he complains of the Zōshikan and Kaiseijo, "be to bring forth men of character, their performance has been most disappointing."

Of mathematics Mori disposes in one terse phrase: "You will not get anywhere without it." English, he explains, would render accessible the literature of America as well as Britain. The American political and legal system, he emphasizes once again, is well worth study, as is the French, and the latter can be approached through texts in English translation: "Without reading some text or other thoroughly, you cannot master any scholarly subject."

Mori reserved his profoundest remarks, however, for the laws of England. Whatever dissatisfaction Englishmen themselves may have felt on the subject, Mori admires English laws for their humanity, their rationality, and their practicality. His favorable comparison of them with those of Japan goes well beyond an exercise in comparative legal systems and suggests that he has begun to grasp something even more fundamental, namely, the concept of society, and beyond that the concept of man, which underlies those laws:

> We have some laws in Japan which are suitable for our traditional way of life, but the great majority of them are cruel and contrary to human sentiment. I suppose they are better than no law at all; and much the same complaint applies to foreign legal systems as well. Of the laws of England, however, I must say that not since my arrival here over a year ago have I seen

or heard of an unreasonable ordinance among them; on the contrary, when I compare them with our laws, which are unreasonable and inhumane, I feel myself unbearably ashamed. Can the renovation of the nation possibly be attempted on the basis of such retrogressive laws? If you, dear brother, could undertake from this moment a study of the laws of the various foreign countries, blending them with the best in our own legal tradition, and working out a new system firmly grounded on the principles of justice, the benefits surely would be felt throughout Japan for ages to come. Of course, in these times there is not much fame in store for this type of scholar, no matter how profoundly he penetrates his subject and contributes to the national weal. The pursuit of fame and the coveting of honor, however, are the marks of a petty man and were deeply despised by great men of the past.

Such dedication to a scholarly task devoid of public acclaim suggests, on the motivational level, that national affairs were to Mori something other than mere raw material for the magnification of his own ego, and the suggestion for "blending" the old and the new betrays an approach to problems of modernization that is pragmatic and instrumental. Mori continues: "If we do not at once undertake a careful investigation of our own [legal] system, it will be difficult to make comparisons with various other systems. If laws do not suit the particular conditions of a given country, they will prove injurious. Would it not be possible, by acquainting ourselves with the laws of Japan and of the West and by blending the two, to establish a legal system consistent with our environment, its integrity assured by firm adherence to the principles of justice?" The passage betrays both enthusiasm for the new and appreciation of the old. "There would be no greater mistake, no greater misunderstanding," Okubo Toshiaki writes on the basis of this quotation, "than to ascribe to Mori an infatuation pure and simple with occidental civilization."[42] The heart of the issue, indeed, transcends the question of old versus new, of East versus West. Mori is interested above all in the workable, and in results, and those in the very near future.

Mori's impression of the humane and rational in the laws of England was reinforced by examples of the same two forces at work in British society at large. After visiting the Institutes for the Deaf-and-Dumb and for the Blind at Newcastle, and after seeing

42. OTM, p. 31.

the systems of sign language and Braille, and the workshops where the handicapped were trained for a useful life, he exclaimed in the "Kōro kikō": "Is this not indeed the very height of Western enlightenment! What a fine thing to take these dumb and blind folk and, instead of casting them aside, teach them the skills which will enable them to earn a secure living! This one instance teaches us a great deal about Western society as a whole. I had heard stories to the same effect while still in Japan, but had not believed them. Now that I have seen it with my own eyes, however, I find myself at a loss for words to express my amazement."[43]

Another source of Mori's admiration of Britain, not discussed with Yokoyama but coming out very strongly in the "Kōro kikō," was her economic and commercial prowess, illustrated respectively by the booming industrial complex in the Newcastle area and by the highly favorable terms of her trade with Russia. Mori was led to conclude: "This is evidence of the clumsiness of Russian traders. The Russians are still, comparatively speaking, the country bumpkins [*inakabito*] of the Occident. Consequently, although fortune has blessed them with great natural resources, they are incapable of turning them into manufactured wares. They sell cheaply to foreign countries, then buy back the finished product at a fancy price; or so I have been told."

Mori's deep distaste for Tzarist autocracy is only partially alleviated by what he has learned of the recent reforms of Alexander II. "The government here runs everything," he concludes after one week in Russia, "just like in China and Japan." Upon landing at Kronstadt this already had been apparent: "We inquired after the chief taboos of the land, and were told 'political discussion,' along with other things too numerous to jot down. In this country everything is left to the discretion of the Tzar, and the common people worship him like a Shinto god or a Buddha, in a fashion very similar to that prevailing in Japan and China—all of which goes to show how unenlightened a land this is." Mori shows intense annoyance at the fire regulations pertaining to Kronstadt harbor which, if unreasonable to begin with, are cynically abused by the port authorities themselves: "They tell us that fire-making, even so much as puff of tobacco, is strictly forbidden on account of the many magazines in the vicinity. Meals, etc., have to be taken on shore. Steamships inside and outside the harbor, however, fill the air with cinders, and when a Russian officer came on deck he was shamefacedly smoking away on his pipe. This is beyond my com-

---

43. Mori, "Kōro kikō," 4 Aug. 1865.

prehension. Secretly I suspect that it is all a Russian stratagem [to force foreign crews to patronize the restaurants ashore.]"[44]

And the strategic warning is sounded once again, too: "A road has already been constructed across northern Asia from [European] Russia to the Amur River, which puts the latter within two months' reach of the Russian capital. They now hope to run a railroad half of the way which would bring to a fortnight or so the travel time between Hokkaido and St. Petersburg. Fearful indeed is the Russian ambition for world empire!"

Mori's attention, however, seemed to focus on a social, more specifically a moral, problem. He was scandalized by the high rate of illegitimate births among the upper classes of Russia, who abandoned their unwanted waifs on the road or quietly put them to death, while the orphanges established by the Tzarina to mitigate the tragedy seemed only to encourage the temptation to license. Reflecting deeply on this, he writes:

> I have heard that precisely the same problem exists in our own country, painful as the admission may be, and that it has greatly vexed our people from ancient times. If we proceed as the Russians do, even if not going to the extent of taking human life, then it assuredly will be difficult to stem the corruption of the entire moral order. This abuse must be brought under control, and I have spent many a sleepless night worrying over the matter. I have decided that sexual passion is something from which it is basically very difficult to escape. Take the Zen or the Shin priests, for instance: they all talk about holding the fort against carnal desire, but I have never heard of one who was capable of abstinence throughout the whole course of his life. How much more so then in the case of ordinary men and women. Possibly we should not condemn too severely what they do innocently or in ignorance. Nevertheless, the mutual fidelity of husband and wife certainly seems basic to the moral order. Although I have already reached the age of discretion, I have not yet, alas, found a satisfactory solution to this problem.[45]

44. This and the preceding three quotations from ibid., 23 and 31 Aug. 1865.
45. Mori uses the phrase *fūfu o betsu ni suru*, which somewhat resembles the classic Confucian maxim, *fūfu betsu ari*, meaning "there should be a distinction between husband and wife." I have followed here, however, the suggestion of Professor Hayashi Takeji to the effect that the distinction intended by Mori would seem to be not between husband and wife but be-

One can only speculate as to how *personal* a problem this may have been for Mori. In the passage just quoted he begins as a patriot searching with a detached, sociological eye for the secrets of national vitality, yet ends up on an unmistakably subjective note. In any case we see here an outstanding instance of a propensity for linking public problems to private behavior and for feeling an unusual degree of personal responsibility for broad civic issues which most people would at least not be likely to lose much sleep over. It is also evidence that it was British morality as well as British politics that gave Mori his sense of homecoming at Hull. He never for a moment lost his respect for battleships or bridges. But there was also emerging in his mind, at the end of the first year, the outline of a national life more securely based on a legal and political structure that we would recognize as rational, humanitarian, and not undemocratic, and on a morality which we might be inclined to characterize as Victorian.

The brief flashes of poetry and humor (including laughter at his own expense) in the "Kōro kikō" suggest that Mori had inherited at least some of his father's generous, good-humored nature. Our total picture, however, is that of a young man as severe in his moral attitudes as he is energetic and thoroughgoing in his studies. There is much here which recalls the Mori we knew in Kagoshima: the puritanism of his reaction to Russian sexual mores; his concern for physical fitness; his imperial sympathies; his preoccupation with naval preparedness; his political awareness and sense of mission, so very much in line with the exhortations of Shimazu Nariakira; and his thoroughly Confucian inclination to view political regeneration in terms of educational and moral reform.

By Mori's own admission, however, he has also "experienced a profound change in spirit" upon arriving in England. He seems to have realized not only, with Godai, that armaments are not enough, but also—going beyond Godai—that wealth itself will not turn the trick either. Moral and spiritual qualities are even more fundamental. In terms of individual morality (i.e., of personal probity and political dedication), the reference is still largely traditional, but in terms of national life Mori has grasped hold of some concepts which can only be explained as a product of English example and of tutoring by Laurence Oliphant.

The master-concept here seems to be that of justice, in its manifold expressions: in the international conduct of nation states; in

---

tween the married couple and all others. Discussion with Professor Hayashi, August 1967.

the relationship of a government to its people; and above all in the system of law determining the mutual relationship of individuals and reflecting the moral character of a nation as a whole. Mori sets out almost at once to translate these insights into practical institutional reform, making the investigation of legal systems the chief end of his educational program and the mastery of English the chief means to that end.

Three other significant concepts, or attitudes, emerge during 1865–1866. One is Mori's strong bent for the rational, as expressed in his admiration of English law and his disdain for Tzar-worship. On a minor, but very tell-tale, point this also comes out in his indignation with the hypocritical no-smoking regulations for Kronstadt harbor. Mori's frustration here, verging on rage, suggests a temperamental impatience with the irrational, encouraged no doubt by his mathematically gifted mind. Another emerging attitude is Mori's humanitarian concern, which, of course, has strong Confucian roots in Mencius, and can also perhaps account for much of his anti-autocratic bias. To the extent, finally, that Mori goes beyond mere disapproval of autocracy to the espousal of something more positively democratic, we may speak of a third emerging concept, as yet somewhat muted and ill-defined, and most safely described as a growing awareness of the value of popular participation in government.

Mori's new enthusiasms are too pronounced and too ingenuous to be brushed aside as mere calculated means to national wealth and military power. It would be fairer to say that Mori, if anything, had not calculated sufficiently the relationship between *fukoku kyōhei* and his new concept of justice, holding on to both viewpoints—his respective legacies from Godai and Oliphant—in an ill-thought-through and potentially unstable amalgam. For Mori subjectively, of course, there were formidable obstacles to perceiving a possible contradiction between the two viewpoints. The Britain he admired, after all, fulfilled admirably all three requirements of *kyōhei, fukoku,* and justice, while his chief tutor in justice, Laurence Oliphant, could at times fret over the strategic exposure of Japan as sympathetically and eloquently as Hayashi Shihei.

It is important, however, to note that at this juncture Mori was as yet under no specific religious influence. His comments on Russian Orthodoxy were those of an intrigued tourist; and, while awaiting departure from Newcastle, he also had occasion to record respectfully, if somewhat distantly, his first encounter with a proselytizing Christian:

Millie, the proprietress of our inn, looked about fifty and, though apparently suffering greatly from a chronic illness, made her living by taking in guests and running her establishment day in day out in a most efficient manner. She was by nature an extraordinarily kind and courteous woman, and we were much taken with her. One day she spoke to us as follows: "Things are never easy in a strange country; so much the less for the two of you who have come to me tonight from so distant a land. If there is anything you lack, no matter how trivial, please let me know and I will do everything I can to help. That is how people should treat one another. For it was the Lord's pleasure to create men living souls distinct from all other creatures, that they might assist each other, and treat each other as they would treat themselves." Thus she spoke plainly from the heart. On the other hand, this exceedingly straightforward person also believed in Christianity, holding forth earnestly on the supernatural and even attempting in all sorts of ways to entice us into accompanying her to church on Sunday. But we were not interested, and went to great pains to wiggle out of the invitation.[46]

It is evident that Mori was far more impressed with what Millie had to say about the human, than about the supernatural, order. He had embraced up to this point the political faiths and the generalized social morality of mid-nineteenth century England: cold baths and chastity, yes; but churchgoing, no. Whereas many Japanese Christians (with Niijima Jō perhaps a good case in point), would be willing to accept Western culture in general as a corollary to their conversion to Western religion, Mori seems to have reversed the sequence, coming upon the religious element last of all, as something which could give greater coherence and deeper personal meaning to the totality of his new interests and enthusiasms.

That new religious element, indeed, was already in the air the moment he returned to London. For Yoshida and Samejima had just come back from America with glowing accounts of a "Living Confucius" whom they had met there. And in Thomas Lake Harris, Mori was destined to find compelling new guidance in his search for what it was that gave a man character, a society health, and a nation the strength to stand on its own against all comers.

46. Mori, "Kōro kikō," 3 Aug. 1865.

Three   *1866–1868*

THE STUDENT
TURNED PILGRIM

That Mori was able to drink so deeply of the Occident was probably due more than anything else to his association during 1867 and 1868 with Thomas Lake Harris' Brotherhood of the New Life, a spiritualist offshoot of Anglo-American Swedenborgianism. The encounter of the young Satsuma samurai with the American visionary and sexual mystic surely constitutes one of the most extraordinary chapters in the annals of East-West cultural relations. Inasmuch as later Japanese historians repeatedly refer to the question of Mori's "Christianity," thereby greatly oversimplifying the matter, it behooves us to establish not only what Mori did imbibe but what he did not. The mainstream of New World culture must have been puzzling enough for a young samurai. The Brotherhood, however, occupies an ambiguous and forgotten niche in the history of American religious and social thought which itself needs considerable illumination before its impact on the Japanese can be evaluated.

It was at Oliphant's invitation that Yoshida and Samejima had crossed the Atlantic during that same summer vacation of 1866, a journey which the Englishman had undertaken in order to gather material for a new book, *On the Present State of Political Parties in America* (London, 1866), visit his mother, who was about to join the Harris community then at Amenia, Dutchess County, New

York, and apply for admission to the colony himself.[1] Harris sent the supplicant packing back to England with instructions to divest himself first of everything he held dear in life, including his political ambitions. On the boat going over to America, however, the discussion had come around to morality and religion. The two Japanese proclaimed themselves good Confucianists, whereupon Oliphant replied: "Confucius is dead and gone; there is nothing left of him but his books. We have however a veritable living Confucius today, by the name of Harris, in New York State. If you'd like to meet him I'd be happy to give you an introduction."[2]

Yoshida and Samejima eagerly accepted the invitation, met Harris, came back to London thoroughly impressed, and immediately communicated their enthusiasm to Mori. Harris, Matsumura recalls, had told the two that modern Christianity was corrupt and should by no means be allowed into Japan in its present unregenerate state. When the American visited England in the spring of 1867, arrangements were made for him to meet Iwashita Hōhei and other high Satsuma officials who had come to Europe in connection with the Paris Exposition, and in early April Mori in the company of Yoshida and Nakamura traveled the 200 miles to Harris' retreat in Wales in order to meet him. Nagasawa, and presumably other members of the party, were introduced to Harris when he came up to London to lecture. "Thus," Kaimon Sanjin concludes, "Mori and his confreres got to see Oliphant's so-called 'Living Confucius,' becoming his disciples, entering upon the study of Christ, and learning to say 'Amen' with great fervor."[3]

    1. Herbert W. Schneider and George Lawton, *A Prophet and a Pilgrim* (New York, 1942), p. 113. The full subtitle of the authoritative study of the Brotherhood of the New Life reads: "Being the Incredible History of Thomas Lake Harris and Laurence Oliphant; Their Sexual Mysticisms and Utopian Communities, Amply Documented to Confound the Sceptic." Lady Mary Oliphant was already a full-fledged member at Amenia when her son was finally admitted on probation in the summer of 1867. *The London and China Telegraph* for 30 October 1866 carried a notice from a recent edition of the *New York Herald* as follows: "Among the arrivals in this city are two Japanese, accompanied by Mr. J. [sic] Oliphant as their friend and interpreter . . . There is something a little problematical to the outside world in regard to the aspect of the visit of these distinguished foreigners to this country. They may possibly be veritable princes *incognito* of whose mission have no intimation . . . secrecy and despatch being a national trait of the Japanese . . . or they may be commercial agents."
    2. KSM, p. 17.
    3. Ibid., p. 17 and *Sappan kaigunshi,* comp. Kōshaku Shimazuke Henshūjo (Kagoshima, 1928), II, 910 and 977. Mori's journey was noted by Nakai Hiroshi in his entry for 8 April 1867 in his *Kōkai shinsetsu* (New light

HARRIS, OLIPHANT, AND THE JAPANESE

Thomas Lake Harris (1823–1906) was, in the words of one biographer, "an American curiosity—an exhibit, not a gospel."[4] Having run away from a home dominated by an unsympathetic stepmother, young Harris had been driven by his sense of personal and theological estrangement first to Universalism, then to the spiritualism of the medium Andrew Jackson Davis, and finally (willing neither to renounce entirely the mediatorial and redemptive office of Christ nor to divest himself of his spiritualistic orientation) to Swedenborgianism, a traditional point of intersection for Christianity and spiritualism.

Orthodox Swedenborgianism had disowned the Harris movement from the start as one of those aberrant spiritualistic heresies with which it is periodically embarrassed.[5] Although Harris borrowed from Swedenborg such doctrines as that of the "Divine Man," of "uses," of "internal respiration," and of the evils of "scortation" (sexual passion) and "proprium" (self-love),[6] he placed himself beyond the pale on two major counts: (1) his claim to direct access to the divinity and to the world of spirits (with a life accordingly punctuated by almost daily visions, convulsions, and trances); and (2) his elaborate sexual mysticism, which many suspected of being nothing more than a device for free love under the banner of chastity.[7] Like Swedenborg, Harris advocated the spiritualization of sex, and preached a doctrine of "spiritual counterparts" and "counterpartal marriage" reminiscent of Swedenborg's "conjugial pairs," except that for Harris the counterpart

---

from across the seas), quoted in Hayashi Takeji, "Bakumatsu no kaigai ryūgakusei" part V, *Nichibei fōramu*, July–August 1964, p. 52. Nagasawa's recollections were recorded in a memorandum of interview by George Lawton, bearing no date, which at the time viewed was located in HOP, Box no. 13, Folder no. 2.

4. Schneider and Lawton, *Prophet and Pilgrim*, p. 40.

5. Marguerite Beck Block, *The New Church in the New World* (New York, 1932), pp. 133, 138.

6. For the concept of "Divine Man" (i.e., God as Universal Man, with individual men as his concrete and particular appearances), see Schneider and Lawton, *Prophet and Pilgrim,* p. xv; for that of "the uses" (the dedication of individual labor and wealth to the service of society), see Block, *New Church,* p. 378; for "internal respiration" (i.e., of the Divine Breath, man's link to the celestial world), see Schneider and Lawton, p. xvi, and Block, p. 138; for "scortation" and "proprium" see Block, p. 141.

7. Schneider and Lawton, *Prophet and Pilgrim,* p. xvi, delivers its verdict on this second count as follows: "Seldom has sexual insanity been cultivated so profusely."

was not another human soul on earth, but the female half of a bisexual divinity with whom the human soul achieved union: "Two-in-oneness," as he expressed it, "between wifehood (Lily Queen) in heaven and husbandhood on earth."[8]

Harris turned his back then on organized religion altogether and set out to establish a model community—the "Brotherhood of the New Life," as he called it, which would be a rebuke both to the established churches and to modern industrial society; for in his social thinking Harris had been influenced by the Christian Socialist writings of Frederick Denison Maurice and above all by what he had seen with his own eyes of the evils of the new industrialism during his first preaching tour of Britain in 1859–60. He had gradually gathered about him a following numbering in the dozens: American Protestants of middle-class extraction and a handful of wealthy, patrician English Swedenborgians, most prominent among whom were William Francis Cowper, later Baron Mount Temple (a stepson of Palmerston), and his wife Georgiana. By the spring of 1867, with the financial backing of the English contingent, Harris was laying plans for the removal of the colony still located at Amenia to a permanent and more pretentious site upstate at Brocton, Chautauqua County, on the shore of Lake Erie west of Buffalo—an area that had been host to the Mormons, the Shakers, the Oneida group, and a variety of less well-known utopian and revivalist communities.

Oliphant had introduced himself to Harris after hearing the American preach in London in 1859 and had at once involved in his new enthusiasm his closest spiritual confidante, his own mother. What attracted Lady Oliphant, a strict and pious Evangelical, to the austere program of the Brotherhood is not so hard to see; the motives of her globetrotting, funloving, lady-chasing, bachelor son are a bit more difficult to fathom. Oliphant had inherited a strong interest in the occult from his father, Sir Anthony, who for years was chief justice of Ceylon and a fascinated student of Indian mesmerism. For analysis, or psychoanalysis, of the crisis which beset Oliphant in the mid-1860's and its resolution, however, the reader may best refer to the arguments presented at length in the two most recent biographies, the general drift of which runs as follows: "While his sensuality in degree and kind was hardly different from that prevalent in the society of his time, Oliphant's evangelical heritage made him attribute to it a much greater importance than it actually possessed. Existing within him side by

---

8. Block, *New Church*, p. 138.

side, therefore, was a 'pagan' sensuality and a Calvinist conscience, and Oliphant's whole life was an attempt to satisfy now one, now the other, and finally, in accepting Harris' theories and practices, to achieve a rationale which would enable him to satisfy both at the same time."[9] And from another author:

> Heroic and saintly as this renunciation may appear from one aspect, it was actually a retreat: a headlong flight from the appalling muddle of his emotional life motivated by a craving for absolute authority and a return to the security of his childhood. He achieved this by sharing his "conversion" with his mother, by feeling that he had his father's approval from beyond the grave, and by finding a father substitute in Harris, who would now punish him for his self-indulgence. This state of psychological muddle had its origin in his mother's dominant influence and to [sic] the fact that he was far too attached to her to achieve anything like a normal or satisfactory relationship with another woman.[10]

Harris was a preacher of dynamic and compelling eloquence, an irrepressible and rather gifted improviser of mystical verse, and a man of almost hypnotic personal presence. If his impact on Oliphant was that of a father figure, it is most likely that the Japanese too were attracted above all by the force of Harris' personality, and that he must have fitted quite closely their image of the *sensei*—the teacher who traditionally holds the allegiance of his disciples less by the sharpness of his intellect than by the strength of his character.

Mori's second year in London may best be classified as a period of growing but indirect Harris influence: of Harris as mediated by Oliphant, an Oliphant who himself has entered upon a period of agonizing self-examination and spiritual crisis. The sudden termination of Mori's letters to Yokoyama after July 1866 leaves a wide gap in the record at just this point. Hayashi Takeji has suggested[11] that nothing speaks more eloquently for Mori's grow-

---

9. Schneider and Lawton, *Prophet and Pilgrim,* p. 119.
10. Philip Henderson, *The Life of Lawrence Oliphant: Traveller, Diplomat and Mystic* (London, 1956), p. 131.
11. Hayashi, "Ryūgakusei," part V, p. 52. Pushing this argument to its cynical limit, one also could speculate that the letters in question, if written at all, might have been destroyed well on into Meiji, either (most improbably) by Mori himself, or (more plausibly) by his biographers, family, or friends, in an effort to cover up an embarrassing incident out of his youthful past.

ing religious involvement than this total silence: that either Mori was afraid to write home at all on the subject, or more plausibly that Yokoyama, mindful of the anti-Christian edicts still in force, destroyed the letters soon after receipt.

The only document we have from Mori's own hand between the "Kōro kikō" and his departure for Japan in June 1868 is a memorial to the Satsuma government dated 10 July 1867, written and signed jointly by himself, Samejima, Yoshida, Hatakeyama, and Matsumura. The purpose of this memorial was to forestall the impending ratification, by the special Satsuma envoy Iwashita Hōhei, of the commercial protocol entered into by Godai Tomoatsu with Count Descantons de Montblanc. This Belgian entrepreneur, the students warn, has his own interests at heart, not Satsuma's, and has even confided to Thomas Glover that the French would use their fleet out of Yokohama if Satsuma defaulted on the loans involved. Westerners, the students sadly conclude, are simply not to be trusted:

> The disasters brought upon the world by the European peoples are beyond enumeration. A certain gentleman told us that it was impossible to find in ancient or modern history a single European who had worked on behalf of others rather than for his own profit. We tried very hard to think of some exception to this rule, but failed . . . When we first came to England our senses were as yet beclouded, and we gasped in rapturous amazement at all that we beheld. Since then, however, we have gradually come to see the negative side of things, having been rescued from our ignorance by an extremely fine friend who has informed us in great detail about Europe and America. We are now of the opinion that the things to be learned from the West are few in number, those to be avoided many. Our friend warns us that although the government of Britain looks fair enough to the untutored eye, the opposite is the case: she is, in reality, all craft and guile. And he is absolutely right: Britain has cast off all morality in her pursuit of selfish interests—there is neither continent nor island that has escaped her pillaging hand. To despise the weak and curry favor with the strong: that is the nature of Europe and America![12]

The second year seems to have brought a fresh look at the nature of international relations, and a corrective of an earlier

12. *Kaigunshi,* II, 979–980.

innocence which, if somewhat hyperbolically stated, must have been a useful lesson in the currriculum of a diplomat-to-be. The "certain gentleman" is of course Oliphant, whose English-language memorandum detailing the rapacious record of the Western powers was forwarded as an attachment to the memorial. Terajima in later years recalled that Oliphant had warned him then that "if foreigners came to Japan for the purpose of trade, they certainly would make off with the wealth of the land," and marveled that "this gentleman was truly concerned for the welfare of Japan; as I look back upon it now, rare indeed was the foreigner who would deliver this sort of warning."[13] Matsumura likewise noted that Oliphant had advised them that "modern diplomacy is necessarily half truth, half lies," and had warned especially that foreign debts would lead inevitably to territorial absorption by the creditor nation.[14]

Glover very likely had his own simple tradesman's reasons for divulging his conversation with his Belgian rival directly to the Satsuma group, but Oliphant's sweeping condemnation of the West, including his own England, suggests some profounder motivation. What a long distance Mori has traveled from the simple Anglophilism and Russophobia of the first year, when the West was neatly divided into sheep and goats! It is clear that Oliphant, too, has traveled the very same distance; and it is not difficult to surmise that the chief propelling force has been this Harris who has pronounced Western civilization and modern Christendom beyond redemption, appointing himself the "Pivotal Man," in his own jargon, of a new regenerative order to be based on his own special principles of chastity and social solidarity.

This drastic sense of disillusionment with the West provides an important clue to Harris' own interest in Japan. As the *philosophes* of eighteenth-century France in combatting their own *ancien régime* had evoked images of a rationalistic, liberalistic, humanistic China which in fact had never quite existed, so precisely did Harris (very possibly on this subject under the instruction of his disciple, Oliphant) turn to Japan—or rather to an idealized image of Japan— for reaffirmation and encouragement in his struggle to reform the degenerate nineteenth-century West.

Global regeneration, Harris had concluded, would have to begin with the Asian countries, with those least penetrated by Christianity. And Japan had two particular attractions for him. First,

13. Ibid., II, 940, quoting Terajima Munenori, "Rirekisho" (A summary of my career), which was written about 1888.
14. Ibid., II, 908.

Harris thought he detected in the traditional Japanese religion and morality certain points in common with his own creed. Secondly, and more practically speaking, here were Oliphant's young friends, the very pick of one of Japan's most powerful clans, who, with the proper indoctrination, might be persuaded to work for the conversion of Japan into the bastion of his new order. As regards the first motive, Harris, who like Swedenborg had conceived of God as bisexual in nature, supposed that a nation which for centuries had worshipped the Sun Goddess, Amaterasu, would be responsive to his own Divine Feminine and most eager to adhere (Harris certainly could not have heard of the Yoshiwara gay quarters) to his own platonic ideal.

To Harris, Christianity and Islam had been vitiated by what he called their "acceptance of the Jewish monotheistic idea in its aspect of arid and cruel masculinity," adding that "the hope of the planet is India, the Japanese Islands and portions of China and Siam."[15]

Standing Anglo-Saxonism on its head, Harris wrote of the Asiatics:

> These races—though mentally more subtle, though structurally more virtuous, though separately more gentle, more cleanly, more abstemious, more genuinely religious, more sympathetic with nature, more docile and governable, more predisposed to solidarity, more capable of the loftier religious impulses, more interior and more intuitive—these races are being crowded back as to their positive manhood, forced into subserviency, and imprisoned into slavery . . . India is perishing, China is perishing, Japan is perishing for a religion that shall reveal paternity in maternity, and both in conjugiality, and this in society . . . [Christ] comes to childlike natures in the swoon of sense and in the dawn of soul. Tell the Anglo-Saxon about the "swoon of sense and the dawn of soul," and he gibbers like an idiot and scowls as if he were an inquisitor. With India in His right hand and China in His left hand, and Japan laid upon His heart between them, our Lord shall come to vindicate himself amid his blessed.[16]

and:

15. Thomas Lake Harris, "Annunciation of the Son of Man" (unpublished manuscript; in HOP), p. 52. A date of 1878 for this manuscript has been suggested by Schneider and Lawton, *Prophet and Pilgrim*, p. 561.
16. Thomas Lake Harris, "The Bridal Word" (unpublished and undated manuscript; in HOP), pp. 213, 216.

The power of the European races over the nations of the East depends upon the sphere of the natural Hell. Not that the Eastern races are in themselves [acquiescent], for they are violent; but they are stricken with a singular paralysis at the sight of these disciplined hosts. And it is impossible for them to acquire discipline to resist them. Since Hell adopted Christendom, its march has been like the sea. Europe must decline with the decline of the infernal power.[17]

These remarks, although probably written a decade later, give some indication of how the Asian nations fitted into Harris' scheme of salvation. He placed particular hope upon Japan because of the presumed fitness of her ruling class for the task at hand. In the words of Harris' disciple and hagiographer, Arthur A. Cuthbert:

While all the aristocracies of the world have proved on the whole, but always with individual exceptions, adverse influences, occultly, to the advancing Divine Breath in the Bosom of the Race; yet the pivotal personality in the Breath—that is, Mr. Harris himself—has always expressed a strong conviction that the ruling Royal Family and the descendants of the old Princely Nobility of Japan, were at this day and would probably prove in the future, the greatest and most notable exception. He earnestly entertained this hope mainly because in the old Shinto religion and traditions the worship of the Divine Mother is the central and most inspiring influence; who from her high altar, Fusiyama [sic] . . . rules supremely over the hearts of all the Japanese people . . . For this Divine Feminine is the great transforming power. She is the "Holy Ghost." From Her, in unison with the Divine Bridegroom, whom Her bosom unveils, flows forth the whole blessed host of the Fays, who at this day are flocking into the bodies of all who truly love and worship Her, to restore the old physical ruins, where Death at present prevails, and in the midst of these ruins to lay the foundation of the new body that "shall never die."[18]

And it was in Mori's group that Harris thought he had found his opening wedge. In a lengthy memorandum dated 2 July 1867 and entitled "A Prophecy of Japan," he wrote triumphantly:

17. Thomas Lake Harris, "The Book of O-I" (unpublished manuscript, 1876; in HOP), p. 81.
18. Arthur A. Cuthbert, *The Life and World-Work of Thomas Lake Harris* (Glasgow, 1908), Appendix "C," pp. xvi–xvii.

I have thus solved the problem of Japan. Its successful outworking depends on finding a Daimio who will carry it out . . . The policy is this: that Daimio will declare himself neutral and a peacemaker in all Japanese conflicts. He will accept the New Life, take the advanced Japanese who are receiving the truths and establish a Military College! He will concentrate the entire revenue to the one end of organizing a Japanese Divine Army. As soon as he has a sufficient force, he will proceed to remove everything that is opposed to order from his dominions. By this means the sphere will become so powerful that nothing can resist it: it will be the nucleus of the New Japan.

The American poet Edwin Markham, a great admirer of Harris' who once collected materials for a biography of the man, made the following editorial note beside the foregoing passage from Harris' "Prophecy of Japan": "Our Seer teaches that the world has reached a plane of disorder where it can be set in order by nothing short of a benevolent military discipline."

The "Prophecy" then continued:

There is a society to be formed in Japan, called the "Brotherhood of the New Life," of which I have at the present time the organization. I will say here only that the external or visible bond of union is a compact to devote all the powers for the regeneration of the Japanese individually and of Japan collectively, making it an open breathing people . . . Through Iwashita I have penetrated to the internal morals of the court of Satsuma, and I am disgusted with the brutality, the arrogance, and the dishonesty of the older politicians . . . The hope of Japan is in the young men . . . From the general wreck and ruin of Japan some province must be saved if possible; this being reorganized will serve as a nucleus for the resurrection of the nationality. Our motto must be "Christ for Japan" . . . It looks as if the fight cannot be carried on to advantage anywhere else than in Japan. Presence is power. When the Daimio is found all the open breathing Japanese will be placed in confidential positions about him; and as fast as a new brother is brought in, he will be brought into a confidential position. Then the palace will be in the hands of the Brotherhood. It will go like lightning.[19]

19. Thomas Lake Harris, "A Prophecy of Japan" (unpublished memorandum, 2 July 1867; in HOP), pp. 1–3 *passim*.

And well might the "Pivotal Man" congratulate himself; for he had just persuaded six of the Satsuma students to cross the Atlantic and enter upon the discipline of the Brotherhood at Brocton.

Harris' invitation came at a most critical juncture, since funds from Satsuma had been terminated as a result of the costly Restoration campaigns. Machida Hisanari called a conference which decided that he and his two younger brothers with Tōgō, Takami, Nagoshi, and Murahashi would return forthwith to Japan leaving Mori, Samejima, Yoshida, Matsumura, Hatakeyama, and Nagasawa free to accept Harris' offer of free passage at least half way home, plus room and board and some additional schooling. As to the students' motivations, Kaimon Sanjin and Kimura Kyō follow Matsumura in emphasizing the financial and academic aspects. There is no doubt that Harris helped them out of a financial impasse, and that the group as a whole, from Machida on down, regretted abandoning studies so well begun. Ōkubo Toshiaki mentions Mori's new admiration for the United States as an additional factor in his particular instance and credits him with a genuine enthusiasm for Harris, the point on which Hayashi Takeji places primary emphasis.[20]

It was no easy life which awaited the six at Brocton; this they knew, and their readiness to participate must have been on the whole sincere. The fact that five of the six were signatories of the memorial of 10 July 1867, suggests a high degree of involvement and enthusiasm. And nothing at that moment could have sustained and fired that enthusiasm more than the magnificent example of Oliphant, who, to the scandal of London high society, resigned his seat in Parliament and sailed for New York and the Harris colony on 27 July 1867. The six Japanese followed shortly thereafter, the five eldest destined to remain with the Brotherhood until late the following spring, and the youngest, Nagasawa, for the rest of his life.[21]

THE RIGORS OF BROCTON

The property[22] of the Brotherhood of the New Life at Brocton, or "Salem-on-Erie," was a tract of land about two and a half miles

20. Hayashi, "Ryūgakusei," part V, p. 46.
21. Hayashi Takeji, *Mori Arinori kenkyū: dai ni: Mori Arinori to kirisutokyō* (Sendai, by the Author, 1968), p. 155.
22. The general description of the Brocton community which follows has been based, except as otherwise noted, on materials in Schneider and Lawton, *Prophet and Pilgrim,* on the letters from Laurence Oliphant to Mr. and Mrs. William F. Cowper, in HOP, and on "A Celestial Utopia," article in *The Sun* (New York), 30 April 1869.

long by one mile in breadth, comprising some twenty former farmsteads, well supplied with wood and water, rising gently from the shores of Lake Erie back along the slopes of a deep valley. Within a year of operation some eighty acres had been planted to the "Salem" grape, the chief source of the colony's income, and several dairy farms ranged the hilltops on the inland side. A sawmill and several homes already stood on the property. Gradually new homes, a wine cellar, a grist mill, a general store, and a small schoolhouse were added, and a barn was remodeled into a gymnasium downstairs with a chapel in the loft. Since the Brotherhood first started moving, in stages, from the old site at Amenia in the late fall of 1867, the Japanese were at the most half a year on the premises, which were still abuilding and in a general state of logistical confusion. Harris lived in lordly seclusion in a thirty-room mansion on the lakeshore, generally attended by two or three ladies of the colony (and later also by Nagasawa). Oliphant, after three months' total isolation by way of probation in a rude shack at Amenia, arrived at Brocton in late November 1867, finding Yoshida and Samejima (still apparently his two closest confidants) already there, and took up residence with the two Japanese and four Americans in a house about two miles distant from Harris. Mori, Hatakeyama, Matsumura, and Nagasawa apparently were kept waiting at Amenia (where the Brotherhood had operated a grist mill and established a bank), until late December.[23]

Harris and Oliphant, with the assistance of the six Satsuma samurai in Mori's group and of the Cowpers in London, had pressed on with the recruitment of additional young Japanese.[24] In September 1867 two Satsuma students, Tanimoto Heimon and Nomura Ichisuke, who had just arrived via California (bound for the Monson Academy in Massachusetts), visited Amenia and were sufficiently impressed to sign up at once. Another Satsuma group of five (Enatsu Sōsuke, Tanegashima Keisuke, Nire Kagenori, Yūchi Sadamoto, and Yoshihara Shigetoshi—the latter a future governor of the Bank of Japan), already enrolled at Monson, had been shaken by the suicide of a fellow Satsuma student (Kido Ichisuke) at the academy. Samejima visited them shortly after the event and persuaded them to abandon their studies at the end of the quarter, which they did, moving directly to Brocton in late November, and taking up residence with a Mr. and Mrs. Leavey.

23. HOP, letters from Laurence Oliphant to William F. Cowper, 1 Dec. 1867 and 29 Dec. 1867.

24. HOP, letters from Laurence Oliphant to William F. Cowper, 27 Nov. 1867 and 1 Dec. 1867; Hayashi, *Mori kenkyū: dai ni,* pp. 119, 141–143.

In Britain meanwhile, friends were making efforts to secure the release of two Chōshū boys, "Dokie" and "Hatori," from the Glovers at Aberdeen, and of a third Chōshū boy "Obah" and his Tosa companion Yūki Yukiyasu from their guardian, a Mr. Hooper, in London. "Dokie" and "Hatori" are known to be cover names for a nephew of the Chōshū daimyo, and the son of one of his *karō;* "Obah" remains unidentifiable. A fourth Chōshū lad, Minami Teisuke, a staunch convert, was already en route to Japan in the brave hope of persuading his daimyo to travel to America and join the Brotherhood at Brocton. As the shogunate tottered toward collapse, there was also a renewed attempt to dislodge fourteen Bakufu students in the English capital from the iron grip of their supervisor, a Royal Navy Chaplain named Lloyd, who had locked one of the boys (Wada Shinjirō) in his room for a week for having visited an English friend after hours. Only Yūki made it to Brocton, in late May, 1868 just as the group was breaking up, and left after a stay of only one week.[25] The Chōshū four, however, had all been eager to come, as had been Wada and his colleague Yasui Shinpachirō. That Harris' projects commanded at least the respect of a large number of those approached is suggested by the reaction of Nakamura Masanao, then with the Bakufu group, who "appeared much impressed and listened attentively" to Oliphant, but concluded with regard to Harris that "there was no use in going to him as he was struggling after the impossible."[26]

By early 1869 there were about sixty adults all told in the community (presumably somewhat fewer during Mori's sojourn), well over half of these women, a good number of children, and a corps of hired laborers, mostly Swedes, to assist with the ambitious construction program. There were five orthodox Protestant clergymen, including a former Virginia slaveholder, but the majority of the faithful were American and British laymen, devout Protestants (perhaps mostly Baptist by affiliation, with two Shakers and one Quaker), hailing preponderantly from the Southern states.[27] Members assumed special names within "The Use," as they called their colony, e.g., Harris: "Faithful"; Oliphant: "Woodbine"; a Mrs. Gallagher: "Tiny Funnyhorns." Aside from this practice, however, the community in no manner, whether by dress or speech or food

---

25. HOP, letter from Laurence Oliphant to Mrs. William F. Cowper, 6 Nov. 1868; Hayashi, *Mori kenkyū: dai ni,* p. 155.

26. HOP, letter from Laurence Oliphant to William F. Cowper, 1 Dec. 1867.

27. Schneider and Lawton, *Prophet and Pilgrim,* p. 150.

or other custom, set itself apart from the ordinary run of citizens, and was in terms of artistic and intellectual interest and ambition a good cut above average.

The Japanese contingent at Brocton entered the new year 1868 thirteen strong. It was a cold winter, during which the self-flagellating Oliphant, up at 4:30 A.M. in subzero weather and lantern in hand, prided himself on hauling the laundry water from a frozen stream a quarter of a mile away in icy, sled-borne barrels.[28] The Satsuma samurai, Nagasawa recalled,[29] worked hard cutting vine poles, chopping wood, baling hay, tending the greenhouse, making beds, washing the dishes, and running sundry errands for "Faithful," or "The Primate," as Harris was also known. Mori seems to have had special duties in the bakery. "Not only," affirms Kimura Kyō, "did he discharge these duties faithfully, but he strove also, as time permitted, to make a collection of American textbooks."[30] Oliphant wrote to Cowper on 26 November 1867 of "a school immediately to be opened," by which he probably meant a one-room affair presided over by himself; and it seems likely that the studies of the Japanese were not entirely interrupted. The bulk of the Brocton schedule, like the atmosphere of "The Use" itself, was in all probability, however, much more that of a work camp than of an academic institution.

Physical exertion and manual labor were not only the substance of everyday life, but were believed to be the chief instruments of moral regeneration as well: a toughening of the body to temper the soul. The idea must have seemed familiar enough to graduates of the Gōjū, the strict discipline of which was also revived in the Brocton routine. William Cowper wrote of the colony in 1868 that: "The practice of implicit obedience in the details of work is imperative in order to break down the Selfhood. Disobedience leads to a state which requires isolation. The discipline of a school is revived, or of a Regiment. It's a test of earnestness, and when a man has learnt to obey in spite of his natural impulses, he can command without any indulgence of his natural love of power and preeminence."[31]

28. HOP, letter from Laurence Oliphant to William F. Cowper, 29 Dec. 1867.
29. In an interview with George Lawton. For the memorandum of the interview see note 3 above.
30. KKM, p. 31.
31. Entry in the hand of William F. Cowper for September 1869, in a notebook kept jointly by Mr. and Mrs. Cowper, entitled "Conversations of Thomas Lake Harris, 1867–1871," Hampshire Record Office (Winchester), Cowper Papers.

The Japanese seemed to be in their element. Although Oliphant was perhaps neither the first nor the last to read into the Mongoloid physiognomy an inward state of beatitude, he may have been reasonably close to the mark when he wrote of them at Amenia: "I see them, dear souls, every day hard at work with their countenances beaming with delight. They feel the effects of the sphere and of the influx that comes with labor, and they say that they never knew what happiness was before."[32] A (New York) *Sun* reporter who visited Brocton in April 1869 came away with the same impression, writing of "those previously idolatrous Japanese" (having most probably met Nagasawa): "We made a short call on one of them, who was engaged in his study (to wit, the corner of the workshop), after his day's work had been done, studying the Scriptures. The tawny pagan actually seemed to have been born again physically as well as spiritually. How happy he was! His face shone as though it were reflecting rays from the Sun of Righteousness."[33]

Unfortunately the record is far less clear regarding the spiritual, as opposed to the physical, regimen of the Japanese. Judging from a report delivered by Mori and Samejima to Yokoi Shōnan at Kyoto after returning to Japan, it seems likely that they underwent at the outset a probationary period of isolation and Carthusian-like silence similar to that of Oliphant. Yokoi later reported: "The two Satsuma lads were at first overwhelmed by the undertaking but at last, and with great effort, managed to enter upon the study of the true spiritual discipline."[34] Beyond an occasional worship service, however, the religious element communicated itself less through organized religious activities than through the daily pre-

32. HOP, letter from Laurence Oliphant to Mrs. William F. Cowper, undated, addressed from Amenia, where Oliphant was "on probation" during September–October, 1867. "Spheres," of which there were various types, were an important part of Harris' mystical jargon, generally representing forces for good or evil originating in the outside world as opposed to an individual's own mental state. They were very like the "vibrations" in our present psychedelic argot. The "sphere" in this passage might best be taken perhaps as a reference to the "celestial sphere," the sphere of love, or the sphere of Harris' own spiritual influence.

33. From "A Celestial Utopia."

34. Letter from Yokoi Shōnan to his two nephews, Saburō and Suketarō (surnames not available), 30 Oct. 1868 (15 IX Meiji 1), quoted in Yamazaki Masashige, comp., *Yokoi Shōnan ikō* (Tokyo, 1942), p. 560. Saburō and Suketarō were at that time studying in the United States, and Yokoi hoped they would have a chance to meet Harris. The visit of Mori and Samejima to Yokoi in Kyoto is mentioned in Yamazaki Masashige, *Yokoi Shōnan den* (Tokyo; 1942), II, 149.

cept and example of the faithful, through casual conversation, through exhortations in Oliphant's "schoolhouse," through occasional audiences with Harris, and (to judge by the *Sun* article) through a certain amount of Bible reading. Seances were strictly barred, although Harris continued to communicate with the celestial realm in the privacy of his own chambers.[35]

Nor were the members of the colony Sabbatarians. Services following a typical "left-wing" Protestant pattern were held on an irregular basis in the chapel loft, with Harris often preaching to an overflow crowd of outside curiosity-seekers.[36] There were sermons, hymns, and occasional outbreaks of mass emotion. Despite the regimentation of daily life, and Harris' own Armageddon approach to world affairs, however, it seems likely that the group expression of religious sentiment at Brocton was on the whole more joyous than morose, lacking something of the inward-looking contrition and conviction of sin which characterized the typical revival meeting. Herein Brocton betrayed its debt to the strongly anti-Calvinistic, Heaven- rather than Hell-oriented tradition of orthodox Swedenborgianism.[37] Oliphant caught the gladsome, even fanciful, spirit of group worship at Brocton when he wrote:

> We have fitted up a beautiful little chapel, with a pulpit so beautifully arranged by Dovie [Miss Jane Lee Waring] that a flood of light comes down upon Faithful's head from a window concealed by scarlet drapery, upon which there is a large sort of embossed red cross. Then it is all so tastefully decorated with evergreens, young hemlock trees arching whole overhead . . . Most delightful of all, Dovie is now receiving music, while Faithful receives the words. It adds so inexpressibly to the sweetness and the solemnity of our singing to know that it has come from the Heavens expressly for us. Faithful saw Sebastian Bach standing by the piano the other day as Dovie was composing. The music comes first and suggests the words to Faithful. It is nearly all of a warlike character: so spirit-stirring that in church many people are moved to tears.[38]

There is abundant evidence that the Japanese brought to the spiritual life of the community the same enthusiasm with which

35. Schneider and Lawton, *Prophet and Pilgrim*, p. 201; Block, *New Church*, p. 127.
36. Schneider and Lawton, *Prophet and Pilgrim*, p. 177.
37. Block, *New Church*, pp. 35–43.
38. Letter from Laurence Oliphant to William F. Cowper, dated "February 6th, Brocton," possibly 1868 but probably 1869, Hampshire Record Office (Winchester), Cowper Papers.

they attacked their daily chores. They displayed a capacity for deep emotional involvement and a high susceptibility, it would seem, to the persuasion offered. Of Tanimoto's and Nomura's instant recruitment at Amenia, Oliphant noted:

> Three days ago two new Japanese arrived—they had just come from Japan via California. They cannot speak a word of English, but heard of our Japanese through the others that I wrote you of last letter. They at once wrote to make inquiries. Our Japanese answered telling about Faithful, but telling them also to wait till they heard from them again. Their impatience was so great however that they came without waiting. Although Faithful was away, they were so struck with our life of labour, and with the love sphere that is here, that they said they felt sure that Faithful's teaching must be true and decided to wait till his return. The same night one dreamt that Faithful appeared to him and said, "Die to self," and the other dreamt that Faithful appeared and said, "Be humble," and set him to wash a tub, so in the morning they said that they had made up their minds to accept the life. They said that their past lives in Japan had been very wicked, and that any punishment which Faithful saw fit to inflict they would willingly bear. They are now learning to wash clothes, make beds, wash dishes and other humble uses. It will be such a joy to Faithful on his return to find them.[39]

Oliphant went on to attribute to the young Japanese certain qualities of character—openness, sincerity, responsiveness to affection—which fitted them in his mind better perhaps than Westerners for the life at Brocton: "The Japanese say that in their opinion nobody can really appreciate Faithful's teaching who has not seen the life here. This proves more to them than all else beside, but that is because owing to their openness they feel the force of the sphere of love and purity which pervades the very atmosphere, but an ordinary closed Western person is not conscious of this subtle influence."[40] He says further:

> If you only knew all these dear souls as I do, and had the experience that I have had of their simple and noble natures you

---

39. HOP, letter from Laurence Oliphant to William F. Cowper, 29 Sept. 1867.
40. HOP, letter from Laurence Oliphant to Mrs. William F. Cowper, 6 Oct. 1867

would feel as I do and as I know you will, that it is a privilege to be permitted to assist in bringing to a knowledge of our Lord these His little ones, whom He is now gathering into His fold, and who by the ardour of their love for Him, and the absolute sacrifice of self which they make to Him, put us who have known Him so long to shame and confusion . . . They accept Faithful's teaching fully as much as they know, and desire only to follow a system which may enable them to lead pure and good lives. You will find Yukee [Yūki Yukiyasu] especially a gentle loving youth. Indeed they are all of tender sensitive natures, and are so very "open" that they are able to judge of a person by his sphere much more readily than we can, and are always amenable to the sphere of love.[41]

The Japanese also took readily to prayer and to the respiratory practices associated with its higher phases. Likening the "Breath of God in Man" to the Pentecostal experience of Christ's disciples, Cuthbert described it as "a concrete and physical reality, and not merely a mystical and spiritual reality."[42] Taking it well beyond the figurative sense of the indwelling of the Holy Spirit in Man, the Brotherhood strove for what is called "open respiration" or "divine respiration" as the climax of organized worship. Harris regarded the physical "influx" of the "Divine Breath" as the surest guarantee of the moral vitality of his community. In his view, "Man in his holy state was, so to speak, directly connected with God, by means of what might be likened to a spiritual respiratory umbilical cord, which ran from God to man's inmost or celestial nature, and constantly suffused him with airs from heaven, whereby his spiritual respiration or life was supported, and his entire nature, physical as well as spiritual, kept in a state of god-

---

41. HOP, letter from Laurence Oliphant to William F. Cowper, 1 Dec. 1867. Oliphant's somewhat treacly terms of endearment for the Japanese samurai here are typical. In a letter to Cowper dated 26 Nov. 1867 he had referred to them as "the dearest boys" and as "little lambs." Along the line of analysis suggested by Philip Henderson (see note 10 above, and corresponding text), it might be asked whether this language is not evidence of a certain sublimated, homoerotic fixation. All evidence, in any case, points to extreme complexity in Oliphant's psychosexual make-up. Oliphant by his own admission had been something of a playboy and a womanizer and did not settle down to married life until 1872, at the age of forty-three. He lived in celibacy with his first wife, Alice le Strange, who died in 1886. His second marriage, to Rosamund Dale Owen, granddaughter of Robert Owen, took place within five months of Oliphant's death in 1888. Both women were prominent spiritualists.

42. Cuthbert, *Life of Harris,* p. 19.

like purity and innocence . . . After the fall of man this spiritual respiratory connection between God and man was severed . . . This divine respiration . . . retains all that is of the natural respiration as its base and fulcrum, and builds upon and employs it for its service . . . Highest prayer with them is attended, not with breathlessness but with breathfulness; and the nearer one approaches the omnipotent Object of his worship, the more copious becomes the river of that diviner atmosphere which, pulsing through the spirit, expands and invigorates the breast . . . and this higher breath, whose essence is virtue, builds up the bodies of the virtuous, wars against disease, expels the virus of hereditary maladies, renews health from its foundations, and stands in the body as a sentinel against every plague."[43]

The Japanese were anything but timid in their "breathing." During a service at Amenia, Oliphant reports: "There came down such an overpowering sphere during the service that I could scarcely bear it. All were more or less affected to tears. The sermon was most searching and quickening, and brought us into states of humiliation and penitence, so that afterwards many embraced each other in tears and yet there was a love and a joy mixed with it, and such an amount of kissing it seemed as though people did not know what to do with their overflowing love. The dear Japanese were especially demonstrative."[44] Writing again half a year after Mori had left, Oliphant further recalled: "It [the breathing] was always deep and silent with myself; with the Japanese it was more demonstrative, you heard from their own lips their experiences."[45] William Cowper likewise noted: "When the Japanese were informed of this doctrine [i.e., the Breath as a manifestation of a new life of selflessness] they were told to pray and, as they did not know what prayer is, they were instructed to address themselves to the Highest Being they could conceive and ask

43. As explained to the author of "A Celestial Utopia." Since the reporter had managed to disguise himself as an applicant for admission, Harris spoke from the heart, revealing a good deal more of his doctrine that he intended for public consumption, and showing great chagrin when it all appeared in print a few days thereafter. The episode is described in HOP, letter from Laurence Oliphant to William F. Cowper, 28 May 1869. This article, which ran to over 7,000 words, was contemporary (within one year) of Mori's sojourn, and as a conscious effort to explain matters to the layman is both more succinct and urbane than most of the prose emanating from Harris or his followers. It will be quoted from frequently below.
44. HOP, letter from Laurence Oliphant to William F. Cowper, 29 Sept. 1867.
45. HOP, letter from Laurence Oliphant to Mrs. William F. Cowper, 6 Nov. 1868.

for the Breath. It came sensibly pulsing through their frames and they at once accepted from their own sensations what was taught."[46]

In terms of Western religious experience, the Brotherhood on this particular point stood close to George Fox and the early Quakers.[47] One is hard pressed, however, to trace any oriental affinities that might have provided a stepping stone for the Japanese. Yoga, with its central emphasis on respiratory exercises, was alien to their native tradition. Regulated breathing was considered conducive to meditation in Zen, and Yoshida and Samejima did upon returning to London in 1866 originally describe the Brotherhood as practicing *zazen*.[48] But the physical and emotional symptoms of the Divine Breath seem a good deal more frenetic than those appropriate to the pursuit and achievement of *satori*.

THE APPEAL OF THE NEW LIFE

It is clear that the Satsuma samurai did not approach "Salem-on-Erie" empty-handed. It is also by and large possible to establish from subsequent biography what each individual got out of Brocton, or saw fit to keep later on in life. It is more difficult to reconstruct precisely what the Brotherhood meant to the Japanese at the time of their sojourn in it, and at the height of their enthusiasm and involvement, in terms of intellectual comprehension and emotional response. Our analysis is complicated by the fact that the Japanese, who surely had their hands full already trying to make sense of the West, suddenly found themselves hermetically sealed, so to speak, for a whole year in a fringe environment.

The Brotherhood was a baffling concoction of the earnest and the eminently sensible with the fanciful and downright preposterous, which left the general public continually speculating, often salaciously, as to what really went on, and which drove its most authoritative chroniclers to despair of rendering a final verdict upon it.[49] It is difficult to establish the precise role which esoteric

46. Undated entry, 1869 or shortly thereafter, in Cowper, "Conversations of Harris, 1867–1871."
47. Cuthbert, *Life of Harris,* p. 48.
48. *Kaigunshi,* II, 909.
49. Schneider and Lawton, *Prophet and Pilgrim,* p. xiii, states that the authors arrived, "at the end at no absolutely clear picture of their characters nor final diagnosis of their madness . . . We had studied spiritualism, Swedenborgianism, utopianism and socialism; we knew something of the theories of mysticism and apocalyptic visions; we tried to explain the whole matter with the aid of psychoanalysis . . . We have told the truth, but ourselves

doctrine and practice played among the Anglo-American membership, but two factors in the case of the Satsuma samurai serve drastically to reduce the area of possible speculation: (1) important secular transformations within the community itself; and (2) the assimilative capacity of the Japanese.

The Brotherhood of the New Life, as Mark Holloway has pointed out, started as a typical early nineteenth-century, pre-Civil War utopian experiment, with its roots in Owenite-Fourierist socialism, in revivalism, and in a spirit of pioneering consciously patterned on the primitive Christian ideal. With the growth of population and the rise of industrialism, the energies in America previously harnessed by simple communitarian utopianism were deflected either into anarchism, cooperation, Marxist socialism, or the trades union movement (all in essence political) or into a new rash of apolitical, esoteric, often pseudoscientific, mysticism of which Theosophy was the prime example.[50] The Brotherhood of the New Life followed the latter deflection. From the 1880's on, Harris' interests turned increasingly to oriental mysticism and occultism, and his prose became in places almost unintelligibly electrochemical. It is possible that some shift in moral tone as well may have befallen the Brotherhood ("Utopia in Decline," as Holloway has characterized it), after its removal to Fountain Grove, Santa Rosa, California, in 1875.

In 1891, at any rate, the Brotherhood became the subject of an internationally publicized scandal.[51] Harris' "inverse Platonism,"[52] i.e., his typically spiritualistic habit of seeing spirits concretely, held within itself the possibility that the sublimating mechanism of his sexual mythology might break down and that some day, to put it crudely, the Divine Feminine might appear in the guise of someone else's wife. That, in essence, was the charge put forward by the press. The town fathers of Santa Rosa came to the defense of Harris and their own good name, but as a former member of Brocton was to write: "Everything of this sort had been forever taboo at Brocton, and the shock occasioned by the loss of faith was very great."[53] Philip Henderson suggests that sexual irregular-

---

scarcely know how much of the story to believe. All we know is that no one could believe it all, and hardly anyone will know why he draws the line where he does."

50. Mark Holloway, *Heavens on Earth: Utopian Communities in America, 1680–1880* (London, 1951), pp. 211–229.
51. Schneider and Lawton, *Prophet and Pilgrim*, pp. 534–558, *passim*.
52. Ibid., p. xv.
53. Ibid., p. 340, quoting Robert Martin.

ities were a feature of the community from the very start, with an inner circle of initiates in vice, and an outer circle of gullible believers.[54] The evidence would seem to point, however, only to the possibility of such irregularities, and that at a much later date, suggesting that Mori's sojourn coincided with the early, vigorous, pristine phase of the Brotherhood's development.

The value system which the Japanese students confronted at Brocton may be analyzed on three levels: at the top, the glittering theological idiosyncrasies of Harris; at the middle, and far less dramatic, the informal generalized Christian and socialistic orientation of the majority of members, typified by Oliphant; and finally at the bottom, as insidious as they were subtle and unspoken, all those assumptions shared by the community as a whole simply by virtue of being English or American in the latter half of the nineteenth century. The assimilative capacity of the Japanese at the first level must have been virtually nil; at the second level, moderate; at the third, possibly immense. Given the intimacy and the intensity of personal relations within the Brotherhood, the exact discipline, the continual self-examination, the dependence on an alien language, and a form of communal living maximizing daily (and "everyday") contact with non-Japanese, Brocton must have provided something of a hothouse exposure to typically Western modes of thought and behavior. Mori was to see much of the world besides Brocton, but his seeming ability so often to identify with the West, to internalize what he had learned of it, probably had its roots here in the intensity (as opposed to the content) of his association with the Harris community.

The following extract from a letter of Oliphant's at Brocton to the Cowpers in London regarding the proselytization of the Bakufu students, suggests the intellectual content of that association:

> Proceed rather slowly and cautiously. You might begin by unfolding to those who desire it, such of Faithful's teaching as seems adapted to their states, dwelling on the power of love and cooperation among themselves as the only protection for Japan against the foreigners . . . I do not suppose you will be able to extract them from Mr. Lloyd at present, but you can be preparing them for Faithful, giving them his views as to living the Life and avoiding the doctrinal points . . . The idea of the necessity of deep humility, and of the absolute extinction of self they always accept at once. They delight in learning how to

---

54. Henderson, *Life of Oliphant,* p. 146.

live better, but they would be dreadfully puzzled by the atonement or the doctrine of imputed righteousness, justification by faith, adoption by free grace, etc. The Sermon on the Mount they are never tired of reading, and of trying to embody in their lives . . . I only give you these hints, but I feel you will not require them, for you will feel their wants and how to get at them so as to draw out their love and confidence.[55]

Three important conclusions emerge from the foregoing: (1) that Harris' appeal to the Japanese was primarily on a simple, straightforward ethical level, a level very possibly devoid of any deep philosophical awareness of, or personal commitment to, the Biblical Christ; (2) that the Japanese had little difficulty in connecting the new ethic with their own native upbringing; and (3) that there was a deliberate attempt on the part of their mentors to link the new faith to the national welfare of Japan.

Assuming that the Japanese were spared the esoteric Harris doctrines as well as such orthodox teachings as Oliphant considered beyond their comprehension, the question remains as to just what sort of Christianity did rub off. Of the Brocton teaching, "very little," in the recollection of Margaret Oliphant "[was] inconsistent with the most orthodox Christianity, slightly transformed by the Swedenborgian theory . . . fervent and living nobility of faith, the high spiritual indignation against every wrongdoing and against all that detracts from the divine essence of the spirit of Christianity."[56] This would seem to bear out Yokoi Shōnan's recollection of what Mori and Samejima had said of Harris: "He maintained that the entire world had fallen into heresy and that humanity would in fact perish in chaos brought about by the pursuit of selfish interests . . . It was Harris' belief that the essence of Christ's teaching was the cultivation of man's conscience and the clarification of his ethical principles."[57] As between traditional evangelical Protestantism with its focus on Christ as personal savior, therefore, and a simpler ethical creed, with Christ reduced to mere exemplar, there is a strong presumption for concluding that Mori's party was presented with the latter. What was involved here was prob-

55. HOP, letter from Laurence Oliphant to William F. Cowper, 1 Dec. 1867.
56. Margaret W. Oliphant, *Memoir of the Life of Laurence Oliphant and Alice Oliphant, His Wife* (London, 1891), p. 4. Margaret was Laurence's cousin.
57. Letter from Yokoi Shōnan to his nephews Saburō and Suketarō. See note 34 above.

ably as much a matter of emotional attitude as of closely reasoned dogma, but it seems likely that the Japanese confronted something a bit different from the typical preaching of the American Board of Foreign Missions, the most significant difference lying perhaps in perception of, and relation to, the person of Christ.

Swedenborgianism scrupulously maintained the dualism of Creator and Creation,[58] and the existence of evil, and Harris took great pains to guard himself against the charge of mystical pantheism, opposing his own "Theo-Spiritualism" to the "Nature Spiritism," as he called it, of Theosophy and Buddhism, and balking at "the acceptance of Lhassa in place of Nazareth."[59] For the majority of his followers, therefore, who hailed from the mainstream Protestant sects, affiliation with the Brotherhood offered not a fresh set of beliefs but rather a scheme for practical living in greater harmony with established faith. In point of emphasis, however, there was a distinct shift away from the biblical fundamentalism, the sacramentalism, the orthodox Trinitarianism, and the Calvinism which would have been encountered in various proportions in the traditional churches. Much of this de-emphasis was inherent in orthodox Swedenborgianism itself,[60] and Harris by breaking even with that, had dramatized his independence of organized religion altogether. His own "Theo-Spiritualism," he explained, meant: "a spiritual culture of man, *de novo,* beginning anew in vital fresh experiences of young and ardent souls, divested from all sectarianism, from all ritualism, souls called and consecrated in all the ardency and intensity of their powers to the following of the Master Christ, and so to the embodying of the love and service of God and the service and culture of humanity."[61]

Swedenborgianism did not go as far as Unitarianism in divesting Christ of his divinity, but it had set its face resolutely against the concept of Christ's vicarious atonement to an angry father for human sin, strongly shifting its emphasis from the Crucifixion to the Resurrection.[62] Oliphant, who in all probability remained the Satsuma group's closest tutor even in points theological, had written to his mother in 1857 that it was the ethics of Christianity which continued to hold him to his faith: "I am a thorough Christian so far as my reverence for and belief in every moral principle

58. Block, *New Church,* p. 40.
59. Thomas Lake Harris, "A Study of Occultism" (unpublished manuscript, 1888; in HOP), pp. 2, 31.
60. Block, *New Church,* pp. 35, 47, 399.
61. Harris, "Study of Occultism," p. 31.
62. Block, *New Church,* pp. 41–42, 288.

Christ has propounded is concerned, but I am utterly opposed to the popular development of Christianity—indeed I think it is quite inconsistent with his teaching." He says further of his own view of Christ: "What papa calls God's invention of Christ does not remove the difficulty: it substitutes another being, whose merit is that you are to think of Him as God. The moment you think of Him as God, He is as far away as ever."[63] The key question put to the Japanese, therefore, was probably not, "Are you saved?" ("Do you accept Jesus Christ as Lord and Savior?"), but rather, "Are you going to shape up?" ("Are you prepared to walk in His Way with joy and gladness?"). And to this latter question, we can almost hear Mori, resolved since London to rid himself of his "backward patterns of thinking and behavior," replying, "Yes! Yes!"

The psychological vectors of a simple ethical (or "Liberal" or "Latitudinarian") Protestantism would seem to run parallel to rather than athwart those of Confucianism, emphasizing the social weal, assuming the basic goodness of man (and by extension of one's own "self") and functioning, in the long and short of it, simply as a reinforcement of previous family and Gōjū commitments and as a call to a fresh round of moral exertion. Christ comes through as little more than *sensei;* "salvation" is viewed as a matter of social- and self-perfection (along lines for which Christ, like the Chinese sages, provides the ultimate model), or in the words of Yokoi, of "the cultivation of man's conscience and the clarification of his ethical principles"; and one skips the more typically evangelical conversion experience in which an oppressive conviction of personal inadequacy and radical guilt leads, through deep contrition, to an intimate awareness of Christ as personal savior.

Such an evangelical, as opposed to purely ethical, experience of Christianity would probably differ significantly, therefore, in its long-range intellectual and psychological impact on a person emerging from a Confucian background. In philosophical terms, Christ as personal savior challenges far more radically the traditional web of family, social, and political obligations, than does Christ as mere moral exemplar. This in turn probably would contribute to a heightened awareness of the transcendent worth of the individual as against society or state. In psychological terms, this awareness of Christ as savior tends to express itself subjectively (as it did with St. Augustine or Luther), in a sense of liberation,

---

63. Letters from Laurence Oliphant to Lady Mary Oliphant, written from China in 1857, and quoted in Schneider and Lawton, *Prophet and Pilgrim*, pp. 89–90.

and as a joyful renovation or transcendence (rather than a suppression) of self. Niijima Jō would give expression to both the philosophical and the emotional aspects of the evangelical experience when he proclaimed: "I wish you would rejoice with me at this triumphant hour, for I am a free man, a free man in Christ . . . I do not care for the esteem of men, but only wish to remain a humble child of God."[64]

There is a story[65] to the effect that Mori once disappeared from Brocton for an entire week, occasioning great anxiety among the ladies of the community, with whom he apparently was a great favorite. Upon returning, he explained that he had gone off by himself to meditate on the Resurrection, and that he had found it extremely difficult to comprehend. Whatever the truth of this tale, it seems clear that the chief appeal of Brocton lay not in the type of freedom that Niijima would find but in the wide resonance between Harris' values of obedience, self-effacement, and self-control, and the traditional samurai ethic of *muga,* or "rising above self."

In terms of objective conduct, *muga* and Christian selflessness made much the same demands. Like the Christian ethic, too, *muga* in its original Buddhist inspiration had pointed the way to a subjective sense of deliverance. Both the practical asceticism of the samurai, however, and the Brocton ethic of obedience and self-control (insufficiently related to the love and forgiveness of Christ), must have promoted less an awareness and liberation of the individual self than a reaffirmation, philosophically, of group ties, and —in psychological terms—a tightening of the screws.

Within this general framework of self-denial, Mori may have found the sexual ethic of the Brotherhood particularly compelling: "For all had one great and terrible enemy in themselves to conquer, and this is that old enemy of the flesh of man, Scortation—the inverted and debased sexual sense and passion . . . and it is this that also constitutes the basis or root of that 'proprium' or debased selfhood."[66] Sexual purity, for which Mori at seventeen first expressed

64. Letter from Niijima Jō to Mr. and Mrs. Alpheus Hardy, 8 March 1872, quoted in Arthur S. Hardy, *Life and Letters of Joseph Hardy Neesima* (Boston, 1891), p. 122.

65. As told to the author in July 1966 by Hayashi Takeji. Professor Hayashi heard the story from Mrs. Hiro Ijichi of Berkeley, California, whose late husband was a nephew of Nagasawa Kanaye and had himself spent some time with the Harris colony in California. Mr. Ijichi, in turn, originally had the story from the elderly ladies at Santa Rosa, who still remembered Mori at Brocton.

66. In the words of Arthur A. Cuthbert, as quoted in Block, *New Church,* p. 141.

concern in his "Points to Be Cultivated by the Samurai," and which had taken on for him national significance during his voyage to Russia, was an important tenet of orthodox Swedenborgianism, and with Harris was absolutely central. "Sexual impurity," Cowper noted, "is the great cause of all the evils that afflict the human race. It is the great disorder of the world . . . The Christian Church has only negative exhortation and no positive effective teaching."[67] Swedenborg's doctrine of "conjugial love," as adapted to Harris' theory of "counterpartal marriage,"[68] aimed to remedy this defect. Whatever esoteric twists this tenet may have taken in the private life of the "Primate" himself, to the majority of the Brotherhood it probably meant nothing more complicated than a reaffirmation of the ethical, at the expense of the sensual, bond in the marriage relationship and, in practical terms, celibacy. The *Sun* reported Harris' explanation as follows:

> In heaven the basis of social order is marital order, and so it must be in this world. There, all the senses are completed and included in the sense of chastity, and so it must be in this world . . . Within this sense of chastity nuptial love has its dwelling-place. So utterly hostile is it by nature to what the world understands by desire and passion, that the waftings of an atmosphere bearing these elements in the bosom affect it with loathing . . . In true nuptial love, which is born of love to God, the nuptial pair, from the inmost oneness of the Divine Being, are enbosomed each in each . . . In possessing each other they possess the Lord, who prepares the two to become one heart, one soul . . . With them [the Brotherhood], marriage is the holy of holies on earth, and family relations are held to be absolutely sacred and inviolate.[69]

Matsumura recalls Oliphant's direct confession to the Japanese of his own youthful extravagances,[70] and there is little doubt that

---

67. From a notebook of William F. Cowper entitled "Conversations of Mr. Harris, May 16 to June 1871," Hampshire Record Office (Winchester), Cowper Papers.

68. At its furthest development, counterpartal marriage involved union with the female half of the Divinity, an achievement Harris claimed for himself. There were intermediate stages of "conjugial" (Swedenborg's term —not to be confused with "conjugal") love, however, that apparently were worth striving for as between ordinary married couples. Schneider and Lawton, *Prophet and Pilgrim*, pp. 16, 179–184, 301–303.

69. From "A Celestial Utopia."

70. *Kaigunshi*, II, 909.

the subject was much discussed between them and their Western mentors. What probably counted most on this score, however, was the object lesson of Brocton itself. Harris, himself a widower remarried, lived in celibacy with his second wife (often as not absent from the community), and generally demanded celibacy of his followers, at least until they had acquired the foregoing "sense of chastity." General segregation of the sexes was not enjoined, but as the community settled down, billeting assignments were usually such as to keep the married partners effectively separated from each other (although during Mori's sojourn several couples lived together under the same roof, very possibly setting excellent examples of traditional Western family life at its best). A few marriages took place within the colony, but only two children were born at Brocton (and these to the same couple).[71] The Brotherhood must also have provided an important object lesson in the respectful treatment of women. Harris deplored the indignities still visited upon womankind, as he did those upon his so-called feminine races, and Brocton, like most of the utopian experiments of the time, was ahead of American society in general in the practical equality granted its female members. Encouraged no doubt by the later rise of the feminist movement, Harris would write in 1903:

> Omens appear of one divine rebellion,
> Uprise of Womanhood from sea to sea;
> Closing of outraged wombs million by million;
> Marriage survives, but not sex slavery.
> Godness in sex, shall sex emancipate:
> The normal pulse in woman recreate.[72]

A samurai's concern for stamina and physical health, finally, could also account for interest Mori might have shown in Harris' tenet. Harris was not a faith healer, and there was a practicing physician numbered among the faithful at Brocton. Nevertheless, Harris' own highly publicized struggles with the "inversive forces" attacking him had the quality of exorcism,[73] and there was a great deal of talk within the Brotherhood, even in the 1860's, about the positive physical benefits conferred by "open breathing" in "demagnetizing against disease" and in "energizing for increase of

71. Schneider and Lawton, *Prophet and Pilgrim*, pp. 180–181.
72. From Thomas Lake Harris, *The Song of Theos* (Glasgow, 1903), II, no. XV, quoted in Cuthbert, *Life of Harris*, p. 413.
73. Schneider and Lawton, *Prophet and Pilgrim*, p. 167.

physical health and strength."⁷⁴ Unstated too, perhaps, both in the Brotherhood's concern with sexual purity and in Mori's condemnation of Russian morals, may have been a dread, far more pervasive then than a hundred years later, of venereal disease.

Harris' greatest appeal for Mori probably lay in the fact that his gospel, for all its striking anomalies, was still in the main dynamically social and historical in aim and awareness, and Harris indeed proclaimed it a practical remedy for the concrete economic, social, and political ailments of the nineteenth-century world, including those of Japan. As mystics go, Harris stood squarely in the theistic, nonpantheistic Western Christian mainstream (e.g., Ruysbroeck, Groote, à Kempis), denying neither the reality of matter (including the human body) nor the social experience of mankind. His was what Schweitzer would have called "a mysticism of ethical world and life affirmation,"⁷⁵ as opposed to the renunciation, the quietism, the *via negativa,* of most oriental mysticism and of the Neoplatonic tradition (e.g., Plotinus, Erigena, Eckhart) in the West. The very person of Harris himself bespoke this aspect of his creed, the New York *Sun* describing him as follows: "Mr. Harris is a tough, wiry, compact man, some forty-five years old, of medium height and much muscular activity. His eye is keen, clear, and firm and his intellect strong and practical. We were surprised, phrenologically speaking, to find his intellect and common sense so predominant over his imaginative and spiritual faculties. Judging from his personal presentation, not even Gradgrind himself had a better appreciation of 'hard facts' nor was less a dreamer."

Schweitzer's further characterization of the Japanese religious nature as "world and life affirming" (which he attributes to the persistent work of the life-affirming animus in Shinto)⁷⁶ suggests the very basic predisposition which the Satsuma group would have possessed for this sort of world view. Mori in particular, as his letters to Yokoyama suggest, was interested in his own self-perfection less as an end in itself than as a means to fulfilling his "great task," which in turn was socially and historically defined.

What recommendations in detail Harris and Oliphant may have

---

74. Ibid., p. 172. Harris in later years would lay claim to having found out, "How, without passing through physical disease, a man shall practically embody and realize the resurrection." (Ibid., p. 454, quoting Thomas Lake Harris, *The Brotherhood of the New Life* [Fountain Grove, 1891]).

75. Albert Schweitzer, *Indian Thought and its Development,* (Mrs.) Charles E. B. Russell (Beacon Paperback edition, Boston, 1957), p. 18.

76. Ibid., pp. 150–156.

made to the Japanese with regard to the future development of their country is not recorded. Judging, however, from Harris' "Prophecy of Japan" and from Mori's farewell letter of June 1868, they dwelt more on moral and ethical than on social, economic, and political matters, and viewed the former as the key to the latter. Political education no doubt continued to progress under the tutelage of Oliphant, with fresh attention perhaps to the American scene. Although Brocton members held their property in common, Harris rejected both the class struggle of the Marxists and what he considered the oversimplified, outmoded methods of the Owenites and Fourierists. His views on the economic order during the 1860's were closest to those of Christian Socialism, but what impressed the Japanese most in economic matters was probably once again the object lesson provided by the community itself. The Brotherhood operated its enterprises in a highly efficient and utilitarian manner, and at a very handsome profit. Max Weber once noted the combination, the functional fusion even, of religious eccentricity and economic rationality in many of the American "fringe" sects. And of this, Brocton was a prime example.[77]

Brocton would have been a "hothouse," a far from normal way of life, for most occidentals too, and it is instructive that Harris failed to keep the allegiance of the children of Brocton members, who with few exceptions broke with the community upon attaining their majority, reviling Harris in later years for their memories of an unhappy childhood.[78] A break was in the making among the Japanese as well: first, a split intramurally, and then the defection of the majority from Brocton. Bad blood originally broke out between Mori and Yoshida during a group confessional. As Mrs. Cowper would recall in 1873: "The Japanese after listening to a sermon agreed that they would tell one another their faults and bound themselves not to resent what was said. Each one was put forward in turn for the others to state to him his faults, but most of them smarted under what they considered the injustice of the charges made against them. Sawai [Mori] condemned Nagai [Yoshida] very severely, and the smothered antagonism that has existed between them broke out fiercely and they quarrelled and a general state of anger and dispute sprung up amongst them, and they all went wrong."[79]

77. Max Weber, "Die protestantischen Sekten und der Geist des Kapitalismus," in *Gesammelte Aufsätze zur Religionssoziologie* (Tübingen, 1920), I, 207–236.
78. Schneider and Lawton, *Prophet and Pilgrim*, p. 218 ff.
79. Cowper, "Conversations of Harris, May 16 to June 1871."

Tension boiled over in May 1868 when the hypothetical question arose as to what their proper attitude should be in the event of a war between Japan and the United States. Nagasawa in later years recalled that some (presumably those who defected, including Yoshida), came out for Japan; others hedged the choice by suggesting neutrality. This second group presumably numbered those who remained loyal to Harris, including Mori, who while in England had decided that Japan and America had a great deal to gain by remaining good friends. Harris, asked for a verdict, poohpoohed the whole issue as unreal, but said he trusted they would all stand firmly on the side of Christ.[80] That was too much for the Monson five, who at once bolted, and for Yoshida, Matsumura, and Hatakeyama, who ran away to Rutgers College, "rescued or escaping," in the later words of William Elliot Griffis, "from this Lake Erie delusion and slavery."[81]

The defection of Yoshida, the great favorite, came as a deep shock to both Harris and Oliphant. His leaving them, however, was perhaps as much a matter of temperament as of patriotism, and certainly not one of religion; for both he and Hatakeyama went on to join churches at New Brunswick.[82] Harris was a puzzling combination of charlatanism and genuine spiritual power. Souls in search primarily of guidance tended to see in him only the latter, and to take his self-proclaimed role at face value. More independent souls, struggling above all for self-expression, were inclined to espy in him something of the former. Yoshida, from what we know of his later personality,[83] probably had the sense of humor which enabled him, at last, to call Harris' number. Mori—this terribly earnest, somewhat literal-minded, increasingly somber young man, who could write essays about paving stones and lose sleep over the problem of illegitimate births—did not.

Mori and Samejima also left shortly thereafter, but under entirely different motivation. Whereas Kimura Kyō attributes their departure to Harris' urgent prompting, Ōkubo Toshiaki judges that the exciting news of the Restoration would have been sufficient

---

80. In the later recollection of Nagasawa, in Washizu Shakuma, "Nagasawa Kanaye den" (Life of Nagasawa Kanaye; unpublished), discussed by Hayashi in "Ryūgakusei," part V, p. 60. Yoshida and Hatakeyama already had left Brocton by 22 May 1868. (Hayashi, *Mori kenkyū: dai ni*, p. 155.)

81. William E. Griffis, "The Japanese Students in America," *The Japanese Student: A Bimonthly for Japanese Students in America*, vol. 1, no. 1 (October 1916), p. 11.

82. *Kaigunshi*, II, 913.

83. See Chapter Six.

reason for Mori's returning home even without Harris' blessing and exhortation to work for the cause in Japan.[84] That Mori was not among the disenchanted in any case, and that he was able to reconcile his religious and patriotic motivations, is attested by a farewell letter which he and Samejima addressed to Yoshida, Hatakeyama, and the five Monson students, all of them still in America. Having left Brocton on 8 June 1868, and having boarded a steamer in New York on the twelfth, they mailed their reproof from Panama on the seventeenth:

> The object of our going at this time is nothing very special, but is simply to discharge our duty to our country . . . We concluded to go, throwing ourselves into the midst of disturbance and darkness, because we felt we should. We should be exceedingly glad and fully satisfied if we could only be worthy to become even the very smallest prey for the sake of the restoration of the kingdom . . . We still feel, yea more and more, inexpressibly grateful towards the Lord our Heavenly Father, for He is through His beloved servant T. L. Harris working so infinitely and so mercifully for the salvation of all the inhabitants of the globe . . . Those who in reality hunger and thirst to find their life in the Lord, and to become his children, or rather to return to their proper and pure state originally ordained, shall doubtless arrive at the state in which they shall be able to bear the true acknowledgment concerning the teaching through Mr. Harris . . . The purpose of telling you all these things is but to make what we acknowledge clearly known to you, lest that you might have taken some untrue impressions, and that you might thereby have felt somehow badly toward the teachings . . . May the Most High guard you against every temptation and attraction of the Prince of the World.[85]

Mori and Samejima wrote the letter as given above, in English. We can only guess whether the kingdom to be restored was the

84. KKM, p. 31; OTM, p. 26.
85. Letter from "Noda" (Samejima Naonobu) and "Sawai" (Mori Arinori) to "Nagai" (Yoshida Kiyonari), "Soogiwoola" (Hatakeyama Yoshinari), "Hisamatz," "Shimada," "Ohara," "Yoshida," and "Kudo," 17 June 1868. The last five names presumably were the cover names for the five Monson students—Enatsu Sōsuke, Tanegashima Keisuke, Nire Kagenori, Yūchi Sadamoto, and Yoshihara Shigetoshi. The letter was written aboard the steamer, *H. Chauncey,* and mailed from Aspinwall (today's Colon), Panama. A typescript copy of the letter, with addressees, may be found in HOP; the full text of the letter is given in Schneider and Lawton, *Prophet and Pilgrim,* pp. 214–215.

emperor's, or God's, or both. It is conceivable, of course, that Harris or Oliphant may have suggested the idea of the letter, perhaps even some of the phrasing, before their departure. But it is clear in any case that Mori has embarked upon the "great task" he set himself while in England, and for which his Satsuma upbringing had predisposed him, and that much of the strength he had been looking for during that first year in London would now come from a source undreamed of prior to his return from Russia.

The most significant long-range function of the Satsuma expedition of 1865–68 probably was the training of a corps of able young diplomats, fluent in the English language, and very much at home in British and American society—Mori, Yoshida, Samejima, Terajima—who traded off among themselves the ministerial posts at Washington and London during the 1870's and into the early 1880's, contributing immeasurably to the relatively smooth and amicable tenor of Anglo-Japanese and Japanese-American diplomatic and cultural relations during the two opening decades of Meiji.[86] For Mori, the first year had brought a vision of a prosperous, modern society, justly and rationally and humanely organized; the second year, among other things a more realistic view of world politics; and the third year, an approach to public and personal problems which was aggressively moralistic in tone.

What Harris and Brocton had essentially done for Mori was to provide his developing vision of a new Japan with both a moral and a more personal, or "existential," dimension which had been lacking during his first year in London. This was accomplished in the main by mobilizing his existing moral sentiment and psychological structure. Mori's concept of justice and his feeling for the rational and the humane, which emerged very strongly in 1865–1866, suggested well enough how society and institutions might, in specific ways, be reformed. But they still fell short of the all-encompassing moral rationale which Mori, by virtue of his Confucian training, was strongly predisposed to seek. And they were strictly speaking social ideals, somewhat impersonal in quality, which had failed among other things to shed light on the nagging problem of sexual ethics.

Oliphant apparently did not broach religious matters, or speak of Harris, until his Atlantic crossing in the summer of 1866. From

---

86. Members of the Satsuma expedition who later served as Japanese ministers at Washington included Mori (1871–1873), Yoshida, (1876–1882), and Terajima (1882–1883); and at London: Samejima (1871–1872), Terajima (1872–1873), and Mori (1880–1884). Mori's immediate predecessor at the London legation was his old English tutor of earlier Kagoshima days, Ueno Keihan.

the autumn of 1866 on, however, Mori gradually came to find in Harris' teaching not only wisdom on the sexual question but also a comprehensive moral framework for the regeneration of Japan. Harris furthermore spelled out for Mori his own individual role in the scheme and reinforced his longstanding sense of political mission—and his craving for political involvement—with the fresh sanction of divine appointment. As to means, Mori was asked to rely on the familiar ethic of self-denial, bolstered by the familiar rigors of physical exertion. As to ends, he was assured that the very existence of his own country was at stake. Neither the new justice to which Oliphant had introduced Mori in 1865–1866 nor the new morality to which Harris and Oliphant led him in 1866–1868 were perceived to be in any way incompatible with the national power and security of Japan.

How deeply Mori had absorbed these new Western elements would not be apparent until he could put them to the test of application which awaited him upon landing in Yokohama in July 1868. His education was far from over. But from now on it would be the highly practical education of a rough-and-tumble involvement in fast-moving national affairs.

Four   1868–1870

IN AND OUT OF THE
NEW GOVERNMENT

On 11 September 1868 (25/VII Meiji 1), barely a month after his return from Brocton, Mori received an appointment as *gaikokukan gonhanji* (assistant inspector) in the foreign ministry, with which he would be officially associated for nearly sixteen years until his transfer to the education ministry on 7 May 1884. Mori's life had entered upon the second of its three phases of student, diplomat, and Monbushō official.

Mori in a sense came home to a foreign land. Photographs for 1868–69 show him in traditional Japanese dress, girt about with the long and short swords, having gone full circle from *hakama* to tweeds to dungarees and back to *hakama* again. However, the chronicler relates,[1] Mori deliberately wore these swords in "reversed" or *sorizashi* fashion, that is to say with the tips thrust frontward through the belt and the grips well out of reach somewhere to the rear, rendering a quick draw physically impossible. With no other sartorial gesture could he have thumbed his nose more dramatically at the feudal heritage of his native land.

In this vignette, which might be called the Anecdote of the Unserviceable Swords, we encounter the first of a series of semi-legendary stories about Mori, many of them compiled by Kimura Kyō in a postscript to his biography entitled "Sensei no hanmen" (Profiles of the man). The proportion of historical truth in these

1. KKM, p. 269.

stories no doubt varies considerably from case to case, but they do help to outline for us the image of Mori in the popular mind of his own times, and we shall introduce them occasionally for this purpose, abbreviating and paraphrasing the Japanese originals and being careful to identify them as "Anecdotes."

How distant and outlandish a figure Mori seemed to local Tokyoites as of New Year's Day 1869, for instance, is suggested by the Anecdote of the Parboiled Pachyderm:

> Mori had no proper court dress in which to pay his respects to the Emperor on New Year's Day. In desperation, he went to Kanda Kōhei for advice. The two decided it would be best to feign illness and repair to Kanagawa. Stopping for lunch at the Kamata Gardens, they asked the waitress what was on the menu. She suggested *umani* [a boiled fish-and-vegetable dish, *ni* meaning boiled, but *uma* being a homophone also for "horse"]. Mori was greatly taken aback. He scolded the waitress roundly, calling her a fool and exclaimed, "Boiled horsemeat indeed! Bring us veal! Nobody eats horses!" Kanda laughed and tried to explain, but Mori only got angrier. The two then decided to drop in on Terajima, then governor of Kanagawa. Kanda at once related the lunchtime incident. Terajima, keeping a straight face all the while, turned to Mori and said, "I have a real Japanese dish here—*zōni*—[boiled rice cakes, *zō* being also however a homophone for "elephant"] to which I'd like to treat you, but don't be disappointed if you don't get elephant!" Terajima then burst out laughing, but Mori merely scratched his head and kept his mouth shut.[2]

Kimura suggests that Mori's isolated Kagoshima upbringing may have been as responsible as his occidental sojourn for such gaucheries as he may have committed upon arrival in the new capital. Mori was far too valuable a person, however—with his knowledge of the West, his linguistic skill, and his Satsuma connections—not to be stretched to the full in a number of official capacities, the variety of which reflected less his own innate versatility than the bewildering scope of diplomatic, political, administrative, and cultural problems which the new government suddenly found itself confronting.

2. Ibid., p. 264, has a brief version of the episode. A fuller account may be found in Tanaka Kazutoshi, *Kinsei ijin hyakuwa* (Tokyo, 1922), pp. 64–66.

POLITICAL APPRENTICESHIP IN TOKYO

Mori and Samejima upon homecoming met with Sanjō Sanetomi in Tokyo and Iwakura Tomomi in Kyoto, and were introduced to Yokoi Shōnan by the latter at that time.[3] "They held forth," Kimura relates, "on the true state of Western civilization and on the urgent need to import it into Japan. Iwakura was most impressed with what they had to say and took a great liking to them."[4] They both stood so high in his confidence, indeed, that William Elliot Griffis reported them as being "dubbed, in the political slang of the capital, 'the legs of Iwakura'."[5]

The two and a half years Mori would now spend in Japan divide into three subperiods: something less than a year (September 1868–July 1869) of sedulous governmental activity in Tokyo, balanced by the relaxed, informal flavor of life at home with his student boarders, and climaxed by his startling proposal for the abolition of sword-wearing; something over a year (August 1869–October 1870) of rustication at Kagoshima, culminating with the suicide of his brother and his own reappointment to the foreign office; and roughly three months' preparation in Tokyo for his new diplomatic post in America.

Mori, Samejima, and Minami Teisuke (T. L. Harris' Chōshū devotee) filled the three posts of assistant inspector under Inspector (*hanji*) Machida Hisanari in the Gaikokukan, as the foreign office was known under the Seitaisho (Edict on the Form of Government) structure in effect from 11 June 1868 to 15 August 1869. This office was initially established at Osaka, and it seems likely that Mori remained in the Kansai until the transfer of the Gaikokukan to Tokyo on 5 December 1868 (22/X). Machida ranked directly under Vice Minister (*fukuchiji*) Higashikuze Michitomi and Foreign Minister (*chiji*) Date Munenari; and below Mori's grade came an apprentice inspector, a secretary, and three scribes; so his duties most likely lay somewhere between the policy-making and the clerical levels. Given the English language fluency of the three young assistant inspectors, it was probably they who carried the burden of ongoing contact with the representatives of the treaty powers.[6] Their task was made no easier, though

3. KKM, p. 32; OTM, p. 27.
4. KKM, p. 32.
5. William E. Griffis, *The Mikado's Empire*, 11th ed. (New York, 1906), I, 399.
6. One Western diplomat impressed with Mori's linguistic ability, although not with the ripeness of his years, was Ernest Satow, who wrote in his

their scarcity value was no doubt enhanced, by the natural reluctance of the new government to make use at the highest level of the seasoned corps of Bakufu foreign affairs specialists. These had been transferred en masse to the new Tokyo municipal customs bureau, or Unjōsho, many of them thereupon resigning and offering their services, in a fit of spite, to the foreign legations.[7] The Meiji government announced very generally in January 1869 its intention of commencing negotiations for a revision of the unequal treaties,[8] but the actual negotiations that were concluded during Mori's first stint at the foreign office served to extend Japan's web of obligation, new treaties being entered into with Sweden and Norway on 11 November 1868, and with the North German Confederation on 20 February 1869, both on terms considerably less favorable than the agreements concluded by the Bakufu in 1858.[9]

A far more challenging task[10] awaited Mori in the Gijiteisai Torishirabesho, or Bureau for the Investigation of a Deliberative Assembly System, which he joined (concurrently with his Foreign Office post) at the rank of *kakari* (Secretary) on 3 November 1868 (19/IX). Here Mori served with five other *kakari* (Akizuki Taneki, Fukuoka Kōtei, Ōki Takato, Kanda Kōhei, and Samejima Naonobu) under the presidency of Yamanouchi Toyonobu, all of them entrusted with the development of plans for a deliberative assembly in conformity with the promise of the Charter Oath that public councils would be widely established and all matters decided by public discussion. The result of their labors was the Kōgisho (Deliberative Assembly), which opened its doors on 18 April 1869 (7/III), with Mori in the chair as Acting Speaker (*tōbun gichō,* or *gichō jimu sekkō*) from 4 through 28 May (23/III-17/IV), when he relinquished that post to Kanda Kōhei. On 28 May the Gijiteisai Torishirabesho was reconstituted briefly as the Seidoryō (Bureau for the Study of Governmental Institu-

---

diary for 28 November 1868: "Parkes and Bishop Alford came up to Yedo, and we had a European breakfast and conversation with Uwajima and Higashikuze at the Setsu-gū-jo. Machida Mimbu and Mori were there. They have both been in England and speak the language, especially the latter, who is a youngster of about one and twenty." PRO, Satow Papers, PRO-30-33-15-3, "Diary, November, 1868–August, 1871."

7. Inau Tentarō, *Nihon gaikōshisōshi ronkō: dai ichi: jōyaku kaiseiron no tenkai* (Tokyo, 1966), pp. 46–47.
8. Ibid., p. 59.
9. Ibid., pp. 48–49.
10. KKM, pp. 32–33; OTM, pp. 28, 37. For Mori's superiors and colleagues, see the materials compiled by Robert A. Wilson, *Genesis of the Meiji Government in Japan: 1868–1871* (University of California Publications in History, vol. 56; Berkeley, 1957), p. 119.

tions) in order to review recruitment policies for government officials. Mori was appointed with Matsuura Akira and Ōhara Shigesane as one of three vice presidents (*fukusōsai*) under the two *sōsai,* Yamanouchi Toyonobu and Nabeshima Naomasa. On 27 June (18/V) this body gave way in turn to the Seido Torishirabesho (similarly translatable as its predecessor) which investigated the governmental structure on an across-the-board basis, Mori serving here as one of the four *goyō kakari* (official secretaries), with Ōhara, Kanda, and Katō Hiroyuki, until his resignation on 28 July 1869 (20/VI). He also continued without break his activity in the Kōgisho, not as the representative of Satsuma, however, but as a representative of the government, particularly of the Gijiteisai Torishirabesho and its successor bureaus, all of which continued to prepare the Kōgisho agenda.

In February 1869 Mori was invested with a court rank of the Junior Fifth Rank, Lower Grade (jūgoi-ge), while appointment to two additional commissions gave him insight into other fundamental questions of the day.

From 17 December 1868 to 23 April 1869 (4/XI/Meiji 1 to 12/III/Meiji 2) he served on the Gakkō Torishirabe, or Committee for the Investigation of the Educational System, and from 27 June to 28 July (18/V to 20/VI) as an inspector (*hanji*) of the Gakkō, forerunner of the ministry of education, which continued the work of the earlier committee. In both instances Mori worked under the chairmanship and vice-chairmanship of Yamanouchi Toyonobu and Akizuki Taneki, respectively, his colleagues including Mitsukuri Rinshō, Kanda Kōhei, Katō Hiroyuki, Uchida Masao, and Hosokawa Junjirō. No records survive of the early deliberations of this group, which not only laid the groundwork for the Monbushō of 1871 and the Gakusei (Fundamental Code of Education) of 1872, but also exercised a general supervisory role over such state-sponsored educational institutions as emerged during the interim.[11] Mori, however, probably took the lead in pressing those arguments in favor of Western learning which eventually weathered the heavy attack from Confucianist and Shintoist quarters from 1868 to 1871.

Finally, Mori, as inspector (*hanji*) in the Gunmukan, or military

11. OTM, p. 37; *Gakusei gojūnenshi,* comp. Monbushō (Tokyo, 1922), p. 22. The Gakkō, or Shōhei Gakkō to use its full name, doubled also as a seat of higher learning, the old Tokugawa college having been revived for that purpose on 17 August 1868. It was renamed Daigakkō on 23 July 1869 and Daigaku on 29 December 1869, which name it retained until its metamorphosis into the Monbushō on 2 September 1871 (*Gakusei gojūnenshi,* pp. 7–8).

affairs office, from 28 February to 28 May 1869 (18/I to 17/IV), recommended patterning the Japanese navy after that of Britain and the army after that of France.[12] It was a point which had also occurred to Mori's former mentor, Godai, in 1865,[13] and the choice of France was natural enough in the years immediately preceding Sedan.

Mori's diplomatic, educational, and military interests, however, were all peripheral to his activities on behalf of the Kōgisho during this busy political year. The Kōgisho (16 April–15 August 1869) and its lineal descendant, the Shūgiin (15 August 1869–13 September 1871), for all their failure to develop into an authentic legislative body, did represent the only experiment of any kind with a "public council widely established" between the Restoration and the convening of the first Diet in 1890. Even accepting George Sansom's verdict that "the assembly proved incapable of any useful discussion or advice,"[14] it is here that one would have to search for evidence of Mori's earliest views on representative government and for his reputedly liberal bias at that time. Since the Kōgisho as such has been adequately described and evaluated elsewhere,[15] the discussion here will be confined to Mori's own actions and intentions with respect to this body. Unfortunately none of the proposals he submitted to the Deliberative Assembly for debate deals with the constitutional question itself, or with the proper role of a legislature. Since no record exists of the deliberations of the Gijiteisai Torishirabesho, where Mori no doubt explained his own views at length, we must infer his ideas from his general attitude toward the new body.

It seems likely that Mori was neither unaware of, nor unsympathetic to, that which has generally been described as the government's own overriding motive in establishing the Kōgisho, namely, the felt need for a safety valve for the feudal and particularist sensitivities that were bound to be hurt in the drive for a modern, centralized state. Having fretted as early as London over the "unseemly commotions" dividing the land, Mori penned, as his first political document upon returning to Japan, a letter to Ōkubo Toshimichi dated 7 March 1869 (25/I; a good month ahead of

12. KKM, p. 32.
13. *Sappan kaigunshi,* comp. Kōshaku Shimazuke Henshūjo, 3 vols. (Kagoshima, 1928), II, 944, quoting letter from Godai Tomoatsu to Katsura Uemon, 29 Nov. 1865 (12 X Keiō 1).
14. George B. Sansom, *The Western World and Japan* (New York, 1950), p. 321.
15. Notably in Wilson, *Meiji Government.*

the opening of the Kōgisho and two days after the return of han registers by the four western clans), in which he urged the speedy establishment of a strong central government:

> It has become my earnest desire of late that we exercise genuine Imperial rule, maintaining the true relations of sovereign and subjects [*taigi meibun*], and clearly establish the principle that the length and breadth of the land is the Emperor's. Now that our own han and its allies have taken the initiative in this matter, it is my silent prayer, day in day out . . . that the way may be prepared for a speedy reversion of authority from the han to the central government, securing thereby the final objective of our Loyalist cause. My colleagues Lord Yamanouchi and Lord Akizuki have been busier than ever of late, and are of the opinion that the future maintenance of our Empire will prove difficult if we do not at this time establish its foundation securely on the *gunken* [county-prefecture] system, returning political power from the han to the center, placing the national authority firmly in one hand and facing up to the foreign powers on that basis.[16]

Since the membership of the Kōgisho, far from answering for "the people" in any Anglo-American sense of the term, actually represented that very feudal power which Mori was so anxious to see broken, his attitude toward the assembly as constituted was probably somewhat ambivalent, pride of parenthood notwithstanding. Indeed, with his proposal on sword-wearing he would tell them, collectively, to go to perdition.

Of Mori's enthusiastic espousal and leadership of the Kōgisho project, however, there is incontrovertible evidence. Regarding the proceedings of the Gijiteisai Torishirabesho, Ōkubo Toshiaki writes that "Mori conducted a one-man show"; Kimura Kyō that "the real authority lay rather with Mori, though he was nominally subordinate to Yamanouchi"; Kaimon Sanjin that the Kōgisho was "in fact the product of the recommendations of two persons, Mori and Samejima, to the power-holding clique"; Osatake Takeki that "the Kōgisho regulations, in particular the layout of the chamber . . . were based entirely on the information which [Mori] . . . had garnered in Europe and America."[17] We also have, for whatever it is worth, the Anecdote of the Squandered Ballot, which

16. OTM, p. 32.
17. OTM, p. 28; KKM, p. 33; KSM, p. 25; Osatake Takeshi, *Nihon kenseishi no kenkyū*, Ichigensha ed. (Tokyo, 1943), p. 361.

suggests that Mori had grasped something very fundamental about the meaning of the vote: "During the balloting for *sangi* [councillors] some time in early Meiji, Mori once cast the single vote for Takasaki Masakaze, a man already quite out of the running who had already returned to Satsuma after incurring the displeasure of the Chōshū group. Asked why he had wasted his vote, Mori retorted: "Come now, the very efficacy of the ballot lies in the fact that it is freely cast, entirely in accordance with the individual's own wishes. There is absolutely no reason for you to go poking your nose into this matter!"[18]

Most influential in establishing Mori's later reputation for having been a political liberal during this period was the wide publicity Tokutomi Sohō gave in 1889 to a brief passage in Yokoi Shōnan's diary for late 1868 in which the latter recounted that he had had "a very pleasant discussion, lasting the whole night through, with Mori Kinnojō, who expatiated at great length on the subject of the United States Congress."[19] What Mori actually told Yokoi, however, how deep his grasp of the American (or British) system in a political-scientific sense actually went, or just how adaptable he felt such institutions might be to Japan, is not recorded. That Mori held the American polity in profound respect, and that he had perceived the importance of resting the political structure on a just and rational foundation, is evident from his letters from London. It is also certain that whatever knowledge on the subject Mori might have brought home with him—textbooks perhaps, mental notes on Oliphant surely, the memory of visits to Westminster (but probably not Capitol Hill)—would have loomed large against the almost total ignorance which surrounded him. Three years, for instance, would pass before the finer and profounder mind of Kido Takayoshi would be able to pronounce on the same topic from first-hand experience; and Mori was at the time, in the recollection of Ijichi Sumimasa, "regarded as the oracle of English parliamentary practice."[20]

Osatake makes the most telling point in Mori's favor when he argues that the opening clause of the Kōgisho hōsokuan (Draft regulations for the Kōgisho) of January 1869, which Mori was

18. KKM, p. 255.
19. Yokoi's diary is no longer extant, but we have reconstructed the passage here from the indirect discourse as given in Tokutomi Sohō, "Mori Arinori kun," *Kokumin no tomo*, no. 42 (February 1889). Tokutomi's article will appear in *Zenshū* II.
20. Smimasa Idditti, *The Life of Marquis Shigenobu Okuma: A Maker of New Japan* (Tokyo, 1940), p. 117.

instrumental in authoring, and which provided the rules of procedure for the new assembly, shows an unmistakable intent to invest the body with genuine lawmaking authority:[21] "1. The making of laws shall be the primary business of the Assembly. Additional functions may be assigned at the discretion of the Speaker. The Assembly shall not concern itself with measures of a temporary or emergency nature."[22] Three considerations are worth bearing in mind here, however, in any attempt to evaluate underlying intentions.

First, the clause quoted states simply that lawmaking is to be the primary activity, taking precedence over other activities, of the Kōgisho, not that the Kōgisho itself is to hold the primary responsibility, vis-à-vis other organs of government, for lawmaking. As a matter of fact, measures the assembly might pass (by a three-fifths majority) were in no way binding upon the Dajōkan, or council of state. The most progressive aspect of the Kōgisho lay simply in its concurrent right, with the Dajōkan, to initiate legislation.[23]

Second, granting the indispensable role which Mori's relative expertise enabled him to play in evolving the details of the project, it is still important to place his own efforts in the broader context of contemporary Japanese constitutional thinking and government policy. The government had already committed itself, in the Seitaisho of 11 June 1868 to the principles that: "The power and authority of the Council of State shall be threefold, legislative, executive and judicial" [Article 2], and that "The legislative organ shall not be permitted to perform executive functions, nor shall the executive organ be permitted to perform legislative functions" [Article 3]. It was the disappointing confusion in practice of legislative and executive functions originally apportioned under the Seitaisho as between the Giseikan (legislative office) and Gyōseikan (executive office), which had led the government to set up the Gijiteisai Torishirabesho for the study of a more effective separation of powers,[24] and to bring together in that bureau (very shortly

21. Osatake Takeshi, *Ishin zengo ni okeru rikken shisō,* 2nd ed., (Tokyo, 1929), II, 430.
22. "Kōgisho hōsokuan" (Draft regulations for the Kōgisho), in MBZ, IV, 3.
23. Even this right was subsequently lost upon transformation of the Kōgisho into the Shūgiin on 15 August 1869.
24. Kyōto Daigaku Bungakubu Kokushi Kenkyūshitsu, ed., *Nihon kindaishi jiten* (Tokyo, 1958), p. 146. The quotations from the Seitaisho follow the translation given in W. W. McLaren, "Japanese Government Documents," *Transactions of the Asiatic Society of Japan,* vol. 42, pt. 1 (1914), p. 8.

after Mori's homecoming as it happened), figures prominently associated with the various constitutional schools of the 1860's: Yamanouchi and Fukuoka for Tosa; Kanda from the former Bakufu side; Akizuki and Ōki from the Kakyoku or Lower House of the Giseikan.[25] Pre-Restoration theory had leaned heavily in the direction of the separation and balance of powers, somewhat superficially understood, and it is possible to view the Kōgisho less as the antecedent of later Japanese constitutional development than as the last gasp of half-baked Bakumatsu-Montesquieu, and as an abortive attempt to introduce a model (i.e., the American) thoroughly unsuited to Japanese conditions and never again to be raised again as an object of serious constitutional discussion.

As concepts, then, the separation of powers and the establishment of a legislature were hardly new with Mori, and we need to ask just how far his own comprehension of the matter went beyond that of his colleagues. The Kōgisho as a matter of fact served not as an independent legislature but merely as an advisory committee to the council of state, which retained effective and undivided possession of legislative, executive, and judicial powers. We must take pains, accordingly, not to reason from Mori's general admiration for the British and American polities, and from his participation in an experiment with little more than a certain typological affinity for the latter, to the conclusion that he was necessarily anxious or willing, with the Kōgisho, to see a genuine legislature on Western democratic lines introduced into Japan at that time. Osatake's evaluation of the Mori of the Kōgisho as a major contributor to Meiji constitutional development certainly holds at the level of procedure: even if the Kōgisho must be brushed aside as a mere debating society which went through the motions of a parliament, those motions were entirely new to Japan and would someday have to be learned; and Mori at the very least knew (as he would know with the Meirokusha five years later) how to set up the club, rules and all. What we lack for Mori at this juncture is evidence of a firm position on representative government at the substantive, or political, level: the level on which any estimate of his supposed liberalism would have to be based. We have, indeed, no detailed statement of his views on a constitutional system until his pamphlet *On a Representative System of Government for Japan,* dated 1884.[26] Third, and most important in evaluating Mori's intentions with respect to the Kōgisho, we must

25. Osatake, *Rikken shisō,* II, 427.
26. See Chapter Eight.

bear in mind his explicit counsel to his brother Yokoyama regarding the adaptation of legal (and by extension, political) institutions to the Japanese environment: a piece of advice which was to remain an important guideline in his own subsequent political thinking.

The Kōgisho occupied itself for the most part with the discussion of social and administrative rather than political practices, ranging from weights and measures to tatooing and cremation; and Mori's own activity in the assembly is most instructive for what it tells us of his envisioning of a modern, as opposed to a feudal, society. He submitted in all five proposals over his own name.

In "Sōzei no gi" (On taxation; April or May 1869; not put to vote), he advocated: (1) that taxes be collectable in either rice or cash at the convenience of the collecting agent; and (2) that no additional levies beyond the fixed amount, and no increases or reductions in the fixed amount, be permitted without prior debate (Mori does not, however, say "approval"), in the Kōgisho.[27] In "Tsūshō o haishi jitsumei nomi o mochiuru beki koto" (On disuse of the popular name, and exclusive use of the true name; approved 7 June 1869), Mori was concerned to encourage a greater spirit of public service. His proposal skirted the problem of commoners' names, but specified that in the case of officials rank and title might be used ahead of the surname (e.g., "Jūgoi Mori Arinori") but never in place of the given name (e.g., "Mori Jūgoi"), thereby eliminating a practice cherished for centuries by bureaucratic show-offs.[28]

In "Keizai wa sono isshin ni todomeru beki gi" (On the confining of penalties to the criminal concerned; June 1869; not put to the vote), Mori castigated as "heartlessly cruel and unjust" the rubric in traditional law which under given circumstances visited punishment upon the "unwitting and innocent" relatives, wives, and children of the accused.[29]

Sometime in June, in "Gokokutai no gi ni tsuki mondai shijō" (Four questions relating to the matter of the national polity), Mori raised the question how long Japan could remain an amalgam of feudally administered han and directly administered prefectures. He requested the Kōgisho to consider the relative merits and feasibilities of reorganizing the entire nation either on a confederated, feudal (*hōken*) pattern, or on a centralized *gunken* basis. This was primarily a trial balloon calculated to bring into open

27. "Gianroku" (Record of legislative bills), in MBZ, IV, 142.
28. "Kōgisho nisshi" (Kōgisho journal), in MBZ, IV, 55.
29. "Gianroku," p. 145.

discussion the eventual return of han registers.³⁰ It evoked a variety of draft proposals. "Gokokusei kaisei no gi" (On the reform of the national structure), which anticipated many of the measures later taken by the government, and which Osatake Takeki takes to be Mori's own revised draft,³¹ called among other things for: the establishment of a *gunken* system; the organization of a new graded aristocracy, ranging from the imperial blood (*kōzoku*) down through the nobility (*kizoku;* including both daimyo and the old court nobility) to two grades of samurai; the transfer of incompetent samurai to commoner status; the appointment of governors in the prefectures (at the beginning, from among the incumbent han rulers); the establishment of schools "for the civil and military arts" and of assemblies "widely chosen" in each prefecture; the location of a naval headquarters in each of the major port towns; and the selection of army and navy officers on the basis of talent.³²

Mori's views in the Kōgisho debate on the treatment of Christians, which commenced on 26 June 1869 and ended with approval of a resolution calling for the expulsion of Roman Catholicism, have not been recorded. The single pronouncement we have on this subject during this period is Mori's suggestion to Ernest Satow at a dinner party that the Japanese Christians be allotted lands in Hokkaido where they might enjoy free exercise of their religion, a suggestion of which the English diplomat did "not see the advantage"—most likely because it evaded the fundamental issue of religious toleration.³³

The climax of Mori's Kōgisho activity, indeed of his entire political novitiate of 1868–69, came with the "Haitōron" (Proposal for the abolition of sword-wearing), which skyrocketed him into national notoriety,³⁴ and which provides important clues not only

30. Wilson, *Meiji Government,* pp. 51–52.
31. Osatake, *Rikken shisō,* II, 480.
32. "Kōgisho nisshi," pp. 63–64.
33. Satow Papers, "Diary, 1868–1871," entry for 14 Feb. 1869. Satow wrote that "[At the dinner both Kido] and Mori talked about the Christians and asked my advice. I counselled moderate measures and long letters to the Foreign Ministers now and then as a quietus. I acknowledged the difficulty of instilling the idea of toleration into the minds of the whole Japanese people by an act of Parliament, and told them of the disabilities under which Protestants lay in Spain until the other day; but I did not see the advantage of Mori's suggestion to allot lands in Yezo, with a free exercise of their religion to the Christians."
34. The five-act play "Mori Arinori," by Osanai Kaoru, opens with a dramatic reconstruction of the "Haitōron" debate. The full text may be found in Osanai Kaoru, *Gikyokushū* (Tokyo, 1926), while the first act, with the "Haitōron" debate, has been reprinted in Harada Minoru, *Mori Arinori,*

to the mainsprings of his character but also to his view of priorities for Japan. Here was political suicide, openly courted. So drastic an impulse would have to originate (one would suppose) either in some personal idiosyncrasy of the individual or in the objective significance of the issue itself, or in some combination of the two.

Mori's proposal, introduced for debate on 6 July 1869 (27/V) advocated that: (1) persons other than civil and military officials should be permitted to dispense with the wearing of swords; (2) civil officials should be permitted to dispense with the wearing of the short sword. In exposition of the foregoing, Mori argued: "In my humble opinion, swords in the past have been worn for the purpose of warding off individual assailants and protecting one's own person, and as such have been indispensable during times of civil upheaval. As we gradually enter, however, upon an era of enlightenment, as our people develop a new respect for moral principles, and as the odious customs of a rude and savage age begin to fade, the wearing of swords becomes empty show. Our land is now at peace, with the prosperity of our Imperial Throne waxing day by day. Internally we maintain order through equitable laws, while warding off external dangers by means of a military system. We now stand at a juncture where it behooves each of us to refine his own manners, turn his back on rude and savage customs, and embrace that enlightened ethic in which every individual takes it upon himself to uphold the principles of morality."[35]

Mori had kicked up a hornet's nest. "The sword," Amamori Kenzaburō yelled out in the course of the debate, "is the very essence of the noble warrior of Imperial Japan and the natural means of his self-expression; . . . as such it deserves our unquestioning respect. Do you think there is anyone with the least bit of the Yamato spirit who would remove his swords?" Meanwhile Yuri Kimimasa edged up to Mori with a menacing, "Say that again, what was that you said?" to which the latter is reported to have replied, with a gesture toward his own abdomen, "Does the spirit of the samurai reside in this murderous carving knife? . . . the spirit of our warriors lies *here!*"[36]

---

a volume in the unnumbered series, Maki Shoten, comp., *Sekai shisōka zenshū* (Tokyo, 1966), pp. 68–80. This drama, with the final assassination scene excised by the government censors, was performed at the Kabukiza in December 1926 with Ichikawa Sadanji in the leading role as Mori. See Matsumoto Sannosuke, *Kyōkoku o mezashite: 1889–1900*, vol. 8 of Tsurumi Shunsuke, gen. ed., *Nihon no hyakunen* (Tokyo, 1963), pp. 20–21.

35. "Kōgisho nisshi," p. 110.

36. Ibid., p. 110, reports the interjection of Amamori. The exchange between Yuri and Mori was later recalled by Koba Sadanaga in "Mori

The proposal was unanimously voted down on 10 July (2/VI) by an enraged company of 376, every one of whom had been attending the sessions girt about with the traditional two swords. Voices were raised throughout the land, and very loudly in Satsuma, against Mori, which even his two most influential patrons, Iwakura and Ōkubo, were powerless to still. Ono Seigorō, who had the temerity to support Mori during the debates, was murdered,[37] and would-be assassins dogged Mori's footsteps the length and breadth of Tokyo, to the point where he never left home in the evening without a bodyguard of his student boarders tagging along beside his mount.[38] On 28 July (20/VI) the government stripped him of all offices and divested him of his court rank, and on 9 August (2/VII) he left Tokyo by steamer for Kagoshima in great haste and confusion, without even taking the time to pay a farewell call on Ōkubo Toshimichi.[39]

"Mori," as Ōkubo Toshiaki puts it, "had picked a quarrel with an ugly fellow."[40] The siege of Hakodate had only been lifted as of 27 June, and the possibility remained of a fresh outbreak of fighting.[41] Soldiers returning from the battlefield were resentful of the way political power seemed already to have been cornered by the civilian bureaucrats.[42] Most importantly the swords (particularly the short sword, the instrument of ritual suicide), were in many respects the focal symbol of the entire feudal ethic and the sentiments attaching to it. They were an object of reverence second only to one's own lord, and were considered to possess intrinsically a virtue that could not be tarnished by the moral shortcomings of the human wearer.[43] By calling into question this cult of the sword, Mori had struck painfully close to the nerve center of the traditional psychology and value system. Seven years, indeed, would pass before the government felt itself sufficiently secure to implement the measure originally proposed by Mori.[44]

Arinori sensei o shinobite," in Sappanshi Kenkyūkai (Society for the Study of the History of Satsuma Han), eds., *Nangoku shisō* (Historical series on the south country, no. 4; Kagoshima, 1939), to be reprinted in *Zenshū* II.

37. Osatake, *Kenseishi*, p. 362.
38. Takahashi Korekiyo, *Jiden* (Tokyo, 1936), p. 107.
39. OTM, p. 36.
40. OTM, p. 34.
41. KSM, p. 26.
42. KKM, p. 38.
43. KSM, p. 26.
44. As of 28 March 1876. On 19 February 1869 farmers and traders who had been permitted by the Bakufu to wear swords had this privilege removed. On 23 September 1871 the wearing of swords by persons in informal dress was decreed optional but was still mandatory for those in full dress. The

The biographers' comments on the incident are mixed. Kaimon sees it as the "clue to his entire life work," as an instance of Mori's "ability to perceive what ordinary people could not see, and to catch other intellectuals off balance"; of his "determination to throw personal considerations to the wind on behalf of a just cause"; and of his "frank and unaffected nature" and the "fearless and outspoken quality of his speech."[45] Kimura, on the other hand, speculates "whether Mori would have brought such distress upon himself with this provocative proposal had he been a bit more versed in worldly affairs," but grants that "it was a special characteristic of Mori that he should have considered the national weal ahead of his own personal fortune."[46] In Ōkubo's judgment, "Mori gave in to impetuousness and therefore missed his mark."[47] It was not the last time in his life that Mori would combine a praiseworthy boldness with a certain problematical brashness. Why did Mori do it? The British Minister, Parkes, in forwarding W. G. Aston's translation of the "Haitōron" to Foreign Secretary Clarendon, surmised: "The discussion of such a question is not well timed at a moment when the country is engaged in the more serious and primary work of organizing a new constitution. On the other hand it is possible that the government may perceive that the work would be accelerated if they had an unarmed instead of a two-sworded population to control."[48]

The evidence would seem to indicate, however, that Mori crossed his Rubicon entirely on his own initiative and in full awareness of what awaited him on the farther shore. A letter to Ōkubo Toshimichi dated 11 June 1869 (2/V), nearly a month prior to the submission of his proposal to the Kōgisho, suggests that Mori already had presented a draft to the highest authorities, which had evoked words of caution and concern in friendly quarters:

> Since receiving your kind advice the other day on the question of sword-wearing, I have thought the matter through afresh several times. As you clearly pointed out, I have indeed expressed myself recklessly, without taking into consideration the temper of the times . . . Nonetheless, resolved though I be

---

government—unlike Mori at this point—moved cautiously, waiting for public sentiment to reach a general state of readiness for the move. (JWM, 8 April 1876).

45. KSM, p. 26.
46. KKM, p. 39.
47. OTM, p. 34.
48. PRO, Japan/General Correspondence, FO-46-113, letter from Harry Parkes to Earl of Clarendon, 8 Oct. 1869.

to reflect all the more earnestly upon myself in the future, I am as you know stubborn by nature, and have the unfortunate habit of sticking obstinately to any idea once it has entered my head. Try as I may to guard myself on this point, I find it difficult to rein in my feelings, much to my distress . . . My failure to bring even myself under control will greatly harm the conduct of national affairs as well. Assailed by such thoughts I find it impossible to carry on my official assignments a day longer. Yet to resign pleading incompetence would be cowardly, and a dereliction of duty as well . . . Until I achieve a new stage [of self control] I earnestly entreat your fatherly guidance and favor at all times.[49]

There is a deep sense of resignation here, even a questing of sorts after martyrdom. That Mori persisted in his project must be attributed, beyond his own admitted stubbornness, to the stakes involved in the issue, those stakes having been very clearly spelled out in his proposal: a society "enlightened" in outlook, upholding order and stability by the establishment socially of "equitable laws," and by the internalization individually of the "principles of morality"—a new ethos which ran very much against the grain of that traditionally evoked by the sword. The transformation of Japan at this level seemed so important to Mori that he was prepared to sacrifice both his political leverage in a variety of institution-building committees and his broad public forum in Tokyo, in order to make his point.

In his letter of resignation Mori explained that he had accepted duties well above his own capacity only in the hope of repaying the debt he owed his country, regretted his "manifold insufficiencies of spirit and errors of thought, errors possibly expiable only by death," but announced nevertheless: "Upon deep reflection I realize that this would be a senseless loss to the world at large. It would be my greatest regret in life to lay it down without having even begun my repayment of life's blessings. I therefore at this time take the unusual step of asking to be relieved of all my offices, together with my court rank. I shall devote myself wholeheartedly to scholarly pursuits, perhaps for four or five years. Then, in the event I should be recalled to some public office befitting my capacities, I would make every effort to atone for my past errors."[50]

---

49. OTM, p. 35, quoting letter from Mori Arinori to Ōkubo Toshimichi, 11 June 1869 (2 V Meiji 2).

50. KKM, pp. 39–40 gives Mori's statement of resignation in full. It is dated 28 July 1869 (20 VI Meiji 2), but gives no addressee. The suggestion

Although Mori "manfully took the blame on himself,"[51] he was in fact dismissed by the government, which found itself unable otherwise to mollify the popular commotion which he had aroused. Far from intending censure, however, the government indicated its own attitude toward Mori by bestowing on him in the emperor's name a farewell honorarium of two rolls of bleached cotton cloth and two hundred yen cash, "in appreciation of remarkable devotion to duty."[52]

MORALIST AND MENTOR
IN KANDA AND KAGOSHIMA

It was not over a political principle, but rather over a social custom and the moral cosmos which it symbolized, that Mori had chosen to forfeit his public career. The emphasis he placed on matters moral, and on setting a personal example, were amply illustrated by his private life, first in Kanda and then in Kagoshima. The tone had been set by a memorial Mori and Samejima presented jointly on 25 October 1868 (10/IX) just before joining the Gijiteisai Torishirabesho, expressing a sense of awe at the high responsibilities with which they had been entrusted, calling attention to the exhaustion of the national treasury and to the sufferings and privations of samurai still on the battle line, and requesting a reduction of salary to thirty yen per month.[53] This early Tokyo period is particularly rich in anecdotes descriptive of Mori's character:

> [On his compassion:] Mori invariably returned home from his office by rickshaw. If the puller was a young chap, Mori would mount. Should he happen to be an old fellow, however, Mori often would refrain from riding and instead would walk alongside the conveyance, plying the old man with friendly questions about his family and worldly circumstances. Upon reaching his destination, Mori would pay the fellow full fare plus tip and occasionally invite him into the kitchen for a meal.[54]

> [On his generosity:] Late in the twelfth month Mori assembled his household servants and student boarders and made over to

---
that it may never have been delivered has been advanced by Hayashi Takeji, *Mori Arinori kenkyū: dai ni: Mori Arinori to kirisutokyō* (Sendai, by the Author, 1968), p. 169 ff.
51. KKM, p. 40.
52. Harada, *Mori Arinori,* p. 81.
53. KKM, p. 41.
54. KKM, p. 254.

them his entire year-end bonus, instructing them to divide it among themselves. He explained that it was through their efforts that he managed an early start every morning and was able to put in a good day's work at the office.[55]

[On his respect for inferiors:] Enroute from Kyoto to Tokyo, Mori once put up at Sekigahara, tired by the long day's journey. Calling in a masseur, he engaged the latter in a lengthy discussion of the famous battlefield there, asking the fellow question after question and showing great delight at the old man's detailed command of the subject.[56]

[On his courage:] At the height of the furor over the "Haitōron" Mori one evening hitched up his carriage and took a ride alone through Hibiya at sundown. As he came to a bridge, an assassin accosted him, fired a volley, but missed. Mori bellowed out, "Idiot!" and then with perfect self-possession stood up from the driver's seat, raised his arms over his head exposing his breast, and yelled across to his assailant, "Well, if you're going to shoot, here's your target!" whereupon the assassin lost his composure, dropped his pistol, and fled.[57]

Simplicity and frugality, together with moral and scholastic fervor, were the keynotes of life at Mori's residence in Nishikimachi, Kanda. Mori had taken into his home as *shosei* (student lodgers) three young Sendai samurai who had just returned from a two-year sojourn in America and were now being hunted down by the *jōi,* or anti-foreign, faction that had seized power in their han with the Restoration: Takahashi Korekiyo, (the future prime minister, age fifteen at the time), Suzuki Tomoo, and Ichijō Jūjirō. These three were soon joined by Naitō Seitarō and Nakahara Kuninosuke, both of Chōshū, making a total of five. Mori, now twenty-one, led a modest bachelor's life, throwing open the *amado* (storm shutters) himself in the early morning, joining his students at their meals, ordering their single cook-housekeeper to dispense with special dishes for himself, and setting up a study routine for them reminiscent of the "Each One Teach One" system of the Gōjū: Ichijō was to instruct his confreres in the Chinese classics; Mori himself set out to teach English to Takahashi only, who in turn would instruct the others; while an outsider was called in for calligraphy.

55. KKM, p. 256.
56. KKM, p. 261.
57. Tanaka, *Kinsei ijin hyakuwa,* p. 67.

By late spring of 1869 the Sendai three had progressed sufficiently in their English to be appointed assistant instructors at the Daigaku Nankō. The capture of Ichijō by Sendai plainclothesmen outside the school gates, and his temporary detention by the han authorities, confronted Mori with a practical instance of the jumble of feudal and central authority to which he had called attention in the Kōgisho. The following morning he stormed into the Sendai han residence, demanding the immediate release of Ichijō and protesting the illegality of the arrest by han agents of a national civil servant, which Ichijō was by virtue of his new teaching position. To prevent any future difficulty, Mori arranged with the Sendai authorities to have all three youngsters transferred onto his own household register. When forced himself to decamp from Tokyo, Mori entrusted to the care of his friends these five *shosei,* who felt they had lost in him a "fatherly master."[58]

Mori's Kagoshima routine may be viewed as a continuation of that in Kanda, although for the fourteen months' exile which now ensued we know only that he established in the temple precincts of the Kōkokuji a school for the English language, and we have for this period only two documents: a memorial to the Satsuma daimyo and a letter to Yokoyama, both dealing with the problems raised by Mori's new educational experiment. On 3 August 1870 (7/VII), Mori complained to his brother of the lamentable deficiency of scholars of Western learning in Kagoshima, explained that he was determined not only to carry on his own education but also to impart as widely as possible his new knowledge to others, and remarked that the unexpected demand for English instruction had crowded his little school beyond capacity.[59]

It was with this same problem in mind that Mori had petitioned his daimyo on 20 June 1870 (22/V) for official assistance within limits permitted by straightened han finances. In "Yōgaku kyōiku ni kansuru jōsho" (Memorial on instruction in Western learning) he touched for the first time on the problem of the linguistic medium through which the learning of an alien civilization could best be transmitted to Japan: a problem which would occupy his own mind, and that of other Japanese educators, for a good many years to come. Over the next two to three decades Japanese education, in appropriating the knowledge of the West, would work its way gradually through the following broad stages: (1) instruc-

---

58. KKM, p. 43. Mori's student boarders are discussed in KKM, pp. 42–43; Takahashi, *Jiden,* pp. 94–96, 111; and in Hayashi Takeji, "Bakumatsu no kaigai ryūgakusei," part I, *Nichibei fōramu,* January 1964, pp. 32–34.

59. KKM, pp. 43–44.

tion by foreign personnel in a foreign language medium; (2) instruction in the Japanese language by Japanese personnel who themselves, however, had first mastered their subjects in a foreign language medium; (3) the enrichment of the Japanese language and the expansion of the body of translated literature to the point where all but the most advanced or specialized areas of Western Learning were available in Japanese.

One gathers from this document that only the first two phases have occurred to Mori. The memorial is concerned specifically with the teaching of the English language (as opposed to substantive curriculum), and since Mori's stated objective here is the achievement of a fluency sufficient to carry on meaningful discussion with foreigners, it is further evident that he is still thinking largely in terms of phase 1. The first step in the whole process, as he sees it, is pronunciation, the corner which must first successfully be turned before one can proceed safely to grammar, composition, and the substantive subjects which lie beyond. He takes a dim view of the ability of native instructors to impart a good English pronunciation, including himself in the indictment, and requests his daimyo to hire foreign instructors for this purpose as soon as possible. Meanwhile, as a stop-gap measure, he announces that he has persuaded William Willis, an instructor at the newly established han medical school, to admit fifteen nonmedical students into his regularly scheduled pronunciation classes, each batch of fifteen to be replaced by a similar group the moment it has reached the required level of competence.[60]

If the scholar in Mori saw language training as the most pressing need of the day, Mori as moralist found in his academy ample scope also for character-building and for edification-by-example, which, as end and means, were coming to form the foundation of his emerging pedagogical philosophy. "Tokyo," he wrote Yokoyama at this time, "teems with all kinds of characters, but you will look in vain for true Confucian scholars or men of profound learning . . . Take my word for it, the publicity-seeking, unproductive types you find around the Shōhei Gakkō[61] are certainly not to be taken as a standard."[62] Mori went on elsewhere to affirm: "When it comes to the education of people it does not

60. Mori Arinori, "Yōgaku kyōiku ni kansuru jōsho, 20 June 1870 (22 V Meiji 3) is quoted in full and discussed in KKM, pp. 44–45.
61. For the Shōhei Gakkō, see note 11 above.
62. Letter from Mori Arinori to Yokoyama Yasutake, undated but written sometime between summer 1869 and summer 1870. Quoted in KKM, p. 46.

suffice to hand down precepts in a dictatorial fashion. On the contrary, this tends to lead them astray. One ought to await the student's inquiry before giving vent to one's own opinion. There is nothing more effective in influencing others for the good than the example of one's own proper conduct."[63]

Mori was with his charges day and night, doubling in the roles of schoolmaster and dormitory prefect, his stress on clean living exemplified by the campaign which he conducted to "curb the vice of sodomy peculiar to Satsuma."[64] Mosquito netting was banned from the sleeping quarters, and tutor and tutees alike suffered heroically through the bug-bitten nights of the long Satsuma summer.[65]

A dramatic convergence of the moral and political realms occurred with Yokoyama's suicide on 22 August 1870 (26/VII), the day before Mori's own twenty-third birthday. Early in the morning, Yokoyama, then enrolled at the academy of Taguchi Bunzō in Tokyo, thrust two documents—a memorial and an attachment—into the fork of a bamboo pole, stood the pole against the outer gate of the Shūgiin (Deliberative Assembly), and then withdrew to the service entrance of the Shimazu residence to rip out his intestines there at break of day.

The memorial condemned the political morality of the new government on nine counts:

> 1. Our officials from the chief ministers on down live a life of luxurious extravagance, beguiling the Imperial Court and ignoring the starving multitude.
> 2. Many officials assume a haughty attitude towards others and have their hearts set on the pursuit of wealth and honor.
> 3. The common people are bewildered by the sudden reversals of government policy, which are far-fetched and have failed to take into careful account the popular mood.
> 4. The increase of rental fees for equestrian mounts and the imposition of a 20% tax thereon, is a cruel measure taken without approval of the common people and in total disregard of popular feeling.
> 5. With clever men honored, and honest men despised, the

---

63. KKM, p. 46, quotes this as "the sort of thing Mori was constantly impressing upon other people at this time," without giving any specific source for the quotation.
64. OTM, p. 38.
65. KKM, pp. 45–46.

code of integrity is increasingly assailed by a spirit of easygoing corruption.

6. In every department of the government, work is pursued with an eye not to duty but to personal profit. Instead of recruiting individuals to suit the offices, offices are sought out for the profit of the individual.

7. Soberer forms of social intercourse are neglected in favor of lavish outlays for food and drink.

8. The careless fashion in which treaties have been concluded with foreign powers has raised public indignation to the boiling point.

9. Promotions have been based not on ability but on personal favoritism.

Yokoyama's attachment attacked the growing sentiment for a punitive expedition against Korea (which had spurned a Japanese request for a treaty of commerce and friendship), warning that Korea was in far better a position to resist attack than in Hideyoshi's day. He also pointed out that Japan's international reputation would suffer irreparably if she undertook such action without legitimate pretext and argued that the government should turn rather to the immense backlog of domestic problems demanding its attention, and do something about the poverty and distress of the common people which lay at the root of much of the anti-Korean sentiment. "The urgent business of the government today," he concluded, "is to establish law and order, bring coherence into its numerous ordinances, create public confidence in its policies, and show concern for the welfare of the masses."

Yokoyama explained in his memorial, and again to Satsuma officials as he lay expiring at the han residence, that a great many petitions of a similar nature by other persons had been pigeonholed by lower-level functionaries, and that he had finally settled on suicide as the only way of getting himself heard in high places. Unfortunately the lack of biographical material on Yokoyama, particularly on the personal circumstances surrounding the suicide, leaves one guessing as to the full scope of his motivation, and as to the involvement of Mori, if any, in events leading up to the incident. The Satsuma authorities, in their testimony to the police, praised Yokoyama for his fine character, describing him as "straightforward and honest, sparing in his speech, but always one to point out faults directly, be it to his friends or to his han government; where he espied error, he could not hold his peace." The court, far from taking umbrage, paid his funeral expenses and informed the Shimazu daimyo that, "Although there were some errors in his perception of the current state of affairs, his action proceeded from a deep concern for the national weal."[66]

Yokoyama's nobility of motive was combined here with a devil-may-care bravado reminiscent of his younger brother's "Haitōron," except that the elder brother had played for ultimate stakes. Political suicides in the United States in connection with the Vietnam War suggest that the phenomenon is not necessarily unknown in a modern—or even a democratic—society; and the Kōgisho, in strong reaffirmation of traditional sentiment on the subject, had only the previous year rejected by a vote of 200 to 3 a proposal for the proscription of ritual suicide. Nevertheless, Yokoyama's action invites analysis, if not along lines of modern psychopathology, then in terms of an unusual hypertrophy of a traditional sense of political obligation.

Kimura claims that Mori sensed the build-up in Yokoyama of suicidal intent and attempted to dissuade him by "gentle admonition."[67] It seems most likely, too, that the fundamental causes for which Yokoyama gave his life—probity in public office; concern for the well-being of the masses; the avoidance of reckless and unjustifiable military adventure—would not be lost on a devoted younger brother. One cannot, however, leave the subject without at least asking to what extent we may have here a case of feedback: i.e., a possibility that Mori, his own early character largely formed by Yokoyama, may have repaid his elder brother many times over with fresh moral fervor and political awareness garnered from London, Brocton, and high political office in Tokyo; and that he may have helped unwittingly, by adding fuel to Yokoyama's fire of indignation, in bringing on his brother's suicide.

With its decision to establish Japan's first permanent diplomatic posts abroad, the government ordered Mori back to Tokyo on 19 October 1870 (25/IX). On 27 November (5/intercalary X) he was restored to his former court rank and appointed at the grade of *shōbenmushi,* or chargé d'affaires, to represent Japan at the new legation in Washington, Samejima Naonobu receiving at the same time a similar appointment covering London, Paris, and Berlin concurrently.

66. Yokoyama's memorial and attachment, the police reports, and other related documents may be found in Nakayama Yasumasa, comp., *Shinbun shūsei Meiji hennenshi* (Tokyo, 1934–36), I, 338–339.
67. KKM, p. 267.

The brief diary, "Bibō daini" (Notebook No. 2),[68] which Mori kept from the time of his departure from Kagoshima until his arrival in San Francisco (22 October 1870–16 February 1871) relates that upon arrival in Tokyo he stayed with Samejima, who, after the death of Yokoyama, had become his most intimate confidant. Five days after arrival, the diary continues, Mori and Samejima and Nawa Michikazu (a Chōshū samurai who was to become assistant secretary of legation under Mori at Washington) enjoyed an outing on the Sumida River in the course of which they consumed six bottles of beer. Kimura Kyō, however, paints a somewhat more earnest picture of the trio: "Mori at the time was deeply concerned about the collapse, due to the recent military upheaval, of the old virtues of circumspection and moral constancy, formerly observed by high and low alike. With Samejima and Nawa [Michikazu] he took under consideration various schemes for retrieving the loss. Whenever the three had time to spare from their official duties, they would get together for a lively discussion of moral problems."[69]

A letter from Mori to Nawa, mailed from Nagasaki on 16 August 1869 (9/VII), suggests how very much Mori and Samejima were still under the direct inspiration of Brocton at this time: "Opinion regarding Harris is even more divided in this region, to my unspeakable regret. When, oh when, will the Lord lead these people to the citadel of the New Life? That, in the fullness of tears, is my silent prayer."[70]

It is not impossible to suppose, on the basis of this letter, that the trio of Mori, Samejima, and Nawa had tried to establish a Japanese branch of the Brotherhood of the New Life with, it would seem, rather limited success. Unfortunately this is the only direct statement we have by Mori for this period either on Thomas Lake Harris or on Christianity, and it is difficult to connect, except in a very general way, Mori's moral crusading with the specific schemes, palace revolution and all, of the American mystic.

What we do have, on the other hand, is evidence that Mori still took Harris very seriously as his foremost moral guide. The frugality of his everyday living in Kanda and his dormitory vigils at Kagoshima repeat familiar Brocton themes, while the stray anecdotes which we have of Mori's generosity and compassion may indicate a conscious effort to put into practice what Harris

68. Mori Arinori, "Bibō daini," to be published in *Zenshū* II.
69. KKM, p. 42.
70. Letter from Mori Arinori to Nawa Michikazu, 16 Aug. 1869 (9 VII Meiji 2), to be published in *Zenshū* II.

and Oliphant had told him was the essence of the Christian ethic. Mori's proposal for resettlement in Hokkaido was evidence of his sympathy with the plight of Japanese Christians, while the best proof of his continuing esteem for Harris lies in the fact that upon returning to America in 1871 he took with him at his own expense, and placed with Harris in Brocton, a young Sendai samurai named Arai Ōsui, who had come under the influence of the Russian Orthodox priest Nicolai at Hakodate.[71]

This esteem, apparently, was fully reciprocated by Harris and Oliphant. The latter, writing to Mrs. William F. Cowper on 28 May 1869, took pride in the high offices Mori and Samejima had assumed in the government of Japan, reporting, "they have sent us some beautiful specimens of Japanese workmanship," and fulminating over the persistent efforts of Yoshida Kiyonari, then still at New Brunswick, to detach Nagasawa Kanaye from the colony.[72] And interestingly enough, if there be any proof of whom *Harris* remembered as the most faithful of his disciples, it was Mori and Samejima who appeared reassuringly to him in a dream during the darker hours of the Russo-Japanese War (years after the two of them had died).[73]

Mori's imminent return to the Atlantic seaboard, in any case, would provide indication of just how far he still looked to Brocton for guidance. The assignment to Washington, and his confrontation there with the functioning original of the constitutional model he had merely dallied with in the Kōgisho, promised to force some resolution of Mori's outlook on political questions as well. Would he attempt to achieve a fuller understanding of the American political system with a view to its eventual adoption by Japan, or would he abandon this model entirely? And, finally, the self-educational project which Mori had taken upon himself in London had been expanded in Kanda and Kagoshima (along lines reminiscent of the Gōjū, and with a mixture of traditional and Western

71. See Chapter Six.
72. HOP, letters from Laurence Oliphant to Mrs. William F. Cowper, 5 April 1869 and 28 May 1869. Nagasawa would not be detached, remaining with the colony for life, succeeding eventually to the title of the Santa Rosa property, and continuing to manage the vineyards and winepress until his death in 1932. See Herbert W. Schneider and George Lawton, *A Prophet and a Pilgrim* (New York, 1942), pp. 487–488.
73. The complete entry in Mrs. Harris' diary for 24 September 1904 is as follows: "Last night Noda [Samejima] and Sawai [Mori] were with Father [Harris] all night holding to him to help them through the Port Arthur crisis. They are both strong men in the New Life holding grandly." The diary is in HOP, Box no. 12, "Letters and Diary 1899–1906."

curricula), to encompass the instruction of like-minded young samurai. In America it would become an enterprise on a national scale: for Mori had been charged, alongside the conduct of diplomatic business, with the supervision of all government-sponsored Japanese students in the United States.

Mori, during this first period of homecoming from the West, emerges as political activist, as moralist, and as educator. His political efforts, however, ended largely in failure, while his moral crusade fared little better. It was perhaps for this reason that Mori would come to focus his interest so strongly on public education during the next two years in America, and keep it there—in effect —for the remainder of his life, in the hope that education would provide the long-range answer to both the political and the moral challenge.

Mori's "Haitōron" best epitomized, perhaps, the interweaving of traditional and Western factors in the unfolding of the young man's personality and thought. The proposal was most obviously an effort to bring Japanese society more into line with the standards of justice, rationality, and humaneness which Mori had appropriated during his first year in London. The perspicacity with which he called for the internalization of ethics and morality, and his scorn for their externalization in the cult of the sword, however, owed much to his pilgrimage to Brocton. Mori recommended the abolition of sword-wearing in the interest not of national wealth or power or security but solely of the ethical quality of Japanese life itself. To that extent, and at this point in time at least, Mori clearly transcended the narrow instrumentalism of *fukoku kyōhei*. He was able to do so because the statesman's admiration for certain Western institutions was undergirded by the moralist's commitment to the ethic behind those institutions; because, for example, the justice which expressed itself in British law or in educational institutions for the deaf and blind was consciously linked, in Mori's mind, to the justice which he himself was attempting to practice in everyday life. Finally, as a legacy of his Kagoshima upbringing, there was something in the audacious, head-on tactics of the "Haitōron" which smacked of old Satsuma *jigenryū;* and the tenacity of his purpose had its roots in a deep-set personality trait very much shared by his ill-starred elder brother.

Five   *1871–1873*

REPRESENTING JAPAN AT WASHINGTON

Mori reached San Francisco on 16 February 1871 and Washington late the same month. His debut as a diplomat coincided with Japan's own first, uncertain entrance upon the stage of modern diplomacy. It was also the era of the first encounter between the Japanese and American peoples on this side of the Pacific, an encounter which produced such unlikely scenes as that of the twenty-nine young samurai bouncing across the Great Plains on the Union Pacific, swords stashed away on the baggage rack overhead, who "when weary of gazing at the corn-oceans" busied themselves with their grammars, lexicons, or phrase-books;[1] or such outlandish scenes as that of the entire Iwakura Mission, in full ceremonial dress, propelling itself backward out of the Blue Room of the White House into the main foyer after taking leave of President Grant.[2] Mori occupied a unique position in that initial encounter, for he knew enough of both cultures to be able to interpret each of them, at least in part, to the other.

The year 1871 passed uneventfully, with Mori heavily dependent on the avuncular Hamilton Fish for instruction in the most elementary of the arts of diplomacy. There was a sudden upsurge of activity in 1872 with the arrival of the mission, which was

1. Charles Lanman, *The Japanese in America* (New York, 1872), p. 68.
2. Ibid., p. 34.

based in Washington from 29 February to 27 July, followed by another lull up to Mori's own departure for Japan, on 18 March 1873, which gave him the time to bring out the last two of the three published English-language works which provide the chief statement of his thought for the period: *Life and Resources in America* (September 1871), *Religious Freedom in Japan* (November 1872), and *Education in Japan* (January 1873).

THE FLEDGLING DIPLOMAT

Perspective on the context of Mori's official life in America is best established for the twentieth-century reader by a drastic cutting-down to size of stage and *dramatis personae* on both sides. Secretary of State Fish, with Assistant Secretary J. Bancroft Davis and Second Assistant Secretary William Hunter, in 1871 presided over a not too terribly overworked corps of thirty-two clerks, one law officer, two messengers, three watchmen, and five laborers.[3] Mori maintained a similarly simple establishment in a large home at the corner of 24th and M streets, which served both as chancery and residence for himself and his Japanese secretaries. The second-ranking position on the Japanese side, secretary of legation, was filled during 1871 by Toyama Masakazu, then by Takagi Saburō, and that of assistant secretary first by Nawa Michikazu and then in 1872 by Magome Tamesuke. Toyama and one of the students in Mori's charge, Yatabe Ryōkichi, would one day as leading professors of Tokyo Imperial University during Mori's ministry be instrumental in expediting the latter's reform of that institution. An American staff consisting of a secretary, one butler, one cook, one chambermaid, and one gardener assisted the young Japanese. The legation maintained consulates at New York and San Francisco, under the honorary consulship of American citizens. Anyone hankering after a less complicated world must read with a certain wistfulness of the matters that agitated Japanese-American relations in the autumn of 1871. Mori in September expostulated to Fish: "The improvements which are going on at the corner of 24th Street and M Street are greatly interfering with my convenience, and I write to ask you that these troubles may be remedied. Not only am I prevented from leaving my house, or reaching it, in a carriage, but this morning the water pipes have been broken, or taken up, so that my house is wholly without a supply of water. Of course these annoyances ought not to be continued, and I trust

---

3. U.S. Government, *Official Register of the United States, 1870–1871.*

that suitable instructions may soon be given by you to the city authorities."⁴

Fish, as a matter of fact, was throughout Mori's tour preoccupied with a more important problem: the dispute with Britain over the *Alabama* claims. The Washington Treaty of 8 May 1871 had turned the matter over to arbitration by an international tribunal at Geneva, but passions aroused as the arbitration progressed threatened, prior to the final resolution of the case on 25 August 1872, to push the two nations to the brink of hostilities. The Iwakura Mission, indeed, was forced to share newspaper headlines in early 1872 with speculation over possible war against a Britain allied with resurgent Southern elements.⁵ Japanese affairs, as Marlene Mayo has pointed out,⁶ were simply not a central concern of the department, while Americans in general, a good three decades short of their own progress to world-power status (and consciousness), adopted an attitude toward the Japanese which was friendly, curious, and above all casual.

Mori arrived in Washington possessed of the highest recommendations from Tokyo. Foreign Minister Sawa Nobuyoshi wrote Fish, in a letter dispelling any lingering doubt of the young man's full reinstatement to official favor, that Mori's appointment had proceeded from "a full feeling of confidence in his patriotism and ability as well as from his well-known honesty and sincere efforts in promoting the political welfare of the Empire of Japan."⁷ The American minister to Japan, Charles Delong, likewise communicated to Fish his belief that, "the authorities of this Empire in making the selection that they have and in sending such an officer first of any to our government have intended thereby to convey to the United States Government a very handsome and marked compliment." Delong continued: "I beg leave to bespeak for Mr. Mori a cordial reception and such attention at your hands as will enable him with the least possible annoyance to discharge the duties of his office which are so new to him."⁸

Such attention the sixty-three-year-old lawyer turned statesman

4. NAW, Department of State, "Notes from the Japanese Legation: 1871–1872," note from Arinori Mori to Hamilton Fish, 27 Sept. 1871.

5. Editorial, *Washington Evening Star*, 12 Feb. 1872.

6. Marlene J. Mayo, "The Iwakura Embassy and the Unequal Treaties" (unpublished Ph.D. dissertation, Columbia University, 1961), p. 305.

7. Department of State, "Notes from Japanese Legation," letter from Nobuyoshi Sawa to Hamilton Fish, 25 Nov. 1870.

8. NAW, Department of State, "Despatches from United States Ministers to Japan: 1855–1906," Microfilm no. M-133, Roll no. 17 (1 Jan. 1871–26 April 1871), dispatch from Charles Delong to Hamilton Fish, 10 Jan. 1871.

was prepared to extend generously to the twenty-three-year-old who presented his credentials on 2 March 1871. Mori asked the Department of State during his first year, among other things, for "a copy of the Diplomatic correspondence of the United States with foreign countries for the past three years";[9] for "advice in regard to the proper size for a national flag, to be used at this Legation";[10] for a set of the International Codes then under discussion at Alexandria, Egypt;[11] for permission to forward his legation's mail pouch together with those of the department free of charge to Japan;[12] and for the favor several times of sending his own official correspondence in American dispatch bags directly.[13] These requests, which bespeak both the professional innocence of the young man and the political innocence (in the first and last requests) of Japanese-American relations, were at once honored.

Fish also proved an indispensable preceptor in diplomatic practice and protocol and in the ways of American politics, careful at all times to spell out for Mori the precise nature and scope of his official function. When the possibility of the return of the Shimonoseki Indemnity became a matter of wide public discussion, for instance, Fish confided in his diary: "He is advised again not to allow private citizens to draw him into conversation about questions or matters which pertain to his official position, and especially not as to questions or matters which are in the course of settlement and may become subjects of diplomatic negotiation."[14] With respect to the same issue, Fish later noted he had also found it necessary to inform Mori that "as a rule Senators are not fond of being spoken to by Foreign Ministers [i.e., envoys] unless there be some intimacy to justify it, but there would be no harm in his introducing the subject should he meet any of them socially. He was at my home last Monday evening."[15]

When Horace Capron in May 1871 brought Fish a memorandum of an agreement entered into with Mori for his own employment by the Kaitakushi, or Development Bureau for Hokkaido, Fish noted in his diary: "I tell him that the engagement on the

9. Department of State, "Notes from Japanese Legation," letter from Arinori Mori to Hamilton Fish, 1 June 1871.
10. Ibid., note from Arinori Mori to J. Bancroft Davis, 21 Oct. 1871.
11. Ibid., letter from Arinori Mori to J. Bancroft Davis, 1 Dec. 1871.
12. Ibid., letter from Arinori Mori to J. Bancroft Davis, 15 July 1871.
13. Ibid., note from Arinori Mori to Department of State, 27 Aug. 1871.
14. LCM, Hamilton Fish Papers, "Diary," vol. 3, entry for 30 March 1872.
15. Ibid., entry for 12 Dec. 1872.

part of Mr. Mori is entirely without his diplomatic character and function, and that I have no means of knowing whether he has any authority from his government to make the engagement on their part . . . that we know but little of Mr. Mori who has been here but a short time—he seems however to be an honorable and upright man."[16]

The Western system of sovereign and independent states, governed in their mutual relations by a highly rationalized, universalized framework of international law and diplomatic etiquette, presented a formidable conceptual hurdle to the traditional East Asian mind.[17] Although Mori had expressed warm admiration for the legal foundations of Western society and had perhaps, thanks chiefly to Oliphant, already cleared this particular hurdle, he was nevertheless fortunate to have for his mentor as he first came to grips with *legalities,* i.e., with the everyday practice of what he had preached, a seasoned attorney who not only was a stickler for punctilio but was also patient and willing to take pains. Fish continued to coach Mori right up to the end, when Mori, preparing for departure, once again sought his advice: "Mr. Mori . . . asks whether he himself, being only a Chargé, can name a Chargé d'Affaires *ad interim.* Is told that if his instructions authorize him to make such an appointment, the statement of the fact in his note will be sufficient, and Mr. Takaki will be recognized."[18]

Mori needed assistance at the less theoretical level of everyday legation business as well, and within two months of his arrival had informed the department that he was ready to "engage for two half-days during the week . . . a gentleman holding an official clerkship who is thoroughly acquainted with the mode of governmental business and departmental etiquette,"[19] a post filled briefly by a W. J. Daplyn,[20] and then from September 1871 through July 1872 by the author Charles Lanman, who was introduced to Mori by the scientist Joseph Henry and was hired primarily with the preparation of *Life and Resources in America* in mind.[21] With the

16. Ibid., entry for 17 May 1871.
17. Mayo, "Iwakura Embassy," p. 6ff.
18. Fish Papers, "Diary," vol. 3, entry for 12 March 1873.
19. Department of State, "Notes from Japanese Legation," letter from Arinori Mori to J. Bancroft Davis, 5 May 1871.
20. Ibid., letter to the Department of State from the Japanese Legation dated 11 August 1871 over the signature of "W. J. Daplyn, Secretary pro-tem."
21. Arinori Mori, *Life and Resources in America,* "prepared under the direction of Arinori Mori, for circulation in Japan," by the actual compiler, Charles Lanman, first edition (Washington, D.C., 1871). The text used in

departure of the Iwakura mission, and for the last half year of his sojourn, Mori apparently felt ready to solo. Lanman, whose release had come as a deep personal disappointment,[22] was not so sure, and Henry in consoling his friend over the matter protested: "I do not see how Mr. Mori can do without you. He has no aptitude for business, and will fall prey to any plausible fellow who has the opportunity to gain his confidence."[23]

Mori's diplomatic activities, aside from the Iwakura-Fish conferences, verged on the picayune. He requested and received from his government powers to negotiate the first postal convention with the United States, which was signed shortly after his own departure for home.[24] He secured on 4 September 1872, after nearly a year's representation, the abolition of a discriminatory tonnage rate levied upon Japanese ships arriving in American ports, having argued that commerce and goodwill would thereby be promoted, and having given assurances that when Japanese bottoms entered the carrying trade to Japan the tonnage rate applied would be no lower than that imposed on incoming vessels of foreign ownership.[25] He arranged the appointments of advisors, among them of E. Peshine Smith to the foreign ministry, of General George B. Williams to the finance ministry, and of Capron to the Kaitakushi. He worked successfully for the admission of additional Japanese cadets to

---

this study is the reprint which appears as part III (p. 137ff.) of Charles Lanman, *The Japanese in America* (New York, 1872). As is apparent from the cards of the Union Catalogue, Library of Congress, Washington, D.C., *Life and Resources in America* was originally published chapter by chapter and finally issued in a single volume before the end of 1871. *The Japanese in America,* similarly written by Lanman at Mori's request, gives a lively account of the Iwakura mission and also contains much useful information on Mori. It was published in 1872 in both New York and London in time for the visit of the mission to Britain. *The Japanese in America,* incorporating *Life and Resources in America,* was reprinted by the Hokuseido Press, Tokyo, in 1931 under the title *Leaders of the Meiji Restoration in America.*

22. Letter from Arinori Mori to Charles Lanman, 5 Sept. 1872, in "Letters: Japanese Legation, U.S.A." (A letter copybook of correspondence addressed by Mori and his subordinates for the most part to private American citizens; personal property of Mori Arimasa, Paris, France; to be published in full in *Zenshū* III).

23. Charles Lanman, *Haphazard Personalities: Chiefly of Noted Americans* (Boston, 1886), p. 20, quoting letter from Joseph Henry to Charles Lanman, 11 Sept. 1872.

24. KKM, p. 61. The convention was signed in Washington on 6 Aug. 1873.

25. Department of State, "Notes from Japanese Legation," letter from Arinori Mori to Hamilton Fish, 21 Nov. 1871 and 30 Aug. 1872; article in *Washington Evening Star,* 11 Sept. 1872.

Annapolis,[26] where his erstwhile colleague Matsumura Junzō had gone before, but was turned down by the Senate on his request to admit six students, all expenses paid by the Japanese government, to West Point.[27] And he fretted over the completion of two vessels at Brooklyn being built for the Kaitakushi. The steamer *Kuroda* set out across the Atlantic without ship's papers or funds for provisioning or coaling en route to Japan, necessitating telegrams to London requesting the hospitality of the British yards in Gibraltar and India; while delay in the transmission from Japan of payments due on the *Capron* brought threats from the shipbuilder to sell the vessel in order to collect his debts. The complications with regard to these two vessels arose after the dismissal of Lanman, suggesting that Henry was not so wide of the mark when he thought it foolish of Mori to have dropped his own pilot.[28]

When the Iwakura mission arrived, Mori proved indispensable to it as chief interpreter, as impresario for a series of well-run and highly praised social functions beginning with the White House reception on 4 March,[29] and as a substantive contributor (at Iwakura's special request),[30] to the discussions with Fish. The diplomatic, social, and investigative activities of the mission have been well and extensively treated in the English language,[31] and

26. Ibid., letter from Arinori Mori to Charles Hale, 24 Sept. 1872; Fish Papers, "Diary," vol. 3, entry for 1 April 1871.

27. The objections raised in the Foreign Relations Committee hearings of the Senate were directed at the problem of church attendance, the privileges which the Japanese would enjoy under their generous government stipends, and the pressures of American applicants for admission. The risk of training a possible future enemy apparently had not occurred to the committee. (*Washington Evening Star*, 10 Jan. 1872).

28. "Letters: Japanese Legation," cable from Arinori Mori to Munenori Terajima, 29 Dec. 1872; letters from Arinori Mori to David F. Baker, 10 Jan. 1873 and 8 Feb. 1873.

29. Lanman, *Japanese in America, passim; Washington Evening Star*, 12 March 1872 and 17 March 1872; *New York World*, 17 March 1872. LCM, Hamilton Fish Papers, "Miscellaneous," has a memorandum from the Japanese legation to the Department of State showing that the White House reception was planned down to the last detail by the Japanese side. The provision for formal bows in lieu of handshaking, for instance, gives evidence of Mori's own initiative, although one is inclined to detect in the dinner parties described by the *Star* as "most recherché" the hand of Mr., possibly of Mrs., Lanman.

30. Mori was especially active at the first and third interviews, on 11 and 16 March 1872, respectively.

31. Notably by Mayo, "Iwakura Embassy," and Lanman, *Japanese in America*. Authoritative accounts in Japanese may be found in Shimomura Fujio, *Meiji shonen jōyaku kaiseishi no kenkyū* (Tokyo, 1962), and (by the

here again, as with the Kōgisho, we shall limit discussion to Mori's own specific role.

The decision of the mission to embark on negotiations for a revised treaty while in Washington, a decision which necessitated the dispatch of Itō and Ōkubo back to Japan for additional powers, and which both altered profoundly the purposes of the mission and protracted greatly the duration of its stay in the United States (all in the end to no avail), was taken on the fervent recommendation of Itō and Mori on the evening following the first interview with Fish at the State Department on 11 March 1872.[32] Mori's initiative here tells us a great deal about his own highly idealistic view of Japanese-American relations. The failure of that initiative, however, would add to the growing annoyance of Kido, and to a lesser extent of Iwakura, with the aggressive self-confidence of the young chargé d'affaires.

Sasaki Takayuki, commissioner for the judicial and administrative surveys of the mission, dubbed Mori and Itō "Arabian horses" for their precipitance.[33] The two were very much in harness, and their lifelong personal and political friendship dates at least from this time if not from the previous spring, when Itō visited Washington during his study tour of Western taxation systems. Itō, upon returning to Tokyo that summer, expressed hopes for revision far

---

same author) in "Iwakura shisetsu no ō-bei hakken to taibei kōshō," in Kodama Kōta, ed., *Nihon shakaishi no kenkyū* (Tokyo, 1955).

32. That the initial pressure to negotiate had come from the American side, an explanation which I have not come across in any of the studies of the mission, was suggested by the *Japan Weekly Mail* on 8 August 1873. The pertinent passage is quoted here in full for its historical interest, but the reader is forewarned that this newspaper and its editor, Capt. F. Binkley, were in the habit, especially in the opening years of Meiji, of putting wherever possible an unfavorable construction upon American actions and motivations with regard to Japan: "In the United States the Presidential election was impending and a new treaty with Japan, granting a reduction of duties on goods carried by American steamers and railways was too good a lever to be used with the great companies and the Pacific states not to be worth striving for. The Embassy were told that the President was ready to make very large concessions to Japan, that the European powers would have to follow such, and that all the ends the most sanguine Japanese diplomat ever dared hope for, might be obtained by simply concluding on the spot a new Treaty with the United States. Full powers were demanded and sent, and after a tedious six months work, during which the Japanese had an opportunity of passing through all the different shades of American temperature, both parties threw up the work in disgust, and the Embassy left for Europe."

33. Quoted in Kiyosawa Kiyoshi, *Nihon gaikōshi*, 2 vols. (Tokyo, 1942), I, 213–214.

more sanguine than those contained in the foreign office's own current model treaty draft. This suggests the possibility of prior consultation (and of a very early meeting of minds) with Mori, who was the more familiar with the American scene.[34]

Mori had addressed *Life and Resources in America* to the Japanese people in hopes of explaining the Americans to them and had opened the volume with the remark that: "enmity and bloodshed are the consequences of storing up prejudices resulting from the want of mutual knowledge of the parties engaged."[35] In the closing paragraph of the same volume, pointing to the imminent visit of the mission to America, Mori had addressed his American readers with confidence: "When they [the Japanese ambassadors] shall have experienced the unbounded hospitality of the American people generally, they will undoubtedly be impressed, and effectually convinced that America and Japan are strongly bound together by the cords of sincere regard and unselfish affection."[36]

What we have here is not empty flattery but a clear echo of Mori's early surmise to Yokoyama that American friendship was most worth cultivating and of his opting for neutrality in the Brocton fracas over a hypothetical Pacific War. Mori's advocacy of immediate negotiations sprang probably therefore from a long-standing predisposition to see American intentions in the best possible light, a tendency abetted by the warm friendship and attention with which he personally had been received in Washington, and by a lingering naiveté concerning the nature of inter-state relations which came to the surface during the Iwakura-Fish interviews and which the Secretary of State did his best to remove. Mori's "of course you can trust *us*" posture at the department was the reciprocal of the "of course you can trust *them*" argument which he had—more successfully—sold his own superiors in the mission. The third interview, on 16 March, included a particularly revealing exchange, in connection with the issue of tariff autonomy for Japan:

> *Mori:* The government of its own accord will be always anxious to fix rates in encouragement of commerce . . . suppose that we give you assurances that our present policy is fixed and permanent?

34. Ōyama Azusa, "Iwakura kaisei sōan to Terajima sōan," *Kokusai seiji*, 3:51–63 (autumn 1957).
35. Arinori Mori, *Life and Resources in America*, part III of Charles Lanman, *The Japanese in America* (New York, 1872), p. 137.
36. Ibid., p. 352. From the closing paragraph of *Life and Resources in America*.

Fish: Presidents, Emperors, Councillors, Ambassadors do not live forever. What may be the policy of your next Emperor, or of your people in the next generation, nobody can tell. You cannot give us any positive guarantee that some change of policy may not come about.

Mori: Then you lack confidence in our government.

Fish: It is but lack of confidence in human nature.

Mori: From the nature and situation of our country, it seems to me that you might have confidence that our present policy must be permanent.[37]

Fish finally found it necessary to cut Mori short with a few words of gentle advice.[38]

Kido Takayoshi soon came to doubt the wisdom of the decision to negotiate. After the first four meetings with Fish, he was ready by 26 March (18/II) to confide to his diary how bitterly he now regretted his abdication of initiative to the two supposed young experts on the West, and his acceptance unthinkingly of the assurances of Itō and Mori that it would be in Japan's interest to have the mission conclude treaties while it was overseas. "The truth of the matter is," Kido wrote, "we stand to gain very, very little from it."[39] There was another and perhaps more important source of Kido's growing irritation with Mori, which blazed forth from the pages of his diary and which exploded from time to time in the conference chambers of the legation from March to July 1872.[40] Unaware how perceptively critical Mori and his student charges could at times be of the United States, he was taken aback by what seemed to him an indiscriminate adulation of American ways at the expense of everything Japanese, and particularly by the expression of such sentiment in public. The *Washington Evening Star* on 26 December 1871, three days after Iwakura left Tokyo, had carried for instance the following notice: "Mr. Mori, the Japanese

---

37. NAW, Department of State, "Japanese Embassy: Minutes of Conferences, Drafts of Treaties Submitted, etc., 1872," minutes of the third meeting, on 16 March 1872, as recorded in English by the American side.

38. Mayo, "Iwakura Embassy," p. 184.

39. Kido Takayoshi, *Nikki* (Tokyo, 1932), II, 149, entry for 26 March 1872 (18 II Meiji 5).

40. That Itō escaped similar censure perhaps may be attributed to the fact that he was an old protégé and fellow Chōshū clansman. Also, having been en route to and from Japan during the interval in question, he was out of sight, *ergo* out of mind.

Chargé d'Affaires, urges his government to interdict the further teaching of Chinese, which is the written language of Japan, and substitute English. Mr. Mori believes that his people will ultimately adopt not only the language but the manners and customs of America." If that was not enough, the mission upon reaching Washington found the guest room of the legation graced by two photographs of Iwakura, one taken of the man in his traditional Japanese costume and the other in prevailing American dress, mounted side by side in a single frame over the caption "Ancient and Modern Japan."[41]

Kido wrote on 7 April (30/II):

> All day long our entire party from the Ambassador on down gathered to discuss the treaty draft, clause by clause ... arguing the merits of each item from the standpoint of the welfare of our country and its people ... I find it deplorable that some persons seem more concerned to advance their own fame than to consider the welfare of the nation or its people. Therefore in today's meeting I brought up the seriousness of this matter ... These First Secretaries [of the Mission] are, as Japanese go, relatively well informed about conditions abroad, and we therefore decided to have them assist us in our task. I had not as yet had the opportunity to express my point of view to them. Today therefore we unburdened ourselves one to another. The discussion climaxed in a dispute between Shioda [Shioda Atsunobu, first secretary to the mission] and Mori, at the end of which Mori jumped out of his chair and left the room. What inexcusable and ill-mannered deportment really! I was apprehensive at the disgrace this would bring upon us all if it became known outside, and therefore thought it best to deal with him leniently. But how exceedingly unfortunate an affair for our country![42]

Complaint then followed upon complaint:

> [8 April (1/III)] Mori without the permission of the Mission has announced his intention to take a trip—arbitrary, irresponsible.[43]
> [15 April (8/III)] For many days now, his conduct has left a great deal to be desired. It is the Americans rather who have

41. Lanman, *Japanese in America*, p. 39.
42. Kido, *Nikki*, II, 154–155.
43. Ibid., II, 155.

a proper understanding of the condition of Japan and a knowledge of her customs. Our students here, on the other hand, have a very shallow appreciation of the foundations of their own native land, and have easily developed an infatuation for the ways of the Americans. Lacking any idea as to how they as Japanese properly should conduct themselves, they speak irresponsibly of "independence" and "republicanism" and similar doctrines too frivolous and addlebrained to bear hearing. Rumors have already come to my attention that Mori, our own official representative here no less, has publicly and wantonly disparaged our native customs before foreigners. There have also been among our officials a good many who have travelled abroad briefly and have seen fit to criticize our country after viewing nothing more than the surface of Western culture. It has been the nature of our world from time immemorial that every good thing entails a certain amount of evil. How much the less reason then to adopt things in an indiscriminate and reckless fashion! What distress must any man feel who loves our country or who cares for its people.[44]

[22 April (15/III)] This evening Mori came over and we discussed the revision of the treaty. The talk went on for hours, and the Ambassador [Iwakura] sharply upbraided Mori for the customary shallowness of his patriotic sentiment.[45]

[26 June (21/V)] The harm done by taking Mori's and Itō's advice on treaty matters has frequently manifested itself up to now. The nation is endangered when we fail to perceive behind the preachments of these young prodigies an opportunistic questing after fame.[46]

[30 June (25/V)] During this evening's discussion Mori showed considerable misunderstanding of the existing treaties, but would not be budged at the end of much argumentation from his jumbled line of reasoning. Mori's discourtesies during the interval were beyond enumeration. Our chagrin defies description. The sweltering heat in recent days has been enough to roast one alive. Today was the worst: 97° indoors, over 100° outside.[47]

[1 July (26/V)] The Secretaries as a group, too, have been put to great inconvenience by Mori's behavior to date. By now everyone is aware of his error. His improprieties have been so

44. Ibid., II, 157–158.
45. Ibid., II, 162.
46. Ibid., II, 193.
47. Ibid., II, 194.

many. Since we were not able last night to accept the conclusions he had presented in his memorandum to the Mission, the meeting ended without reaching any agreement. The Ambassador therefore asked him over today to question him on points in yesterday's memorandum. He finally arrived here in the evening, but since he continued to insist on his own viewpoint, we still have no agreement.[48]

[2 July (27/V)] Mori came over this morning to express his views on the clause relating to courts of law. Try as I would, there was no meeting of minds.[49]

What had brought the emotional temperature up to the level of a Washington summer from 26 June throughout the ensuing week was the revelation to the mission on that day by the Prussian minister to Japan, Max von Brandt, that other powers, simply by invoking the Most Favored Nation principle, would be in a position to garner all the privileges gained, without making any of the concessions granted, by the United States in any treaty concluded bilaterally between that country and Japan.[50] It was galling to Kido that Mori should have persisted in his original optimism even now when the wisdom of continuing the negotiations had been called radically into question. But it was only the last of a long series of provocations.

One senses, however, behind the substantive points of dispute over negotiations or over the merits of westernization, something that was basically a clash of character, or rather of temperament. This is suggested above all by the high esteem in which Kido, at the time profoundly hostile to Christianity, held Niijima Jō, who had been persuaded by Mori to join the mission as interpreter. Kido wrote on 1 April (24/II): "When I had my first talk with Niijima upon arrival here, I could see that his kindness and sincerity differ greatly from the frivolity and superficial knowledge of those fellows now recklessly preaching enlightenment. In our dealings he seems like an old friend. There is much to be learned from him, and he is one we can depend on in the future."[51] It seems likely, therefore, that it must have been to some extent the manner in which Mori put forth his ideas and proposals which rubbed Kido the wrong way. On the other hand, it would be unfair to Mori not to mention Kido's high-strung nature and proverbial irritability, or the word

48. Ibid., II, 195.
49. Ibid., II, 195.
50. Mayo, "Iwakura Embassy," p. 279.
51. Kido, *Nikki*, II, 152.

which Fish used in his diary to describe the attitude of the Mission toward Mori: "jealousy."[52]

THE "VOICE OF JAPAN"

"By his intercourse with our official representatives and by his visits to different parts of the country," Charles Lanman wrote of Mori in his account of the Iwakura mission, "he has gained the confidence and esteem of very many distinguished Americans."[53] Megata Tanetarō, one of Mori's students at the time, would also at a later date hand Mori the chief credit for the good will toward Japan which existed in America at that time.[54] He made on the whole, at ages twenty-three to twenty-five, a youthful and energetic and engaging representative of his country. Mori's more important achievements, indeed, lay in the realm of what goes nowadays by the sobriquet of "government-to-people diplomacy." He anticipated in many ways the role of the modern twentieth-century cultural or information attaché, a role for which no need existed as yet among the traditional Western powers, but which had been created for Mori by the sudden confrontation of radically different cultures and by Japan's need to explain, if not "sell," herself to important and almost totally ignorant customers.

We find Mori-as-press-attaché, for instance, briefing the Foreign Affairs and Appropriations Committees of both Houses of Congress (in written memoranda prepared by Lanman under his direction), shortly before the arrival of Iwakura, on the course of Bakumatsu politics and on the Restoration, ending with assurances of the reconciliation of the former warring parties and the forward-looking nature of the new government.[55] We see Mori-as-cultural-officer making a collection of oriental literature for the legation library;[56] sponsoring translations of Japanese poetry;[57] helping American orientalists with the importation of Japanese books;[58] preparing a fifty-page English-language summary of Japanese history (off the

52. Fish Papers, "Diary," vol. 3, entry for 10 July 1872.
53. Lanman, *Japanese in America*, p. 41.
54. Ko Megata Danshaku Denki Hensankai, eds., *Danshaku Megata Tanetarō* (Tokyo, 1938), p. 188. The portion of this biography relating to Mori will be published in *Zenshū* II.
55. Lanman, *Japanese in America*, pp. 26–29.
56. Ibid., p. 127.
57. Lanman, *Japanese in America*, has a chapter on "Japanese Poetry" by Mori's First Secretary, Takagi Saburō.
58. "Letters: Japanese Legation," letter from Arinori Mori to Addison Van Name, 2 Oct. 1872.

top of his head) in his "Introduction" to *Education in Japan;* publishing, according to Lanman, a good many pamphlets,[59] which unfortunately have disappeared without a trace; and welcoming every speech-making occasion which came his way as an opportunity to cure the Americans of their annoying habit of mistaking the Chinese they saw around them for Japanese.[60] It was not a matter at all of disdain for China or the Chinese as such. Indeed, Fish noted: "Mr. Mori is anxious to elevate the Asiatics and with this view would [wish] the Chinese to establish a legation and consulates in the U.S. and in the other Powers, and desires my opinion 'personally' on the subject."[61]

It was simply that, at a time when Japan was sending to the United States her best brains and her top officials, the vast majority of Chinese in America happened to be manual laborers or laundrymen, and to have the two confused naturally undercut the image of Japan which Mori was endeavoring to promote.[62] Occasionally, too, there were embarrassing circumstances which indeed needed "explaining," such as the time when "a Japanese scholar in one of the New Haven schools having been insulted by a schoolmate . . . sent a note to one of the instructors requesting permission to kill the offender,"[63] or when Mori found it necessary to assure the contractor for the *Capron:*

> I do not attribute this delay on the part of my government to any desire to avoid the settlement of the claims of these gentlemen . . . I think that the delay is merely caused by the great distance of my country from the United States and to delays arising from the introduction of new methods of transacting business. The ways of the West are yet new in Japan and do not operate with that facility that they do in the countries from which they have been lately taken. It will be well for you to assure the gentlemen in the name of this Legation that Japan has no intention of dishonoring her contracts and that every penny justly due will finally be paid.[64]

59. Charles Lanman, *Japan: Its Leading Men* (Boston, 1886), p. 136.
60. *Megata Tanetarō*, p. 188.
61. Fish Papers, "Diary," vol. 3, entry for 13 Feb. 1873.
62. John F. Howes, "Japan's Enigma: the Young Uchimura Kanzō" (unpublished Ph.D. dissertation, Columbia University, 1965), p. 86, mentions that Uchimura took offense at the same phenomenon.
63. *Washington Evening Star,* 11 Sept. 1872.
64. "Letters: Japanese Legation," letter from Arinori Mori to David F. Baker, 15 Jan. 1873.

Lanman had also written that Mori was "greatly interested in the progress of knowledge, earnest and desirous of promoting the advancement of his country in all good things,"[65] and the publication of works intended for the Japanese also in the English language shows how concerned he was, while attempting to enlighten his own countrymen, to instill in his Western readers through the same texts a sympathetic interest in the problems of Japan, and some confidence that she was determined and able to solve them.

Of far greater symbolic value and public impact than the two Iwakura photographs, for instance, was the presentation to the Smithsonian Institution of a Japanese sword originally intended for Mori's own assassination. The repentant owner, "convinced," as Mori wrote Secretary of War William W. Belknap, "of the uselessness of that custom [i.e., sword-wearing]," had showed up sheepishly at the legation and turned over the weapon with apologies, remarking how after the "Haitōron" he had waited in ambush time after time only to miss his quarry. The sword, an *objet d'art* in its own right, was displayed together with an account of its recent history and seems to have drawn great crowds to the museum.[66]

When rumors of a conservative coup d'état in Tokyo arose during the autumn of 1872, Mori took to the pages of the *Washington Evening Star* to pronounce them "a fabrication concocted in Washington." The edition of 4 October continued: "He admits that the path of the progressives is beset with difficulties, but feels that his government will soon rest on secure foundations. He does not disguise the fact that many of the present officers of the government are young and inexperienced and will have to 'make haste slowly' in the great work of reform. He believes, however, that they will be successful in effecting a peaceful revolution, and finally of placing Japan on a par with the first rate powers of the world."

It is important to bear in mind, in evaluating Mori's pronouncements in Washington on the future of his country, the duality of focus inherent in his position. He had not only to convince his own government *of* the need for progress, but also a sceptical Western audience *that* progress was indeed coming, and that he and not the so-called non-progressives (as the *Star* put it) represented the wave of the future. Without intending any slur on Mori's sincerity, it is worth asking whether this propagandizing requirement does not to some extent account for the positive, unqualified flavor of his public appreciations of the West.

65. Lanman, *Japanese in America*, p. 41.
66. Ibid., p. 42.

Mori's command of English, his style of living, and his excellent network of contacts contributed immensely to the effectiveness of his mission. "Where did your 'chief' learn the English language so as to speak it fluently and read it understandingly?" asked the Rev. Octavius Perinchief of his intimate friend Charles Lanman on 27 September 1871.[67] Megata has described Mori as able, and eager, to deliver himself of impromptu speeches in English when given the opportunity,[68] while personal letters in Mori's own handwriting testify, despite the little errors so unmistakably his, to a remarkable command of appropriately florid Victorian written English as well.[69] Letters in English between Mori and his subordinates suggest that he encouraged the use of the foreign tongue within the legation itself,[70] and he also is reported to have sent his own dispatches to Tokyo in English.[71]

Life within the legation, according to Kimura Kyō, in many respects reproduced the atmosphere of Kanda, or of "Mr. Harris' seminary": "Mori and his Secretaries slept and ate and laughed together, just like one big family . . . Conduct and behavior had to be above reproach; rather, they scoffed at the moral shortcomings of the Americans . . . Mori, being fond of learning, read extensively while at the Legation, placing special emphasis on literature and ethics, reading Spencer on philosophy and John Stuart Mill on economics."[72] This air of self-help and simplicity was bound to appeal to contemporary Americans, themselves shy of traditional diplomatic ceremonialism, and Mori once delighted the entire capital by appearing at a White House reception in an ordinary frock coat and silk hat. He explained that he could not fancy appearing in his own Japanese ceremonial robes of the Heian period; that the swallow-tail on the other hand was "not the formal dress of Japan"; and that he therefore had settled upon ordinary Western dress.[73]

Fish and Henry were in all probability the initial points from

67. Charles Lanman, *Octavius Perinchief: His Life of Trial and Supreme Faith* (Washington, D.C., 1879), p. 279.
68. *Megata Tanetarō*, p. 188.
69. See the letters not only signed but also written by Mori in his own hand, e.g., "Letters: Japanese Legation," Arinori Mori to Charles Lanman, 5 Sept. 1872, or Arinori Mori to Birdsey Northrop, 26 Dec. 1872.
70. See, for example, ibid., letter from Tamesuke Magome to Arinori Mori, 26 Dec. 1872.
71. Robert S. Schwantes, "American Influences in the Education of Meiji Japan" (unpublished Ph.D. dissertation, Harvard University, 1950), p. 124.
72. KKM, p. 62.
73. *Megata Tanetarō*, p. 188.

which Mori's political and cultural contacts ramified. As the former had opened the young man's eyes to the world of international law and diplomacy, so must the latter have given him a new vision of the world of modern science and scholarly endeavor. Lists of Mori's supposed "friends"[74] probably have been padded by obvious line-of-duty acquaintances such as "Vice President Wilson" or "President Grant," although Kimura claims that the latter was very fond of Mori and would receive him in the White House outside of official visiting hours.[75] One also suspects that reports of his friendship with Longfellow[76] or any of the other New England greats have been exaggerated and probably stem from the farewell dinner for the Iwakura mission in Boston on 2 August 1872, which was attended by Longfellow, Emerson, and Oliver Wendell Holmes. Kaimon Sanjin has described Charles Sumner as Mori's "closest friend," surmising that the influence of the elderly abolitionist on the young envoy was considerable, and that his discourses on "slavery" may have contributed to Mori's developing views on the role of women in Japan.[77]

The evidence of Mori's proximity to Joseph Henry is well documented and much firmer. It was Henry who introduced Mori to Lanman and who first suggested and took up with the envoy of Japan the return of the Shimonoseki Indemnity,[78] and it was to this world-renowned physicist, director of the Smithsonian Institution and veritable dean of American science, that Mori first broached his radical ideas on the Japanese language. The following report by Henry to the Joint Committee on the Library of Congress on 10 January 1872 suggests the possible origin of this close friendship: "Gentlemen: The Smithsonian Institution, in its mission for the 'increase and diffusion of knowledge among men,' has entered into friendly relations with the authorities of Japan for the exchange of specimens of natural history and ethnology, and for the establishment of meteorological, magnetic and other physical observations. In relation to these matters, I have had frequent intercourse with Mr. A. Mori, the Japanese Minister, and have been informed as to his various plans for elevating the intellectual condition of his people."[79]

Between the two of them, Henry and his friend Lanman no

74. As given, for instance, in KKM, p. 63.
75. KKM, p. 64.
76. OTM, p. 43.
77. KSM, p. 33.
78. Lanman, *Japanese in America,* pp. 42–43.
79. Ibid., pp. 42–43 has the quotation.

doubt did a great deal to ease Mori's entrée into the world of American letters and education. Charles Lanman, who returned to serve the legation under Mori's successor, Yoshida Kiyonari, and remained in its employ until 1882, was no doubt after Oliphant the most colorful figure in Mori's life: a "handsome man of genial presence," popular in society and an excellent raconteur, author in his lifetime of thirty-two distinct works, painter and member of the National Academy of Design, explorer of the Mississippi valley, and the first to popularize canoeing as a recreational activity. Before coming to Mori he had worked as a newspaper editor, as private secretary to Daniel Webster, and as librarian of the House of Representatives.[80]

Octavius Perinchief, rector of the Old Swedes' Church at Bridgeport, Pennsylvania, and an Episcopal clergyman of outspoken "Low Church" views, was in later years very close to Yoshida and a regular host to Japanese passing through the United States. It is quite possible, judging from his intimacy with Lanman and his contribution to *Education in Japan,* that he may have had more than a passing acquaintance with Mori as well. Perinchief had continued in his letter to Lanman of 27 December 1871, discussing Mori and his students: "These men may do us much good by cordially and considerately criticizing our civilization. That fellow who signs his name 'Pagan' must be an original. Indeed, I know these men have a keen eye with respect to our follies." And again on 23 January 1872:

> These young Japanese manifest a decided talent for observation, and their remarks have a sarcastic ring to them which might be very salutary to us as a people, if we could only get our people to hear them . . . I observe, too, what you say about [Mori's] desire to "have the facts, even if against us." That is a very special point, to give him the facts, and not let him take facts merely for appearances, as they strike a stranger. As, for example, what Mori deplores, is, I doubt not, far more deplored by us—the abusive language in our legislative halls and newspapers. But what is the fact there? Simply the fact of an *abused* privilege or right—that of *free speech* . . . There are those who carry the country, but unhappily there are those whom the country has to carry. We feel it, as I said before, more sadly than Mori. All honor to him that he does see it; he is, therefore, the safer guide for his people.[81]

80. *Dictionary of American Biography,* 1943 ed., X, 606.
81. Quoted in Lanman, *Perinchief,* pp. 283–284.

Perinchief in his lengthy letter argues, basically, that Mori has become if anything too critical, missing the forest of American freedoms for the tree of an occasional (and inevitable) abuse. He bears out Kimura's description of the high, and perhaps a bit prudish, moral ground from which the legation looked out upon local manners and mores, and indicates a far more selective and qualified enthusiasm for American ways than is suggested by many of Mori's publicly reported statements. When we come to his students, and the delightful collection of essays which Mori solicited from them and edited only slightly for publication in Lanman's account of the Iwakura mission, *The Japanese in America,* we find them pulling very few punches in their censure of everything from political demagoguery, sham Christianity, and the money-making animus, to the petty campus conspiracies of boarding school life. The forthrightness of the criticisms, on the other hand, must have proved still another asset in dealings with Americans.

NEW EDUCATIONAL HORIZONS

The Washington tour marked Mori's transition from simple pedagogue to educational statesman, at least in the scope of his thinking if not as yet in the official station from which he could give effect to his views. It started out simply enough, with Mori keeping close tabs on some 200 Japanese students in the United States, including ten who had accompanied him across the Pacific on the *Great Republic,* a small group which he had selected personally, less with a view to their English language fluency than to their "unimpeachable moral character."[82] The great majority of students were on government stipends of about $1,000 per person per year, funds which Mori transmitted while seeing to it that the recipients kept in touch with the legation.[83] Kanda Naibu, Kōhei's son and at fourteen the youngest of the group, wrote home on 10 March 1871, in beginner's English: "Every month I must send letter to Mr. Mori, which I want to send to Japan, and beside the former I

---

82. Included in this group were Magome Tamesuke, Yatabe Ryōkichi, and Kanda Naibu. The considerable scope of Mori's supervisory responsibility is suggested by the following figures. Lanman, in *The Japanese in America,* p. 55, estimated the total number of Japanese students in America in 1872 at approximately 200. The Senate hearings on the Shimonoseki Indemnity during January of the same year mentioned a figure of "about 300." (*Washington Evening Star,* 10 Jan. 1872). Monbushō, *Monbushō dai-ichi nenpō* (Tokyo, 1873), p. 176 gives a total figure of 373 students in Europe and America, 250 of them supported by the government.

83. Lanman, *Japanese in America,* p. 55.

must send any composition, or record of anything which I saw, and any which I hear, or visit, to Mr. Mori." And on 20 June 1871: "I was told by Mr. Mori to send him an English composition every week. He is very kind in regard to every matter."[84]

Mori watched the students' progress carefully. Lanman describes them as having "fallen into the habit of sending [Mori] some of the results of their school education,"[85] and it was from these that the aforementioned essays were culled. Correspondence with guardians or headmasters shows Mori's concern with money matters and with the good health of his charges as well. Mori wrote to the president of the Collegiate Polytechnic Institute at Brooklyn: "I authorize you to enforce your rules in such a manner as you may think will induce these young students to desist from such extraordinary exertion. Please advise them to regard their health as one of the objects which is worthy of their care and development."[86]

With *Life and Resources in America,* Mori took all Japan for his classroom. The purpose of the volume, a straightforward across-the-board description of the United States in the early 1870's, was, according to Kimura, to counter the antiforeign feeling in Japan by depicting an advanced Western society in detail,[87] and "to invite all lovers of their race, in Japan," as Mori himself put it, "to join in the noble march of progress and human happiness."[88] Mori's original intention seems to have been to translate the English manuscripts directly into Japanese as they emerged from Lanman's hand, "for exclusive circulation in Japan."[89] This task, in the press of official duties, he never accomplished, but at the suggestion of his American friends (and with little resistance one would imagine from Lanman himself), Mori authorized the immediate publication of Lanman's original. This, although Lanman's in point of research and expression, was Mori's in overall concept, with his editorial hand clearly visible on points of judgment, especially as regards religion and politics.

The editing of this volume no doubt made Mori the Japanese

---

84. Kanda Memorial Committee, ed., *Memorials of Kanda Naibu* (Tokyo, 1927), pp. 11–12 and 283.

85. Lanman, *Japanese in America,* p. 57.

86. "Letters: Japanese Legation," letter from Arinori Mori to D. H. Cochran, 1 March 1873.

87. KKM, p. 64.

88. Mori, *Life and Resources in America,* p. 137.

89. Lanman, *Japanese in America,* "Preface," p. i; Lanman, *Haphazard Personalities,* p. 19; Charles Lanman, *Recollections of Curious Characters and Pleasant Places* (Edinburgh, 1881), p. x.

best informed on America in 1871–1872. But neither the training of individual students nor the writing of individual texts would take Japan very far, and Mori early in his tour began to grapple with the problem of education as a system. On 15 May 1871, barely three months after arrival at the legation, we find him inviting Niijima Jō to Amherst, where he himself had taken a young Japanese for placement in the Agricultural College. Niijima reported that: "the main idea of his inviting me is that he was intending to establish schools at home after the American system and desired me to take charge of it."[90] One searches in vain for any official authorization for this early initiative. It preceded by three months the establishment on 2 September of the Monbushō (ministry of education), which after a year's deliberation in Tokyo promulgated the Gakusei (Code of Education) of 5 September 1872, very much on a French model; it preceded by half a year the setting up of the Iwakura mission with its educational study commission under Tanaka Fujimaro, with instructions to investigate and report the educational question first hand; and it preceded by nearly a year the first official offer to an American educator of employment as advisor to the Monbushō, an offer extended after the arrival, and apparently on the instructions, of the Iwakura mission. Mori may well have been kept informed of general developments within the Daigaku (formerly the Gakkō), of which he himself had previously been an inspector,[91] but it seems likely that the proposal to Niijima, made before Mori had settled down to his own study of American schools, was quite unauthorized and premature.

It bears repeated emphasis that Mori, until 1884, remained an outsider to the official educational establishment of Japan, and that it was essentially an indirect contribution that he made toward the educational researches of the Iwakura mission which did so much to bring about the "Americanization" of the Gakusei during the 1870's. Particularly difficult to apportion is the responsibility, as between Mori and Kido, for the appointment of Prof. David R. Murray of Rutgers College as superintendent of educational affairs (*gakkan*), and chief overseer of Japanese education from August 1873 to December 1878. It has often been implied that this appointment stemmed from Mori's favorable response to the letter which Murray contributed to *Education in Japan*.[92] Mori doubtless

---

90. Letter from Niijima Jō to Mrs. Alpheus Hardy, 7 June 1871, quoted in Arthur S. Hardy, *Life and Letters from Joseph Hardy Neesima* (Boston, 1891), p. 103.

91. See note 11, Chapter Four.

92. See, for example, Horimatsu Buichi, *Nihon kindai kyōikushi: Meiji*

participated in the decision and had provided the initial contacts, first with Birdsey G. Northrop, secretary of the Connecticut State Board of Education, who declined the offer,[93] and then with the Rutgers mathematician, who had taken an interest in the Japanese students at New Brunswick and was on particularly close terms with the renegade Broctonian, Hatakeyama Yoshinari. It was Kido, however, who interviewed Murray in Washington and again in Boston, and who dispatched the official orders for the American's appointment from England, after the mission's arrival there.[94]

Kido would serve as education minister (*monbukyō*) upon returning to Japan until leaving the government altogether (January to May 1874). And as Tanaka's supervisor in command of the educational investigations of the mission, he was deeply interested in education in his own right. After visiting schools in San Francisco in late January 1872, he had written: "Schools are more important than anything else for the advancement of our civilization,"[95] and "We do not at the moment possess a true civilization . . . there is but one way to forestall great national weakness a decade hence, and that is by promoting schools."[96] It is possible that even Mori's circular letter to American educators of 3 February 1872, the point of departure for *Education in Japan,* may have had some prompting from Kido. Murray himself recalled in 1897: "At this time Mori was Chargé d'Affaires . . . and under his guidance the Embassy made extensive and fruitful visits to the Departments of Education and institutions of learning in the different States of the United States."[97] It is instructive, however, that Murray should have gone on to attribute the successes of Meiji education in its early years to the investigations of Kido and Tanaka (not mentioning Mori) in 1872. Those investigations led

---

no kokka to kyōiku (Tokyo, 1959), p. 59; Yoshida Kumaji, "Dabitto Morurē shinpō kaidai" in MBZ, X, 24; and Kaigo Tokiomi, "Morurē," in Tsuchiya Tadao, ed., *Kindai Nihon kyōiku no kaitakusha* (Tokyo, 1950), pp. 17–19.

93. *Memorials of Kanda Naibu,* pp. 136–137; *Washington Evening Star,* 1 March 1872.

94. (Mrs.) David Murray, comp., *In Memoriam: David Murray, Ph.D.* (New York: by the compiler, 1915), p. 3; Marlene J. Mayo, "The Iwakura Mission to the United States and Europe" (unpublished M.A. thesis, Columbia University, 1957), p. 77.

95. Kido, *Nikki,* II, 126–127.

96. Kido Kō Denki Hensanjo, comp., *Shōgiku Kido kō den* 2 vols., (Tokyo, 1927), II, pp. 1506–1508, letter from Kido Takayoshi to Sugiyama Takatoshi, 25 Jan. 1872 (16 XII Meiji 4).

97. LCM, David Murray Papers, "Education in Japan," lecture delivered at Johns Hopkins University on 15 Nov. 1897.

to the publication of Tanaka's *Riji kōtei* (Progress of the commission) in fifteen volumes from 1875 to 1877, which in turn provided much of the basis for his Kyōikurei, or Education Ordinance, of 1879. Tanaka was also immensely aided by the services of Niijima Jō as interpreter and co-worker. But here again Mori's role was simply to have talked Niijima, very adroitly, into accepting the job. He shared neither in the research nor in the conclusions of the Tanaka commission.[98]

Mori's educational activities during the Washington tour were significant rather as reference material from which he would draw (as he pleased) in later years. Discussion of the Shimonoseki Indemnity revealed the types of schools and the kind of education which held his attention. The replies from American educators to Mori's circular show, in the pages of *Education in Japan,* the sort of advice he was getting. He best stated his own emerging educational philosophy, however, in a lengthy aside in *Religious Freedom in Japan* in late 1872. Reports differ as to just what Mori had proposed to do with the indemnity in the event of its return to Japan (which eventually transpired in 1883). Fish noted on 4 January 1872: "Mr. Mori suggests that the Japanese indemnity fund may be very beneficially appropriated in the establishment of a Public Library, or a Hospital, or some public institution for the benefit of the education and elevation of the general masses."[99]

In his statement to Congress previously quoted, Joseph Henry on 10 January elaborated on the young chargé's (and very possibly in origin his own) proposal, describing Mori's "Library" as: "a National Institution in the city of Jeddo for educational purposes, to be furnished with a Library in which shall be represented the science and literature of Western Europe and the United States, with specimens, apparatus, and models to fully illustrate all the principles of abstract science, as well as their application to the practical uses of life. This Institution is designed to be a great central University, and to serve as a normal school, in which teachers may finish their education as rapidly as a knowledge of the English language is disseminated throughout the country."[100]

Mori's plans shifted somewhat after he had discussed the matter with the Iwakura mission. On 30 March, in outlining "unofficially

---

98. cf. Harada Minoru, *Mori Arinori*, a volume in the unnumbered series, Maki Shoten, comp., *Sekai shisōshi zenshū* (Tokyo, 1966), p. 93: "We may well say that *Riji kōtei* . . . was the product of Niijima's diligent efforts which were traceable entirely to Mori's own recommendation."
99. Fish Papers, "Diary," vol. 3, entry for 4 Jan. 1872.
100. Quoted in Lanman, *Japanese in America*, p. 43.

the views of his government," he told Fish: "the money will be used for establishing schools in the Treaty Ports for the education of both Japanese and foreigners."[101] Fish, in reporting his talk with Mori to Edward Thornton, the British minister, further explained the proposed schools as establishments "in which Japanese and foreigners should be educated together, the former learning the foreign languages, and the latter being instructed in the Japanese language."[102]

Lanman's description of the project later in the year suggests that Mori eventually reverted to his original concept: "He would take about one-third of the amount, and erect in Japan a number of appropriate buildings in the leading cities and furnish them with all the necessaries, including libraries and scientific apparatus, for a complete course of education; he would have them supplied with professors and subordinate teachers, taken from the United States; and would then have the balance of five hundred thousand dollars invested in U.S. securities, and kept in Washington, the interest of which should be used to support the institutions of Japan."[103] If his indemnity proposals show a concern for what might be called higher education, Mori's travels and the company he kept show a strong interest in basic popular education as well. Kimura relates: "He made the rounds of schools in Connecticut and Massachusetts, and made a point of sounding out educators on their views. At a time when even Americans had not yet taken much interest in the subject, Mori very positively set about the study of kindergartens."[104]

The choice of the two New England states was not haphazard. Massachusetts under Horace Mann as secretary of the state board had led the nation in the establishment of a state-operated system of free and compulsory primary schools. Connecticut under Henry Barnard was not far behind, and Mori had in Barnard's successor, Birdsey Northrop, not only an expert professional advisor but also a good personal friend who assisted with the supervision of local Japanese students and who joined Joseph Henry in a publicity campaign on behalf of the indemnity, sending out on 1 January 1873 a petition for signatures which was later presented to the

101. Fish Papers, "Diary," vol. 3, entry for 30 March 1872.
102. PRO, Granville Papers, PRO-30-29-250. Letter from E. Thornton to Earl Granville, 8 April 1872.
103. Lanman, *Japanese in America*, p. 43. Written probably during the summer or fall of 1872, in any case in time to reach the British public while the Mission was still in their country.
104. KKM, p. 63.

Senate.[105] At the secondary level, America was still in the first stages of the transition from private academies to public high schools, and the legality of supporting the latter out of public taxes had only been established in 1870.[106] The Land Grant Act of 1862, which laid the foundation of a system of federally aided public institutions for higher education had, on the other hand, already borne fruit in certain states. The Agricultural College at Amherst (later the University of Massachusetts), which Mori had visited in 1871, came under this category—a universal feature of which, then as now, was the provision of a Reserve Officers' Training Corps program.

John Eaton, United States commissioner of education and indefatigable supplier of official reports and statistics to Mori and the mission, on 23 May 1872 sent the former a letter of introduction to Dr. J. M. Gregory, president of the Illinois Industrial University (later the University of Illinois), strongly urging him to meet this leading exponent of industrial education.[107] We do not know whether Mori seized this opportunity, but the fact that he included in his *Education in Japan* circular Peter Cooper, manufacturer and inventor and founder of the Cooper Union in New York City, suggests that he was interested in exploring the fields of technical and vocational training.

Several decades would pass, however, before the United States developed the closely articulated system of tax-supported, free, and secular elementary, secondary, and higher education under public control which is so familiar today. The institutional model for that system as it began to emerge was largely provided by the pre-1850 Prussian scheme, and Americans whom Mori knew were quite ready to acknowledge the debt. Mori, Kaimon tells us,[108] was on close terms with the septuagenarian Charles Brooks, a Unitarian clergyman and educationist who returned from a trip to Europe in 1833–34 so impressed with Prussian schools that he had at once set about campaigning on behalf of Mann's primary school movement in Massachusetts, and had called for the state support of teacher training.[109] He made known to Mori, according to

105. *Dictionary of American Biography,* XIII, p. 565–566.
106. I. N. Thut and Don Adams, *Educational Patterns in Contemporary Societies* (New York, 1964), p. 237.
107. NAW, United States Commission on Education, "Letter Books," no. 12, letter from John Eaton to Arinori Mori, 23 May 1872.
108. KSM, p. 34.
109. Charles Brooks died on 7 July 1872 at the age of seventy-seven. He ought not to be confused with the younger Charles Walcott Brooks, honorary Japanese consul at San Francisco, who accompanied the Iwakura mission to Washington.

Kaimon, both his admiration for Prussian education and the importance above all of a first-rate normal school system.

Lanman, too, writing for Mori in *Life and Resources in America,* admitted that "Prussia is far in advance of the United States" in teacher training,[110] and also handed Prussia the top grade among nations "for the investigation of abstract science."[111] Murray likewise in his letter in *Education in Japan* had written: "Germany, since the days of Frederick the Great, has been patiently perfecting her system of education, so that every German child, whether peasant or noble, may receive a thorough education; and it was Germany's education, Germany's universal culture, which triumphed over France in their recent struggle."[112] If Waterloo had been won on the playing fields of Eton, the outcome at Sedan (many observers were beginning to conclude) had been decided on the schoolbenches of Brandenburg, and the events which focussed the attention of the entire world on the Prussian schoolmaster had occurred the very year before Mori's arrival in Washington.

The five questions which Mori addressed to American educators on 3 February 1872 showed not only the general connection which he drew between education and national welfare but also more specifically the priorities and purposes which were beginning to take shape in his mind. Mori wrote (making use of the Spencerian triad): "I wish to have your views in reference to the elevation of Japan, intellectually, morally and physically, but the particular points to which I invite your attention are as follows: The effect of education: (1) Upon the material prosperity of a country; (2) Upon its commerce; (3) Upon its agricultural and industrial interests; (4) Upon the social, moral and physical condition of the people; and—(5) Its influences upon the laws and government."[113] The replies to this circular form the body of *Education in Japan,* published in English on New Year's Day, 1873, at New York. Only a small portion of the Japanese version which Mori had promised in his circular saw publication, and that many years later, under the title "Nihon kyōiku saku," (An educational scheme for Japan) in the *Meiji bunka zenshū* of 1928.[114]

110. Mori, *Life and Resources in America,* p. 268.
111. Ibid., p. 295.
112. Arinori Mori, *Education in Japan: A Series of Letters Addressed by Prominent Americans to Arinori Mori* (New York, 1973), p. 101.
113. Ibid., pp. 1–2.
114. In MBZ, X. Only the letters from Garfield and Whitney and the U.S. Commissioner's report were translated and published. Kaigo Tokiomi estimates the date of the translation, written down on official Sain and Dajōkan stationery, at 1874 or 1875. No indication of the translator's identity

Between Mori's introductory summary of Japanese history and two "Additional Papers" ("On the Adoption of the English Language in Japan," by Professor William D. Whitney of Yale, and "On Education in the United States," a report prepared by the U.S. Commission on Education) were printed, in order of date of receipt, replies from the following:

1. Theodore D. Woolsey, retired president of Yale College; scholar of classical Greek, political science and international relations; Congregational clergyman.
2. William A. Stearns, president of Amherst College; member of the Massachusetts board of education; Congregational clergyman.
3. Peter Cooper, founder of the Cooper Union; owner of the Canton Iron Works and constructor of the first American locomotive.
4. Octavius Perinchief, Episcopal clergyman; rector of Old Swedes' Church, Bridgeport, Pennsylvania.
5. Mark Hopkins, president of Williams College; philosopher and president of the American Board of Commissioners for Foreign Missions.
6. Julius H. Seelye, professor of philosophy at Amherst (succeeding Stearns to the presidency in 1876); Dutch Reformed clergyman.
7. James McCosh, president of the College of New Jersey at Princeton; trained in philosophy; Presbyterian clergyman.
8. Joseph Henry, director of the Smithsonian Institution; physicist and president of the National Academy of Science.
9. David Murray, professor of mathematics and astronomy at Rutgers College; former headmaster of Albany Academy, Albany, New York.
10. Birdsey G. Northrop, secretary of the Connecticut State Board of Education; former pastor of the Congregational Church at Saxonville, Massachusetts.
11. Charles W. Eliot, president of Harvard College; trained in mathematics and chemistry.
12. George S. Boutwell, Secretary of the Treasury; specialist in international law and former Congressman from Massachusetts; author of *Thoughts on Educational Topics and Institutions,* 1859.

---

is afforded by the original copy, which in any case was not in Mori's hand. See Kaigo Tokiomi, "Nihon kyōiku saku kaidai," MBZ, X, 18.

13. James A. Garfield, Congressman from Ohio and later President of the United States.[115]

Some of the respondents, like Northrop, thought they could help most by summarizing American educational experience and outlook; others, notably Peter Cooper, went into great detail on the educational sectors with which they themselves were most familiar; still others could not resist the temptation to proselytize, as did Stearns when he urged upon Mori that "Japan has the opportunity, one of the grandest offered to the nations of men, to introduce a pure Christian civilization, the principles and inspiration of which shall be drawn, not from the formalism of the old Churches, but *directly from the New Testament*."[116] All were handicapped by massive ignorance of Japan. Murray, one would imagine, plied his Japanese students at Rutgers for first-hand information, and it is not surprising that it was his exposition, by far the lengthiest and the most systematically directed to the case of Japan, which most impressed Mori and the Iwakura mission. The burden of Murray's advice, indeed, had been that tradition be utilized and built upon wherever possible.

Six of Mori's respondents, including four among his six college presidents (incumbent, retired, or prospective) were ordained clergymen, and it is not surprising that the most common denominator of the replies taken as a whole seems to be the great attention given to Mori's fourth question, particularly to the impact of education on individual and social morality. In the letters of Stearns, Hopkins, McCosh—and Henry—the advocation of Christianity was most specific. Others had something more general in mind. Woolsey warned: "Morality, then, including the duties of the family, of society, toward the state, and toward God, cannot be left out of education with impunity."[117] Seelye pointed out: "The direct foes to law and liberty, and social order, and moral purity, have ever been men of education who lacked moral inspirations. The sad, sad fact is that education does not make men virtuous."[118] As to solutions, however, Seelye could suggest no more than "the instruction of the true religion." Boutwell, getting very much

---

115. *Education in Japan* gives the addressee as "the Hon. John A. Garfield, House of Representatives." This seems to be a printer's error. There was no such Garfield in the House in 1872. James A. Garfield was at the time second in command of the Republican Party leadership of the House.
116. Mori, *Education in Japan*, p. 13.
117. Ibid., p. 6.
118. Ibid., pp. 69–70.

down to specifics, forwarded Mori an essay of his own entitled "Education and Crime."[119]

Many of the respondents mentioned the matter of women's education, and Perinchief, Henry, and Murray gave it particular emphasis, calling attention to the role of the mother as the most determinative influence in the development of the child.[120] In this area, Mori had already made a small start—if only at the level of social graces and piano lessons—with the party of five Japanese girls who had come over with the mission: Yoshimasa Ryō (age 15), Ueda Tei (15), Yamakawa Sutematsu (12), Nagai Shige (10), and Tsuda Umeko (8). Tsuda and Yoshimasa had been placed with the Lanmans upon arrival, the other three in a nearby family. A short while thereafter a house was rented and all five were placed together with an English instructor, a Miss Haynes, though still under the general supervision of Mrs. Lanman and Mori. In the fall of 1872 they were reassigned to separate American families. Three of them eventually would go on to graduate from American colleges: Tsuda from Bryn Mawr, and Yamakawa and Nagai from Vassar.[121]

The initiative for the dispatch of this party seems to have been taken by Kuroda Kiyotaka, with the approval of Mori. Kuroda, in Washington during early 1871 in connection with the hiring of Horace Capron, had been impressed with the happy lot of American womanhood, and had memorialized his government on the subject of women's education, suggesting the dispatch of a delegaton of young girls to the United States as a starter. Mori, "if a little less enthusiastic," in the words of Lanman, "was quite as deeply interested as the commissioner," when he had seen a copy of Kuroda's memorial.[122] Mori's "personal views" on the education of the delegation, Lanman noted, "have been freely expressed in Washington society," and were summarized by the latter as follows: "He would in the first place have them made fully acquainted with the blessings of *home life* in the United States, and in the second place, he would have their minds fully stored with all those kinds of information which will make them true ladies."[123] Perinchief, who baptized Tsuda in a nonsectarian ceremony at the Old

119. Ibid., p. 118ff.
120. Ibid., pp. 40, 85, 103.
121. Lanman, *Leaders of the Meiji Restoration in America*, p. 375; Robert S. Schwantes, *Japanese and Americans: A Century of Cultural Relations* (New York, 1955), p. 197.
122. Lanman, *Japanese in America*, p. 46.
123. Ibid., p. 48.

Swedes' Church on 12 July 1873, wrote in his diary for that day: "While it was understood that the instruction of these girls in matters of the Christian faith was unavoidable, it was not desired that they should adopt the tenets of any particular sect. This is in harmony with a prevailing sentiment in this respect among the Japanese in the United States."[124]

The problem of Japanese marital ethics became closely (and in the long run unnecessarily) involved during the early years of Meiji with suggestions for racial intermarriage. Kaneko Kentarō, at the time a student in America, recalled in later years a speech given by Mori to the assembled Japanese boys in New York in which the latter had said, in Kaneko's recollection: "It will take more than the mere abolition of the Japanese language to advance our country to the heights of civilization and enlightenment. The first requirement is to improve the race. It will be necessary for Japanese in the future, therefore, to marry with Westerners. You fellows should associate with American girls during your studies here, marry them, and take them home with you."[125]

The evidence suggests, however, that Mori held such a view very briefly, if at all, and that he was not nearly as skeptical of the qualities of Japanese womanhood as Kaneko had made him out to be. Within two or three years, Mori would heap ridicule upon such proposals for intermarriage,[126] while Lanman as early as 1872 argued, on behalf of Mori, that the upper classes of Japan had resisted the Chinese (i.e., Confucian) influences which had led to the degradation of oriental women; that the reign of eight empresses in ancient Japan was proof of the high respect in which Japanese women had once been held; and that: "Japan need not hesitate now to enforce among all classes that respect and consideration which has never been wanting about her Court and among her better families."[127] It seems probable, indeed, that the exhortation reported by Kaneko, if ever seriously entertained by Mori, had

---

124. Quoted in Lanman, *Perinchief,* p. 147. The baptism was performed according to the Book of Common Prayer, simply for the sake of some formula. Perinchief's church had been selected for its nonsectarian tradition. Since breaking with the Church of England at the time of the Revolution, it had remained unaffiliated as to sect, although it had uniformly called clergymen of the Protestant Episcopal Church to its pulpit (see ibid., p. 148).

125. Cited by Ōmura Kakichi in "Mori Arinori: Eigaku o sasaeta hitobito: dai-roku," *Eigo Shōnen,* July 1965.

126. See the discussion of Mori's "Saishōron," in Chapter Seven.

127. Lanman, *Japanese in America,* p. 52. Lanman quotes "a Japanese," whom we may safely take to be his own employer.

first been put into his head by Kuroda. Again, it is Lanman who explains: "With his friend Mr. Arinori Mori, [Kuroda] held several long discussions on the subject, and took the advanced ground that the Japanese ought to intermarry with the people of the more enlightened foreign nations, and, in his zeal went so far as to insist that Mr. Mori should marry an American lady without delay. To this the youthful minister replied that he considered himself a true patriot and would like to oblige his friend, but did not think it necessary for him to go into the marrying business quite so suddenly."[128]

Buried under recommendations explicit or implicit on behalf of Christianity in *Education in Japan* was, in the reply of the Low Churchman Perinchief, a clearcut admonition to keep organized religion out of the schools: "The one work there is intellectual training. Let that be well done, and in doing recognize no religious sect, and have nothing whatever to do with any . . . Experience has shown that, whenever a state compels a special form of religion, it is invariably not the best."[129] It was this latter advice which Mori took to heart. In the closing paragraphs of *Religious Freedom in Japan* he describes as the "principal characteristic" of the "educational organization" which he now envisions for Japan, "an entire absence of any particular religious influence." As for the "scope" of the system, he thinks it "should comprehend universal learning and include all classes and kinds of persons without distinction and with perfect impartiality."[130]

Arguing from the major premise of his pamphlet that "religious faiths are purely matters of individual conviction," Mori concludes that "it is wrong for the state to usurp, as a function within its province, the introduction of religious influences into the educational administration."[131] This, however, he immediately goes on to say, does not absolve the state of responsibility for education as such. Persons "who hold that it may reasonably be asserted that education is entirely a subject for personal and private determination," he is not prepared to oppose, "so long as parents or guardians are faithful to their trust." Nevertheless: "If the state has any authority at all to punish criminals, or, correctly speaking, to protect its people from violence, it certainly has equal authority

128. Ibid., p. 45.
129. Mori, *Education in Japan,* pp. 45–46.
130. Arinori Mori, *Religious Freedom in Japan: A Memorial and Draft of Charter* (Washington, D.C.: by the author, 1872), p. 11. Reprinted in MBZ, XI, interleaved between pp. 532–546.
131. Ibid., p. 11.

to assure their peace. No, the state cannot possibly disclaim its responsibility. It can best discharge its obligations by assisting in the diffusion of a knowledge of facts in science and art, and thus it shall establish peace upon a solid foundation of enlightenment."

This knowledge, furthermore, is to be dispensed widely: "Everyone, whether male or female, without exception, shall be its recipient. The mode of giving everyone in the community an opportunity to receive an education may vary according to his or her condition in regard to age and occupations."[132]

Unfortunately, Mori does not elaborate any further while in America on his basic concepts of secular, universal, state-supported education which have taken root here. As to the urgency of the project and its basic purposes, however, he is a bit more specific: "While the laws are the best protection for our liberty, its greatest security depends wholly upon the character and potency of our popular education. The value and urgency of an interest in education is at once manifest. Every one of us must be profoundly convinced that our present position is one of awful responsibility. We are charged with the task of moulding the destiny of our nation."[133] Mori's own sense of destiny, of his participation in the "great task" which he first mulled over in his letters to Yokoyama, is also gradually coming into focus. His objectives remain politically and morally defined, but he has now settled with finality on national education as the most promising instrument available. Murray, in his lengthy letter, had pointed out: "Good and intelligent populations need but little government . . . What is spent on education will be saved a hundredfold in armies, and police, and courts of justice."[134] Mori echoed this sentiment, quoting Horace Mann: "Education is our only political safety; outside of this ark, all is deluge."[135]

132. Ibid., p. 12.
133. Ibid., p. 11.
134. Mori, *Education in Japan,* pp. 88, 100.
135. Mori, *Religious Freedom in Japan,* p. 11.

Six   1871–1873

THE
EXTRACURRICULAR
HARVEST OF AMERICA

The educational question, Mori's central preoccupation during his Washington tour, led inevitably to more general considerations of Japan's impending transformation, ranging from the status of women to the role of language. The latter lay close to the heart of the educational challenge, and Mori attacked his own native tongue much as he had attacked the wearing of swords, creating a furor this time in scholarly circles, and raising a good many eyebrows among Western intellectuals as well. Unlike the language proposal, Mori's developing views on religious liberty and his own personal faith, as far as it can be ascertained, were much closer to what the average American would have endorsed, although they bear a careful reading to establish the exact proportion of approval or participation, as opposed to mere toleration, as regards Christianity.

Mori's political position, by contrast, turned out to be a criticism of much that he found in America, and was given the briefest public expression. Much of it has to be grasped obliquely through his evaluation of the contemporary American polity, and through his reflections, historically, upon that of Japan.

These three topics are presented here in descending order of their "radicalism" and of the public interest which they evoked at that time: this being the ascending order of their long-range impact on Mori's life work. The two puzzling matters of Mori's attempted resignation and of his clash with Yoshida Kiyonari over the flotation of a foreign loan deserve attention, in conclusion, for the light they shed upon Mori's personality and character.

ON THE ABOLITION OF THE JAPANESE LANGUAGE

Mori's "Kokugo haishiron," more properly speaking his "Kokugo haishi eigo saiyōron" (Proposal for the abolition of the Japanese and adoption of the English language), is not the title of a document but rather the popular designation of Mori's general idea, which found its final, its fullest, and its most drastic expression in the closing paragraphs of the introduction to *Education in Japan,* in which Mori proclaimed, as of 1 January 1873:

> Without the aid of Chinese, our language has never been taught or used for any purpose of communication. This shows its poverty. The march of civilization in Japan has already reached the heart of the nation—the English language following it suppresses the use of both Chinese and Japanese. The commercial power of the English-speaking race which now rules the world drives our people into some knowledge of their commercial ways and habits. The absolute necessity of mastering the English language is thus forced upon us. It is a requisite of our independence in the community of nations. Under the circumstances, our meagre language, which can never be of any use outside of our islands, is doomed to yield to the domination of the English tongue, especially when the power of steam and electricity shall have pervaded the land. Our intelligent race, eager in the pursuit of knowledge, cannot depend upon a weak and uncertain medium of communication in its endeavor to grasp the principal truths from the precious treasury of Western science and art and religion. The laws of state can never be preserved in the language of Japan. All reasons suggest its disuse.[1]

Herewith Mori abandoned an intermediate position, apparently held as of the spring of 1872, though neither very well developed nor clearly expressed, to the effect that the Japanese vernacular might still be maintained and put to some good use through Romanized transcription. Herewith he also turned a deaf ear to

1. Arinori Mori, *Education in Japan: A Series of Letters Addressed by Prominent Americans to Arinori Mori* (New York, 1873), p. lvi.

the advice of the American scholar whose opinion on the subject he had most earnestly solicited: William D. Whitney, professor of Sanskrit languages and literatures at Yale.

The report of the *Washington Evening Star* of 26 December 1871 regarding Mori's desire to "interdict the further teaching of Chinese," shows how early he had come to concern himself with the issue. As the argument developed in 1872, it became clear that "Chinese" as Mori uses it in this context refers not to the language of nineteenth-century China but to Sino-Japanese, i.e., the written language of Japan as it had existed before the welding of the spoken and written languages into an identity (*genbun itchi*), which gradually took place during the Meiji period. His definition seems to include not only the classical (and most genuinely "Chinese") *kanbun*, but also the more Japanized written styles such as the epistolary (*sōrōbun*), all of which depend heavily for their vocabulary on words of Chinese origin pronounced in the Sino-Japanese (*on*) fashion, and for their writing on Chinese characters (*kanji*).

Mori's letter to Whitney of 21 May 1872 went out under cover of another letter from Joseph Henry dated the following day. That Mori had long been in touch with Henry with regard to the language problem is suggested by the latter's reply to the *Education in Japan* circular, dated 4 March 1872, in which he noted: "Prior to the elaboration of your system of education, an essential question will arise as to what written language you shall adopt as the vehicle of thought, your own, as we are informed, being too cumbrous and difficult of acquisition to suit the wants of higher education of your own people, or to be adapted for communication with foreign nations; . . . the English language would be the best for you as a commercial nation."[2] It is difficult to believe that Henry, himself anything but a professional linguist, could have been the originator of these ideas. His informant obviously has been Mori himself. It is quite possible, however, that Mori's plans took on a clearer shape in the course of discussing with the Smithsonian director various schemes for disposal of the Shimonoseki Indemnity. Henry had assumed in his testimony to Congress on 10 January that the projects would go forward "as rapidly as a knowledge of the English language is disseminated throughout the country."[3] And his letter of 4 March confirms the impression that it was only the written language of Japan that Mori was originally concerned

2. Ibid., pp. 82–83.
3. Quoted in Charles Laman, *The Japanese in America* (New York, 1872), p. 40.

with, and that this concern had arisen from difficulties foreseen (or personally experienced by Mori himself) in appropriating the higher thought of the West, or in dealing with it in business matters, through any medium other than one of its own leading languages.

Mori wrote Whitney that: "all the schools the Empire has had, for many centuries, have been Chinese; and, strange to state, we have had no schools nor books in our own language for educational purposes. These Chinese schools, being now regarded as not only useless, but as a great drawback to our progress, are in the steady process of extinction."[4] Mori's position on the vernacular at this juncture is at best puzzling. He seems to contradict himself flatly in mid-letter. Having written at the outset of "the spoken language of Japan being inadequate to the growing necessities of the people of that Empire, and too poor to be made, by a phonetic alphabet, sufficiently useful as a written language,"[5] he then goes on in the very next page to assert: "Schools for the Japanese language are found to be greatly needed, and yet there are neither teachers nor books for them. The only course to be taken, to secure the desired end, is to start anew, by first turning the spoken language into a properly written form, based on a pure phonetic principle. It is contemplated that Roman letters should be adopted."

Taking Mori at his latter, not his former, word, it seems reasonable to suppose that as of May 1872 he still thought the native tongue might be retained in some secondary role, analogous perhaps to that of Welsh, which even today retains currency in the family circles of Wales, ceding to English the realms of modern science, government, commerce, and education. By New Year's Day 1873, however, even this modest proposal for Romanization had been abandoned. Mori concluded in *Education in Japan* that: "there are some efforts being made to do away with the use of Chinese characters by reducing them to simple phonetics, but the words familiar through the organ of the eye are so many, that to change them into those of the ear would cause too great an inconvenience, and be quite impracticable."[6]

It may, nevertheless, have been Mori's brief flirtation with Romanization which prompted the peculiar development of the other

---

4. Yale University Library, Historical Manuscripts, Whitney Manuscripts, letter from Arinori Mori to William D. Whitney, 21 May 1872, p. 2 of the letter.

5. Ibid., p. 1.

6. Mori, *Education in Japan*, pp. lv–lvi.

half of his linguistic proposal—the appropriation by his countrymen of English. He had written Whitney: "It is very important that the alphabets of the two languages under consideration—Japanese and English—be as nearly alike as possible, in sound and powers of the letters."[7] And it is very possible that it was the consideration of a phonetic Roman alphabet suitable to Japanese which brought to a head his own long-standing frustrations, as expounded to Whitney, with the irregularity of English inflections and orthography, and which led him to advocate the adoption by Japan of a "Simplified English."[8]

Mori's letter, Henry's covering letter, and Whitney's reply all as a matter of fact assume the importation into Japan, more or less massively, of the English language, and are directed far less at the problems of Japanese than at those bedevilling the English tongue. Mori warned: "It would be . . . nearly useless to make an effort . . . in behalf of the English language in its present form—a language so difficult to be learned, that by far the larger proportion of persons, with whom it is vernacular, speak and write it incorrectly . . . I could not conscientiously recommend my countrymen to cause their children to devote six or seven years of their lives to learning a language so replete with unnecessary irregularities . . . and rendered so difficult by a fantastic orthography."[9] The chief purpose of this letter, indeed, was to solicit Whitney's comment on Mori's own proposals for reform of *English*. Henry, as a matter of fact, had gone so far as to ask the Yale scholar whether he would be willing to undertake the creation of a new "Simplified English" for use in Japan, pointing out that: "it ought to be done under the direction of some competent philologist and I would suggest to [Mori], if it would be agreeable to you, that he employ you for the purpose."[10]

Mori's suggestions for verb inflections included, for example, the substitution of *seed* for saw and seen, *speaked* for spoke and spoken, *bited* for bit and bitten. The spelling of "phantom," "inveigh" and "receipt" Mori would have changed to "fantom," "invey" and "receit," taking as his standard the orthography in

---

7. Whitney Manuscripts, letter from Arinori Mori to William D. Whitney, 21 May 1872, p. 2 of the letter.

8. Ibid., p. 3.

9. Ibid., pp. 3, 4, 8.

10. Whitney Manuscripts, letter from Joseph Henry to William D. Whitney, 22 May 1872. Since Henry asked Whitney for a separate and confidential reply to this question, it is not clear whether the initiative for this offer was a joint one, or Henry's alone.

"fancy," and "convey" and "deceit."[11] Whitney was primarily a grammarian and had attempted to apply to Sanskritic studies the principles of modern linguistic science. Corresponding secretary of the American Oriental Society as well as president of the American Philological Association, he had been chairman of a committee set up under the latter to study the problem of English spelling,[12] and he now welcomed Mori's proposals for spelling reform as something which would profit the entire English-speaking world. But he drew the line there, and warned: "Any alteration, in the process of adoption, of the essential structure of English, would constitute an interference. You cannot join the community of English speakers without frankly accepting English speech as they have made it, and now use it."[13]

Whitney also surmised of the Japanese that: "by coming to speak English, they would, in a manner, make themselves a part of those races, having immediate access to all that was done by them; uniting, so far as civilization was concerned, the destinies of the two peoples."[14] Taken out of context this reads like an endorsement of the wildest schemes of westernization. Actually the passage is conditional. Whitney is saying that *if* Mori intends to adopt English for purposes of international communication (as he does), *then* he should by all means stick to the current, if somewhat cumbersome form. The letter to Whitney, in retrospect, might well have been dubbed Mori's "Eigo haishiron": a proposal for the abolition of the English language.

Whitney went on not only to encourage Mori's suggestion for a Romanization of the vernacular but also to plead for the retention of the Japanese language and the "ennobling and enriching of the native speech so that itself shall become a means of the increase of culture." He suggested: "Let the English language be studied as much as possible; let it take in Japan the place so long occupied by the Chinese; let it become the learned tongue, the classical language . . . but let the beneficial effect of all this be felt in the Japanese tongue itself . . . Accept the English language in its form as spoken and understood by those to whom it is native, for the standard and classical language of the new Japanese culture." He warned, however, against the displacement of Japanese: "[It] would be likely to result in the formation of a learned class, of

11. Whitney Manuscripts, letter from Arinori Mori to William D. Whitney, 21 May 1872, p. 4.
12. *Dictionary of American Biography*, 1943 ed., XX, 166–169.
13. Mori, *Education in Japan*, p. 146.
14. Ibid.

limited numbers ... with a wholly ignorant lower class, separated from the other in nearly all its sympathies."[15]

Whitney anticipated the actual course of events both with his call for enrichment of the native tongue and in his willingness to see a simplified English spelling introduced in the initial stages of learning the language (as it is used today by Japanese schoolchildren, in the form of the International Phonetic Alphabet). From the very positive terminology Whitney used in describing the future function of English, however, one is inclined to ask if the situation he actually envisioned was not really closer to that of modern India than to that of modern Japan. It was the example of India, implicit in Whitney's warning, which brought forth the most notable attack on Mori's proposal. Baba Tatsui, at the time a student in England, explained in the preface to his *Elementary Grammar of the Japanese Language,* published in London in 1873, that he intended his little treatise both as a guide to spoken Japanese and as a refutation of the position Mori had taken in *Education in Japan.*[16] "There is not the slightest proof," Baba protested, "about the impossibility of establishing popular education through our native speech."[17] He accused Mori of unqualified and unproved statements and echoed Whitney's fears about creating a dual culture. Above all, he tried to illustrate with his textbook that Japanese was sufficiently sophisticated and regular from the standpoint of grammar and syntax to be taught in the schools according to modern linguistic methods and to serve as the vehicle of national, popular education, for which he, like Mori, was deeply concerned.

All available evidence suggests that the reception of Mori's proposal was overwhelmingly unfavorable, both in Japan and abroad. Nishi Amane, although in favor of Romanization, was quick to dissociate himself (in the very first issue of the *Meirokuzasshi*) from any scheme to abandon the native tongue.[18] The famous Oxford Sanskritist, Friedrich Max Mueller, was equally forthright in his disapproval.[19] The *Japan Weekly Mail* spoke of "Mr. Mori's much and properly ridiculed scheme,"[20] and sum-

---

15. Ibid., pp. 150–152.
16. Tatui Baba, *Elementary Grammar of the Japanese Language: Easy Progressive Exercises* (London, 1873), p. iii.
17. Ibid., p. vii.
18. Nishi Amane, "Yōji o motte kokugo o shosuru no ron" (The argument for writing the Japanese language with Western letters), MRZ no. 1 (March 1874), reprinted in MBZ, XVIII, p. 51.
19. Takahashi Tatsuo, "Kokugo kokubun kara mita Fukuzawa sensei" *Shigaku,* 13. 3:387 (November 1934).
20. JWM, 2 Aug. 1873.

marized what it took the British reaction to be, grumbling that: "Mr. Mori has proved himself so unpractical and reckless a visionary in his educational views, that little apology need be offered for our having paid no attention in England to his vagaries."[21] And the greatest irony of all for Mori must have been to have his proposal quashed with finality, at the ministry of education, by none other than David Murray in his Report of 1873.[22] Ōkubo Toshiaki, otherwise favorably disposed toward Mori, characterizes the "Kokugo haishiron" as an extreme example of utilitarian thinking: "The expectation that national independence can be promoted by throwing away the national cultural heritage, is a doctrine which for the sake of means has forgotten ends and which will result, on the contrary, in the negation of true independence."[23]

Mori had known both England and America in an era of dramatic industrial and commercial expansion, an expansion wherein one could well have thought the chief challenge and danger to Japan lay. On another level, if one seriously gives priority to a full and free exchange of ideas with the Western world, then the modern Indian and Pakistani intelligentsia, moving with immense ease through the world of Western ideas and values, emerges less as a disaster than as proof positive of Mori's insight into the power of language.

One suspects, however, that a very fundamental motivation for Mori's proposal was the sense of inevitability to which he clearly gave vent. As regards the possibility of acquiring the sophisticated culture and technology of the Anglo-American world through any medium other than English, Mori had not moved beyond the position taken in his memorial to the Satsuma daimyo in 1870. No alternative plan seemed practicable at the time, and if the switch of languages had to come, then the sooner the better.

IN DEFENSE OF RELIGIOUS LIBERTY

The chapter on "Religious Life and Institutions" in *Life and Resources in America* had dealt with all aspects of American religion in a neutral, textbook fashion. In conclusion, however, Mori addressed his readers in the third person, thinking it proper "that the writer should submit a few particulars . . . which are somewhat personal to himself":

21. JWM, 19 July 1873.
22. David Murray, "Dabitto Morurē shinpō: Meiji rokunen," tr. anon., in MBZ, X, 127–128.
23. OKM, p. 179.

After his return to Japan from Europe, some years ago, he was frequently questioned by his countrymen as to his opinions about the Christian religion. In his replies, he took the ground, that, as far as he could understand it, the Bible was a good and wise book, but that it contained many things he did not understand. That while the people who called themselves Christians claimed to have the only true religion, and pretended to be better than all other men, they did not, in that particular, differ from the Chinese or Japanese, who assert the same claims for their religions. He thought it advisable that those who desire to form any opinion on Christianity, should acquaint themselves with it by close and attentive study, and then to judge for themselves . . . Whatever may be his private opinions on matters of such great importance, he has not thought it proper for him either to oppose or advocate them . . . It would be a very wonderful thing, should the time ever arrive, when the so-called Christians, who profess the faith, but do not live up to it, shall cease to boast of the superiority of their religion, and regard themselves as worse than all other people, because of their guilt in making insincere professions. True Christianity may not be considered as identical with the general sense of civilization—in which the good and the bad participate—but true philosophy would seem to teach that it should be a leading element in such a civilization.[24]

Despite the diplomatic silence which Mori maintains regarding his own private beliefs, this is very clearly not the profession of a sectarian enthusiast. Yet the statement is not hostile to Christianity in what he calls its "true" aspect, and much of his very frank stricture on the religion as actually practiced would have met with heartiest approval among Christians themselves. But was it the criticism of an insider or of an outsider?

The arrival of the Iwakura mission gave Mori the opportunity to show that he favored very strongly the toleration of Christianity in Japan and that he was prepared to intervene personally on behalf of individual Japanese Christians who anticipated difficulties with their government on account of their new faith. The repressive measures against Christians in Kyushu had been widely publicized in the West, and the issue was one which neither the press nor the

24. Arinori Mori, *Life and Resources in America* (originally published in 1871), part III of Charles Lanman, *The Japanese in America* (New York, 1872), pp. 243–245.

host governments in America and Europe would permit the mission to forget. Iwakura in the course of the third interview at the State Department had asked whether a demand was to be made for freedoms of religion, press, and speech for native Japanese (as opposed to foreign residents only), to which Fish had replied that such assurances would be desirable. The mission was reluctant to write into the text of a revised treaty anything which might imply foreign dictation of domestic policy, and an embarrassed silence then followed, which Mori was the first to break by insisting that the government of Japan was a liberal government; that it would bestow freedom of thought as fast as it could, consistent with national safety; and that there was accordingly no need to lay down such a stipulation. Mori's very adroitness here in arguing the question of religious freedom, Hayashi Takeji has surmised, may have deepened the mission's suspicion of his own personal belief in Christianity.[25]

Mori, in his capacity of student overseer, had first told Niijima Jō in mid-March 1871 that if he would inform the Japanese government in a brief letter who he was and what he had been studying, Mori would provide a passport which would enable him to return to Japan. Mori had also offered to pick up the young convert's educational expenses, an offer which Niijima refused for reasons confided to an American acquaintance: "I shall be bound up to the Japanese government by that sum of money. I would rather remain a free Japanese citizen and consecrate myself wholly to my Master's business."[26] Mori was sympathetic to the predicament of his Christian friend, four years his own senior, and when Niijima as of mid-June was still trying to compose the requested letter, and was in doubt as to the wisdom of informing the authorities of his Christian faith, Mori had advised him (Niijima recalled) that "he did not know whether it would be safe for me to do so or not, but I might try that."[27] Niijima, thereupon, had decided not to contact the Tokyo authorities at all for the time being, and had concluded that: "while I am studying I do not wish to be hindered by the government's affairs . . . Yet I will try to keep up a friendly relation

25. Shimomura Fujio, *Meiji shonen jōyaku kaiseishi no kenkyū* (Tokyo, 1962), p. 166. See also Hayashi Takeji, "Mori Arinori kenkyū: dai-ichi: Mori chūbei dairikōshi no jinin," reprinted from *Tōhoku daigaku kyōiku gakubu kenkyū nenpō*, 1967, pp. 5–6.
26. Arthur S. Hardy, *Life and Letters of Joseph Hardy Neesima* (Boston, 1891), p. 102, quoting letter from Niijima Jō to Mrs. Flint, 21 March 1871.
27. Ibid., pp. 103–104, letter from Niijima Jō to Mrs. Alpheus Hardy, 13 June 1871.

with the minister at Washington, so that when I get ready to go home he might be of some help to me."[28]

The following March, when asked to join the Iwakura mission as interpreter, Niijima was anxious that his participation in no way be construed as an obligation due the government from one of its students, but only as a hired service contracted for in the usual manner. "Mr. Mori stood very favorably for me," Niijima reported to his American sponsors, recalling Mori's words to the mission at that time as follows: "Mr. Neesima came here not as a bondsman, but with his kindness to give you some advice concerning education. So you must appreciate his kindness and willingness to do such a favor for you. As Mr. Neesima has such a relation to his Boston friends, he cannot commit himself to the Japanese government without their consent, neither has the government any right to lay claim on him, or to command him to do this or that, but the things ought to be done by a contract between him and you. Fortunately he has three weeks' vacation, and will do some good service to you if you treat him as a friend. He is a lover of Japan, but not a slave."[29]

The right of the individual to the free choice and exercise of his religious convictions, so well defended in the highly practical case of Niijima, was the central theme of Mori's fifteen-page English-language memorial, *Religious Freedom in Japan,* and of the two-page draft of a "Religious Charter of the Empire of Dai Niphon" appended to it. Although nominally addressed to the prime minister, Sanjō Sanetomi, the pamphlet was never translated into Japanese. This fact led Yoshino Sakuzō to surmise that Mori intended it for circulation among Western readers and a few select English-reading Japanese statesmen, not for the Japanese people or government at large, and that its main purpose may have been to reassure the American public with regard to Japanese religious policy.[30] It is, however, as Yoshino himself admits, an honest, hard-hitting document. Far from trying to whitewash the situation, it attacks the current government policy in unmistakable terms, and can be taken only in the most peripheral sense as a public relations gesture.

Mori first showed his draft to Fish on 8 October 1872, a good

28. Ibid., p. 104, letter from Niijima Jō to Mrs. Alpheus Hardy, 13 June 1871.
29. Ibid., p. 120, letter from Niijima Jō to Mr. and Mrs. Alpheus Hardy, 8 March 1872.
30. Yoshino Sakuzō, "Nihon shūkyō jiyū ron kaidai" in MBZ, XI, 59. A rough translation of the pamphlet "by a friend" of Mori's was eventually prepared for inclusion in Kimura's biography, as Chapter 18.

month ahead of the 25 November publication date. On the twenty-ninth Fish returned the copy Mori had left with him. Fish had described it in his diary as "a dispatch to his [Mori's] Government."[31] Fish noted in his covering letter: "I have read with much interest and return herewith, the paper you kindly permitted me to peruse. On some doctrinal points there will of course be difference of opinion, but there can be no question as to the soundness of the position it assumes on the great questions of religious toleration, and freedom of thought and conscience which are sustained with clearness, ability and philosophic argument."[32]

Mori's "Religious Charter" states three premises: (1) that matters of conscience are not amenable to force; (2) that society has no right to impose religious beliefs on the individual; and (3) that Japan would be wise to avoid sponsoring any particular religion by the state. It proceeds then to six resolutions disavowing any attempt by the state to: (1) pass laws in restraint of religious liberty; (2) interfere with any religious body "not in conflict with the laws of the state"; (3) treat religious institutions as different from "any other kind of social institution"; (4) favor any particular sect; (5) confer ecclesiastical title or rank; or (6) countenance any action contributing to religious animosity within the realm.

Unlike Nakamura Masanao's article only two months earlier, positively advocating the adoption of Christianity as the quickest means of absorbing Western culture,[33] Mori's memorial in its fundamental logic went no further than simple toleration and argued for a rigid separation of religion and state which if consistently applied would leave no room for any official encouragement of the Christian faith. The practical consequences of toleration, however, as missionaries hoped, and as traditionalist Japanese feared, would be the revival in strength of the long-proscribed religion. The fact that Mori could not find "too severe condemnation" for the current government support of Shintoism and Buddhism, and that he took great pains to argue away the fears held by Japanese regarding the influx of Christianity, must have strengthened any impression that he was actively in favor of the latter.

Mori opens the argument of the memorial as follows: "In all the enlightened nations of the earth, the liberty of conscience, especially in matters of religious faith, is sacredly regarded as not only

31. LCM, Hamilton Fish Papers, "Diary," vol. 3, entry for 8 Oct. 1872.
32. Ibid., entry for 29 Oct. 1872.
33. Nakamura Masanao, "Gitaiseijin jōsho" in *Shinbun zasshi*, no. 56 (September 1872).

an inherent right of man, but also as a most fundamental element to advance all human interests."[34] These two aspects of religious freedom—as a right of the individual and as a factor favorable to social progress—form, then, the primary and secondary reasons for its espousal. Mori complains that the current religious policy of the Japanese government will in effect "crush the very soul of man": "Every one that lives is himself solely responsible to his Creator for all his thoughts and deeds. He who is deprived of the knowledge of this responsibility, and the freedom to exercise it, can no longer be rightly called a man in the proper sense of the term. The notion of making a new religion or precept by the authority of the state, which now prevails in our country, has a strange appearance in the light of reason. Religion can neither be sold to, nor forced upon, any one. It is, if set forth in a word, a duty of man as a rational being; and according to the internal conception of its light, we, independently of each other, are enabled to know and to enjoy the happy life of faith, and insight into spiritual truths."[35]

The expression "right" or "rights" appears ten times in the memorial, described alternately as "inherent," "sacred," "inalienable," and "of man," but never as "natural." The inspiration of the document would seem to derive less from the French Enlightenment than from Anglo-American Protestantism in its liberal nineteenth-century development, and particularly from the unqualified disestablishmentarian sentiment which characterized its American branch. Mori could not have read Mill in his legation study very long without encountering *On Liberty,* and it is possible that the secular liberalism of English Utilitarianism underlies some of his hostility toward the intervention of the state in this realm. But occupying the background most clearly are the figures of Mori's devout American Protestant mentors: Harris, Henry, Perinchief, Lanman, Sumner; and the concrete model he seems to be recommending is the one he has had all along right before his own eyes: the American, with its axiomatic separation of Church and State.

In his introduction to *Education in Japan,* Mori tells his American readers that Buddhism, Shintoism, and Confucianism (the latter having provided Japan with her "social statics") are now "suffering a decline and are ebbing away before the new lights of science and art, which are being introduced from Europe and Amer-

---

34. Arinori Mori, *Religious Freedom in Japan: A Memorial and Draft of Charter* (Washington, D.C.: by the author, 1872), p. 3. Reprinted in MBZ, XI, interleaved between pp. 532–546.

35. Ibid., p. 4.

ica."³⁶ And in *Religious Freedom in Japan* he urges the Japanese to expose themselves also to the stimulus of Western religion, advancing counterarguments to what he takes to be the three basic objections to a toleration policy. Addressing the party which looks upon Christianity as "bad and superstitious" and remembers "our experience of Christian troubles in the past," he inquires, leading still from his basic premise of freedom of conscience: "Who can be found with the requisite authority to perform the awful and responsible duty of separating the good from the evil? To dare to undertake the task one should possess qualities essentially equal to those of Christ himself."³⁷

In reply to those who fear that the introduction of Christianity will "produce a sad discord between superiors and inferiors in our class system of society,"³⁸ he advances an instrumental defense of the foreign faith viewed from the social, as opposed to the individual, standpoint:

> Progress without revolution is impossible. A discord in society is often a blessing . . . The society which receives the addition of a new knowledge, and a power of the character of the Christian morality and faith, will necessarily better its condition by becoming both wiser and stronger. This is no mere assertion. It is fact, demonstrated by the history of the nations of the earth, among which none have so grandly advanced to the head of civilization as those whose religion has been Christianity . . . Progress can only be achieved through revolutions and trials, inasmuch as such is the law of nature. The benefits of social revolution have been amply experienced by our people now for many centuries, especially within the last twenty years.³⁹

Kōsaka Masaaki has called attention to this passage as "one of the earliest statements in which the Meiji Restoration was equated to a social revolution."⁴⁰ In view of the modern connotations of the phrase, it bears pointing out that what Mori seems to have had in mind was at best rapid social change, not a violent class upheaval. That he was no equalizer is suggested by one of

36. Mori, *Education in Japan*, pp. liv–lv.
37. Mori, *Religious Freedom in Japan*, pp. 5–6.
38. Ibid., p. 6.
39. Ibid., pp. 7–9.
40. Kōsaka Masaaki, *Japanese Thought in the Meiji Era*, trans. David Abosch (Tokyo, 1958), p. 67.

the arguments used to explain the inevitable diversity of religious views, namely that: "irrespective of our class organization of society, nature or the Creator distributes human qualities unequally among us."[41] More importantly, Mori envisioned the changes, however breathtaking, as occurring within an orderly framework to be provided by "the establishment of proper laws . . . and the organization of an educational system."[42] This was the argument he turned against persons who foresaw immediate and short-term difficulties in the toleration of Christianity and was also the point at which he digressed into his brief summary of his educational philosophy. "The precaution that forbids an attempt to undertake the task," Mori inveighed against this third group of objectors, "is not precaution; it is rather neglect."[43]

RENEWED SEARCH FOR A SOCIAL ETHIC

"I observe," Perinchief wrote Lanman on 23 January 1872, "that Mori desires to get the distinguishing characteristics of the sects, and especially how the sacraments are administered."[44] This was several months after Mori had worked through, with Lanman, the rather detailed chapter on religion in *Life and Resources in America*. It suggests that he continued to be an extremely interested observer of Christianity. But we still lack, even back here again in America where the opportunity existed in abundance, any evidence of Mori's active social participation in the faith.

Mori's relationship to Thomas Lake Harris in particular becomes as problematical during this second American sojourn as does his relation to Christianity in general. The moralistic tone of legation life, the attack on Christian hypocrisy in *Life and Resources in America,* the antisectarian animus of *Religious Freedom in Japan,* and even Mori's occasional enjoyment of wine and beer, reflect specific and traceable influences of Harris.[45] Kaimon speaks

41. Mori, *Religious Freedom in Japan*, p. 8.
42. Ibid., p. 9.
43. Ibid., p. 8.
44. Charles Lanman, *Octavius Perinchief: His Life of Trial and Supreme Faith* (Washington, D.C., 1879), p. 283, quoting letter from Octavius Perinchief to Charles Lanman, 23 Jan. 1872.
45. Tobacco had been forbidden at Brocton, but not alcohol, at least not wine, as befitted a community in the grape-growing business. Harris himself was evidently very much the connoisseur, as pointed out in Herbert W. Schneider and George Lawton, *A Prophet and a Pilgrim* (New York, 1942), p. 187. Our evidence suggests that Mori himself was no teetotaler. In Chapter Four, we found him enjoying beer on a Sumida River outing, and in Chapter Seven we will see that he liberally plied the guests at his own

of Mori's "numerous trips to the shores of Lake Erie" during this period,[46] but the only hard evidence we have for this pertains to early 1871 and the placement of Arai Ōsui with Harris.

Arai, a promising young scholar and samurai from Sendai, had fought for the Bakufu cause in Hokkaido under Enomoto Takeaki and had developed an earnest interest in Christianity after meeting the Russian Orthodox priest Nicolai at Hakodate.[47] In late 1870 he had been introduced in Tokyo to Mori, who was then busily packing for America. Arai, one year Mori's senior, was not particularly interested in going to America, but Mori, struck at once with his intelligence and character, determined that Arai belonged in Brocton. Since Arai was still on the Sendai blacklist, Mori first had to take the trouble to secure his pardon, and to agree to bear all travel and tuition expenses, since Arai could not be taken along as an official government student.

Arai boarded the steamer *Great Republic* listed as Mori's servant, and he spent a couple of months living in the legation "on probation" after experiencing (like Oliphant before) a first refusal at the hands of Harris. By May of 1871, however, he had been admitted, and a letter which he wrote on the eighth of that month describes a visit by Mori to the community. Arai relates that on that day he asked Mori why he had brought him to Harris. Mori replied that he did not know why; that he had had a premonition, however, that he was doing the right thing; that he himself in 1867 had not understood his own reasons for entering Brocton; but that he trusted both his own move and Arai's had been prompted by God's will.[48]

We then face the puzzling fact that the chapter on religion in

---

wedding with an assortment of whiskies and wines. And on 13 December 1872 we find him forwarding payment for "five boxes of wine" from the legation to a firm with the improbable name of Wilson & Woodrow. See "Letters: Japanese Legation, U.S.A." (A letter copybook of correspondence addressed by Mori and his subordinates to private American citizens; personal property of Mori Arimasa, Paris, France; to be published in full in *Zenshū* III).

46. KSM, p. 40.

47. Otis Cary, *A History of Christianity in Japan*, 2 vols. (New York 1909), I, 384–386.

48. Arai's letter, addressed to his nephew, Arai Ichirō, is quoted by Hayashi Takeji, "Kindai kyōiku kōsō to Mori Arinori," *Chūō kōron*, August 1962, p. 215. The original letter may be found in Nagashima Tadanobu, *Arai Ōsui sensei* (Tokyo, 1933), p. 194. Hayashi has treated the relationship between Mori and Arai in the following articles as well: "Mori Arinori to Tomasu Rēku Harisu," *Nichibei fōramu*, March 1963; "Bakumatsu no kaigai ryūgakusei," part I, *Nichibei fōramu*, January 1964; "Mori Arinori to Arai Ōsui ni kansuru oboegaki," mimeographed manuscript, Sendai, n.d.

Life and Resources in America, published some time between September and December of the same year, contains no reference whatsoever to Harris. Swedenborgians, Shakers, Hicksites, Millerites, Dunkers, Free Masons, Odd Fellows: all are mentioned; but not so much as a breath about The Breath. Mori eventually must have discovered how the great majority of Americans who had heard of it viewed the Brocton colony: skeptically, or contemptuously, or worst of all, as something of a joke. And it might have taken precisely the half year between March and September, and the cooperation with Lanman on the chapter in question, to open Mori's eyes for the first time to the extreme fringe position which Brocton occupied on the religious map.

Given Mori's usual outspokenness and forthrightness, it seems unlikely that the total silence regarding Harris which henceforth ensues could have been purely diplomatic. One suspects that it represents a genuine cooling of Mori's earlier unqualified enthusiasm and also a gradual severance of personal ties, not in conscious repulsion and deliberate defection, but simply through participation in broader social circles, and in wider intellectual realms, than were inhabited by the members of the Brotherhood: a gentle but inevitable weaning away. This impression is strengthened by Kimura's report to the effect that Mori removed Nomura Ichisuke from Brocton, where he had been "worked so hard he had not had the time to study a single day." Mori "took pity" on the poor fellow, put him up temporarily at the legation, and arranged to have him sent back to Japan.[49] Kaimon Sanjin concludes that although Mori's "practical- and logical-mindedness found no room for the weird, wooly doctrines of the spiritualist," he continued to regard Harris as his "benefactor" [*onjin*] and "exemplar" [*shi*].[50] One's *sensei* after all, in the traditional Japanese teacher-pupil relation, was not so easily forgotten. And Hayashi Takeji has concluded that "the influence of Harris lived on in Mori right up to the end of his life."[51]

Harris' long-term contribution to the formation of Mori's personality and basic fund of ideas becomes apparent with the further passage of time. This, however, should not be confused with the question as to whether partisan loyalty and conscious allegiance continued, or ceased, beyond 1871–1872. It also would seem the better part of wisdom not to attempt any extrapolation of Mori's personal faith from events or persons connected with the Harris

49. KKM, p. 265.
50. KSM, pp. 37, 40.
51. Hayashi, "Oboegaki," p. 2.

community in the years after he had lost all verifiable contact with the sect. Hayashi Takeji has suggested that the impact of Brocton on Mori possibly might be illuminated by its impact on Arai, who stayed on until 1899, when, driven away by Harris, he returned to Japan, collected a small band of disciples and continued in a very quiet and unobtrusive way to communicate his faith to others until his death in 1922. The decline of the community at Santa Rosa from the 1870's onward, if not morally then certainly in terms of social and intellectual relevance to the world around it, contrasts sharply with Mori's activist and international career— so sharply, indeed, as to cast almost insuperable doubt on the relevance of Arai's case to that of Mori. The former's faith and outlook were formed by twenty-seven years of an increasingly esoteric Harris, in virtually total isolation from both the Japanese and the American everyday world. Mori's sojourn in the community, in its very first months of operation at the Lake Erie site, lasted less than a year, and whatever he picked up there would inevitably be challenged by and adjusted to a whole spectrum of thought and experience which to Arai remained a closed book.[52]

52. See Hayashi, "Ryūgakusei," part I, p. 44. Materials on Arai in addition to those mentioned in note 48 above may be found in two other works by Nagashima Tadanobu: *Arai Ōsui sensei no omokage to sono danwa* (Tokyo, 1929); *Ōsui goroku* (Tokyo, 1931). There is some discussion of Arai also in Schneider and Lawton, *Prophet and Pilgrim,* and in the diary of Mrs. Thomas Lake Harris in HOP, Box 12, "Letters and Diary: 1899–1906." The latter has entries for 25 June and 14 July 1899 mentioning Arai's "indiscretions" and "sad failure" as background for his mysterious dismissal from the colony. A reporter who visited Santa Rosa in 1891, however, found Arai a most humble, self-effacing and gentle character who had "let fall remarks concerning doings in the community of which I cannot speak, so vile are they" (quoted in Schneider and Lawton, *Prophet and Pilgrim,* p. 539). An American lady of eighty interviewed by Nagashima, on the other hand, recalled that she had detested Arai; that he was always in "filthy clothes like a beggar," and that he avoided other people, as if they were snakes (Nagashima, *Arai omokage,* pp. 3–4). Arai, who upon returning to Japan lived, and preached that one should live, as a "willing slave to Christ," (Hayashi, "Oboegaki," p. 2) had for years lived as a virtual slave to Harris, setting type for his books and essays and totally subservient to the latter's command. The final break, I would suggest, may have occurred as a result of Arai's at last having seen through Harris' growing charlatanry, and having at last had the temerity to challenge his master on some point of personal conduct. This is only a guess. Arai recounted to his disciples in Japan virtually nothing of his life in America, while they in turn left virtually no comment on the life of their master in Japan. Uchimura Kanzō, Miyake Setsurei, and Kuga Katsunan, however, all knew, and apparently thought very highly of, Arai (Hayashi, "Mori to Harisu," p. 99). But the man seems

There is good evidence as a matter of fact that Mori, however willing still to take Harris as a guide to personal conduct, was already looking for some creed philosophically more comprehensive, and intellectually more satisfying, than that offered by the Brotherhood of the New Life. On a fresh page following the final diary entry of "Bibō daini" (17 February 1871 [28/XII/Meiji 3]) Mori penned the following: "ON THE PRINCIPLES OF HUMAN RELATIONS: (Based primarily on citations from the work of Herbert Spencer). *Chapter One: A Reliable Creed:* (A) Among the major faiths which heretofore have commanded the greatest respect and allegiance of mankind—Buddhism with its Compassion; Confucianism with its Benevolence; Christianity with its Love—none so far has [met this criterion]."[53] Mori probably entered this undated notation at the legation in Washington, where he read up on "ethics," including the "philosophy" of Herbert Spencer.[54] What looks like the beginning of a series of notes on Spencer, or an outline of an essay of Mori's own based largely on Spencer, goes this far and no further. It provides, however, the first indication of a line of ethical thinking which would resurface dramatically in the Monbushō's *Rinrisho* (Ethics textbook), prepared under Mori's direction in 1888.[55] And it also provides, incidentally, an excellent example of Mori's failure to keep any written record of his own intellectual development, or to leave posterity with anything but the most fragmentary clues as to the texts or thinkers or personal friends who influenced him most.

Spencer's *Principles of Ethics* would not have been available until 1879 at the earliest. Spencer's intention to find a scientific basis for the principles of right conduct, and to ground the truths of ethics on the findings of all other fields of knowledge, however, was clearly spelled out in the *First Principles* of 1860–1862 (which formed the basis of his entire system), and also in his very first

---

quite deliberately to have hid his light under a bushel. Extinction of the self was a very basic and ancient ideal common to the samurai class as a whole. But Arai's particular brand of quietism, his withdrawal from the world, and his passive contemplation of God sets him if anything poles apart—certainly in psychological terms—from Mori. *Prophet and Pilgrim* tells a fascinating tale of Harris' continued preoccupation with Japan, his excitement over the Russo-Japanese War, and his abortive attempt at one point to set up a colony for immigrant Japanese in Lower California: all of which, like the story of Arai, has been omitted here for its lack of relevance to the case of Mori.

53. Mori Arinori, "Bibō daini," to be published in *Zenshū* II.
54. KKM, p. 62.
55. See Chapter Ten.

work, *The Proper Sphere of Government* of 1842.⁵⁶ Mori would have had access to either of these, as well as to Spencer's *Social Statics* of 1850. The fact that Mori in his introduction to *Education in Japan* could write that "our social statics have been the precepts of the Confucian school,"⁵⁷ suggests not only that he was familiar with (at the very least) the last of these three texts but also that the "reliable creed" sought for was one which could supplant Confucianism in the realm of "human relations," i.e., of social ethics.

This was an area in which Harris—so plausible on individual, and particularly sexual, morality—was perhaps beginning to prove a bit too flamboyant and apocalyptic to be of much use. However much Mori personally may have continued to think in the Broctonian idiom of regeneration and the New Life, it was a fact that his talk of Harris had suffered a cool reception in Japan and a high probability that it had been greeted with muffled snickers in Washington. Mori's own attention, too, had now turned to the practical development of a national system of education, and it was natural that he should begin to look for some broad social ethic more modern than Confucianism and more marketable than Harris.

The fact that Mori did not turn for this purpose to the ample literature of orthodox Christianity, provides additional insight on his relationship to organized Christian religion. Mori's own principles as argued in *Religious Freedom in Japan,* of course, would have ruled out any promotion of Christian teaching by the state or in the public schools of Japan. The fact, however, that Mori—despite numerous recommendations on behalf of Christianity—turned so readily for his social ethics to the secular and would-be-scientific philosophy of Herbert Spencer, suggests a basic intellectual dissatisfaction with the orthodox faith.

I proposed in Chapter Three that Mori's encounter with Christianity at Brocton lacked both the philosophical and the emotional depth of the typical evangelical experience. The intellectual shallowness of that encounter shows through both in *Life and Resources in America,* where he admits that the Bible "contained many things he did not understand," and in his curiously inarticulate reply to Arai's query as to why he had been placed in Brocton. And to Mori's own lack of intellectual commitment would

---

56. Also available to Mori at the time would have been Spencer's *Principles of Psychology* (1855), *Education* (1858–59), and *Principles of Biology* (1864–67).

57. Mori, *Education in Japan,* p. liv.

have been added positive pressures from Western friends who no longer found orthodox Christianity intellectually respectable and were seeking to bring their own belief more closely into line with modern scientific knowledge.

One of Mori's erstwhile Brocton colleagues, Matsumura Junzō, eventually rejected both Harris and Christianity outright.[58] Another, Hatakeyama Yoshinari, moved away from Harris but directly into the Christian mainstream, receiving baptism into the Dutch Reformed Church at New Brunswick.[59] Mori seems to have followed still a third course, remaining loyal to Harris—and to Christianity, as far as he understood it—at the level of moral sentiment, but looking beyond both Harris and Christianity to Spencer for an articulate social philosophy and for intellectual sustenance generally. And the lack also in Mori's Brocton experience of a personal, or "existential," commitment to Christ would certainly have eased the transition.

Mori remained impressed with the civilizing aspects of Christianity as a social force and with the personal rectitude of individual Christians who lived up to their profession of the faith. He had also for so many years counted so many English and American Protestants among his closest friends and advisors that it would have been unusual if he had not retained some imprint, in his general character and bearing, of that lengthy association. The keen concern for religious liberty which constitutes their most lasting legacy to Mori, however, needs to be put in proper perspective.

In *Religious Freedom in Japan* Mori had asserted that "according to the internal conception of [religion's] light, we, independently of each other, are enabled to know and enjoy the happy life of faith." Mori's tract was above all an attack on intolerance. It was written in support not of religion but of freedom of conscience. Mori's own personal religion, to the extent that he can be said to have had one, was an eminently private affair. His social thinking had already to some extent been detached from it and entrusted to a secular ethic, which Herbert Spencer may have explained in fuller detail to Mori when the young chargé sought him out in London on his return to Japan in the spring of 1873. And with the social ethic excised, it was not surprising that Mori would draw little, if any, connection between his personal religion and his political thought.

58. *Sappan kaigunshi,* comp. Kōshaku Shimazuke Henshūjo, 3 vols. (Kagoshima, 1928), II, 913.
59. William E. Griffis, *The Rutgers Graduates in Japan* (New Brunswick, N.J., 1916), pp. 22–23.

A RETICENCE POLITICAL

Political liberty in several of the leading Protestant nations of the West was the offspring of a quest for religious liberty, or, as Robert N. Bellah has put it, "the application of the principles of the Reformation from the Church itself to society as a whole," or "the application of church democracy to political democracy."[60] Mori's views on religious freedom, I have suggested, stem rather from this older Protestant tradition than from the eighteenth-century secular, natural-rights persuasion which provided the second major fountainhead of political liberty for the modern Western democracies. But did Mori's defense of individual conscience, his plea for religious toleration, and his call for the separation of religion and state, therefore imply an enthusiasm also for the political framework which historically accompanied the progress of religious liberty in the West?

The introduction to *Life and Resources in America* warned Japanese readers:

> While we entertain an exalted opinion of what is called a Republican form of government, we confess that it is not without its disadvantages and dangers. For any nation fully to understand them must require time and much careful study. The Japanese people have been somewhat fascinated by what they have seen of the American government and institutions, and it is of the utmost importance that they should well consider the subject in all its bearings, before adopting any of its features into their own form of government. The evils resulting from the misuse of freedom in America, are among the most difficult to correct or reform, and ought carefully to be avoided ... A prosperous, happy and permanent Republican government can only be secured when the people who live under it are virtuous and well educated.[61]

Mori, whose term in Washington spanned the latter half of the first Grant administration (1869–1873), had the misfortune to view the American political system operating at one of its all-time lows and to witness in the Grant-Greeley presidential contest of 1872 some of the most vicious mud-slinging and political lampoon-

---

60. Robert N. Bellah, "Values and Social Change," *Asian Cultural Studies*, 3:20–21 (Tokyo: International Christian University, October 1962).

61. Mori, *Life and Resources in America*, in Lanman, *Japanese in America*, pp. 141–142.

ing in the history of the Republic. Dedicated as *Life and Resources in America* was to an honest account of its subject, it is not surprising that it should have presented, in the chapter entitled "Official and Political Life," an account virtually unmitigated in its censure of the current scene.

Of Congressmen, for instance, the reader is told: "That the large portion of them are mere time-serving politicians is a fact that cannot be questioned."[62] The chapter goes on to deplore what Mori calls "mere politicians or demagogues": "This class of citizens has greatly multiplied of late years, and it is safe to say that nearly all the troubles which befall the country are the result of their petty schemes and selfish intrigues. There is not a village in the land in which they do not congregate or pursue in secret their unpatriotic designs."[63] The spoils system and the frequent rotation of office, furthermore, "interfere with the proper and regular working of the machinery of the Government, and are the primary cause of the bitter political dissension."[64]

There is much in Mori's criticism which suggests a general familiarity with Alexis de Tocqueville's *Democracy in America,* a text which Mori is known to have possessed.[65] He also may have read John Stuart Mill's *Considerations on Representative Government,* which drew heavily on de Tocqueville's classic, but lacked much of the latter's favorable appraisal of the American scene. Kimura Kyō tells us simply that Mori read Mill on "economics" while in Washington. That Mori read *Representative Government* is therefore a probability rather than a hard fact, but if Mori did read it, he would have found much to strengthen his negative impression of American political behavior. He also would have found, by way of contrast, rather favorable evaluations of monarchy for its "energy," of aristocracy for its "sustained mental ability and vigor in the conduct of affairs," and of "the conduct of

62. Ibid., p. 148.
63. Ibid., p. 151.
64. Ibid., p. 158.
65. See Alexis de Tocqueville, *Democracy in America,* ed. Phillips Bradley, Vintage Paperback ed., 2 vols. (New York, 1954), especially vol. 1, chap. 13 ("Government of the Democracy in America") on the instability of the administration (pp. 216–219) and on the corruption and vices of the rulers (pp. 233–235); vol. 1, chap. 15 ("Unlimited Power of the Majority in the United States and its Consequences") on the instability of both legislation and administration (pp. 264–267) and on the tyranny of the majority (pp. 269–272, 276–281); and vol. 2, chap. 6 ("What Sort of Despotism Democratic Nations Have to Fear"). Mori presented Kanda Kōhei with a copy of de Tocqueville's book. See Kanda Memorial Committee, ed., *Memorials of Kanda Naibu* (Tokyo, 1927), p. 8.

affairs" in bureaucratic systems "by skilled persons, bred to it as an intellectual profession."[66] If one was to have democracy, on the other hand, then education was for Mill its prime prerequisite: "universal teaching must precede universal enfranchisement."[67] Voting, he urged, should be weighted in favor of the educated man, and it was the virtual exclusion of brains and trained talent from the political leadership of the nation which had most turned Mill against the American example.[68]

Life and Resources in America does not tell us what kind of government Mori is *for,* only what he is against, and although he levels his criticisms specifically at "a Republican form of government" and at its concrete abuses in the United States, what seems to concern him are the difficulties of representative government in general, not just of republican as opposed to constitutional-monarchical or of presidential as opposed to parliamentary systems. With the exception of the following brief passage, *Life and Resources in America* is silent also regarding the relation of the center to the localities (an issue on which Mill came out very clearly in favor of vigorous and enterprising local government with wide popular participation):[69] "The secret of the unparalleled growth and the daily increasing power of the United States is, that the Government, in its practical working, is confined to the narrowest limits; that it is the agent, not the master, of the people; and that the latter initiate all changes in its political and social life."[70]

The proportional responsibility for any given passage of this book as between Lanman and Mori is not always easy to determine. It seems difficult to believe, nevertheless, that the chapter "Official and Political Life," on a subject so sensitive and with a viewpoint so outspoken, could represent anything but Mori's own personal political conviction as of late 1871, however much abetted or informed by that of his compiler. The introduction, in which the admonition on republican government appears is, furthermore, indisputably Mori's personal pronouncement. And as final evidence of his hand in the chapter on American politics we have the streak of moral disgust which runs through its pages: that disgust which

66. John Stuart Mill, *Considerations on Representative Government,* ed. Currin V. Shields (New York, 1958), pp. 86, 87, 91. Mill of course went on to balance the advantages against the disadvantages of the various types of government. For Mill's debt to de Tocqueville, see ibid., pp. xxiii and 129.
67. Ibid., p. 132.
68. Ibid., pp. 137 and 129.
69. Ibid., pp. 212–228.
70. Mori, *Life and Resources in America,* in Lanman, *Japanese in America,* p. 169.

Perinchief had feared would blind Mori's eyes to the basic strength and nobility of the American system.

On the other hand, there is little reason to suppose that Lanman, and a good many other concerned Americans, would not have sympathized with Mori's scruples regarding contemporary American politics, scruples which do not necessarily require Mill or de Tocqueville for their explanation. There is a strong presumption in favor of the conclusion that Mori in his views on politics, as in his views on religion, was heavily influenced by the general intellectual climate and by the concrete examples of religious liberty and of political corruption which presented themselves for his consideration at that time. Far from recapitulating in his own mind, so to speak, the last 300 years of Western intellectual history, and deriving a political creed from a religious persuasion, Mori seems to be following out both questions simultaneously, along independent and virtually unrelated lines.

Of Mori's political position it would perhaps be more correct to say that it had not as yet, except in a negative sense, been formed. The polity which Mori would espouse as best suited to Japan had not yet taken shape in his mind. Nevertheless, his introduction to *Education in Japan,* if read carefully between the lines, does reveal attitudes and predispositions—straws in the wind, so to speak—regarding the throne, popular government, and political leadership.

Mori's fifty-seven page survey of Japanese history, from the ancient legends down to the Restoration, was the first account of its kind to be presented to Western readers, and perhaps the most important generalization that can be made about it is that it is not apologetic. The darker aspects of Japan's history Mori readily acknowledges, but he places great emphasis on the redeeming ability of the Japanese nation to learn, to adapt, and to transform itself in response to outside stimuli. Of Japan's previous borrowing from China Mori writes, for instance: "Among many peculiar and interesting characteristics of our people, the most remarkable was their noble and appreciative disposition with which continental civilization was received. Not only were its benefits appreciated, but so ready and apt was then our nation as a pupil that it soon equalled its master in the versatility of its knowledge."[71] In a later passage, he characterizes the appearance of Perry's "black ships" as "a severe trial of the national capacity for sudden revolution,"[72] a phrase which substantiates the impression that what Mori means

71. Mori, *Education in Japan,* p. xvi.
72. Ibid., p. xxxvii.

by "revolution" is rapid (i.e., "revolutionary") change, very broad in content and unspecified as to means, rather than something like the Paris Commune, which was making headlines during his first year in Washington. By identifying innovation as a major theme of Japanese history, as one of its *traditions* in effect, Mori was able to assure his American readers of spectacular changes in the offing without divesting himself of his own patriotic Japanese identity.[73]

The Restoration Mori attributes to "two principal causes": to the "influence of Western civilization," the most recent of the outside stimuli; and to "the peculiar reverence of our people for the throne."[74] As to the political aspect of the imperial institution, Mori takes his stand as a loyalist partisan, affirming the legitimacy of the Southern over Northern Court, describing the shogun as a usurper and the throne as "the only legal authority," and characterizing the Restoration as an *ōsei ishin,* which he translates as "restoration of the government of the kings."[75]

Mori mentions the veneration which the throne popularly evokes, but strikes us as a rather distant observer, divulging very few clues as to whether he himself shares, sympathizes with, or merely approves of the quasireligious feeling of the common people for their emperor. "We must loyally revere the ancient and glorious dynasty of our Imperial family," he affirms, and he displays for the loyal Kusunoki Masashige an admiration as patent as his distress for the humiliations and disturbances which have afflicted the throne down through the centuries.[76] But Mori most disappointingly refrains from any comment or evaluation when he notes the fact that during the Tokugawa period "the throne was an object of profound reverence, and came to be regarded as a sacred thing, having supernatural origin. Under this system, and at this stage of affairs, the relation between the sovereign and the subject grew mythical."[77] The early historical records of his country, Mori admits, were "filled with traditional and fabulous descriptions of events and persons," but he attempts no historical criticism with

---

73. There is one instance in "Letters: Japanese Legation" in which Mori departed from his usual habit of signing nondiplomatic correspondence simply with his name, or with his name plus the title "Chargé d'Affaires." Writing to the agent of the Bank of Montreal at New York on 28 December 1872 to ask for a credit of $30,000, he added the phrase, "Of the Empire of Japan," penning this in with his own hand at the bottom of a letter prepared for his signature by one of his secretaries.

74. Mori, *Education in Japan,* p. xxxv.

75. Ibid., pp. xxvi, xxv, iv.

76. Ibid., pp. xvii, xxvii, xx.

77. Ibid., p. xxxv.

respect to the "strangely long lives," as he puts it, of the early emperors.[78]

Mori's reluctance to pass judgment on the phenomenon of emperor-worship seems the more deliberate when we consider that the sentence just quoted immediately follows one in which his attack on Tokugawa Confucianism is clear cut and unrestrained. "The doctrine of obedience, the leading feature in the Confucian school of morals, was one of the most important levers of the central authority. Its evil effect upon society was seen in the manner in which it retarded the development of the vital spirit of self-reliance, destroyed the happiness of domestic life, and cultivated the feeling of subjection."[79]

The attack on the repressive features of the Tokugawa polity was as close as Mori came, however, to supporting a more popular form of government; and the explicit statements he makes are not on behalf of more democratic, but of more humane government, in a fashion reminiscent of his brother Yokoyama. Hideyoshi's invasion of Korea, for instance, he describes as "a rude incursion into a peaceful land," in which "the invaders, without cause or excuse, rode over the innocent and inoffensive people and devastated their homes."[80] Mori also insists that the great changes brought about by the Restoration have all been "in the cause of humanity."[81] But it is interesting that in giving his own translation of the Charter Oath of 1868 he should have rendered the first article simply as "All the affairs of state shall be guided by public opinion," leaving out entirely the additional phrase in the original to the effect that "Public councils shall be widely established."[82] Mori gives us the five articles "in substance," and it is possible that he did not have a copy of the original before him at the time of writing. On the other hand, this very important omission may represent a deliberate effort to discourage premature expectations in the West of the establishment of representative institutions in Japan. For the Shūgiin had been dispensed with upon the final abolition of the han in 1871, and a full decade would pass before the emperor's promise in 1881 of a national assembly to be established in 1890.

Mori writes approvingly of progress in Japan: "It is difficult to comprehend the power and energy of the impulse which is rolling our nation forward in the path of progress. The leaders of the

78. Ibid., pp. iv, ix.
79. Ibid., p. xxv.
80. Ibid., p. xxx.
81. Ibid., p. liii.
82. Ibid., p. xlvii.

country are amazed to find themselves unconsciously involved in the advance without wish or invitation." He immediately, however, issues a word of caution: "Our youths, educated abroad, are returning with their faces flushed with enthusiastic sympathy with the modern civilization of Christendom. Their opinions and ideas are influencing and bending the actions and desires of their leaders and patrons. One of the difficult problems for our solution is the restraint of our youths, so that their little knowledge will not prove a danger, but will become, in its maturity, a powerful weapon of defense . . . Wise advice from abroad on this vital question is called for. Education has become imperative."[83] Since Mori a few pages later would pronounce with finality on the language issue, and since this statement followed by a mere six weeks his eloquent defense of religious liberty, it seems most probable that the matter requiring "wise advice" is the political one. Mori here speaks of his own students in much the same vein as had Kido Takayoshi, suggesting either that his own political views had shifted rapidly in the course of 1872, or that Kido had too easily lumped Mori and the students together in his own mind, or that he had failed to distinguish significant shades of emphasis within the young chargé's overall progressivism.

The latter two explanations seem the most likely. Mori's political caution was apparent, in *Life and Resources in America,* as early as the autumn of 1871. Kido's English would not as yet have been equal to a mastery of that text, and he may well have been misled by sweeping statements, such as that reported in the *Washington Evening Star* in December 1871,[84] in which Mori talked of adopting the "manners and customs" of America, a phrase which could be taken under a broad interpretation to include the political realm. The most superficial survey should have sufficed to reveal how varied were the political alternatives among the nations of late nineteenth-century Europe and America, many of which in cultural, economic, social, and intellectual terms would have considered themselves "modern," and all of which certainly were "Western." Kido in his criticism of the students had seen the need for selectivity and caution as a general principle. He had not as yet, however, sorted out in his own mind the levels at which the West might safely be approached, or at what speeds, and this may have rendered him less perceptive to the differential that had already emerged in Mori's mind between political as opposed to nonpolitical matters.

This was not the last time that Mori's espousal of radical

83. Ibid., p. lii.
84. See Chapter Five.

measures at the cultural, educational, or social levels would be assumed erroneously to apply to the political mechanism as well. And at this stage of Mori's career the misunderstanding was perhaps natural enough: memories of the Kōgisho were still fresh in the public mind; the flamboyant nature of the changes which he did espouse certainly smacked of a wholesale embrace of the West; and, most importantly, he had not as yet committed himself, publicly and at length, to a specific and positive political formula for Japan.

Foregoing for the moment any ideological evaluation of Mori's differential approach, it may be said that it was inherent to some extent at least in his subject matter. A principle such as freedom of conscience, or a specific policy such as religious toleration, was something which Mori could enunciate simply enough, and with full sincerity. If he conceived a bit naively of language as nothing more than a tool of any given culture, he might conclude that it could be imported painlessly enough along with other species of machinery. But Mori had from his days in London, well before the Kōgisho, viewed the legal and political system as something requiring considerable study, together with appropriate adaptation to the Japanese environment.

"The many radical changes that are and have been in operation in Japan," Mori continues in the same paragraph, "have produced a transition period, for which allowance, sympathy and assistance are solicited."[85] He seems to rest his hope for the future on three points: on "education"; on "wise advice from abroad," for which he himself would turn to Herbert Spencer in London en route home that March; and on the fact that the radical changes "are suggested and supervised by the aristocracy, at great sacrifice of their own interest, for the national glory and prosperity."[86]

TRUEHEARTED BUT BULLHEADED

Mori had repeatedly emphasized the close relationship between education and good government, and at that moment and for the immediate future it was clear that the educated political leadership of Japan would have to come from the samurai class. His concern for this class, as an indispensable reservoir of short-run talent, was fully shared by Iwakura and Kido, and all three were puzzled and alarmed by the appearance of Yoshida Kiyonari in Washington on 14 May 1872 (8/IV) with instructions from Tokyo to float a loan

---

85. Mori, *Education in Japan*, p. liii.
86. Ibid., p. liii.

for the purpose of abolishing the stipend system by means of a lump sum payment to the samurai. Despite their misgivings, however, and despite the fact that the caretaker government by dispatching Yoshida had in effect broken a promise not to launch any new domestic programs without first consulting the mission, Iwakura and Kido did not deem it proper to interfere with the business of the deputy vice minister for finance.[87] Mori thereupon took matters into his own hands, engaging Yoshida in a bitter personal exchange, circularizing his prominent American friends on the subject, and generally making things so difficult for the special envoy that the poor man despaired of collecting any money in America and left New York for England on 8 June, after a stay of a little over three weeks.

Mori's tiff with Yoshida, which Ōkubo Toshiaki calls "his most world-shaking exploit" while in Washington,[88] provides, like the "Haitōron," an example of great moral courage combined with considerable impetuosity. In this case, however, Mori's intellectual rawness and personal brusqueness went a good deal further in taking the luster off the nobility of his action. Mori displayed splendid pluck and initiative in standing up to higher authority on behalf of his own convictions. But much of the difficulty was brought on by Mori's substantive misunderstanding of the issue at stake, and most men in public life probably would have made some effort to prevent personal animosities from reaching the pitch which they did.

On 16 May Mori sent Yoshida a note asking the special envoy for a summary of the purposes of his mission, which Mori pronounced to be within the purview of his own official responsibility. Yoshida replied the following day, stating the content and the official nature of his business and asking Mori's reasons for his unwarranted intervention. And with that, the fur began to fly.

On 18 May Mori wrote Yoshida that as chargé he would share responsibility for any "diplomatic contract" signed in the United States; that the flotation of a foreign loan for the liquidation of the stipend system was the pursuit of an unjustifiable end by injurious means; and that even if the scheme had received the sanction of

---

87. The following incident is covered in KKM, pp. 51–60; OTM, pp. 41, 53–55; Hayashi, "Mori kenkyū: dai-ichi," pp. 1, 14–15; dispatch, *New York Tribune*, 8 Nov. 1872, with the dateline "Yedo, September 6"; and in *Zenshū* I, 81–113, which gives in its entirety the correspondence between Mori and Yoshida and most of the letters between Yoshida, Williams, and their superiors in Tokyo.

88. OTM, p. 41.

the sovereign authority, Yoshida ought to keep himself open to fresh advice and be willing to revise his objectives if he could be shown that they were harmful to the interests of Japan. Yoshida replied on 19 May that he was under government orders which he was in no position to revise, whatever his own opinions on the subject; that there was really no use in carrying the discussion any further; but that he would visit the legation that afternoon to disabuse Mori of his misconception of the government's policy. On 21 May, two days after the interview (which had served only to widen the quarrel), Yoshida replied at length to fourteen questions which Mori had posed in a memorandum dated 20 May. He explained to the chargé that the sum required could not be raised from domestic sources; that the money saved by the commutation of stipends would benefit the nation as a whole, and would not go into the pockets of a few favored individuals; that the principle of commutation would be applied fairly and uniformly to all grades of samurai; that the trust of the foreign powers would best be maintained by setting Japan's financial house in order; and that the decision had been fully debated at the highest level and could hardly be considered "rash."[89]

Yoshida then tossed the ball back with four questions of his own, to which Mori responded on 23 May:

> Should he not at least have refrained from giving their dispute a wide public airing?
>> Except where under a specific prohibition, a diplomatic representative is under no restriction as regards public discussion of matters affecting the welfare of his country. It goes without saying that in cases in which he is without official instructions, he takes upon himself full responsibility for his own statements.
>
> Had he not been in error in describing the stipends as private property, and government plans for their liquidation as thievery?
>> My reference to "government robbery" certainly holds good from the standpoint of logical analogy; and if you don't fancy the phrases "plunder by purchase" or "burglary by curtailment," you can turn to the literary men for a more precise definition. You say something to the effect that, "If one considers these amounts (*taka*) as allowances (*roku*), etc." Well, as for myself, I don't know what prin-

---

89. The correspondence up to this point is in *Zenshū* I, 81–87.

ciple you go by—probably one of the unprincipled principles so popular in the Orient—certainly not by the principle of human sympathy.

Could he not more properly have expressed his disagreement in a memorial to the home government, or sent a personal messenger, or even gone home himself to plead his cause?

Where a moral principle is at stake, I deem it a virtue to act in accordance with my own conscience.

And finally, were Yoshida's orders not tantamount to a law requiring a subject's, certainly an official's, obedience and support? No, Mori again replied: it was still a matter of conscience.[90]

Mori on 9 July also wrote a rather harsh letter to General George B. Williams, who had accompanied Yoshida in an advisory capacity. Mori stated his disappointment that Williams, whom he personally had recommended for the finance ministry post, should have gotten involved in a matter so far removed from the original objectives of his appointment. Williams replied on the same day that he was in no position to pass on the merits of a policy already decided prior to his arrival in Japan, and that he intended to abide by his orders. He sent copies of the exchange to Saigō Takamori and Inoue Kaoru in Tokyo, stating that due to Mori's intervention he and Yoshida had been forced to proceed forthwith to Europe.[91]

Yoshida had already on 22 May registered his own complaint in a letter addressed to Inoue Kaoru, Ueno Kagenori, and Shibusawa Eiichi at the finance ministry. Intimating that Ōkubo Toshimichi and Itō Hirobumi upon arrival in Tokyo would present a proposal for Mori's appointment to a high post in the ministry of education, he declared on behalf of himself, and also of Kido:

If a chap of his ilk should get a foothold in the educational administration, then the future of our country will be wholly in the dark . . . After arriving here in Washington he found himself praised on all sides, and the American authorities seem to think (to an extent which truly surprises me) that Japan's progress to date has been brought about entirely by this one man's effort. If the enlightenment of Japan is to be the "enlightenment" sponsored by this kind of fellow, then the sooner

90. *Zenshū* I, 88, letter from Mori Arinori to Yoshida Kiyonari, 21 May 1872 (15 IV Meiji 5).
91. KKM, pp. 58–59 quoting letter from Mori Arinori to General George B. Williams, 9 July 1872 (4 VI Meiji 5), and a reply from Williams to Mori dated the same day.

I get out of the picture the better . . . During our interview he sighed for grief over the "peril to the Japanese Government" and expressed his hostility and contempt for my official mission. I suggested, "Well, if you are really all that worried about it, why don't you go back to Japan and do your best for your country there, and apply your enlightenment theories not only to finance but to all levels of government; I should think you would find it distressing to have to remain a moment longer on this distant shore, moaning over the condition of our "barbarous country" [English in the original]; so hurry on home and go to it." After I had pressed the point two or three times, he fell into great perplexity and had nothing more to say.[92]

Correspondence between Yoshida and his superiors reveals particular dismay over Mori's construction of the samurai stipend as private property in the typical Western sense and of its gradual repeal as a forcible violation by the government of a sacred individual right.

Mori in two English-language circulars[93] had appealed directly to Western principles of jurisprudence and economics in describing the stipends as inherited wealth which had achieved the status of private property with the passage of time and in likening their "confiscation" to the nationalization of land. Consistently confusing the *roku* allowances with landed property, Mori argued that the best way to create a powerful and enlightened nation was to give land to the people and encourage them to work it for their own profit; that the government should be selling and distributing land, not snatching it up; and that funds for railway and other projects should be raised internally, as an additional means of encouraging private initiative and enterprise.[94]

The inspiration here of economic liberalism is clear enough, but that Mori should have attempted to apply the concept of private property so literally to Japan suggests a lingering ignorance of countrywide conditions in his own native land. The samurai of Kagoshima city, like the vast majority of samurai throughout the

92. *Zenshū* I, 98–100, *passim*, letter from Yoshida Kiyonari to Inoue Kaoru, 22 May 1872 (16 IV Meiji 5).

93. George B. Williams in a letter to Ōkuma Shigenobu, Ōkubo Toshimichi, and Inoue Kaoru, dated 4 July 1872, forwarded two English language circulars by Mori which he claimed had been widely read in the West and had seriously damaged the confidence of Japan's prospective creditors. *Zenshū* I, 107.

94. *Zenshū* I, 89–94, has the Japanese translations of the two circulars. The English-language originals are no longer extant.

other han, were stipendiaries (*kuramaitori* or *fuchimaitori*) who received a fixed amount of rice via their daimyo's storehouse from lands under the daimyo's direct control. The *chigyōtori,* who had been granted land directly, together with control of peasants, were generally to be found only in the uppermost ranks of retainers. Was it the independent American farmer whom Mori had in mind? Or was it Satsuma, again the exception, where numerous warriors, the *gōshi,* tilled with their own hands the fields from which their wealth accrued? This superficial resemblance to private real estate possibly may have misled Mori, who, except for a year in Tokyo and perhaps a month in the Kansai, had seen virtually nothing of Japan outside of his own native han.[95]

The relative proportion of impertinence as opposed to *Zivilcourage* in Mori's attitude depends entirely on one's evaluation of the matter at stake. If every appointed official were to feel free to countermand any order no matter how trivial which did not meet his own personal approval, the machinery of government and of diplomacy would quickly come to a halt. Ōkubo Toshiaki credits Mori with great honesty and resolution where, rightly or wrongly, he thought a great moral principle was at stake.[96] It may also be said in Mori's favor that, with powers somewhat ambivalently divided between the caretaker government in Tokyo and the mission in Washington, he may have felt that he was not flaunting the highest authority as long as Iwakura and Kido issued no specific injunction to him to desist. Hayashi Takeji, on the other hand, has probably drawn too severe a dichotomy between the "moral" basis of Mori's action and the "strictly bureaucratic logic and ethic" of Yoshida's position. Much as this evaluation may hold true for Mori, it seems a bit too harsh for Yoshida.[97]

In this instance, as earlier at Brocton and also in later years, Yoshida Kiyonari provides us with something of a foil to Mori's own character. Yoshida may or may not have been something of a "smoothie," but one gets the impression that in any case he must have been a considerably easier person to get along (to say nothing of relax) with, than was Mori. Lanman, in *Japan: Its Leading Men* of 1886 expressed respect for Mori, but betrayed both respect and affection for Yoshida, whom he served as private secretary from 1876 to 1882. Lanman wrote of the latter's "quiet

95. I am indebted to Mr. Inoue Isao of the Graduate School (Japanese History) of Tokyo University for suggesting a possible interpretation of Mori's misunderstanding along this line.
96. OTM, p. 41.
97. Hayashi, "Mori kenkyū: dai-ichi," p. 15.

and unobtrusive influence in Washington," of his "high character and agreeable manners," and of his "popularity not second to any diplomat in Washington ever."[98] We get bucolic scenes, too, of Yoshida fishing the waters of southern Pennsylvania in the company of the Reverend Mr. Perinchief.[99] The temperamental polarity which probably underlay much of the bitterness both at Brocton and in Washington was best suggested by the chronicler of ex-President Grant's trip around the world in 1878–79. Reporting on a farewell dinner which Grant gave for high Japanese officials in Tokyo in September 1879, John Russell Young wrote of Itō, who "gives you a hearty American greeting," of Yoshida "with his handsome, enthusiastic face," and of Mori: "who looks as though he had just left a cloister."[100]

Letters from the finance ministry to Yoshida reveal a steadily hardening attitude toward Mori on the part of the Tokyo authorities: Sanjō was outraged and wanted him punished (29 July [24/VI]); the matter had been taken up by the Seiin (Central Chamber: 21 August [18/VII]); and the government had decided that some sort of disciplinary action would have to be taken.[101] Joseph Henry, too, writing at about the same time to solace Lanman upon his dismissal, admitted: "I participate in your feelings regarding Mr. Mori. He stands on a dangerous elevation. If all the plans which he advocates and attempts to reduce to practice do not produce the anticipated results, he will be denounced . . . I know that you have been of great service to Mr. Mori, and have sustained the character I gave you when I recommended you for the place. It is evident that he is acting under some improper influence, and it is a very unfortunate condition."[102] Henry, who had abetted Mori's educational, and particularly his language, schemes does not tell us just which dangerous plans he has in mind, but

98. Charles Lanman, *Japan: Its Leading Men* (Boston, 1886), pp. 246, 249.
99. Lanman, *Perinchief,* p. 247.
100. John Russell Young, *Around the World with General Grant,* 2 vols. (New York, 1879), II, 592.
101. *Zenshū* I, 104, letter from Ueno Keihan and Inoue Kaoru to Yoshida Kiyonari, 29 July 1872 (24 VI Meiji 5); ibid., I, 113, letter from Ueno Keihan, Inoue Kaoru, and Shibusawa Eiichi to Yoshida Kiyonari, 21 Aug. 1872 (18 VII Meiji 5); Hayashi, "Mori kenkyū: dai-ichi," p. 16, citing letter from Inoue Kaoru and Ōkuma Shigenobu to Ōkubo Toshimichi, Itō Hirobumi, and Yoshida Kiyonari, between 3 Sept. and 2 Oct. 1872 (VIII Meiji 5), day of month not given in original letter.
102. Charles Lanman, *Haphazard Personalities: Chiefly of Noted Americans* (Boston, 1886), p. 20, citing letter from Joseph Henry to Charles Lanman, 11 Sept. 1872.

the passage confirms the air of tension that was building up around Mori toward the end of his Washington tour. Lanman also in later years would recall of Mori: "It would seem indeed that the more his facetious countrymen criticized his political opinions, or his tastes as a private gentleman, the more indifferent did he become to their carping criticisms; and when they found that they could not make him angry, the more angry did they themselves become."[103]

Forthrightness had always been one of the cardinal samurai virtues, and, if necessary, forthrightness unto death, which usually meant (as it had meant for Yokoyama Yasutake) ritual suicide in defense of one's principles. On the other hand, the culture into which Mori had been born traditionally placed great emphasis, particularly in the everyday conduct of affairs, on harmony and on consensus and on the avoidance of explicit and humiliating personal confrontations. It was not a society in which one could go through daily life maintaining an unbending showdown posture and hope to remain popular for very long. Mori's retribution was bound to come, and it is my surmise that it came in a more indirect, and for Mori far more devastating, guise than commonly has been supposed.

The general understanding, as given by Ōkubo Toshiaki, has been that Mori was duly punished by means of recall from his post in Washington; that Itō and Ōkubo Toshimichi, who saw the trouble coming and recognized Mori's interest in education, thought to do him a favor by easing him gracefully out of the Gaimushō into the Monbushō; but that Mori's case was forgotten in the confusion over Korean policy, so that he squeaked through "very luckily" to the post of secretary (*dajō*) in the foreign ministry on 12 December 1873.[104]

Hayashi Takeji has shown, however, that Mori had already attempted to resign his post well in advance of the dispute with Yoshida; that the government kept him on in Washington, however, and that orders for recall were first officially mentioned as late as 22 January 1873; that talk of transfer to the ministry of education probably had originated at Mori's own eager request; but that this was rejected, with the result that Mori "had to wait a full ten years for the realization" of that ambition.[105]

Could not this phrase properly be revised to read: "*forced* to wait"? Was not Mori's real punishment, possibly, his exclusion for

103. Lanman, *Japan: Its Leading Men*, p. 137.
104. OTM, p. 54–55.
105. Hayashi, "Mori kenkyū: dai-ichi," pp. 2, 3, 16, 18, 19.

over a decade from the path he wished most to travel? If Yoshida's protestations, backed by those of Kido, found wide sympathy, there may well have been a deliberate decision to retain Mori in the Gaimushō, where he represented a positive asset by virtue of his English, his knowledge of the West, and his way with foreigners; and to keep his itchy fingers a safe distance from the strategic levers of internal change wielded by the Monbushō. Mori was forced to look on as a bystander while David Murray and Tanaka Fujimaro made all the exciting educational innovations of the 1870's. He would not reach the minister's chair in that department until the accession to the prime ministership of a man who could more than forgive him—his own fellow "Arabian horse," Itō Hirobumi.

Aside from the specific proposal for Mori's transfer, carried from Washington to Tokyo by Ōkubo and Itō, his interest in a Monbushō post at this juncture is not so much proved as simply inferred from the immense interest he had shown, while in Washington, in the future education of Japan. The evidence for his dissatisfaction with his diplomatic role is, by contrast, detailed and concrete.

Sometime between the ninth and twentieth of March 1872, Mori composed a letter of resignation, requesting to be relieved no later than 1/VIII (3 September).[106] In view of the growing importance of Japanese-American relations he asked his government to appoint a personage of the highest rank in his stead, with credentials of envoy plenipotentiary similar to those held by the American minister to Japan. He realized that he was "too young" for the position but he had tried to do his best. His letter was presented to the Seiin by Itō and Ōkubo a few days after their arrival on 30 April 1872.[107] The government, however, far from accepting the resignation, issued Mori powers to participate as plenipotentiary in any international conference which might (as it was hoped) be called for treaty revision, and on 25 May Komatsu Terumori left for Washington bearing Mori's promotion to the senior fifth rank (*shōgoi*) and to the diplomatic grade of *chūbenmushi,* the equivalent of minister resident.[108]

---

106. Mori's letter of resignation is reproduced in full in Inau Tentarō, *Nihon gaikō shisōshi ronkō: dai-ichi: jōyaku kaiseiron no tenkai* (Tokyo, 1966), p. 15. It is dated simply II Meiji 5. The first day of the second lunar month was 9 March 1872; Itō and Ōkubo left Washington for Japan on 20 March 1872.

107. Hayashi, "Mori kenkyū: dai-ichi," p. 4.

108. Ibid., pp. 9–10.

Mori turned down both promotions. The government apparently accepted his refusal, for in the reorganization of the foreign service of 14 November 1872 (14/X), in which both Terajima Munenori at London and Samejima Naonobu at Paris received promotions, Mori was simply reappointed (under the new nomenclature of *dairikōshi*) to his previous grade of chargé d'affaires, the title he continued to use in his English language correspondence right up to the day of his departure.[109] The promotion of May, and the government's rejection of his resignation at that time, make sense in terms of the role he was expected to play in the hoped-for treaty negotiations. Mori's retention at his post a full half year after the collapse of those hopes, despite his earlier desire to resign and despite the growing demand in Tokyo for his recall, has been explained by Hayashi Takeji in terms of Mori's own unfinished business: the preparation of *Religious Freedom in Japan,* and *Education in Japan,* all very much delayed by the mission's unexpectedly long sojourn in America.[110]

Among his motives for resignation, the one which Mori made most explicit was his consciousness of being "too young" for his task. It was the central theme of his official letter of resignation, and it was a sentiment which he conveyed indirectly to Hamilton Fish shortly after receipt of his promotion in late June 1872. Theodore W. Dimon, disbursing clerk of the Department of State and a personal friend of Mori, wrote Fish on 27 June:

109. Mori and Samejima, as Japan's first resident diplomatic representatives, had been appointed to the lowest of three grades established by the table of organization of 27 November 1870 (5 X [intercalary] Meiji 3): *daibenmushi* (Ambassador), *chūbenmushi* (Minister Resident), and *shōbenmushi* (Chargé d'Affaires). In the reorganization of November 1872 these grades were redesignated as *zenkenkōshi, benrikōshi, and dairikōshi,* respectively. Samejima continued to represent Japan at Paris and Berlin after being relieved of his duties in London by Terajima in the summer of 1872. In November of that year Terajima was promoted from *chūbenmushi* to *zenkenkōshi,* and Samejima from *shōbenmushi* to *benrikōshi.* By then the repercussions of the Yoshida incident had made themselves felt in Tokyo, and there had been talk in the Gaimushō, put down only by the personal intervention of Ueno Keihan, of begrudging Mori even a reappointment to his current rank of chargé. (Hayashi, "Mori kenkyū: dai-ichi," pp. 10–11.)

110. Hayashi, "Mori kenkyū: dai-ichi," p. 13. It seems likely that Mori would have had little difficulty in securing the extension required in view of the government's difficulty in finding an appropriate successor. Ueno was appointed to Washington in November but was transferred to a foreign office position the following month. Japan was represented in America by Chargé *ad interim* Takagi Saburō until the arrival of Yoshida as Minister Resident in 1876.

> Mr. Mori has not accepted the promotion yet, because he is desirous of ascertaining whether he is perfectly acceptable to you and the administration generally before he takes any steps toward presenting his credentials in his new capacity. The crime of being a young man seems to embarrass him. He says he has been received here with so much affection and general attention that he is in some doubt whether he is regarded as altogether acceptable to this government. There is a refinement of sentiment in this that is as clear and pure as crystal. He is prepared to adhere to his resignation if it can be thought that a person of greater age or rank could transact the business of his country with greater effect.[111]

Fish replied to Dimon on 29 June: "I should have been glad to hear that his government had made him an Envoy Minister Plenipotentiary. He has made himself *very* acceptable to the Government at Washington and to the people of this country . . . The "crime of being a young man" is a daily growing less [sic]—if it be a "crime" it is one, you may assure him, of which all old men have at some period of their lives been guilty."[112] It does not from the evidence available, however, seem likely that Mori was ever very seriously worried about the American government's attitude toward him. He was "criminally" young only in the eyes of certain of his Japanese superiors, and it seems most likely that he passed on his sentiments to Dimon either in a moment of personal dejection or perhaps in a deliberate effort to evoke additional proof for the mission of how very well he stood with the United States authorities.

Both the original resignation and the Dimon letter coincided with the cresting of tension between Mori and the mission over treaty negotiations: in early March as to whether they should be attempted and in late June as to whether they should be continued. Inau Tentarō has suggested that Mori may have attempted to resign in response to sufficient chiding by Iwakura and Kido, or possibly even as a propitiatory gesture after winning his point on the treaty issue.[113] Hayashi has seen behind the attempted resignation also Mori's desire for a different type of work and perhaps an element of the self-denial which had characterized his petition in

---

111. LCM, Hamilton Fish Papers, "Correspondence," vol. 88, letter from Theodore W. Dimon to Hamilton Fish, 27 June 1872.
112. Ibid., "Letter Copybook," no. 5, letter from Hamilton Fish to Theodore W. Dimon, 29 June 1872.
113. Inau, *Gaikō shisōshi*, p. 116.

1868 for a reduction in salary. Nor is the ostensible reason at all to be discounted: the British government in 1871, offended by such a youthful appointment, had given Samejima an extremely cool reception in London; and even Itō, in an oblique reference to Mori and Samejima, had written home from Washington that same year of the "callow youths" and "beardless schoolboys" who had been entrusted with the representation of Japan overseas.[114]

Despite the professional and intellectual immaturity which Mori occasionally exhibited during the course of his Washington tour, it is necessary to make, as does Hayashi Takeji, the very important point that, as regards the fundamental issue of change versus status quo, the new Meiji government had unequivocally opted for the radical transformation of Japan, and that, "If there was a point on which Mori could be taken to task, it was simply that he believed and persisted in, more honestly and more sincerely, the type of reformation [which had been decreed]."[115] Mori had clearly expressed his awareness, in *Education in Japan,* of the problematical nature of the "transition period" which lay ahead; he had been particularly careful to guard his words on the political or constitutional question; and the warning which Herbert Spencer passed on to the young chargé on his way through London must have given Mori more than a little pause for reflection. The English philosopher recalled in his diary during the spring of 1873: "He came to ask my opinion about the reorganization of Japanese institutions. I gave him conservative advice—urging that they would have eventually to return to a form not much in advance of what they had, and that they ought not to attempt to diverge widely from it."[116]

It was in his political views, specifically in his total abandonment of the American model, that Mori had traveled furthest since his first return to Japan from the West in 1868. This, however, had not shaken his faith in the United States as a diplomatic partner, nor his idealism regarding interstate relations. Similarly, the moralist in Mori, while personally bearing the permanent imprint of association with Thomas Lake Harris and scores of more or-

114. Hayashi, "Mori kenkyū: dai-ichi," pp. 10–11, 4 and 6 respectively.
115. Ibid., p. 8.
116. From an undated entry in Spencer's unpublished diary, reprinted between letters dated 2 March and 3 June 1873 in David Duncan, *Life and Letters of Herbert Spencer* (London, 1908), p. 161. Mori left Washington on 18 March and arrived in Yokohama via Suez on 23 July 1873. It would be most reasonable to suppose that the meeting with Spencer took place during April or May.

thodox Christians, had, in shifting to Herbert Spencer for a secular social ethic, reverted in a sense to his earlier, nonreligious, grasp of the principles of justice and humanity as of 1865–1866. What was freshest in Mori's stock of ideas by 1873 was the vast quantity of data on educational affairs and on matters closely related to them. How far would Mori get with his language proposal, for instance, or be able to give expression to his concern for the elevation of women? What sort of education would he now recommend for Japan as a whole, and what could be done about it, anyway, from his offstage position in the Gaimushō?

It is most probable that Mori's interview with Spencer took place at the Athenaeum Club on Pall Mall, where the philosopher was in the habit of spending most of his waking hours.[117] Mori may or may not have at this juncture sensed that the doors of the Monbushō would be closed to him. But the sight of the literary, scientific, and artistic flower of the entire British Empire assembled under one roof must have been a thought-provoking one. And perhaps by the time Mori arrived in Yokohama on 23 July 1873 via Suez, he had already struck upon a more direct and personal means, if necessary, of taking his message of enlightenment to the Japanese people.

117. Duncan, *Life of Spencer,* p. 494.

Laurence Oliphant

Thomas Lake Harris

The Satsuma Students in 1865

Left to Right:
Seated: Mori Arinori, Matsumura Junzō, Nakamura Sōken
Standing: Hatakeyama Yoshinari, Takami Yaichi, Murahashi Naoe, Tōgō Ainoshin, Nagoshi Heima

Seven   *1873–1876*

APOSTLE OF ENLIGHTENMENT

The young diplomat, just turned twenty-six upon his second homecoming, was no less disposed to startle his countrymen with new proposals and innovations than had been the globetrotting student who returned to Japan from the West for the first time five years earlier. The Mori of 1873, however, unlike the Mori of 1868, had gained by virtue of his official representation of his country in one of the major capitals of the Occident a far more sophisticated and comprehensive view both of the requirements of Japan and of the possible uses of the West. The difference, in a word, was an emerging sense of the possible. The yoke of bureaucratic office, though still chafing, was beginning to settle on him, and the increasing responsibilities of high office required of Mori that he envision the national interest far more clearly and appropriate his means to his ends far more rationally than had been the case in his earlier student and post-student days.

The "Kokugo haishiron," boldly enunciated on the eve of Mori's second homecoming, and perhaps the most quixotic proposal of his entire career, had made him—if one may trust the *Japan Weekly Mail*—the laughingstock of the foreign community in Tokyo and Yokohama.[1] It may well have been this signal lack

1. The *Japan Weekly Mail* attacked Mori mercilessly on the subject of the "Kokugo haishiron" in two editorials written just before and just after his arrival in Japan, on 19 July and on 2 August 1873 respectively. "When

of encouragement for the scheme on the part of his Western confidants that led Mori to abandon it upon his return to Japan. For the remainder of his life he would continue ardently to promote the study of English, but the record we have shows no further defense or even mention, by Mori himself, of his "Kokugo haishi eigo saiyō" proposal subsequent to January 1873. During the exceptionally creative two-and-one-half years which elapsed between his return from Washington and his assignment to Peking, Mori managed to set aside more grandiose blueprints for the remaking of Japan and to channel his enthusiasm into three institutional vehicles, of modest and manageable proportions, all of which took firm root in the cultural and intellectual development of his country.

First, for the general intellectual edification of the public, Mori introduced with the Meirokusha (Meiji Six Society) and the *Meiroku zasshi* (Meiji six magazine) the traditions of the academic society and of the critical journal, both of which survived the rather early demise of Mori's own particular originals. In the field, secondly, of moral uplift Mori concentrated on the marriage relationship, developing his ideas at great length in his "Saishōron," or "Discourse on wives and mistresses," and giving concrete commitment to those ideas in his own contractual wedding ceremony. And thirdly, Mori did something about the great concern he had shown in America for Japan's commercial viability, turning to the otherwise neglected field of commercial education and establishing with his Shōhō Kōshūjo (Commercial Institute) the forerunner of today's Hitotsubashi University.

The expansion of the public's intellectual horizon could scarcely fail to stimulate a heightened political awareness, and in response

---

a man has seriously made a proposition to carry over the English language bodily to Japan and then tinker it for easy adaptation to the wants of the people," it wrote, "there is no further necessity of arguing with him." The *Mail* went on to talk of Mori's "ludicrous incapacity" to treat of educational matters in general, heaping scorn on *Education in Japan* and on the "kindly tolerance" with which Americans had greeted it. That Mori had succeeded in inciting the *Mail*'s latent anti-American animus suggests how pro-American he was assumed to be in at least one quarter. Two years later, on 22 May 1875, the *Mail* relented, praising Mori for his achievements on behalf of the enlightenment of Japan, and reminiscing that "we all had our laugh over his [language] scheme." The paper refused to let Mori forget his early foible, however, for as long as he lived. Reporting on a recent speech by the minister of education, the 12 January 1889 edition of the *Mail* noted with mock relief, a bare month prior to Mori's assassination, that "he does not intend to carry into effect his supposed hobby of rendering English the national language of Japan." The *Mail* continued to gnaw a very, very old bone.

to this Mori was forced increasingly to take some sort of stand regarding the relationship of the individual and the state. His statements for this period, however, revolving as they do around the role of the scholar in society and the proper function of the Meirokusha, remain highly generalized, suggestive rather than indicative of a political philosophy; and he still does not oblige us throughout the 1870's with any explicit, constructive proposals regarding the Japanese polity.

With the suspension of the *Meiroku zasshi* in late 1875 Mori's official identity as foreign ministry bureaucrat advances once again to the fore. His initial appointment to the grade of secretary (*dajō*) in 1873 was followed by a promotion to deputy vice minister (*shōyū*) on 9 June 1875, and up to that time he concerned himself chiefly with the minor issue of travel by foreigners in the Japanese interior. Mori's appointment as ambassador to China that November, however, and his role in helping to settle the Korean crisis of 1875–1876, would put to the test not only his long-held concept of diplomacy but his entire apostleship of enlightenment as well.

MEIROKUSHA:
THE MEIJI SIX SOCIETY

The act which gave Mori his firmest niche in the intellectual history of Meiji Japan was his conception and sponsorship of that society of intellectual luminaries, named after the year of its founding, which stood at the very center of the Enlightenment Movement (*keimō undō*) of the 1870's.

It may have been providential for the establishment of the Meirokusha that the government forced Mori to mark time for nearly five months in Tokyo upon returning from America, while it made up its own mind what to do with, about, or to him. The replacement of Fukushima Taneomi by Terajima Munenori as foreign minister on 28 October 1873 signified not only the resolution of the Korean question in favor of the peace party but also the advent to that office of an old Kagoshima friend and London mentor who would be inclined to take a lenient view of Mori's controversial behavior in Washington. On 24 November Terajima finally got around to asking Iwakura for the final disposition of Mori's case, which led to his appointment three weeks later.[2]

Finding himself out of touch with scholarly circles in Tokyo

2. Inau Tentarō, *Nihon gaikō shisōshi ronkō: dai-ichi: jōyaku kaiseiron no tenkai* (Tokyo, 1966), p. 117, letter from Terajima Munenori to Iwakura Tomomi, 24 Nov. 1873.

after two-and-one-half years abroad, Mori first of all sought out Nishimura Shigeki, who in his *Ōji roku* (Account of things past) has left the best record of Mori's original motivations for establishing Japan's first modern learned society:

> In the summer of 1873 Yokoyama Son'ichirō introduced to me Mori Arinori of Satsuma, who had just returned from America and had asked to see me. Mori was at that time staying at the house of Takashima Tokuemon in Kobekichō-rokuchōme. "Scholars in America," Mori informed me, "set up learned societies in their respective fields of interest in which they deliver lectures and through which they engage cooperatively in the study of the arts and sciences, all to the great benefit of the public. Scholars in Japan however live in isolation, without mutual intercourse, and contribute therefore very little to the general welfare. I should like to see our scholars organize a society, along American lines, in which they could gather for discussion and research. Moreover, the morals of the Japanese people have in recent years shown a steady decline, with the bottom not yet in sight, and it is precisely our senior scholars who must come to the rescue. The society which I propose therefore should on the one hand promote learning, and on the other set an example of moral conduct."[3]

The Kaiyakusha, a fellowship of Western learning scholars attached to the Bakufu's Kaiseijo, which had flourished in the years immediately preceding the Restoration, and which in terms of orientation may be viewed as the lineal ascendant of the Meirokusha, had been disbanded in the confusion of events, and nothing had emerged to take its place.[4] A comprehensive seat of higher learning, too, would have to await the constitution of Tokyo University in 1877, out of a jumble of pre- and post-Restoration institutions. Ever since his discussion with Joseph Henry of the Shimonoseki funds, Mori had shown a keen interest in the promotion of higher education. The development, institutionally, of a modern university was properly the task of the Monbushō, but Mori clearly envisioned as one of the two great purposes of his new society the stimulation of scholarship at the highest level which eventually would be provided by the research and graduate facilities of Tokyo University. Mori's original concept of the

3. Nishimura Shigeki, *Ōji roku* (Tokyo, 1905), pp. 164–165.
4. OTM, p. 64.

Meirokusha, however, both in the expansion of this first function to include popularization of new learning and in the second function of moral bellwether, went far beyond the purely scholarly role of the typical Western academic society.

Mori's American models in this latter, highly limited sense, come readily to mind: Joseph Henry had been serving at the time as president of the American Association for the Advancement of Science, of the National Academy of Science, and of the Philosophical Society of Washington; William Whitney was president of the American Philological Association; Charles Lanman was a member of the National Academy of Design. And, for a prototype near at hand, there was the Asiatic Society of Japan, to which Mori himself was elected on 22 December 1873 as its first (and until the following year, only) Japanese member.[5] The closest thing in America to the Meirokusha in its aspect of a small band of intellectual elite committed to the propagation and popularization of a broad school of thought, was the Transcendental (or "Hedge") Club founded by Emerson and his friends in 1836 for the discussion of the new "German" philosophy. Mori probably had heard of this group, and possibly may have met in the course of his several trips to New England the surviving members (such as Emerson, George Ripley, Frederic Hedge) who continued to meet in Boston from time to time. This club, however, had long since passed its heyday of the early 1840's, when it set the in-

---

5. Mori at the time of his election to the Asiatic Society of Japan was the only Japanese among the 114 society members. A second Japanese, Sanjō Junrō, joined in April 1874 and a third, Hatakeyama Yoshinari, in 1875. By 1879, nine Japanese members were listed, including Mori's old Meirokusha colleagues, Nakamura Masanao and Tsuda Sen. At the fourth annual meeting on 14 July 1876, Mori was elected one of the ten councillors of the society (again, the only Japanese so honored), and he maintained membership throughout his life. W. G. Howell, in welcoming Mori to his first meeting, was reported to have remarked that "whatever we might bring to the Japanese it was certain that much of the information which we sought here must come from them." Mori promptly obliged by jumping into a discussion of R. H. Brunton's paper on "Constructive Art in Japan" with useful remarks on the evolution of thatched-house architecture. Mori's election to the society coincided with the very period during which the regulations and format of the Meirokusha were under discussion by its prospective members. The Asiatic Society of Japan, in the general style of its proceedings and in its rules of membership, did not differ significantly from the societies Mori may have remembered from America; but it may possibly have provided a convenient point of reference for Mori in his attempt to organize his own group at the time. (See membership lists in the *Transactions of the Asiatic Society of Japan*, Vols. I (1872–73), II (1873–74), III (1875) and VII (1879), and the *Japan Weekly Mail* for 3 January 1874 and 5 August 1876.)

tellectual world astir through the pages of its provocative journal, *Dial.*

It is more difficult to identify any specific Western inspiration for the moral leadership enjoined by Mori upon his new society. The realms of knowledge and of morality continued to overlap in the Tokugawa intellectual cosmos to a degree the West had not known since the High Middle Ages, and the impulse here would on the face of it seem to be purely traditional. Beyond that one could only suggest perhaps the Athenaeum in London. Strictly speaking a social club for the literary, scientific and artistic great rather than an academic society (and serving perhaps the function of mutual admiration better than any other), the Athenaeum did nevertheless regularly extend extraordinary membership to judges, cabinet ministers, and bishops as a group; and the impressive combination of intellectual, political, and moral authority wielded collectively by the nominal membership of this one club may possibly help to explain the ambitious breadth of Mori's own concept.

The great emphasis which Mori placed upon moral leadership is suggested by the fact that out of sixteen pages of original essay material which he contributed to the *Meiroku zasshi,* fully eight were concerned with a moral issue (the marital relationship).[6] The political and social turmoil of recent years had taken their inevitable toll in private and public morality, and Fukuzawa, in one of the few estimates of Mori's character based on intimate personal acquaintance as opposed to the official biographer's praise, has left the best account of his younger friend's effort to breast the current of the times: "Everyone recognized the moral character of Mori's conduct. It was in the immediate post-Restoration period that Mori entered upon manhood. This was a time of great change and confusion, a time when many persons of high station were giving themselves over quite publicly to dissipation, debauchery, gambling, and every conceivable form of vice. There, however, steadfast against the raging billows stood Mori—alone—maintaining against the flood the moral integrity of his conduct. Here was one aspect of Mori which never failed to arouse my deepest respect."[7]

The "Anecdotes" which Kimura Kyō has recorded for this period reinforce Fukuzawa's characterization and confirm Mori's streak of sober frugality. He would occasionally visit the bazaars

6. This page count excludes Mori's annual report in MRZ no. 30, which was not an essay, and the bulk of "Shūkyō," in MRZ no. 6, which—being for the most part a translation from Western texts—was not original.

7. KKM, p. 289.

of Peking, we are told, to track down *go* boards for his father, but would never return with purchases for personal, family, or embassy use; in the late 1870's as vice foreign minister he indignantly rejected the request of the London legation for suitable ornamentation of its official carriage; and he refused to carry along the customary *mimaihin,* or "sympathy gifts," when calling on the sick, attacking the custom as a burden on the poor which often prevented them from carrying out visits to which they were inclined by natural sympathy.[8] Mori's reaction to Kabuki, too, was predictably "puritanical": "Mori had occasion at this time to visit the theater, but since he had no particular appreciation of the Japanese stage he sat there straight-faced, unable to make any sense of it, with people weeping and wailing or roaring with laughter on every side. After only two acts he fled the premises and returned home."[9]

Nishimura had enthusiastically accepted Mori's proposal and was instrumental in recruiting the other eight charter members of the Meirokusha: Fukuzawa Yukichi, Katō Hiroyuki, Nishi Amane, Nakamura Masanao, Tsuda Masamichi, Sugi Kyōji, Mitsukuri Shūhei, and Mitsukuri Rinshō. After three or four informal meetings in the autumn of 1873 the group decided to proceed with the formal establishment of a society, and by early February 1874 a set of bylaws, reflecting a compromise between original drafts submitted by Mori and Nishi, had been agreed upon and the first official meeting held in what was to become the regular venue of the society: the upper story of the Seiyōken, a Western-style restaurant in the Tsukiji quarter often patronized by the foreign community. The bylaws contained the usual stipulations with regard to membership, officers, dues, finances, election, expulsion, and revision of the bylaws, and stated: "This society is established for the purpose of discussion by interested parties of means appropriate to the advancement of education in Japan, and for the promotion of knowledge through the exchange of opinion among the assembled members."[10] The revised bylaws of May 1875 confined the statement of purpose to the second of these two clauses. Both versions excised the pretensions to moral leadership in Mori's original concept, and shifted the emphasis from the scholarly research central to the Western model to the role of popular en-

8. KKM, pp. 256, 259, 281.
9. KKM, p. 268.
10. For the original and revised bylaws of the *Meirokusha,* see Ōkubo Toshiaki ed., *Meiji keimō shisō shū* (Tokyo, 1967), volume III of Chikuma Shobō, compilers, *Meiji bungaku zenshū,* pp. 403–404.

lightenment in which the Meirokusha in fact was to make its mark.

The society held its meetings on the first and sixteenth of each month. Members assembled at 11:00 A.M., discussed club business until noon, lunched together from twelve to one, then devoted the afternoon to speechmaking and discussion. Fukuzawa was offered the presidency but declined, whereupon Mori assumed the position. This he held until the first annual meeting on 1 February 1875, when Mitsukuri Shūhei was elected to succeed him. In his annual report to the society on that day, Mori extended his thanks to Sera Ta'ichi and Shimizu Usaburō for their services as secretary and treasurer respectively, and announced that five additional regular members, five corresponding members, and ten extraordinary members had been added to the rolls during the preceding year. In view of the steadily increasing number of invited guests, Mori went on to suggest that the meetings be thrown open to the public, with the imposition of an admission fee, reservation of seating, and advance notices in the papers.[11]

The suggestion was adopted, and it was at this point that the Meirokusha achieved its immense popularity and renown as a public lecture forum, with scholars and government officials flocking to the biweekly meetings in great numbers. For this it had entirely to thank the success of Fukuzawa in prodding its members into the making of formal, prepared public speeches. This was an activity totally lacking in the native tradition, which members naturally approached with considerable shyness, and which Mori had explicitly opposed on the basis that it could never be done in the Japanese language. It is ironic that the founder of the society should have scorned a method which did so much in fact to promote his own objective. The impression that Mori no longer advocated the abolition out-of-hand of the Japanese language is strongly confirmed by his failure to join the discussion of the language problem which occupied the first issue of the *Meiroku zasshi,* but it is clear from Fukuzawa's recollection of the matter that Mori still harbored a deep pessimism regarding the construc-

---

11. Mori's first annual report was printed in MRZ no. 30 under the title "Meirokusha dai-ichi nenkai yakuin kaisen ni tsuki enzetsu" (Speech delivered on the occasion of the first annual election of officers of the Meiji Six Society), in MBZ, XVIII, 198–200, and provides much of the detailed information which we have on the Meirokusha. The description of the society here has been based on this speech and on general information contained in Ōkubo Toshiaki, "Meirokusha no hitobito," in Konishi Shirō, ed., *Nihon jinbutsushi taikei* (Tokyo, 1960), V; in Nishida Chōjū, "Meirokuzasshi kaidai," in MBZ, XVIII, pp. 10–13; and in Asō Yoshiteru, *Kinsei Nihon tetsugaku shi* (Tokyo, 1942), pp. 267–281.

tive possibilities of his own native tongue, in this instance the spoken form: "Mori . . . young as he was, put forth an opinion opposed to my own, maintaining that speechmaking in the Western fashion could be conducted only in a Western language and that Japanese, although suitable for conversation or discussion, was not a language in which one could give expression to one's thoughts before an assembled audience."[12]

Fukuzawa first started to coax his fellow members into speechmaking in the spring of 1874,[13] but Mori in his annual report was still far from satisfied with the results, complaining that: "although with introduction of public speechmaking last spring we began to take on the true form of a 'society' [original in English], we have not yet reached the stage of criticism and debate following our speeches. The difficulty here is probably that the speakers employ too many Sino-Japanese compounds which listeners do not understand, and that we are not yet well versed in the proper speechmaking technique."[14] The society made a less dramatic but in the long run even more significant impact on the public mind with the publication of the *Meiroku zasshi* (actually entitled *Meirokusha zasshi*), which appeared first twice and then three times monthly and ran for a total of forty-three issues (with sales of approximately 3,200 copies per issue) between March 1874 and November 1875. Mori's signature as editor first appeared on the flyleaf of the magazine with the fortieth issue, in compliance with the new press law, but his overall editorial responsibility presumably dates from the very start.[15] The journal originally was designed to make public the substance of the discussions at the Seiyōken, but most articles seem to be essays prepared either in anticipation of, or subsequent to, discussion at the society's meetings.

Mori's ten articles (counting by installments) represented an average contribution in terms of length far less prolific than that of Tsuda Masamichi, Nishi Amane, or Sakatani Shiroshi (with 30, 25 and 20 articles to their credit respectively) but more active than several others, including Fukuzawa, who had other outlets for his writing. With the exception of his lengthy "Saishōron," which appeared in five installments between May 1847 and February 1875, Mori's contribution fell entirely within the first four months

12. Cited in Takahashi Tatsuo, "Kokugo kokubun kara mita Fukuzawa sensei," *Shigaku,* 13.3:387 (November 1934).
13. Ibid., p. 387, and Kōsaka Masaaki, *Japanese Thought in the Meiji Era,* trans. David Abosch (Tokyo, 1958), p. 64.
14. Mori, "Dai-ichi nenkai enzetsu," MBZ, XVIII, 199.
15. Nishida Chōjū, "Meirokuzasshi kaidai," p. 11.

(or first seven issues) of the publication. There is no evident reason for this concentration of output in the early numbers of the journal. The "Saishōron" later appeared at leisurely two-to-three month intervals, and perhaps with the pressure of foreign ministry business Mori felt that this lengthy essay and his general editorial guidance represented a fair share of the work. Taking as a yardstick, however, the number of subjects treated—in Mori's case only six—the contrast with the giants (as we well may call them) of the *Meiroku zasshi* is even more striking. Tsuda for instance swept over the whole range of human culture, touching on matters as variegated as constitutional government, freedom of the press, trade balances, torture, capital punishment, prostitution, and earthquakes. Mori with *Life and Resources in America* had produced an informative treatise on the West inviting favorable comparison with Fukuzawa's *Seiyō jijō* (Conditions in the West; 1866), but he does not come through in the *Meiroku zasshi* as one of those zealous retailers of fresh information who did so much, through the pages of this journal, to expand their countrymen's knowledge and appreciation of the outside world. Mori's role here, as with the society in general, was preeminently that of a promoter, an organizer, a mover of men: less the professor than the administrative dean.

Mori's essays included: (1) "Gakusha shokubunron no hyō" (A critique of arguments concerning the role of the scholar), in MRZ [*Meiroku zasshi*] No. 2 (March 1874), a rejoinder to the viewpoint advanced by Fukuzawa in *Gakumon no susume* (On the encouragement of learning); (2) "Kaika daiichi wa" (Civilization: part 1), in MRZ No. 3 (April 1874), a brief exposition of Guizot's theory of the three-stage evolution of civilization; (3) "Minsen giin setsuritsu kengonsho no hyō" (A critique of the petition for the establishment of a popular assembly), in the same issue; (4) "Shūkyō" (Religion), in MRZ No. 6 (May 1874), a translation of excerpts pertaining to the relation between religion and law in the West, taken from treatises on international law by Emerich de Vattel and R. J. Phillimore; (5) "Dokuritsu kokken gi" (The meaning of national sovereignty), in MRZ No. 7 (May 1874), a basic statement of Mori's views on international law and diplomacy; and (6) the "Saishōron" (Discourse on wives and mistresses), which appeared in five installments, "Saishōron/I" through "Saishōron/V", in Nos. 8, 11, 15, 20, and 27 of the *Meiroku zasshi* for May, June, August, and November 1874, and February 1875, respectively.

The *Meiroku zasshi* sold at such a profit that Mori submitted elaborate plans in his annual report for the eventual construction by the society of its own meeting hall, a multipurpose cultural center which would be available to the public for concerts, literary forums, and business meetings on days when the Meirokusha was not in session.

These plans were very much in keeping with Mori's conception of the Meirokusha as a purely cultural institution. He went out of his way in his annual report to interpret the charter as having in no way suggested the discussion of current political problems: "The matters to be discussed by our society are, as stated in Article One of the bylaws, exclusively those which relate to education, such as literature, technology, physics, science, etc.: in other words, those things which are necessary for the enrichment of human talent and for the promotion of good conduct. Since we have our sights set on the future, it is altogether probable that we shall incur the ill will of the present generation—but that is inevitable. However, the discussion of political affairs does not fall within the original intention of our society. It is something which ought to be avoided since it would only use up our energies to no avail, and might possibly bring unnecessary harm upon our society."[16] Here was an extremely arbitrary definition of the two words in Article One, "education" and "knowledge," around which Mori's gloss revolved. Perhaps as a ranking official he could see the press and libel laws coming; perhaps he felt that the society was bound to strike so many sensitive nerves at the level of traditional social relations and morality that it simply could not afford to alienate also the political authority, an authority which Mori may have tended to view more as a probable ally than as a potential enemy, since the government at that time was committed to many of the aims and much of the viewpoint of the Meirokusha in the nonpolitical realm. In any case the formula of political taciturnity, coupled with loquaciousness on practically every other subject, was one which Mori himself by and large had followed since 1870.

The political interests and responsibilities of the individual members, however, inevitably drew the society and its magazine into the political debates which had been sparked by Itagaki Taisuke's presentation on 16 January 1874 of a petition for the establishment of a popular assembly. It was Mori, ironically enough, who first trespassed on political territory with his criticism of the petition in the third issue of the *Meiroku zasshi*. Attacks on the proposal by Nishi and Katō in the third and fourth issues re-

16. Mori, "Dai-ichi nenkai enzetsu," MBZ, XVIII, 199.

spectively, and arguments in favor of a popular assembly by Tsuda in his lengthy "Seiron" (On politics), extending intermittently from the ninth to the sixteenth issues (June to August, 1874), show how involved the society had been in this specific problem from the very start; and a much higher proportion of the articles (on diplomacy, taxation, or religious freedom for instance), touched indirectly on the political sphere. Mori's insistence in his annual report on the original nonpolitical orientation of the Meirokusha smacks either of a loss of memory or of considerable insincerity.

There is another possible explanation, however, which would view the chief change as having occurred in outside circumstances rather than in Mori's own mind, and his exhortation to political neutrality in 1875 as a response to an exacerbation of the relationship between the government and the press which nobody perhaps quite foresaw as of early 1874. With the exception of Fukuzawa and Nakamura the charter members of the Meirokusha were all in the employ of the Meiji government, and such political dialogue as they might choose to pursue retained in essence the form of an intramural bureaucratic debate: embarrassing perhaps if widely aired—a bit like the members of the Richard Nixon cabinet taking to the pages of *Ramparts* magazine to discuss national policy—but a game in which even totalitarian communist regimes, in complete control of their mass communications media, have in recent years found it possible to indulge. The Meiji government at the time, however, was far from being in control of the Japanese press, which itself was in the immediate postnatal stage, with its role and identity and relationship to the government as yet largely undefined.

When Mori himself saw fit to comment on the Itagaki petition in MRZ no. 3, that relationship was governed by the relatively toothless press law of October 1873, directed at a relatively somnolent adversary;[17] but by early 1875 the government confronted a press, particularly in the vernacular dailies, which had turned not only aggressively political but also intensely and almost uniformly hostile.[18] It was under these new circumstances that the govern-

17. The "Shinbunshi jōmoku" (Stipulations for newspapers) of 19 Oct. 1873. See Nishida Chōjū, *Meiji jidai no shinbun to zasshi* (Tokyo, 1966), pp. 85–86.

18. Not only did the regulations of 1875 carry clearcut penalty provisions absent in those of 1873, but the object of the government's concern also had shifted in the course of two years from the leakage of confidential information by government officials, to the incitement of public hostility toward the government by the vernacular dailies. Alongside the journals of general opinion, of which the *Meiroku zasshi* was the foremost example, had ap-

ment promulgated the Press and Libel Ordinances ("Shinbunshi jōrei" and "Zanbō ritsu") of 28 June 1875, and it was against this background of heightened political tension that the society assembled on 1 September 1875 to consider its response to the new regulations. Mori insisted that there was still important work for the society to accomplish in the cultural and educational sphere and argued for continued publication of the *Meiroku zasshi* in compliance with the law. Fukuzawa on the other hand called for suspension of publication in protest against the new restrictions, arguing that the bylaws implied the discussion of politics, that the members could continue to write within the framework of the ordinances only by compromising their intellectual and personal integrity, and that the only real alternatives therefore were self-degradation, imprisonment, or suspension under protest. He also made the point that academic societies in the West could afford to be purely "academic" because the citizenry there had already learned to shoulder its political burdens: an end toward which he felt the Meirokusha should continue to furnish its invaluable leadership and guidance.[19]

In the vote for or against suspension Fukuzawa carried the day, with only Mori, Tsuda, Nishi, and Sakatani in favor of continued publication. We have no transcript of the proceedings of 1 September and therefore do not know whether the voting for or against suspension necessarily represented support for the contrasting rationales presented by Fukuzawa and Mori.[20] The motives for instance of Katō, who had turned official government

---

peared in March 1875 the *Hyōron shinbun,* the first magazine devoted exclusively to direct political criticism. Up to the end of 1874 political discussion in the newspapers, too, was to be found primarily in letters to the editor, or in feature articles by paid contributors, whose chief merit lay in a talent for writing rather than in the possession of any fixed political opinion. With the advent in the latter half of 1874 of men of pronounced political views like Kurimoto Jōun, Narishima Ryūhoku, and Fukuchi Gen'ichirō to the staffs of the *Yūbin hōchi,* the *Chōya shinbun* and the *Tōkyō nichi nichi,* politics became the standard preoccupation of the editorial page. And by 1875, in the words of Nishida Chōjū, "eighty to ninety percent of the papers in the Tokyo-Yokohama area had been turned entirely into vehicles for political discussion" (Ibid., pp. 39–41, 77–79, 84–91; quote from page 41).

19. Fukuzawa developed his viewpoint at length in an editorial over his name in the *Yūbin hōchi shinbun* for 4 September 1875. Reprinted in Ōkubo, *Meiji keimō shisō shū,* pp. 410–411.

20. I am indebted to Mr. Jerry K. Fisher, Department of History, Carroll College, Waukesha, Wisconsin, for calling my attention to this distinction, which has been overlooked in extant accounts and analyses of the vote on the suspension of the *Meiroku zasshi.*

apologist on the popular assembly issue, may have been somewhat different from those of Fukuzawa. Regarding the three members who voted with Mori, it would seem more than coincidental that they happened to be also the three most active contributors to the journal: a point which oddly enough never has been raised in general accounts of the matter. The votes for continued publication may very possibly be explained simply in terms of vested interest, with an added pride of parentage in Mori's case.

Fukuzawa certainly had principle all on his side, but it is worth attempting to reconstruct Mori's own probable view both of the feasible alternatives and of the issue at stake. It was never remotely contemplated that the members of the Meirokusha, individually, would cease to publish generally, or even to write specifically on political topics. Involved was nothing more than a decision to abandon the *Meiroku zasshi* as a common vehicle of expression.[21] At stake therefore was not whether the members would continue to be heard but rather whether they would continue to be heard collectively: and that went right back to Mori's original motive in establishing the Meirokusha. The society, as Okubo Toshiaki has pointed out, was a fellowship of prima donnas. Each member was already an established authority in his own right, quite capable of looking out for himself and making his own particular impact on the times. So the society was fated from the very start to a certain lack of solidarity.[22] But that, however ephemeral, had in Mori's mind been all along the major point: the exploration mutually, and the presentation jointly, of new intellectual (and as he himself would have had it, "moral") realms.

Mori's line of argument on 1 September, not recorded at the time, may be surmised from the admonitions in his earlier annual report, and from allusions by Fukuzawa in an editorial in the *Yūbin hōchi* three days later: "Certain persons have suggested that the government has some other object in mind with its press and libel ordinances; that these will not in the least affect the publication of the *Meiroku zasshi* or similar magazines; and that although these laws appear quite stringent on the face of it, they are not really intended to be so."[23] Fukuzawa's use here of the term *naijitsu,* in the sense of "inside information" or "concealed circumstances," brings to mind the Tokugawa legal tradition in which the published codes were backed up by secret clauses intended

21. Ōkubo, "Meirokusha no hitobito," p. 150.
22. Ibid., p. 150.
23. Ōkubo, *Meiji keimō shisō shū,* p. 410. See note 19 above.

solely for the guidance of judges.[24] Even today the police and the judicial authority in Japan enjoy unusually wide discretion in the application (or more properly speaking in the nonapplication) of stated law. It is conceivable that Mori, close as he was to the inner government circle, had good reason to believe that if only the *Meiroku zasshi* could avoid the temptation to emulate the dailies in the field of political polemics, all would be well. The libel ordinance, it was true, contained distressingly broad and imprecise definitions of libel and slander; but Mori may have reasoned that the *Meiroku zasshi* even at its most political had surely never come anywhere near the advocacy of revolution in government, the subversion of the state, the stirring up of rebellion, or the incitement to lawbreaking and riot covered by the crucial clauses, Nos. 12–14, of the press ordinance.

Perhaps Mori also correctly foresaw that the suspension of the journal would inevitably entail the demise of the society itself. Two final, politically innocuous issues of the *Meiroku zasshi* appeared in October and November 1875; and although some of the members would gather together under the name of the society to reminisce about old times until as late as 1900, the final meeting of the Meirokusha in its historical form was held on 1 February 1876. But by 24 November 1875 Mori had already left Tokyo for his new post in Peking.

"SAISHŌRON": ON WIVES AND MISTRESSES

During Mori's discussion of the Korean crisis with Li Hung-chang at Paoting on 25 January 1876, the following digression (as given in the official English transcript), occurred:

> *Mori:* Though an Asiatic man, I must confess that there will, in my humble opinion, be a very long time or some centuries before Asia to become [*sic*] capable of competing with Europe. The Asiatics as a people live so low and degraded a life only little better than that of beasts.
> *Li:* How so?
> *Mori:* The position ordained for woman to occupy is one of the highest and most sacred ever created by the will of the Supreme Being. It is that of the mother of mankind in general, and of a country and family in particular. Now look at the

---

24. George B. Sansom, *Japan: A Short Cultural History,* rev. ed. (New York, 1943), p. 460.

actual condition of the woman [sic] everywhere in Asia, and the position they occupy. They are both regarded and treated as little better than some other [sic] animals. You will see without my telling any further, the truth of what I said before, respecting the low life of the Asiatic people.[25]

From his supervision of the Tsuda Umeko group in Washington to speeches on female education in the closing months of his career, the elevation of women was a theme in which Mori over the years maintained both a high level of interest and continuity of viewpoint. The inadequacies of the old dispensation and Mori's proposed remedies were most fully spelled out in the "Saishōron." The first installment considered the relationship of the spouses; the second, the fate of the offspring; the third, the problem of mutual fidelity; the fourth, the role of the mother; and the fifth presented a draft marriage contract.[26]

"The relationship between husband and wife is the fountainhead of all morality. It is the basis of virtuous conduct. And virtuous conduct, in turn, is the starting point of national strength and stability. When two people marry, they are joined in a mutual relationship of rights and duties, in which neither party has the upper hand ... When one looks at the present marriage customs of our country, one sees that wives are entirely given to the service of their husbands without any attention being paid to their own wishes, and that our laws long have permitted the husband to divorce his wife at will. A context of rights and duties is missing here. Call the couple 'husband and wife' if you will, but it is a far cry from the true meaning of the term. To my mind the foundation of morality has yet to be established in this country." Opening on this dual note of national welfare and genuine humanitarian concern, the "Saishōron" taken as a whole was a plea for a marriage relationship of mutual love and fidelity, backed by the legal

25. From Mori's second interview with Li, for which we have both an English and a Japanese transcript, given in *Zenshū* I, 177–181 and 162–166, respectively. Mori spoke in English, which was translated into Chinese for Li by his interpreter Huang Hui-lien. (See *Zenshū* I, 181.) The English, therefore, is the original.

26. The five installments of the "Saishōron" may be found in MBZ, XVIII, as follows: "Saishōron/I" (from MRZ no. 8, May 1874), pp. 93–94; "Saishōron/II" (from MRZ no. 11, June 1874), pp. 110–111; "Saishōron/III" (from MRZ no. 15, August 1874), pp. 127–128; "Saishōron/IV" (from MRZ no. 20, November 1874), p. 153; "Saishōron/V" (from MRZ no. 27, February 1875), pp. 184–185. The entire essay has been conveniently assembled both in OTM, p. 167ff., and in *Zenshū* I, 241ff.

guarantees of a contract entered into at the time of the wedding.

That not only a moral but also a legal reformation was required is clear from the closing paragraphs of the first installment, in which Mori pointed to the equal recognition extended under the old codes to wives and "mistresses" (and to their respective offspring), and noted that husbands generally were inclined to favor the latter. The *shō,* written with the Chinese character for "concubine," rendered also in the native Japanese as *mekake,* and translated here for want of a better term as "mistress," was a creature peculiar to the traditional Japanese social scene. She was neither a respectable secondary wife, a true "concubine" in the Chinese or Moslem fashion nor simply a "mistress" in the Western sense of a "kept woman" (kept often as not by an unmarried man). The *mekake* was a partner maintained (usually but not necessarily) secretly in addition to the "wife" received through the above-board process of go-between negotiation and parental consent. Her sons, however, if favored by the father, might be chosen to continue the official family line or *kakei,* which led Mori to exclaim that "a great many of our aristocratic and wealthy families, therefore, owe their perpetuation to harlots."

This muddying, so to speak, of one's pedigree was the central theme of "Saishōron/II," in which Mori traced the evil not only to the *mekake* but also to the *mukoyōshi,* or adoptive son-in-law. He pointed out: "Throughout Europe and America great emphasis is placed on the proper maintenance of one's own bloodline [*kettō*]. It is the foundation of their morality. This is not always the case in Asia; and especially in Japan has disregard for the bloodline been carried to deplorable extremes." Mori gives a genuinely moving description of the unhappiness which invades a home when a *mekake* intrudes upon the scene, particularly in cases where her offspring is elevated to the position of heir. No one is more wretched than the child himself, who is forced to regard as his mother his father's official wife, to whom he bears no blood relationship. Nor are things any easier for the nominal mother: "In the home [such a child] is deprived of the friendship, based on love and respect, which exists between parent and child, while in society at large he never comes to taste the real joys of social intercourse and is deprived of his fundamental human happiness. There may be some shame attached to the adoption of an heir from a strange family, but to go to the extreme of recognizing as one's own child the offspring of a mistress is, I must say, the very limit of heartlessness and injustice."

Mori's line of argument with regard to the *mukoyōshi,* the

young man adopted as heir into a family with female offspring only, is more difficult to follow. The practice is one which is still widespread and perfectly respectable in Japan today. Since the adoptive son legally came to consider his wife's parents as his own, Mori concluded with a literal-mindedness verging on the quaint that something akin to incest was involved: "The partners stand in the relationship of brother and sister; one cannot say that a law which permits the marriage of brother to sister has as yet achieved the proper respect for morality."

Mori did put his finger on the very important fact that there tended to be far more divergence in Japan than in the West between the legal pedigree (*kakei*) and the actual bloodline (*kettō*), and he seems to be arguing for a maximum congruence of the two. It is clear enough how the transfer of a mistress' child to the tutelage of a nominal mother would disrupt the normal parent-child relationship attendant on the bloodline. In the case of the *mukoyōshi*, however, there was no real anomaly either in the relationship between the spouses nor between the partners and their own offspring, but only between the adopted son and the adopting parents. Yet this seemed to bother Mori a great deal, and he apparently would have preferred to see the rule of strict male succession supplemented by some codicil for female or joint succession whereby the *kakei* of a family without sons could be preserved through a daughter married to a husband retaining his own parents and his own family name.[27]

The motive for Mori's preoccupation with pedigree was the reasonable assumption that the natural blood relationships were the source of the natural affections from which, in turn, a natural morality would flow: "Unless one first establishes the proper relationship between husband and wife, how can one possibly expect the proper relationships to flourish between parents and children, between brothers and sisters, or between relatives?" "Saishōron/III" returned accordingly to the attack on the contemporary connubial relationship, likening it to that which existed between "master" and "slave," and describing the Japanese wife as a "lifeless creature" treated as a "subhuman animal" in a fashion reminiscent of "barbaric" cultures. Here was a crime, Mori judged, which "in terms of natural law would not be overly punished by the sanctions appropriate to premeditated murder."

Mori in his first installment had defined the ideal relationship in terms of rights and duties in a framework of mutual respect and

27. This is what I take to be the sense of the extremely opaque passage at the end of the first paragraph of "Saishōron/II."

affection. The wife had a right to her husband's protection and he a right to her never-failing help; the duties were simply the reciprocals of those rights. Katō Hiroyuki in *Meiroku zasshi* No. 31 (March 1875), and Sakatani Shiroshi in the following issue, pounced on Mori for having advocated *equal* rights, that is to say, an equality of authority, between husband and wife. In a postscript to Sakatani's article Mori denied this: "In my recent 'Discourse on Wives and Mistresses' I argued that the status of husband and wife was equal (*dōtō*), and that while the former was not justified in any assumption of superiority, the latter should experience no feeling of inferiority; but I said not a word about equality of rights (*dōken*)."[28]

The participants in this debate in effect had been talking past each other. Katō was afraid of feminism, symbolized for him by the Western "ladies-first" etiquette which he thoroughly abhorred; Sakatani wondered, in essence, whether Mori really was out to reverse the primeval order of mankind; and both of them had put into his mouth a phrase, *fūfu dōken* or "Equal Rights of Husbands and Wives," which Mori never once had used. The equality he intended was one of love and respect and of obligation to uphold the other partner's rights, those rights themselves being quite differently defined. Indeed the new code which Mori envisioned would be, he explained in the fifth installment, "for the most part based on traditional practice." It was the emotional and sexual content rather than the political structure of the traditional system which he sought to reform.

Fidelity was the heart of the problem: traditional Japan had required it only of the wife. This was unfair to her; under such circumstances, how could she possibly display the true love and devotion which her husband demanded and which was the foundation of healthy family life? "Saishōron/III" continued: "When husband and wife are joined in marriage by a contract, they are expected to devote themselves wholeheartedly to each other, guarding against the transfer of their affection to any other person . . . if on the contrary the husband chooses to abandon himself, like dogs and pigs or horses and cattle, to the pursuit of any number of mates, how can he possibly repay the devoted affections of so many wives?" The great practical problem, in other words, was how to induce the Japanese male to spend his nights at home. "Saishōron/IV" deplored the traditional notion that romantic love was to be had only in the gay quarters: "Popular thinking . . . has it that pleasure is to be gained from a thoughtless indulgence in

28. MRZ no. 32 (March 1875), in MBZ, XVIII, 211.

sake, sex, *samisen* and song, and that if women do not join with men in these activities then they are not truly 'falling in love.' Foreigners regard Japan as leading the world in debauchery, and this probably is no empty charge."

The degradation of woman as wife took its deadliest toll in handicapping her even more important function as mother; and here we have reached the heart of the "Saishōron," the ultimate end toward which Mori's arguments regarding humane treatment, unsullied pedigree, and mutual fidelity have been directed. The fourth installment explained:

> The child reflects its mother precisely as a mirror reflects its own surroundings. If the mother is of pure character, so inevitably will be the child. Therefore, if one hopes to see fine qualities in the latter, one must first assure that they have been cultivated by the former. Honesty is the basis of trust; if the child wholehearedly trusts his mother, he will follow her to the last detail. If the mother on the other hand is false-hearted, how can one expect the child to maintain faith in her? The child who has played a game of mutual deception with his mother will, upon attaining his majority, deceive in turn society at large, and bring great harm upon it.

Mori discussed solutions in the third, fourth, and fifth installments. In "Saishōron/III" he dissociated himself from two remedies currently being bruited about. One was the introduction of a religion, presumably Christianity, which automatically would eradicate the old morality as it began to take root among the people. Another was to encourage Japanese to marry Westerners who understood true marriage, and to have them set forth in their own married lives an example to the rest of the nation. Mori vehemently protested:

> Such suggestions are chimerical, and certainly have not been well thought out. They may be traced no doubt to the fact that we have not yet established a suitable marriage code in this country, and to the feeling that such a code will be a long time in coming. To accept such a premise, however, is tantamount to admitting that we are a people without independent spirit, and that rather than expect such a listless crowd to work toward its own enlightened culture we had better rely entirely on foreigners for the task. Can you just imagine the indignation such a proposal would provoke among our people, who

speak of "the Imperial Realm" or "the Land of the Gods," and who pride themselves on their true heart and on their heroism?!

Ōkubo Toshiaki, on the basis of this statement, finds it impossible to believe that Mori ever could have advocated the far more drastic proposal that Japanese intermarry with Caucasians in order to improve their racial stock, as Kaneko Kentarō one day would recollect.[29] There were two approaches which Mori positively espoused: the education of women and the contractual marriage. "Saishōron/IV" argued that the good wife and mother had to be healthy, virtuous, and intelligent; that women were well endowed with the power of love, which they often, however, did not know how to use; and concluded: "women therefore should first receive a broad general education, expand their intellectual horizons and learn how best to apply their ample fund of affection."

"Saishōron/V," finally, contained specific proposals for a new marriage code. Mutual consent was the central provision. Men twenty-five or over, and women twenty years of age or over, were permitted to contract marriage of their own free will; cancellation was allowed for specified contingencies (e.g., misrepresentation of age); there were prohibitions against inbreeding; infidelity and gross misconduct were grounds for divorce, which could be sought through application to a local official; there was provision for alimony amounting to anywhere up to two-thirds of the husband's property; and the procedures for witnessing and attesting the contracts were carefully spelled out. It was, all in all, a remarkable testimonial to Mori's belief in the rationally ordered life and to his faith in the moral efficacy of the law.

On 26 February 1875, in the same month as the publication of "Saishōron/V," Mori with the full courage of his convictions was married to Hirose Tsuneko in a Western-style civil ceremony without precedent in the land. Generally taken to be the first "free and contractual marriage in Japan"[30] it was the talk of all Tokyo:

---

29. OTM, p. 62. See Chapter Five.
30. In the words for instance of Fujiwara Kiyozō in *Kyōiku shisō gakusetsu jinbutsu shi: Meiji zenki hen* (Tokyo, 1942), p. 769. Actually, the *Tōkyō nichi nichi* account of Mori's wedding (in the 7 Feb. 1875 issue) mentioned a very similar ceremony which had taken place in Tokyo only a few days earlier, on 23 January, with the marriage of a scholar of Western learning from Chōshū by the name of Tsuboi Kōzō. Tsuboi, too, had recently returned from the West and, at his wedding, rings were exchanged and

which was precisely what Mori had intended it to be. On the morning of the twenty-sixth over a hundred distinguished guests, Japanese and foreign, in everything from tuxedo to *haori*-and-*hakama* to Tokyo Governor Ōkubo Ichiō's hunting costume *à l'anglaise,* made their way through a duststorm to Mori's residence at No. 13, 10-chōme, Kobekichō, just behind the Seiyōken in Tsukiji. The ceremony was held on the ground floor of an imposing two-story red-brick structure, adjacent to Mori's own small Japanese-style home, which was being erected to house his prospective Commercial Institute. The white pillars of the double-storied front portico had been decorated with clusters of flags, garlands of green foliage, and strings of paper lanterns for evening illumination; while the interior had similarly been festooned with the national emblem and with sprays of camellia. At eleven o'clock Mori, in tuxedo, entered the outer parlor, where the guests had assembled, his bride-to-be on his arm. Tsuneko, daughter of a Shizuoka samurai family, appeared in a light grey Western-style dress, with white veil. The couple advanced to the front of the room, where an elderly Kagoshima gentleman by the name of Higo read out to them and the assembled guests the following marriage contract:

1. From this time forth Mori Arinori takes Hirose Tsuneko as his wife; Hirose Tsuneko takes Mori Arinori as her husband.

2. Both parties to this contract undertake, as long as they shall live, and as long as this contract is in force, to love and respect each other whole-heartedly and to maintain the proper relationship of husband and wife.

3. The property which the couple now own, or shall come to own, shall not be loaned or sold to third parties without the consent of both partners.

4. In the event of a unilateral breach of this contract, the injured party may appeal to the authorities for redress.

The couple then stepped forward to sign the document, which briefly comprised the essence of the "Saishōron/V" draft; and Fukuzawa added his signature as witness. All then retired to the inner parlor and helped themselves copiously to the occidental fare that weighed heavy on the tables—cold meats, pastries, fruits,

---

a homily read before the couple by the go-between. Mori however was by far the better known of the two, and it was his wedding which received all the publicity.

whiskies, and wines—eating and drinking on their feet. The reporter from the *Tōkyō nichi nichi,* on whose account of 7 February this description has been based, complained that there was hardly room to stand; but then, of course, he ended on a note of resignation, both host and guests alike were members of the "Western Enlightenment Set."[31]

The reference to "national strength and stability" in the opening phrases of the "Saishōron" harks back directly to Mori's "Kōro kikō" entries for St. Petersburg in 1866. There is, however, not a trace of spiritual esoterism here; nor has Mori attempted to defend the sanctity of marriage in the transcendental terms of orthodox Christianity. The influence of Brocton comes through in the intensity of emotional attitude, in the virulence of Mori's condemnation of marital irregularities and in his almost apocalyptic vision of the regenerative powers of a new sexual ethic, rather than in the form of explicit doctrine. If one had to produce an explicit source of inspiration, it is striking—virtually beyond the possibility of mere coincidence—what one could find in John Stuart Mill. Mori's recommendations were in line with general social practice throughout the Western world, but the secular premises of his argument find a wide resonance, if not necessarily a one-to-one correspondence, in the pages of *The Subjection of Women,* which had appeared five years before the "Saishōron."

"The legal subordination of one sex to another," Mill writes on the first page of his treatise, with the same mixture of utilitarian and humanitarian values as Mori, "is wrong in itself and now one of the chief hindrances to human improvement."[32] He goes on to speak of marriage as a "partnership," averring that it is "not true that in all voluntary associations between two people one of them must be absolute master," and cites business partnerships as an example of the fact.[33] The role of the mother in character formation is touched upon,[34] as is the importance of female education, which would promise "doubling the mass of mental faculties avail-

---

31. David Murray's wife, Martha, wrote to her "Cousin Lucy" on 8 February 1875 that "I think you would have been entertained if you could have peeped in on Mr. Mori's wedding . . . It was entirely in foreign style—bride dressed in grey silk and tulle veil—but I have written all about it to Alice so will not repeat to you." The message to Alice, unfortunately, is not to be found in the collection which includes the letter to Lucy, namely, LCM, David Murray Papers, Box no. 4.
32. John Stuart Mill, *The Subjection of Women* (New York, 1911), p. 1. The original edition was published in London in 1869.
33. Ibid., p. 85.
34. Ibid., p. 185.

able for the higher service of humanity,"[35] but in the specific rights he would extend to women Mill is more generous than Mori, going beyond that of property to those of occupation and suffrage as well: to the full *dōken* which Mori had disavowed.[36]

Mill's ethic was part of his broader belief that humanity was gradually passing from the "law of force" to the "law of justice," and that marriage was the social institution which most needed changing in line with this general trend.[37] It was imperative to have "the most universal and pervading of all human relations" regulated by justice instead of injustice: "All the selfish propensities, the self-worship, the unjust self-preference, which exist among mankind, have their source and root in, and derive their principal nourishment from, the present constitution of the relation between man and woman."[38] Mill's specific linking of marital matters with the problem of egoism in general must, at least distantly, have echoed Thomas Lake Harris in Mori's mind, and smoothed his transition to a less overtly Christian marital ethic. The "Saishōron" had dealt drastically with what Mori had termed a "barbaric" morality, and like Mill he had, in the course of talking about women, in effect said something very important about Man.

SHŌHŌ KŌSHŪJO: THE COMMERCIAL INSTITUTE

The building in which Mori's wedding had taken place was finally opened as the Shōhō Kōshūjo, literally the "Commercial Short-Term Training School," on 1 October 1875. This Commercial Institute did not hold the original priority among the educational projects Mori had thought about while in Washington. A large collection of books which he shipped home from America, appraised by a foreign trader at 7,000 yen and enough to fill a good many shelves, was probably intended at first for the library which had figured so centrally in his discussions with Americans of the Shimonoseki indemnity. He soon sold the volumes, however, to the ministry of education, hoping to invest the proceeds in the establishment of a girls' school on newly reclaimed land in downtown Tokyo. But since the government had just preempted this field with the establishment of the Tokyo School for Girls (Tōkyō

35. Ibid., p. 182.
36. Ibid., pp. 102–112.
37. Ibid., p. 180.
38. Ibid., p. 175.

Jōgakkō) in 1872, Mori finally decided to invest his money in the cause of commercial education.[39]

So confident had Mori been of the demand for this sort of training that shortly before leaving America he had on his own initiative contracted for the services of an American expert, in full expectation that the Japanese government would appropriately employ him. William C. Whitney had been operating a business college in Newark which Mori had visited to inspect the studies of Tomita Tetsunosuke, who had been enrolled there.[40] The government, however, having in April 1874 opened its own Ginkōgakukyoku (bank training section) within the finance ministry, turned a deaf ear to Mori's entreaties, arguing that no further initiatives were required in the field, and leaving Whitney without a job.[41] This is not to suggest that the Commercial Institute was built in effect for Whitney, but the various turns that Mori's mind took before hitting upon the establishment of this particular institution do show how very much his energies and ambitions outstripped his actual opportunities and how much he remained a frustrated outsider to the world of official education.

Mori, with the help of Tomita, then turned to the enlistment of private support. Katsu Kaishū, Shibusawa Eiichi, the two Mistukuris, and Fukuzawa have been listed as prominent contributors. Fukuzawa wrote a prospectus entitled "Shōgakkō o tateru no shui" (Basic reasons for establishing a Commercial School), dated 1 November 1874, in hopes of obtaining additional private donations, while Shibusawa managed with the approval of Governor Ōkubo Ichiō to transfer to the use of the institute a sizeable proportion of the Tokyo Common Fund, of which he recently had been appointed custodian.[42] So Mori was not without friends in high, though nonofficial, places; and with Shibusawa and Fukuzawa he had made partisans of the two men who in their respective roles, as entrepreneur and as apologist, would come most to symbolize the emerging world of Japanese private business enterprise.

Instruction at the Commercial Institute proceeded along the latest American lines and entirely in the English language, using

39. KKM, p. 78; OTM, pp. 62–63.
40. Robert S. Schwantes, "American Influences in the Education of Early Meiji Japan" (unpublished Ph.D. dissertation, Harvard University, 1950), p. 195.
41. Karasawa Tomitarō, *Kindai nihon kyōikushi* (Tokyo, 1968), pp. 123–126.
42. KKM, p. 78; OTM, p. 63; *Zenshū* I, 323, letter from Mori Arinori to Takagi Saburō, 10 Sep 1875; Kyugoro Obata, *An Interpretation of the Life of Viscount Shibusawa* (Tokyo, 1938), p. 155ff.

Bryant and Stratton's *Bookkeeping* and *Commercial Arithmetic,* Wayland's *Political Economy,* and the Spencerian system of penmanship. The school was not exactly swamped with applicants. The opening class, including several transfers from Fukuzawa's school (later Keiō University) numbered about twenty-three, and only ten of these could be described as having applied under positive motivation.[43] Mori was bucking not only a general public ignorance regarding the value of modern commercial education but also a deep-seated traditional prejudice against commercialism and all its ways.[44]

Mori upon assignment to Peking turned over the superintendency of the school to Yano Jirō, whom he continued to advise by mail. Yano retained the directorship until 1893. General management (including financial responsibility) was turned over in November 1875 to the Tokyo Chamber of Commerce, whence it passed to Tokyo Prefecture in 1876, thence to the agriculture and commerce ministry in 1884, and finally to the ministry of education in 1885, where it has rested ever since. Mori's Commercial Institute was four times renamed: as the Tōkyō Shōgyō Gakkō (Tokyo Commercial School) in 1884; as the Tōkyō Kōtō Shōgyō Gakkō (Tokyo Higher Commercial School) in 1885; as the Tōkyō Shōka Daigaku (Tokyo Commercial University) in 1920; and as Hitotsubashi University in 1949. Despite this bewildering devolution of nomenclature and management, and notwithstanding the fact that it is Yano's statue which graces the new postwar campus at Kunitachi, the Hitotsubashi student today still looks upon Mori as the original founder of his school.[45]

Mori in the passage on language in his introduction to *Education in Japan* had written almost frantically of the commercial challenge that had been thrust upon his country. Joseph Henry had described Mori as having "no aptitude for business," and one can imagine how keenly Mori must have felt his own inadequacies in the long-drawn-out and embarrassing hassle with the contractors for the steamers *Kuroda* and *Capron.*[46]

Fukuzawa's prospectus gives eloquent expression to the spirit in which the Commercial Institute was conceived.[47] The bene-

43. Schwantes, "American Influences," p. 153; Karasawa, *Kindai nihon kyōikushi,* p. 126.
44. Alfred Stead, *Great Japan: A Study of National Efficiency* (London, 1906), p. 198.
45. Personal testimony of several Hitotsubashi students and graduates.
46. See Chapters Five and Six.
47. *Zenshū* I, 319–320 has an undated memorandum, filed here between documents relating to the Commercial Institute of 1874–1875 and giving Mori's reasons for the establishment of commercial education. This memo-

ficial competition between individual Japanese merchants, he begins, must now give way to competition between Japanese merchants as a whole and foreign traders as a group. Western merchants have achieved an economic stranglehold on native business reminiscent of the control long exercised by the big city wholesalers over the country general stores, or *yorozuya*. The *yorozuya*, however, at least know the rules of the game, and can write proper letters to the wholesalers, which is a lot more than the Japanese merchant can do in his dealings with foreign traders. Fukuzawa speaks with scorn of the foreign merchants as parasitical middlemen who must be driven from the port cities before Japanese commerce will be able to stand on its own feet. He looks forward to the day when native importers will be able to deal directly with wholesale houses in London and Paris; but this will require a knowledge of bookkeeping and of modern business correspondence in the English language. Reflecting on the fact that schools have proliferated in every field except commercial education, he warns: "The Western nations as a rule have commercial schools for the training of their businessmen, just as we in feudal times had places where a samurai could learn the martial arts. In a military struggle one does not proceed to the battlefield without having first learned the art of swordsmanship. By the same token we cannot take on our foreign opponents in commercial warfare without a prior study of commerce. The man of commerce must ever keep his eye fixed . . . on the trade struggle in which our entire nation is engaged."[48]

Mori's major surviving comment on the school was delivered in a letter written to Yano Jirō from London on 25 October 1882, in which he expressed his immense satisfaction that a graduate of the institute, Watanabe Senjirō, had arrived to take over the London office of the Mitsui Bussan Company from the Englishman who had been managing it. Mori shook his head at the "commercial malpractices" rampant since the opening of the country, but trusted that: "our Commercial Institute will become the bastion of sound business education in Japan, and its graduates will in the future

---

randum so closely follows a speech Mori gave before the Osaka Chamber of Commerce in 1885, however, that it would seem on the face of it to be an outline, or a set of notes for, that later speech. Like the speech, the memorandum emphasizes the challenge specifically to the Osaka merchant, and its knowledgeable points with reference to Chinese commercial acumen suggest a date subsequent to Mori's stay, 1876–1878, in Peking. See Chapter Ten.

48. KKM, pp. 78–82 gives the full text of Fukuzawa Yukichi, "Shōgakkō o tateru no shui" (Basic reasons for establishing a Commercial School), 1874. Quotation from p. 81.

very likely play the leading role in commerce both domestic and foreign."[49] Mori's "malpractices" included ethical as well as professional shortcomings. He enclosed a sum of money to be spent on prize books for graduating students who had "excelled in moral conduct," and urged Yano to choose them carefully.

Nagai Michio has seen the Shōhō Kōshūjo as a symbol of progressive, rationalistic, efficient, technologically oriented education, but an education pursued neither for its own sake nor for the sake of the individual, but purely for the extrinsic purposes of economic development and national power.[50] These are profound questions which can and should be raised, but preferably at a somewhat later date, perhaps from the mid-1890's onward when Japanese technical and vocational education first begins to flesh out its skinny frame and give the analyst a reasonable amount of data to work with. It is possible that Mori's valiant band of two or three dozen, wrestling with the latest elementary texts from America, may have harbored the consequences Nagai has described. The emphasis on national need was clear enough. But there was no suggestion at the time that the benefit of the individual was not also involved; and business education never has been something to be pursued for its own intrinsic delight, like art or philosophy.

What may most safely be said of the Commercial Institute is that its orientation was intensely practical. It attempted to come to grips with the economic challenge in a concrete and realistic fashion. It is not perhaps entirely coincidental that Hitotsubashi University today should have taken the lead in developing an island of Keynesian economics in a sea of academic Marxism. The term "practical" of course harbors an ambivalence: Nagai in effect suggests that Mori's approach was *too,* i.e., too narrowly, practical. But in the mid-seventies the problem perhaps lay elsewhere: in the fact, as Mori and Fukuzawa saw it, that in matters commercial nobody was being practical *enough.*

INDIVIDUAL AND STATE: CONTINUING AMBIGUITIES

Of Mori's three institutional innovations, the Commercial Institute afforded the least likely point of departure for speculation on the nature of Man. The contractual marriage, on the other hand,

---

49. KKM, p. 83, citing letter from Mori Arinori to Yano Jirō, 25 Oct. 1882.

50. Nagai Michio, "Chishikijin no seisan rūto," in *Kindai nihon shisōshi kōza,* vol. 4: *Chishikijin no seisei to yakuwari* (Tokyo, 1959), p. 203.

with its respect for the personality of woman, would seem to rest on a concept of the dignity of the individual as explicit and as profound as any contemporary Anglo-American liberal could possibly have hoped for. The latter, however, would have been hard put to applaud wholeheartedly the rationale which Mori advanced in connection with the political activities of the Meirokusha.

The typical Western liberal derived his view of Political Man from some still more fundamental concept of Man *sub specie aeternitatis*. Mori on the whole, however, maintained during his Meirokusha years the disconnection, already evidenced in Washington, between his view of politics and his concept of the individual as expressed in his concern for freedom of conscience. "Shūkyō" and "Minsen giin setsuritsu kengonsho no hyō" (hereinafter "Minsen giin"), contributed to the *Meiroku zasshi* within a month of each other, echo both his earlier defense of religious liberty and his earlier cautiousness with respect to representative government. "Minsen giin" made some mention of the relation of the people, as a whole, to their government; so did "Gakusha shokubunron no hyō" (hereinafter "Gakusha shokubun"), which commented also on the role of the scholar in government service; and the annual report to the Meirokusha touched on the even broader question of the intellectual in politics. Mori did not go so far, however, as to stage a confrontation between an abstracted individual and an abstracted state, on behalf of political liberty, to match his disquisition on religious liberty.

The relatively greater difficulties attendant upon the achievement of political as opposed to religious liberty have been amply illustrated by the history of Germany, where a subjective sense of intellectual freedom and of the sanctity of one's private thoughts has long flourished within the interstices of objective political despotism, whether feudal or imperial or fascist. "Lutheranism," in the words of A. J. P. Taylor, for instance, "though it preached the absolute supremacy of the individual conscience within, preached an equally absolute supremacy for the territorial power without."[51] The genesis of political liberty in modern Japan was complicated not only by the practical difficulties inherent in the rapid transformation of a feudal society but also by conceptual hurdles peculiar to the Confucian cultural orbit. Political liberty as an operative political formula only made sense upon the prior philosophical assumption of the value of the individual in his own right, quite apart from his value to society or to the state. In the Confucian world-view, however, the social nexus was all; and the

51. A. J. P. Taylor, *The Course of German History: A Survey of the Development of Germany Since 1815* (New York, 1946), p. 19.

political realm, that is to say the state, was coterminous with it. The philosophical "leap" required of the early Meiji intellectual aspiring to a true understanding of Western democratic principles was, therefore, an enormous one.

The most serviceable conceptual handle was the doctrine of natural rights, or *tenpu jinken,* which provided the theoretical basis for the Popular Rights Movement, or *jiyū minken undō,* from the mid-1870's onward. On even firmer ground perhaps was the Japanese Christian who through a conversion experience had moved beyond mere intellectual to a fuller emotional and psychological awareness of individuality. In any case it was necessary to grasp quite consciously some principle, whether sacred or secular in inspiration, which placed the individual beyond the claims of the social or political collectivity. This was the yardstick against which Mori's political and quasipolitical pronouncements would have to be reckoned.

Mori's comments on women provoked a reasonable question by Li Hung-chang at Paoting: "I am greatly struck with your remarks. Do you belong to the Christian religion?" To this Mori replied: "I profess none of those so-called religions: the Christian, the Buddhist, the Mohammedan or anything else. I am a plain man, just as appearing now before you. The aim of my life is simply to live an honest and harmless life. I nevertheless find it extremely difficult to so conduct myself, in consequence of the constant interference of this same self of mine against it."[52] When the Reverend Dr. W. A. P. Martin, head of the Imperial College at Peking, asked Mori at a diplomatic function whether he was a Christian, he had received an essentially similar, and in the words of one observer "characteristic," answer: "I endeavour to live so that men may think that I am a Christian."[53] Here in 1876 (or possibly 1877-78 for the second quote) we at last have an explicit confession of the nature of Mori's own personal faith: a private ethical code which had drawn copiously on the moral insights of Christianity while rejecting the church in its dogmatic and organizational aspects, and which perceived Christ at the most as exemplar, not as personal saviour.

Such political consequences as Mori was able to draw from his

52. From the second Li-Mori interview, *Zenshū* I, 178. English in the original.

53. The quotation, and the description of the same as "characteristic" of Mori, appear in Marquis L. Gordon, *An American Missionary in Japan* (Boston, 1892), p. 191. Mori upon arrival in Peking, Gordon further relates, had presented Dr. Martin with a Japanese translation of the latter's *Evidences of Christianity,* by Nakamura Masanao.

religious view were inevitably affected by this duality of focus: a profound respect for the individually held belief or opinion, coupled with a certain suspicion and disdain for the great historical creeds. "Shūkyō" followed *Religious Freedom in Japan* unswervingly in its defense of private conscience; but there was evident in this article an important shift of emphasis in Mori's view of the political context conducive to that end. The earlier pamphlet had been concerned with the freedom of religion *from* the secular authority and had attacked the organization of religion by the state, specifically the official promotion of Shintoism and Buddhism. "Shūkyō," by contrast, seems more concerned to define the proper limitations on freedom *for* religion as related to the general interests of the state, and turns a wary eye this time on organized religion as such, including by implication Christianity. It is, specifically, a rebuttal of previous articles in the *Meiroku zasshi* by Tsuda calling for the adoption of Christianity as the national faith, and by Nishi suggesting that politics and religion were two totally unrelated realms and that the government therefore would do best not to concern itself with religious affairs at all.[54]

In a brief introduction to the translated excerpts from Phillimore and Vattel which made up the bulk of his article, Mori wrote:

> Mr. Tsuda argues that it would be the wisest policy to choose the loftiest religion in the world and introduce it into this country as our national faith. Mr. Nishi believes that the right to freedom of worship may best be established for all ages by severing all connection between politics and religion, on the premise that they derive from entirely different sets of principles. My opinion of the matter is that the proper function of the government lies solely in the protection of the person and property of the people; that therefore religious matters, generally speaking, should be left to the free choice of each individual person; but that in instances where belief leads to overt actions harmful to other persons the government may properly formulate laws to control the same.[55]

The excerpts which follow seem to be offered primarily in elucidation of this last premise. Vattel's *Law of Nations* is quoted

---

54. Tsuda Masamichi, "Kaika o susumeru hōhō o ronsu" (On a method for advancing enlightenment), MRZ no. 3 (April 1874), in MBZ XVIII, 65; Nishi Amane, "Kyōmon ron" (On religious sectarianism), MRZ no. 4 (March 1874), no. 5 (April 1874) and no. 6 (May 1874), in MBZ, XVIII, 70–71, 74, and 82–84.

55. Mori Arinori, "Shūkyō" MRZ no. 6 (May 1874), MBZ, XVIII, 83.

to the effect that religious freedom does not comprise the further right wilfully to disturb the public order, which it is the proper duty of governments to secure. This is to be achieved, however, not by the repression of religion but simply by the control of publicly harmful conduct. The best way to avoid sectarian strife indeed, Vattel suggests, is by a policy of across-the-board toleration. This eighteenth-century Swiss philosopher of international law, writing in 1758, with papal claims and sectarian strife no doubt very much on his mind, insists nevertheless on the inviolable sovereignty of the state over all foreign churches and all domestic factions. The nineteenth-century English jurist, Sir Robert J. Phillimore, also seems to have been quoted in defense of that sovereignty, with a passage from his *Commentaries upon International Law* (1854–1857) which chiseled away at the purported rights of the Western powers to intervene on behalf of Christian subjects of the Porte.[56]

Both authorities were in favor of religious freedom in principle but—in the very passages excerpted by Mori—advanced numerous instances, in the realm of public policy, where that principle would have to be bent to preserve the still more fundamental principle of national sovereignty. Phillimore cited cases where the state might properly proscribe an alien religion in the interest of public safety, and Vattel was quoted as investing the sovereign with the exclusive right to adopt, or to revise, the national faith.

The nation states of Europe had emerged after a long contest with religious power. The process had little parallel, and the problem little relevance, in the historical context of Japan. Mori's excerpts, however, were deliberately and carefully selected from various portions of the authors' works, and it is clear that he now required that the sanctity of conscience be adjusted to the security of the state: an adjustment painlessly enough effected, perhaps, with a simple and private creed like his own which made few if any demands on the state either politically or theoretically and asked of the state in turn no more than to be left alone. Mori's concern for public order and the harmony of the realm were reflected even more strongly in his comments on purely political questions.

56. It would be reasonable to suppose that Mori used a popular American edition of Vattel's *Le droit des gens,* originally published in London in 1758, namely, Emerich de Vattel, *The Law of Nations; or, Principles of the Law of Nature Applied to the Conduct and Affairs of Nations and Sovereigns;* translated from the French with notes by Joseph Chitty and E. D. Ingraham (Philadelphia, 1859). The excerpts from Phillimore likewise would have come from an early edition, perhaps from Robert J. Phillimore, *Commentaries upon International Law* (Philadelphia, 1854–1857).

The only members of the Meirokusha who came out in favor of Itagaki's proposal for an assembly were Nishimura and Tsuda. Mori expressed his opposition promptly, together with Nishi and Katō; and even Fukuzawa, ever a staunch admirer of Anglo-American political institutions, found much fault in both parties to the dispute and did not lend his unequivocal support to the establishment of a Diet until 1879.[57] Nishi's criticism was primarily on the philosophical plane: he could not accept the doctrine of the social contract which the petitioners seemed to be propagating. Katō's perspective was essentially historical: he drew on the theories of J. C. Blüntschli and of F. K. Biedermann to argue the prematurity of an assembly given the contemporary customs and conditions of Japan. Fukuzawa's scruples were primarily practical: the petitioners did not yet really know what it was they were after; the only purpose of participation in government, after all, was to secure individual rights, but the petitioners had no sense yet of what those rights might be; they merely wanted to share in the same, old, oppressive governmental power.[58]

Mori's "Minsen giin" stands closest to Fukuzawa in orientation, but of all the disputants his arguments come through as the most patently—or perhaps one could say the most honestly—political. "It goes without saying," Mori commences, "that broad discussion by the public of national political affairs is a sign of the true achievement of national independence and of the advancing prosperity of the people." He puts forward, however, three objections to the present petitioners and to the form of their petition. First of all, he questions their motivations. They have called for an assembly as the best means of healing the rift that has arisen between the governing and the governed as a result of the suppression of public discussion. But who is to blame for the latter? The petitioners were for the most part in office when the press ordinance of October 1873 was promulgated and must share responsibility for it with their former colleagues still in office: "When we look into the matter closely we discover that most of these gentlemen were of the party which formerly advocated the invasion of Korea. They say that if their policy had been carried out, there would be no restraints on public discussion today; but I find that impossible to believe."

"Sour grapes" is the essence of Mori's accusation. He questions the sincerity of the petitioners' liberal protestations, and views them

57. Carmen Blacker, *The Japanese Enlightenment: A Study of the Writings of Fukuzawa Yukichi* (Cambridge, England, 1964), p. 117.
58. Ibid., p. 114.

primarily as government "outs" wanting back in. Mori's second criticism regards the extravagance of the language used to attack the government, "words which I never should have expected from such well-known gentlemen of intelligence as the signers of this petition." Mori's first two objections are, strictly speaking, *ad hominem* rather than substantive. It is his third point which deserves serious attention, in which he surmises that the petitioners have not given sufficient consideration to the method of establishing their assembly:

> Will they establish it by fiat of the government to the people? Or will they have the people establish it of their own accord after notifying the government of such intention? Or will they establish it upon securing the prior permission of the government? Considering the phrase in the petition, "We trust that you will give these remarks due consideration," it looks as though they want the assembly established by the government on behalf of the people. If that be the case, then what we have is not a people's assembly, but a government assembly. Despite the sobriquet "popular," the representatives will be selected from among the people by the government. The government, which has selected the representatives according to its own liking, will be free again whenever its displeasure has been incurred to abolish the assembly, even after it has been properly constituted.

Such an assembly, Mori concludes, would end up being a mere mouthpiece for the government.

Mori's rejoinder was not entirely relevant to Itagaki's proposal. The petition had stated clearly in several places that the representatives were to be chosen by the people. Under contemporary circumstances the first step in any case had to be a willingness to consider the matter at the highest government level. And in the long run *what* was to be established was the fundamental question, not *how*. Given basic agreement as to the objective, method would probably not deserve quite the same prominence as Mori seemed to attach to it. The most flattering construction that can be placed on Mori's line of argument is that he is holding out for some more ideal procedure, such as a constitutional convention, to which he has given serious thought; the least flattering, that he is simply running indiscriminate theoretical interference on behalf of the team already in power. In absence of corroboration for either of these two extreme interpretations, or of any concrete proposals of Mori's own, it seems reasonable to assume that he still held to his previous reservations on representative government; that he felt sufficient and sincere attention was being given the matter in the Sain (Ministry of the Left), which since 1872 had been discussing the very same proposals Itagaki was now proclaiming as his own;[59] and that in any case he would have preferred to see the project entrusted to somewhat more disinterested hands.

Where Mori's views on representative government at the national level tended to work away from his earlier enthusiasm for the American model, his opinion on the relationship between the localities and the center at this point took a turn away from the centralization urged upon Ōkubo Toshimichi in 1869 toward a more decentralized concept. The evidence is in an informal discussion which took place between Fukuzawa, Katō, and Mori before the regular proceedings of the 1 May 1875 meeting of the Meirokusha, as recorded in English for the *Japan Weekly Mail* of 19 June. The fact that the *Mail* was forced to print a retraction the next week, on the grounds that the article "was not authorized by the Society and contains several errors of an important nature," would not affect the substance of the point Mori was beyond doubt making.

Katō had been arguing that it was no use giving the people representative institutions until they had developed sufficient "recoiling power" to seek such liberties on their own initiative. To this Fukuzawa had replied that the initiative of the government in abolishing the han had not prevented the people from grasping at the liberties thereby established. Katō countered that the *ken* (prefectures) had been created out of a feeling for national unity rather than for liberty, to which Fukuzawa rejoined that the samurai, as a part of the people, had seized the han on behalf of the nation and out of a thirst for liberty, much as the English barons had forced Magna Charta on King John. It was a rambling postprandial chat, full of non sequiturs. It ended on a final interjection by Mori, as follows:

> I rejoiced indeed at the time of the abolition of the han and the creation of the *ken*. But I cannot now feel as I felt then, for this recoiling power of the people has become so weak that it has almost disappeared. A man from Satsuma becomes the governor of Kaga, and a man from Choshiu becomes the governor of Oshiu. But these men, not being natives of the provinces they are appointed to govern, take no sufficient pains to

---

59. Ōkubo, "Meirokusha no hitobito," p. 148.

acquaint themselves with the state of affairs of the provinces they are thus sent to govern. I judge therefore that the power of the people today is weaker than it was during the time of the daimios, and in proof of it I adduce this fact that the people of a province cannot choose their governor from among the natives of that province, but rest contentedly under the rule of a man who comes from another province. This seems to me like a person living in a house submitting to have his housekeeping affairs controlled by his neighbor. Surely this cannot be called independence! I am a man of Satsuma, and I would not permit a man of any other province to rule over me. I would . . . have a man of Satsuma put in his place. The government of a province can only be accomplished with success by a native of that province. But if the people obey men from other provinces who are appointed to rule over them, it cannot be said that they understand their rights, and thus I infer that the abolition of the han and the creation of the *ken* came too soon.

Mori would seem to be upholding Katō's admonition against premature institutional change, arguing (against Fukuzawa) that the *ken* actually represented a regression from the standpoint of liberty. What we have here probably is an unconscious survival of traditional han loyalties, strengthened by a recent reading of Mill on local government. In any case, however, it is clear that Mori is ready to contemplate a far greater degree of local autonomy than had been granted within the new national structure, or than he himself had advocated in 1868–69.

Mori comes closest to defining the relationship of the individual to the state in his rebuttal of Fukuzawa's assumption of an antagonism—albeit a creative one—between the people and their government. To Fukuzawa, the great driving force in the history of any nation was the spirit of its people, and it was in the reactivation of the initiative of individual Japanese—so long accustomed to direction from above—that he placed his greatest hopes for the future progress of Japan. Hence his consistent emphasis on the creation of a broad private sector—in religion, education, publishing, agriculture, commerce—free of government meddling or control.[60] In the fourth serial pamphlet (i.e., chapter) of *Gakumon no susume,* Fukuzawa had taken a broad swipe at the age-old propensity of educated Japanese to rush to the government for employment; and in an attempt to define more precisely just what the

60. Blacker, *Japanese Enlightenment,* pp. 96, 97, 108.

proper relationship between the government and the people should be, he developed the analogy of a living organism which maintained its health by virtue of an equilibrium between external pressures and internal responses. The nation was the organism; the government, its vital inner forces; the people, its indispensable outside stimuli. The relationship between the latter two was ideally a harmonious one, but the difference between their respective functions was very clearly defined. Each had its own proper sphere of activity. It was essential, however, that the stimuli should stimulate, and that was why Fukuzawa urged scholars and intellectuals to remain in the private sector, enlightening the people and acting as a goad to the government.[61]

Mori wrote "Gakusha shokubun" to defend the scholar's usefulness inside the government, and in the course of doing so put forth a concept of the fundamental harmony and identity of government and people which contrasted markedly with the social discords he had so openly welcomed in *Religious Freedom in Japan:*

> When it comes to formulating the rights of the people, it shall be sufficient to have sincerity of purpose, wisdom in argument, and the active interest of our educated classes. Some persons, however, are not content with this point of view. What are we to make, for instance, of the doctrine that, "the rectification of the entire national structure can proceed only when the government and the people confront each other"? It is the public duty of the people to respond without fail, in matters civil and military, to the requirements of the nation, and it goes without saying that every person must comply to the best of his abilities. If you ask what is meant by this "people," it refers to those persons who have the right to bear this responsibility. Accordingly, officials too are "the people"; so are the nobility; so are the commoners. Every single person whose name appears on our registers as Japanese belongs to "the people" and is obliged to shoulder its burdens. The "government" therefore is the government of all the people, established for the people, and maintained by the people.[62]

After thus challenging Fukuzawa's theoretical premises, Mori proceeded to question Fukuzawa's practical advice to scholars, sur-

61. Fukuzawa Yukichi, *Gakumon no susume,* Iwanami Shoten (Tokyo, 1966), p. 39ff.
62. Mori Arinori, "Gakusha shokubun ron no hyō," MRZ no. 2 (March 1874), in MBZ XVIII, 59.

mising that: "if they would give careful consideration to the station they ought to occupy in conducting the affairs of the world, every one of them should be able to find the position best suited to himself for advancing the public welfare: some of them going into government and some of them into private life, with no particular distinction between the two." What Mori feared specifically was that: "if we ever maintain that the public good can better be served in private occupations than through official service, then we are in effect saying that the national weal will first be promoted when our scholars have left their government posts and entrusted them to incompetents."

The Confucian notion of the unity of thought and action had created a traditional bias in favor of official careers. Mori had been raised in that tradition, and there would have been relatively little in his own professional experience to have challenged the essential soundness of its premises. As a member of the government and of the diplomatic service practically from the very first days of their establishment, he was acutely aware of the shortage of good talent, especially of people with knowledge of and interest in the West, within official ranks. Mori's argument therefore derives largely from a practical consideration. There were important theoretical assumptions implicit, however, in his attack on Fukuzawa's somewhat crude but highly suggestive analogy. Where the latter viewed the relationship between the government and the people in terms of a fundamental dialectic, Mori seemed to conceive of them as a pair of harmonious, parallel, coordinate forces.

The debate, it is true, revolved around the *government* and the people rather than the individual (or the people) and the *state*, and was not properly speaking addressed to the issue of sovereignty, which would come to occupy the attentions of the best political minds in Japan during the 1880's. In the democratic ideal the line between the governing and the governed was indeed drawn as lightly as possible, and Mori's definition of the government here was virtually a direct translation of Lincoln's famous original. Mori elaborated: "The 'confrontation' of the government and the people, therefore, is a thing neither known to theory, nor visible in fact. In Europe there were many countries where the power of the king had been unlimited, and where political authority had been wielded by a single family. This incurred the displeasure of the people, who accordingly dissented and rebelled. Thereafter limitations were placed upon power, political authority was placed in multiple hands, and the political structure changed into a constitutional monarchy or a republic. But I have yet to hear of a theory, much less an example, of the people and the government confronting each other as external stimulus and internal response."

Fukuzawa's analogy invited a certain amount of ridicule, but it had been the essence of Western philosophy to make, rather than to slough off, distinctions. The historical democratization of power described by Mori had been mightily abetted by a theoretical discourse which had posited the individual, the people, the government, and the state as distinct entities the mutual relationship of which constituted the heart of the political debate. Lincoln after all stood on the shoulders of Harrington, Locke, and Montesquieu, among others. The facile, rather self-complacent definitions of the "government" and the "people" which Mori gives us in "Gakusha shokubun" in February 1874 go a long way toward explaining the equanimity with which he would view the press and libel laws and his readiness to see the Meirokusha shunted off onto an apolitical siding in 1875. Fukuzawa chose to view the continued publication of the *Meiroku zasshi* in terms of political principle. Mori, however accurate his surmise as to the government's actual intentions, either failed to see or refused to admit that a principle was—certainly up to a point—at stake.

Mori in his *Meiroku zasshi* articles did not so much as once use the term *tenpu jinken,* or "natural rights," which flowed so freely from the pens of his fellow contributors and which, as Motoyama Yukihiko has pointed out, provided a philosophical common denominator for writers as diverse as Fukuzawa, Nishi, Tsuda, and (at that time) Katō.[63] Neither had he placed his individual in a transcendental framework, as had Niijima Jō. Nor had he as yet developed a definition uniquely his own. Against this background of theoretical ambiguity, Mori's pronouncements on domestic politics during 1873–1875 take on the color of transitional, ad hoc, opinions: inching away somewhat from a typical "liberal" position on religion and the state, moving toward a more liberal one on local autonomy, and simply marking time on representative government. They would be subjected to further revision by fresh information, new experiences, and changed circumstances.

DIPLOMACY: NATIONAL SOVEREIGNTY AND THE RULE OF REASON

It is not surprising that Mori should have revealed more of his mind to us through statements on international, as opposed to

63. Motoyama Yukihiko, "Bunmei kaika ki ni okeru shin chishikijin no shisō: Meirokusha no hitobito o chūshin to shite," *Jinbun gakuhō,* 4:19–20 (February 1954).

domestic, political affairs. Foreign affairs was the field in which he exercised an ongoing, daily responsibility and the area in which he was at last, in the winter of 1875–76, permitted to exercise a dramatic personal initiative. Mori's view of interstate relations tells us, curiously enough, a great deal about his concept of interpersonal relations as well, and about the general moral-ethical context in which his apostleship of "enlightenment" was conducted.

Nothing is known of Mori's possible involvement in the territorial disputes over the Ryukyu and Kurile Islands which occurred during his assignment as secretary in the foreign ministry, beyond Kimura Kyō's supposition that he may have worked to promote the exchange of Sakhalin for the Kuriles (Treaty of St. Petersburg, 1875) after learning from his old friend Kuroda that it would be an advantageous deal.[64] Mori's recorded statements for the period have to do rather with the general problem of the unequal treaties and with the specific issue of residence and travel in the interior of Japan by members of the foreign community.

Mori as a student in London had been imbued, through Laurence Oliphant, with an immensely idealistic view of what diplomacy ought to be: an idealism which had been strengthened by Oliphant's tirades against diplomacy as it actually was. This had manifested itself at Washington primarily in a naive optimism, which Hamilton Fish had taken some pains to correct. By 1874 we find Mori resting his idealism more soundly on what might be called the traditional Western precepts of international law of the pre-, or at most semi-positivist school. These in turn revolved for Mori around the two fundamental concepts of national sovereignty, and of *jōri,* or "reason" both as a normative principle and as a practical method of conducting diplomatic business.

In a memorandum written in early 1874 and entitled "Gaikoku kōsai ni jōjitsu o mochiizaru beki no gi" (On the avoidance of sentiment in diplomatic intercourse),[65] Mori juxtaposed *jōri* with *jōjitsu,* and urged that in dealings with the foreign representatives reliance be placed exclusively on the former. Each of these two terms, given here as "reason" versus "sentiment," but equally renderable in this particular context as "impersonal principle" versus "personal considerations," harbored a wide range of nuances. *Jōri* in the narrowest definition referred to "reason" as logic, or logical sequence; a bit more broadly, to the "reasonable" or what squares with reason; and, in the broadest sense, to the fundamental principles of order in the universe. *Jōjitsu* referred to

64. KKM, p. 67.
65. *Zenshū* I, 114–116.

sentiment, particularly to sentimental considerations, special connections, and favoritism in the conduct of public affairs, and evoked the entire cosmos of personalism in which Japanese social and political relations traditionally had been grounded. *Jōri* it is true had some roots in Confucian universalism, but Mori seems to be using it in a fully Western sense, in an appeal to impersonal, universalistic "reason" as a mode of argument and as a guide to interpersonal and interstate relations. Mori begins: "In our dealings with the foreign representatives, it is not only useless but positively harmful, no matter what the subject, to bring appeals to sentiment into the discussion. That is a clumsy and unreliable method . . . If you argue from reason, you leave no further room for complaint or for resentment. On the contrary, the other party will respect your point and deepen his liking for you."

Mori warns that *jōjitsu* places its user on the defensive and puts Japan, the weaker party, in the position of begging the treaty powers for favors. He also points out that the use of *jōri*, to be convincing, cannot be dragged in at the last moment, after the *jōjitsu* game has already been played and lost. He lines up all the arguments that the opponents of interior travel and mixed residence have ever thought of, then shows how the foreign envoys with their superior logic will no doubt proceed to bowl them all over. Mori apparently had great faith in the amenability of Westerners to *jōri*, and this served to keep alive his trust that treaty revision would begin to move off dead center if only the Japanese would learn to counter the West with its own mode of argument. On 10 February 1874 the Jōyaku Kaitei Torishirabe Kyoku, or Investigative Bureau for the Renegotiation of Treaties, was established in the foreign ministry, and on 20 May Mori was appointed to its directorship. Already from early January he had been working, together with the ministry's American legal advisor, E. Peshine Smith, on a new treaty draft, and on 25 March had produced a model Japanese-American treaty over his own name, which he shortly thereafter submitted to the American Minister John A. Bingham for comment and annotation.[66]

Mori's was a treaty for full judicial and tariff equality, "far more

66. Mori submitted his draft to Bingham some time after 29 April 1874, although it is not clear who actually took the document to the American minister, or whether it was forwarded before or after it had been viewed by Foreign Minister Terajima. In any case neither Terajima nor Bingham had seen it before the twenty-ninth, and although Mori acknowledged his debt to Peshine Smith for portions of his draft, it is clear that the document was very much the product of his own initiative and his own particular point of view. (See Inau, *Gaikō shisōshi*, pp. 117–121.)

radical" in the words of Inau Tentarō[67] than the very liberal treaty eventually negotiated by Yoshida Kiyonari and William Evarts in 1878. It called, in its most striking clauses, for the abolition of the consular courts, for the rescinding of all previous treaties, and for a ten-year time limit on the new treaty with provision for unilateral abrogation upon two years' advance notice. Mori's gumption here derived largely from his definition of Japan as a fully sovereign state, entitled to all the rights and privileges pertaining under international law to full sovereignty.

This was the burden of his "Dokuritsu kokken gi" in the *Meiroku zasshi* of May 1874. Mori complained: "There are persons who object to the idea of our Empire as a free and independent country. They point out that our culture remains primitive, our military strength insignificant, our political system as yet to be developed, and that we are as a result still bound by the treaty system. They contend that much as we would like to exercise the rights and responsibilities of independence, we are under the circumstances in no position to do so. Such opinions are sheer nonsense, and unworthy of refutation. It would not be difficult however to do so, and to make a clear case for the sovereign independence of our country." The essay begins with a definition of a sovereign state as one which possesses *dokuritsu kokken*, or "the sovereign rights of independence," and is in complete control of both its domestic and its foreign affairs. Mori then describes various degrees of dilution of sovereignty in the cases of tributary states such as Tibet, autonomous entities such as Hungary, or states like China or Persia bound by treaties imposed upon them by virtue of *force majeure;* and he places Japan alongside the United States in the category of full sovereignty.

States voluntarily surrender a portion of that sovereignty, Mori continues, when they make treaties. These if freely entered upon may, however, be discarded upon expiration of the time limit, or abrogated at will if no time limit has been specified. The treaties binding China, he points out, were forced upon her as a result of military defeat; they cannot be revised without the consent of the Western powers, and have placed her under restraint indefinitely. Japan by contrast, Mori argues—in a fashion which, historically speaking at least, smacks of special pleading—entered upon her treaties with the West of her own free will. "Due to the many inconveniences which beset us upon the opening of the country," nearly half of Japan's judicial and tariff autonomy has temporarily been made over to the treaty powers, but all this will be retrieved,

67. Ibid., p. 127.

either through revision or through abrogation of the treaties, as soon as the time limit has expired. "Even without new treaties" [i.e., in the event of abrogation], Mori concludes rather sanguinely, "we still have the law of nations, and that should suffice to sustain our international intercourse and trade on an ever more cordial and increasingly advantageous basis."

Mori seems to be directing his arguments both at the Western envoys and at pussy-footers on the Japanese side. The one difficulty he is willing to concede is the immaturity of the Japanese legal system, and here he goes straight back to his advice to Yokoyama in 1865, calling once again for the development of laws consistent both with foreign codes and with the best in the native Japanese tradition. The implicit point of the essay, however, was that the internal conditions of a particular country strictly speaking were irrelevant to the question of its sovereignty under international law, and Mori in the early summer of 1874 accordingly urged the foreign minister to feel free to take the high ground in his dispute with the resident envoys on the interior travel issue.

The Japanese government on 31 May had issued a new set of passport regulations, against which the envoys had jointly protested on 8 June. Mori, fearing that Terajima would waver in his defense of the new code, on 12 June composed still another memorandum, this time "Gaikoku kōsai o tadasu no gi" (On the reform of our diplomatic intercourse),[68] in which he urged the foreign minister to take his stand on the principles of international law and to refuse to give in to pressure: "When Perry made his incursion at Uraga and forcibly demanded that we conclude a treaty of commerce and navigation, we had neither a knowledge of the principles of international law with which to counter these demands, nor the courage to refuse them. So we heedlessly gave in to him, parting with a portion of our sovereign rights and condemning our country to a long period of troubled circumstances. When I was serving in Washington, an American once criticized me to my face for our lack of courage in confronting Perry. His comment went through me like a knife, and I have never been able to forget it."

68. *Zenshū* I, 117–121. Inau, *Gaikō shisōshi,* p. 127, sees something of a contradiction between "Gaikoku kōsai ni jōjitsu o mochiizaru beki no gi," which seems to argue in favor of foreign travel in the interior as a logical necessity, and "Gaikoku kōsai o tadasu no gi," which seems to argue against it as an infringement of national sovereignty. Consistency is reestablished, however, if one takes the former primarily as a warning as to the sort of arguments the Japanese negotiators must be prepared to meet, and the latter as being opposed not to interior travel in the long run but simply to the revision of the Japanese regulations under foreign pressure.

Mori went on to urge a four-point program: to establish the achievement of full independence as the goal of Japanese diplomacy; to place carefully screened officials of the foreign ministry in all the treaty ports; to dispatch intelligent men to the West to learn the "sophisticated arts of diplomacy"; and finally, "to take the law of nations as our shield, fulfilling our responsibilities, and resolving to make it the firm foundation of our policy in circumstances both favorable and unfavorable, and in times both of quiet and of danger."

Mori's familiarity with international law derived certainly from R. J. Phillimore, in whom Tabohashi Kiyoshi describes him as having been "thoroughly versed";[69] also from Emerich de Vattel, whom he had translated in his article, "Shūkyō"; and possibly from other authors of whom we have no record. Phillimore, although writing in an increasingly historical-minded, positivistic age, had in the words of one twentieth-century authority, a "conception of the natural law . . . perhaps nearer to that of the Schoolmen than any modern writer since Grotius," and tended to speak of custom and usage "as outwardly expressing the consent of nations to things that are naturally, that is by the law of God, binding upon them."[70] This may well have been one source of Mori's extraordinary faith in *jōri*.

Vattel, on the other hand, may have contributed a great deal to Mori's concept of the sovereign state. Although unwilling to abandon the lore of natural law or the habit of a priori moralistic reasoning, Vattel had dispensed with the notion of an international commonwealth, had likened nations to individuals living in a state of nature, and had propounded the concept of "the abstract personality of the State as the subject of international rights and duties."[71] By making a distinction between a *jus naturale* (natural law) in which right and wrong stood out beyond a doubt, and a *jus gentium voluntarium* (voluntary law of nations) to cover less clear-cut cases, he had also opened the door to much future mischief by describing "a lower plane of imperfect rights, in which the precepts of the law of nature were accommodated to the duties of the state to itself."[72] Mori's rather free and easy attitude toward the abrogation of treaties would also have found some theoretical support in Vattel.

69. Tabohashi Kiyoshi, *Kindai nisen kankei no kenkyū* (Tokyo, 1940), I, 531.

70. Charles G. Fenwick, *International Law* (New York, 1948), p. 57.

71. P. E. Corbett, *Law and Society in the Relations of States* (New York, 1951), p. 29.

72. Fenwick, *International Law*, p. 56.

Upon his assignment to Peking, Mori applied *jōri* both as a principle of persuasion with the Chinese authorities and as a general context within which Japanese policy regarding the opening of Korea should operate. And here was the ultimate test of his professions: would he continue to be guided by them when Japan held the upper hand? F. Hilary Conroy has viewed the resolution of the crisis of 1875–1876 as the definitive triumph of the anti-war party over elements which had been calling for military action against Korea ever since 1873.[73] Kido Takayoshi on 8 October 1875 had set the basic policy that there would be no move by Japan against Korea unless China disavowed her responsibility, as suzerain, for the bombardment of the Japanese surveying ship *Unyō* by Korean shore batteries on 20 September.

Mori had studied and had submitted an opinion on the incident, and when the question arose as to whom to send to sound out Chinese intentions, the choice fell on him. On 10 November he received his credentials as envoy extraordinary and plenipotentiary, and on the fourteenth he submitted a memorial to the Seiin arguing: (1) that it was important to maintain friendly relations with China; (2) that demand should be made for the opening of two ports and for permission to make coastal surveys, recognizing Korea as an independent state; if China refused her assistance in the capacity of a friendly neighbor, Japan would take appropriate measures on her own; and (3) that Japan's attitude should not be vindictive, and that any apology which might be extracted from Korea would be purely ancillary to Japan's main objectives—the surveys and the ports. In conclusion, Mori warned: "Even though Korea is a backward country, she is a sovereign state, and in dealing with her we must base our actions squarely and without regret on the principles of justice [*kōsei no jōri*], doing nothing to disgrace ourselves in the eyes of other nations, even though we may have to await the future judgment of posterity. Not only is our national reputation obviously at stake, but our sole hope for the retrieval of the sovereign rights *we* have lost lies in an adherence to the principles of justice. Therefore if we proceed against Korea in reckless disregard of these principles, we are in fact injuring and destroying ourselves."[74]

Mori accordingly was upset when orders issued by Terajima included a demand for an indemnity. In the belief that his philosophy had yet to penetrate to the highest seats of power, he addressed the Seiin once again on the twenty-second, spelling out more specifically

---

73. F. Hilary Conroy, *The Japanese Seizure of Korea, 1868–1910* (Philadelphia, 1960), p. 67.
74. Tabohashi, *Nisen kankei*, I, 515–518.

the conciliatory posture to be assumed by the government's mission to Korea, and adding arguments about the depletion of the national coffers, the confidence of the common people, and the dangers of commencing hostilities without sufficient pretext, which could have been lifted straight out of his brother Yokoyama's suicide note of 1870.[75] The offending clause was as a result excised, and his official instructions of 20 November were entirely in line with his own proposals, which led the *Chōya shinbun* of 28 December to attribute the government's Korean policy in the main to Mori.

Mori arrived in Peking on 4 January 1876, engaged the Tsungli-yamen (foreign office) in an unproductive round of visits and exchange of notes from 10 January to 14 February, but managed to make his point to Li Hung-chang[76] during two interviews at Paoting on 24 and 25 January. The unproductive discussion had revolved around the definition of Korea's status, with Mori's arguments from Western international law butting against a wall of traditional concepts about the Chinese tributary system. The point successfully made was not regarding Korean sovereignty but rather with respect to Japan's peaceful intentions. Li, convinced on that score by Mori, finally counseled the Tsungli-yamen to advise the Koreans to negotiate.[77]

In the first interview Li and Mori dealt with diplomatic issues proper. Li, suggestively, began by praising the nonaggression clause of the Sino-Japanese Friendship Protocol ("Nisshin shūkō jōki") of 1871. Mori, overriding Li's protestations to the effect that China would "forever" be faithful to her treaty commitments and that the protocol was to hold good for ten years, insisted that "what has been written down in a general fashion will give rise to various interpretations unless clearly defined"; that "the expression 'forever' is a most unfortunate one"; that, "[treaties] stand to be revised sooner or later in accordance with the trend of events"; and that the protocol was far from perfect, since it contained ambiguities on the status of Korea and the Ryukyu Islands. Mori hastened to reassure Li, however, that Japan intended to send a purely diplomatic mission to Korea, although she easily could have sent a punitive one. She was interested primarily in the maintenance of

---

75. See Chapter Four. Mori's second memorial on the subject may be found in Tabohashi, *Nisen kankei*, I, 519–520, and in an English translation (in part) in the *Japan Weekly Mail* of 1 Jan 1876.

76. Li Hung-chang was at the time governor-general of Chihli Province and *de facto* foreign minister of China.

77. Tabohashi, *Nisen kankei*, I, 524–544; Conroy, *Japanese Seizure of Korea*, p. 66.

her national honor and in the protection of her fishing fleet, the same issues that involved her in Taiwan in 1874. Had conquest been her object there, she could easily have held on to the areas occupied at that time.[78]

The first interview was not without its lighter side. Li had marveled at Mori's worldwide travels, to which Mori replied: "My period of study abroad did not last very long; therefore I did not really master any single subject, as Your Excellency will have perceived. My life has been devoted to the public service."[79] When Li asked him to compare Europe and Asia, Mori estimated the relative ratio of progress for the two continents as seven versus three on a scale of ten, and when asked for his advice on China had replied that the most essential thing was to train talented young men for national leadership, send them abroad for study, and see to it that they secured responsible positions after returning to China.

The second interview was entirely in an informal vein. Li disapproved of the Japanese adopting Western dress; it was, among other things, disrespectful to one's ancestors. Mori argued as follows, in English, addressed to Li's interpreter, Huang Hui-lien:

> You may have ever [sic] seen our old-fashioned costume. It is a very loose and comfortable one, and excellent for those who pursue a life of ease and idleness, but wholly unsuitable to one of activity . . . If our ancestors were still living they would without a doubt do exactly what we have done . . . Our ancestors about a thousand years ago adopted the Chinese costume as they then found it better than the one they had. It is one of our national characteristics to readily take in anything that is both good and beneficial . . . The Chinese costume appears to our eye not half so good nor convenient as the European. The long tail that hangs down from the head, the shoes so big and awkward and almost impossible for our people to get used to . . . Activity, you know, is the principle element of wealth and prosperity, and indolence that of poverty and ruin . . . Our new European costume suits that of activity.[80]

Here was Mori once again defining Japanese tradition in terms of adaptation and change, and he told Li that he considered the relation between Europe and Asia to be "a question concerning

78. From the first interview, *Zenshū* I, 153–161, *passim*.
79. Ibid., p. 154.
80. Ibid., pp. 180–181.

the competition for supremacy between the races and the religions, as well as for intelligence, power and wealth between two of the great divisions of the world."[81] This had led directly to the previously quoted remarks on the treatment of women which had led Li in turn to ask Mori whether he was a Christian.

Mori's China assignment was the climax of his apostleship of enlightenment, for now he had taken it upon himself to lecture Japan's own cultural progenitor. Our image of the Mori of the Meirokusha and the "Saishōron" rests uneasily beside characterizations of his Peking mission as an exercise in a cynical, two-faced sort of *Realpolitik*,[82] and fits more readily with interpretations such as Conroy's, to the effect that Mori was making a sincere effort to hold China to the principles of modern international law which he himself held to be basic.[83] He was no easy bargainer; he had an acute sense of international competition; he made no apologies in pleading for—or in exercising—the sovereign rights of Japan. But the concept of natural law, which comes through rather faintly in his statements on the individual, is pronounced in Mori's insistence on both sovereignty *and* the rule of reason in international affairs. The professional diplomat, to do full justice to his calling, is forced to look at the world from both the national and the rational point of view and effect the optimum adjustment between the two. And Mori was no exception.

Mori's Peking mission, however, was not only the first but also the most successful of the diplomatic tasks with which he was entrusted between 1876 and 1884. Dealings with the Western powers would prove increasingly difficult and frustrating, and it would be against a growing awareness of Japan's weakness, internationally, that Mori's thinking on politics and education would grow to maturity.

81. Ibid., p. 179.
82. For example, in George H. C. Wong, "Mori Arinori's Mission to China, 1876," in *Chung Chi Journal*, November 1963.
83. Conroy, *Japanese Seizure of Korea*, p. 67.

Eight 1877–1884

THE DIPLOMAT AS KIBITZER ON POLITICS

With Mori's promotion to vice foreign minister (*taifu*) on 27 June 1878 and his appointment as minister at the Court of St. James on 6 November 1879, his public identity gradually shifted from that of intellectual and cultural innovator to that of prominent diplomat and official spokesman for Japan. He would maintain his intellectual pursuits without flagging, but quietly now, and on the side; and he would bring his "extracurricular" researches to focus almost exclusively from 1877 to 1884 on the two areas of politics and education.

At the level of official duties, there were negotiations in Tokyo over cholera quarantine in 1878–1879, and in London over treaty revision on and off throughout 1880–1883, in which Western diplomats at times could show themselves exasperatingly unamenable to *jōri*. In this third period of residence abroad, however, Mori was as quick to join the social whirl in London as he had been in Washington, and there were Englishmen—private citizens, among some of Victorian England's most respected thinkers—who were ready with sympathetic advice on the political and educational future of Japan. As a result, Mori's London years, 1880–1884, would stand in much the same relationship seminally to his views on the Constitution and educational reform during 1884–1889 as did his Washington assignment of 1871–1873 to the more heterogeneous cultural enterprise of his Meirokusha years, 1873–1875.

DIPLOMATIC FRUSTRATIONS

From 1876 to 1878, the least recorded and least interesting years of his career, Mori operated on a shuttle between Tokyo and Peking. Illness in his family brought him home for the summer of 1876, and home leave in 1877 was extended over the better part of the year, during which he served as acting vice foreign minister under Terajima Munenori, whose time was much taken up by the Satsuma Rebellion. Little is known of Mori's Peking duties except for his alleged friendship with the Russian and German ambassadors, and the good will which accrued to Japan during his tour as a result of private contributions of Japanese to the China famine relief fund. Letters home reveal that Mori spent many evenings lecturing on "political ethics" to his own legation staff and that he appreciated the amenities of his Western-style residence with beds, furniture, and heated chambers for the severe North China winter. Breakfast apparently consisted of eggs, coffee, and bread; lunch of Japanese dishes; and dinner of soup, meat, and pastries. Mori wrote that he was appalled, however, by the dust and smells and constant threats of robbery on the streets of the capital and that one member of his party was keeping a pistol handy at all times.[1]

The cholera epidemic[2] which left 101,000 dead[3] in 1879 alone had first made its appearance in Japan in 1877, and when Mori returned from Peking to assume the duties of vice foreign minister in June 1878, he found the Japanese government engaged in an attempt to impose a system of strict quarantine on incoming shipping, supervised exclusively by Japanese officials and subject only to Japanese courts of law. To this the European envoys were adamantly opposed, insisting instead on a system of medical inspection in line with the Vienna International Sanitary Conference of 1874. The real issue, however, was that of jurisdiction over foreign vessels and personnel, and the British minister, Harry Parkes, viewed the whole affair as an underhanded attempt by the Japanese to reassert jurisdictional powers in violation of the treaties.

In this dispute the American Legation took the side of the Jap-

---

1. KKM, pp. 105–106; JWM, 5 Aug. 1876, 21 Oct. 1876, 30 March 1878; letters from Mori to his parents, 19 Nov. 1876, and from Mori's nephew Ishūin Kaneyoshi to his own parents 25 Jan. 1877, to appear in *Zenshū* II.

2. The following account of the cholera quarantine controversy has been based on PRO, Granville Papers, PRO-30-29-314, *Correspondence respecting Quarantine Laws in Japan* (printed for the Foreign Office, 1880), pp. 1–6, 24–29, 92–98, 141–142.

3. Inoue Kiyoshi, *Jōyaku kaisei shi* (Tokyo, 1956), p. 42.

anese. At a meeting of the envoys on 3 July 1878 Minister John A. Bingham had insisted on the "right of the Japanese Government to make what Quarantine Regulations they liked," and on placing "all jurisdiction in the matter" in their hands.[4] In 1879 President Grant, whose visit to Japan that summer became one of Mori's chief diplomatic chores, told the Japanese that they would have been justified in firing on a German vessel (the *Hesperia*) which had forced its way past the Japanese quarantine patrol under protection of a German cruiser.[5]

On 26 July 1879 the Japanese Government established a Superior Board of Health, with three foreign and three Japanese doctors under the presidency of Mori, to consider a revised set of quarantine rules. At the first meeting, on 28 July, Mori barred from the deliberations an Englishman (Wilkinson) who had presented himself as Parkes' "delegate" to the meeting. Parkes complained to London that: "Mr. Wilkinson . . . was told by Mr. Mori that the Board was not appointed at the suggestion of the British Minister, that the draft Regulations of the Japanese Government had not been officially communicated to the foreign Representatives, and that the sanction of the latter to any Regulations of the Japanese Government was not required. He also informed the members of the Board that they need not take into consideration the quarantine systems of other countries, as Japan ought to frame and adopt her own system."[6] The Japanese in the end settled for a medical inspection system after finding quarantine administratively too cumbersome to enforce. The incident showed, however, how ready Mori was to take the high ground in dealing with the most stubborn of the treaty powers, Britain, sustained both by American sympathy and by belief in the theoretical rightness of his position as expounded in "Dokuritsu kokken no gi." Mori's long-standing conviction of American good will no doubt was confirmed by the signing in 1878 of the Yoshida-Evarts treaty, a document which, although not to come into force until ratified by the other powers, displayed the willingness of the United States to push Japan rapidly forward to full tariff autonomy.

This impression of American support and fair play would have two important consequences for Mori. First, it very likely accounts

4. Granville Papers, *Quarantine Laws,* p. 3, letter from Sir H. Parkes to the Marquis of Salisbury, 29 March 1879.
5. Tadao Johannes Araki, *Geschichte der Entstehung und Revision der ungleichen Verträge mit Japan: 1853–1894* (Marburg, 1959), p. 98.
6. Granville Papers, *Quarantine Laws,* p. 5, letter from Sir H. Parkes to the Marquis of Salisbury, 29 March 1879.

for the unusual idealism with which he continued to view interstate relations throughout his life: for international justice was not a chimera as long as some states, some of the time at least, actually managed to adhere to it. No matter how tough the going, Mori somehow managed to avoid the cynicism which finally overtook Fukuzawa, who could already declare by 1878 that "A hundred volumes of international law are not like a few cannon, nor any number of treaties like a keg of gunpowder."[7] Secondly, it raised Mori's level of expectations and, with that, his level of impatience with the British. Acting on the belief that loud and persistent appeals to *jōri* would be effective, he all but destroyed what little effectiveness he might have had with the British foreign office.

Mori arrived in London on 4 January 1880 as part of a fresh ambassadorial brigade dispatched to Western capitals by Inoue Kaoru, who had replaced Terajima Munenori as foreign minister in September, 1879. Terajima's policy of dealing separately with the various powers, and of concentrating on the tariff issue, had proved a failure; and Inoue had decided to press both the jurisdictional and the tariff questions gradually, through a joint conference of the powers in Tokyo. Tangible evidence of Japan's steady modernization was taken to be the key to successful negotiations, and a forced-draft westernization—of everything from legal codes to ballroom dancing—was hopefully embarked upon by the government. It was the assignment of Mori in London, of Samejima Naonobu in Paris, of Yoshida Kiyonari in Washington, and of Aoki Shūzō in Berlin, to promote the idea of a joint conference and to publicize these efforts at westernization.[8]

Mori's diplomatic activity in London divides into three broad phases. From the time of his arrival through 1881 he worked to elicit a response to Inoue's conference proposal (and a revised treaty draft) from the foreign secretary, a post held until 28 April 1880 by Robert Cecil, Third Marquess of Salisbury, and thereafter (until 1885) by George Leveson-Gower, Second Earl of Granville. During most of 1882, with the conference under way in Tokyo, treaty matters were largely taken out of Mori's hands. With the suspension of the conference, however, Mori in 1883 resumed his badgering of the foreign office, this time for a response to Inoue's treaty proposals of 5 April 1882, which the conference had recessed to consider.

7. Fukuzawa Yukichi, "Tsūzoku kokkenron," in *Fukuzawa senshū* (Tokyo, 1951–1952), IV, 108.
8. KKM, p. 112–113; OTM, p. 85; Araki, *Revision der Verträge*, p. 102; F. C. Jones, *Extraterritoriality in Japan: and the Diplomatic Relations Resulting from its Abolition* (New Haven, Conn., 1931), p. 87.

Mori was working against far greater odds in London than those he had once faced in Washington. Britain, with the greatest vested interest in her treaty rights, was least responsive to Japanese hopes for revision. Powerful commercial interests, whom Mori did not hesitate to approach directly,[9] were fearful of repercussions which concessions to Japan would have on the even more lucrative China trade. Mori found social life in the capital inordinately expensive, yet London society hardly noticed him. He met many important people, but was dwarfed by all the greatness surrounding him, and received very few of the attentions which had been showered on him in America. British foreign policy under the second Gladstone administration (1880–1885) remained, on the whole, passive. The attention of the aging Granville was focused during 1880 on the Afghan War, in 1881 on the French annexation of Tunis and on German and Belgian moves for colonial bases in Africa, and in 1882–1883 on the occupation of Egypt. Japan, with her demands for treaty revision, had little more than nuisance value.

It was against this inauspicious background that Mori attempted to develop the major themes of his approach to the foreign office. In his basic premises he continued to insist on Japan's sovereign independence, and to appeal to the rule of reason as embodied in the principles of international law. On 9 August 1881 he explained to Granville: "The general wishes of Japan . . . amounted to a demand for a resumption by my country of the rights and privileges which are inherent to every sovereign State, which had been placed for a time in abeyance by the Treaty of 1858 . . . Great Britain, as I firmly hope, must regard with pleasure any steps which, even if accompanied by some possible loss in money or in privileges to her traders (though this apprehension I venture to believe to be visionary), would lead to the execution of a Treaty on which both Powers could look with satisfaction as equitable and consistent."[10] Two years later, on 11 October 1883, Mori was still making the same point: "The inherent right of Japan to enjoy full equality and perfect freedom in her Treaty arrangements with other Powers has never been surrendered by her. There is no clause in her Treaties which can be rightly interpreted as an admission that any perpetual control with respect to them has been granted to other Powers, nor

9. See for instance Mori's correspondence with Jacob Behrens, representing the Bradford Chamber of Commerce, over the matter of tariff revision: PRO, Granville Papers, PRO-30-29-312, *Further Correspondence Respecting the Revision of the Treaty between Great Britain and Japan* (printed for the Foreign Office), part 3, p. 105, no. 18, letter from Jacob Behrens to the Marquis of Salisbury, 10 March 1880, with enclosures.

10. Ibid., Part 4, p. 101, no. 90, letter from Jushie Mori to Earl Granville, 9 Aug. 1881. "Jushie" for *jūshii*, the Junior Fourth Rank.

under any circumstances would such a contention be at present equitably maintained."[11]

Mori placed great faith in the law of nations. Writing to the British minister, J. G. Kennedy, just before leaving Tokyo for England, Mori insisted that: "the Government of Japan regards as past, never to return, the time when any nation can with safety or with benefit withdraw itself from free intercourse with others . . . [Japan] has in good faith entered the comity of Western nations; and while she is willing to assume the obligations which that comity imposes upon her, she reasonably expects to be allowed the full enjoyment of the privilege which it likewise confers." Mori also mentioned that: "His Majesty's Government confidently expects that the friendly Powers will be disposed to separate Japan from its former general classification with the other Asiatic nations."[12]

Mori's lengthy "Statements of Facts" periodically addressed to Granville were largely concerned, therefore, to publicize the progress which set Japan aside from other Asiatic states—especially from China—and entitled her to the sort of treatment the Western powers normally accorded one another. On 12 March 1883 he wrote Granville of Japan's "sincere determination to enjoy all the benefits of Western civilization,"[13] and on 11 October 1883 he dilated on Japan's "steadily increasing progress, without parallel in Asia," and called attention to the "facts" that "all feeling of animosity against foreigners has entirely died out," that in the civil and military services "freedom from venality and corruption will bear comparison with those of almost any country," that "justice is also well administered throughout the Empire," and that "liberty of conscience and toleration of religious worship are now in fact fully enjoyed by everyone."[14]

The delay of the British government in responding appropriately to these evidences of progress, coupled with the fact that Mori's own letters to the foreign office often went unanswered for weeks

11. PRO, Granville Papers, PRO-30-29-313, *Further Correspondence Respecting the Revision of the Treaty between Great Britain and Japan* (printed for the Foreign Office), part 5 (continued), p. 14, no. 12, letter from Jushie Mori to Earl Granville, 11 Oct. 1883.

12. Granville Papers, PRO-32-29-312, *Further Correspondence,* part 3, p. 18, enclosure in no. 10, memorandum from Mr. Mori to J. G. Kennedy, 12 Nov. 1879.

13. Granville Papers, PRO-30-29-313, *Further Correspondence,* part 6, p. 99, enclosure in no. 17, memorandum from Jushie Mori to Earl Granville, 12 March 1883.

14. Ibid., part 5 (continued), p. 15, no. 12, letter from Jushie Mori to Earl Granville, 11 Oct. 1883.

or even months, on two occasions drove the still somewhat youngish envoy (now in his mid-thirties) over the brink of diplomatic decorum. On 12 July 1881 Mori wrote Granville a brief but forceful note inquiring as to the status of a letter he had sent the foreign secretary on 22 March.[15] J. G. Kennedy complained in Tokyo to Inoue Kaoru that Granville had been "much disquieted" by the "language and attitude" of Mori's letter, which seemed "dictatorial and presumptuous." Inoue, referring apologetically to Mori as "a very young man," had to assure Kennedy that Mori's language to Granville was "unauthorized."[16]

Mori, however, had not learned his lesson. In another memorandum to Granville, on 12 March 1883, Mori closed with a heavy-handed warning to the effect that the "serious consequences" which would follow any collapse of the Tokyo negotiations would be the "whole responsibility" of Britain and the other treaty powers.[17] Inoue was again required to disclaim Mori's "unauthorized and objectionable" language, this time to Minister Harry Parkes.[18] How quick Mori was to show emotion emerges from a note to Granville, dated 4 January 1884, from F. R. Plunkett, who was about to leave for Tokyo as the new British envoy: "Mr. Mori, who seemed much mortified at my reply, argued at great length and with some warmth, that our proposal to make the recognition of eventual Tariff autonomy contingent on the previous success for three years of the new arrangements was humiliating to Japan, and would never be accepted . . . Mr. Mori was evidently too much mortified at my suggestion that Tokyo and not London was the proper seat of negotiation to be able to continue our conversation with calmness. I therefore, as soon as possible, turned to other topics."[19]

15. Granville Papers, PRO-30-29-312, *Further Correspondence,* part 4, p. 88, no. 75, letter from Jushie Mori to Earl Granville, 12 July 1881.

16. Ibid., part 5, p. 19, no. 33, letter from J. G. Kennedy to Earl Granville, 10 Oct. 1881; ibid., part 5, p. 38, no. 51, letter from Kennedy to Granville, 21 Dec. 1881; PRO, Tenterden Papers, FO-363-1, letter from J. G. Kennedy to Lord Tenterden, 28 Sept. 1881. Kennedy wrote Tenderden, the Permanent Under Secretary, that, "I have relieved Inouye's mind somewhat since the receipt of last correspondence between Lord Granville and Mr. Mori. I have told Inouye that the style and context [*sic*] of Mori's note is offensive and would indispose H. M. Gov't. to oblige Japan."

17. Granville Papers, PRO-30-29-313, *Further Correspondence,* part 6, p. 99, enclosure to no. 17, memorandum from Jushie Mori to Earl Granville, 12 March 1883.

18. Ibid., part 6, p. 118, no. 39, dispatch from Sir H. Parkes to Earl Granville, 14 May 1883.

19. Ibid., part 7, p. 1, no. 1, memorandum from F. R. Plunkett to Earl Granville, 4 Jan. 1884.

Mori's impatient and high-handed posture stems from three sources, the first of which was purely temperamental. The second source was continued American support, in particular as regards the right of denunciation (upon expiry of a treaty's time limit)—a right proposed by Inoue in 1882 but never before granted to a non-Christian power.[20] The American Minister Bingham, J. G. Kennedy complained to Granville on 16 August 1881, had suggested that "in case the Treaty Powers do not restore to Japan her independence in Tariff matters . . . Japan should simply denounce the existing Convention of 1866 and defy the Treaty Powers."[21] The third source of Mori's high-handedness might best be described as the haunting nightmare of Egypt—spiralling foreign debts, financial disarray, rebellion, massacre of Europeans, a foreign occupation, loss of independence—all of which transpired while Mori was accredited to the government which conducted that occupation. The Western powers seemed to have a different set of rules in dealing with non-European states, and Mori took great pains to set Japan apart from other Asiatic countries. When in 1880–1881 there had been talk of an exchange of orders between the Meiji Emperor and Queen Victoria, Mori insisted that the Japanese, who were prepared to bestow their highest order, the Chrysanthemum, would settle for nothing less than Britain's highest order, the Garter. The lower-ranking Star of India would not do. Undersecretary Julian Pauncefote reported to Granville on 11 May 1881, after consulting Mori: "The Emperor, who thinks that the progress made by Japan entitles her to rank with the most civilized Powers, is very susceptible about being treated as an *Asiatic* [underlining in the original] Prince."[22]

Under such pressures, it is all the more striking that Mori's outlook did not take a militaristic turn. In terms of sheer bulk, it is true, most of the correspondence between the Japanese legation and the foreign office (often forwarding for the admiralty) during 1880–1884 concerned naval matters: the purchase and refitting of two small cruisers; the training of Japanese cadets at the Royal Naval College and aboard British warships; visits to dockyards and arsenals; and requests for information on everything from specifications for rope and chain to the proper format for inventory

20. Jones, *Extraterritoriality in Japan*, pp. 101–102.
21. Granville Papers, PRO-30-29-312, *Further Correspondence*, part 5, p. 4, no. 7, dispatch from J. G. Kennedy to Earl Granville, 16 Aug. 1881.
22. PRO, Japan/General Correspondence, FO-46-278, letter from J. Pauncefote to Earl Granville, 11 May 1881.

of sea stores.[23] Mori's strategic thinking—as befitted one with his own early background—remained entirely naval in concept. But it also remained defensive and, on the whole, self-confident.

It was the economic and commercial, rather than any naked military threat, which seemed to worry Mori the most. The evidence for this is in an hour-and-a-half interview which he gave a reporter from the *Pall Mall Gazette* on 25 February 1884, the very day before his departure for Japan. The reporter's paraphrase of the discussion, carried in the following day's issue (under the heading, "The Japanese Ambassador on Public Affairs"), provides Mori's lengthiest statement on general matters during his London tour of duty. At one point he had noted: "Japan is very fortunately situated. In many respects her geographical position resembles that of England, with this difference—that a much greater extent of sea rolls between us and our nearest Continental neighbor. That, however, increases our sense of security. At the present moment we have absolutely nothing to fear from any hostile Powers. At home we are in perfect peace. Abroad we have for the last fifteen years resolutely pursued a pacific policy . . . Great credit is due to the resolution with which Japanese statesmen have resisted every temptation to embark on a policy of warlike adventure, and as a result we are now on most excellent terms with everybody."

Mori then went on to add: "You ask me about standing armies, and the impression which is produced on the Oriental mind by a continent converted into an armed camp. That spectacle, I am free to confess, impressed me far less than the war of commerce which, under the name of 'competition,' goes on unceasingly. In military warfare you sometimes have peace . . . but the war of commerce never stops. The competition of nation with nation for the monopoly of the trade and industry of the world is constant and cruel. I don't complain; nor do I affect to censure. I am taught that the progress of the race is by the survival of the fittest and the elimination of the weak by a process of natural selection; and the commercial competition is one form by which superior organisms triumph over the lower. In that competition I hope Japan will now take a much more prominent part than she has hitherto done."

Many Japanese in the 1880's, impressed by the "standing armies" of Europe, particularly the German, were quick to em-

23. See for example PRO, Japan/General Correspondence, FO-46-262 ("Domestic: Various"), *passim* and FO-46-278 ("Domestic: Mori"), *passim;* and, regarding the purchase of men-of-war, LCT, 10 April 1883, 16 April 1883, 2 May 1883, 15 May 1883, 19 June 1883, 9 Nov. 1883 and *The Times* (London), 14 July 1883.

brace a military-oriented doctrine of *Machtpolitik*. What Mori came away with after more than four years in London, however, was Social Darwinism in its original, commercially oriented, English guise. For Herbert Spencer, while foreseeing the possibility of an "untoward incident" which could plunge the world into a "generation" of military conflicts, was more inclined to a vision of a long global peace during which expanding industrial and commercial activity would serve gradually to erode man's war-making institutions.[24] Mori in his letters home, too, consistently reassured his father that Europe was at peace "as usual," and in a paean to electric power—which was about to "transform the face of the entire earth" to everyone's convenience—he revealed a typical mid-Victorian faith in the unlimited peaceful potentialities of scientific discovery.[25] And when Mori said, "I am taught," he meant just that: for Herbert Spencer was both the most famous, and perhaps the most intimate, of his prominent social contacts.

MAN ABOUT LONDON TOWN

Mori as vice foreign minister had been one of the most familiar figures to foreign residents of Tokyo in the late 1870's. Miss Isabella L. Bird, intrepid lady explorer of Japanese back country, wrote on 11 October 1878 that she had attended an "afternoon entertainment" given to the diplomatic body by Mori in the Shiba Pavilion: "Mr. Mori is one of the most progressive of Japanese politicians, and, under an Oriental despotism, is an 'advanced Liberal.' He would tolerate everything . . . His wife dresses tastefully in English style, and receives his guests along with himself . . . He was in America for some years, speaks English tolerably well, and, unlike most of his countrymen, knows how to wear the European dress . . . Mr. Mori complimented me with much *bonhommie* on my 'unprecedented tour' [of northern Japan] . . . A mere imitation of an English reception, and had nothing distinctively Japanese about it."[26]

There is every indication that Mori felt thoroughly at home in London. Ernest Satow wrote in his diary for 5 April 1883: "Called on Mori at 9 Cavendish Square, a fine house. Lunched with him; his wife as bashful as ever; two little boys Kiyoshi and Hide age

---

24. Herbert Spencer, *The Principles of Sociology*, 3 vols., 3rd. ed., New York, 1921–1925), I, part V, p. 648.

25. Letters from Mori to his father, 5 Oct. 1881 and 20 Jan. 1882, *Zenshū* II.

26. Isabella L. Bird, *Unbeaten Tracks in Japan*, 2 vols. (London, 1880), II, 202–204, letter no. 50, dated 11 Oct. 1878.

7 and 6 have entirely forgotten their Japanese, and speak English quite naturally. He said Herbert Spencer wished very much to see me, and I promised to call at the Athenaeum Club whenever it might be convenient."[27] Satow had originally written that Kiyoshi and Hide had "quite" forgotten their Japanese, then crossed out the expression and entered the word "entirely." Mori may or may not have attempted to enforce his "Kokugo haishiron" within his own family, but the vignette indicates how very anglicized his style of living had become.

The newspapers occasionally reported Mori's excursions into the provinces—to Ramsgate in 1882 for the fresh sea air, to Hampshire in 1883 to inspect a workhouse, and to Manchester and Birmingham in 1884 to visit spinning mills and a stock exchange[28]—but the pivot of Mori's social life was the Athenaeum Club. He apparently made full use of the honorary membership to which his diplomatic rank entitled him. The *Japan Weekly Mail* of 1 September 1883, indeed, wrote disapprovingly: "It cannot be said that Mr. Mori has achieved signal success as a diplomatist. His talents seem to be rather of a literary order. Indeed, there are rumours that his reputation as a philosophical disputant is quite formidable at the Athenaeum Club and that some of his theories have attracted considerable attention. Doubtless this is all very agreeable, but it is scarcely quite what Japan expects of her Minister in London." Mori got around to introducing Satow to Spencer (anxious for information on Shinto) at the Athenaeum on 9 April 1883, and on 28 April he assembled Spencer, Satow, and the author Andrew Lang at the Savile Club to meet Itō Hirobumi.

Spencer, who had a deep interest in Japanese history and culture, was during 1880–1881 engaged in the preparation of Part V ("Political Institutions") of his *Principles of Sociology,* and his need for first-hand information would seem to explain his initial motive in cultivating the friendship of the Japanese minister. In Part V, as in Parts II and III of his study (issued during 1874–1877), Spencer frequently cites the instance of Japan in support and development of his own theories.[29] Spencer on at least one occasion gave a dinner at the Athenaeum in Mori's honor. The

---

27. PRO, Satow Papers, PRO-30-33-15-7, "Diary, January 1882–March 1884," entry for 5 April 1883.

28. LCT, 3 May 1882 and 23 July 1883; *Manchester Evening News,* 16 Jan. 1884.

29. Satow Papers, "Diary, 1882–1884," entries for 9 April and 28 April 1883. See Spencer, *Principles of Sociology,* I, parts II and III, and II, part V; and Herbert Spencer, *An Autobiography* (New York, 1904), II, 416–443, *passim.*

date was 19 May 1881, and the guest list included Professor Alexander Bain, the rector of Aberdeen University and a pioneer of association psychology; Dr. David Masson, biographer and editor; and John Morley, editor of the *Pall Mall Gazette* and *Fortnightly Review* and author of *The Struggle for National Education* (1873), who was a strong proponent of secular public schools.[30] And on 12 April 1883 we find Spencer writing to Edward L. Youmans that he has spoken to Mori about the Japanese version of his *Data of Ethics*.[31] The Athenaeum was for Spencer more of a home than his own residence: "There he could frequently—for many years almost daily—see his friends. When in London he used to go to the Athenaeum almost daily, and occupied himself in looking at the weekly papers, glancing at the magazines and skimming the new books . . . He used the library for purposes of reference . . . An hour or two every afternoon was passed at the billiard table."[32]

It seems highly probable that Mori and Spencer were brought rather frequently into contact through regular use of the Athenaeum. Makino Nobuaki, then an attaché at the legation, later recalled that Mori spent much time there.[33] The volumes in the club's superb library could not be borrowed but had (then as now) to be read on the premises.[34] And Mori no doubt indulged at the club, perhaps in Spencer's company, the only hobby which his widow would recall him as ever having pursued: billiards.[35] Of Mori's prominent scholarly acquaintances, many (like Thomas Huxley) were members of the Athenaeum, but, except for Spencer and Matthew Arnold (who wrote many of his letters there), it is not known how frequently they may have used the club's facilities. Another source of scholarly contacts would have

30. David Duncan, *Life and Letters of Herbert Spencer* (London, 1908), p. 215, citing entry in unpublished Spencer diary for 19 May 1881. Also present at the dinner were Prof. Edward Frankland, Sir Henry Thompson, and Lord Arthur Russell. Despite an exhaustive search of the major London libraries, including the Athenaeum, and inquiries addressed to several British scholars who recently had worked on Spencer, I failed to unearth Spencer's diary, which may possibly contain additional references to Mori.
31. Ibid., p. 231, quoting letter from Herbert Spencer to Edward L. Youmans, 12 April 1883.
32. Ibid., p. 494.
33. As told to me in July 1966 by Makino's nephew, Ōkubo Toshiaki.
34. As explained to me by Miss A. Elise Walker, librarian of the Athenaeum Club, in April 1966.
35. Mori Hiroko (as told to Mori Arimasa), "Mori Arinori no omoide," *Mikuni*, 4.3 (March 1938); to appear in *Zenshū* II. Hiroko was Mori's second wife.

been the Royal Asiatic Society, which Mori at once joined in time for its meeting of 16 February 1880, at which he felt no compunction in "criticizing . . . in free terms" a paper just delivered by Professor Friedrich Max Mueller of Oxford on a "Sanskrit Text Discovered in Japan": a subject on which Mori knew next to nothing.[36]

Mori called occasionally on Gladstone at 10 Downing Street and on Granville at Walmer Castle,[37] met the politically prominent at royal levees, and took his family and several Japanese students along to the consecration of the first Anglican missionary bishop of Japan at Lambeth Palace Chapel.[38] Mori also supervised the steady progress of Japanese dignitaries through the British capital; but the only one of these who was of any consequence to Mori, personally, was Itō. Sometime between 29 August and 3 September 1882[39] Mori crossed the Channel to pay his respects to Prince Arisugawa, who had arrived in Paris on his way to the coronation of Tsar Alexander III. Itō Hirobumi had come up from Vienna for the same purpose, and the discussions which he and Mori held on that occasion would prove largely determinative of the course of Japanese education from 1885 to 1889.[40] It seems that political matters, however, were first discussed between the two during Itō's visit to England from 3 March to 5 May 1883.

Upon returning to London, Mori had written Itō on 12 September 1883: "I should by all means recommend that, when you have finished your work in Vienna, you make an investigation of the Italian political achievement. England is the most respected country in Europe; there are many things of which Englishmen themselves are thoroughly entitled to boast; there is much to be learned from them, especially in making good the deficiencies in our own national character. I would urge you to come and see things here at first hand when you have completed your study of Austria and Germany."[41]

Mori did not specifically recommend the British political system, but he did recommend that of Italy; and the Kingdom of Italy

36. *Court Circular* (London), 21 Feb. 1880.
37. LCT, 11 Nov. 1882 and 13 Oct. 1883.
38. The consecration of Arthur W. Poole is described in LCT, 26 Oct. 1883.
39. See note 49, Chapter Nine.
40. See Chapter Nine.
41. OTM, p. 89, quoting a letter from Mori Arinori to Itō Hirobumi, 12 Sept. 1882. The entire Mori-Itō correspondence for 1882–1883 has conveniently been assembled in OTM, pp. 88ff. In the *Zenshū*, it is scattered throughout volumes I and II according to topic.

(1861–1922), like Britain and unlike Germany, represented a genuine constitutional monarchy with the supremacy of the parliament and the fundamental rights of the individual citizen firmly established. Italy also possessed (unlike Britain) a highly centralized and fairly efficient bureaucracy inherited from the Napoleonic era.[42] This suggests three things: that Mori's constitutional thinking as of 1882 may not have stood too far from that of the "English" school represented by Fukuzawa Yukichi and Ōkuma Shigenobu; that Itō at Paris had not revealed to Mori how definitely he himself had already opted for the German model; and that Mori was only dimly aware of the depth of the political crisis of October 1881 in which Itō had driven Ōkuma from power, or of the decisiveness of the former's triumph.[43]

By the time Itō left London the following spring, however, it was clear that Mori had at least been brought around to sharing his view of Itagaki Taisuke, the Popular Rights Movement (*jiyū minken undō*), and the more radical "French" school. After introducing Itagaki to Spencer, Mori reported to Itō sometime in early May 1883: "Itagaki had his interview with Spencer—the central idol of his researches—three days ago, with Kawakami along as interpreter. He went into it as though approaching the Emperor, but in the actual discussion master and pupil traded places, with the disciple doing all the sermonizing and putting forth his usual empty and unfounded theories. Finally the central idol lost his patience, got up in the middle of the conversation muttering "no, no, no" [English in the original] and took his leave of Itagaki, just like that."[44] Mori also wrote in the same letter that he hoped to join Itō for a few days in Berlin as soon as he could get away. This would have been his third trip to Germany, which he first visited briefly after attending the funeral of Samejima Naonobu in Paris on 7 December 1880, and again in early October 1881.[45] Accord-

42. Mario Einaudi, comp., "Italy," *Encyclopedia Americana*, 1964, XV, pp. 549ff.

43. Inagaki Tadahiko has written in Kaigo Tokiomi et al., "Mori Arinori no shisō to kyōiku seisaku," *Bulletin of the Faculty of Education, University of Tokyo*, 8:35, 43 (1965) that "Mori was free of Fukuzawa's distrust of authority; the outsider's spirit of Fukuzawa also was foreign to Mori; nor did Mori have any direct experience of the political crisis of 1881 . . . Mori, without perceiving the contradiction between his own position and Itō's, cooperated with Itō and established the basic structure of statist education."

44. OTM, p. 96, letter from Mori Arinori to Itō Hirobumi, May 1883, no day of month given, but written sometime between Itō's departure from London on 5 May and his arrival in Berlin on the eleventh.

45. LCT, 8 Dec. 1880. Letter from Mori to parents 15 Oct. 1881, *Zenshū* II.

ingly, the intellectual background against which Mori, in the latter half of 1883 at long last set about drafting a specific constitutional proposal included the ready availability of Herbert Spencer and the pervasive influence of the English intellectual circles in which Mori constantly moved; the brief, but intimate, discussions with Itō; and three short visits to Germany, the details of which have been lost to history.

What would not figure in Mori's political thinking now were his religious beliefs, or even the concept of the individual (defined in terms of the sacredness of conscience) of which *Religious Freedom in Japan* had in 1872 shown considerable promise. The record does not tell us whether (and, if so, on what terms) Mori may have seen something of Laurence Oliphant, who had broken with Harris in 1881 and who found himself in London in May–December of 1880, in May 1881 and in January–March of 1882. Some of his letters at the time were written from the Athenaeum, of which he long had been a member. Mori's resort to Harris' terminology (in the expression, "uses") in his English-language peroration at Samejima's funeral, suggests at any rate how very much the two of them had remained soul brothers in the lingering influence of their Brocton pilgrimage: "Samejima! Ever since you began your uses in this world righteousness has found you a most faithful servant. You worked hard and well thirty-seven years worthily spent. No more, O precious soul! no more, O noble labourer! no more, O bright star! Still you live, still you work, still you shine in the bosom of your friends. You know me well!"[46]

We also know that Mori continued to assist, and to sympathize with, individual Christians who had difficulties with the state authorities on account of their religion. The evidence is to be found once again in Mori's assistance to Niijima Jō, this time in securing passports for some of the foreign staff at Dōshisha College in Kyoto. Mori told Niijima: "You have a right to exist and also to employ foreign teachers if you use your own fund instead of that of the Board. The Foreign Office objects to your depending upon the American Board altogether." In Niijima's further recollection: "Mr. Mori stood up for us nobly, and persuaded [Foreign Minister Terajima] to grant our application. At the same time he sent me word by a friend to be cautious, and advised me to raise a permanent fund at once."[47]

---

46. Philip Henderson, *The Life of Laurence Oliphant: Traveller, Diplomat and Mystic* (London, 1956), p. 222 and *passim*. LCT, 8 Dec. 1880.

47. Arthur S. Hardy, *Life and Letters of Joseph Hardy Neesima* (Boston, 1891), p. 226, quoting letter from Niijima Jō to the Prudential Committee

Mori's defense of a Christian's right to education of his own choice, coupled with his distaste for foreign control of a Japanese school, neatly reflects the conflict of religious freedom and national sovereignty with which his *Meiroku zasshi* article, "Shūkyō," had come to grips. William E. Griffis in his second edition of *The Mikado's Empire* (1877), quotes statements by Mori—not on Christianity, but on Shinto—which indicate, however, how far Mori had shifted his balance in favor of state power. Mori explained to Griffis: "The leading idea of Shinto is a reverential feeling toward the dead./ As to the political uses of it, the state is quite right in turning it to account in support of the absolute government which exists in Japan./ The early records of Japan are by no means reliable."[48]

Mori we know was consistently opposed, not only in *Religious Freedom in Japan* but also later as minister of education, to the establishment of the traditional creeds as a state religion. What we have in the foregoing quotation are replies to three questions specifically posed by Griffis, not information volunteered at Mori's own initiative; and this statement, rather out of character with both the earlier and later Mori, is perhaps best seen as a defense not of state-supported Shinto but of the right of the state (as previously asserted in both "Shūkyō" and *Religious Freedom in Japan*) to make rules for religion where it impinged on the public safety and welfare. The previously quoted Miss Bird also asked Mori in 1878 about the government's religious policy and noted that "he regards Shinto only as a useful political engine."[49]

One can well imagine that foreigners in Tokyo were more than ready with advice on religious policy. Mori as envoy in Washington had found it necessary to convey the sentiments of the American people to the Iwakura mission and to give assurances on the religious question to the government to which he was then accredited. His position now was somewhat different. The ban on Christianity had in effect been lifted in 1873, and Mori's overriding concern now was to assert, as against Western pretensions, the sovereignty

---

of the American Board of Foreign Missions, February 1879; day of month not given.

48. William E. Griffis, *The Mikado's Empire*, 2nd ed. (New York, 1877), p. 100. The quotation appears in a footnote to Griffis' tenth chapter, which dealt with "Ancient Religion." Other comments were solicited from Harry Parkes, Ernest Satow, and J. A. von Brandt, and included in the same footnote. The preface to this second edition was dated 10 May 1876; Mori's remarks therefore probably date from late 1875 or early 1876.

49. Bird, *Unbeaten Tracks in Japan*, II, 202.

of the Japanese state in all internal matters, from religious policy to cholera quarantine.

PREMISES FOR A "REPRESENTATIVE" GOVERNMENT

Sometime in early 1884 Theodore D. Woolsey, retired president of Yale College, received a letter from London, dated 10 January, in which Mori announced that "Japan is going to engraft on her political institutions a Representative System of Government in 1890," and enclosed a "short, and in some respects preliminary, paper on the subject . . . confidentially, with my particular solicitude that you will kindly peruse it, and give me any criticisms or observations on it."[50] The enclosure was an English-language pamphlet in nine parts entitled *On a Representative System of Government for Japan,* marked "Strictly Private," and prefaced with the following note: "This Paper is the First of a Series intended to contain Suggestions as to the development of Constitutional Government in Japan. The first three parts of the Paper are therefore to be regarded as introductory not only to this particular Paper, but also to the whole Series."[51] Two warnings require posting, however, before this document may safely be approached. First, we do not have the complete original text. Second, Mori not only gives us a title that is misleading but also fails to state his most important premise. For the latter, we fortunately have the *Pall Mall Gazette* interview, in conjunction with which Mori's *Representative System* (as we conveniently may call it) needs to be read.

Unfortunately there are extant neither replies to this pamphlet, which presumably was transmitted to a number of Mori's Western friends, nor any subsequent "Papers" in Mori's contemplated "Series," nor for that matter copies of any of the last five (out of nine) parts into which the pamphlet received by Woolsey had been divided. What we do have is a complete, nine-part Japanese-language version of *Representative System,* entitled "Nihon seifu daigi seitairon" (On a representative polity for the government of

50. Yale University Library, Historical Manuscripts, Woolsey Manuscripts, letter from Arinori Mori to Theodore D. Woolsey, 10 Jan. 1884.
51. Arinori Mori, *On a Representative System of Government for Japan* (London: by the author, late 1883). A reprint of the sole extant copy of the original pamphlet, now in the personal possession of Ōkubo Toshiaki, will appear in *Zenshū* III. I am indebted to Professor Hayashi Takeji for a photocopy of Professor Ōkubo's original.

Japan; hereinafter "Daigi seitairon").[52] Written in hasty, unpolished Japanese, inferior in comparative style to the rather passable English of *Representative System,* it would seem to be either an original Japanese draft of, or a later translation from, the English pamphlet. The conclusion of "Daigi seitairon" with the stock phrase, *tei suru* (I present), also suggests the possible preparation of a quick translation, upon Mori's return to Tokyo, for further circulation among Japanese authorities. And there is still a third possibility, namely, that "Daigi seitairon" may represent a translation prepared not by Mori himself but by some other Japanese, versed in English but no stylist in his own language, for the use of the biographer Kimura Kyō, (who read no English), some time after Mori's death. In any case, we cannot be sure whether the Japanese expression in any given instance is Mori's own or that of another Japanese translating from *Representative System.*[53]

52. Mori Arinori, "Nihon seifu daigi seitairon" (On a representative polity for the government of Japan; unpublished manuscript, undated but probably 1883 or thereafter), to appear in *Zenshū* III. I am indebted for the evaluation of the style of this document to Hayashi Takeji, who believes it difficult to conclude, on the basis of that style, that the document could be either Mori's original draft, or his own translation—however hurried. Unfortunately we do not know in whose hand the original copy of "Daigi seitairon" was made, i.e., whether in Mori's or in someone else's. This original copy, formerly in the possession of Kimura Kyō, has since been lost. Kimura in any case made no reference to the document in his biography of 1899. With the Meiji Constitution established, and the emperor's status clearly defined, Kimura may possibly have felt some hesitation in publishing materials which dealt so freely with the emperor. None of the three Japanese biographies, indeed, discusses either *Representative System* or "Daigi seitairon." Kimura had a copy of the latter prepared for Ōkubo Toshiaki in 1938, from which the *Zenshū* III reprint will be taken.

53. The single extant copy of *Representative System,* comprising the first four parts only, is in the possession of Ōkubo Toshiaki. Professor Ōkubo does not recall how the pamphlet originally came into his collection. It is possible, of course, that these first four parts were all that Mori ever mailed to Woolsey and other Western friends, and that he never completed an English-language version of parts V through IX, corresponding to the latter half of "Daigi seitairon." There is, however, nothing at the end of part IV in the English version— either of a stylistic or typographical nature—to suggest the end of the essay; nor is there in the the text or in the covering letter to Woolsey any reference (which courtesy would require) to a later mailing of the remaining parts of this paper. (Mori informs Woolsey that he has enclosed his first paper—in a projected series—not just the first four parts of his first paper). Part IV belongs topically to the succeeding five, not to the previous three, parts, and a break between parts IV and V seems particularly abrupt. The simplest explanation, on the face of the evidence, would be the disappearance—for some unaccounted reason—of parts V

References, however, to the year 1884 as the present time in Part II (both versions) and Part VIII (Japanese version) suggest the completion of the entire English original by late 1883 in anticipation of publication ("just prepared," as Mori wrote Woolsey on 10 January) in early 1884. Starting with the extant Parts I–IV of *Representative System,* and taking Parts V–IX of "Daigi seitairon" as a fair translation of the lost portions of the English pamphlet, we have here the lengthiest political essay of Mori's entire career, breaking the silence maintained on the subject since his "Minsen giin" of 1874, and revealing a basic philosophy to which his later remarks on the Constitution, while minister of education, would provide no more, really, than footnotes.[54]

Mori in this essay is firmly committed to the introduction of a national assembly in some form or other by 1890. The task is one which he approaches with a basic optimism deriving both from his long-standing faith in his country's adaptive capacities and from his fresh discovery of serviceable elements in the existing political tradition. What he offers, however, is not a scheme of representative government in the most commonly accepted sense of the term, i.e., government by the people through their elected deputies, but rather the "engrafting" (in Mori's own favorite expression) of a certain representative element onto a structure which, as a whole, remains highly unrepresentative. The very title of his essay is in this sense misleading, and much confusion would have been avoided had Mori—in his title, in his letter to Woolsey, and throughout the document—characterized as "representative" not the "system of government" but simply the one political organ to which the term applied: the national assembly.

Parts I through III of the essay provide theoretical underpinning for the specific institutional proposals in Parts IV through IX. Part I, advancing fourteen "General Historical Facts," grapples with some of the classical problems of Western political science; Part II lists eleven "Special Historical Facts" characterizing the political tradition of Japan; and Part III presents twenty-one points in "General Conclusion" based on these foregoing "facts." Part IV deals with the national assembly; Part V with the function, and

---

through IX of the copy of *Representative System* which eventually found its way into Professor Ōkubo's hands. Each part of the English-language pamphlet starts afresh from the top of a new page, rendering all the parts easily detachable from the rest of the essay.

54. See the Appendix for reasons for not attributing authorship of still another pamphlet, *The Proposed National Assembly in Japan: by a Japanese,* to Mori.

Part VI with the selection, of two legislative bodies, a senate and a house of councillors; Part VII with the cabinet; Part VIII with the emperor. Part IX, finally, provides a brief summation, the key sentence of which tells us: "According to the system proposed in this paper, the Emperor (*kōtei*) will remain, as in the past, the most exalted head of the nation (*kuni no chizon naru tōshū*), while the organs (*kikan*) acting to fulfill his command may be summarized as follows: (1) the Cabinet (Naikaku): for administration (gyōsei); (2) the House of Councillors (Sangiin) and Senate (Genrōin): for legislation (*rippō*); (3) the National Assembly (Kokkai): for representation (*daigi*)."[55]

The three introductory parts present justifications for the powerful executive and the separation of legislative and representative functions which highlight Mori's proposed structure, together with elucidation of three traditional elements, ready-made for incorporation into the new political process: the emperor, the family system, and local government.

Mori assumes, as his point of departure for both Parts I and III, the "human inequality as regards the intellectual, moral and physical faculties" (Part I/Point 1, Part III/Point 1). The consequent need to "restrain the strong from injuring the weak" (I/2) gives rise to "justice which has been more or less recognized as the only impartial standard" (I/4), and this in turn gradually improves "following the development of the intelligence of the people" (I/3). Mori's own emphasis on general wisdom and on professional or specialized qualifications for the conduct of political affairs crops up in every single part of the essay. "Human intelligence," he tells us, "has been regarded as one, if not *the* most important, of the sources from which all useful work is obtained"; in "the most advanced countries" it has become so "necessary for public purposes, that its development in every youth is made compulsory at public expense."(I/6).

This concern for wisdom and expertise gives Mori's differentiation of "legislation" and "representation" a superficial resemblance to John Stuart Mill's suggestion that lawmaking would best be protected against ignorance and jobbery by entrusting its preparation entirely to a permanent appointive professional commission, leaving to parliament simply the final sanctioning, or enacting, power.[56] The ultimate control, as opposed to the performance, of

55. Quotations from parts V through IX are my own translations from "Daigi seitairon." Quotations from parts I through IV are taken directly from Mori's *Representative System*.
56. John Stuart Mill, *Considerations on Representative Government*, ed. Currin V. Shields (New York, 1958), pp. 68–84, *passim*.

both legislative and executive functions was reserved by Mill, however, to the people's representatives. With Mori, by contrast, the latter retain neither a performing nor an enacting role in legislation.

In preparing his readers for a sympathetic consideration of his purely deliberative national assembly, one would expect Mori to have argued from the standpoint either of prematurity or of sovereignty, i.e., either (in line with Katō Hiroyuki, for instance[57]) that the popular intelligence had not yet reached the point at which it could be entrusted with the framing and approval of legislation or (in line, for instance, with typical German constitutional theory) that sovereignty lay elsewhere than with the people. Instead, Mori argues unconvincingly and unnecessarily against direct popular representation *in principle,* attacking it as a political process which tends inherently to negate the popular will. He reiterates his distaste for "politicians" and "party politics"—disdainfully rendered in quotation marks—all familiar enough from his *Life and Resources in America* of 1871.

One may accept as historically valid Mori's contention that the popular election of legislators brings party politics in its train; and one may admit the abuses (simply alluded to by Mori, not defined) to which the party-political system is prone. What one cannot accept is Mori's implied conclusion that popular election and party politics *necessarily* frustrate the popular will. And it is on this ironical assumption, most inadequately demonstrated, that Mori's essay as a whole would seem to turn; for the substantive proposals which follow represent above all an effort to provide supposedly more faithful representation of the popular will through devices such as indirect election and coöptative selection. The crucial passages in question are worth quoting in full here; the first and second deal with the exclusion of popular representatives, and the third with the inclusion of officials, in the legislative organ.

> It is a fact that under a system of direct representation, the elected body does not necessarily represent the majority of the electors; and that there are many national affairs of importance, in which political parties are not as such directly concerned (I/11) . . .

> Since the system that allows the people to select *directly* the legislators of the state has been invariably followed by the creation of what is called "party politics," which prejudicially and even injuriously operate against the free expression of a political opinion, it may be concluded that such a system is entangled

57. See Chapter Seven.

with some radical errors, which ought to be avoided by Japan (III/6) . . . Since judges and soldiers in constitutional countries are generally excluded from having a voice in any political affairs of the day, it may be concluded that if not thus excluded they would either endanger political interests, or act injuriously in connection with the interests of their respective professions, or create both these results; and that this exclusion from politics is an arbitrary arrangement justifiable, if at all, in such countries as are governed in politics by the direct voice of the people, who are deemed open to any unfair influence of these professional classes; but that it is not at all justifiable in a country that adopts a representative system, which permits the people to exercise their voice in politics in such an *indirect* manner as to be not in the least degree affected by any external influences of that kind (III/7).

Queries and objections leap to mind. Is it gerrymandering, or bossism, or the non-pledging of the elected body which makes Mori so skeptical of direct representation? And what other system, indeed, better represents the majority of electors? How, furthermore, can party politics be said to hamper in any fundamental way the freedom—as opposed to the wisdom or the decorousness—of political expression? And if the politically articulate citizen is a *desideratum* (as Mori implies), how is he better created than involving him in the political process through the direct vote; and is the occasional tergiversation of the party candidate really too high a price to pay for that? And, finally, what is the use of protecting the popular voice against undue influence by judges and soldiers when the popular voice has so little say vis-à-vis the judiciary and the military in the first place?

It is on this shaky theoretical foundation that Mori proceeds to build his constitutional edifice. Much of what has just been quoted looks like special pleading he could have avoided simply by not trying quite so hard to square his system with the popular will or to maintain the fiction of its over-all representativeness. Mori is to be faulted less for intellectual dishonesty than for a failure to think through to, or at any rate to make explicit in this essay his true, underlying objection to a popularly elected legislature. For he does have a premise more plausible than his juxtaposition of party politics versus the popular will; but we have to go to the *Pall Mall Gazette* interview of 25 February 1884 to find it: "Not that I have very much faith in Parliaments . . . I doubt whether parliamentarism can be successfully grafted on Japanese habits of thought.

It is hardly in the line of our historical development . . . In the Europe of which you form a part, parliamentarism with universal suffrage as its ultimate outcome is in the line of your development: you cannot avoid it; but I doubt whether we shall find it equally inevitable in Japan."[58]

This is an argument neither from sovereignty, which Mori does not treat at all, nor from prematurity, since the development is in any case not in the direction of parliamentarism, but from what might best be described as a doctrine of historical particularism, or of special historical evolution. Mori leans so heavily on this rubric elsewhere in *Representative System* that one wonders why, in his preliminary statement of principles, he was not content to rule out a popular legislature on these grounds alone, but felt he had to attack it in its native Western context as well. It is almost as if he were unwilling to admit in so many words, either to his English and American addressees or to his own Anglo-American-trained self, how very far he had placed himself from the genuine parliamentary tradition.

Mori's introductory parts make it clear that although a portion of the people's representatives are to be included in the legislative organ (III/11), their role in their own assembly will be simply to "express their individual opinions on legislative subjects," and to have a voice in the "fair imposition" or "apportioning" of taxation, but not in fixing its purposes or amounts (III/9, 11). Considering that "there are many requirements for the efficient working of government, such as communication, transportation, education and sanitation" (III/10), and that "every important object can best be cared for by those who are specially qualified," Mori wants his national assembly "composed of members, each of whom should represent bodies of national importance . . . first, the local assemblies, and second, any association . . . of sufficient importance to justify its official recognition as an electoral body" (III/21). These representatives, as we shall call them in conformance with the *daigisha* of the Japanese version, rather than the less descriptive "members" of the English original, are "responsible to those whom they represent," to whom their opinion "ought to be made known" (III/13). Their opinion, furthermore, "ought to be regarded as that of their constituents" (III/14).

Mori takes a dim view of the extension in some countries, under the maxim of "Taxation and Representation," of "a voice in effectively approving, or disapproving, the political conduct of their rulers," to "almost all classes, without any correct assessment of

58. *Pall Mall Gazette* (London), 26 Feb. 1884.

their wisdom and of their other qualities for the exercise of such an important power" (I/8). He seems to regret the historical processes by which "the actual framers of laws were, in early times at least, nominally advisers to the head person of the State, but . . . have gradually become practical rulers" (I/9); and by which "the legislative power has been generally vested in more than one body of men, but . . . has by degrees become absorbed by one body known as the 'Representatives of the People' " (I/10).

The first cardinal principle for Mori's legislative arm, therefore, is its very careful selection. Indeed, the "selecting persons themselves can be found only through the operation of a certain system of selection" (III/1). The second principle is the exercise of its powers "under the mutual check of two or three differently organized legislative bodies" (III/2), subject of course to "safeguards" against their becoming "inoperative through their disagreement" (III/3). The system of selection, "proper for adoption in Japan, will be one best suited to her own political development and circumstances" (III/5); objects of legislation are to be classified in order to secure for each class "one or more members possessing such knowledge and skill as are required for efficiently pursuing their respective objects" (III/4); and any enactment of the legislature must protect "all the legal rights of every person, especially those relating to possession of property and liberty of conscience" (III/8).

Mori finds that "the President's enormous power of administration" in America obviates some of the difficulties of the British executive, where "the legislators . . . who thus control the administration, are themselves dependent for their position on the pleasure of the electorate, and are therefore unable to ensure the successful working out of many important administrative measures." The Prussian administration, "appointed by, and . . . responsible to the King alone," is listed without comment as a third alternative (I/12). Communication, transportation, sanitation, and education are specifically "to be controlled by the government." Mori wants these areas "clearly defined," however, "in order to let the people understand that they are free to pursue any object of their desire, so long as they do not thereby disturb the due application of these measures of government" (III/10).

Mori makes a great deal once again of Japan's "aptitude for appreciating, and readily making use of, foreign ideas, manners and things"; and as she once "engrafted on her political institutions many features belonging to the highly developed systems of her Asiatic neighbors," so will she now learn from the systems of

Europe and America (II/2). Mori insists, however, that Japan's own system be established "on the soundest principle of politics which can be found to be in harmony with the historical character and development of the Empire" (III/20).

Mori's identification of this adaptiveness itself as a traditional feature and his sense of Japan as a separate historical case are more amply stated in the *Pall Mall Gazette,* and with an unmistakable note of national pride. After characterizing the Tokugawa seclusion as a 200 years' aberration, Mori affirmed: "People imagine here that Japanese progress during the last ten or fifteen years is a new thing to us. It is, on the contrary, but a return to her historic role, the only difference being that, whereas we formerly borrowed from the East, we now borrow from the West . . . You think that this importation of ideas and institutions from foreign and alien civilizations will weaken and impair our strength. I have too much confidence in the Japanese heart. Go all over the world, take any Japanese you like, no matter how Americanized or Europeanized he may be, and you will find in him the same stout heart which beats in the breast of every native of Japan." A consideration of the causes of "this intense attachment of the Japanese to their country—an attachment which neither time nor distance can weaken," led Mori directly into an appreciation of the emperor: "I think that two of its great causes are—first, the fact that for twenty-five centuries Japan has never passed beneath the rule of a conquering race—for all that period Japan has been free and unconquered . . . The second is that during the same period—for 2,500 years—we have remained under the same dynasty . . . No other state can point to such a record, and it is but natural that we should feel a pride in our country—a pride that makes us smile with amusement at the idea that our importation of steam engines, telegraphs or parliaments can in any way affect our Japanese heart."

Representative System identifies these same two causes, referring to "the Throne being the center of our national existence," and noting in the Japanese "a profound and unqualified respect for the Imperial Throne, and a peculiarly strong love for our country" (II/1). The initiative for establishing the new political system, therefore, lies with the emperor: "Since the Imperial Throne . . . is the center of our national existence, and the Sovereign is paramount, it may be concluded that, having regard to the historical development of the country, He should remain as He has hitherto been, the supreme authority of the State, and that He should establish a system, in accordance with which the selection of legislative councillors is to be made for our country . . ." (III/15). Mori, however, does not hesitate to pick and choose within the Japanese tradition to support his contention that all subjects should be equal before their emperor. He avers that the events of 1868 have "thoroughly restored the ancient form of the Imperial Government [meaning, one gathers, the Taika polity in its pristine form], which was constituted of two factors only, the Sovereign and His people, the latter having no political class-division." The fact that "at present political power remains almost entirely in the hands of those men who have been militarily brought up," is for Mori an unfortunate legacy of the feudal past, and he concludes that "no administrative or legislative office, on the basis of its hereditary occupation by any particular class or family, can be regarded as recommendable" (II/5, III/19).

The people are to participate in the political process not as individuals, however, but as family units. Mori argues that "the whole political system of Japan has always been based, essentially, on the principle that the head of every family is responsible for the conduct of its members . . . The political unit of Japan has always been identified with the head of every family, and no other unit can take its place" (II/3, III/17). Or, as Mori would elaborate in the *Pall Mall Gazette:* "In Japan our social system would enable us to adopt a different political unit from that of the male adult, or of the property-qualified elector. The head of the household with us would alone exercise the right of suffrage, no matter how many otherwise properly qualified adult males lived under his roof." As a fundamental principle of politics, *Representative System* continues, the family thus displaces wealth and property, which have "never been regarded by the Japanese so important in connection with politics as has been the case in Europe." Perhaps this alleged casualness toward property helps explain Mori's otherwise unelucidated contention that "the principle governing taxation in Japan has always been based only on the necessities of the State, without reference to the people's willingness or unwillingness to pay taxes" (II/3, III/17).

Mori pointed out to the *Pall Mall Gazette* reporter with pride, however, that the ratio (to total population) of paupers dependent on charity in London was thirty times the Tokyo figure. His expression suggests that the family system is more than a mere political instrumentality for him, and that he retains an attachment for it which is basically ethical in inspiration: "I must say there is one thing in Japan which you have not here, and which I miss . . . I refer to the sense of brotherhood which binds together all the members of one family, and which extends from them to all dwellers in one district . . . When I am in Tokyo, for instance, there is no man from my native village, no matter how poor, how mean, or how destitute he may be, who would not have the utmost confidence in coming to me for assistance. Nor can I refuse it him. There is nothing like that here; and that you may say if you like is one great element of practical religion among my people. Thus it is that we keep the second commandment of Christ: 'Thou shall love thy neighbor as thyself.' "

The third utilizable legacy of the past, Mori maintains, is Japan's regional political centers, "properly answering all the purposes of local politics," with some experience already in a "local Representative System," and ready to play a vital role in the selection process for his national assembly (II/4, II/8, III/18). Other factors, finally, which augur well for Japan's political stability include natural resources, an energetic population, an insular strategic position, an achievement of religious toleration, and a nation "so homogeneously formed as to remove any fear that race questions will disturb her politics" (III/10, 11).

MORI'S CONSTITUTIONAL SCHEME

Turning to the details of Mori's system (diagrammed in Figure 1), its most interesting and original feature in many ways is the selective mechanism which binds the representative, legislative, and administrative bodies into one single, interlocking whole. The structure is not "popular," but neither is it arbitrary, and it is above all testimony to Mori's overriding concern for quality in personnel. Up through the ninety-man national assembly (Kokkai), the selective mechanism is what Mori calls "graduated elections," or what we today would call "indirect" elections. As described in Part IV, the sixty representatives for Mori's "provincial" interests (in effect the political, or "popular" element in the national assembly), are elected by—and out of—the prefectural (*fu-ken*) assemblies, the membership of which in turn has been elected by, and out of, the county or ward (*gun-ku*) councils, and so on down through the town and village (*chō-son*) councils to the family heads at the base line. An identical procedure obtains for the thirty national assembly seats reserved for functional representation, i.e., for the special or professional interests which Mori suggests should include agriculture, industry, commerce, sanitation, education, science, and art. Here the members for the commercial interest, for instance, would be elected by and out of the national chamber of commerce, itself

Fig. 1: Mori's Constitutional Scheme

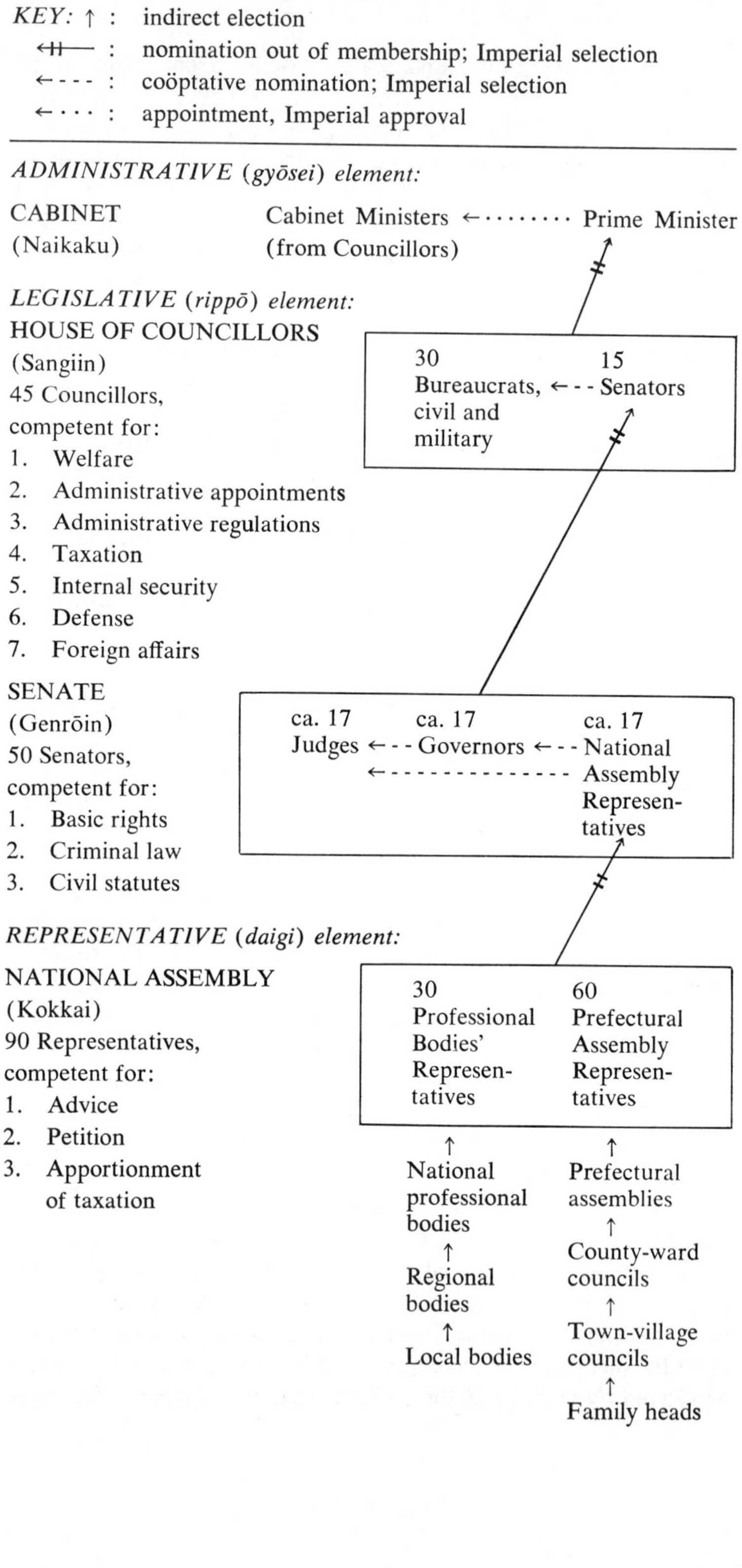

KEY: ↑ : indirect election
    ⇤ : nomination out of membership; Imperial selection
    ←--- : coöptative nomination; Imperial selection
    ←··· : appointment, Imperial approval

ADMINISTRATIVE (gyōsei) element:

CABINET   Cabinet Ministers ←········ Prime Minister
(Naikaku)   (from Councillors)

LEGISLATIVE (rippō) element:

HOUSE OF COUNCILLORS
(Sangiin)
45 Councillors,
competent for:
1. Welfare
2. Administrative appointments
3. Administrative regulations
4. Taxation
5. Internal security
6. Defense
7. Foreign affairs

30	15
Bureaucrats, civil and military	←-- Senators

SENATE
(Genrōin)
50 Senators,
competent for:
1. Basic rights
2. Criminal law
3. Civil statutes

ca. 17	ca. 17	ca. 17
Judges ←--	Governors ←--	National Assembly Representatives
←--------------		

REPRESENTATIVE (daigi) element:

NATIONAL ASSEMBLY
(Kokkai)
90 Representatives,
competent for:
1. Advice
2. Petition
3. Apportionment of taxation

30	60
Professional Bodies' Representatives	Prefectural Assembly Representatives

    ↑   ↑
National   Prefectural
professional   assemblies
bodies   ↑
  ↑   County-ward
Regional   councils
bodies   ↑
  ↑   Town-village
Local bodies   councils
               ↑
               Family heads

elected by and out of regional or local chambers of commerce constituted in the first instance by heads of mercantile houses.

Starting however with the two houses of Mori's legislature—the senate (Genrōin) and house of councillors (Sangiin)—and up through the prime minister (*dajōdaijin*), a different scheme obtains. Described in Parts VI and VII, it bears no particular name, but is in effect a system of imperial selection out of slates of nominees put together through both "graduated" (i.e., indirect-election) and coöptative processes. Its general function is to maintain a progressively diluted "popular" element against ever heavier infusions of bureaucratic, nonpolitical membership. Mori's fifty-man senate, (more "popular" in this scheme than his "House"), is to be divided evenly between representatives (i.e., from the national assembly), prefectural governors and judges (these latter two either incumbent or retired); his forty-five councillors are to include fifteen senators and thirty high-ranking civil and military officials; while his prime minister is to be nominated by—and out of—the house of councillors.

In each instance the lower (i.e., more "popular") body nominates, out of its own membership—that is to say, in "graduated" fashion—the first constituent portion of the body immediately superior to it: the representatives nominate from their own number the first third of the senate, the senators from their own number the first third of the councillors, the councillors from their own number the prime minister. The remaining two-thirds of senate and house of councillors are nominated, by contrast, in coöptative fashion: the first (i.e., representative) third of the senate coöpts the third reserved for governors, and these two together then coöpt the remaining third reserved for judges; while the first (i.e., senatorial) third of the councillors coöpts the remaining two thirds out of the civil and military bureaucracy.

In each instance, a slate of nominees double the membership required is submitted to the emperor, who, after consulting the cabinet (*naikaku ni komon shi*), selects (*chokusen*) half the slate in question. In selecting the prime minister the emperor chooses among three nominees (all councillors) and, when filling vacancies in the senate and house, among two names which must be submitted from the appropriate category: e.g., judges to replace judges. The prime minister, finally, selects his entire cabinet, subject to imperial approval (*chokkyo*), out of the house of councillors. The assembly, the senate, and the house are all represented (presumably by their respective speakers) in the cabinet, alongside the nine executive ministry chiefs for foreign affairs, interior, finance, justice, army, navy, education, industry and agriculture, and commerce. The interlocking of the system is further guaranteed by provision for concurrent service, which would make it theoretically possible for a representative in the assembly to hold seats simultaneously in the senate, house, and cabinet as well.

Of the ninety-five seats of Mori's combined bicameral legislature, two-thirds are reserved for governors, judges, and bureaucrats, with the imperial prerogative of final selection extending to the whole. Some popular counterweight is created by filling the first third of each chamber with members from the body next below, and entrusting that first third with the coöptation of the remainder; but the most significant balance is provided by restricting the field of nomination in each instance. In line with Mori's injunction against hereditary political classes, neither royal family nor peerage nor any persons ex officio (save for the emperor) play any role in his system. Neither the emperor nor the prime minister is permitted to recruit, either for legislative or for administrative posts, outside of closely defined categories. Neither pedigree nor wealth but professional qualification alone provides the selective yardstick, while countervailing against the massive intrusion of executive elements into the legislature is the requirement that the prime minister and all his cabinet be nominated out of the house of councillors.

As regards powers and competencies, Mori in Part IV describes those of the national assembly as three: tax apportionment, deliberation ("advice to the government on any question"), and—not mentioned in Part III—petition ("complaint as to the political conduct or legislative acts of the government"). With respect to tax apportionment, the government is to be bound by a two-thirds majority and to be liable for explanations whenever it rejects a majority decision short of two-thirds. The two chambers of the legislature, as explained in Part V, divide between them the matters in which they are to originate and process legislative proposals. Mori's senate is entrusted with the area of criminal and civil law and with the protection of the fundamental rights to life, property, and freedom of worship. With the preparation of Japan's own civil and criminal codes still pending, and with the absence in his scheme of an independent judiciary, Mori may have envisioned for the senate the tasks both of legal codification and of judicial review. To the councillors, by contrast, is reserved—in addition to matters affecting foreign affairs, defense, internal security, taxation and administrative procedure—the entire field of positive legislation on behalf of the "people's welfare" (*kokumin no kōfuku*).

Legislation originating in either chamber must be considered and voted on by both bodies, and Mori presents elaborate safeguards against stalemate, a recurring feature of which is his preference for two-thirds majorities. Bills failing of a majority in both chambers must be shelved for at least one year; bills receiving majorities in both chambers but less than a two-thirds majority in either chamber must be submitted to the emperor for a decision; following that, if a simple majority of the two chambers jointly assembled is not satisfied with the cabinet's explanations, the cabinet must resign; and, finally, a two-thirds majority in both chambers is binding upon the emperor. This last provision is probably the most "progressive" feature of the entire essay, even though Mori's legislature is not really—it bears repeating—"representative."

The nomenclature of the two legislative chambers is the most confusing item in the essay. Mori consistently refers to his senate and house of councillors as "Genrōin" and "Sangiin," respectively, except for one instance apiece in Part V in which he refers to his senate as "namely the Upper House" (*sunawachi* Jōin) and his house of councillors as "namely the Privy Council" (*sunawachi* Sūmitsukaku). Mori's councillors seem a bit too numerous for a privy council, but his use of the term certainly seems to underline their nonrepresentative character. The two chambers furthermore are clearly intended as coordinate legislative organs, which means that it is the councillors, not the representatives of the assembly, who correspond to the "lower" house. The quasijudicial aspect of the senate, together with the judges and governors who sit in it, do endow this chamber with a certain augustness lacking among the bureaucratic councillors with their more prosaic assignments. Yet, in terms of the selection procedure, Mori's senate is both the more numerous and the more "popular" of his two chambers.

Mori begins Part VIII by expatiating, in a crescendo of purple prose, on the charismatic (as opposed to the constitutional) role of the emperor in the Japanese polity:

> The Imperial Throne of Japan has remained in the same dynasty continuously now for 2,544 years. Over this period of time our people have ever (*tsune ni*) revered (*sonsū suru*) their Emperor (*tennō*) and looked upon Him as the axis [or pivot] of government (*seifu no kijiku*), the source of all honor (*eiken no minamoto*), and the father of his people (*jinmin no chichi*). When the moment arrives, therefore, to put into effect the proposed constitutional polity, presided over by His

Majesty (*heika hōtai shite*), He will continue to occupy as in the past the most exalted rank (*hōi*). The Emperor stands ever (*tsune ni*) at the center (*chūshin ni shite*), surrounded on all sides by His officials and His people. The position of the Emperor with respect to Japan may be likened to that of the sun, providing the central point for the revolving energy of the entire universe and commending the movement of the myriad stars in their courses.

Mori had referred very pointedly as early as 1873, in *Education in Japan,* to the affection in which the Japanese people held their sovereign. What is new here is not the assertion itself but the political consequences which Mori is now prepared to draw from it. His argument here again is neither from sovereignty nor from universal political evolution, but from Japan's own particular historical case. Mori's central "fact" is no less "historical" for its being entirely subjective, a matter of popular sentiment rather than of the emperor's objective historical powers. The subjective, or sociopsychological, factor would seem to constitute the core, indeed, of Mori's concept, and it is the stability which Mori attributes to this factor which renders his view, "historical" though it may be, one that is "evolutionary" only in a very limited sense. The key expression, *tsune ni* (clearly intended here in the sense of "continually" rather than of "ordinarily"), appears twice in the preceding quotation, while in the *Pall Mall Gazette* interview "Japanese habits of thought" are proclaimed to be impervious to a parliamentarism "hardly in the natural line of our historical development." Mori acknowledges and describes the historical evolution of Japan's political and social institutions yet seems to take this affection of the people for their sovereign as a virtually static facet of Japanese history. Nor does he suggest that the role, either constitutional or charismatic, which he now ascribes to the emperor is transitional to something more Western or to something more modern or sophisticated in a Japanese mode, or that it is anything less than permanent.

Mori's entire "representative system," indeed, is nowhere described as a stage preparatory to something more genuinely representative. On the contrary, Mori affirms in Part IX the value of "carefully retaining the most reliable and most essential portions of the present political system." In principle, of course, Mori does leave the door open to subsequent development through an amendment provision, briefly mentioned in Part III, Point 15: "Since no arbitrary changes in such a system is consistent with any constitutional government, the responsibility for any alteration of that system ought to be borne by His political advisers—the Ministers of State—this responsibility consisting in their being accountable to His legislative councillors." Mori is referring here to revisions in the selection mechanism for the legislature, but inasmuch as this is the only reference in the entire essay to an amendment procedure, one perhaps might reconstruct Mori's intended rule for constitutional amendment as follows: initiative by the cabinet, sanction by the legislature, promulgation by the Emperor. Mori does not tell us, however, in what direction (if any) he would like to see his proposed system develop.

The emperor is further described in Part VIII as "Himself taking the initiative, opening and leading the way" in the establishment of constitutional government, and the first of his two great constitutional functions is to serve, or rather to remain, as the "axis of government," as the center not only of the people's affection but of the political structure as well. This rather nebulous assignment is given substance through the appointive powers which constitute the emperor's second, and more tangible, constitutional function. He is described in Part VIII as the *saijōkan* of Mori's complex selection process. This expression, written with the characters for "uppermost" and "official," suggests an incipient "organ" theory, implicit also in much of Itō Hirobumi's thinking, and explicitly developed later by Minobe Tatsukichi. Unfortunately, Mori's original English equivalent for *saijōkan* (where it appears also in Part III, Point 15), is simply "the supreme authority of the State," referring it would seem more to a degree of power than to a status as "highest ranking official."

GENERAL IDEOLOGICAL AFFINITIES

In the closing paragraph of Part IX of "Daigi seitairon" Mori recommends his system as one which relies on qualified personnel at all levels, which reserves to each branch of the government full scope for its proper function, and which preserves a fine balance between each of the succeeding elements of the structure. He points out that in his national assembly, for instance, the "practical experience" of the members coming from prefectural assemblies will balance the "scientific specialization" of the representatives of professional bodies, while in his two legislative chambers the "knowledge" of the "ruled" will balance the "experience" of the "rulers," i.e., of the bureaucratic element.

For all its alleged internal balances, however, Mori's "representative system" as a whole leans rakishly in the direction of limited constitutional monarchy, with the emperor and the executive enjoying an overwhelming preponderance. The tightly categorized nominating procedure protects the system, it is true, against the whimsy of a Wilhelm II. Mori also avoids introducing the extracabinetal bodies or powers of Japan's actual prewar polity, such as the privy council (Sūmitsuin) or imperial household ministry (Kunaishō) or army and navy general staffs possessed of the right of direct appeal to the throne (*iaku jōsō*). Furthermore, neither of Mori's two legislative chambers reserves seats for the nobility as would the house of peers (Kizokuin). On the other hand, the house of representatives (Shūgiin) of the Meiji Diet would not only start with, but would rapidly add to, effective powers well beyond those ever contemplated by Mori as appropriate for directly elected representatives of the people. Finally, with his prospective uses of the emperor and of the family system, Mori anticipates two of the central features of the coming political orthodoxy.

Whatever the progressive component in *Representative System* and "Daigi seitairon," it is clear that Mori's political views as of late 1883, when this essay was written, had shifted in a conservative direction since September of 1882, when he could still urge upon Itō the value of investigating the Italian polity. We know (as Chapter Nine will explain) that Mori and Itō at Paris in 1882 were in basic agreement on matters political as far as they affected educational affairs. What most likely happened in London in the spring of 1883 was that Itō, winding up his own researches at that time, finally spelled out for Mori the precise area within which constitutional proposals would still be entertained, and that Mori spent the remainder of the year preparing his essay with these guidelines in mind.

There are two points in *Representative System* which may have taken some inspiration from Central European models. The selection procedure for Mori's assembly, for one, finds an echo in that of the contemporary Abgeordnetenhaus (house of representatives) of the Austrian Reichsrat (parliament), which was elected by four separate constituencies or *curiae* corresponding to socioeconomic classes: (1) large landowners; (2) chambers of commerce; (3) towns; and (4) rural communities. Directly elected after 1878, the Abgeordnetenhaus had up to the reforms of that year been elected indirectly by the provincial diets of the seventeen crown lands, which in turn had been chosen by the same four *curiae*.[59]

59. Edwin R. A. Seligman and Alvin Johnson, eds., *Encyclopedia of the Social Sciences* (New York, 1948), V, 519; E. C. Helmreich, "Austria," *Encyclopedia Americana*, 1968, II, 793ff.

Mori's bicameral legislature, secondly, is not entirely without resemblance to the Bundesrat, or federal council, of the German empire. This body, although nominated by the various *Länder* (State) governments, could by no stretch of the imagination have been called representative. Not only was it clothed with the final sanctioning power over legislation and with that of constitutional amendment, but it also enforced, through the imperial bureaucracy under its control, legislation at the federal level within those very same areas staked out by Mori for his house of councillors. The dual executive-legislative nature of the Bundesrat ("the pivot on which the entire Imperial system turned"[60]), might very well have been realized in the actual practice of Mori's model, given the umbilical attachment of his cabinet to his house of councillors; while the popularly elected Reichstag (parliament) in its virtual impotence must have come very close to what Mori had envisioned for his national assembly.[61] Mori makes no effort, however, to derive his system from, or accommodate it to, the sort of abstract, organic theory of the state which one would expect if he had put himself to school with any of Itō's own advisers—Rudolf von Gneist, Albert Mosse, Lorenz von Stein—or otherwise committed himself in any fundamental way to German political theory. Mori's essay does not ring Teutonic, and as a constitutional model his scheme is most safely tagged as *sui generis*.

Many of Mori's fundamental premises are, to begin with, not only distinctly his own but also of very long standing. The need to adjust new institutions to Japan's historical heritage was stated as early as 1865 in the letters to his brother Yokoyama; the inadvisability of rushing to representative institutions vitiated by party politics as early as 1871 in *Life and Resources in America;* the peculiar capacity of the Japanese for adaptation, together with their affection for the emperor, as early as 1873 in *Education in Japan;* and the plea for specialized talent in government as early as 1874 in "Gakusha shokubunron no hyō." Much of what remains can be more easily traced to English (or American) than to German sources, adjusted of course to fit the area presumably acceptable to Itō.

Mori's faith in bureaucratic expertise, for instance, required

60. Harold Zink, *Modern Governments,* 2nd ed. (New York, 1962), p. 408.
61. Ibid., pp. 405–409; Karl Loewenstein, "Germany: Government to 1945," *Encyclopedia Americana,* 1968, XII, 535–536; A. J. P. Taylor, "The German Empire, 1867–1871 and 1871–1918," *Encyclopaedia Britannica,* 1968, X, 316–326.

neither Itō nor Prussian efficiency for its inspiration. The second lengthiest document of Mori's London tour was his memorial on the civil service, "Kanri tōyōhō narabi ni taikyūhō seido kengon" (Memorial on the rules for appointing, and the system for pensioning, government officials), addressed to the prime minister (*dajō daijin*) Sanjō Sanetomi on 16 March 1881.[62] In this essay, Mori argues that Japan is at last ready for a career civil service; that a proper pension system is the best guarantee of an honest and hardworking officialdom; and that recruitment and pension policies need to be in thorough alignment "like the two wings of a bird or the two wheels of a chariot."[63] He then proceeds to lavish praise on the British civil service, both in India and in the home islands: "The most brilliantly effective system of this type that comes to mind in the recent history of the world, is the pension system for the government officials of British India . . . Once the ruling authority in India was transferred to the government of the British Crown, and a first-rate pension system established throughout India, the ethical conduct of officials saw a dramatic improvement . . . The governments of almost all the advanced nations of Europe today have recruitment and pension codes . . . I consider those of Britain to have the fewest glaring faults. Nevertheless, legal systems need to be well adjusted to actual conditions in any given country if they are to be of any service at all. The British codes therefore, however splendid, ought not to be transferred directly to Japan."[64]

This essay refers neither to Germany nor to Prussia. The United States is mentioned, but negatively, in connection with the spoils system. Mori's attachment of a working paper, "based in the main on current British pension codes," shows where his focus of attention still lies.[65] Mori obviously has given the matter a great deal of careful thought. He opens with a most convincing psychological portrait of the official faced with an insecure old age, goes on to attack current recruitment methods, and ends by making many specific recommendations: the appointment of a special committee to investigate foreign systems and devise one suitable for Japan; the establishment of an examination system; the clear demarcation of civil service and political appointments; the careful spelling out

62. Mori Arinori, "Kanri tōyōhō narabi ni taikyūhō seido kengon," *Zenshū* I, 23–29.
63. Ibid., p. 25.
64. Ibid., pp. 25, 27.
65. Ibid., p. 27. Mori's attachment dealt specifically with the appointment and pensioning of judicial officials, and follows the memorial in *Zenshū* I, 30–33.

of numbers and grades of officials and of rules for calculating raises and pensions;[66] and the creation of judicial officials genuinely independent of the government.[67] Throughout the argument, one can sense the practical, methodical mind of a born administrator at work.

If pensions were required to raise the ethical standards of officials, recruitment by examination seemed to Mori necessary not only to boost the quality but also to limit the quantity of applicants: "Our officialdom has gradually grown to the point where we now have supernumerary members. If we want to reduce personnel and save the government's money, it will do no good simply to close down part of a ministry or change the names of bureaus and sections. For until we set up a designated gateway for the recruitment of officials and establish fixed numbers for them, the [i.e., ex-] samurai throughout the land will continue to aim indiscriminately (pensions or no pensions) for high office, and to struggle and compete with great fervor for government service. Shoo them away as you will, they come swarming back like flies on a bowl of rice."[68]

Referring in his conclusion to the seven out of ten who do not survive this free-for-all, Mori remarks that: "If we had an equitable code for government appointments in this country, which automatically would limit the number of officials, these young fellows would not suppose from the day they were born that good fortune was to be sought for solely in government service, but would turn to some suitable employment in the private sector, in line with their respective talents . . . Is it not an immense waste of the nation's resources to force [these youths] to repeat, after one failure, their entire preparation for life's work?"[69] In "Gakusha shokubunron no hyō" in the *Meiroku zasshi,* Mori had begged trained talent—against the enticement of Fukuzawa—to stay in government service. Here, in "Kanri tōyōhō taikyūhō," he asks all but the most highly qualified to stay away. It was not Mori's principle so much as the times that had changed. With the gradual spread of education and the rise of political consciousness, it had become necessary to devise an appropriate sorting mechanism. Mori's elitism is explicit, and the scorn with which he brushes aside the political aspirations of the multitude suggests that it rests not only on economic considerations but on a strong temperamental bent as well. This elitism carried with it important implications

66. Ibid., p. 27.
67. Ibid., p. 31. From the attachment.
68. Ibid., p. 26.
69. Ibid., pp. 28–29.

not only of a political but also of an educational nature: for the turnstile of civil service examinations could only be but the last of a series of progressively narrowing wickets built into the whole sweep of the school system.

Mori's emphasis on specialized talent resembles—but does not necessarily reflect—the technocratic, bureaucratic biases of German statism and French positivism. He echoes much that could be found in chapters 5 and 14 of John Stuart Mill's *Considerations on Representative Government*,[70] and there was also at hand in England, besides Mill and besides the civil service legislation Mori so admired, the whole Benthamite and Utilitarian canon to provide philosophical justification for a specialized elite.

There was much, indeed, in the general English intellectual climate which finds resonance also in the historical, as opposed to abstract, quality of Mori's political thinking. Walter Bagehot (d. 1877), Benjamin Disraeli (d. 1881) and Sir Henry Maine (d. 1888) all, for instance, interpreted society and the state in evolutionary, historical terms.[71] Bagehot and Disraeli furthermore both identified and emphasized what they called "national character."[72] And Disraeli had written not only of the charismatic properties of the Crown (as had Edmund Burke much earlier) but also of its functional headship in an increasingly divided nation.[73] Bagehot and Maine shared Mill's apprehension of the rule of the common man, and Maine's *Popular Government* of 1885 would go much further than Mill in its low estimation of party politics and the democratic principle.[74]

OVERCOMPENSATING CONSERVATISM: SPENCER AND GRANT

Mori possibly may have met Disraeli and Maine as fellow members at the Athenaeum. It is a certainty, however, that Herbert

70. Mill, *Representative Government*, pp. 68–83, 194–211.//
71. Crane Brinton, *English Political Thought in the 19th Century*, Harper Torchbook ed. (New York, 1962), pp. 130–148, 180–198, 266–282; John Bowle, *Politics and Opinion in the Nineteenth Century: An Historical Introduction*, Galaxy Book ed. (New York, 1964), pp. 248–264.//
72. Disraeli in "Vindication of the English Constitution," (1835) in W. Hutcheson, ed., *Whigs and Whiggism* (1914), p. 120; and Bagehot in "Physics and Politics," (1872) in Mrs. R. Barrington, ed., *Works* (1915), VIII, 24. Both cited in Brinton, *English Political Thought*, pp. 135 and 190, respectively.//
73. Brinton, *English Political Thought*, p. 139.//
74. Ibid., pp. 275–279; Bowle, *Politics and Opinion*, p. 255.

Spencer personally read and commented on Mori's constitutional scheme, and his influence on several important points is beyond question. Spencer had upon their very first meeting in 1873 given Mori extremely conservative advice regarding the reorganization of Japanese institutions.[75] That Mori had shown *Representative System* (or some preliminary English draft of the essay) to Spencer in London in the early 1880's, and that the latter had found even Mori's scheme too radical, emerges from Spencer's own recollection as addressed to Kaneko Kentarō on 21 August 1892: "Probably you remember I told you that when Mr. Mori, the then Japanese Ambassador, submitted to me his draft for a Japanese constitution, I gave him very conservative advice, contending that it was impossible that the Japanese, hitherto accustomed to despotic rule, should all at once become capable of constitutional government. My advice was not, I fear, duly regarded, and as I gather from the recent reports of Japanese affairs, you are experiencing the evils arising from too large an installment of freedom."

Spencer would elaborate in another letter to Kaneko, dated two days later: "My advice to Mr. Mori was that the proposed new institutions should be as much as possible *grafted* upon the existing institutions, so as to prevent breaking the continuity—that there should not be a *replacing* of old forms by new, but a modification of old forms to a gradually increasing extent. I did not at the time go into the matter so far as to suggest in what way this might be done, but it now occurs to me that there is a very feasible way of doing it."[76]

Kaneko had struck up a personal acquaintance with Spencer in London in the spring of 1890, when the English philosopher had arranged to have him made an honorary member of the Athenaeum.[77] At that time, too, Spencer had alluded to his earlier advice to Mori, as reported (in direct quotation) by Kaneko in a memorandum dated 2 March 1890, entitled "Supensā shi to no danwa" (A talk with Mr. Spencer):

> Unless the constitution of Japan and the laws adjunct to it possess a spirit and character in conformity with Japan's history and polity (*kokutai*), there will be great difficulty in putting them into effect, and in the long run it will prove impossible to carry out the purposes of constitutional government.

75. See Chapter Six.
76. Duncan, *Life of Spencer,* p. 319, quoting letters from Herbert Spencer to Kentaro Kaneko dated 21 and 23 Aug. 1892.
77. Ibid., p. 292.

I once expressed my opinion on this subject to the Japanese Minister in England, Mori. I expressed the hope that Japan would summon up the spirit to establish its constitution as follows: to be guided by the principle of gradualism and conservatism (*zanshin hoshu no shugi*); to take the history and customs of the land as its foundation; to introduce at the same time the constitutionalism of Europe and America and accommodate the traditional form of government (*seitai*) to it; and to avoid by all means erecting the new system on the ruins of the old. I explained how botany teaches that vegetation transplanted from a foreign land will not produce the same flowers and fruit as in its native soil; that constitutions follow a principle identical with this botanic law; that constitutions in Europe and America had developed according to the polity, history and customs of each individual country; and that it certainly would be an immense mistake to hope that a constitution of foreign origin, translated and promptly put into practice, would bear the same fruit as in its native land. However, after a brief perusal of your Constitution, it is clear from the text and from the notes that it was drafted according to gradualist, conservative principles, with Japan's ancient history and customs as its base.[78]

Spencer's enthusiasm as of 1890 was considerably lessened, one gathers from the letters of 1892, by the performance of the first three Diets. Spencer in his *Principles of Sociology* had described Japanese history in general, and the Tokugawa period in particular, as an instance of a society in its "militant" phase, as "an organization completely militant, under which political freedom was unknown."[79] Spencer accordingly foresaw great difficulties in Japan's transition to the "industrial" phase which inevitably would follow according to his general scheme of evolution, but his go-slow advice to the Japanese constitution builders was so out of line with his own liberal reputation, that he felt it necessary to caution Kaneko in a third letter, on 26 August 1892, that: "I give this advice in confidence. I wish that it should not transpire publicly, at any rate during my life, for I do not desire to rouse the animosity of my fellow-countrymen."[80]

78. Kaneko Kentarō, "Supensā shi to no danwa," in Itō Hirobumi, ed., *Kenpō shiryō*, 3 vols. (Tokyo, 1936), I, 211.
79. Spencer, *Principles of Sociology*, I, part III, p. 742. Similar statements may be found in volume I, part II, p. 562 and part III, p. 752.
80. Duncan, *Life of Spencer*, p. 323, quoting letter from Herbert Spencer to Kentaro Kaneko, 26 Aug. 1892.

Liberals and conservatives in Meiji Japan made quite opposite uses of Spencer's liberalism and of his Social Darwinism at the level of theoretical debate. To this influence should be added perhaps a third, namely, the direct, ad hoc, behind-closed-doors tips which Spencer was in the habit of giving Mori, Kaneko, Itō, and other "leading Japanese statesmen, resident in or visiting London," who, in the words of Spencer's biographer, David Duncan, "were wont to consult him on matters bearing on the changes their country was passing through."[81] That Spencer, who met so many Japanese, should in 1890 and 1892 (nearly a decade later) specifically have remembered Mori suggests the intimacy of their acquaintance and the depth of their political conversations at that time. That Spencer strengthened Mori's concern for historical continuities and provided him with the expression "engrafting," seems beyond question. The "feasible way," furthermore, which "now occurs" to Spencer corresponds very closely to some of the salient features of *Representative System*. One would not expect Spencer to have remembered exactly what he told Mori ten years earlier, and the simplest explanation of points of resemblance between Mori's essay and the letters to Kaneko, is that Spencer is repeating points he forgot he had already made to Mori. Another possibility, of course, is that Mori originally may have put some ideas in Spencer's head—rather than the other way around.

Spencer's "feasible way" may be summarized, in his own words, as follows: "You have, I believe, in Japan still surviving the ancient system of family organization . . . This organization should be made use of in your new political form. These patriarchs or heads of groups should be made the sole electors of members of your representative body . . . I suggest that, for three or four generations, the assembly formed of representative men elected by these patriarchal heads of groups should be limited in their functions to making *statements of grievances* . . . This would be a function completely on the lines of the function of our own representative body in its earliest stages . . . After three or four generations

---

81. Ibid., p. 318. Nagai Michio, in "Herbert Spencer in Early Meiji Japan," *Far Eastern Quarterly,* 14. 1:55–64 (November 1954), has covered the first two instances of Spencerian influence in considerable detail and has also mentioned Spencer's advice to Mori and Kaneko. I should like to suggest simply that the direct, personal advice was in effect a third type of influence, essentially pragmatic, as opposed to the theoretical, polemical uses —whether liberal or conservative—made of the man in literary, scholarly, or journalistic circles. This advice, which got through to the actual framers of the constitution, was perhaps in the long run the most important aspect of Spencer's highly variegated influence.

... they should have the further power of suggesting remedies—not the power of passing remedial laws ... And then, after this had been for generations the function of the representative body, there might eventually be given to it a full power of legislation, coordinate with that of the other two legislative authorities."[82]

Spencer's identification of the family as the political unit, his separation of representative and legislative functions, and his "other two legislative authorities" as distinct from the representative assembly, all appear in *Representative System*. Mori's scheme is at first glance the more progressive in that it accords the representative body at the outset not only the right of petition but also the second, advice-giving function for which Spencer would have it wait "three or four generations." In the long—if very long—run, however, Spencer unlike Mori foresees the representative organ assuming legislative powers. Spencer's concept, however dilatory, is genuinely evolutionary, working along a universal line of growth, the model for which seems to be England's own leisurely constitutional development. Mori's framework, although similarly historical, places Japan by contrast not only in an earlier phase, but also in a different line, of development from that of the West.

Spencer, in the passage just quoted, argued in 1892 that the conservative leanings of household elders, and above all the reduced number of the electorate, "would at once do away with the possibilities of those quarrels from which you are now suffering."[83] Kaneko's memorandum reported a similar distrust of popular power on Spencer's part in 1890, when the latter admitted that "*laissez-faire* is the ultimate goal of government," but warned that it was the final fruit of a lengthy process of political evolution no intermediate phase of which could be omitted. Kaneko recalled that Spencer spoke with irritation of things having "gotten to the point where the right of participation in government is held without the corresponding duty to pay taxes," and of "governments taking the initiative to press the right of political participation on their citizenry." That Spencer at least confirmed Mori's Washington-bred anti-party bias, is suggested by his admonition to Kaneko about what happened a few decades after the establishment of the Constitution of the United States: "Politics in America gradually fell into the hands of political parties, most of which are dominated by the self-interest of politicians. Good citizens came to lament these abuses, but in the end were forced to despair of

---

82. Duncan, *Life of Spencer*, pp. 319–320, quoting letter from Herbert Spencer to Kentaro Kaneko, 23 Aug. 1892.
83. Ibid., p. 320.

ever securing in actual practice the equality of rights guaranteed by the Constitution."[84] Spencer's emphasis on native institutions may have encouraged Mori in his willingness to make full political use of the popular reverence of the Japanese for their sovereign. What we do not possess is a provable (or even probable) Spencerian lead for Mori's concept of, and proposals for, the emperor.

The traces of Spencer in *Representative System,* taken together with Mori's total acceptance of Social Darwinism in the area of national commercial competition, amount to an impressive tutelage by a man still widely reputed to be not only the oracle but also the arch-liberal of his age. And if a liberal of Spencer's stature could give such conservative advice, what theoretical defense was left for such liberalism, nascent or residual, as Mori himself may have possessed? Spencer's advice, as a matter of fact, represents only the most conspicuous example of a more general phenomenon in Mori's political tutelage by Westerners. This might be described as an overcompensating conservatism on the part of his tutors, a tendency to lean over backward away from their own liberalism in order not to push Japan too rapidly down the road of progress. Perhaps because of their own typical nineteenth-century faith in the inevitability of progress, the danger which presented itself most plausibly to their minds was simply chaos, rather than the authoritarian reaction which their own overcompensating posture in fact abetted.

The London press from 1880 to 1889, for instance, showed less concern that Japan would opt for a German constitutional model (to which, one gathers, she was more than welcome) than that she would attempt the too ambitiously progressive. The most authoritative reporter on Far Eastern affairs, the *London and China Telegraph,* in an editorial on 15 March 1880, very soon after Mori's arrival, cautioned: "No one who has really the good of the country at heart would wish to see the contemplated reforms very long delayed if they are desired by a large proportion of the people, though their best friends will trust that they may act with caution. *Festina lente* should be their motto." As of 7 June 1884, shortly after Mori had left, the *London and China Telegraph* still had not changed its mind: "It may seem to us, even now, that the endeavour to introduce full-blown Parliamentary Government among a people who have hardly yet shaken off the last trammels of feudalism is, to say the least, a premature step on dangerous ground."

The indulgent skepticism with which the British press as a whole greeted the Meiji Constitution in 1889 suggests, finally, how per-

84. Kaneko, "Supensā shi to no danwa," p. 212.

vasive Mori must have found the posture of overcompensating conservatism in London:

> [*Manchester Guardian:*] The great hope of the friends of Japan in this tremendous leap in the dark must be the character of the Japanese people themselves . . .
>
> [*Morning Post* (London):] It is impossible not to see that Japan is progressing so fast that it seems very likely to trip in its hurry . . .
>
> [*Daily Telegraph* (London):] Parliamentary institutions will be on their trial in Japan, and that for a good while to come. Manhood suffrage is a leap in the dark . . . Japan has got its Parliament, however, and we can only hope it may prove a useful as well as an amusing toy.[85]

Nor had Mori's American mentors, beginning with personal friends such as Charles Lanman or Joseph Henry, been any different. Ex-President Grant, whom Mori had known in Washington and whom he had accompanied during the former's visit to Japan in 1879, went out of his way to advise the emperor in a lengthy interview in Tokyo that: "[elective] assemblies are very good for all countries in due time . . . The people shall know that it is coming and they should be educating themselves for the responsibility. But you must always remember that privileges like this can never be recalled . . . Consequently in establishing such an assembly too great caution cannot be taken . . . You do not want to see anarchy as the result of any premature creation of an assembly . . . It seems to me that the first step should be an advisory assembly, a council of the leading men in Japan with power to debate but not to legislate."[86]

Outlandish as the choice may seem to us today, Herbert Spencer and Ulysses S. Grant were probably the one Englishman and the one American most trusted and most admired by the Japanese in their day as dispensers of political sagacity; and Mori had been as close to either of these two men personally as had any other Japanese. Mori indeed is one of the most applicable cases of what George Sansom must have had in mind when he noted: "A study

---

85. As reprinted in LCT, 18 Feb. 1889.

86. From the English-language transcript, "Memorandum of the Conversation between His Majesty and General Grant, August 10th, 1879, at Hama Rikiu," in *Guranto Shōgun to no Gotaiwa hikki,* Kokumin Seishin Bunka Kenkyūjo ed. (Tokyo, 1937), pp. 16–17.

of what we may call literary influences, though tempting to the historian, may be misleading, for often they do not penetrate beyond intellectual circles and find little response in practical life. It is probable that, despite the great number of Western books circulated in Japan during the first twenty years of Meiji, their effect was not so great as the aggregate influence of individuals consulted by Japanese on their journeys abroad and of foreign advisers employed in Japan, who were in close touch with officials and students destined later to hold important posts."[87]

This dichotomy between indirect "literary" influences and direct personal influences was magnificently epitomized by Spencer's walking out on Itagaki when he could no longer stand the playback of his own liberal philosophy from the Japanese visitor. The typical intellectual of the Popular Rights Movement worked from books, many if not most of them in Japanese translation. Mori's contact with Western thinkers was, by contrast, both literary and social, and conducted entirely in the original Western-language (i.e., English) medium. The advice given was often, as the case of Spencer illustrates, piecemeal, ad hoc, and specially tailored for the Japanese inquirer. It was the sort of influence one could not surmise from the published works of Western thinkers, but could only be reconstructed from letters or diaries or other specific accounts of the personal encounter in question. This suggests an added dimension of complexity in evaluating the intellectual development of Japanese like Mori, for whom the impact of such informal, personal, and largely unrecorded Western influences may have been as instrumental in inducing political conservatism as any failure to bridge the philosophical or psychological gap between the Confucian and the Western concepts of society and the individual. Similar personal—and primarily English—contacts were meanwhile proving to be equally important for Mori in the development of his educational viewpoint.

87. George B. Sansom, *The Western World and Japan* (New York, 1950), p. 362.

Nine   *1879–1884*

THE MAKING OF AN EDUCATION MINISTER

Diplomacy continued to provide Mori with his daily vocation until 1884, but his avocation lay very clearly in the contemplation of Japanese education, a matter of far greater interest to him personally than the constitutional question. Both Mori's thinking as it developed during this period and the general trend of Japanese education as well require some discussion as a prelude to the years when Mori himself would at last be able to set that trend.

SOME USEFUL COORDINATES

Such a discussion entails something at once broader and narrower than a survey of early Meiji education. Much of what held Mori's own attention lies properly speaking in the field of comparative education, while that in the Japanese educational trend which may be essential for our understanding of Mori omits a great deal that would belong in a comprehensive survey of the subject. There are, however, four rough coordinates (entirely hand-drawn) along which virtually all significant material on education, whether historical or comparative in approach, can be arranged, and which are suggested here as aids to navigation over the billows, so to speak, of statistical profusion and organizational complexity inherent in any institutional study, namely (1) basic values and specific purposes (the normative coordinate); (2) control and finance (the administrative coordinate); (3) organization and scope of the system (the structural coordinate); and (4) subject matter and teachers (the instructional coordinate). This paradigm might further be elaborated as follows:

I: NORMATIVE:
    A. Basic Values
        (1) View of Man
        (2) Attitude toward knowledge
    B. Specific Purposes
        (1) Material
        (2) Intellectual and spiritual
        (3) Social and Political

II: ADMINISTRATIVE:
    A. Control
        (1) Locus and channels of authority
        (2) Implementation of authority
            (a) Supervision (of instruction)
            (b) Management (of plant)
    B. Finance

III: STRUCTURAL:
    A. Organization of Schools
        e.g.: primary, secondary, university, normal, technical and vocational, women's schools; public and private sectors
    B. Scope of Opportunity
        e.g.: Single-, dual-, multiple-track

IV: INSTRUCTIONAL:
    A. Subject Matter
        (1) Curriculum
        (2) Textbooks
    B. The Teacher
        (1) As Pedagogue
        (2) As Exemplar

The *normative coordinate* (I) subsumes both those basic values (I-A) of the general culture most relevant to an educational philosophy—notably its view of Man (I-A-1) and its attitude toward knowledge (I-A-2)—and also those specific purposes (I-B) which the educational system has been established to serve in the material (I-B-1), or intellectual and spiritual (I-B-2) or social and political (I-B-3) realms. Societies generally reveal distinct preferences regarding such fundamental polarities as individualism versus collectivism, egalitarianism versus elitism, or liberalism versus authoritarianism (to take three of the most obvious examples), as well as certain biases toward knowledge both in its epistemological aspect (e.g., idealism, rationalism, empiricism) or in its social dimension (e.g., relative valuations of character as opposed to intellect, of functional as opposed to nonfunctional information, of the innovative as opposed to the conservative mentality). These basic values may give rise directly to specific purposes (e.g., as egalitarianism would generate a demand for social mobility) or may serve simply as limiting factors, circumscribing or suggesting the ways in which specific purposes may be carried out (e.g., as individualistic and liberalistic values tend to restrict the educational measures that may legitimately be taken to increase the wealth or power of the state).

Since public instruction necessarily involves a balance of collective and individual interests, it is not surprising that the specific purposes of education all tend to throw that balance one way or the other. On the material plane, an educational system may be geared primarily toward the attainment of national wealth or, conversely, toward the maximization of individual economic opportunity; to the extent that it promotes physical health, on the other hand, it may contribute simultaneously to both individual and collective well-being. The same dual benefit adheres, in the intellectual and spiritual realm, to the increase of knowledge and the development of character. Some educational systems, however, have been committed beyond that to the imposition of religious or political conformity, while others have deliberately sought the self-realization of the individual. At the social and political level, finally, the individualistic goals of social mobility and education for citizenship stand in sharp contrast to attempts to allocate human resources according to national need, or to create a leadership elite.

The *administrative coordinate* (II) involves above all the control (II-A) of the educational system. Arguments about the locus and channels of authority (II-A-1) have produced such classic debates as that between centralization and decentralization, or the public versus the private sector, or the separation of education from (versus its manipulation by) political or religious interests. The implementation of such authority (II-A-2) may be analyzed in terms both of the supervision of instruction (II-A-2-a) (e.g., inspection, curriculum control, textbook authorization, teacher certification) and of the management (II-A-2-b) of the physical plant of the school establishment.[1] The actual disbursement of money

1. "Supervision" and "management" as used here are, strictly speaking, technical terms corresponding to the distinction made between *Oberaufsicht* and *Verwaltung* in Prussia, where the control of teaching traditionally had

falls properly under management, but the problem of its collection, i.e., the financing (II-B) of education (through taxation, philanthropy, tuition fees, or other means) constitutes a high-level policy question closely linked, as often as not, to the debate on authority.

Although the administrative coordinate on the whole reflects the values and purposes of the normative coordinate, which it seeks to implement, the correspondence is to some extent deflected by considerations only distantly if at all related to the beliefs and goals of a given society. There are, for instance, the pressures of "objective" factors of a geographical, demographical, or economic nature, and the imperatives peculiar to the administrative coordinate itself—such as administrative efficiency or operational economy. Nations with values and purposes as different as the Soviet Union and modern France, for instance, have centralized their control of education to a high degree, and one must be careful not to jump from administrative practice to ideological conclusions.

Along the *structural coordinate* (III) the organization (III-A) of the system into various levels and types of schools, easily enough classified and described, tells us what sort of education has been established in fulfillment of the material, intellectual, and spiritual purposes of the normative coordinate. The social and political effects of an educational system, however, are determined less by the classification of schools than by the scope of opportunity (III-B) provided by them; and this is in turn a function of their number and capacity, and above all of the method of their articulation within the whole. The so-called single-, dual-, and multiple-track systems represent three of the most basic patterns of articulation, the former serving to promote economic and social mobility, the latter two operating by contrast to produce economic, social, political, bureaucratic, and technological elites.[2]

---

been entrusted to the state, and the control of physical plant to the localities. See A. D. C. Peterson, *A Hundred Years of Education: A Comparative Study of Educational Patterns in Western Europe and the United States,* Collier Books Edition (New York, 1962), p. 54; and Lorenz von Stein, *Handbuch der Verwaltungslehre* (Stuttgart, 1870), p. 122.

2. The multiple track is, strictly speaking, a variant of the dual track pattern, and the terms often have been used interchangeably. The significance of the single, dual, and multiple track systems lies in the way in which they serve to widen or narrow the access to university education, which in turn commands the road to political and/or economic power. They thereby determine also the social prestige attaching to various types of education. Universal primary education is basic to both patterns. Secondary education in the dual track caters to a very limited portion of the population, however, and functions solely as the "preparatory" stage of university train-

The *instructional coordinate* (IV), finally, covers the content of education: both its subject matter (IV-A) or *what* is taught, i.e., curriculum (IV-A-1), textbooks (IV-A-2), and *how* it is taught by the teacher (IV-B). The latter needs to be considered as pedagogue (IV-B-1), i.e., in terms of what he *does* as a teacher (e.g., methods of instruction, educational psychology), and as an exemplar (IV-B-2), i.e., in terms of what he *is* as a human being (e.g., his own social origin and status, and his own training, character, and ideals). The values of the normative coordinate are most obviously apparent in the instructional coordinate, painfully so in systems deliberately committed to ideological indoctrination. As in the case of administration, however, the instructional coordinate has certain independent imperatives of its own, i.e., strictly educational imperatives, which should not be lost sight of. It may be desirable, for instance, to keep an eye on textbooks with no more sinister motive than quality control. One may wish also, out of a simple sense of decency, to require of teachers that they adhere to certain minimum moral standards. And the adoption of a scientific curriculum does not necessarily in and of itself imply (as classicists fear, or feared), the abandonment of a humanistic outlook.

These four coordinates have been suggested solely to facilitate the classification of data, and no further functional or theoretical validity is claimed for the paradigm. Two points might be made, however, regarding the interrelationship of the coordinates themselves. First, with due allowance for autonomous imperatives in the administrative and instructional coordinates, the normative generally tends to govern the other three: value preferences to some extent determine methods of control and finance; purposes directly

---

ing. In the single track, where it approaches (at least at the lower secondary level) universality, it serves by contrast both as the terminal stage of common education and as the preparatory phase not only for university but other types of specialized training (e.g., normal, technical and vocational, women's education) as well. In the dual track, such specialized training builds directly on the primary level, enjoys no lateral mobility vis-à-vis the academic (i.e., secondary and university) track, and is distinctly inferior to the latter in terms of prestige. In the single track, specialized education builds by and large upon the secondary level and enjoys both a high degree of lateral mobility into, and coordinate prestige with, the academic track. The dual track, strictly speaking, emerges when the segregation of students destined ultimately for the university takes place as early as the lower primary level, the multiple track when the segregation occurs subsequent to the primary (or at least lower primary) level. Classical examples of the single, dual, and multiple track systems may be found respectively in modern America, in France of the Third Republic, and in Japan prior to World War II.

dictate what sort of schools shall be established and for whom; and both values and purposes help determine what shall be taught and by whom. The second point is that the administrative, structural, and instructional coordinates enjoy by contrast very little fixed or necessary relation with respect to each other, and that even under an identical normative rubric an almost kaleidoscopic variety of combinations in administration, structure, and instruction is conceivable. To take a simple example: centralization can be imposed on either the single or the dual track, and the ensuing combination can in turn be oriented either humanistically or technologically as to curricular content.

The foregoing paradigm may be profitably utilized to illustrate the probable shape of Mori's information on American education, the one Western system with which he was thoroughly familiar prior to 1880. At the normative level, American education was as to basic values individualistic, egalitarian, and liberalistic in its view of Man, and in its attitude toward knowledge by and large empirical and utilitarian. It had among its specific purposes (although not necessarily stated in so many words) the self-fulfilment of the individual in both material and nonmaterial terms, the achievement of maximum social mobility, and the preparation of citizens for participation in a political democracy, while its secular principle (i.e., the separation of religion and education) may be viewed in effect as a "negative" purpose. Along the administrative coordinate, authority was vested in the states and local communities; the Americans had to an unusual degree succeeded in involving the local citizenry in the supervision and management of their own schools; and free public schooling was entirely supported out of state and local taxes. As to structure the American system had, in line with its ideal of equal opportunity, pioneered the single-track pattern and was distinguishing itself by its early effort to organize technical, women's, and general secondary education within that pattern. Finally, at the instructional level, American education in the 1870's and 1880's was quick to reflect the impact of modern science and technology; pedagogical theory was shifting from Pestalozzi to Herbart; and the yardstick of competence characteristically applied to teachers (whose status in society remained, unfortunately, relatively low compared to what it was in other lands), was purely professional and devoid of explicit political or ideological criteria.

The further application of this paradigm to Meiji education is particularly helpful in forestalling sweeping generalizations about the Japanese system as a whole, based on developments actually relating to only one or two of the four coordinates. Unfortunately, a fifth coordinate, the "statutory" (seldom congruent with all, or even most, of the other four), must also at times be borne in mind in connection with official ordinances and codes of education and their nomenclature. Thus Mori's new decrees, the Gakkōrei, or School Ordinances of 1886, constitute the third great statutory watershed, following the Gakusei or Fundamental Code of Education of 1872, which first established the modern system, and the Kyōikurei, or Education Ordinance of 1879, which was twice revised: as the Kaisei kyōikurei, or Revised Education Ordinance of 1880, and as the Shin kyōikurei, or New Education Ordinance of 1885.

Mori's regime may safely be viewed as the third major phase of Meiji education, but the clearest demarcation between a first and second period, if periodize one must, occurs not with the great statutory break of 1879 but gradually, and for the most part along the normative and instructional coordinates, following the statutory *amendments* of 1880. The first period, 1872–1879, has generally been characterized as "progressive" because of the predominance of a Western liberal viewpoint in the attitudes of educators and in the material which they taught. Conversely, the eventual emergence of statist or traditionalist features along these same two coordinates has led most authorities to characterize the following period, 1880–1885, as one of "reaction." The centralistic features of the Kaisei kyōikurei of 1880 have easily enough been viewed as part and parcel of that "reaction," but it should be recalled that, along the administrative coordinate, the so-called progressive period had experimented both with extreme centralization in control and finance under the Gakusei of 1872 and with extreme decentralization under the Kyōikurei of 1879, and that the Kaisei kyōikurei is therefore properly speaking an instance of re-centralization.

In terms of structure, finally, Japan during the years of the Gakusei managed to organize schools representative of nearly every type, the chief omissions being in the field of women's secondary and higher education and, as Mori's Commercial Institute testified, in the area of technical and vocational training. The scope of the system, that is to say the entire question of educational mobility and opportunity, however, remained ambiguous and up in the air from 1872 to 1886, pending Mori's clearcut decision in favor of a multiple track. The statutory changes and the educational controversies which ran on from the late 1870's into the mid-1880's had to do almost exclusively with primary education (understandable enough for an early phase of modernization), and Mori would be the first educational statesman since the early authors and implementers of the Gakusei to give serious and comprehensive attention to the other components of the educational structure as well.

The 1870's, and with it the progressive—or what might well even be called the "American"—decade in Japanese education, all but went by without any further comment from Mori after his *Education in Japan* of 1873. Finally, in 1879, he expressed himself in an essay on physical education and in a written opinion on the Kyōikurei of the same year, in which he indicates the general drift of his thinking on instructional and administrative matters. His thoughts as of 1879 regarding the ministry of education itself can further be deduced, retrospectively, from a letter addressed to the Tokyo Academy in 1882.

Mori's assignment to London took him out of the country for all but the tail end of the educational countertrend. The mutual antagonists of that second period (although not entirely at odds with each other), were Motoda Eifu and Itō Hirobumi, and it was Itō who, meeting Mori in Paris in 1882, would provide the latter with the mandate to prepare for the third era of education, i.e., Mori's own. Itō would arrive at that meeting after counseling by advisors in Berlin and Vienna; while Mori would return from it to London, where he would review the entire panorama of European education, taking the leading authorities of contemporary Britain as his guide.

MORI AND THE "PROGRESSIVE" DECADE

There is perhaps no better example of the difficulties incurred by overhasty, wholesale cultural borrowing than the first phase of Japan's modern education, when American advisors, an Anglo-American philosophical viewpoint, and a French administrative model held sway. These were the years when Mill, Spencer, and Pestalozzi (the latter through the mediation of the Oswego Movement in America) were in vogue; when textbooks were often translated without regard to their applicability in a Japanese context; when the old didactic Confucian texts were dropped in favor of American or French primers in translation; when foreign consultants and instructors were legion throughout the system; when the system itself was effectively in the hands of Vice Minister Tanaka Fujimaro, an outspoken enthusiast for American practice;[3] and when Americans in particular, such as David Murray as Tanaka's chief

---

3. Tsuchiya Tadao, *Meiji zenki kyōiku seisakushi no kenkyū,* rev. ed. (Tokyo, 1968), p. 111.

adviser at the ministry (1874–1878) or Marion M. Scott at the Tokyo Normal School (1872–1874) were honored with positions of the highest trust.[4]

This period had opened with an attempt to reproduce in toto on Japanese soil the French university-district system of the Third Republic. The Gakusei called for eight such districts, each with its own university and inspectorate, and each controlling thirty-two middle schools. Each middle school in turn was to serve 210 primary schools, for a grand total of eight universities, 256 middle schools, and 53,760 primary schools throughout Japan. Reminiscent of the ambitious city plan of ancient Kyoto (imported virtually intact from Ch'ang-an in China), barely half of the Gakusei grid had been fleshed out by the end of the decade. This first era closed, finally, with the collapse within less than a year of the Kyōikurei experiment with a highly decentralized American-style model.

More significant than administrative and structural arrangements, however, were the utilitarian, egalitarian, individualistic presuppositions of the period. The Dajōkan decree of 4 September 1872 (2/VIII/Meiji 5) which served as a philosophical preamble to the Gakusei of the following day, and the opening chapter of Fukuzawa's *Gakumon no susume* (On the encouragement of learning), published earlier that year, both echoed the same themes: the purpose of education was to promote the welfare, in particular the economic welfare, of the individual; the state would of course benefit from all this too, but in the final analysis the strength and independence of the nation would have to rest on a

4. The most important works consulted here and in Chapter Ten with respect to education in early and mid-Meiji Japan may briefly be listed as follows. For a general treatment of the period 1872–1879 see Tsuchiya, *Seisakushi*, pp. 111–146 (emphasizing personalities and policy-making); Horimatsu Buichi, *Nihon kindai kyōikushi: Meiji no kokka to kyōiku* (Tokyo, 1959), pp. 13–61 (correlating education with intellectual and political trends, and quoting from the most important documents); and Karasawa Tomitarō, *Kindai nihon kyōikushi* (Tokyo, 1968), pp. 21–62 (for a general overview). For more detailed treatment, statistics and specific facts, the following three—in ascending order of thoroughness—may be consulted: *Gakusei gojūnenshi*, comp. Monbushō (Tokyo, 1922), pp. 18–88; Nakajima Tarō, *Kindai nihon kyōiku seidoshi* (Tokyo, 1966), pp. 28–93 (with particularly thorough treatment of regulations and ordinances); and *Meiji ikō kyōiku seido hattatsushi*, ed. Kyōikushi Hensankai (Tokyo, 1938–1939), I, 273ff. and II, 1–136 (the most basic, official account). The aforementioned six volumes may similarly be consulted with reference to the succeeding phases of Japanese education. The most convenient compendium of primary documents is Matsumoto Kenji and Suzuki Hirō, *Genten: kindai kyōikushi* (Tokyo, 1962).

strong, independent citizenry; the socially exclusive, impractical learning of the past would have to make way for a new utilitarian education available to every citizen without distinction of social or economic status or sex; and finally, the Dajōkan decree promised and exhorted: "We look forward confidently to a time when there shall be no village with an untutored household, no household with an untutored member. Parents and guardians should take this purpose to heart, cultivating a spirit of tender care for their children, and sending them without fail to school."[5]

The liberal spirit of this decree of 1872 and the administrative localism of the 1879 Kyōikurei were both predicated, however, on a popular enthusiasm and initiative for education which failed to materialize, and herein lay the greatest hope and the greatest disappointment of the period. The anomaly of a government urging (and in good faith, too) an individualistic philosophy upon reluctant individualists, was bound to break down one way or the other: either the people would rise to the initiative, as they had so notably done in America, or the government would move toward a more conscious, and thoroughly unreluctant, paternalism.

It was less a failure to appreciate the value of education, however, than sheer economic privation which kept attendance rates, and the actual length of the elementary course itself, down to a mere fraction of what the Gakusei had envisioned. For primary education, although effectively "universal" and "compulsory" after 1886, did not become "free" until 1900, and it had taken a good deal of wheedling and cajoling and pressuring on the part of officials charged with the spread of education to get things moving under the Gakusei. Common complaints included excessive fees, the removal of children from gainful employment, and the teaching of subjects of little relevance to workaday life; and with the revival of the Popular Rights Movement in the late 1870's, the school system readily provided one important focus for antigovernment sentiment.

The government, still reeling from the effort of the Satsuma Rebellion, was in no mood to provoke such sentiment unnecessarily, and this circumstance accordingly combined with Tanaka's preference for the American model to produce the Kyōikurei, often

---

5. The Dajōkan decree may be found in Matsumoto and Suzuki, *Genten*, pp. 50–51. The decree is addressed entirely to the individual benefits of education, and it was Fukuzawa who pointed out the intimate connection between individual and national welfare. To Matsumoto, the decree "reflected very powerfully" the influence of Fukuzawa's educational philosophy (ibid., p. 49).

dubbed the *jiyū* or "liberal" Education Ordinance, in effect from 29 September 1879 through December of the following year. According to it, the rigid university-district grid of the Gakusei was abolished and the period of (nominally) compulsory education reduced from eight years to only four months per year over a four-year period, i.e., to a mere sixty-four weeks. Supervisory responsibility for primary education, which had rested with the superintendents (*torishimari*) of the middle school districts (*chūgaku-ku*), working under the close supervision of the university-district inspectorates (Tokugakukyoku) and of the ministry itself, was now transferred to the prefectures (*fu* and *ken*), while the managerial responsibility for the establishment, operation, and financing of the primary school plant was taken from these same superintendents and placed in the hands of popularly elected school boards or Gakumuiin at the town and village (*chō-son*) level. And in an extraordinary series of amendments Itō (in his capacity as *sangi*) and the Genrōin (Senate) between them managed to revise Tanaka's original draft in an even more progressive direction, excising all exhortations to morality and patriotism and obedience to teachers, and inserting a specific prohibition against corporal punishment.[6]

David Murray himself had been basically in favor of the centralistic features of the Gakusei,[7] and Tanaka's ordinance, far from stimulating local initiative, produced a slackening of effort all down the line. Lack of pressure from the center was mistaken for lack of interest. More significant than a slight drop in total attendance rates was the heavy transfer of elementary students from public to private schools, which tended to be cheaper and to teach the traditional, pre-Meiji subjects in the traditional manner, while some public schools were closed down and plans for new ones abandoned.[8] Tanaka, in considerable discredit, was transferred out of the ministry on 15 March 1880, shortly after the appointment on 28 February of a new minister of education, Kōno Togama, who set about at once preparing the Kaisei kyōikurei, which came into effect on 28 December and which effectively reestablished central control over primary education.

6. Ibid., pp. 61–62, gives the text of the Kyōikurei. For a discussion see ibid., p. 60, and Horimatsu, *Kyōikushi,* pp. 59–60. The full text of the Genrōin debate is given in Ōkubo Toshiaki, ed., *Meiji bunka shiryō sōsho: kyōiku hen,* vol. 8 of Meiji Bunka Shiryō Sōsho Kankōkai, gen. eds., *Meiji bunka shiryō sōsho* (Tokyo, 1961), pp. 99–151.
7. Horimatsu, *Kyōikushi,* p. 59; Matsumoto and Suzuki, *Genten,* p. 59.
8. Horimatsu, *Kyōikushi,* p. 63.

Mori, it will be recalled, remained an "outsider" to the official educational establishment throughout the 1870's. His comments therefore are of a piecemeal nature and afford at best indirect evidence of his attitude toward the general trend of the decade. Mori's "Kyōikurei ni kansuru ikenshoan" (Draft of a written opinion on the Education Ordinance; hereinafter, "Kyōikurei ikenshoan")[9] opens on an apologetic note: he does not even know whether Tanaka's proposals have been acted upon, and admits that: "if the matter has not yet been decided, I shall not escape the charge of having trespassed on another's territory." He supports, however, the chief intent of the ordinance to transfer responsibility for primary education to the prefectures and local school boards and, in Point Two of five "additional suggestions" of his own, endorses Tanaka's basic philosophy of decentralization: "The Ministry should take under advisement the general plans developed by the primary schools under the encouragement of the prefectural authorities. The people themselves should play the major role in this process, avoiding as much as possible control by persons involved in politics."

Mori as of 1876 was still (together with Tanaka, Kido, Iwakura, and Hatakeyama Yoshinari) on Commissioner John Eaton's distribution list for publications of the United States Commission on Education,[10] and there is every reason to believe that the American school system, which he had viewed at first hand and which formed the model for Tanaka's ordinance, was the only one at the time with which Mori was generally familiar. Point Five, in which Mori suggests that the local boards be empowered to fix school rates in accordance with local economic conditions, likewise reflects American practice and a typically American hope that "this will do the most to enourage them to be self-supporting."

Mori's remaining three suggestions, however, depart from the typical American pattern. In Point One, he wants to leave the establishment and operation of secondary schools entirely to the private sector: an idea in accordance with the actual situation

---

9. Mori's written opinion on Tanaka's Kyōikurei has been preserved in draft form only, given in *Zenshū* I, 324, and should not be confused with his lengthier and better known "Kyōikurei ni tsuki iken" (Opinion on the Education Ordinance), pertaining to the revision of the Kaisei kyōikurei in 1885. The latter is discussed in Chapter Ten. The former bears no date, but from the content may safely be said to have been written in 1879.

10. See for example NAW, United States Commission on Education, "Letter Books," no. 12, letter from John Eaton to Yoshida Kiyonari, 1 Feb. 1876, transmitting five copies of the Annual Report for 1874 for forwarding to the five Japanese mentioned.

throughout much of the United States, but hardly with the gradually emerging American ideal of public high schools available to all.[11] In Point Three, Mori argues that, "in establishing our [national] educational system we should bring together persons with broad experience in educational matters and base our final arrangements on their deliberations." And in Point Four he calls for suspension of subsidies to the prefectures and the reservation of central funds "exclusively for the universities and for the training of scholars." Neither the third nor the fourth point was relevant to the American pattern, where the federal government (West Point and Annapolis aside) held neither policymaking nor financial responsibility for education. The Kyōikurei was addressed for the most part to primary education, and what Mori's "Kyōikurei ikenshoan" in effect reveals is his own ideal concept of the total structure: local autonomy at the elementary level; private initiative at the secondary level; and central responsibility for higher education and for general direction of the whole.

Mori showed a distinct inclination to rely on professional expertise in matters of education administration, and his concern to involve the best brains of the country in the policymaking process was fully shared by Tanaka and Murray at the ministry, who on 15 January 1879 had established the Tōkyō Gakushi Kaiin, or Tokyo Academy, with the dual functions of a scholarly society and of a board of inquiry on government educational policy. In this latter capacity the academy (forerunner of the Imperial Academy, or Teikoku Gakushiin of 1906) was to report directly to the ministry, taking into special consideration the complaints of the people regarding the educational system. The seven charter members chosen by the ministry were all former members of the Meirokusha: Fukuzawa (the first chairman), Katō, Tsuda, Nishi, Nakamura, Kanda, and Mitsukuri Shūhei. Mori himself was elected to membership at the tenth session on 28 May 1879, and from the 15 June meeting until his departure for London regularly attended the monthly deliberations. Educational questions, after sufficient debate, were put to the vote, and majority decisions were forwarded to the ministry in the form of specific proposals.[12]

The academy in a sense had institutionalized one of the functions originally intended by Mori for the Meirokusha: the encouragement and guidance of modern education. With the dismissal of Tanaka and the appointment of Kōno, however, the advisory function of the academy was gradually dropped, and Mori himself

11. Peterson, *Hundred Years of Education*, pp. 169–170.
12. OTM, pp. 75–81.

would write from London on 23 June 1882, in a letter "respectfully addressed to the Honorable Members of the Academy" ("Kyōtei gakushi kaiin shoken"), recommending that the academy limit its educational activities to the administration of a national library system and the awarding of prizes in encouragement of good literature. The academies of Europe, he would report, had long since surrendered to education ministries such supervisory powers over national education as they had once possessed; and the Tokyo Academy would be wise to follow suit and to model itself as much as possible on the Académie Française.

Mori's most original suggestion prior to departure for England lay, however, in the field of pedagogical rather than administrative theory. It is his essay "Shintai no nōryoku" (On physical fitness), which best reveals his views as to both the purposes and techniques of education, and which constitutes, after *Education in Japan,* his lengthiest statement on education during the 1870's.[13] Mori opens with an invocation of the triad made famous by Herbert Spencer's *Education: Intellectual, Moral and Physical* of 1861: "The chief aim of education, generally speaking, is to nourish and to develop the several faculties with which man is endowed and by so doing to increase the pleasure [*kairaku*] to be gained from them. These faculties may be distinguished as three: the intellectual, the moral and the physical . . . They correspond to our three traditional virtues of 'wisdom,' 'benevolence' and 'courage.' Man's greatest pleasure is achieved when these three virtues are brought together into harmony and balance." Here Mori seems to have imbibed not only Spencer's psychology but his utilitarian and individualistic philosophical bias as well.

The essay was read before the Tokyo Academy in September 1879. Addressing its members as a body collectively responsible for the future of Japanese education, Mori warns that the faculty most neglected at the time in Japan is the physical and that even the former samurai are beginning to show signs of the enfeeblement which has long characterized the population as a whole. Seven sources of debility are noted, their respective relevance in the case of Japan analyzed, and their cures prescribed. "Fertile soil" and a "benevolent climate" are dismissed as minor factors: whatever indolence they may have induced in the workaday world of the past will be sufficiently countered by the imperatives of the new international competition. "Food," "shelter," and "clothing" —Mori's third, fourth, and fifth factors—present less tractable

---

13. The following quotations from Mori Arinori, "Shintai no nōryoku" have been taken from *Zenshū* I, 325–329, *passim.*

drawbacks, "not easily weeded out by the force of law or by argument and admonition." He insists on the debilitating effect of a vegetarian diet (abetted by intemperance in drink) on the muscle, blood, and bone structures, and faults the custom of sitting or squatting on tatami mats for crooked backbones, bowleggedness, and a general preference for physical ease; while the traditional kimono, with its long sleeves and shapeless fit he finds (as he had explained to Li Hung-chang) unsuited for energetic movement.

Mori's severest criticism, however, is reserved for the sixth and seventh factors, namely "literature" and "religion":

> Regarding my sixth point, literature: all excellence or profundity of Confucian doctrine aside, the writing system of China which was imported along with that doctrine requires many years of hard and diligent work, from the initial step of learning to copy the characters to the final stage of sophisticated exegesis, before it can be put to any use. Therefore those who study it generally ruin their health with long hours of passive sitting and end up by being, I regret to say it, utterly enfeebled bookworms . . . Not only does the study of the Chinese classics thus weaken the body, but its pedagogical approach as such is mistaken. By luring its devotees into a life of unproductive study (asserting that there is no other way to govern the world except through the grasp and application of its own doctrines of statecraft), [Confucian scholarship] has been the major source of effeteness in today's world.
>
> As for my seventh point, religion: since the introduction of Buddhism into our country, the adoration of the Buddha has so engrossed the minds of the faithful as to turn their thoughts away completely from the actual problems of everyday life, with the result that people who subscribe to this faith place their hopes entirely on the impossible promises of a world to come, making light of all that pertains to their corporeal bodies.

The debilities arising from "literature" (i.e., Confucian studies) and "religion" (i.e., Buddhist faith) are past remedy in the older generation, but Mori reasons that: "if we can put an end to traditional educational practice—the reading of the classics by rote, and attending temple schools—and can bring into use from the very start easy-to-read sentences combining Chinese and Japanese [scripts], and can set up a program of physical exercises, there is good reason to hope that young folk in the future will be spared the worst of these debilities." Mori herewith repudiates the *sodoku* of his own Gōjū training. His call for an interspersion of Chinese characters (*kanji*) and Japanese syllabary (*kana*) involves the replacement of the old Confucian texts, which were written entirely in *kanji,* and implies abandonment not only of the style but of the content of the classics themselves. It is the third reform, however, upon which Mori pins his greatest hope, and which occupies the remainder of the essay.

The ministry had already done a good deal to introduce a system of gymnastics, stressing marching and calisthenics with dumbbells, patterned after that which Tanaka Fujimaro had seen at Amherst in 1876. A new corps of physical education instructors was at the time in school at the Taisō Denshūjo (Physical Training Institute) established by Dr. George A. Leland, chief exponent of the method involved, and introducer to Japan of rowing and baseball during his four-year stay 1878–1881.[14] Mori gives the ministry full credit for what it has achieved to date, but expresses scepticism whether "games" will suffice to promote his own *desideratum:* "the strength of good health plus courage (*yūki*)." The term allotted the educator to influence the lives of his charges is, Mori laments, distressingly brief. Spencer himself had emphasized the interrelationship of the three faculties, and Mori is clearly interested in forms of exercise which will contribute not only to physical, but also to moral, growth: "The function . . . of physical fitness . . . is, in the main, to provide the individual with the strength to practice virtue [*zen o okonau*]. However, such strength does not emanate from bodily health alone; it cannot attain perfection without the addition of a fearless courage."

In casting about for a technique which would simultaneously elevate both the physical and moral capacities, Mori suggests: "In my view the best thing would be to introduce, upon the widest possible basis, compulsory physical training along military lines. A program suitable to Japan may be established after consulting the systems of military-type schools now in effect in Switzerland and other foreign countries. I should at once add a word of caution, however: the military style, I should like to make clear, is to be adopted solely for the purpose of physical education, not for the sake of military service, or for the encouragement of militaristic thinking." "Shintai no nōryoku" concludes with a request to the members of the Academy to weigh the pros and cons of military drill. Mori believes that the former outweigh the latter, and that this one single technique will go a long way in remedying the

---

14. Robert S. Schwantes, "American Influences in the Education of Early Meiji Japan" (unpublished Ph.D. dissertation, Harvard University, 1950), pp. 161–162.

effeteness traceable to the last five factors of food, shelter, clothing, literature, and religion: but he is willing to listen to counterarguments. What Mori calls the "military-style" schools of Switzerland refers simply to the regular schools of that country where then, as now, physical education programs were geared to the preparation of the citizen army on which Swiss defenses have traditionally rested. Under instructors trained and maintained by the military department, all boys underwent various types of paramilitary training to prepare them for their future army duties. Gymnastics and competitive games were also taught by the same instructors, but from the standpoint of emphasis physical training or "athletics," in the narrow sense, served as an adjunct to paramilitary drill, rather than the other way around.[15]

Mori's concern with physical fitness had long been a matter of record. One need only be reminded of the anti-intellectual bias of Zen Buddhism, or the unity of thought and action preached by the Ōyōmei School, to appreciate how much there was in the native tradition itself that was opposed to the sessile, scholastic brand of Confucianism. Mori's attitude is more directly explicable, of course, in terms of his own rugged physical and paramilitary training in the Gōjū. His regimen of rope-climbing and cold baths in London, and the remorse with which he admitted to Yokoyama his neglect of athletic routine, show how deeply these values already had been instilled. Brocton, finally, would have provided the specific link, as ends to means, between physical training and moral regeneration. By the time Mori inquired anxiously of the president of Collegiate Polytechnic at Brooklyn regarding the health of his Japanese students, his general bias on the subject was moving in the direction of an explicit educational theory.

There would have been much in contemporary Britain and America, as well, to accelerate this development. "Muscular Christianity" was much in vogue; there was a new emphasis on organized sports both inside and outside the schools; and, on a more scientific level, Alexander Bain's *Mind and Body* of 1872 had drawn attention to the physiological basis of many of the so-called mental processes. Finally, Mori would have gotten an earful from Western advisers in Tokyo on the underexercised, tubercular-prone condition of the average Japanese student.[16] The direct Western inspiration of "Shintai no nōryoku" as far as it can be traced, however,

---

15. I. N. Thut and Don Adams, *Educational Patterns in Contemporary Societies* (New York, 1964), pp. 229–230.

16. See William E. Griffis, "Education in Japan," an article contributed to JWM, 10 Feb. 1874.

would seem to be Herbert Spencer, either through Mori's reading of *Education: Intellectual, Moral and Physical*,[17] or through personal discussions in London in 1873, or most likely, by virtue of both. Spencer, as Josiah Royce has pointed out,[18] had come to take an intense interest in physical training as a result of his own growing nervous invalidism which had given him a hypochondriac concern with his bodily sensations: a motive of which Mori, as far as we know, was totally devoid. Quite apart from the triad of faculties, however, there are numerous correspondences of viewpoint between Mori's essay and the portions of Spencer's text pertaining to physical education.

Spencer delivers a broadside attack on what he calls "overstudy" —sedentary, desk-bound education—and like Mori is hedonistic in his approach to diet and clothing and to the body in general.[19] Spencer finds his enemy, however, not only in bookworming but also in certain ascetic prejudices carried over from early nineteenth century evangelicalism: a battle which Mori, in his native context, was largely spared.[20] The human body under various rubrics of the Japanese tradition, including the samurai code, was something to be controlled, even severely controlled, but had never properly been an object of abhorrence or mortification. Even Buddhism had wreaked its damage chiefly by preaching the futility of worldly exertion, rather than by instilling a disgust with the body as such. Spencer, although not at all athletically inclined himself, put the case well for a whole generation of late Victorian gentlemen in the process of discarding certain of their fathers' and grandfathers' inhibitions, and one can readily imagine the psychological rapport and mutual respect at this level which must have existed between a Gōjū-trained samurai and Westerners of a robust, adventuresome disposition such as Laurence Oliphant or Charles Lanman.

The greater portion of "Shintai no nōryoku," concerned as it is with physical well-being, may be viewed as an extended footnote on one facet of the development and happiness of the individual which had been proclaimed with the Gakusei to be the goal of education; and to that extent, Mori may be taken to have been in sympathy with the values and purposes dominating the Japanese school system during the 1870's. The closing paragraphs, however,

---

17. Herbert Spencer, *Education: Intellectual, Moral and Physical* (London, 1949). Originally published in 1861.

18. Josiah Royce, *Herbert Spencer: An Estimate and Review* (New York, 1904), p. 151.

19. Spencer, *Education*, pp. 180–203 and 211–228, *passim*.

20. Ibid., p. 179.

reveal a concern with the forced-draft production of virtue—of the courage conducive to virtue—so profound as to leave one wondering whether this has not superseded individual happiness as Mori's primary goal. The more precise nature of that courage and virtue, the goals which they in turn should serve, and above all the reasons for supposing that moral qualities could be instilled through military drill, were matters Mori would only gradually reveal in the course of the 1880's. So what starts out ostensibly as a crib from Spencer winds up quite open-ended as to ultimate purposes.

ITŌ, MOTODA, AND THE COUNTERTREND

Mori left for England at the height of Tanaka's Kyōikurei experiment, and the second phase of Meiji education which ensued in the early 1880's would concern him directly only after his return to Japan, as the immediate inheritance of his own administration. This countertrend[21] is more significant for what it may tell us of Itō Hirobumi, whose educational philosophy by the time of his meeting with Mori in Paris in 1882 would have been formed largely by two factors: by trends in Japan prior to his own departure for Europe, and by the advice of his constitutional consultants in Germany and Austria.

Itō's precise connection with the Kaisei kyōikurei of 1880, and the recentralization of Japanese education along the administrative coordinate, is somewhat obscure; in any case there were sufficient reasons of a strictly educational (as opposed to political) nature to account for the Revised Education Ordinance. Along the normative coordinate, by contrast, a battle royal was waged between Itō and the emperor's tutor Motoda Eifu in the fall of 1879 over the purposes of education, the documentary evidence for which commences with Motoda's "Kyōgaku taishi" (Great principles of education), continues with Itō's rebuttal in "Kyōikugi" (Opinion on education), and closes with the counterrebuttal in Motoda's "Kyōikugi fugi" (A reply to the "Opinion on education"). Both men were sufficiently alarmed, however, by the politicization of

21. Herbert Passin, in *Society and Education in Japan* (New York, 1965), pp. 81–86, has given the first extended treatment in the English language of this countertrend, the significance of which apparently was lost on earlier authorities such as Hugh L. Keenleyside and A. F. Thomas, *History of Japanese Education and Present Educational System* (Tokyo, 1937), or Baron Dairoku Kikuchi, *Japanese Education* (London, 1909), but which has been made a great deal of by postwar Japanese writers.

education through the Popular Rights Movement to permit what looks like a tacit entente regarding the instructional coordinate, along which the countertrend most strikingly occurred. The Public Assembly Ordinance ("Shūkai jōrei") of 5 April 1880 restricting the political activities of teachers and students, and the succession of Confucianizing regulations, formularies, and textbooks which emanated from the ministry from 1880 to 1882 combined (if from rather differing philosophical premises) to undo the liberal spirit of the preceding decade as regards curriculum, texts, and teachers.

The Kaisei kyōikurei, in response to the virtually unanimous complaint of responsible officials in the field, reasserted first of all the principle of government intervention in primary education.[22] Secondly, it extended the period of compulsory attendance to thirty-two weeks a year over a period of three years for a total of ninety-six weeks (as opposed to sixty-four weeks in the Kyōikurei), and required the permission of the head county or ward official (*gunkuchō*) for elementary education conducted outside the public schools or under the itinerant teachers recognized by the Kyōikurei. And thirdly, and most importantly, it shifted to prefectural officials (i.e., to lower echelons of the ministry of the interior or Naimushō), under general direction of the Monbushō, many of the powers which had been wielded originally by ministry of education bureaucrats under the Gakusei, and had then been surrendered at least in part to the local school boards under the Kyōikurei.

With the initiatives it entrusted to the prefectural governors, the Kaisei kyōikurei represented something short of the total centralization of the Gakusei. The chief difference between these two centralizing ordinances, however, lay in their channels of authority. In the case of the Gakusei, the channel was preponderantly educational, running in a direct line from the ministry of education through its inspectorates at the university-district level and its superintendents in the middle school districts down to the primary school principals. Under the Kaisei kyōikurei, however, authority was deflected into the essentially political channels of the Naimushō, which henceforth enjoyed a direct involvement in educational affairs.

22. Accounts of the Kaisei kyōikurei may be found in *Gakusei gojūnenshi*, pp. 89–93; Matsumoto and Suzuki, *Genten*, pp. 72–73; Horimatsu, *Kyōikushi*, pp. 65–66; Shimada Saburō, "Kaisei kyōikurei no happu," in Kokumin Kyōiku Shōreikai, ed., *Kyōiku gojūnenshi* (Tokyo, 1922), pp. 29–32; and in Tsuchiya, *Seisakushi*, pp. 193–236.

The new educational prerogatives of the prefectural governor were wide indeed: public primary schools were now established under his direction (*shishi*), private schools and itinerant classrooms with his approval (*ninka*); private school regulations, over which the ministry had formerly enjoyed little control, were now established by him with ministerial approval; the compilation of primary school regulations was transferred from the schools themselves (where Mori in his "Kyōikurei ikenshoan" had been content to leave them) to the governor's office; teachers were appointed by the governor on recommendation of the school boards and their salaries fixed by him with ministerial consent. It was an immense accretion of authority over his chief function under the Gakusei, namely, the appointment of the middle school district superintendents, who had gone on, however, to report directly to their respective inspectorate, with which the governors were to "hold consultation" [*kyōgi suru*] in carrying out the directives of the ministry of education. The school boards, which under the Kyōikurei had been elected by the localities and which had held responsibility for the establishment and management of primary schools and for the enforcement of attendance, were now appointed [*sennin*] by the governor upon recommendation [*senkyo*] of the localities. To the board was now added, as *ex officio* member, the local syndic, or *kochō*, the lowest official of the Naimushō hierarchy. Under the Shin kyōikurei of 1885 the residual powers of the boards were transferred to the office of the syndic entirely and the boards themselves abolished. "Thus," in the summation of Matsumoto Kenji, "by according due recognition to the longstanding habits of autonomy exercised by traditional community organization, it was possible to put the latter to good use within the framework of bureaucratic control."[23]

In matters of finance, the Kaisei kyōikurei eliminated all subsidies from the center for primary education. With the national economic retrenchment decreed by Finance Minister Matsukata Masayoshi in 1881, and with the ensuing deflation and depression, alternative sources of school income, such as local taxes, tuition fees, and gifts were also severely strained, and as a result primary education continued right into the 1880's to be plagued with the same problems of finance and attendance which had beset it in the 1870's. Finally, the Kaisei kyōikurei retained the curriculum of the Kyōikurei, but moved *shūshin,* or "moral training" from the bottom to the top of the order in which authorized subjects were listed

23. Matsumoto and Suzuki, *Genten,* p. 72.

in the wording of the ordinance (namely, *shūshin,* reading, writing, arithmetic, geography, history as basic subjects; and—with allowances for local conditions—drawing, singing, gymnastics, physics, physiology, natural history, and sewing for girls). Apart from this amendment and the assertion that "persons morally unfit may not qualify as teachers," the Revised Education Ordinance offered little that was new at the instructional level. The nature of moral unfitness it did not bother to elaborate or define.

The Genrōin debates over the Kaisei kyōikurei draft make it clear that the purpose of recentralization was to establish the viability of the educational system and that it did not proceed from any crude expectations of political or ideological control. After rejecting a motion for the inclusion of military drill in the primary school curriculum, the debates revolved for the most part around the feasibility of local autonomy and initiative. Kanda Kōhei, Tsuda Masamichi, and Mitsukuri Rinshō, all former members of the Meirokusha, attempted to preserve, especially in the area of teachers' salaries, some of the authority of the school boards and town and village councils (*chōsonkai*) vis-à-vis the prefectural governors and county or ward officials, but were outvoted.

The majority position was defended by Education Minister Kōno Togama and his chief ministerial secretary, Shimada Saburō. Not a word was said about the political biases, if any, of the school boards. The complaint was directed entirely at their lack of qualified and interested members and at their shirking of fiscal responsibility. Professional standards and prestige had already suffered from the tendency of the boards to hire teachers on the cheap, and it was felt that only a higher authority could guarantee the establishment throughout the land of a fair and adequate salary scale.[24] Shimada, reflecting in 1922 on the minority position, attributed it to a misapplication to Japan of the laissez-faire, noninterventionist principles of Herbert Spencer and Alexander Bain, popularized by Japanese students recently returned from England. In philosophical terms the Genrōin debates over the Kaisei kyōikurei boiled down to the question of compulsion, for which Shimada stated the classic argument that although the individual certainly was to be educated to be free, freedom did not comprise the option not to be educated.[25]

Like the role of Itō in the Kaisei kyōikurei, the responsibility generally for educational policy in the years intervening between the regimes of Tanaka and Mori is unusually difficult to fix. The

24. Ōkubo, *Sōsho: kyōiku hen,* pp. 152–172.
25. Shimada, "Kaisei kyōikurei no happu," p. 32.

post of minister (still known as *monbukyō*), which nobody seemed particularly anxious to fill,[26] was held successively by Kōno Togama from February 1880 to April 1881, by Fukuoka Kōtei to December 1883, and by Ōki Takato until Mori's appointment in December 1885.[27] The staff of the ministry itself seems to have been divided between a majority of westernizing modernists, for the most part veterans of the Bakufu's Kaiseijo, and a minority of traditionalists, judging from the lament of Egi Kazuyuki, a scholar of the Mito school and a proponent of *kōdō shugi* (The Imperial Way) who had belonged to that minority and who would draft two of the most important "reactionary" formularies of 1881.[28] Both the Kyōikurei and its successor, as we have seen, were considerably revised at the hands of the Dajōkan and the Genrōin, and it would seem on the face of it likely that educational policy during the years 1880–1885 was subjected to unusually heavy extra-ministerial pressures including those emanating from Motoda Eifu and the court.

Itō's most obvious *démarche* on the educational front was of course the Public Assembly Ordinance, article 7 of which denied to both pupils and teachers, in public and private schools alike, the right "to attend or to join as members in assemblies organized for the purpose of political lectures and debates."[29] Primary school teachers, as adepts in the new learning, had been in great demand with the Popular Rights Movement, which (unlike the samurai rebellion of 1877) made a great point of attacking the government from the philosophical and theoretical side. In local areas teachers had often been instrumental in founding political societies and had provided political rallies with their readiest source of speakers, the *sensei* often as not cheered on as he mounted to the podium by his own primary school charges and their mothers in the audience.[30]

This ordinance, the precise political intention of which is at once apparent, swept away not only formal rights such as free speech and assembly but also a type of activity which, if at times precocious, must have been for students and teachers alike in the truest sense of the term instructive and educational. However, this political activity was, strictly speaking, extracurricular, and the blow

26. Tsuchiya, *Seisakushi*, p. 193.
27. The post previously had been held by Saigō Tsugumichi (May–December, 1878) and Terajima Munenori (September 1879–February 1880), who served as Tanaka's superiors during those two brief periods.
28. Horimatsu, *Kyōikushi*, 78–79, 80, 86.
29. Quoted in Karasawa, *Kindai nihon kyōikushi*, p. 71.
30. Ibid., p. 32; Kinoshita Naoe, *Kami, ningen, jiyū* (Tokyo, 1934), pp. 322ff.

was struck entirely from outside the educational establishment. To what degree, or with what expectations, Itō may have approved or condoned the Confucianizing trend concurrently exhibited by the ministry of education is less easily stated. That trend was at least as much the product of a mounting philosophical and cultural reaction to westernization as it was a deliberate device to provide ideological props for the political power which Satsuma and Chōshū had managed to corner by the end of 1881. Although Itō (as he would tell Mori the following year) was keenly interested in the political ramifications of education, he was no Confucianizer, and whatever the political gain accruing from the educational countertrend, his great debate with Motoda in 1879 suggests that he would have been in less than total sympathy with its methods and purposes.

Motoda's "Kyōgaku taishi,"[31] the earliest statement of a point of view which eventually would triumph with the promulgation of the Imperial Rescript on Education in 1890, was itself issued in august rescript form, conveying the emperor's distress at the decline of traditional values in education as witnessed in the course of a tour of several prefectures in the fall of 1878. It also echoed many of the popular complaints regarding the Gakusei, but its basic premises were three: (1) that the chief end of education was the transmission and maintenance of traditional values; (2) that the degeneration of the moral clime was traceable to faulty education, the chief fault lying in an undue attachment to superficial, technological Western knowledge; and (3) that the solution lay in the restoration of the "ancestral teachings," and particularly the "study of Confucius," to the head of the curriculum. In the appended "Shōgaku jōmoku niken" (Two items on elementary education) Motoda advocated specifically the display of inspirational portraits in classrooms and the cultivation of practical and vocational subjects in lieu of "high-flown, empty theories," which were as inapplicable to everyday living as they were politically precipitate and disturbing.

Upon being presented with this document personally by the emperor in September 1879, Itō, then doubling as *sangi* and as *naimukyō* (minister of the interior) at once set Inoue Kowashi to drafting a rebuttal.[32] "Kyōikugi" called into question all three of

31. English translations of Motoda's "Kyōgaku taishi" and of Itō's "Kyōikugi" may be found in Passin, *Society and Education in Japan*, pp. 226–233, and the Japanese originals (together with "Kyōikugi fugi") in Matsumoto and Suzuki, *Genten*, pp. 65, 67 and 70. Portions quoted here have been translated by the present author.

32. Matsumoto and Suzuki, *Genten*, p. 66.

Motoda's foregoing premises. Itō gave, to begin with, no definition of the ultimate purposes of education, beyond supporting the guidelines already laid down by the government, but he issued an unequivocal warning against "giving shelter to the mistaken customs of the past." Alterations in the moral climate, he furthermore insisted, had been generated not by the educational system but by the breathtaking pace of social change since the Restoration, and in part by radical political-party ideas imported from Europe. And, finally, the establishment of a single "national doctrine" (*kokkyō*) for propagation through the educational system he considered "beyond the proper competence of the government." Itō urged that history, literature, customs, and language, as fundamental elements of the national polity, be carefully studied, but his "Kyōikugi" was a good statement of what in Western parlance would be called the secularist position, in spirit very close to Mori's argument for the separation of religion and education in *Religious Freedom in Japan*.

Actually, Itō was more worried than Motoda about the philosophical and ideological preoccupations of contemporary students, the chief difference between the two lying in Motoda's tendency to view as a moral phenomenon what to Itō was purely and simply a political problem. Confucianism indeed was to Itō less a remedy than a cause of the ailment, and he blamed much of the current political disputatiousness directly on the tradition of the Confucian schools. His own solution lay rather in the widespread promotion of industrial education and in the severe limitation of admissions into courses on law and politics. The educational system, Itō surmised, had not done badly, considering the very brief period of its operation: "Very little time has passed since its establishment, and no doubt there have been some errors of form, some lapses of spirit, and some overconcern with detail at the expense of essentials. But if the government from this moment can make a sincere effort to promote and expand [the educational system], applying corrective pressures as needed, we should be able to hope for a civilized condition within a few years." Itō consequently had very little to suggest in terms of specific reforms of the system, contenting himself with some extremely general suggestions with regard to teachers and texts: "Teaching regulations for the greater part should follow current practice; use should be made of readers, well chosen, dealing with ethics and manners; teachers should be hired on contract and regulations for the profession put into effect; and one should expect teachers of their own accord to maintain the prescribed standard of conduct, to be modest in speech, and to serve as worthy models for their students."[33]

33. Ibid., p. 68.

In his counterrebuttal, Motoda reiterated the case for an official national doctrine and warned that industrial education though indeed desirable would nevertheless require a moral foundation. "Kyōikugi fugi" leaped, however, at the foregoing suggestions of Itō as evidence of common ground. Motoda immediately went on to elaborate that the ethics texts would, of course, have to be primarily Confucian but trusted it would not be necessary to rely on the "bigoted, long-winded" Confucianists of the old school in order to have them taught. Motoda's argument in "Kyōikugi fugi" in effect established the guideline for the ministry's innovations in instructional matters from 1880 through 1882, and in the "Gakusei ni tsuki chokuyu" (Imperial instructions regarding the educational system) of 11 February 1882, those innovations received the emperor's explicit approval.[34] It was a purely tactical victory, however, attributable to Motoda's immense personal influence with the Meiji emperor. On the strategically central issue of a national doctrine, Itō still held the upper hand. In October 1879 he managed to have Motoda's post of *jiho* (Court Attendant) struck from the table of organization,[35] and when Motoda in August 1884 presented his argument once again in the polished form of an essay entitled "Kokkyōron" (On a national doctrine), Itō in his capacity of minister of the imperial household (*kunaikyō*) chose simply to ignore it.[36]

The significance for Itō of his conflict with Motoda transcended educational matters and impinged vitally on the constitutional question; it might, in fact, be argued that what aroused Itō to such swift rebuttal of the "Kyōgaku taishi" was less what Motoda had said than the fact that he had presumed to say it at all. All aspects of a personal power rivalry aside, there was a world of theoretical difference between the modern if limited constitutional monarchy envisioned by Itō and the personal imperial rule (*tennō shinsei*) which dominated the constitutional thinking of Motoda, Tokudaiji Sanenori, and other functionaries at the court. In practical terms, the unity of court and government implicit in Motoda's approach meant the involvement of court officials in politics and in the actual running of the state. Itō's new cabinet system of December 1885 at last made the separation of "court" (*kyūchū*) and "government" (*fuchū*) explicit, but Motoda's efforts from 1879 onward to inter-

34. Horimatsu, *Kyōikushi*, p. 87.
35. Watanabe Ikujirō, *Nihon kenpō seiteishi kō* (Tokyo, 1937), pp. 177–178; Tsuchiya, *Seisakushi*, pp. 172–174.
36. Watanabe, *Nihon kenpō seiteishi kō*, pp. 175–178. Motoda Eifu, "Kokkyōron" (On a national doctrine) may be found in Kaigo Tokiomi, *Motoda Eifu*, vol. 19 of Ishikawa Ken, gen. ed., *Nihon kyōiku sentetsu sōsho* (Tokyo, 1942), pp. 202–207.

fere in educational policy had clearly represented the opening wedge of a rival interpretation of the national polity.[37] Despite its political conservatism, Itō's "Kyōikugi" was unmistakably oriented toward Western learning and in defense of the general trend of Japanese education under the Gakusei, and it seems likely that the traditionalistic aspects of the countertrend, which may now be briefly summarized, would have offended both Itō's concept of modern education[38] and his view of the proper function of the entourage at court.

As to the purposes of education, Motoda, in line with his belief that it should aim first of all to instill the traditional values and virtues, had begun in 1879 the compilation of *Yōgaku kōyō* (Essentials of learning for the young), a guide to moral instruction listing twenty of those virtues, briefly elaborated in Japanese and further illustrated with *kanbun* quotations from the Chinese classics. On 3 December 1882 this text, with a preface by Motoda, was personally "granted" (*gokashi*) by the emperor, in a solemn court ceremony, to the assembled prefectural governors. The imperial instructions (*chokuyu*) accompanying the presentation opened with the phrase "Ethics and morality being the chief foundation of education," and conveyed the emperor's positive wishes, as contrasted to the essentially negative admonishment against excessive westernization previously delivered in his "Gakusei ni tsuki chokuyu" of February 1882. The emperor's "donation" of *Yōgaku kōyō* was given wide publicity in the press, and by 1884 this text was in use throughout the school system.[39]

At the level of curriculum and texts, two special developments accompanied a movement, already overdue perhaps, to shake free of simple imitation or direct translation of foreign books. One trend, a fresh, positive emphasis on native history and traditional

37. Watanabe, *Nihon kenpō seiteishi kō*, pp. 161–184, *passim*.
38. A modernist view of education was already apparent in Itō's memorial of 11 February 1869 (1 I Meiji 2). In "Kokuze kōmoku" (An outline of national policy) Itō called for the education of all citizens according to their natural talents, drawing upon the "useful" knowledge of all nations. He suggested specifically that two universities be established, at Tokyo and Kyoto, along with modern schools in every corner of the land. "Old abuses" were to be abandoned, and the government if necessary was to force its enlightened policy upon the recalcitrant in order to bring Japan up to the level of European civilization. The memorial may be found in *Itō Hirobumi den*, Shunpō Kō Tsuishōkai comp. (Tokyo, 1940), I, 422–423.
39. Horimatsu, *Kyōikushi*, pp. 74, 87. Kaigo, *Motoda Eifu*, pp. 155ff. has the *Yōgaku kōyō* minus the *kanbun* illustrations.

morality, was represented by the establishment within the Ministry of the Hensankyoku or Compilation Bureau in March 1880. The other trend, a negative effort to weed out materials favorable to the Popular Rights Movement, was represented by the appointment of a *torishirabe kakari,* or investigation officer, in June of the same year. Both developments had followed quickly upon Kōno's appointment and Tanaka's dismissal.

Nishimura Shigeki, now in charge of the Hensankyoku, had since 1875, when he published his "Shūshin chikoku hinitoron" (Moral training the only way of governing the country) in the thirty-first issue of the *Meiroku zasshi,* been moving toward a viewpoint very close to Motoda's. In April 1880, within a month of his appointment, he brought out what may be regarded as the forerunner of the *shūshin* texts: his *Shōgaku shūshin kun* (Moral primer for elementary schools), replete with traditional maxims cast in the traditional language and with instructions for memorization in the traditional fashion.[40] Even more significant in their broad effect on the curriculum were the "Shōgakkō kyōsoku kōryō" (General rules of instruction for primary schools), drafted by the aforementioned Egi Kazuyuki and published on 4 May 1881. Article 10 of the new regulations upped the required hours for *shūshin* from one to two per week during the third and fourth year only under the Gakusei, to six hours a week for grades one through six, and three hours a week for grades seven and eight, of the full eight-year primary course.[41] Article 15, relating to classes

40. Horimatsu, *Kyōikushi,* pp. 85–86; Yoshida Kumaji and Kaigo Tokiomi, *Kyōiku chokugo kanpatsu izen ni okeru shōgakkō shūshin kyōjū no hensen* (Tokyo, 1934), p. 63.

41. Horimatsu, *Kyōikushi,* p. 84. More significant of course than the limited time allotted to *shūshin* under the Gakusei was the nature of its content, which was Western-oriented and largely conveyed by the teacher orally, drawing freely from a wide range of sources, rather than being tradition-oriented and acquired through memorization of prescribed texts. Inatomi Eijirō, in *Meiji shoki kyōiku shisō no kenkyū* (Tokyo, 1956), pp. 166ff., points out that *shūshin,* which in pre-Meiji times had referred to the ethical self-perfection of the mature scholar, first came to refer to the moral training of young children with the establishment of the Gakusei, and the provision of the latter for a *shūshin* course in the primary school curriculum. The educational system of the early Third Republic, which the Gakusei had copied, made provision for moral instruction, the content of which was Roman Catholic in orientation. The Japanese, however, had no national faith which would qualify undisputably as the content of such instruction, and educators at first were at considerable loss as to how to treat this new subject in the curriculum, turning in the 1870's to Western ethics and in the 1880's back to their own rather diverse tradition which Motoda and others

in history, shifted the emphasis drastically from world history to virtually exclusive concern with Japanese history, and pronounced it "particularly important to cultivate a spirit of reverence for the Emperor and love for one's country (*sonnō aikoku*)."[42]

Textbooks were brought under closer scrutiny and control of the ministry during the early 1880's, but a stable and thoroughgoing system of ministerial authorization (*kentei*) would not be established until 1886, under Mori, and a system of state-prescribed (*kokutei*) texts not until 1904.[43] What the *torishirabe kakari* (assigned to the Chihō Gakumukyoku, or Provincial Educational Affairs Bureau) in effect did, was to read and evaluate texts used in the primary, middle, and normal schools and prepare lists (in three categories of unsuitability) of books "preferably not used" (*saiyō shinai hō ga yoi*). These lists were distributed to prefectural education officials, and Minister Fukuoka Kōtei in December 1881 asked the assembled governors in Tokyo for their cooperation pending the establishment of a formal authorization system. Category "B" (books unsuitable from the nature of the text for use in primary schools) included the better-known political treatises of Fukuzawa Yukichi and Katō Hiroyuki. One may well ask whether such difficult texts belonged at the elementary level in the first place. The spread of the Popular Rights fervor right down into the primary schools inevitably cast the ministry, however political its own motivations, in the role of guardian of pedagogical common sense.[44]

Finally, with respect to teachers, Egi Kazuyuki's "Shōgakkō kyōin kokoroe" (Rules for primary school teachers), published on 18 June 1881, spelled out proper attitudes for the profession in terms many of which would have appealed to Itō as well as to Motoda. The Confucian relationships and the primacy of moral education received, it is true, great stress; but there were also calls for a spirit of *sonnō aikoku* among teachers, for their abstention

---

like him were attempting to define. In the pre-Meiji period the moral message (in the parlance of Marshall McLuhan), had been inherent in the medium of the classical texts themselves and the differentiation of academic and ethical subject matter and the establishment of a specific course for moral training took place originally under a Western, not a traditional impetus.

42. Matsumoto and Suzuki, *Genten*, p. 73; Karasawa, *Kindai Nihon kyōikushi*, pp. 65–66; Horimatsu, *Kyōikushi*, pp. 84–86.

43. Karasawa Tomitarō, *Kyōkasho no rekishi* (Tokyo, 1956), pp. 148, 192.

44. *Meiji ikō kyōiku seido hattatsushi*, II, 493–497; Horimatsu, *Kyōikushi*, pp. 83–84, 258.

from the discussion of religious and political matters, and for an awareness of primary education as an important factor in the prosperity and stability of the state.[45] Similarly, if Motoda would have been pleased with the revisions in teacher certification of 8 July 1881 which permitted established Confucian scholars to teach *shūshin* without sitting for a formal license,[46] Itō would not have overlooked the potential political uses of the "Gakkō kyōin hinkō kentei kisoku" published the twenty-first of the same month. These "Official Regulations for the Moral Conduct of School Teachers" closed the loophole of the Kaisei kyōikurei by defining what was meant by "morally unfit" to include "drunkenness, violence and all other disgraceful conduct unbecoming to a teacher."[47]

Particularly with respect to teachers, but also in its general outlines, the countertrend of the early 1880's represented a considerable overlap and coexistence (with what degree of stability only time would tell) between the moral and the political traditionalism of Motoda and the modern, rationally oriented statism of Itō. The willingness of Itō at the time to countenance a certain degree of Confucianization is perhaps best explained in terms of the advice of his close confidant, Inoue Kowashi, to whom he had entrusted the drafting of his "Kyōikugi" in 1879. Inoue on 7 November 1881 had addressed to Itō, Sanjō, and Iwakura a memorial in which he presented a five-point plan for dealing with the Popular Rights Movement, including controls over the press, the organizing of retired officials in the provinces, the establishment of vocational-oriented middle schools for sons of ex-samurai to coax them away from the politically oriented private academies in Tokyo, a fresh emphasis on Chinese and Japanese classics to balance "revolutionary" French and English thought, and the promotion of German studies and the German language throughout Tokyo University.[48] Since Inoue was at all times close to Itō, and later also to Mori, it will require particular attention, when the time comes, to determine to what extent (if at all) Mori actually followed the traditionalizing, Germanizing prescription of Itō's chief Japanese braintruster.

45. Karasawa, *Kindai Nihon kyōikushi,* p. 77; Tsuchiya, *Seisakushi,* pp. 251–254; Horimatsu, *Kyōikushi,* p. 66.
46. Horimatsu, *Kyōikushi,* p. 80.
47. Ibid., pp. 79–80.
48. Inoue's proposal may be found in Ōkubo Toshiaki, "Meiji jūshinen no seihen," in Meiji Shiryō Kenkyū Renrakukai, ed., *Meiji seiken no kakuritsu katei,* vol. 1 of *Meijishi kenkyū sōsho,* rev. ed. (Tokyo, 1968), pp. 149–154.

ITŌ, GNEIST, AND STEIN

The exchange of educational views between Itō and Mori at Paris occurred sometime between 29 August and 3 September 1882.[49] By that time Itō would have received lectures from Rudolf von Gneist and Albert Mosse in Berlin (late May to early August) and from Lorenz von Stein in Vienna on alternate days from 9 August until his departure for the French capital. Although we have no record, it is reasonable to assume that educational matters were again discussed by Mori and Itō during the latter's sojourn in England from March to May 1883. By then Itō would have built up his Central European backlog even further. For from Paris he would return directly to Vienna for additional lectures from Stein running straight through to the end of October 1882 and proceed thence to Berlin for a resumption of instruction by Gneist and Mosse continuing until the following February.[50]

What had impressed Itō even more than Gneist's lectures on constitutional theory was the wisdom the man brought to problems of administration and the practical workings of government, and it was the opportunity to hear more on that subject which motivated Itō to return to Berlin.[51] Writing to an unidentified addressee just before his second visit to the German capital in early November 1882, Itō had remarked: "If you want to have good administration, you must firmly lay down its organization and its standards."[52] While in Europe, Itō was at least as involved in investigations that led to the establishment of the cabinet system in December 1885 and to the reorganization of the bureaucracy in February 1886 as he was in the pursuit of theoretical ammunition on the constitutional question.

Gneist had insisted on the necessity of developing the polity in harmony with Japan's historical experience, and Stein, with his wider-ranging sociological approach, had urged Itō to take into account general social conditions as well.[53] Stein's one recorded lecture on education, the seventeenth and last of the series, was delivered on 31 October 1882, and followed rather closely the

49. Itō left Vienna on 28 August, visited Prince Arisugawa at his hotel on the thirtieth, and addressed his first letter to Mori (obviously written after their meeting) on 4 September 1882.
50. Yoshino Sakuzō, *Kandan no kandan* (Tokyo, 1933), pp. 159–185.
51. Ibid., pp. 170, 174–175.
52. Quoted in ibid., p. 184. Written from Vienna; neither date nor addressee.
53. Ibid., p. 171–173; Shimizu Shin, *Doku-ō ni okeru Itō Hakubun no kenpō chōsa to Nihon kenpō* (Tokyo, 1939), p. 21.

material in his *Handbuch der Verwaltungslehre* of 1870 in which education had been taken up alongside census-taking, sanitation, and the police, as an aspect of *Innere Verwaltung* or "domestic administration."[54] It seems highly probable that Itō, too, would have been primarily interested, as regards education, in knowing just how it might properly be fitted into his new administrative and political structure, with adjustments for the historical and sociological condition of contemporary Japan.

Itō's letter of 27 August 1882 to the *sangi*, Yamada Akiyoshi, recommending the invitation of Lorenz von Stein to Japan as chief educational advisor,[55] indicates not only that the subject had already been under discussion well before Itō met Mori but also that Itō had already embraced with enthusiasm Stein's point of view. Stein in November finally declined the offer on grounds of advanced age,[56] but correspondence Itō had addressed to the home government in the interval gives a clear picture of what he had hoped for from Stein. To Yamada, Itō had suggested putting Stein "in charge of the University" and having him "lay down our educational policy." To the Foreign Minister Inoue Kaoru he would write on 23 September 1882 of "bringing this man to Japan primarily for the purpose of having his views, on the spot, regarding the establishment and organization of schools and on methods of education;" and on 22 October (again to Inoue) of having him "reform our educational system."[57] The September letter had mentioned employing Stein concurrently as an advisor on governmental matters, while the October letter alluded to Stein's further value as a scholarly counterpoise to the "democratic" theorists of the Popular Rights Movement. The educational assignment, however, was in Itō's mind foremost. "To set aright the spirit of our people, we must needs begin with the reform of our schools," he had concluded in the latter letter.

Stein's advice to Itō can be reconstructed directly from Itō Miyōji's transcript of the October 1882 lecture, preserved in Japanese as the *Shutain-shi kōgi hikki* (Transcript of Mr. Stein's

---

54. The material in Stein's *Handbuch der Verwaltungslehre* of 1870 would be covered more fullly in his monumental *Die Verwaltungslehre*, which appeared in eight parts between 1869 and 1884 (Stuttgart). Part V, dealing with education, was first published in 1883.

55. *Itō Hirobumi den*, II, 305, letter from Itō Hirobumi to Yamada Akiyoshi, 27 Aug. 1882.

56. Yoshino, *Kandan no kandan*, p. 178, quoting letter from Itō Hirobumi to Sanjō Sanetomi and Iwakura Tomomi.

57. *Itō Hirobumi den*, II, 318 and 321, letters from Itō Hirobumi to Inoue Kaoru, 23 Sept. 1882 and 22 Oct. 1882, respectively.

lectures; hereinafter *Hikki*),⁵⁸ and also indirectly from the general point of view indicated in *Handbuch der Verwaltungslehre* (hereinafter *Handbuch*). In the former, Stein begins by identifying education as a province of domestic administration. He then proceeds to describe the structural differentiation of education into *Elementarschulwesen* (*ippan kyōiku,* or primary education), *Berufsbildungswesen* (*senmon kōtō no kyōiku,* or professional education), and a third category of *Allgemeine Bildung,* or "general education," by which Stein means the public media, particularly the press. Professional education is further subdivided into *Vorbildung* (*nitō kyōiku*) and *Fachbildung* (*kōtō kyōiku*), which refer to secondary and higher education as we nowadays understand those terms, and Stein spends considerable time explaining to Itō the relationship of the several parts of the articulated whole. As to administrative practice, he contrasts the laissez-faire attitude toward education of the British government with the virtually total centralization in France, and concludes by drawing Itō's attention to the paramilitary value of the military drill, with weapons, in the *Realgymnasien* (semiclassical secondary schools) of Germany.⁵⁹ The *Hikki* covers in summary some, but not all of the points brought up in the *Handbuch,* and for Stein's educational philosophy as a whole one does best to turn directly to the latter.

The pertinent portion of the *Handbuch* begins by stating that education (*Bildung*) "as the sum total of intellectual/spiritual properties" (*geistigen Güter*) attained by an individual person, "has the highest value for every individual . . . its breadth and its depth constitute the very measure and worth of the individual." Thus far, neither Fukuzawa nor Ben Franklin could have put it better. But Stein immediately goes on to add that the individual in his education is "no self-sufficient entity," that he is "neither able nor supposed to acquire or retain his education all by himself," and that education's "most important conditions, like its most important consequences, lie outside the sphere of one's individual life."⁶⁰ "The community of education," Stein continues, "we call moral culture (*Gesittung*): moral culture is the education of all the individuals [taken] as the most important fact of public life."⁶¹

---

58. Shimizu, *Doku-ō kenpō chōsa* carries the complete Itō Miyōji transcript, as translated into Japanese by the transcriber after returning to Japan. Stein's lectures and Itō Miyōji's original notes were in English (ibid., pp. 19–20).

59. Ibid., pp. 331–335.

60. Stein, *Handbuch der Verwaltungslehre,* pp. 107–108.

61. Ibid., p. 107.

And it is the state which is responsible for "the totality of public ordinances governing the activity of the administration in maintaining and developing a nation's culture." By virtue of this duty, "the administration reaches deep into the intellectual/spiritual (*geistige*) life of the individual, and the resulting restrictions on the freedom of the individual define the content of our public education law."[62]

The German word *Geist*, like its Japanese equivalents *seishin* or *kokoro*, comprises the concepts both of "mind" and of "spirit" as dichotomized in the English. The full moral quality likewise of *Gesittung*, renderable as "culture" or "civilization," is brought out by the additional meanings of "morality," "good breeding," "refinement," and "etiquette"; and the impending discussions between Mori and Itō would range far beyond the mere intellectual uplift of Japan and would assume, with Stein, some responsibility of the state for the moral and spiritual development of the nation as well. As means to fulfillment of that end the state, according to the *Handbuch*, is responsible in particular for the secondary and higher educational establishment. After describing the complex variety of institutions involved, Stein concludes: "The unity of this great whole is therefore the task of the government; the true meaning of a Ministry of Education is first achieved when one holds fast simultaneously to the idea of a unified [establishment for] professional education, and to the principle of autonomy for each teaching faculty."[63]

Stein is of the opinion, however, that the central authority should involve itself directly only at the level of *Fachbildung*, i.e., with the universities and the higher technical schools, leaving secondary and primary education to lower seats of government.[64] He points with pride to the local control of primary schools in Prussia and Austria in financial and managerial matters, with the responsibility of the ministry limited to supervision (*Oberaufsicht*) and coordination (*Einheit*).[65] This achievement of a flexible autonomy within a coordinated whole represents to Stein the crowning merit of the German pattern of education, which he straightforwardly recommends as the most advanced in Europe, combining "the internal and external unity of France with the free and individualistic education of England." In France he sees "the free movement of the mind/spirit (*Geist*) crammed into a narrow drawer" by virtue of

62. Ibid., p. 113.
63. Ibid., p. 132.
64. Ibid., pp. 115, 118.
65. Ibid., p. 122.

the "weakness of local government and of local associations," and he faults England for a "great lack of education among the lower classes."[66]

These broader considerations—the purposes of education, the nature and extent of the state's responsibilities, the balance of central and local authority (i.e., the normative and administrative coordinates)—would have been of much greater interest to Itō than detailed information on European schools, the likes of many of which had already been established in Japan. These fundamental principles, the burden in other words of the *Handbuch,* must have been divulged to Itō prior to the latter's letter to Yamada and hence prior also to the meeting with Mori; and it seems likely that the *Hikki* of October simply covered, according to formal lecture plan, material long since broached in informal conversation.

Itō was deeply disappointed by Stein's inability to accept his invitation, writing Sanjō and Iwakura on 30 November 1882 that he earnestly hoped "to find some other suitable man" for the position. And this no doubt was the motive behind the appointment in August 1883 of Hermann Techow, *Regierungsrath* (counselor) of the *Provinzialschulkollegium* (provincial school board) for Prussia at Berlin, as advisor to the cabinet on educational, legal, and local government affairs. Techow, a competent specialist though hardly a personage of Stein's stature, would serve in Japan until June 1886.[67]

MORI AND ITŌ AT PARIS

With Itō having gone so far by August as to think of employing Stein as an advisor, it is reasonable to assume that he came to Paris on the twenty-eighth with educational matters well on his mind, perhaps even mulling over whom on the Japanese side it would be suitable to appoint as education minister in his projected new cabinet. Although Yoshino Sakuzō is doubtless correct in surmising that "Itō was not necessarily of a mind with Mori in the latter's fanatic insistence on the importance of education,"[68] the passivity of Itō has probably been overdone in the account of their encounter left by Koba Sadanaga, a member of Itō's party who later became Mori's private secretary:

66. Ibid., p. 116.
67. Tsuchiya, *Seisakushi,* pp. 285–289; Otto Schmiedel, *Die Deutschen in Japan* (Leipzig, 1920), p. 45; *The Times* (London), 1 September 1883; Nakayama Yasumasa, comp., *Shinbun shūsei Meiji hennenshi* (Tokyo, 1934–36), V, 49, 401, 411, 420.
68. Yoshino, *Kandan no kandan,* p. 179.

Viscount Mori called on Prince Itō at his Paris hotel and engaged him in an earnest discussion of the future course of the nation. Mori stressed the importance of promoting education, and went to great length to explain that the advancement and spread of education constituted the single most important prerequisite for the establishment of constitutional government in Japan. The discussions between the two men continued over a period of several days, but the upshot of it was that Itō was brought over wholly to Mori's views. Itō considered no one better suited for this momentous task than Mori himself, and promised Mori that when the opportunity should present itself at some future date, he would certainly entrust him with that undertaking. Mori was requested to return for the time being to the English capital, to carry on the necessary investigations and make a study of the European and American educational systems. Mori at first declined the offer but, sensing Itō's enthusiasm and moved by his entreaty, finally agreed to it and returning to London worked harder than ever on his educational researches.[69]

Okubo Toshiaki has characterized this encounter as the critical turning point in Mori's career as an "educational statesman," or *bunseika,* and as the occasion of a firm if confidential commitment by Itō to give Mori the education portfolio in his first cabinet.[70] Mori, back in London, on 12 September mailed Itō (as an attachment to his letter recommending a consideration of the Italian polity) a "memorandum of points I made to you verbally the other day," which he entitled "Gakusei hengen" (A few words on educational administration).[71] This provides us not only with clues as to the substance of the talks at Paris but also with the fullest statement we have of Mori's educational philosophy in the early 1880's prior to his appointment to the Ministry. Mori begins on a note familiar enough from "Shintai no nōryoku": "Man is en-

69. Koba Sadanaga, "Mori monbudaijin no kaikaku," in *Kyōiku gojūnenshi,* pp. 91–92.
70. OTM, pp. 86, 90.
71. *Gakusei,* written in this instance with the characters for "learning" and "government," refers to the government's "educational administration," i.e., to the administering of and the policymaking for the school system. This ought not to be confused with the term Gakusei, or "educational system," which refers as a rule to the system of schools in effect from 1872 to 1879, or, more properly speaking, to the *ordinance* of 1872 establishing that system, and which may best be rendered as the "Fundamental Code of Education." To round out this homophonic horror, neither term is likely to be confused, fortunately, with the *gakusei* meaning "student."

dowed with capacities mental, moral and physical. These three capacities are developed and brought into balance by training and by instruction: and this we deem to be the central purpose of education."

The pronounced historical orientation which emerges in Mori's political thinking while in England shows up at once, however, in the second paragraph; he expresses a dismay with current political trends in Japan, which would have set well with either Itō or Motoda; and he places an emphasis on the moral and spiritual training of the nation which would hardly have raised an eyebrow from Stein:

> First of all we must take under consideration the temperament of our people and their traditional customs; distinguish between the merits and the defects of educational methods in effect up to now; and take measure of what is suitable and what is not. Having gotten that far, there will be one point which will require our very special attention: namely, that we conform to the characteristic political heritage of our land . . . The long road ahead is beset with hardship, and there are many defects which lie athwart our immediate path . . . [the latter] we must by all means speedily remedy, and root out in advance the seeds of future trouble. The most urgent requirement is a method of training: by which I mean a method of disciplining the character and the physique of our people. Character training aims chiefly to develop a steady and trustworthy nature, and manners that are simple and honest—the importance of which has certainly not been lost on intelligent persons in positions of authority. I am afraid, however, that the popular sentiment of late has taken a frivolous and roistering course; that politics have been thrown into confusion by empty theorizing; and that commerce has been impaired by [reliance on] mere guesswork—instances whereof could be enumerated at length. These evils feed upon each other, and there are signs that our nation stands upon the brink of some impending disaster.

Turning then to physical training, Mori repeats the basic arguments of "Shintai no nōryoku" as regards its beneficial effect on the individual but links this now specifically to the welfare of the nation as a whole. No conflict however is assumed, nor is any priority stated, as between the two: "To begin with, the maintenance of the individual's bodily health is certainly the primary basis of national strength, and is very probably a prerequisite for individual happiness. If the body is strong, the spirit will advance of its own accord without flagging. Physical training is an indispensable element for character training." Finally, with respect to educational administration proper, Mori notes that: "the rightness or wrongness of our educational policy will have a bearing upon the ebb and flow of politics as a whole, and its merits and its demerits will make themselves felt for years to come." He urges accordingly that educational policy be placed as much as possible beyond the vicissitudes of party politics: "The person entrusted with the administration of our education should not be looked upon as a politician beholden to party organization and subject to sudden appointments and dismissals. Although his involvement in current politics may to some extent be unavoidable, he ought as much as possible to be placed in the position of a consultant. If a need should arise for his participation in state affairs, this should of course be accomplished according to established rules. Such need conceivably would arise in the event the cooperation of the educational administration were required in meeting a severe national crisis, or in the event it were decided to reestablish the educational administration itself on a new set of principles."[72]

This latter rubric would cover the justification for Mori's own appointment to the first Itō cabinet, but it is clear that he envisioned the educational system as functioning ideally outside the realm of politics altogether. The ministry of education (one gathers) would operate apart from the regular cabinet structure, as something of an autonomous corporation; while the minister, as something of a Japanese David Murray, would in normal circumstances enjoy a politically neutral status analogous to that of a foreign adviser.

In concluding the body of his letter of 12 September 1882, Mori revealed how far he had already thought his way into the details of his future position: "I have omitted from my discussion here the importance of teaching arithmetic and the methods for the efficient collection of school fees since, vital though they be, they are peripheral to the main discussion. I am pursuing my investigation of European educational systems without stint, and of course the longer I am stationed here, the more thorough my survey will be."[73] Sometime between the twelfth and the twenty-sixth, when he wrote once again to Vienna, Mori received a message from Itō

72. Mori Arinori, "Gakusei hengen," is given in its entirety in OTM, pp. 185–186.
73. OTM, p. 89.

dated 4 September, formally requesting acceptance of a high educational post, and developing reasons for the invitation.[74]

Itō reiterates much of the philosophy of his "Kyōikugi." Education he argues (implicitly against the Popular Rights party) should not be confused with the "aimless promotion of intellectual prowess" or with "the struggle to get ahead." Its essence rather is to "train the child to know what it is that makes a man," and by so doing to "elevate the spirit of the entire nation." He admits on the other hand, implicitly in distinction to Motoda, that "it goes without saying that the thought of a given individual or of a given nation is not something readily amenable to restraint by system or by a set of rules." Nevertheless, "the administration of national education and the guidance and training of children and young folk means laying down, to some extent, proper directions for them."

Admitting, in turning to Mori, the political nature of his concern, Itō writes: "Although there are persons who preach the necessity of basing political progress on education, I find no one willing to shoulder the burden energetically himself . . . Although there are among the scholars of Japan quite a few persons who are interested in the educational question, I do not find anyone with the vision to establish the foundations of education with an eye to the future political stability of the nation." The person Itō is looking for "would be a man capable of administering the national system of education, possessed of the vision to establish its foundations in such a fashion that the common people, in the future, would have their guidelines laid down for them while they are young." Other qualifications are that this person be "fond of learning himself" and not "overly enamored of Western learning, or excessively devoted to Chinese learning, or unduly bound to any religion."

"Therefore," Itō concludes, "I am placing my hopes on you, and trust you will not refuse the responsibility."[75] To this entreaty Mori responded affirmatively on 26 September 1882, assuring Itō of "my full support, of course, for the chief burden of your letter, namely that the foundations of education be established with a

---

74. OTM, p. 89, takes Mori's letter of 12 September 1882 to be a reply to Itō's of the fourth. Mori first acknowledges receipt of the latter, however, in his letter of the twenty-sixth, which also (unlike his letter of the twelfth) replies substantively to Itō's message. The "Gakusei hengen" therefore precedes, rather than responds to, Itō's written invitation, and provides additional evidence of Mori's persistent initiative on the subject of education.

75. OTM, pp. 88–89.

view to the future political stability of the nation." He then accepted the proposed appointment subject to the condition that he be given a free hand and sufficient time to accomplish his task:

> The government should not . . . place any hope whatsoever on immediate results; the full effect probably can not be hoped for within anything less than thirty years . . . If policy for the system can be laid down in advance, and a person chosen to hold responsibility for it, then that person should be extended full confidence as well as constant and sincere cooperation. However, he should be expected to produce results only gradually over an agreed period of time. Upon appointment he should be treated with favor and should not be forced to produce results within any shorter interval; and as long as he applies himself diligently ought by no means to be replaced. The correction of deficiencies of custom and character of course cannot be effectively accomplished within a short period of time. In order to prevent persons already in adulthood from straying down the wrong path, we shall have to rely on more than our educational administration alone. The direct impact of the latter falls rather upon young children and youths; and even at that it can do little more than train the mental and physical powers of the former and perhaps deflect the latter from their first false step. Nevertheless, if you can develop proper guidelines for the system and find a talented person to fill the office, the whole political life of the nation stands to be improved, and manners and customs elevated—and that is saying a great deal.[76]

Mori thus shares Itō's appreciation of the political implications of education. Both, however, remain far less sanguine than Motoda as regards the explicit ideological uses that should, or could, be made of the system. Mori, judging from his language, promises nothing more than a general stabilization of the moral and political clime, while Itō clearly does not want an ideologue of any pronounced hue for the responsible office. If Mori's political discernment constituted a *sine quā non* from the standpoint of Itō, then Itō's assent to the autonomy of the educational system within the new constitutional framework, and its protection against political influence and manipulation, would seem to represent the basic condition insisted upon by Mori. Any commitment to Itō's frame-

76. OTM, pp. 90–91.

work was of course manifestly political to begin with, and Mori's reluctance to see party men head the ministry may perhaps partly be explained in terms of an aversion to the Popular Rights Movement, as well as his general anti-party bias. It would be mistaken, however, to see that reluctance wholly or even primarily in terms of political motivation. Mori on the twelfth had written of "sudden appointments and dismissals" to which party men were subject, and it seems probable that this handicap, as much as anything else, threatened in Mori's mind the continuity and stability of the educational system—*quā* system—for which he pleaded at such great length in his acceptance letter of the twenty-sixth.

The agreement at Paris would seem to derive less from Itō's sudden conversion to the cause of education, or from Mori's subservience to the political plans of Itō, than from a felicitous reciprocity of priorities, each man approaching the problem of educational administration from his own characteristic angle: Itō from that of politics and Mori from that of education, with each relinquishing to the other the initiative in the field of secondary interest to himself.

For the few remaining years of his life Mori would remain thus in harness once again with his fellow "Arabian horse" of earlier Washington days. Still in step with each other they had both slowed down, on the political track at least, to the pace of an old grey mare, while Mori, viewing the rutty road of educational affairs that stretched before him, seemed reconciled to proceeding with all the slow but steady footwork of a water buffalo.

MORI'S FIELD OF VISION

Mori writing on 5 April 1883 from the London legation to his old friend Birdsey Northrop, secretary of the Connecticut State Board of Education, announced: "There are many things I have been observing in Europe which may interest you to hear; but I have to postpone writing you this time about them until some future occasion."[77] It seems reasonable, in view of the addressee, to attribute Mori's excitement to his new discovery of European (as opposed to American) education; and his postponement of writing to the vastness of the field—the education of an entire continent, as well as of the British Isles—which he hoped to cover before returning to Japan.

77. Kanda Memorial Committee, ed., *Memorials of Kanda Naibu*, (Tokyo, 1927), p. 137, quoting letter from Arinori Mori to Birdsey Northrop, 5 April 1883.

A thumbnail sketch of European education in the early 1880's tells us, of course, no more than what Mori would have perceived had he had the eyes to see. Studies in comparative education tend to focus on recent or contemporary developments, and it is not unnatural that the images popularly evoked by "German education" or "American education" or similar references to national school systems should apply with greater accuracy to the twentieth than to the nineteenth century. What we need to recreate, therefore, is not merely the comparative but, so to speak, the historical-comparative context in which Mori set about the reform of Japanese education. The fact that Mori left an account neither of his survey nor of what it was that he may have borrowed or adapted from Europe when he was minister makes such a sketch the more rather than the less necessary: both as a yardstick by which that borrowing or adaptation can be measured and confirmed and as sufficient background for descriptive or value statements about Japanese education in comparative context.

Mori, surveying the scene from London, would have perhaps been most struck[78] by the contrasts along the normative and administrative coordinates as between England, France, and Germany—contrasts in the purposes and in the power structure of public education which reflected the widely differing ideological heritage and historical experience of the three leading nations of Europe. Mori would have found these contrasts further worked out along the structural coordinate in specific institutions of various types and levels. He also would have noticed, however, thanks to the common imperatives of a scientific and industrial age, and to the intellectual interchange of an unusually cosmopolitan era, a tendency of the various national systems to grow toward each other, especially along the instructional coordinate, and a widening area of agreement among educational statesmen and theorists of all countries as to what was progressive, modern, and worth working for.

The English tradition Mori would have found marked by a deep-seated ideological preference for private initiative and a distrust of government action in the educational field, with both

78. Except as otherwise indicated, the following account has been drawn from the very basic materials presented by Thut and Adams, *Educational Patterns,* pp. 76–171; Vernon Mallinson, *An Introduction to the Study of Comparative Education* (London, 1957), pp. 1–233, *passim;* W. H. G. Armytage, *Four Hundred Years of English Education* (Cambridge, England, 1965), pp. 119–171 and *passim;* W. H. G. Armytage, *The Rise of the Technocrats: A Social History* (London, 1965), pp. 61–182, 319–327 and *passim;* and Peterson, *A Hundred Years of Education,* in its entirety.

sectarian fervor and social class structure operating as additional deterrents to forceful government initiatives. The vast majority of primary schools operating at the time would, for instance, have been the so-called voluntary schools established by the Church of England, while the new city and provincial colleges (such as those at Manchester and Liverpool, established in 1880 and 1881 respectively), which had arisen in response to the new technology, owed their founding to local initiative and to private capital provided by the new captains of industry. The nine great secondary or "public schools" and the two traditional universities Mori would have found the closed preserve of the ruling class, whose basic attitude toward the education of the nation had been one of almost total neglect. And had the Japanese minister asked his English friends wherein lay the chief pride of their national education, they would have been hard put for an answer, so conscious were they rather of its deficiencies.

England was very slow in organizing a modern school system. She would not have her Local Educational Authorities until 1902, or her ministry of education until 1944. Mori would have found such central control as existed largely confined to the power to dispense or withhold treasury grants: the authority of the carrot, so to speak, without the stick. Grants were made on the recommendation of a central inspectorate reporting to the Education Department, first established in 1856 and presided over by what has aptly been described as an "embryo Minister of Education": the vice president of the Committee of the Privy Council on Education.[79]

Government responsibility for primary education had gotten off to a fitful start with William E. Forster's bill of 1870, which provided for the establishment of secular or "board schools" (alongside the church schools) under the control of local boards, supported by a combination of tuition fees, local taxes, and grants from the center, and empowered with the establishment of curriculum, the licensing of teachers, and the option to enforce attendance. This "permissive compulsion," as it was called, proved unequal to the avalanche of school-age children produced by population growth and the gradual effectiveness of the Factory Acts; and with the Mundella Act of 1880, enforcing attendance for all children under ten, England had at long last achieved the stage of universal and compulsory (but not until 1891 "free") primary education. There was as yet little formal training, however, for the teachers of these same schools beyond the establishment of so-called pupil-training centers by some of the more progressive

79. Armytage, *English Education*, p. 119.

school boards, bucking great opposition from the voluntary schools, which traditionally had trained their staffs on the job.[80]

At the highest rung of education, Anglican control over the professions had ended with the abolition of the university tests in 1871, and Mori would have also found women at Oxford, Cambridge, and London (since 1879, 1869, and 1870 respectively). Although the latter institution, like the new city colleges, had opened its curriculum to the new scientific and technological disciplines, the former two universities, like the public schools which prepared for them, still leaned heavily toward the classical humanistic tradition.

The basic function indeed of Oxford and Cambridge, of Eton and Harrow and Winchester, lay less in the realm of the advancement of human knowledge than in the molding of Britain's political, military, and moral leadership. The student community at the two universities consisted entirely of "undergraduates" (to use the twentieth-century term) studying for the bachelor's degree, and here as in the "public schools" great emphasis was placed on the cultivation of human relations and responsibilities within a community framework. The model for the public schools had been largely provided by Thomas Arnold at Rugby, where the "Christian Gentleman" had supplied the conscious ideal, athletics the means to both physical and moral robustness, and the prefect system an effective training device in the giving and taking of orders. The ethos of this ladder to national leadership was in its essence profoundly humanistic, individualistic, and liberal-minded. Very few however were privileged to enter upon it, admission being a matter not of a boy's ability but of his birth into the hereditary ruling class.

The antithesis of the English pattern, as Stein would point out to Itō, was not Germany but rather France. The centralist tradition which Mori would have found across the Channel had its roots in the very early encroachment of the monarchy upon feudal power, a process in which the former traditionally had enjoyed the support of elements (notably the emergent middle class) oppressed by the latter. Frenchmen had developed a bias in favor of strong central government as a guarantor of, rather than a threat to, individual liberties, and in the nineteenth century monarchists and republicans alike were equally committed to the highly centralized pattern in national education which the Bourbon kings, the Jesuits, and finally Napoleon had created for them.

80. W. H. G. Armytage, *A. J. Mundella, 1825–1897: The Liberal Background to the Labour Movement* (London, 1951), pp. 213–214.

A second distinctive feature of French education lay in its unique ethos: a conscious dedication to the preservation of French culture (a *culture générale* participated in by the entire nation), coupled with a pronounced intellectualistic bias in true Cartesian fashion, i.e., an enormous faith in the powers of the logically trained mind and in the efficacy of formal examinations. This ethos profoundly affected the third characteristic of the French system: its structural organization for the production of a ruling elite, an elite in which political and intellectual leadership were assumed to go hand in hand, and the chief passport to which, unlike the English system, was the possession not of pedigree but of brains. If Mori had asked where the distinctive achievement of French education lay, it would have been proper to inform him: "in the fostering of an intellectually well-trained elite."

The administrative framework of French education in the early 1880's was that established by Napoleon in 1806 under the misleading designation of Université de France, which, like the seventeen *académies* subordinate to it, was an administrative rather than a teaching body. Subsequently redesignated Ministère de l'Instruction Publique, it established policy for all branches and levels of French education, the implementation of which was assured by the intimate coordination of the two ministries of education and of the interior at their various respective subordinate levels. Orders passed from the ministry of education directly to the *recteurs* (rectors) of the seventeen *académies* (i.e., the "university districts" which the Japanese had borrowed directly for their Gakusei), under whose immediate control stood the universities and the state secondary schools known as *lycées*. The line of educational authority passed thence from the rector to the prefects, subprefects, and mayors (all officials of the ministry of the interior) of the *départements, arrondissements,* and *communes* located within a given rector's university district. Normal schools were operated at the level of the *département,* the municipal secondary schools (*collèges*) and the elementary schools at the level of the *commune*. A general division of responsibility throughout the university district was maintained as between the functionaries of the interior, who managed the physical plant, and the ministry of education inspectors (reporting directly to the rector) who supervised all instructional matters. Both prefects and mayors were provided with elected advisory councils on education, but these (as Stein pointed out) were largely moribund in the context of such massive bureaucratic initiative.

The authoritarian implications of this symmetrically neat pyramid of control are significantly relieved, however, if one bears in mind the fact that it all rested under another, inverse, pyramid: namely that of the French people pressing its will, through a parliament responsible to it, upon the ministry, which stood (in diagrammatical terms) at the narrow waist of the hourglass. The educational system was also saved, at least at the upper levels, from bureaucratic dry rot by the activity of the Conseil Supérieur de l'Instruction Publique, or Higher Council on Public Instruction, a blue-ribbon board of political and intellectual luminaries, of a status coordinate with that of the ministry itself, which acted as a court of appeal on behalf of teachers and the consultation of which by the ministry was mandatory on matters of a supervisory (as opposed to managerial)[81] nature.

Napoleon had established his system with only secondary and higher education in mind. A national system of elementary schools was first established by Guizot in 1833, but primary education had just (to Mori's eyes) become free and compulsory and secular (with the expulsion of all clergy from the schools) with the laws of 1881 and 1882, for which the ardent nationalist and anticlericalist Jules Ferry had worked, first as minister of education in 1879 and then as premier in 1880–81.[82] The more remarkable aspect of French primary instruction lay rather in its preparation of teachers. France by 1856 had seventy secular *écoles normales* throughout the country and by 1879 could boast one normal school for men and one normal school for women in each of her *départements*. The state bore all the expenses of the teacher trainees, who were housed residentially at their training institutes with a view to inculcating the values of community life and instilling an awareness of the future role they would be called upon to play in society. Upon graduation they were licensed by, and took an oath of loyalty to, the state and remained responsible directly to the ministry.

Secondary and higher education in France presented a well-articulated and tightly coordinated production belt for the political, technological, and cultural leadership of the nation, with a typical dual-track pattern[83] by which the majority of elementary school graduates could proceed if desired to higher levels of vocational or teacher training, but where those seeking entrance to the bureaucracy or the professions via the universities and the *grandes écoles* (specialized higher schools) had to pass first through the very narrow gates of the state *lycées* or municipal *collèges* at the second-

81. See note 1 above.
82. Alfred Cobban, *A History of Modern France,* vol. 3: *France of the Republics, 1871–1962,* Pelican Books (Harmondsworth, 1965), pp. 24–27.
83. See note 2 above.

ary level. A considerable element of privilege was retained in a system nominally based on performance, due to the fact that it was much easier to get into the *lycées* and *collèges* from certain private primary schools known as *classes préparatoires* than it was from the public primary institutions. The ultimate sorting mechanism, however, remained a strictly scholastic one: the *baccalauréat* examination, administered uniformly on a nationwide basis, which marked the progression from the secondary to the university level. State inspection and control over curriculum and examinations in all private schools further insured that privilege, too, would ultimately be judged by performance.

The organizational disarray of university-level education in contemporary France had led Stein to write that "France simply does not have a university in the German sense."[84] The typical *académie* or university district in the 1880's possessed several university-level faculties of the conventional type, but the complement was seldom full, and the faculties would not be integrated into regional universities until 1896.[85] Many of the more exciting developments on the scientific and technological side, meanwhile, had taken place not in the universities but in the *grandes écoles,* most of which were under the control of other ministries (e.g., agriculture, public works) anxious to train their own technicians. The quality of both types of institutions was beyond reproach, however, and collectively their graduates ran France. Particularly prestigious were the Ecole Normale Supérieure (higher normal school), which trained the staffs of the university-district inspectorates and of the departmental normal schools, and Napoleon's Ecole Polytechnique (higher polytechnical school), which had blazed the first trails into the coming technological age and fired Saint-Simon with his vision of a new technocratic society.[86] Nor with the Technical Education Law of 1880 was France without provision for the organization of the lower levels of technical and vocational education as well. University professors throughout the system, finally, were civil servants; but freedom of teaching and research was zealously cherished and on the whole very well guarded.

Turning to "German" education, a great deal would have depended on whether one was discussing Prussia or the Second Empire as a whole. Administrative and structural patterns in the several *Länder,* or states, of the empire were heavily influenced by, and after 1870 tended increasingly to approximate, the Prus-

84. Stein, *Handbuch der Verwaltungslehre,* p. 131.
85. Peterson, *A Hundred Years of Education,* p. 211.
86. Armytage, *Rise of the Technocrats,* pp. 64–66.

sian model. Control over educational affairs remained in the hands of the *Länder,* however, producing a congeries of *Kultusministerien,*[87] or ministries of education, and a national pattern of regional authority far more pronounced than in England, and in ways reminiscent of the United States except for the preponderant example of one of the *Länder,* namely Prussia.

The answer to Mori's hypothetical question regarding the distinctive achievements of German education would have been: "at the extremities of the organizational ladder: in primary education and in the graduate schools." Both achievements, originally those of Prussia, may be viewed as responses to the basic challenge of national reconstruction imposed by the defeat at the hands of Napoleon in 1806. A system of universal, compulsory, and civil-controlled primary education, which remained the cynosure of educational circles in Europe and America throughout the century, had been established in that year, while the forced march of Prussia from an agrarian to an industrial state, well accomplished by the 1880's, had been enormously aided by the development of the University of Berlin as a model for higher scientific research and instruction. In the intervening area of secondary education, Germany like France placed heavy emphasis on formal intellectual performance. In the case of Prussia in particular, however, access to the better schools was in effect largely monopolized by the Junker class and in that sense resembled the instance of England more closely than that of France in perpetuating hereditary privilege.

The administrative and structural resemblances between French and Prussian education provide an apt reminder of how such similarities may nevertheless hide substantial differences along the normative coordinate: differences both in the basic values and purposes of education and in the historical or sociological context in which the administrative and structural arrangements have been placed. Historically speaking, the highly centralized model which the French people had chosen for themselves was imposed on the people of Prussia by fiat of their King. Sociologically speaking, the French were willing to entrust their national fortunes to the survivors of the academic mill, whatever their class of origin; whereas in Prussia the Junker class in alliance with the crown was determined, as a class, to maintain its control of the state by various means, of which a monopoly of access to the bureaucracy and the professions was only one. Finally as to values, the individualism of a nation of small-scale farmers, shopkeepers, and manufacturers

---

87. Germany has had a nationally centralized system of education during only one period: that of the Nazis.

greatly reinforced in France the ideals of liberty and equality to which the Republic was formally committed, counterbalancing the authoritarian aspects of the administrative pattern.[88]

The Prussian pyramid of authority had taken its cue from the French. The universities stood under the direct control of the ministry of religion, education and health (the *Kultusministerium*) which had been established in 1817, while other types of education were administered through subordinate levels of the ministry of the interior from the *Provinz* down through the *Bezirk* and *Kreis* to the *Gemeinde,* or local community. With the inverse pyramid of popular sovereignty missing, however, the total Prussian pattern was indeed "authoritarian": the bottom half only of our diagrammatical hourglass.

Functionally however, in the relationship between the center and the localities, considerably more initiative and responsibility was entrusted to the latter in the Prussian than in the French instance. This is because the advisory councils and committees attached to the responsible officials of the interior at various levels from the *Provinz* on down, though appointive rather than elective, were far from moribund. Staffed with knowledgeable local personnel, they played an active role in the administrative process, reflecting the relative vitality of local government in Germany as opposed to France: a phenomenon which in turn had its deep historical roots in (among other things) political decentralization, the absence of Roman law, and Protestant parish life.

The *Oberpräsident* (superior president) of the *Provinz,* who was responsible for normal and secondary schools, was assisted by his *Provinzialschulkollegium,* or provincial school board, which certified teachers and administered university examinations throughout the province. The *Präsident* of the *Bezirk* (district), and the *Präsident* of the *Kreis* (county) as well, likewise had their respective school councils; to the former was attached the *Schulrat* (counsellor for schools), responsible for elementary education throughout the *Bezirk,* and to the latter the *Kreisschulinspektor,* responsible for the inspection of primary schools throughout the *Kreis.* It was incumbent upon the *Gemeinde,* finally, to establish their individual schools in accordance with directions issued by the center. Each community had its *Schulvorstand,* or school committee, in which supervision of instruction and management of plant were divided as between the clerical and lay members respectively. Members of the *Gemeinde* were also organized into *Schulvereine,* or school associations, which collected the taxes to support

---

88. Mallinson, *Comparative Education,* p. 36.

the primary schools. For elementary schooling in Prussia was a duty—*Schulpflicht*—not a privilege or a right, and it would not be free of cost until the following decade.

The control over primary schools, seemingly relinquished in Prussia by the center in terms of supervision and financial responsibility, was to a significant degree reestablished through control of normal education. The state-run universities and *Lehrer-Seminare* (teachers' seminaries) produced the staffs for the secondary and primary levels respectively. As in France, teachers were licensed by the state, expected to serve as models of morality to the young, and as trainees were if anything more regimented and more thoroughly drilled in the virtues of order and method than their colleagues across the Rhine. The seminaries had been pruned of politically oriented subject matter as early as the royalist reaction of 1849, and the minute regulation of their curricula enabled the government gradually, over the course of the Bismarck era, to turn primary school teachers as a group into effective propagandists for its own point of view.[89] It should not be forgotten, however, that it was also the German, and particularly the Prussian, schoolmaster who during these very same decades had pioneered the most significant professional frontiers: accepting, testing, and further developing the pedagogical theories of Pestalozzi, Froebel, and Herbart.

Had Mori been looking for examples of the direct encouragement of patriotic feeling, he would have found records of one in the practice of the Second Empire of France, which had formally displayed a crucifix and a bust of Napoleon III in all the major schools, and had conducted prayers prior to morning classes with another break for the same at midday.[90] The encouragement of nationalistic feeling, however, was hardly an issue in Europe. Rather it was a trend, and a growing one, visible on all sides to a greater or lesser degree. What was an issue, and a bitter one, was the relationship of the churches to the schools. The Third Republic, at the very time of Mori's investigation, had just expelled the bishops from the Conseil Supérieur de l'Instruction Publique and the priests from the schools, and had excluded religious instruction in all state institutions: it had been the coming, in the words of Albert de Broglie, of the "école sans Dieu."[91]

Although Britain was spared the severe polarization of clerical and anticlerical sentiment which characterized France, Mori would

89. Thut and Adams, *Educational Patterns*, p. 87.
90. Peterson, *A Hundred Years of Education*, p. 22.
91. Cited in Cobban, *France, 1871–1962*, p. 25.

have found educational progress considerably hampered by incessant squabbles between the secular and church schools, to say nothing of intersectarian rivalries. Prussia by contrast presented in this area the greatest picture of stability. Lutheran clergy were well represented both in the schools and in the educational administration, but they operated as officials of an obedient state church which, in the Prussian table of organization, was in itself no more than a subordinate department of the *Kultusministerium*. A high proportion of schools throughout the German Empire as well had retained a denominational character. Unlike Britain or France, however, in Germany the clash between the religious and the secular authority was greatly mitigated by the religious homogeneity within the individual *Länder,* which controlled their respective educational systems (e.g., Roman Catholic Bavaria, or Protestant Prussia).

The dual-track structure and the elitist spirit of secondary education characteristic of France was repeated in the several states of Germany, the chief differences lying in the fact that the *Abitur* examinations (equivalent of the *baccalauréat*) were prepared by the schools individually, and that the *Realgymnasium,* with its scientific and modern language curriculum had, since 1870, achieved an equal ranking with the traditional classical *Gymnasium*. Both were nine-year schools and offered at their upper reaches instruction which, in modern American terminology, would be called "college-level" or "undergraduate."

The university, on the other hand, which von Humboldt had established at Berlin in 1810 had been a pioneer (to continue the same terminology) of the modern graduate school, introducing among other things the seminar, the research paper, and the doctoral dissertation.[92] Students at Berlin were enrolled in pursuit of doctoral or professional degrees exclusively. Whereas "higher education" in England was dedicated to the additional refinement of a hereditary elite, and that in France to the creation of a national leadership of all the talents, the orientation in Germany was toward the pursuit of knowledge itself. The German universities were models for modern scientific research and were, in Mori's time, attracting great numbers of students from England and the United States, where similar facilities were lacking.[93] The professional staffs were appointed and paid by their respective *Kultusminis-*

---

92. Friedrich Paulsen, *German Education Past and Present,* tr. T. Lorenz (London, 1908), p. 187.

93. America's first graduate course, on the German model, had been established at Johns Hopkins University in 1876.

terien, but *Lehrfreiheit* and *Lernfreiheit* (freedom of teaching and freedom of learning) were still in Mori's time an exciting reality in the German universities. Both Germany and France, finally, had in 1880 passed laws reorganizing technical education, and both countries (unlike Britain) had developed an integrated system of terminal trade and vocational schools and, with their *Technische Hochschulen* and *grandes écoles,* an imposing array of technical universities.

PROBABLE DIRECTION-FINDERS

What in Mori's field of vision specifically arrested his attention can only be inferred from what he would do with Japanese education between 1886 and 1889. One would expect him, however, to have used in his studies such commonsense guides as: (1) a preference for institutional models in their most highly developed form, which would have led him quickly to the universities of Germany or the normal schools of France; or (2) a search for patterns most readily adaptable to the political and social structure of Meiji Japan, which would have inclined him to skip quickly over systems emphasizing extreme decentralization (e.g., as in America) or the perpetuation of hereditary privilege (e.g., as in Britain). Fortunately Mori does give us some hints as to who the persons in London were who helped him find his directions. In his letter to Itō of 22 June 1883 he had remarked in passing: "The other day I met with Mundella, the leading educational official of the British Government, and learned a great deal about the current state of British education and politics. I have also gradually managed to have talks with Huxley and others of great scholarly stature like him who have had a close connection with educational matters up to now. As a result I have been able to gather in, and reflect upon, the opinions of a good many people, all with great profit to myself. Incidentally, the uniform application of the compulsory education act throughout Britain is beginning to bear fruit. The high juvenile crime rate of previous years has gradually fallen, according to the official reports of judges in courts throughout the country, and the papers again and again have raised their voices in praise of this law." [94]

If Mundella and Huxley were the sort of people Mori was seeking out, what point of view did they represent? What would have been their probable advice to Mori, the hypothetical reading lists which they would have presented him, and the colleagues to whom

94. OTM, pp. 93–94.

they in turn might have been inclined to refer him? Anthony John Mundella, author of the compulsory education act of 1880 which Mori so much admired, was vice president of the Committee of the Privy Council on Education in the second Gladstone cabinet (1880–1885). The son of an Italian refugee, Mundella had risen from the lowest rank of apprentice to a lucrative partnership in a hosiery firm, and from there had gone on into politics. He has been described by his authoritative biographer as "the pre-eminent Lib.-Lab. of his generation," as "Shaftesbury's spiritual legatee," and as a "Fabian before the Fabians."[95] Having risen from the laboring classes and having participated in the earlier Chartist movement himself, he remained a friend of the trades union movement. Specifically, he was the original author of the labor arbitration board which would contribute so much over the coming years, in both Britain and America, to the industrial harmony of which he was an outspoken advocate. Mundella's early hardships had taught him what the want of an education meant, while as a manufacturer he keenly felt the national need for technical training. The advance of labor and the progress of education were inextricably linked in his mind, and we have here, in contrast to the monarchical-bureaucratic initiative and the statist concern with national unity and power so characteristic of continental education, a pressure for educational reform stemming from the democratic, humanitarian, and quasisocialistic impulses of English Radicalism.

Mundella has been characterized as "one of the two or three who established the British state system of popular education."[96] Most successful in his establishment of compulsory primary education, and in his revision of the Education Code in 1882 to broaden the elementary school curriculum in the direction of play, manual work, and modern science, Mundella fought in vain for the establishment of an education ministry. He did what he could to reorganize his department—districting the inspectorate and consolidating and publishing the inspectors' instructions—but none other than Forster himself (in the framing of whose act of 1870 Mundella had assisted) expressed the prevalent English attitude toward the creation of such a ministry: "The real objection . . . probably is that it is undesirable to make too much of education. If we were to have a Minister for Education, he might be pushing things on too quickly."[97]

Mundella kept in close touch with the avant garde of educational thought in England, in America, and on the Continent. Matthew

95. Armytage, *Mundella*, pp. 335, 328 and 322.
96. *Dictionary of National Biography,* 1917, XXII (supplement), p. 1084.
97. Quoted in Armytage, *Mundella*, p. 220.

Arnold, for instance, served as one of his own inspectors, and in 1870 (in the company of Thomas Hughes, the author of *Tom Brown's School Days* and leading apostle of athletics and "muscular Christianity"), Mundella had visited America and struck up a lifelong friendship with two educational authorities also well known to Mori: John Eaton and Birdsey Northrop. Mundella's firm owned a branch plant in Chemnitz which provided a window on German affairs as well and excuse for an occasional continental excursion. "The contrast," he had remarked in 1869 in reference to primary education in Saxony, "is something to make an Englishman blush for his country."[98] He was in the habit of urging travelers to Central Europe to visit the German schools and of providing them with the necessary introductions. In 1880 Mundella had returned from an extensive tour of Germany, Austria, and Belgium to investigate technical education, and the publication in 1881 of *Technical Education in a Saxon Town* by his own business manager in Chemnitz (H. M. Felkin) created such a stir in England that Mundella as vice president for education was authorized in 1882 to establish a royal commission (the Samuelson) which spent the next three years investigating the subject in Europe and America.[99] And in 1885 Mundella would be back in Munich and Berlin again for still another look at the primary school system.

Critics were not slow to attack Mundella's apparent Teutophilism. Lord Norton in 1884 accused him of "essaying a flight into continental bureaucracy," of harboring "strongly avowed German preferences," and of failing to take account of "the English Spirit."[100] To such criticism, Mundella's remark a propos of compulsion in 1870 continued to apply: "It is said that compulsion is un-English; but things which are un-English today become English tomorrow."[101] His basic premise, often repeated, and at one and the same time a warning and a hope, was that "the grandest mine this country possesses lies in the intelligence of its inhabitants,"[102] and that the foremost need of the day was to organize the national intelligence, as France and Germany so remarkably had done.[103]

98. Quoted in ibid., p. 73.
99. Armytage, *English Education*, p. 169; W. H. G. Armytage, *A Social History of Engineering* (London, 1961), p. 239.
100. Quoted in Armytage, *Mundella*, p. 221.
101. Quoted in ibid., p. 79.
102. Quoted in ibid., p. 327.
103. The A. J. Mundella correspondence, viewed in its entirety at the Sheffield University Library, revealed no letters to or from Mori. It is likely that any correspondence between the two would have been retained in the official records of the ministry (then department) of education, the greater part of which was destroyed during the Nazi blitz.

Mori would have heard a great deal on the subject of technical education also from Thomas Henry Huxley,[104] who with much encouragement and assistance from Mundella had arranged the establishment in 1881 of the Normal School of Science at South Kensington, in which he was immediately installed as dean. This institution, forerunner of the Imperial College of Science and Technology, was at the time the first and only institute of higher technology in all Britain. Huxley, as a founding member of the London School Board in 1872, had played a prominent role also in the national movement for universal primary education. The London board would for years continue to set the pace for the rest of England, and Huxley had made himself heard on behalf of better moral and physical training, and had given his strong support to the normal school movement.[105]

Despite the immense contribution it was destined to make to the advancement of national industry, technical education in Britain had received curious opposition from manufacturing circles, who feared the revelation of trade secrets.[106] Huxley in his *Report on the Promotion of Technical Education* of 1878 had pointed to developments in Germany and Switzerland and lamented that "the condition in England in these matters is simply scandalous."[107] Particularly admired in Britain at the time was the *Polytechnikum* of Germany (originally secondary level, but gradually being upgraded to the status of *Technische Hochschule*), and in 1883 two technical colleges patterned after the *Polytechnikum* at Charlottenburg were at last established at Finsbury and South Kensington with the private resources of the wealthy London guilds. The staffs of the new technology-oriented municipal colleges had also, to a high proportion, been trained in Germany.[108] Technical education was a favorite theme also of Mori's friend Sir Edward James Reed, M.P., a naval architect and chief constructor of the Royal Navy between 1863 and 1870, who had visited Japan at the invitation of

---

104. A viewing of the Huxley Papers in their entirety at the Lyon Playfair Library at the Imperial College of Science and Technology, University of London, likewise failed to reveal any correspondence with Mori. Huxley was on very close terms with Mundella, however, and was of course a member of the Athenaeum.

105. Armytage, *English Education*, p. 158; *Dictionary of National Biography*, 1909, XX, 896.

106. Armytage, *English Education*, p. 162.

107. Thomas H. Huxley, *Report on the Promotion of Technical Education* (London, 1878), p. 16.

108. Armytage, *English Education*, p. 165; Peterson, *A Hundred Years of Education*, p. 245.

the Japanese government in 1878–79, and upon returning had defended the Japanese position on treaty revision in a verbal free-for-all with Harry Parkes in the letters-to-the-editor columns of the London papers.[109]

Huxley may very possibly have responded to Mori's inquiries on a self-deprecatory note, for the engineering department of Tokyo University had in the early 1870's established the first laboratory in the world for applied chemistry under Henry Dyer and W. E. Ayrton, whom Huxley was able only eventually to lure back to England with his new college at South Kensington.[110] The journal, *Nature,* had remarked as early as 17 May 1877 on the lead Japan had stolen on England in that particular field; and even a full ten years later, in 1887, the foreign office would conclude with a sigh of relief that Japanese students of technology were flocking to Germany not on account of pro-German sympathies but simply because the schooling was so much better there.[111] In that same year Huxley would write in the *Times:* "We are entering, indeed we have already entered, upon the most serious struggle for existence to which this country was ever committed. The latter years of the century promise to see us in an industrial war of far more serious import than the military wars of its opening years."[112]

It is not certain, of course, that Huxley necessarily used the same striking metaphor to Mori, who very likely had already heard it from Spencer. But the very same note sounded loud and clear in Mori's *Pall Mall Gazette* interview, and one can well imagine that there would have been overtones of it in any Mori-Huxley encounter. Huxley's concern for physical training and character building would have found a more flamboyant exponent in Thomas Hughes, whom Mori may possibly have met as a fellow Athenaeum member, or through his diplomatic colleague (and Hughes' own intimate social friend) James Russell Lowell, the American minister to England.[113] Even without a personal meeting, Hughes' vulgarization of the ideals of Thomas Arnold and Charles Kingsley into a cult of athletics and "muscular Christianity" would have been very much in the air.

109. LCT, 8 June 1881; KKM, p. 114.
110. Armytage, *A Social History of Engineering,* p. 233; Armytage, *Rise of the Technocrats,* pp. 116, 325.
111. PRO, Japan/General Correspondence, FO-46-375, letter from Russell Robertson to Philip Currie, 10 March 1887.
112. *The Times* (London), 21 March 1887, quoted in Armytage, *English Education,* p. 170.
113. Edward C. Mack and W. H. G. Armytage, *Thomas Hughes: the Life of the Author of "Tom Brown's School Days"* (London, 1952), p. 186.

Military drill, which Mori had mentioned in "Shintai no nōryoku" in connection with Swiss practice, and which by convention suggests something distinctively Prussian, was conducted in simple form in a good many of the English schools, and was a feature on which the inspectors tended to report with considerable enthusiasm. The great public schools had introduced officer-training programs after the war scare of 1859, and military formation drill had been introduced into the elementary board schools on a voluntary basis with the Code of Education for 1871. Each annual (i.e., academic year) "Report of the Committee of the [Privy] Council on Education" carried extensive comment by the inspectors on the progress of this activity. These reports, together with the annually published codes, constituted the most informative departmental literature which Mundella could, if so inclined, have given Mori to peruse—much as Eaton had once provided Mori with appropriate materials in Washington. Even without the reports, however, Mori would have seen at first hand in the schools he visited the military drill which the roving district inspectors uniformly applauded, though differing as to the actual extent of its practice.

The inspector for the Ipswich and Edmonton district, for instance, wrote with respect to military drill in his Report for 1879–1880: "In several schools military drill is taught, and very well taught. It is desirable that it should appear more often in school timetables. Exercises smartly performed in the playground generally betoken good order in the schoolroom, and they improve the health and carriage of boys and girls."[114] And the inspector for the Oxford district would write for 1882–1883 that: "[at Chipping Norton Junction the visitor] will see a corps of some thirty or forty boys who will go through everything required from a voluntary corps to prove itself efficient, including skirmishing drill."[115] The reports for

114. PRO, "Minutes and Reports of the Committee of the Privy Council on Education, 1839–99" (hereinafter "Reports on Education"), ED-17-50, "Report" for 1879–1880.

115. "Reports on Education," ED-17-53, "Report" for 1882–1883. Instances of this sort of report could be cited at length, e.g.: "It is to be regretted that military drill is not more frequently taught . . . the managers of schools within a certain area might combine to obtain the services of an army instructor. Many teachers, too, who have been volunteers, might . . . secure the requisite certificate" (ED-17-50, "Report" for 1879–1880, Durham District); "I find in those schools in which no such system is practiced, little or no order is maintained" (ED-17-51, "Report" for 1880–1881, Taunton District); "Military drill and marching in the playground is occasionally practiced, sometimes under some old soldier, sometimes under the master— but very few schools practice military drill" (ED-17-51, "Report" for 1880–

1880–81 and 1882–83 would also have carried the biennial "general reports" of Inspector Arnold, England's most eloquent advocate of education, Continental style. Matthew Arnold, in the words of W. H. G. Armytage, "worked from the Athenaeum rather than the Education Department,"[116] and it seems virtually impossible to believe, in view of their common interests, that he and Mori would never have met.

Arnold was a confidant of Mundella, of whom he had written in 1880 as having "more chance of influence with him than with any Vice-President we have ever had,"[117] barring not even Arnold's own brother-in-law, W. E. Forster. He had been dispatched under government authority to investigate elementary schools in France, Holland, and Belgium in 1859–60 and secondary and higher education in France, Italy, and Germany in 1865–66; and he would be sent once again in 1885–86 to view the progress of primary education in France, Germany, and Switzerland. Even if Mori had not had access to Arnold's original reports in the departmental archives, he could have read them in the book form in which Arnold had long since published their substance: *Popular Education in France,* 1861; *A French Eton,* 1864; *Schools and Universities on the Continent,* 1868; and *Higher Schools and Universities in Germany,* 1874. *Culture and Anarchy* of 1869, and *Friendship's Garland* of 1871 also contained important philosophical asides on the subject. Mori, as far as we know, did not read French or German, and these were the most authoritative English-language texts on the subject he had set out to explore.

Arnold was the intellectual heir of Coleridge and Carlyle rather than of the Utilitarian tradition, with which Mori had been more familiar. One of the chief proponents of "collectivism in education" as it came to be known, he stood close to Mundella in prac-

---

1881, Worcester District); "It would be a good plan if teachers and pupil teachers could be formed up in the supernumerary rank and act as sergeants . . . In the use of the younger teachers the knowledge and experience thus gained could hardly fail to be of service to them in the future" (ED-17-51, "Report" for 1880–1881, Bristol District); "A short manual of elementary military exercises and drill, which has been adopted in the Army schools for soldiers' children . . . may be found useful in the civil schools" (ED-17-53, "Report" for 1882–1883, district unidentified).

116. Armytage, *English Education,* p. 163. Roughly a third of Arnold's letters for the period 1880–1884, as compiled in George Russell, *Letters of Matthew Arnold, 1848–1888* (London, 1895), were written from the Athenaeum.

117. Ibid., II, 174, quoting letter from Matthew Arnold to Miss Arnold, 15 Sept. 1880.

tical policy and shared with T. H. Green and Bosanquet an idealist image of the state. Arnold characterized his own country as having "a working class not educated at all, a middle class educated on the second plane, and the idea of science absent from the whole course and design of our education."[118] He therefore outlined, in his conclusion to *Schools and Universities on the Continent,* a "plan of reorganization for English instruction which is suggested almost irresistibly by a study of public instruction in other European countries, and of the actual condition and prospects of the modern world."[119]

Arnold, in *Schools and Universities on the Continent,* had found British education wanting both as to system and as to substance. With respect to administration, his discomfiture extended beyond education to the lack generally in Britain (as opposed to the Continent), of "a civil organization which has been framed with forethought and design to meet the wants of modern society."[120] Arnold's emphasis on an integrated educational establishment ran parallel to that of Stein, and in comparing the schools of Britain to those in Rome he complained of: "the same easy going and absence of system on all sides, the same powerlessness and indifference of the State, the same independence in single institutions, the same free course for abuses, the same confusion, the same lack of all idea of *co-ordering* things, as the French say."[121] At the instructional level, "the want of the idea of science, of systematic knowledge," Arnold argued, "is, as I have said again and again, the capital want, at this moment, of English education and of English life."[122]

With respect to primary education Arnold lavished praise on the French *commune* with its state-appointed mayor and pointed out that a rational municipal organization (which Britain would first achieve with the Municipal Corporations Act of 1882) was the key to an effective system of public-operated schools.[123] The superiority of Continental elementary education was generally acknowledged, however, and public argument revolved chiefly around feasible means of applying it to the British context. It was in the fields of secondary and higher education, rather, that Arnold was most con-

118. Matthew Arnold, "Schools and Universities on the Continent," in R. H. Super, ed., *The Complete Prose Works of Matthew Arnold* (Ann Arbor, 1960–1965), IV, 313.
119. Ibid., IV, 328.
120. Ibid., IV, 304.
121. Ibid., IV, 304.
122. Ibid., IV, 318.
123. Ibid., IV, 306.

cerned to shock the public into an awareness of the inadequacies of the native educational establishment.

This concern was in keeping with Arnold's historically familiar role as apostle of culture, as arch enemy of "Philistinism": a term he had borrowed originally from Heinrich Heine (*Philistertum*).[124] The chief beneficiaries of the reorganization and expansion of secondary and higher education would be the British middle classes, whom Arnold found intellectually depressed and educationally deprived in comparison with their French or German counterparts. At the most obvious level of commercial competition, Arnold pointed to the Swiss and German *Realschulen* and *Polytechniken* warning that "in every part of the world their men of business trained in these schools are beating the English when they meet on equal terms as to capital."[125] More significantly, however, he found the middle classes "cut off from the aristocracy and the professions, and without governing qualities."[126] Therein lay the greatest danger to England's future: the intellectual unpreparedness of the class that gradually was assuming the chief political power in the land. Furthermore, if the middle classes could be rescued, the emerging working class would have a model on which to form itself.[127]

Robert Lowe (a former vice president for education under Disraeli) had warned the House of Commons as early as 1867 that "it will be absolutely necessary that you prevail on our future masters to learn their letters."[128] What we see in Arnold, in short, is an educational program informed by the idealist viewpoint and by a tradition of *noblesse oblige,* which dovetailed closely with a vision inspired, in the case of Mundella, by the Radical tradition. Both men were committed to the gradual extension of political and social democracy in Britain, and it should be remembered that this provides the fundamental ideological context in which their specific proposals, for all their seemingly authoritarian overtones, must be placed.

Since Arnold was chiefly concerned with secondary and higher education, and since like Stein he assumed that this was an area best entrusted to state authority, the centralizing note is even more pronounced in his case than in that of Mundella. In his call

124. Johannes Renwanz, *Matthew Arnold und Deutschland* (Greifswald, 1927), p. 27.
125. Arnold, "Schools and Universities on the Continent," IV, 310.
126. Ibid., IV, 309.
127. Armytage, *English Education,* p. 136; W. F. Connell, *The Educational Thought and Influence of Matthew Arnold* (London, 1950), p. 246.
128. Quoted in Armytage, *English Education,* p. 139.

for the appointment of an education minister, he had written: "The intervention of the State becomes especially necessary in superior instruction, because here the body of public opinion educated enough to discern what is wanted gets smaller than ever, while the importance of organizing your instruction well and committing it to first-rate men becomes greater than ever. It is not from any love of bureaucracy that men like Wilhelm von Humboldt, ardent friends of human dignity and liberty, have had recourse to a department of State in organizing universities; it is because an Education Minister supplies you, for the discharge of certain critical functions, the agent who will perform them in the greatest blaze of daylight and with the keenest sense of responsibility."[129] Arnold then went on to characterize an education minister as "directly representing all the interests of learning and intelligence in this great country."

From France, Arnold would have had his country adopt the Conseil Supérieur de l'Instruction Publique, "comprising without regard to politics the personages most proper to be heard on questions of public education, a consultative body only, but whose opinion the minister should be obliged to take on all important measures not purely administrative;"[130] and from Germany, the *Provinzialschulkollegium*. The Provincial School Board, of which he would have established "eight or ten" throughout Britain, was, he argued, "well suited to our habits, supplies a basis for local action, and preserves one from the inconveniences of an over-centralized system like that of France."[131] Arnold, though deeply attracted to (and perhaps the most eloquent popularizer of) German culture, was temperamentally even more at home in France,[132] but he assumed the German educational model to be more readily adaptable to the English context because of the local autonomy built into it at various levels between *Gemeinde* and *Kultusministerium*. Arnold apparently took the German educational system to operate in antiseptic isolation from political influences (an educational ideal reminiscent, if perhaps not even to some extent provocative, of Mori's own), and in the criticism of one biographer, seems to have been "strangely unaware" of the pronounced political guidance, particularly in Prussia, at the very time of his investigation.[133]

At the secondary level, Arnold wished to see the establishment

129. Arnold, "Schools and Universities on the Continent," IV, 325.
130. Ibid., IV, 314.
131. Ibid., IV, 315.
132. Renwanz, *Matthew Arnold und Deutschland*, p. 45.
133. Connell, *Matthew Arnold*, p. 90.

of the equivalent of the *lycée* or *Gymnasium,* chiefly "by the absolute appropriation by public authority for the purposes of a better application,"[134] of the majority of endowed schools: schools which, though established by their original charters for the sake of indigent but talented local youths, had gradually become the preserves of privilege. The newly constituted schools would prepare for an examination comparable to the *Abitur,* on which admission to the universities and access to the higher public offices would henceforth depend. They would "be under the direct control of the Education Department and the Provincial Boards," with "regulations for management, fees, books, studies, methods, and examinations, devised by public authority as most expedient."[135] Arnold, finally, was hardest of all on the English universities, likening them to mere *"hautes lycées,"* offering "no real university instruction, therefore, at all,"[136] and leaving native education with "an entire absence of the crowning of the structure."[137] Arnold called for "eight or ten" regional universities with their faculties appointed entirely by the ministry.[138]

Arnold and Huxley and Mundella in their day represented the vanguard of progressive, modernist educational thought in England. That they were a minority is amply shown by the very slow pace at which English education gradually did develop in the direction they had indicated. The majority view, however, was a negative one, more a visceral abhorrence of central authority than an articulated educational philosophy, with virtually no concrete program for Mori to grasp. The greatest exponent of laissez-faire in educational as in other matters was of course Herbert Spencer, whose classic pronouncement on the subject, *The State and Education,* would first be published in 1890. Mori in "Shintai no nōryoku" had leaned heavily on Spencer's educational psychology, but at the level of governmental educational policy it would be evident from the course Mori followed either that he ignored Spencer's viewpoint or, what is more likely, that Spencer in his private advice to the Japanese reversed his laissez-faire position on educational, as he had on political, matters.

One is struck by the correspondence at many points between the point of view of Arnold, Huxley, and Mundella, and that of Lorenz von Stein: by the wide area of agreement in other words through-

---

134. Arnold, "Schools and Universities on the Continent," IV, 317.
135. Ibid., IV, 317.
136. Ibid., IV, 319.
137. Ibid., IV, 320.
138. Ibid., IV, 322, 326.

out Europe as to what constituted modern education, and by the propensity of the progressive English thinkers to look to the Continent for their models. Kaimon Sanjin has given us the following surmise: "At that time [while minister in London] Mori travelled to Prussia and took up once again his observation and study [of educational systems], having recalled most likely the advice given him while in America by his friend Brooks. When he later became Minister of Education, Mori established his policy along statist lines, in German fashion, while the organization of the normal schools (among other things) was patterned on the German model. The successful prospects of his administration were already established at this earlier time."[139] Charles Brooks, whom Mori met while in Washington, had been active alongside Horace Mann in the pre-Civil War movement for public-supported primary and normal schools.[140] More recent influences, however—and all of them English—would have been sufficient to fire Mori with enthusiasm for what Kaimon (who partook of a very common misconception) would have done better to call a "Franco-German," or "mixed-continental," rather than a "German" educational model. Mori was eminently at home in English intellectual circles and was sufficiently impressed with the English spirit and the English way of life to commend them highly to Itō. Mori's three brief visits to Germany in 1880, 1881, and 1883 may have enabled him to visit schools first hand, but the bulk of his investigation would have depended on materials and on informants in London.[141]

Viewed from the standpoint of respective European influences, therefore, the Itō-Mori entente on educational matters appears less as a conversion of Mori to "German" ideas under the prodding of Itō than as a convergence of educational viewpoints common to leading thinkers in both Central Europe and England. Any "German" element in Mori's thought would seem, as far as the years 1880–1884 are concerned, to have been mediated by his English mentors in the limited and ad hoc form of a specific educational program. Although conformable enough to the sort of political conservatism evident in *A Representative System of Government for Japan,* it would not have been derived from a prior commitment to characteristically German *political* theory. If Mori did view Germany primarily through English eyes, it would be significant to know just how Germany looked at that time to the English and to divest that image of twentieth-century accretions owing to

139. KSM, p. 73.
140. See Chapter Five.
141. See Chapter Eight.

two world wars, the first of which occurred a full three decades after Mori left London. In England of the early 1880's there was a fresh awareness of Germany (and of America) as a serious industrial competitor but not the cultural and political antipathy that would come to characterize a later era. "Representative British thought of the day," up to 1870, had been in the words of G. M. Trevelyan, "all for the German civilization and against the French."[142] The Franco-Prussian conflict had produced some second thoughts[143] but nothing like the twentieth-century revulsions which would cast in a sinister light aspects of Germany's culture—her technology, her efficiency, her schools—which an earlier generation of Englishmen had taken, and largely admired, at face value. The Anglo-German naval rivalry was in Mori's day still a thing of the future, and Germany as the chief Continental military power, devoid as yet of naval ambitions, was a natural equipoise against France and Russia, with which Britain more often came into conflict during the remainder of the century.[144] English diplomacy during the second Gladstone administration was particularly passive and deferential to the diplomatic initiatives of Bismarck.[145] All of which simply suggests that any new admiration which Mori might have developed for Germany would not necessarily have struck him as a defection from such kinship as he may have felt for English, or for Anglo-American, ways.

Mori's two brief references to Germany, indeed, reflect a mixed appraisal and do not even mention military prowess. In April 1880 he had warned Kuroda Kiyotaka that Bismarck's designs for national unity were threatened by party opposition and provincial loyalties and that if he lost control it would alter the power balance of Europe overnight. And Mori's recommendation of Germany to Itō in May 1882 had been couched entirely in economic terms: he praised the Prussians as "the Chinese of the West" for their superior "commercial" abilities and predicted that Germany eventually would become the "wealthiest" nation in Europe, even though Bismarck was still having trouble with some of his fiscal policies.[146] Finally, two other facets of Mori's ideological prism while in England need to be scrubbed free of the insight of hind-

142. George Macaulay Trevelyan, *British History in the Nineteenth Century and After (1782–1919)*, Pelican Books (Harmondsworth, 1965), p. 352.
143. G. M. Young, *Victorian England: Portrait of an Age*, Doubleday Anchor (Garden City, 1954), p. 156.
144. Trevelyan, *British History*, p. 355; Young, *Victorian England*, p. 158.
145. "Granville," *Encyclopaedia Britannica*, 1968, X, 687.
146. Letters from Mori to Kuroda Kiyotaka, 27 April 1880, and to Itō Hirobumi, 27 May 1882, to appear in *Zenshū* II.

sight, so to speak, inherent in twentieth-century historiography. The first regards military power, i.e., national power in its crudest and most limited sense. A reporter in Hong Kong wrote in the *London and China Telegraph* for 20 May 1884: "H. E. Arinori Mori, Japanese Minister to London, with Mrs. Mori, left here for Japan ... on April 8. His Excellency had been the guest of the Governor, and at about eleven o'clock he drove down to the Murray Pier with Mrs. Mori ... A Guard of Honor of fifty men of the Buffs with the band of the regiment were drawn up on the cricket ground, and saluted as H. E. passed them, and salutes were fired by the shore battery and by H. M. S. "Audacious."

The *Audacious* was the flagship of the British fleet on China station, and the gesture provided a finishing touch, symbolically, to a lifetime's work on behalf of the naval power of Japan. It is important to bear in mind, however, that military power, militarism, and political authoritarianism may, but do not necessarily, constitute an inseparable trinity. There are serious limitations, in the first place, on the ability of a navy to meddle in the domestic affairs of any given country. The British, who were delighted to have their fleet, which Mori so much admired, rule the waves, did not extend to it the deep distrust with which they traditionally viewed large standing armies; and Mori's own strategic thinking, as we have seen, was in essence naval and insular, like that of Britain. In the second place, British naval firepower, which dominated the Far East, rested ultimately in the hands not of a hereditary and restless military elite but of a prosperous, complacent, and steadily expanding middle class. It would have been just as easy, if not easier, for Mori therefore to have associated military prowess (or "preparedness") with British as with Prussian institutions and to have disassociated it in his mind from militarism or political reaction.

With regard to the second facet, namely that of national power in its overall sense, it needs to be pointed out that this was a common obsession by no means confined to Bismarck's Germany and that Mori's English advisors would have been as capable as any Prussian of making the connection between education and national power thoroughly explicit. None other than W. E. Forster, for instance, had told the House of Commons as early as 1870: "On the speedy provision of elementary education ... depends our industrial prosperity, the safe working of our constitutional system, and our national power. Civilized communities throughout the world are massing themselves together, each mass being measured by its force: and if we are to hold our position among men of our own race or among the nations of the world, we must make up for the smallness of our numbers by increasing the intellectual force of the individual."[147]

147. Quoted in Young, *Victorian England,* p. 175. William E. Forster (1818–1886), the brother-in-law of Matthew Arnold, and the colleague and predecessor of Mundella, may well have been among those Mori consulted on the educational question.

Ten   1884–1889

MORI AT THE MONBUSHŌ

On 7 May 1884 Mori received appointment as *gikan* (counselor) in the Sanjiin,[1] together with orders to serve simultaneously in the Naimushō (ministry of the interior) and, as *goyō kakari* (commissioner), in the Monbushō (ministry of education). Mori seldom attended the Sanjiin deliberations except to argue on behalf of the patent law proposals put forward by his former student boarder, Takahashi Korekiyo, now head of the patent office in the ministry of agriculture and commerce.[2] His time was devoted almost entirely to the Monbushō, where he began his long series of inspection tours throughout the country and assumed, in August and September of 1885 respectively, the superintendency of the Higher Normal School and of the Tokyo Commercial School—his own former Commercial Institute.

As *goyō kakari,* however, Mori still was not listed on the official table of organization of the ministry. The fact that his extensive proposals were not reflected in the Shin kyōikurei (New Education Ordinance) of August 1885[3] suggests that he did not, prior to

---

1. The Sanjiin (secretarial board) was established in 1881 for the purpose of preparing a new legal code, and for reviewing specific legislative proposals submitted by the various ministries. It worked closely with the Genrōin, and was absorbed into the legislative bureau of the cabinet in 1885.
2. Takahashi Korekiyo, *Jiden* (Autobiography; Tokyo, 1936), p. 219.
3. See below, this chapter.

1886, have the de facto control of policy that Koba Sadanaga one day would attribute to him.[4] Mori's year and a half in this subordinate position did give him the time and opportunity, however, to familiarize himself with the actual state of Japanese education and to develop his own thinking and plans in such detail that his Gakkōrei, or School Ordinances, could be promulgated within four months of his joining the first Itō cabinet and his accession to the ministerial chair on 22 December 1885. Except for his participation in the privy council discussions on the constitution in 1888, his official activities after 1886 were limited to the educational field exclusively.

There was stiff opposition to Mori's appointment as *goyō kakari* in 1884 from the then Minister Ōki Takato, under pressure from his deputy vice minister, Kuki Ryūichi, a prominent figure in artistic and museum circles, whose traditionalism later would lead him to attacks on Western-style painters and to the defense and encouragement of Okakura Kakuzō. Objecting to Mori's alleged Christianity, Motoda Eifu likewise made a determined effort to block Mori's appointment as *monbudaijin* (education minister) in 1885. In both cases it took the personal intervention of Itō—with Ōki in the first instance, and with the emperor himself in the second—to secure Mori's appointment.[5] In terms of our four basic images of Mori, it is clear that he entered the Monbushō firmly identified as Westernizer Reprehensible in a good many minds. His reputation as nationalist—reprehensible or otherwise—rests by contrast for the most part on the work of the last three or four years of his life. Before we can evaluate Mori's life as a whole or pick out the various continuities in his thought, it will be necessary to analyze the three elements which did the most to create the nationalist image: Mori's statist philosophy; his elitist restructuring of the educational system; and his introduction of military drill and a military atmosphere in the normal schools.

It will also be necessary to explore two traits, much less generally known and appreciated, which to some extent balance and alleviate the statist reputation, namely, Mori's ethical individualism as exemplified in his policy on *shūshin* (moral training), and his economic rationalism as displayed in his policies on textbook authorization and educational decentralization.

4. Koba Sadanaga, "Mori monbudaijin no kaikaku," in Kokumin Kyōiku Shōreikai, ed., *Kyōiku gojūnenshi* (Tokyo, 1922), p. 92; Tsuchiya Tadao, *Meiji zenki kyōiku seisakushi no kenkyū*, rev. ed. (Tokyo, 1968), pp. 287–288.

5. OTM, pp. 98, 105; Tsuchiya, *Seisakushi*, p. 233.

PERSONAL AND PROFESSIONAL STYLE

Mori's educational point of view is well documented, both in half a dozen written statements and in several dozen lengthy speeches delivered in the course of his extensive inspection tours. It is not however, and most unfortunately, presented to us in a systematic fashion. The speeches in particular contain a great deal of exhortation, and therefore hyperbole, together with much reiteration. Nor does Mori relate his educational ideas in a consistent fashion to his general philosophy or reflect during the late 1880's upon many of the topics which held his interest in the early 1870's. As Ōkubo Toshiaki has put it: "He was a man who customarily thought about the actual educational problems of the day, rather than one who developed his own learned system. Although he was an educator, he was no pedagogist."[6]

This lack of a more explicit and more systematically articulated philosophy of education accounts for much of the ambiguity of Mori's administration, just as important silences regarding his general philosophy have contributed to the ambiguity of the man himself. The student of Mori finds himself teased with an abundance of anecdotal trivia (for example, Mori's unusually great fear of earthquakes—the one thing in the world he apparently did fear—and his alleged attribution of the Japanese incapacity for profound or logical thinking to the volcanic instability of their archipelago);[7] and then finds Mori's second wife reminiscing to the effect that her husband never once spoke to her of his own religious beliefs.[8] The fact that Mori's personality was such as to rub many people the wrong way to begin with meant that he paid a doubly high price for not making his ideas and his underlying intentions absolutely clear.

Mori continued to exhibit all the morally upright and humane qualities which had caught the attention of many Japanese after his first return from the West in 1868. While inspecting schools in Shiga prefecture he paid a visit, unprecedented for a cabinet minister, to an Eta (outcast) village; he turned over his semiannual bonuses to charity, and rerouted complimentary barrels of *sake* received at New Year's from Mitsui and other leading firms to the homes of the poor; and he expressed, upon his elevation to viscount in the new peerage of 1884, a fear lest his own descendants become fools on account of their privileged status. He also dis-

6. OTM, p. 106.
7. KKM, pp. 277–278.
8. Mori Hiroko (as told to Mori Arimasa), "Mori Arinori no omoide," *Mikuni*, 4. 3 (March 1938). To appear in *Zenshū* II.

appointed the spectacle-loving crowds in 1886 by carrying out with the greatest simplicity the funeral of his father, Yūjo, of whom he had been taking exceptionally solicitous care ever since the death of his mother, Osato, in 1881.[9]

Mori, altogether true to his own stated principles, seems to have been very much the family man; indeed, this is perhaps the most attractive aspect of his character. His divorce from Tsuneko, his bride of the contract marriage, on 28 November 1886 has been little illuminated; Koba Tadashi has surmised that Tsuneko "did not keep good faith" with her husband;[10] and Mori's grandson, Mori Arimasa, has intimated that there had been rumors of an affair between Tsuneko and one of the English employees of the legation in London.[11] In any case, the divorce like the marriage was carried out by written contract, with the prior consent of both parties. And in June 1887 Mori was remarried, this time in the traditional fashion, to Hiroko, the youngest daughter of Iwakura Tomomi.[12]

Mori's second wife recalled him as having been very patient, and sparing of harsh words, with his two eldest sons, Hide (b. 1875) and Ari (b. 1877). (The third son and Hiroko's child, Akira, was born in 1888.) Mori seldom ate out, taking his evening meals together with his family, after perhaps treating the boys to a late afternoon carriage ride. A typical evening then would be spent playing cards with his wife and would nearly always no matter what the weather conclude with a walk, in the company of his bodyguard, to the Kōjimachi billiard parlor, where he would play a game or two "for his health." These, together with the game of go, were apparently his only pastimes. Mori would also on occasion for the sake of his health forego certain foods, but Hiroko has described their table as having been quite luxurious, with a menu seldom found outside the foreign legations.[13]

Koba Sadanaga, Mori's private secretary, would insist after the assassination that Mori had very faithfully visited local Shinto shrines during his inspection tours and that he was in fact a "respecter of the [Shinto] gods."[14] The evidence, particularly, as

9. KKM, pp. 248–276, *passim*.
10. OTM, p. 60.
11. Interview with Mori Arimasa, Ivry-sur-Seine, June 1965.
12. OTM, p. 60.
13. Mori Hiroko, "Omoide"; Mori Hiroko (as told to Mori Arimasa), "Mori Arinori no omokage," pts. 1 and 2, *Mikuni*, 4.4 (April 1938) and 4.6 (June 1938), respectively. To appear in *Zenshū* II.
14. Koba Sadanaga, "Mori Arinori sensei o shinobite," in Sappanshi Kenkyūkai, ed., *Nangoku shisō* (no. 4; Kagoshima, 1939), to appear in *Zenshū* II.

we shall see, in his educational policy, suggests however that Mori's dutiful shrine visits were inspired by no more than a sense of political propriety. Hiroko recalled that her husband had been an earnest reader of the Bible and that "in his daily life he was as strict as any believer,"[15] and there is strong reason to suppose, despite Mori's outward reticence, that there was a strong ethical Christian influence at work in the family. Hiroko was converted to the faith (after Mori's assassination) by Uemura Masahisa, and her son Akira became an ordained clergyman, who for years held the pulpit of a small church (Presbyterian) in Sakuragaoka, Tokyo.[16] And yet Mori's reluctance to discuss his beliefs with his own wife dramatically confirms the utterly private nature of his faith.

This brings us to one of the major personality traits which must have offended many people, namely, Mori's hardy independence and ability to keep his own counsel. This was one of his most Western aspects, and in broad social or political terms it could be most admirable. He had an amazing knack for neither giving nor taking patronage, showing little of the popular adulation of Saigō and Ōkubo, and working, as far as we can tell, quite free of any Satsuma pressures or commitments while at the Monbushō. He claimed, indeed, that it would be "a great error" for Satsuma and Chōshū to suppose that their achievements in the Restoration entitled them to permanent leadership, and suggested that the cultivation of han cliques threatened to replace one Bakufu with another.[17] The people who seem to have been among his better friends—Nishimura Shigeki, Fukuzawa Yukichi, Kuroda Kiyotaka, Toyama Masakazu, for instance—were for the most part those who had shared his early cultural efforts and enthusiasms; they do not represent regional or political allegiances. Likewise, although Mori joined the Japan Philosophical Society, and continued to attend the meetings of the Asiatic Society of Japan, he was apparently not a member of the Rokumeikan,[18] with its socially pretentious and faddist approach to Western culture.

On the other hand, Mori's independence combined with a certain laconism could give the impression of aloofness; and aloofness combined with a certain air of moral superiority might seem insulting. It sharpened the edge of his frequent personal criticisms of others, which could be very direct and unflattering. What might

15. Mori Hiroko, "Omoide."
16. Interview with Mori Arimasa, Ivry-sur-Seine, June 1965.
17. KKM, 288–290.
18. Hayashi Takeji, personal communication to the author, August 1967.

have been forgivable if rendered in the heat of passion was not so easily accepted when delivered as a sober, rather Olympian, moral judgment. Sometimes Mori was merely misunderstood, as when his refusal to tip was taken as a sign of stinginess.[19] At other times he seems to have flown directly and deliberately in the face of established etiquette and social sensibilities, as in his attack on some of the formalities of the Japanese language which, for all their nominal linguistic absurdity, did nevertheless convey to most Japanese certain sentiments which were the essence of social intercourse. To take one particular instance which also exhibits his literalism, Mori could not abide the phrase *somatsunagara* (literally, "shabby though it be"), used in forwarding gifts. If the present was really shabby, Mori argued, it should never be sent in the first place.[20]

Mori's streak of social aloofness might well have gone unnoticed, however, had it not been combined with so much aggressiveness and pertinacity in his professional style. Kimura Kyō in one of his anecdotes has related that Mori, having engaged an opponent far more proficient than himself in a game of go one evening, insisted on playing for the following three days and three nights running, until he finally managed to win one game.[21] Mori in other words had a compulsion to win, and a childhood friend would later recall of him: "He was never one to yield second place to someone else. In his dealings with people, he would attempt to swallow them whole. No matter who it was, he would fix the other fellow with a stare, and take the higher ground for himself."[22]

No other education minister in modern Japan comes any where near Mori in the extent of his personal imprint upon the entire school system. That Mori was able to have so much of his own way and leave such a distinct mark, was in part due to special advantages that were his: he enjoyed the full confidence and longstanding personal friendship of the prime minister, Itō; and, with neither the Diet nor local government system as yet in operation, a policy once agreed upon by the cabinet could be carried out with great dispatch through strictly administrative channels. More significant, however, was Mori's own sense of destiny and mission to

19. Mori Hiroko, "Omoide."
20. *Zenshū* I, 511, SPM : 1887 : "Kyūshū kakuken/shōgakkō." An abbreviation of the extremely lengthy title given in the *Zenshū*. Titles of Mori's speeches (SPM) will all be abbreviated in a similar fashion to indicate as briefly as possible location of speech and nature of audience only.
21. KKM, p. 259.
22. Kawashima Jun, quoted in KKM, 290.

discharge, in educational statesmanship, the "great task" of national transformation to which he had first felt himself called in London in 1865.

Mori, thirty-eight years of age at the time of his appointment, was both the youngest and the most intellectual member of the cabinet. He was also one of the few ministers of education who was an educator, in the broad sense of the term, and not an appointee (reluctant, as often as not) from some other field. Ernest Satow, calling on Mori in July 1886, noted that he had "talked nothing else" but education,[23] and in a memorandum outlining the order of precedence which he thought the various ministers should enjoy in cabinet decisions, Mori divided all government affairs into three areas, foreign and domestic and cultural, and assigned himself the chief responsibility for all cultural affairs.[24] His School Ordinances embodied his own ideas almost exclusively; indeed, most of them were drafted by Mori himself, checked briefly by one or two trusted subordinates, and presented directly to the cabinet, without traveling through, much less originating in, the regular ministry channels.[25]

Mori's inspection tours, undertaken approximately every half year, lasted nearly two months at a time and involved several prefectures of a given region in each instance. The records of the Fukuoka Normal School have it that "the Education Minister visited the school, and came into our classroom. He looked most splendid, with the air of a Westerner about him. He stood there, swinging his familiar walking stick, and addressing various questions in a loud voice to our principal, Tokuda, who was showing him around."[26] There are other reports, too, of Mori storming up to the head of classrooms to berate teachers whose methods seemed to be less than satisfactory. These provincial excursions gave Mori not only the advantage of first-hand information, but also an opportunity to promote his own philosophy of education among the rank and file of the profession. Wherever he went he would speak at length before students, teachers, administrators, and local government officials, often giving the same address over and over again from town to town. As the first cabinet minister in history to have cultivated the art of public speaking, he had come a long way since the Meirokusha days when he told Fukuzawa it could not be done

23. PRO, Satow Papers, PRO-30-33-15-10, "Diary, November, 1885–December, 1886," entry for 12 July 1886.
24. *Zenshū* I, 342, Mori Arinori, "Kakushō daijin sekinin jūkei no shidai."
25. OTM, pp. 123, 126.
26. Karasawa Tomitarō, *Kyōshi no rekishi* (Tokyo, 1956), p. 41.

in the native tongue. Mori was, in a very real sense, campaigning. Many of his speeches have the flavor of a pep talk, and tend therefore to be couched in his most extreme idiom.

MORI'S *KOKKA:* POLITICAL STATISM

It should be borne in mind that it was Inoue Kowashi, in his posthumous defense of Mori in March 1889,[27] who first characterized Mori's thinking as *kokutai no kyōiku shugi:* "a philosophy of education based on the national polity." Mori himself had never placed any such ideological identification tag on his educational views and policies. Yet the label of "statist education" stuck and provided the chief basis of Mori's two images, favorable and unfavorable, as nationalist. It is a simple matter to collect statements by Mori, particularly from his speeches, which reveal—with a rather dull repetitiousness—an extreme, almost a rabid, statism: a statism which would seem to subordinate and bend to its purposes both the educational system and the individual himself in equal measure. To begin with, the school system as such existed first and foremost to serve the state. As Mori would remark to the directors of the centrally administered University, Higher Normal School, and Higher Middle Schools on 28 January 1889, only two weeks before his assassination: "There is no need for me to go into any great detail as to the purposes of our government educational administration. The government, to begin with, established the Ministry of Education and charged it with the responsibility for administering the system and for supporting various schools from the national treasury. They serve, after all, the purposes of the state. The goal of our educational administration is likewise purely and simply the service of the state. In the case of the Imperial University, for instance, the question may arise as to whether learning is to be pursued for its own sake or for the sake of the state. It is the state which must come first and receive top priority. The administrators of our various schools, therefore, should at all times be mindful of the fact that the undertaking is on behalf of the state, not on behalf of the individual student. This is the most important point, and I insist that you take it thoroughly to heart."[28]

In a similar vein, Mori had admonished *gun* (county) and *ku* (ward) officials throughout Kyushu in 1887 that: "it is fair to say that the [prefectural normal] schools up to now have been erected

27. See Introduction.
28. *Zenshū,* I, 663, SPM : 28 Jan. 1889 : "Monbushō/chokkatsu gakkōchō."

for the sake of the students themselves rather than for the training of teachers to serve the prefectural school system. The new ordinance by contrast emphasizes that the purposes to be served are not those of the students, but exclusively those of county and ward education. This distinction must by no means be forgotten."[29]

Teachers and administrators in the centrally administered schools likewise were exhorted to make the state their *honzon* (main image; i.e., the central idol in a Buddhist temple). Mori implied that those who failed to do so were not fit for employment.[30] Turning from the school facilities, then, to the young people who went through them, Mori told local officials and educators in Wakayama in November 1887: "Reading, writing and arithmetic are not our major concern in the education (*kyōiku*) and instruction of the young . . . Education is entirely a matter of bringing up men of character. And who are these men of character?—they are the good subjects required by our Empire. And who are these good subjects? —they are those persons who live up fully to their responsibilities as Imperial subjects. The fulfillment [of these duties] requires a steady disposition in carrying out the tasks of the nation and in exerting oneself to the full extent of one's capacities."[31]

Thirdly, with respect to the state itself, Mori could declare: "There has indeed been some perplexity within the Ministry concerning moral training (*shūshin*) and education in the home (*katei kyōiku*). I believe, however, that the most appropriate way, and our shortest road, to the solution of this problem lies in making our Sovereign the means of inspiration . . . The best policy available to us is to make the state the ruling and inspiring principle in both our daily work and our academic studies, and to treat the state— formless though it be—as reverently as the Buddha or the [Shinto] gods. We have in fact no other choice. Some have advocated making religion our guiding principle. But this is not easily accomplished. The best way is to focus on the state alone."[32] Fourthly and finally, as regards the Japanese state among the other powers, Mori's most strident nationalist pitch was perhaps reached in an

29. *Zenshū* I, 493, SPM : Feb. 1887 : "Kyūshū/gunkuchō."

30. *Zenshū* I, 663, SPM : 28 Jan. 1889 : "Monbushō/chokkatsu gakkōchō."

31. *Zenshū* I, 581, SPM : 15 Nov. 1887 : "Wakayamaken Jinjō Shihangakkō."

32. Quoted in KSM, p. 81. Kaimon renders the passage in quotation marks, as the words of Mori, but does not indicate his source. This particular quotation appears in the middle of an unbroken string of quotations, all the rest of which are identifiable as quotes from Mori's speeches as education minister.

address to the teacher trainees at the Saitama Normal School on 19 December 1885, three days before his appointment to the cabinet:

> When you stop to think about it, warfare is the daily condition of all mankind. For instance, on the international level, the commercial and industrial struggle; or, on an intellectual plane, the battle of ideas. We too this day, by establishing ourselves in our profession, and taking a firm resolve, are engaged in the battle to render our own Empire an excellent nation. If you say that there is nothing to worry about if Japan takes her place at the tail end of the Great Powers, then of course there is no need to prepare for this struggle. But in such a case, even though we have the expression, "Empire of Japan," our country would decline to the point where we would hardly deserve to be called a nation. I say to you now: is this the intention of the young men of Japan? Anyone who is the least bit Japanese must try to advance Japan from the third rank, where she now stands, to the second; and when she achieves the second rank, then to the first; and finally to the foremost position in the entire world.[33]

It is not unnatural that many people should have jumped from the hyperbolic idiom of some of Mori's speeches to the conclusion that his philosophy included also the militarism, the traditionalism, or the Teutophilism which a later age would assume went together almost as a matter of course with a statist, or even a nationalist, point of view. A more careful investigation of Mori's thought and his specific policies reveals, however, some important qualifications. The diplomatic, the political, and the educational dimensions of Mori's statism present an ascending order of analytical complexity. We will deal at once with the implications of Mori's statism for international and domestic political affairs, seeking to reconstruct his thinking on the constitution, on the emperor, and on the nature of the Japanese nation or state (*kokka*). The remaining subchapters will then deal with the consequences for education of Mori's statist viewpoint.

There is hardly a speech of Mori's which does not refer to *bankoku kyōsō* (the competition of nations), or advance *dokuritsu* (independence) as the most pressing of all national goals. So insistent indeed are the appeals of this ex-diplomat to *dokuritsu*—

33. *Zenshū* I, 483–484, SPM : 19 Dec. 1885 : "Saitamaken Jinjō Shihangakkō."

his leading theme in many ways for nearly fifteen years—that one is almost led to believe that everything for him, from the abacus to the emperor, was no more than an instrument to be used in achieving this one great objective. And yet, for all the emphasis on struggle, Mori's competitive impulses remain economically rather than militarily defined: "In view of the ever-growing precariousness of our international position, we shall have to make full use of our agricultural, industrial and commercial capacities in meeting our foreign competition . . . Will our education and our learning suffice to withstand the severe pressure of this competition when it comes? . . . our indifferently trained human talent is not in all probability . . . equal to the national emergency."[34]

Similar exhortations to peaceful competition could be given at length. Mori remains very much Spencer, not Treitschke, in his view of the global struggle. In April 1885, in a speech before the Osaka Chamber of Commerce advocating the establishment of a commercial school in the Kansai, Mori outlined at great length the commercial dangers and opportunities awaiting Japan. He did, it is true, characterize commerce as the "advance guard of the military," but warned that Japan's army and navy would not avail her one bit unless she hastened to make up her great deficiencies in "agriculture, industry and commerce . . . which constitute the fundaments of any nation." Britain, already overtaken by France and Germany, was now scrambling to build those commercial schools which the Americans, for instance, had had the good sense to provide from the very start, and which had enabled them to shake free, in about seven decades, of European economic domination. Arguing that geographical location and configuration placed Japan in the best position to dominate the water-borne East Asian trade, he chided the Osaka merchants for their conservatism and timidity, and praised the Chinese trading class, which he had held in great esteem ever since his years, 1876–1878, in Peking.[35]

The privy council deliberations on the Meiji Constitution in June 1888 revealed the final development of Mori's political views. In the debate over the legislative "consent" of the Diet he at last indicated his position on the issue of sovereignty and showed how very conservative he had become in his concepts of the emperor and of the constitutional structure. In the subsequent discussion of the "Rights and Duties of the Subject," Mori also revealed how thoroughly dichotomized his concept of the individual had become,

34. *Zenshū* I, 535, SPM : 21 June 1887 : "Miyagi Kenchō."
35. *Zenshū* I, 463, SPM : April 1885 : "Shōgyō kyōiku no hitsuyōsei ni kansuru enzetsu." Delivered before the Osaka Chamber of Commerce.

with its implicit cleavage between inner freedom and outer authority, between natural and political rights. The proposed wording of Article 5 ("The Emperor exercises the legislative power with the consent of the Imperial Diet"), elicited from Mori a number of objections, most of which had been anticipated in his *Representative System* and "Daigi seitairon" of 1883. At the morning session of 20 June 1888 he argued for nearly a quarter of an hour without interruption that "the entire structure and spirit" of the constitution would turn on whether the term "consent" were adopted or not and argued that the phrase be revised to read, "The Emperor exercises the legislative power following discussion by the Imperial Diet."

Mori warned that the original wording would in effect divide the sovereign power equally between emperor and Diet and that, "despite the existence of the Cabinet, the Imperial Diet will hold the greater power, and will in fact come to hold the supreme authority under this constitution." This, Mori further avowed, "would bring about an enormous alteration in the time-honored polity of Japan, and give it the figuration of what is known as a [limited] constitutional monarchy . . . taking into consideration our traditional political system, it is not proper to grant this right of consent which is so very much out of harmony with it." Mori went so far, indeed, as to suggest in the presence of the Meiji emperor, who had been attending the privy council meetings, that "I respectfully appreciate that His Majesty might want to ponder deeply, before his illustrious ancestors, this [proposed] division of sovereignty."

Mori also argued that "in establishing a national assembly for the first time, prudence must be piled upon prudence," and warned: "It is no false charge to assert that [our people] up to now have all lacked [the requisite] habits, experience and learning. It cannot be said that those who have a smattering of this—who have done no more than sit in prefectural, town or village assemblies—have had sufficient practical experience to be relied upon in the future." Mori accordingly insisted: "the Diet should be made no more than His Majesty's advisory organ. Since its opinion is to be sought simply for the Emperor's information, it will be a consultative assembly, and should only be thought of as something to be called into session at times when the opinions of the Privy Council can be deferred temporarily and matters considered from a broad political angle."

The original purpose in establishing a constitution, Mori suggested, was "simply to conduct political affairs in accordance with reason." The key word here—appearing nine times in a single sentence—is *kōhei:* i.e., justice, equity, impartiality. There must be justice in taxation, in the making and enforcement of laws, and in administrative procedure, and since a small handful of officials are not always in a position to judge what is fair or unfair in these matters, the Diet must be permitted to express its opinion. Furthermore, since the emperor from time immemorial has been anxious to promote this sort of justice, Mori sees nothing untraditional about an advisory assembly. He does draw a distinction, however, between the maintenance of basic justice and the making of government policy—of which he mentions treaty negotiations as a prime example. With policymaking, the people's representatives are not to be concerned: "If the subjects of our Empire thus receive justice in all things, they will expect little more. Persons who are not satisfied with this, but insist on having the right of consent at any cost, cannot be said to understand the proper role of the subject."[36]

Finally, arguing a related topic on a later day, Mori contended that the provision in Article 47 for simple majorities in both houses of the Diet would rapidly lead to the realization of parliamentary sovereignty, as in Great Britain. He drew copiously on historical example for his defense of two-thirds majorities, and spoke on, one could almost say "lectured," at such length that the chairman, Itō Hirobumi, finally had to cut him off in mid-sentence.[37] Mori's view of sovereignty had been spelled out also in a memorandum (undated but on cabinet stationery) entitled "Seitō naikaku no hi o ronsu" (The argument against party cabinets), in which he noted: "Party cabinets represent the principle of divided sovereignty. However, in the traditional system of our land, sovereignty—the full control of political affairs—has been imputed to the Emperor alone . . . Therefore party cabinets go against the fundamental code of our country."[38]

Divided sovereignty, Mori had continued in this same memorandum, was in fact a theoretical fiction, and nations differed only as to the locus of undivided sovereignty. These differences in turn were entirely a matter of individual historical development; and since in Japan (as in Germany) sovereignty had al-

36. Inada Masatsugu, *Meiji kenpō seiritsushi* (Tokyo, 1960–1962), II, 595–596, gives Mori's arguments on the question of the Diet's consent, on 20 June 1888. Major portions of the section of *Zenshū* I relating to the privy council discussions were missing from my proof copy at the time of writing.

37. *Zenshū* I, 74, from the privy council session of 22 June 1888.

38. *Zenshū* I, 43, Mori Arinori, "Seitō naikaku no hi o ronsu," undated, but from 1886–1889.

ways rested with the emperor, Mori found it appropriate to leave it there. Mori admitted that it was inevitable that political parties would be formed. Political opinion, after all, would quite naturally differ from one individual to another, and the like-minded could be expected to band together. But he hoped that divisive party influences would not reach as high as the cabinet, which was entrusted with "the great task of our nation today and in the future," namely "the complete realization of national independence both in name and fact." Should party cabinets appear, Mori feared that "not only the general administration, but officials in the military services, police, and educators as well, will all lose their bearings," and that havoc would be wreaked with the nonpartisan spirit which had enabled the present cabinet to achieve so much for Japan.[39]

There was considerable support in the privy council for some revision of Article 5, with Mori's proposed wording receiving specific support from Yamada Akiyoshi, the minister of justice, and from Motoda Eifu.[40] Itō, in a sharp rebuttal, argued however that the consent of the legislature was, along with proper limitations on executive power, one of the two indispensable elements of constitutional government.[41] Ōkubo Toshiaki has noted that "Mori's concept of the state was by and large historical rather than abstract,"[42] and in terms of ideological influences the privy council debate presented a curious, and telling, confrontation between the sincere, if limited, constitutionalism of Gneist and Stein and the hoary, and in essence fatuous, advice of Herbert Spencer.[43]

In the morning session on 22 June, Mori confronted Itō once again, this time with a proposed revision in the title of Chapter Two of the constitution ("The Rights and Duties of Subjects"). Mori's logic here was two-pronged, at once more liberal and more

39. Ibid., I, 44–45.
40. Inada, *Meiji kenpō seiritsushi*, II, 593.
41. Ibid., II, 594.
42. OTM, p. 141.
43. The "overcompensating conservatism"—as we have called it—of Englishmen sympathetic to Japan was perhaps more pronounced among diplomats stationed in Tokyo than commonly has been realized. Sir Francis Plunkett (a former British minister at Tokyo) wrote the foreign office in 1888 that, "The growth of advanced democratic views among the rising generation of Japan is a source of danger to which both the Japanese Government and all the Foreign Representatives are quite alive." Plunkett concluded that he did not consider the views of Itagaki Taisuke, head of the Liberal party, "to be either sound or practical." See PRO, Japan/General Correspondence, FO-46-379, letter from Sir Francis Plunkett to Philip Currie.

conservative than that of Itō. Mori argued first that "subjects, in the English-language sense of the term," possessed only station (*bungen*) and responsibility (*sekinin*) as against the sovereign, and that the phrase *kenri gimu* (rights and duties) therefore should be replaced by *bunsai,* which Mori defined as the equivalent of the English word "responsibility."

To this Itō retorted, "I must say [Mori's] proposal amounts to an expulsion order for constitutional and legal science," and repeated that it was the essence of constitution-making to limit the power of the ruler and protect the rights of the subject. Mori, in reply to that, then took up a different tack, arguing: "Freedom of property, freedom of speech, and other freedoms of the subject are the natural endowment of the people, and to guarantee them within the framework of law places them under a limitation . . . It is improper to assert that these rights first come into force through the constitution . . . Since the Cabinet is supposed to work for the protection of the people's rights, subjects will still have their rights to property and freedom of speech . . . even if we delete the expression 'Rights and Duties.'" Then, returning to the matter of *bunsai,* Mori pointed out that although the conceptual distinction which had emerged in the West as between the state and the sovereign had permitted the definition of a certain number of rights of the subject as against both of them, "it is one of the great differences between Japan and the West that 'the rights and duties of Japanese subjects toward their Emperor' are not only without currency as an expression, but are something which our subjects ought not to have."

To all this Itō replied (encouragingly, in effect) that subjects were going to have rights not as against the emperor but simply "as against the law, and within the framework of the law, by virtue of this constitution," and added (in admonishment) that Rousseauvian natural rights were not up for discussion. Mori finally rested his case rather lamely by asking why Chapter Two alone should be embellished with an extra phrase ("Rights and Duties of . . .") when the other chapters were to be entitled simply "The Emperor," "The Imperial Diet," and so forth.[44] Maruyama Masao has written that "Mori's argument bears a striking resemblance to the natural law viewpoint running from Hobbes to Spinoza, resting as it does on a dualism of public authority and the inviolable natural rights of the individual."[45] Mori's allusion to the inviolability of a spe-

44. The Mori-Itō exchange regarding *bunsai,* on 22 June 1888, may be found in Inada, *Meiji kenpō seiritsushi,* II, 629ff., and in *Zenshū* I.
45. Maruyama Masao, *Nihon no shisō* (Tokyo, 1961), p. 41.

cified private sphere indeed represents the survival of the viewpoint expressed sixteen years earlier in *Religious Freedom in Japan*. Mori, in Maruyama's analysis,[46] failed, however, to resolve his dualism or to identify the ultimate source of authority for enacting the constitution, or to perceive that the only foolproof protection of the private sphere against public power lay in placing the latter squarely in the hands of the people. But Maruyama credits Mori with a basically sounder instinct than that of the Popular Rights advocates, who were content to seek formal political rights while ignoring the "civil" realm, i.e., that whole area of social relationships and practical, everyday personal freedoms in which Mori had shown himself such a progressive, and on which any modern political structure inevitably would have to rest. Mori, in Maruyama's view, saw the constitution, and Japan's *kokutai* (polity), as governing only the outer realm of formal political and legal authority, not as something which eventually (thanks in great measure to Itō's construction) would penetrate to the inner realm of personal freedoms in the name of "protection and surveillance" of the people.

Mori's all-too-brief aside on inviolable natural rights gives us the best clue we have as to just how narrowly political, i.e., how purely legal and constitutional, his statism really was and how far it stood from the sweeping religious and social statism of the later orthodoxy, which came to define the *kokutai* in terms of Shinto legend and of the family-state. This point is all the more important because, within his narrowly political-legal realm, Mori had moved to such a conservative position. One only wishes Mori had not left it to others to pick out the threads implicit in his thought and that he had woven together for us the two strands of his dichotomy. One suspects that Mori himself had given the matter little philosophical attention and that he probably (in typical Anglo-American fashion) took the "civil" realm for granted, i.e., even if the natural rights of the individual were not yet a fact of everyday life in Japan, as they already were in the United States and Britain, they soon would be—with a little more education.

In political scientific terms it seems difficult indeed not to charge Mori with a certain naivete. His odd trusting in the cabinet to work for the protection of individual rights is of a piece with his entrusting of those same rights in "Daigi seitairon" (Part VI) to the wisdom of the judges and governors in his proposed senate.

Mori's digression on natural rights is, unfortunately, no more than an afterthought and is not his real reason for objecting to *kenri gimu*. This digression is not necessarily insincere, but its

46. Ibid., pp. 39–42.

function viewing the discussion as a whole, is essentially tactical. Mori wants the word "rights" deleted not in order to enhance their sanctity but because Japanese simply do not have rights vis-à-vis their emperor. That is the point on which he opens and to which he again returns, having brought up the matter of natural rights only in response to Itō's accusation that he knows nothing of constitutional and legal science.

Mori's overriding concern in the debates both over *kenri gimu* and over legislative consent seems, indeed, to have been the maintenance of the charismatic and institutional preeminence of the throne, as presented in *Representative System* and "Daigi seitairon," against any dilution even by Itō's limited constitutional monarchy. His view of the emperor rests squarely on what we have called the historical particularism of his 1883 essay, and although it partakes to some extent both of the instrumentalism of Itō and of the absolutism of Motoda it needs to be distinguished from both.

Itō, in opening the privy council discussions, had dwelt at length on the need, in the absence of any powerful native religious tradition, to make the emperor the ideological fulcrum of national politics, using the very same term, *kijiku* (axis), that had appeared in Mori's "Daigi seitairon" (Part VII) of 1883.[47] This identical vocabulary, together with Mori's call for "making our Sovereign the means of inspiration" in education, suggests that Mori and Itō had discussed (perhaps as early as 1883) and largely agreed upon the uses which might be made, ideologically, of the emperor institution. What to Itō however must have seemed primarily a political convenience, an artificially, even opportunistically, constructed device, was for Mori more of an historical necessity. Itō feels free, so to speak, to "use" the emperor, whereas Mori feels obliged.

From his characterization in 1873 of the Meiji Restoration as an *ōsei ishin* (restoration of the government of the kings; in the introduction to *Education in Japan*) to his references in 1884 in the *Pall Mall Gazette* to the traditional affection of the Japanese people for their emperor, Mori had shown an acute awareness of the imperial institution in its historical dimension, which was all normal enough for a young Satsuma loyalist who was also the son of a *kokugaku* scholar. And it was Herbert Spencer's glacially slow-paced doctrine of political evolution which probably provided Mori with his final philosophical sanction for revitalizing and utilizing the imperial institution within a political framework which

---

47. Inada, *Meiji kenpō seiritsushi*, II, 567.

perhaps stood closer to the (idealized) Taika polity than it did to the modern constitutional monarchism of Itō. That still does not place Mori in the same camp as Motoda, who supported him in the debate on consent. As we shall see when we come to Mori's policies on *shūshin,* it is in the political realm only (as Maruyama has suggested) that the emperor retains for Mori his absolute character. He is not the final arbiter, the absolute standard, and the indispensable linchpin of the moral order as well, which Motoda and other good Confucianists would have made him.

One of the most disappointing of Mori's many reticences was his failure to develop in explicit detail his concept of the state, particularly as he wished to have it presented to the younger generation in the schools. In one of the few descriptive passages we do have, Mori maintained (three weeks before his death): "The state is a living body with an unlimited span of life, not something with the brief destiny of the individual. Its fortunes rise when all its members keep their common national interest firmly in mind; its fortunes wane when individuals seek their own personal advantage."[48] Mori then continued with his familiar simile of the state as *honzon;* but here, as elsewhere, he is simply stating *that* the state is most important, without telling us to our satisfaction just *what* the state is. Our "central idol" remains by and large without a face, and in the absence of proof positive, the best we can do is assume that, like the constitution and the emperor, the state also remained for Mori conceptually confined to the realm of formal political and legal authority.

We do have some evidence, however, that Mori, although rummaging the antique shop for his means, was in terms of his objectives seeking both with his emperor and his state to promote a modern political consciousness and a typically Western form of nationalism among the Japanese, worrying, as he had confided to Inoue Kowashi, whether his own rickshaw puller had "any [i.e., political] notion in his head of what we call Japan."[49] In his draft cabinet proposal (*kakugian*) of 1887 Mori noted, for instance, that "from medieval times onward the conduct of our national affairs, both civil and military, has been the concern exclusively of the samurai class. The leadership of today's movement for progress likewise rests in the hands of a very small minority. The great majority of our people probably have only the vaguest idea of what

48. *Zenshū* I, 663, SPM : 28 Jan. 1889 : "Monbushō/chokkatsu gakkōchō."
49. See Introduction.

is involved in establishing a state. Looking at Europe or America, however, we see that in every nation people of all classes, both men and women alike, possess a love of country and an unshakeable [national] unity." The spirit of cooperation and endurance required to meet Japan's challenge could only be assured, Mori continued, if the Japanese were "taught—to the very marrow of their bones—to feel a fervent spirit of loyalty and patriotism [*chūkunaikoku*], to maintain a steadfastness of character and a constancy of purpose, to be ashamed of cowardice and to hold all servility in contempt."[50]

Inagaki Tadahiko has observed that Mori makes far more frequent use of the expressions *dokuritsu* (independence), *kyōsō* (competition), *teikoku* (empire) and *shinmin* (subject), none of which are of Confucian origin, than he does of *chūkun* (loyalty: the cardinal virtue of Tokugawa Confucianism) or of *kokutai* (national polity: the central principle of the later orthodoxy). Inagaki suggests that Mori in his own mind had not established any necessary link between the modern concept of "patriotism" or *aikoku* (a term which first acquired its present meaning in the Meiji period), and *chūkun* with its traditional ideological burden.[51] The *kakugian* (the actual wording of which, it may be recalled, was that of Inoue Kowashi) is indeed one of the few instances in which the expression *chūkun* does appear. And it might also be said that, unlike the later orthodoxy, Mori's *kokutai* focusses not on the Shinto gods and on the emperor as their flesh-and-blood descendant but on the emperor as the central figure both in the traditional and in the anticipated governmental structure. This further supports our conclusion that Mori's statism was rather narrowly political. In terms of our normative coordinate for education, Mori's specific purposes were almost entirely dominated by this political statism, with immediate and far-reaching consequences for the structural coordinate. As for his basic values, however, an ambiguity was carried over from the unresolved dichotomy in his view of the individual, with important implications for the instructional coordinate. For, willing as Mori was to force the Japanese into all sorts of physical and moral rigors in the name of character-building, he also took care to leave the intellect and the conscience of the individual free rein.

50. *Zenshū* I, 344–345, Mori Arinori, "Kakugian," 1887.
51. Inagaki Tadahiko in Kaigo Tokiomi et al., "Mori Arinori no shisō to kyōiku seisaku," *Bulletin of the Faculty of Education, University of Tokyo*, 8:40–41 (1965).

GAKUMON-VERSUS-*KYŌIKU*: EDUCATIONAL ELITISM

Mori's most lasting impact on Japanese education was made, in the realm of the tangible, with the several Gakkōrei (School Ordinances) of 1886, which restructured the entire system in a form basically to be retained through the Pacific War. It is worth keeping in mind the general background of the school reforms of 1886. Politically speaking, it was a year during which an extensive reorganization and streamlining of government administrative machinery was carried out under the first Itō cabinet. Economically, Japan was just emerging from the depression of the early 1880's, while the effects of the first major industrial boom (spearheaded by textiles) in the late 1880's would not make itself felt in terms of educational demand until the early 1890's.

Educational demand in mid-decade, indeed, displayed a certain perversity. In the primary sector, on which the government since 1872 had expended so much effort and placed so much hope, the elementary school attendance rate had dropped steadily from a combined average of 51.0 percent for boys and girls in 1883 to 46.3 percent in 1886.[52] At the secondary level, by contrast, there was more demand for general and liberal arts education than the schools at the time could provide or the nation practically utilize, and a greater thirsting after politically oriented subjects than the government, still preparing the constitution, was inclined to quench. Finally, Japanese education up to 1885 had relied on a series of ordinances, all of which (the Gakusei, the Kyōikurei, the Kaisei kyōikurei and the Shin kyōikurei alike) had dealt for the most part with elementary education, with some reference to normal schools, while leaving secondary and higher education to develop without detailed statutory guidance.

It was predictable from Mori's commitment to Itō at Paris that he would impose a greater unity and coordination on the school system as a whole; it was predictable likewise from economic necessity that money from the national treasury would have to be applied where it could count for most in terms of a national need, which in Mori's mind had come to revolve around the international economic competition; and it was predictable from his essay on the civil service, written in London, that he would be prepared to allocate human resources rather ruthlessly, if need be, in line with the

---

52. Horimatsu Buichi, *Nihon kindai kyōikushi: Meiji no kokka to kyōiku* (Tokyo, 1959), p. 68. The respective rates for boys and girls were 67.2 and 33.6 percent in 1883; 62.0 and 29.0 percent in 1886.

foregoing requirements. It is also instructive, however, to note how clearly Mori's basic formula would still correspond with that of his "Draft Opinion" of 1879: higher education directly, and elementary education indirectly, under the control of the center, with the burden of secondary education foisted for the most part onto the private sector.

Mori already had stated his basic guidelines while still a *goyō kakari* in the ministry. In his "Kyōikurei ni tsuki iken" (Opinion on the Education Ordinance) of July 1885 he had pointed out the deficiencies of the existing statute:

> Up to now opinions have been exceedingly vague on the following points, and we have not yet had a clearcut answer and detailed exposition of them: What is the relationship between education and one's livelihood? Where lies the distinction between popular education and higher forms of scholarship? What type and what degree of education is required for each of our individual citizens? To what extent should the state provide facilities and assistance for education which redounds primarily to the benefit of the individual? There are many other pressing points, in addition to the foregoing, which have been neglected. For instance, the matter of planning our educational enterprise entirely in accordance with sound economic principles . . . In order to achieve the foregoing it will not be enough just to make a few changes in the wording of the existing ordinance. We must contrive a new statute, the essence of which would be to establish, first of all, completely separate sets of regulations for each type of school: university, secondary, primary, etc.[53]

The questions raised here were in a general fashion answered in Mori's "Gakusei yōryō" (Essentials of the government educational administration), an undated memorandum from his *goyō kakari* period, which laid down the general principles governing the proper role and optimum proportions of each unit of the system.[54]

Mori begins by identifying "national education" (using the English term, and meaning the schools established at state or public, as opposed to private, initiative), as the predominant element in the Japanese school system, and remarks that it should be

---

53. *Zenshū* I, 339–340, Mori Arinori, "Kyōikurei ni tsuki iken," July 1885.

54. *Zenshū* I, 355–356, Mori Arinori, "Gakusei yōryō," undated, but from 1884–1885. Pages 355–356 give the final draft; pp. 351 and 352–355 two earlier drafts.

administered in accordance with the principles of "national economy" (English in the original). The good of the individual and the good of the state, he continues, are to be promoted "equally." But the remainder of the memorandum in effect shifts the balance very clearly in favor of the state. Mori then introduces the two basic distinctions which would guide him in his reorganization of the school system: first, as between *gakumon* and *kyōiku,* and secondly as between pure and applied *gakumon. Gakumon,* or "scholarship," is in this context perhaps better rendered as "higher learning"; and *kyōiku,* or "education," as "common learning." *Kyōiku* (as most succinctly explained in a speech in 1887) is for Mori "that intellectual, moral and physical education which is imparted entirely by older persons to younger persons who have not yet achieved maturity and are still in a dependent status," whereas *gakumon* is "for men of maturity, a matter in which one follows one's own inclinations, freely choosing a subject and performing research on it."[55] This stark distinction helped to justify theoretically the dual track, or, in more precise technical terms, the multiple track, as it eventually developed, which was to give Japanese education its "dumbbell" configuration: a small corps of highly, even liberally, educated scholars, technicians, and bureaucrats on one end; on the other an entire population trained to basic literacy and economic usefulness and political obedience, up through the primary level; and very little in between.

The distinction between *junsei gakumon* and *ōyō gakumon* (glossed in English as "pure science" and "applied science") would be equally determinative of Mori's approach to higher education. "Pure science," i.e., research, the memorandum continues, will contribute to the long-range benefit of Japan and of the world at large and should be engaged in only by the most highly qualified scholars. By "applied science" Mori means not only technology in the narrow sense (e.g., engineering) but also any knowledge (e.g., legal or commercial or medical) which has immediate practical social application. "Professional education" would be a more accurate rendition of *ōyō gakumon,* which is to produce civil servants, entrepreneurs, doctors, and other professional talent to meet the national requirement. Both *junsei gakumon* and *ōyō gakumon* are to be strictly subordinated to the national need; and, "given the present condition of our country,"[56] pure science will have to yield precedence to applied science.

Turning then to *kyōiku,* Mori explains that the purpose of pri-

55. *Zenshū* I, 580, SPM : 15 Nov. 1887 : "Wakayamaken Jinjō Shihangakkō."
56. In the wording of the first draft of "Gakusei yōryō," *Zenshū* I, 351.

mary education is "to provide such training as will enable the young to understand their duties as Japanese subjects, to conduct themselves in an ethical fashion, and to secure their own individual well-being." The emphasis here is clearly on character-building and on the creation of patriotic and morally upright subjects rather than on the training of the mind or the acquisition of specific skills. The "most urgent task of all," however, is to secure teachers for the required elementary schools. "The character of the pupils must first be trained and brought into decent shape, so that they can make proper use of their studies." The importance placed here on character guidance would prove determinative of Mori's policy for the normal schools, where the teachers themselves were trained. So well had Mori thought out his policy beforehand that his comprehensive new ordinances were ready for promulgation early in 1886: the Imperial University Ordinance (Teikoku Daigakurei) on 2 March, and the Primary School Ordinance (Shōgakkōrei), Middle School Ordinance (Chūgakkōrei), and Normal School Ordinance (Shihangakkōrei) all on 10 April. The Imperial University Ordinance would proclaim the elitist nature and the state-oriented purposes of higher education; the Middle and Normal School ordinances would settle with finality the ambiguous status of secondary education; while the Primary School Ordinance, preoccupied with methods of financing and representing in fact a holding action, would exemplify the economic difficulties which precluded any progress at all, during Mori's administration, in the fields of women's or technical/vocational education.

The Imperial University

The first two decades of Meiji had seen a remarkable growth of private institutions of higher learning. These fell into three broad categories: the seminaries maintained by the Buddhist and Shinto sects; the Christian schools such as Dōshisha or Aoyama Gakuin; and the secular colleges (later universities) such as Hōsei, Meiji, or Chūō, which had their precursor in Fukuzawa's Keiō and had proliferated in connection with the Popular Rights Movement as nongovernment (or even as antigovernment) schools specializing in law, political science, and economics. For all their variety, these schools had at least three things in common. Although not graced with the title of "university"—a term reserved for the government university at Tokyo—these *senmon gakkō* or "Special Schools," as most of them were known, had borne their fair share of the burden of higher education in this period. Secondly, they had in many ways given it a liberal, free-wheeling tone. Finally, they were beyond the reach of state control: Waseda, indeed, had emerged as a result of Ōkuma's fall from power in 1881: a symbol of independence, if not defiance, of the ruling clique.[57]

George Sansom's suggestion that Tokyo Imperial University was the government's retort to Waseda and Keiō[58] generally holds provided one does not overdramatize the gesture by losing sight of the fact that this institution, for all its subsequent changes in structure and nomenclature, had already long been in existence and had enjoyed an intimate relationship with the government from the very early days of the Restoration. Its origins dated from the Daigaku (university) of 1869, an amalgamation of the former Shōheikō (Confucian Academy), the Kaiseijo (School for Western Studies) and the Igakusho (medical college), all carryovers from the Edo period. The purpose of this institution from the very start had been to train a leadership elite, which (it was at that time assumed) would have to come from the children of the existing educated class: the samurai.[59] In 1877 it had been reorganized into the four departments of law, literature, science, and medicine and rechristened Tokyo University. Although the ambitious Gakusei had envisioned the establishment of seven other state universities, Tokyo remained the sole institution in its category until the establishment of the Imperial University at Kyoto in 1897. It was Mori's achievement in 1886 to restructure Tokyo University once again, to grace it with the "imperial" (*teikoku*) sobriquet, to define its role as the service of the state, and to endow it with that exclusive character, as the gateway to high bureaucratic office, which it still retains today.

The reorganization of the University into five new colleges (*bunka daigaku*) of law, literature, medicine, science, and engineering, each in turn subdivided into numerous departments and possessing its own research-oriented graduate school (*daigakuin*), represented a broader and more sophisticated structure than that of 1877. But what would give Tokyo and the other five imperial universities eventually established their edge over the private schools was their *teikoku* status. The private institutions, no matter

---

57. Ōkubo Toshiaki, *Nihon no daigaku* (Tokyo, 1943), pp. 373–374; Japanese National Commission for UNESCO, *Development of Modern System of Education in Japan* (Tokyo, 1960), pp. 14–15; George B. Sansom, *The Western World and Japan* (New York, 1950), pp. 457–459.

58. Sansom, *The Western World and Japan*, p. 460.

59. Japanese National Commission for UNESCO, *Development of Education*, p. 8.

how advanced or excellent the education they actually dispensed, labored under the designation of *senmon gakkō* and were not recognized as *daigaku,* or "universities," until 1919.[60] From July 1887 onward graduates of the law and literature colleges of the Imperial University were permitted to enter directly, without examination, upon duty as higher civil service probationers (*kōtōkanshiho*). The diplomas of the private universities were not valid as passports to government service, and although their graduates distinguished themselves in commerce, the arts, and in party politics, they were excluded from the center of power: the bureaucracy.

The graduate schools were to be the dispensers of pure science, the colleges purveyors of applied science. Taken together, as Article 1 of the Teikoku Daigakurei put it: "The Imperial University shall have for its objects the teaching of such arts and sciences as are required for the purposes of the state, and the prosecution of original investigations in such arts and sciences."[61] Two points should at once be made in extenuation of that statist pronouncement. First of all, the Imperial University was to be supported (as were the Higher Normal School and the Higher Middle Schools) entirely by the central treasury, which certainly gave the state some say as to how those funds were to be used. Secondly, it did not imply any sort of crude ideological intervention in terms of faculty or subject matter, once the basic curriculum had been set. One of Mori's first acts was to replace all foreign deans in the colleges with young Japanese, some of them only slightly prepared for their positions, as an expression of Japanese sovereignty, so to speak, over the entire administrative framework.[62] Perhaps no other single appointment, however, better revealed Mori's ideological position than that of Basil Hall Chamberlain, a historical positivist who interpreted the ancient legends straightforwardly as myth, to the chair of Japanese literature.[63] Meanwhile, among Mori's closest friends and collaborators on the faculty were such staunch Westernizers as Yatabe Ryōkichi, Kikuchi Dairoku, and Toyama Masakazu, the latter an outspoken advocate of women's rights, a supporter of Christianity, and founder of the association which sought to Romanize the Japanese language.[64]

Mori's university policy was attacked in his own day less for its

60. *Gakusei gojūnenshi,* comp. Monbushō (Tokyo, 1922), p. 372.
61. Matsumoto Kenji and Suzuki Hirō, *Genten: kindai kyōikushi* (Tokyo, 1962), p. 85.
62. JWM, 3 April 1886.
63. JWM, 27 March 1886.
64. OTM, p. 126.

orientation toward national requirements than for its interventionism and, above all, its elitism. The 1886 ordinance severely restricted the university's autonomy by placing all appointments to the governing council (*hyōgikai*) in the hands of the education minister, and strengthened the relative position of the law college —and hence the University's ties with the bureaucracy—by specifying that the president of the university serve concurrently as dean of the law college. When the civil service legislation of 1887 rendered those ties obvious to all, a storm of protest was raised in nongovernment circles, with calls for "university autonomy" and charges of subservience to bureaucracy which would find an astonishingly faithful echo in the massive campus upheaval of 1968–1969.[65]

The Imperial University had only 738 students and 128 faculty members on its roster in 1886.[66] In 1888, at the last commencement during Mori's administration, it graduated 59 students in the law college (English law, French law, politics); 36 in the engineering college (civil, mechanical, and electrical engineering; architecture; naval architecture; applied chemistry; mining and metallurgy); 29 in the medical college; seven in the science college (astronomy, geology, mathematics, physics, zoology); and two in the college of literature—one in Japanese literature and one in philosophy.[67] The low figures are attributable both to Mori's elitism and also of course to the early historical phase represented here. The relative proportions between the figures, however, reflect very clearly the preeminence of *ōyō gakumon*.

Middle and Normal Schools

The Gakusei of 1872 had called for the establishment of a total of 256 middle schools, as the connecting link in what was then envisioned as a three-stage but direct progression from primary to higher education. The number of schools involved indeed seems small for the country as a whole, and the number of public middle schools established by 1885 was no more than 107.[68] Yet at the outset secondary education had been conceived of largely within the framework of popular education, its function being to "impart education

65. OTM, pp. 143–144.
66. Japanese National Commission for UNESCO, *Development of Education*, p. 14.
67. JWM, 14 July 1888.
68. Japanese National Commission for UNESCO, *Development of Education*, p. 13.

of a general nature to graduates of the primary schools."⁶⁹ During the 1870's the middle schools (then a six-year course divided into upper and lower sections of three years apiece), had tried to encompass a variety of vocational as well as academic objectives, generally overextending themselves while straining the local financial resources on which they were for the most part dependent.⁷⁰ Already by 1881 there were moves in the direction of a dual-track system. Candidates for secondary education were selected out after the sixth year of the primary course (their less talented fellow classmates being left to round off their education with the last two years of the eight-year primary school), and the middle schools were redefined as places which would "dispense a higher level of general education and teach those subjects necessary for admission to the higher schools or for entry into professions requiring more than an average degree of talent."⁷¹

Secondary education in Meiji Japan evolved along a particularly tortuous course, and the social implications of Mori's elitism would be even profounder here than in the case of university education. Mori did not start the elitist trend, nor did his administration see the end of it. It is the Middle School Ordinance of 1899 which generally is viewed as having constituted the final severance of vocational from general secondary education, relegating the former to an inferior position in terms both of academic credentials and of social prestige, and leaving the latter the sole road leading on ultimately to the coveted university degree.⁷² But it was Mori who first unequivocally proclaimed secondary education to be the privilege of the few, not the prerogative of the many. And even here within these walls of privilege Mori drew a further line of demarcation between ordinary and higher secondary education, a line which was perhaps even sharper than the one he had drawn between secondary education as a whole and all that lay beneath it.

The Middle School of Ordinance of 1886 established a five-year Ordinary Middle School (Jinjō Chūgakkō) course the general, nonprofessional character of which was indicated by a curriculum that included ethics (rinri), Japanese language, the Chinese classics, two Western languages, history, geography, mathematics,

---

69. Matsumoto and Suzuki, *Genten*, p. 56. From Article no. 29 of the Gakusei.

70. Hugh L. Keenleyside and A. F. Thomas, *History of Japanese Education and Present Educational System* (Tokyo, 1937), p. 90; Miyahara Seiichi, *Nihon gendaishi taikei: kyōikushi* (Tokyo, 1963), pp. 86ff.

71. Matsumoto and Suzuki, *Genten*, p. 74.

72. Japanese National Commission for UNESCO, *Development of Education*, pp. 33–34, 58–59.

natural history, physics, chemistry, agriculture, calligraphy, drawing, singing, and gymnastics.[73] Graduates of the Ordinary Middle Schools might proceed to the next higher level or enter directly into practical life, but at this stage the end of education was the same in either case: the instilling of a proper set of ethical and patriotic attitudes, the making of a good Japanese subject.

The Higher Middle School (Kōtō Chūgakkō) course of two (and later three) years' duration partook of both *gakumon* and *kyōiku*. It was professionally oriented and its separate courses in law, literature, science, medicine, engineering, agriculture, and commerce funnelled directly into the various corresponding colleges of the university. Although this higher secondary school was originally intended to prepare not only for the university but also, if the student desired, for immediate entry into gainful employment, the demand for university education was so great that these schools by 1900 had to all intents and purposes become preparatory institutions for the university. According to Mori: "The Higher Middle Schools are intended to train, among people of superior talent, those who will be competent to guide and direct the thinking of the broad masses of society: be they bureaucrats, then those of the highest echelon; be they businessmen, then those for the top management; be they scholars, then true experts in the various arts and sciences."[74] The Ordinary Middle Schools by contrast represented the final phase of *kyōiku*. A few of their graduates, Mori indicated, might proceed to the Higher Middle Schools or perhaps to the Special Schools, but the great majority of them would belong "neither to the upper nor to the lower ranks of society," and would be "expected to devote themselves to the most useful sort of activity" directly upon finishing the lower secondary course. Mori chided the typical middle school student for his aversion to practical subjects and warned that unless he changed his attitude he would be less of an asset than a burden to Japan in the "competition between nations."[75] In an era before the widespread establishment of technical and vocational schools, Mori had no other choice than to turn to the middle schools for his clerks and accountants and foremen and assistant plant managers: the "noncoms," so to speak, of his industrial "war."

Mori's Higher Middle Schools are better known to posterity as the Kōtōgakkō (Higher Schools), his Ordinary Middle Schools simply as Chūgakkō (Middle Schools), in accordance with the new terminology which came into effect in 1894. Of the former there

---

73. *Gakusei gojūnenshi*, p. 167.
74. *Zenshū* I, 535, SPM : 21 June 1887 : "Miyagi Kenchō."
75. *Zenshū* I, 546, SPM : 22 June 1887 : "Fukushimaken Gijidō."

were authorized only five (and later seven) in the entire country (roughly the same number, in other words, as the imperial universities, for which they were in effect preparatory). They were under the direct supervision of the Monbushō and were financed entirely by the central government. Of the latter there were roughly ten times as many: a numerical imbalance which further underscored the gap between the two secondary-school levels. The central government assumed no financial responsibility for the Ordinary Middle Schools, while the prefectures were permitted to maintain only one such institution apiece out of public taxes. Establishment of additional institutions in the prefectures by other financial means was not ruled out; the limitation itself was rescinded in 1891; and in 1899 the various lower units of the prefectures were permitted to establish their own Ordinary Middle Schools provided this did not interfere with the orderly advancement of primary education. Accordingly, by 1900 there were 217 such schools, and by 1910 their number throughout Japan had risen to 309. The immediate effect of Mori's ordinance however was to bring about a sudden halving of their number from 107 in 1885 to a mere 58 in 1886.[76] The keynote of Mori's action here was economy. Private schools, subject to supervision and final control by prefectural governors, continued to provide much of the available secondary education.[77] But priorities had been redefined in favor of the national interest; public resources were strained at all levels; and in terms of the narrow base which Mori deemed sufficient for the leadership of Japan, secondary education as he found it in 1885 was overextended. Hence the pruning.

Mori's normal school policy, at the instructional level, is a story in its own right. In structural terms, however, it may be viewed as an extension of his middle school policy, inasmuch as the Ordinary Normal Schools in effect provided one form of secondary education. The normal schools already had been divided into two types: the prefectural Ordinary Normal Schools (Jinjō Shihangakkō), which trained teachers for the elementary schools; and the single Higher Normal School (Kōtō Shihangakkō) at Tokyo, which provided teachers and directors for the Ordinary Normal Schools and (together with the literature and science colleges of the university) instructors for the various middle schools.[78]

As with the middle schools, Mori's reform initially entailed an

76. *Gakusei gojūnenshi*, pp. 105, 169, 224, 278; Dairoku Kikuchi, *Japanese Education* (London, 1909), pp. 205–206.
77. KKM, pp. 192–193.
78. Matsumoto and Suzuki, *Genten*, p. 91; Kikuchi, *Japanese Education*, p. 298.

economy measure. The prefectures, which were supporting 76 Ordinary Normal Schools (65 for men, 11 for women) in 1882, were henceforth permitted to maintain out of public taxes only one such institution per prefecture, although subsidies from the central government might contribute in part to its maintenance. Their number accordingly dropped to 46 in 1886; following the rescinding of Mori's restriction in 1897, the number would climb once again to 69 by 1907. Admission procedures for the four-year course, open to young persons between the age of seventeen and twenty who had completed the eight-year primary course or its equivalent, were tightened up considerably. Candidates were accepted only upon recommendation of the prefectural governor, county head, or ward mayor and were subjected to a probationary period of up to three months. They were placed under an obligation to serve in the primary schools for at least ten years following graduation, the first five years at an institution not necessarily of their own choosing. This provision was aimed at checking the practice, popular with students ever since these schools were founded in 1872, of enrolling without any intention of ever teaching, thus utilizing the normal schools as a form of general secondary education not available elsewhere. The assumption finally of all students' expenses by the prefecture not only heightened the prestige of normal school education but also removed the financial barriers to a field which had been largely dominated by members of the former samurai class.[79]

The Higher Normal School of August 1885 represented an amalgamation (again, for reasons of economy) of the original Tokyo Normal School of 1872, an institution for men, with the Tokyo Women's Normal School of 1874. A course of three years' duration was prescribed for male graduates of the Ordinary Normal Schools, with a separate course of four years' duration for women who had completed two years at the ordinary level. This institution was under the direct control of the ministry and its expenses, including free tuition and maintenance for all students, were carried by the central government. It was the only institution of its kind in Japan until the establishment of a similar school in Hiroshima in 1902.[80]

Primary Schools

While on an inspection tour of Kyushu in 1887, Mori remarked, "Since parents and guardians indisputably have the duty, not only

79. OTM, pp. 131–132; *Gakusei gojūnenshi*, pp. 191–194.
80. *Gakusei gojūnenshi*, pp. 117, 196–197, 245.

toward their offspring but also toward the state, of sending their children to school, it is perfectly reasonable to hold them liable for the cost of their children's education."[81] Here we find repeated not only the guiding ideology of the Primary School Ordinance, namely, that of the subject's responsibility to the state, but also two of its most important technical provisions: that of compulsory education at the primary level and that of financing primary education by means of tuition fees (*jugyōryō*) levied directly on the parents. *Jugyōryō* was a term originally coined by Fukuzawa in his effort to dispense with the traditional method of reimbursing teachers by means of annual gifts, i.e., in kind, and to put the financing of Keiō on a rational cash basis.[82]

The concept of compulsory education was not new with Mori. The Gakusei of 1872, as has already been noted, conceived of its eight-year elementary course as the privilege of every youngster in the land. In response to economic necessity the Kyōikurei of 1879 had authorized a minimum course of sixteen months' duration (with a further option between a four- or eight-year course depending on local circumstances), and with the Kaisei kyōikurei of 1880 required elementary schooling had been raised to thirty-two weeks each year for three years. Mori set up a compulsory Ordinary Primary School (Jinjō Shōgakkō) course and an optional Higher Primary School (Kōtō Shōgakkō) course, each of four years' duration. He was nevertheless forced to make provision for a Simplified Course (*Kan'ika*) of only three years' duration which might, according to local circumstances, be adopted. This loophole was retained as late as 1900, when the full four-year course (extended to six years in 1907) at last became mandatory.[83] As for the actual enforcement of attendance, Mori had even less success than his predecessors if one is to judge by the rates, which dropped from a previous high of 51.0 percent in 1883 to a low of 45.0 percent in 1887 and even by 1890 had only recovered to 48.9 percent. It was not until the turn of the century that attendance rates passed the 80 percent mark (81.5 percent in 1900), reaching 95.6 percent in 1905 and 98.1 percent by 1907,[84] although this was fast work compared to Western countries, which had taken most of the nineteenth century to cover the same ground.

Considerable economic hardship was of course imposed by Mori's method of financing. This method again was not entirely

81. *Zenshū* I, 497, SPM : Feb. 1887 : "Kyūshū/gunkuchō."
82. Keenleyside and Thomas, *History of Japanese Education*, p. 96.
83. *Gakusei gojūnenshi*, pp. 141, 210–211, 271.
84. Horimatsu, *Kyōikushi*, pp. 68, 268.

new with him, but he now made it the chief fiscal support of the elementary schools. In a variety of ways, differing greatly from one locality to another, the actual burden on parents had in the past been eased: by means of local taxation, through subsidies from the prefectures (in the Kaisei kyōikurei) or from the center (in the Gakusei and Kyōikurei), by voluntary contributions of the wealthy, or even by remission of fees by the teachers themselves.[85] With the Primary School Ordinance of 1886, however, any deficit in the primary schools remaining after the collection of *jugyōryō* and voluntary contributions would have to be made up by the town and village assemblies out of such other local resources as might be available.[86] Critics, however, generally view Mori as having acted here entirely out of necessity. His *kan'ika* in particular is viewed as an earnest of his ultimate goal of free public elementary education, a goal finally reached by Japan in 1900. This Simplified Course was intended for children whose parents could not afford tuition, and although it was widely shunned as a poor man's school, it established the first primary schools in Japan entirely free of charge to the student and financed exclusively by prefectural and local taxes.[87]

Technical/Vocational and Women's Education

What was missing in the house that Mori built? Fujiwara Kiyozō has characterized Mori as the man who founded and Inoue Kowashi as the man who completed Japan's prewar educational structure.[88] It was Inoue who during his tenure as minister in 1893–1894 first gave serious attention to the lag in *jitsugyō kyōiku* (technical and vocational schooling) and in women's education. Government experiments with trade schools during the 1870's and 1880's had met with little success. Low-level technicians managed to receive adequate training on the job in the factories, while members of the former samurai class who might have sought out the more highly skilled positions showed a marked preference for the sort of education which would open for them the doors of the bureaucracy rather than those of industry.

85. Matsumoto and Suzuki, *Genten*, pp. 57, 62, 75; Japanese National Commission for UNESCO, *Development of Education*, p. 55.
86. Matsumoto and Suzuki, *Genten*, p. 87.
87. *Gakusei gojūnenshi*, p. 213; Koba, "Mori no kaikaku," p. 95; Nakajima Tarō, *Kindai nihon kyōiku seidoshi* (Tokyo, 1966), pp. 192–193.
88. Fujiwara Kiyozō, *Kyōiku shisō gakusetsu jinbutsu shi: Meiji zenki hen* (Tokyo, 1942), p. 777.

Economic take-off during the 1890's, however, created a pressing need for medium-grade technicians, and in great numbers. Inoue's Continuation Schools (Jitsugyō Hoshū Gakkō) of 1893 and his Apprentice Schools (Totei Gakkō) of 1894 provided a low-grade technical and vocational training, much of it on a part-time or seasonal basis, for children who had completed at least six years of primary education. The Continuation Schools were attached to the existing primary schools, the Apprentice Schools in many instances directly to the factories. The Diet in 1894 became alarmed at the lack of formal technical and vocational education at the secondary level, and in 1899 Technical Middle Schools (Jitsugyō Chūgakkō) offering a three-year course were established at the prefectural level, while the government undertook through the Special Schools Ordinance (Senmon Gakkōrei) of 1903 the establishment of higher technical schools, which in their variety included not only the government schools for foreign language, for music, and for fine arts in Tokyo but also six state-supported higher schools for industry, two for agriculture, four for commerce, and five for medicine, throughout Japan.[89]

The important thing to remember about all this as regards Mori, however, is that the whole structure of technical/vocational education, for all its impressiveness and for all its contribution to the economy, stood apart from that privileged avenue of general education which led to the state universities and eventually on to the bureaucracy. Japanese education as it entered the twentieth century represented a typical instance of the "multiple-track" system, with an academic track (Chūgakkō, Kōtōgakkō, Daigaku), a normal track, a technical track, a girls' track, and (after 1935) a youth-school track. Fast trains, so to speak, ran only on the academic track, however. The other lines were strictly local. Mori with his Imperial University, Higher Middle and Ordinary Middle schools had installed a limited express on the academic rails and cut the switches to the other tracks. All Inoue did was to hook up a slow-moving freight on the technical track.

Militating against the rapid spread of women's education meanwhile were the deep-seated prejudices regarding the role of women in society, as well as poverty in the home and the variety of domestic chores which traditionally fell to a girl's lot. Even at the primary level attendance rates for girls had shown a steady lag: 15 percent in 1873, 31 percent in 1890, 88 percent in 1899, as

---

89. Japanese National Commission for UNESCO, *Development of Education*, pp. 32–35, 60–62.

opposed to rates during these same three sample years of 40 percent, 65 percent, and 96 percent respectively for boys.[90] Attempts during the 1870's to provide girls with an education equal and similar to that of boys had in effect been abandoned, and Mori's Middle School Ordinance took no notice of women's secondary education whatsoever. By 1899, however, there were twenty-eight girls' high schools in operation with a total of 3,020 students. The fact that only eight of these were publicly maintained indicates the predominance of private (and particularly Christian) efforts in this field prior to the late 1890's. It was not until 1895 that, at Inoue's behest, the first Girls' High School Regulations ("Kōtō jogakkō kitei") were promulgated, establishing a separate six-year course (corresponding to the Ordinary, rather than the Higher, Middle School for boys), open to girls after the fourth year of primary school.[91] These institutions were in effect finishing schools for the few, imparting "the general education and culture necessary for those destined to be of middle or higher social standing."[92]

In this area too, Mori's hand was stayed by financial difficulties. He continued to praise women's education very loudly and, in terms taken directly from the "Saishōron," to describe women as natural-born teachers. He preferred indeed to have the Ordinary Primary Schools staffed wherever possible with women rather than with men, an ideal which stood closer to American than to Japanese practice as it gradually developed. He encouraged dancing at the women's branch of the Higher Normal School. The "emancipated" younger wives, however, were advised by Mori to bear bravely and sacrificially with their mothers-in-law,[93] and were repeatedly told: "The foundations of national prosperity rest upon education; the foundations of education upon women's education. We must remember that the safety or peril of the state are related to the success or failure of women's education. It is extremely important to foster the spirit of thinking of the nation in our education of women."[94] Mori had a tendency to tell whatever audience he might be addressing that *they* were the indispensable cog in the great educational wheel; but in the schooling of women he actually did little more than administer an encouraging pat on the back and

90. Ibid., pp. 10, 16–17.
91. Ibid., pp. 16–17; *Gakusei gojūnenshi,* p. 171.
92. Kikuchi, *Japanese Education,* p. 273.
93. *Zenshū* I, 497 and 626–628, from SPM : Feb. 1887 : Kyūshū/gun-kuchō" and SPM : 20 Jul. 1888 : "Tōkyō Kōtō Jogakkō." Yumoto Takehiko, "Dokusho nyūmon," in *Kyōiku gojūnenshi,* p. 116, to appear in *Zenshū* II.
94. *Zenshū* I, 611–612, SPM : Fall, 1887 : "Daisanchihō gakuji junshi."

a little shove in the right direction. When Mori told the normal school students that they were indispensable, however, he meant it.

HEISHIKI TAISŌ:
PEDAGOGICAL FOLLY

Mori's influence upon teacher training was epochal. "Mori," in the words of Nakajima Tarō, "may be called the father of our normal schools."[95] In the realm of the intangible, Mori no doubt made his greatest impact on Japanese education with the introduction into the normal schools of *heishiki taisō*—"military drill" or, in its full literal translation, "military-style physical training." Indeed, in the broadest terms of Japanese social and intellectual history, Mori's normal school policy may be viewed as his most profound and permanent and distinctive legacy to future generations. What we have here is the indisputable influence of one man's ideas upon an institution and the influence of that institution, in turn, upon the thinking and behavior of an entire nation. There is a high degree of impersonality which attaches to institutional systems, but if one were to ask in what way Mori most influenced Meiji education, in the sense that Itō Hirobumi left his own particular mark upon the constitution, or Yamagata Aritomo his upon the armed forces, it is to the spiritual reorientation of the normal schools that one would first have to turn. Unfortunately, as Fujiwara Kiyozō has suggested, Mori's policy here was a failure to be recorded alongside his many achievements.[96]

Mori had already suggested the usefulness of *heishiki taisō* as early as 1879 in "Shintai no nōryoku" and in his correspondence with Itō in 1882 had referred again (in his "Gakusei hengen") to the need for "a method of training the character and physique of our people." With military drill, Mori thought he had found it. Its military serviceability was strictly incidental, and even its health-building function secondary, to the moral discipline it was supposed to instill. The method here lay not in the reiteration of precept, a technique so familiar in traditional Confucian education, but—as with a monastic order, or a military unit, or an English "public school"—in the imposition of a routine which by itself was deemed capable of producing the required virtues. These virtues, of course, would include a fresh conceptual grasp of the modern

95. Nakajima, *Seidoshi,* p. 236.
96. Quoted in Karasawa Tomitarō, *Kyōkasho no rekishi* (Tokyo, 1956), p. 53.

state and of the subject's duties to it, but this, like the will to persevere in the contest of nations, would all follow from the "training [forging, disciplining] of character [spirit, frame of mind]" (*katagi no tanren*) which was the ultimate end of military drill.

Mori of course was not operating in a sociological vacuum. His policies need to be viewed in terms of immediate practical pressures as well as in terms of some future ideal, and as a response to the incipient breakdown not only of traditional rules of behavior but also of the social context in which those norms had operated. The students who had left their families and villages for the prefectural capitals or for Tokyo in order to attend middle or normal schools, or the university, were even more uprooted than their Western counterparts (armed from the start with a more universalistic, less personalistic, ethic) would have been under similar circumstances. The problem of "Student Bohemianism," as the *Japan Weekly Mail* felicitously put it,[97] was one which plagued and irritated Mori to the end of his career, right down to that last high-handed and ungracious scolding delivered to the university students in the falling snow outside the engineering college shortly before his assassination.

From time to time there were student protest strikes (with occasional political overtones) over such issues as coarse food or excessive punishments, but the problem lay deeper than specific or deliberate misconduct. Arrogant intellectualism, absence of common courtesy, inattention to health and hygiene, a general lack of system and order: these were much more basic. To aggravate the matter, there had been little in Tokugawa education to prepare either teachers for the giving, or students for the taking, of the rather cut-and-dried, impersonal system of punishments by which discipline in Western schools traditionally had been maintained.[98] The typical Tokugawa teacher held sway over his students by means of personal respect and affection, not formal status and authority. Robust and expansive by nature, he had as a generational type survived on into the second decade of Meiji. Because of the very personal nature of his approach, he had lent great strength, together with a certain humanism, to the earliest stages of educational modernization. This species of teacher was by the mid-1880's, however, fast dying out.[99] *Heishiki taisō* was calculated to produce not only a new generation of teachers with a new

97. JWM, 2 Feb. 1889.
98. JWM, 28 May 1887, 7 April 1888, 15 Sept. 1888, 2 Feb. 1889.
99. Hayashi Takeji, "Kyōshokukan no rekishiteki haikei," in four parts (unpublished mimeographed manuscript; Sendai, n.d.), pt. 2, pp. 6–7.

dispensation of authority but also a whole new disciplinary framework for everyday school life.[100]

As a result of his inspections of the Tokyo Normal School during 1884–1885, Mori had been greatly perturbed by what seemed to him the unregulated life and bad manners of the students,[101] and in May 1885 he introduced military drill there on a trial basis. Obviously impressed with the results, the ministry in May 1886 ordered the men's department of the Higher Normal School (as it had been renamed) to reorganize the entire life of the school outside the classroom along military lines. Colonel Yamagawa Hiroshi was transferred from the war ministry to become director of the institution, and a Lieutenant Matsui and a staff of noncommissioned officers were put in charge of physical education, i.e., military drill, and of discipline in general.[102] By 1888, military drill was represented in the curriculum of the primary and middle schools as well,[103] but it was in the central and prefectural normal schools that it made its real impact as a way of life.

Mori's thinking on *heishiki taisō* was fully explained in three documents: in his address at the Saitama Normal School on 19 December 1885; in a draft of a memorial to the emperor, "Heishiki taisō ni kansuru kengon" (A memorial concerning military-style physical training) dating from approximately the same time; and in the "Draft Cabinet Proposal" (*kakugian*) assigned to Inoue Kowashi for the writing, probably in the summer of 1887.[104] It may be recalled that it was at Saitama that Mori had called on future teachers to "advance Japan . . . to the foremost position in the entire world." Mori then had continued: "The accomplishment of the foregoing will be no easy task. Truly it depends on whether the normal schools, which constitute the foundation of popular education, exert themselves to the utmost in the performance of their duties . . . Although there are many ways in which we can advance the welfare of the nation, eight or nine tenths of it depends on the

100. JWM, 28 May 1887.
101. Yokosuka Kaoru in Kaigo et al., "Mori Arinori no shisō to kyōiku seisaku," p. 139.
102. Horimatsu, *Kyōikushi,* p. 154.
103. Yokosuka Kaoru in Kaigo et al., "Mori Arinori no shisō to kyōiku seisaku," p. 138.
104. Neither the memorial (which may or may not have been submitted) nor the draft cabinet proposal are dated. The former, however, refers to the several school ordinances (of 1886) as being about to take effect. For the date of the latter I have followed Inagaki Tadahiko, in Kaigo et al., "Mori Arinori no shisō to kyōiku seisaku," p. 37.

effectiveness of these normal schools."[105] It was likewise in the Saitama speech that Mori first mentioned those three traits of character which he thought should mark the teacher, namely, obedience (*jūjun*), friendship (*yūjō*), and dignity (*igi*): the attitudes which should govern the teacher's behavior toward his superiors, his equals, and his inferiors, respectively. These reappear in the Normal School Ordinance of 1886 somewhat revised by the hand of Motoda Eifu as obedience (*junryō*), trust-and-affection (*shin-ai*), and dignity (*ijū*)—the revisions in each case having added a few extra ounces of specific moral gravity to Mori's original wording.[106]

The relationship between military exercises and character-building, to Mori's mind, was as follows:

> This military-style physical training is something to be used entirely as a means for promoting the three qualities of character I have just mentioned, as a tool for hammering them into shape. We are not adding it to the curriculum with the thought of producing officers and enlisted men for the defense of our country, on the chance that the nation might someday find itself in need of soldiers. The things we hope to achieve by means of this training are three: first, to instill—with the sense of urgency possessed by actual soldiers—those habits of obedience which are appropriate in the classroom. Secondly, as you know, soldiers are always formed into squads, each squad possessing its own leader who devotes himself, heart and mind and soul, to the welfare of his group. And thirdly, every company has its commanding officer who controls and supervises it, and who must comport himself with dignity. By the same token our students, by trading off the roles of common soldier, squad leader and commanding officer, will build up the traits of character appropriate to each of these three roles.[107]

With *jūjun* Mori had in mind very specifically conformity to school regulations, warning the normal school students that they were to follow their teachers' commands, since they were not yet sufficiently mature (at ages seventeen to twenty, it may be recalled)

---

105. *Zenshū* I, 484, SPM : 19 Dec. 1885 : "Saitamaken Jinjō Shihangakkō."
106. Kaigo Tokiomi, *Motoda Eifu,* vol. 19 of Ishikawa Ken, gen. ed., *Nihon kyōiku sentetsu sōsho* (Tokyo, 1942), pp. 146–147.
107. *Zenshū* I, 482–483, SPM : 19 Dec. 1885 : "Saitamaken Jinjō Shihangakkō."

to distinguish the right from the wrong by themselves. The normal school staff, in turn, were to obey the orders of their principals in the conviction that "school directors, who enjoy the trust of the prefectural governor, will not err in judgment."[108] *Yūjō,* on the other hand, meant especially the "spirit of mutual assistance," which Mori described as the foundation of all public morality and as the chief measure of a civilized nation. *Igi,* finally, referred to something like assurance or composure in speech and manners at all times, whether in superior or inferior station. Mori went out of his way to explain that his purposes with *heishiki taisō* were purely pedagogical, that he did not foresee any war in the immediate future, and that in any case there were better places to train professional soldiers. And it was with this very important prior qualification that he then went on with his aggressive talk about warfare being the "daily condition of all mankind" and about advancing Japan to the "foremost rank."

In the two other documents, however, the possible military usefulness, if not necessarily military intent, becomes more apparent. "Heishiki taisō ni kansuru kengon"[109] recommended that the entire responsibility for physical education from the Ordinary Middle Schools on up be transferred from the Monbushō to the war ministry, and that military drill in the schools be supervised by career officers, themselves well trained in the desired qualities of bravery and obedience. Meanwhile, in order to improve the physique and instill a proper sense of the subject's responsibilities in the vast majority of the population who would never get to middle school, Mori recommended in this memorial that all able-bodied men be organized into local militia units which would drill every week or so under army or navy supervision. His *kakugian*[110] was even more specific: the local *kochō* (syndics), he suggested, should assemble all men ages seventeen to twenty-seven once or twice a month on the local school grounds for instruction in "the spirit of defending the fatherland"; the war ministry could then conduct elementary military drill, while the education ministry would publish simple and appropriate texts to be read aloud or expounded in lectures at these assemblies. These two documents, the memorial and the *kakugian,* also happen to contain Mori's chief references to *chūkun aikoku:* the spirit of "loyalty [the traditional term] and patriotism

108. Ibid., p. 481.
109. *Zenshū* I, 347–350, Mori Arinori, "Heishiki taisō ni kansuru kengon," undated but probably late 1885 or early 1886.
110. Mori, "Kakugian," p. 346.

[the modern expression]" required by the state in confronting the international challenge.[111]

During his provincial inspection tour Mori made a point of visiting army establishments to view real military drill at first hand and was in the habit of requesting local commanders for assistance in carrying out *heishiki taisō* in nearby schools.[112] The initiative here was entirely that of Mori, who finally had his way against a cabinet that was seriously divided over the scheme, and an army very reluctant to spare the required personnel for it.[113] On the other hand, Mori, in a move which best proves his nonmilitary intent, won important exemptions from compulsory military service (normally three years in the army, or four years in the navy) for most Japanese educated beyond the primary level. The revised conscription regulations of January 1889 in Article 11 (inserted at Mori's insistence) introduced a system of only six months' active duty for normal school graduates and of one year's volunteer service for graduates of all state and prefectural, and of many private, schools from the secondary level on up.[114] Mori, after all, was building his own type of army for his own type of war and was equally reluctant to part with his own men. That Mori and the Army were to some extent working at cross purposes, that Mori chose *heishiki taisō* without any pressure whatsoever from military circles, serves simply to underline the irony—and the tragedy—of an extremely clumsy choice.

The damage was not perpetrated on the parade ground. The military exercises themselves built on elements of calisthenics and infantry-style marching already present in the curriculum,[115] and one may imagine that the long hikes, the overnight bivouacs, and the simulated war games which were an important part of the program[116] contributed very definitely to physical health and stamina, very probably to social mixing and camaraderie, and very possibly, for students of a certain temperament, to downright good fun. The harm occurred, rather, when the ethos of the parade

111. Ibid., pp. 345, 346; Mori, "Heishiki taisō," pp. 348, 349.
112. Koba, "Mori no kaikaku," p. 101.
113. In the recollection of Koba Sadanaga, who once intruded on a heated discussion of the matter between Mori and Katsura Tarō, then vice minister of war. See Koba Sadanaga, "Mori Arinori shi," *Taiyō*, 18.9 (13 June 1912). To be reprinted in *Zenshū* II.
114. Neither category, however, was exempt from up to ten years' service in the reserves (KKM, p. 216; JWM, 2 Feb. 1889).
115. Yokosuka Kaoru in Kaigo et. al., "Mori Arinori no shisō to kyōiku seisaku," pp. 138–139.
116. Karasawa, *Kyōshi no rekishi*, p. 45.

ground was deliberately extended to the dormitory, refectory, and study hall of the normal school, whence it eventually spread to infect the classrooms of an entire nation.

The normal schools from 1886 onward went by the bugle.[117] Sometimes the bugle brought the teacher trainees, who were all now required to live on campus, tumbling out of their drafty, barrack-like dormitories in the dead of the night for an emergency roll call. A shoe unlaced, a button missing, a cap askew, a bayonet unfixed, or a salute sleepily delivered could entail confinement to quarters, segregation at meals, last turn at the common bath, or even a humiliating trial before the entire student body. So great was their anxiety, indeed, that some students slept uncomfortably under their regulation blankets in full uniform, anticipating the bugle that never blew.

The dramatic shift from the traditional quilted *futon* to bed-and-blankets, and from *geta, hakama,* and shaggy hair to military caps, standing collars, and uniforms (provided, like everything else, at state expense) suggests a frontal attack on the two physically debilitating factors of traditional "shelter" and "dress" as explained by Mori in "Shintai no nōryoku." Tatami mats were conducive to indolence, while young men in wooden clogs never could be expected to make the bugle. Students before 1886 had performed calisthenics with the sleeves of their kimonos held back by armbands; but that would hardly do for *heishiki taisō*. The military style, which involved saluting of teachers and older students, a certain amount of fagging by the lower classmen, and strictly regulated off-campus leave, was carried to picayune extremes. Clothing was folded and piled by the ruler; sneezing, coughing, opening of drawers, and even visits to the toilet were forbidden during the two-hour evening study hall; and to crown and epitomize this pedagogical folly, a student was required to align all of his textbooks very neatly, according to *height*.

Mori, who had scoffed at the externalized morality of the sword cult, should have known better than to attempt the internalization of virtue through such a formalistic type of discipline. What small chance there may have been of developing any real sentiments of dignity, friendship, or obedience within this framework to begin with was finally precluded by placing disciplinary authority in the

---

117. The following account of normal school life has been based, except where otherwise indicated, on Karasawa, *Kyōshi no rekishi,* pp. 44–66, *passim,* which has drawn voluminously on normal school records and histories, and on the testimony of late-Meiji eye-witnesses such as Fujiwara Kiyozō and Noguchi Entarō.

hands of noncommissioned army officers, retired or transferred, of far lower intellectual (and probably social) attainments than the students themselves. Dormitories were supervised by sergeants and corporals who bullied their charges into a false and grudging obedience with the assistance of upperclass prefects who reported on their juniors, while the gateman who clocked a returning student in late from town was likely as not a mere army private. Prospective salary differentials based on graduating marks, and a probationer system according to which the lower third of an incoming class was eventually weeded out, served in the end to raise competitive tensions and limit any sentiment of mutuality among the teacher trainees themselves. The upshot of this system was the emergence of the so-called *shihan taipu* or "normal school type," who, as instructor and as exemplar, did so much (more, one would suspect, than any structural arrangements or even the formal ideology) to set the tone of prewar Japanese education. By many writers, from late Meiji down to the present, he stands seriously condemned.

Noguchi Entarō, who entered one of the prefectural normal schools in 1886 and who later rose to become both a normal school principal and a director of the Imperial Education Association, recalled in 1922: "We wretched pedagogues-to-be were, as a matter of fact, inwardly on tenterhooks. Among colleagues of an even more timorous nature than myself, I can remember several who went quite out of their minds."[118] Of Mori, Noguchi had to say: "It may in one sense be said that Mori's reforms in teacher training, while displaying a great esteem for education and especially for the education of the masses, in fact made education more rigid and placed it under a restraint."[119] One of the earliest chroniclers of Meiji education, Fujiwara Kiyozō, in 1909 wrote of Mori's normal school reforms that: "the result was to turn graduates from then on into servile, listless creatures of a vacillating, obsequious, dejected nature, and to produce a type of person who supposed that he could qualify as a teacher simply by patching up his faults with the plaster of hypocrisy—delighting in formality, striving to mend his façade of outward dignity while ignoring the inner cultivation of his thoughts . . . These graduates, in the end, were trained to complacency, other-worldliness and passivity, and were out of touch with the society around them.[120] This last complaint of aloofness was a common one. It is explained, however, not only by the

118. Noguchi Entarō, "Shihan kyōiku no hensen," in Kokumin Kyōiku Shōreikai, ed., *Kyōiku gojūnenshi* (Tokyo, 1922), p. 371.
119. Ibid., p. 366.
120. Quoted in Karasawa, *Kyōkasho no rekishi*, pp. 52–53.

military-style matrix from which the "normal school type" emerged but also by the privileged position which Mori had secured for teacher trainees within the educational system, and which the civil service status granted to teachers after 1891 would assure them with respect to society as a whole.

The catalog of incriminations could be continued almost ad infinitum, from Lafcadio Hearne's description of the "military and severe" discipline of the austere, rather disconcertingly efficient Matsue Normal School where his students snapped to attention "with a springing movement as if moved by machinery,"[121] to a report of the Japanese National Commission for UNESCO in 1960, which described the normal school type as submissive to authority, aloof from the community, and possessed of a "kind of external goodness different from natural humanity."[122] The ultimate damage, of course, was done in the classrooms where the teacher trainees themselves eventually taught. One American educator who visited Japan in 1899 wrote, for instance: "Japanese primary school children submit willingly to the stern discipline of the classroom, but dillydally with their studies. In America, children may sometimes be noisy in the classroom. But their attitude toward their studies is certainly more active than that of the Japanese primary school children."[123] George Sansom, too, has concluded that: "it would not be difficult to make a case against the modern educational system of Japan, showing that her history would have taken a different turn if her rulers, even at the expense of what was deemed efficiency, had encouraged rather than repressed originality or at least diversity in academic life."[124]

Lack of spontaneity, one of the cardinal weaknesses of modern Japanese education, would continue to bedevil the reformers of the New Education Movement in the 1920's[125] and of the postwar occupation period. Causative factors were of course multiple and no doubt involved a complex of attitudes, habits of thought, and

121. Lafcadio Hearne, *Glimpses of Unfamiliar Japan* (New York, 1894), pp. 430–439.

122. Japanese National Commission for UNESCO, *Development of Education,* p. 45. Nakajima Tarō, in *Seidoshi,* p. 236, takes a more favorable, if somewhat exceptional view of the matter, arguing that the "normal school type" was not considered to be a problem until several decades after he had made his great contribution to the modernization of Japanese education.

123. Japanese National Commission for UNESCO, *Development of Education,* p. 41.

124. Sansom, *The Western World and Japan,* p. 464.

125. Karasawa Tomitarō, *Kindai Nihon kyōikushi* (Tokyo, 1968), pp. 149–162.

interpersonal relations which would have had to be reckoned with in any case. But one may certainly ask what spontaneity might reasonably be expected from children entrusted to teachers whose own spontaneity had systematically been wrung out of them. It is hard to believe that the result was in line with Mori's original intention, however, or that he did not in fact hope to create that genuine originality and spontaneity of spirit which he himself so amply possessed. We seem to be confronted here with an instance of massive miscalculation.

The root of Mori's error lay in his pedagogical, or psychological, assumptions; and these in turn are entirely explicable in terms of his own distinctive education and character training. Mori's first mistake was to make too much of the idea, which crops up in all cultures and in all ages, that outer discipline can be translated into inner discipline, or the body hardened to toughen the spirit. This insight of course has its merits, but only up to a point—a point the more quickly reached as one attempts to apply the formula to large numbers of people. A. D. C. Peterson has written of Thomas Arnold of Rugby, a classical exponent of this approach: "Arnold's system was admired, not for the type of boy and man which it produced, but simply because it was a system for producing types —and was therefore corruptible to . . . totalitarian uses . . . Supposing Arnold was wrong and there *was* a cleavage between the spiritual development of the individual and the production of socially desirable types. The English system was clearly the one which in practice had produced "the public school type" and from which any nation bent on educating an officer class could learn . . . Arnold . . . admitted no problem in balancing the educational needs of society and those of the individual, for [he] held that the Christian gentleman was the answer to both demands."[126]

Mori, whose loyal and energetic Japanese subject was the moral equivalent of Arnold's Christian gentleman, and who shared Arnold's blind spot regarding the potential cleavage of individual and social needs, had the misfortune (we may say) to have been himself the product of two institutions, the Gōjū and the Brotherhood of the New Life, which operated on the principles of outward discipline, physical exertion, and formal obedience. Although thoroughly versed in martial skills, most samurai youngsters would have been spared the intense social discipline of the Gōjū, where, given the intimate, neighborhood aspect of the fraternity, Mori's

126. A. D. C. Peterson, *A Hundred Years of Education: A Comparative Study of Educational Patterns in Western Europe and the United States*, Collier Books Edition (New York, 1962), pp. 124–125.

three traits of obedience, friendship, and dignity actually may have been realized among the members. Most young samurai dispatched to the West, likewise, managed to find their way into social circles more relaxed than those in which they themselves had grown up. Brocton however revived, redoubled, and sanctified the ethos of the Gōjū.

We have indeed in *heishiki taisō* and Mori's normal school policy what may be viewed as the long-range fallout of his earlier association with Thomas Lake Harris and of his failure to find an emotional or psychological liberation in Christianity, rather than an affirmation merely of his own Confucian moral fevor. The methods of bodily austerities and of total obedience and total denial of self, the apocalyptic conception of the challenge, the essentially moral rather than political nature of the undertaking, and the vision of a regenerated Japan: all this was now carried over from Mori's Brocton experience into his plans for teacher training. The simile of a Divine Army (Harris' term) may not have been consciously present to Mori's mind, but the likeness was there. If *heishiki taisō* had its evil genius, it was the Pivotal Man—not the Iron Chancellor.

Mori's second mistake was related to the first. The literalistic cast of his mind shows up in his assumption that the three attitudes formally inherent in the positions of footsoldier, squad leader, and commanding officer could be internalized by trading off these roles on the parade ground. Something indeed might have come of it if he had left the teacher trainees free to develop these relationships by and among themselves, in the autonomous and self-disciplinary fashion for example of the Gōjū. All this was wrecked however by subjecting them to the purely external authority of noncommissioned officers. Mori's further assumption here that actual soldiers necessarily display the "soldierly" virtues likewise suggests a streak of stubborn, unimaginative literalism.

Mori's third mistake, involving the long social and historical perspective, is perhaps more forgivable. Although in organization and style the Japanese normal schools most resembled the *écoles normales* of France and the *Lehrer-Seminare* of Germany, it was the (to Mori no doubt highly familiar) "public schools" of England which best exemplified the Arnoldian principle. Hayashi Takeji sees the public schools as "very probably one of the models" for Mori's normal school policy but points out that most public school pupils in England came from a solid aristocratic background and were assured of their future social standing. Psychologically they were tough, and their secondary-school drubbing did them no harm. Most Japanese teacher trainees, by contrast, had little either in their social origins or in their future prospects to warrant much self-confidence, so that the psychological beating they got in school drove them into the very spirit of "slavish servility" Mori was aiming to eradicate.[127] The differences between Japan and England were not only sociological, of course. The regimentation of the public schools was leavened with the humanism of a classical curriculum and of a conscious Christian orientation, while the tempering instrument here was provided simply by athletics, not military drill. It is against the very long perspective of intellectual history, or of social psychology indeed, that the full tragic implications of Mori's policy become apparent.

The peculiar fusion of feudal and Confucian values during the Tokugawa period had placed the Japanese of Meiji under a double psychological burden which would weigh upon any effort to achieve an individualistic spontaneity or sense of self along Western lines. In terms of psychological tension, we may say that Confucianism in China was significantly relieved by placing emphasis on the (natural) kinship rather than the (artificial) political tie; that feudalism in medieval Europe was lightened, and constantly challenged, by surviving elements of Christian universalism and natural law; but that the Japanese, with the absolute nature of their feudal obligation, and the primacy of political loyalty in their Confucian scheme, had given themselves the worst of both worlds. If spontaneity was Mori's objective, his task was to work his countrymen out of that double bind, not twist them even more tightly into it.

The material Mori had to work with was not altogether unpromising. Along with Fukuzawa and most of the Restoration leaders, he himself was an excellent example of what might be called the "temperamental individualism" of the Tokugawa warrior class. One has only to think of the competitive, aggressive connotations of *risshin shusse* (making one's way in the world), or of the intense self-discipline and self-reliance (*jiriki*) of Zen, or of the rugged activism of men like Kumazawa Banzan (1619–1691) or Yoshida Shōin (1830–1859), who took their inspiration from the Wang Yang-ming (Ōyōmei) intuitionist school of Confucianism, to realize that there was much in the native tradition which could provide the basis for a powerful awareness of self: an "individualism" which, although lacking the political, philosophical, or religious bases of its Western counterpart, nevertheless reproduced a reasonable facsimile of it at the level of everyday personal behavior and emotional response.

127. Hayashi, "Kyōshokukan no rekishiteki haikei," pt. 2, pp. 6–7.

It must also have been this trait which at once established such an extraordinary temperamental rapport and mutual regard between the early Meiji Japanese and their individualistic Western contemporaries. That rapport was short-lived. The Western world went on to even greater psychological emancipation after 1900, but the typical Japanese overseas student of the interwar period—diffident, introverted, and far less at ease socially than (for instance) his Chinese or Indian colleagues—provided a disappointing contrast to his Meiji predecessors and symbolized perhaps as well as anything else the ultimate price of Mori's miscalculation. Other factors such as mass education for an industrial society, or the more explicitly military spirit which invaded the schools after the victories over China and Russia, or the imposition of an official ideological orthodoxy in the 1890's, all contributed of course to the dampening of the "temperamental individualism" possessed by earlier generations of Japanese. And Mori's own emphasis on political loyalty helped to tighten that particular screw. But Mori threw away the most promising instrument in his hands for emancipating the individual Japanese personality: his teachers.

It was all so unnecessary. The Army had not pressured him for it. It was not required by the Herbartian pedagogy popularized from 1888 at the Imperial University by Emil Hausknecht, nor even by the eventual Confucian perversion of Herbartism.[128] And it even went against the better instincts of the Mori who worked hard to simplify and rationalize textbook materials,[129] who was the terror of pompous or long-winded or ineffective pedagogues, and who could urge that: "when pupils are called upon to recite in class, teachers should give them as much freedom as possible to express themselves fully, make sure that they comprehend the answer, and see to it that they do not cringe in delivering their replies. On the other hand, pupils should be taught to obey at once the orders of teachers and administrative staff, and the dignity of the teacher must be fully maintained."[130] Mori thus drew a clear distinction between conduct, which was to be strictly regulated, and thought, which was to remain unfettered. *Heishiki taisō* and normal school discipline, however readily they in fact played into hands of later efforts at thought control, were in Mori's original scheme confined to the realm of conduct. And with this concern for the

---

128. Horimatsu, *Kyōikushi*, pp. 214–224.
129. Inagaki Tadahiko in Kaigo et al., "Mori Arinori no shisō to kyōiku seisaku," pp. 127–129.
130. *Zenshū* I, 508, SPM : Feb. 1887 : "Tozen chihō gakuji junshi."

freedom of the mind we come to Mori in his most enlightened, common-sensical, modern aspect.

JITAHEIRITSU:
ETHICAL INDIVIDUALISM

Mori's solicitude for freedom of conscience would prove determinative of his policy regarding *shūshin,* or "moral training" as formally provided for in the primary and secondary curriculum. Here, in the nonpolitical realm of the individual's private thoughts and of his ethical relationship to other individuals, we find the most important qualification of Mori's educational statism, an aspect which confirmed for many contemporaries his image as out-and-out westernizer, which most outraged his traditionalist enemies, and which probably did the most to create the public mood which led eventually to his assassination. Indeed, Hayashi Takeji has described Mori as the "last resister"[131] (which he certainly was in high government circles) of the traditionalist tide which swept to triumph with the Imperial Rescript on Education in 1890. This rescript added to the purposes of education the inculcation of a specific ideological code and, as a means to that end, set in train the development of appropriate *shūshin* textbooks over the two following decades.

Mori's secularist approach to education, his belief that religion, including Christianity, should be kept out of the schools, was evident as early as 1872 in *Religious Freedom in Japan*. Addressing prefectural officials at Fukushima in June 1887, Mori still found it necessary to press the point home:

> All persons possess religious feelings to a greater or lesser degree. This is quite natural. The outward expressions of faith, however, vary greatly—some worshipping trees and stones or the sun and stars, others revering human beings or gods or a moral code. Since the individual person is free to make his own choice, teachers too should be free to follow any doctrine provided they do no harm to the national interest. However, any teacher who attempts to indoctrinate his primary or middle school students with his own religious beliefs is in effect forcing his own faith upon persons who have not yet achieved intellectual independence. Not only does he fail to understand the purpose of school education; he becomes an obstacle to the

---

131. Hayashi Takeji, "Mori Arinori to nashonarizumu," *Nihon,* April 1965, p. 86.

free development of his pupils' religious sentiment. Teachers of this sort should by all means resign their posts.[132]

With the revulsion against westernization and the fresh search for Japan's traditional identity which characterized the intellectual and cultural climate of the late 1880's, Mori's position became increasingly difficult to maintain. Motoda Eifu, with the "Kyōgaku taishi" of 1879, had been the first to call for a return to traditional values in education, but the issue by now had been caught up in a far broader debate over a definitive national faith. Katō Hiroyuki, for instance, who agreed with Motoda that moral instruction in the schools should be based on a specific national creed, was arguing in 1887 that the new code should include not only Confucianism but equal elements of Shinto, Buddhism, and Christianity as well.[133] The secularist concept of education was poorly understood by a generation reared on the broad doctrinal verities of the late Tokugawa period, and many of Mori's contemporaries mistakenly assumed that his hostility to traditional orthodoxy masked an intention to introduce his own allegedly Christian beliefs into the educational system. Neither his pedagogical philosophy nor the strictly private and personal nature of his own faith would have permitted that. What Mori opposed was the imposition of any official creed upon the schools.

The conflict over principle came to a head in Mori's confrontation with two court councilors (*kyūchū komonkan*): with Motoda Eifu, who had very specific ideas about what the definitive national faith should be, and with Nishimura Shigeki, who had disturbing suggestions for the administrative and instructional reform of moral education (*tokuiku*). Upon appointment as minister in 1885, Mori had acted quickly to remove Nishimura from his strategic position as head of the ministry's compilation bureau, replacing him with Izawa Shūji, a young official who had just returned from the Bridgewater Normal School in Massachusetts full of enthusiasm for the theories of Pestalozzi and J. Johonot.[134] Personal relations between Mori and his erstwhile Meirokusha colleague, however, remained cordial. In 1886 Mori asked Nishimura to accept the presidency of the imperial university and assist him with his wide-ranging reforms of that institution—an offer which Nishimura declined out of a feeling that there probably were too many points

---

132. *Zenshū* I, 549, SPM : 22 June 1887 : "Fukushimaken Gijidō."
133. Kaigo Tokiomi, *Kyōiku chokugo seiritsushi no kenkyū* (Tokyo, 1965), p. 385.
134. Horimatsu, *Kyōikushi,* p. 93, 97.

on which he and his minister would never agree. In 1887, too, Mori showed a keen appreciation of Nishimura's privately circulated tract, *Nihon dōtokuron* (On Japanese morality), which openly attacked the government-sponsored craze for ballroom dancing and other Western fads and fashions and lamented the decline of traditional virtues. Mori even went so far as to recommend publication of the treatise for use as a reference text in the middle schools and university, and when Itō flew into a rage over what he considered Nishimura's attack on his own administration, Mori did his best to pacify the prime minister while persuading Nishimura to soften the language of his tract sufficiently to permit its publication.

Nihon dōtokuron had presented, in fact, a reasonably argued, well-balanced appraisal of the relative strengths and weaknesses of East Asian and Western morality, and this incident suggests that Mori was as ready to entertain serious discussion of the sounder virtues of the past as he was willing to have the more superficial aspects of Westernization criticized. During the same year, however, Mori adamantly quashed a proposal by Nishimura to establish a definitive moral code through the promulgation of an imperial rescript patterned after the "Sacred Edicts" of the two Ch'ing emperors K'ang-hsi and Yung-cheng and to entrust the preparation of appropriate *shūshin* texts to a committee of scholars reporting directly to the emperor. Implicit also in the proposal was Nishimura's well-known desire to see the responsibility for moral education transferred from the ministry of education to the imperial household. Nishimura had received the backing, successively, of his fellow councilors Soejima Taneomi, Sasaki Takayuki, and Sano Tsunetami; of Sanjō Sanetomi (the privy seal); and of Imperial Household Minister Hijikata Hisamoto, who took the idea to Mori.

Mori told Hijikata that he would sooner resign than consider their suggestion and reacted with such indignation that no one in Nishimura's circle could muster the courage to approach him again on the subject. It was not until February 1889, after Mori's death, that Nishimura resubmitted his proposal, this time in a more elaborate form calling for the establishment of an imperially sponsored Institute for the Clarification of Ethics (Meirin'in), to be composed of leading scholars who not only would write the *shūshin* texts but would also supervise moral education throughout the school system. We have no record as to which element of Nishimura's concept angered Mori the most. But any suggestion for court supervision would have represented a massive raid on Monbushō authority; the idea of a morally definitive imperial edict was at odds with Mori's secularist philosophy; and the texts which Nishimura had in mind were clearly out of line with Mori's known *shūshin* policy.[135]

Mori did make some effort, however, to meet the popular criticism that education since 1872 had neglected moral training, and commissioned Nōsei Sakae to prepare under his own direction a primer on ethics, which was published by the ministry in March 1888 under the title *Rinrisho* (Ethics textbook).[136] This primer was intended, however, only for use in the graduating classes of the Ordinary Middle and Ordinary Normal schools, as a guide simply to the most basic principles or "common-sense ethics" as Mori was accustomed to describe them in English.[137] The preface opens by stating: "The sole purpose of teaching ethics (*rinri*) according to this textbook, is to furnish [the student] a standard for judging right and wrong in conduct arising from the attitudes which individuals hold toward one another."[138] The primer, it is further explained, is concerned neither with attitudes toward "things" (*mono*) nor with morality (*dōtoku*). Ethics and morality are related to each other as are fundamental principles (*genri*) to the (i.e., corollary) rules (*hōsoku*) deducible from them. The moral teaching of the young, the instilling of the sense of right and wrong "in the heart of man" by concrete illustrations and detailed explanations is left entirely to the discretion and ingenuity of the teachers trained according to this manual.

The rather abstruse, philosophical nature of the *Rinrisho* (much of the terminology of which had to be glossed in English) is suggested by the table of contents:

1. *General Theory*
2. *Purposes*
3. *Sources of Action:* (a) physical appetite; (b) desire; (c) emotion; (d) association; (e) habit.
4. *Will:* (a) meaning of "the will"; (b) involuntary actions; (c) relation of the will to other faculties; (d) proper application of the will; (e) freedom of the will.

135. Nishimura Shigeki, *Ōji roku* (Tokyo, 1905), pp. 193–198; Kaigo, *Kyōiku chokugo*, pp. 375–377; Kōsaka Masaaki, *Japanese Thought in the Meiji Era*, tr. David Abosch (Tokyo, 1958), pp. 122–127.

136. Ibid., p. 195. The complete text of Monbushō, *Rinrisho* (Ethics textbook), prepared by Nōsei Sakae under the direction of Mori Arinori, 1888, may be found in *Zenshū* I, 419–454. There is a lengthy English-language review in JWM, 29 June 1889.

137. JWM, 29 June 1889.

138. From the *Rinrisho*, in *Zenshū* I, 419.

5. *Standard of Conduct:* (a) meaning of "standard"; (b) the Cooperation of Self and Other: (i) social aspect, (ii) rational aspect, (iii) emotional aspect.[139]

The first four chapters present theoretical justification for the standard of conduct which is the real point of the book. "The Cooperation of Self and Other" was Mori's own English translation of *jitaheiritsu*—written with the characters "self-other-equal-standing"—which he also himself had coined. The *Japan Weekly Mail* in a lengthy review of the primer on 29 June 1889 suggested "coequality" or "coordination" as a more exact equivalent for *heiritsu,* but Mori's "cooperation" comes closer to the practical intention of his standard, which was no more than a simple call for mutual respect and assistance among free-standing equals: a Meiji bureaucrat's version, so to speak, of the Golden Rule. At the theoretical level, of course, in its assumption of a stark horizontality of interpersonal relations, *jitaheiritsu* cut mercilessly across the whole vertical, hierarchical structure not only of Confucian ethics but of actual Japanese social relations as well. Since the textbook by its own admission did not undertake to define the individual's relationship to "things" (including presumably society at large, and the state), *jitaheiritsu* afforded less than a complete concept of the individual. But as a guide to interpersonal relations it expanded on Mori's long-standing devotion to *jōri* and represented perhaps the most profoundly "Western" concept developed by him.[140] Nōsei Sakae, writing in 1890 in his own *Tokuiku chinteiron* (On the suppression of moral education), recalled Mori's viewpoint: "[He thought it] silly to preach the doctrines of Mencius and Confucius in today's world; religion had no place in education proper; and as for philosophy, no matter which school one adopted, there was always a counterargument. Therefore, relying neither on religion nor on philosophy, he took a broad look at human society and perceived that there would be nothing but strife if men were to work at cross-purposes, whereas if everyone were to work together in mutual support one of another, all would be peace and harmony. And he accordingly produced his concept of *jitaheiritsu.*"[141]

139. Ibid., I, 419.
140. Kaigo Tokiomi, in *Kyōiku chokugo,* p. 387, has placed Mori's *jitaheiritsu* on the same level as Fukuzawa's concept of *jishu dokuritsu* (independence and self-help) as a new moral and ethical rubric, breaking completely with the old Confucian order, and suitable for a new, modern society.
141. OTM, p. 136, quoting Nōsei Sakae, *Tokuiku chinteiron* (Tokyo, 1890).

The philosophical argument of the primer revolves around the relationship of the ego and non-ego, of egoism and altruism, and in so doing practically gives away the source of its inspiration. The *Japan Weekly Mail* review noted: "Careful readers of Mr. SPENCER's Data of Ethics will remember how clearly he shows that pure egoism and pure altruism are alike illegitimate . . . that a compromise is the only practicable course. Viscount MORI was an intimate friend and great admirer of HERBERT SPENCER, and we have good authority for stating that the Standard of Ethics adopted by the late Minister was intended to be in entire accordance with Spencerian principles."[142] This review was clearly based on inside information from the Monbushō, and Mori's *jitaheiritsu* indeed comprises Spencer's two central ethical norms of "justice" ("in which every member [of society] achieves his ends without preventing others from achieving theirs") and of "beneficence" ("in which members give mutual help in the achievement of ends").[143] Mori had at last, it seems, found his simple and secular social ethic, his "reliable creed" for "human relations" first alluded to in the back pages of his "Bibō daini" in 1871 or 1872.

Mori at no time went into detail as to the method or content of the moral instruction to be developed by teachers under the guiding ethical rubric of *jitaheiritsu*, but his prescription for oral instruction and his banning of the Confucian-oriented texts which had gradually come into use from the early 1880's reversed the Confucianizing countertrend in the *shūshin* courses. The ministry's regulations for the primary school curriculum (25 May 1866) specified with respect to *shūshin*: "In the primary schools, instructors should teach their pupils the conventional manners and speak to them, in a suitable and easily comprehensible fashion, of the commendable words and deeds of great men past and present, both Japanese and foreign. Teachers should themselves be models of speech and conduct and make every effort to educate children to that standard."[144] In speeches before primary school teachers throughout Kyushu in early 1887 Mori had characterized the *Analects* as "more of a political treatise than a *shūshin* text," described the books put out by the ministry's own Compilation Bureau under Nishimura Shigeki as inappropriate for the growing child from the standpoint of both substance and level of difficulty, and cautioned the teachers that

142. JWM, 29 June 1889.

143. As summarized in Frank Thilly, *A History of Philosophy* (New York, 1914), p. 546.

144. Monbushō Ordinance no. 8, 25 May 1886, quoted in Kaigo, *Kyōiku chokugo*, p. 381.

"None of the current *shūshin* texts is without serious flaws."[145] In May of that same year Mori stopped the use of written texts in *shūshin* courses entirely,[146] and from 1887 through 1892 the publication of *shūshin* texts dwindled to a mere trickle.[147]

The ultranationalistic *shūshin* texts of pre-1945 notoriety, far from owing their origin to Mori, first made their appearance on a wide scale during the opening decade of the twentieth century following the establishment of a general system of state-prescribed textbooks in 1904 and important revisions in content carried out under the influence of Hozumi Yatsuka during 1908–1911.[148]

How badly the Confucianizing party had been hit by Mori's policy, and how deeply they regarded him as their enemy, was testified to by the steady stream of reproaches from Motoda Eifu. In 1886 Motoda complained directly to the emperor, for instance, that "with the Imperial authorization of *Yōgaku kōyō* [Essentials of learning for the young; 1882] the evils of American-style education were gradually being corrected, and the nation was turning once again to the ideals of loyalty and patriotism . . . but since year before last the Western tendency has reemerged and today the reversion to Western studies is complete. Persons concerned with these matters all fear that Chinese and Japanese Learning are on the verge of extinction."[149] And in 1888 Motoda wrote of the *Rinrisho* that although it "deals broadly with social ethics and is very clever in its fine distinctions between will and action," it failed entirely to mention the ethical relationship between sovereign and subject which should have headed the list.[150]

Motoda's own purposes, and his deepest suspicions of Mori, were best revealed however in a memorandum addressed to Mori sometime during 1887, picking up the threads of a recent discussion with the education minister at the court. Mori, it seems, had argued during their meeting that the imperial house, historically,

---

145. *Zenshū* I, 509, SPM : 1887 : "Kyūshū kakuken/shōgakkō."
146. Kaigo, *Kyōiku chokugo*, p. 73; Kishii Isao in Kaigo et al., "Mori Arinori no shisō to kyōiku seisaku," p. 136; Yoshida Kumaji and Kaigo Tokiomi, *Kyōiku chokugo kanpatsu izen ni okeru shōgakkō shūshin kyōju no hensen* (Tokyo, 1934), p. 73.
147. Kaigo, *Kyōiku chokugo*, p. 381.
148. Kōsaka, *Japanese Thought*, pp. 385, 388.
149. Motoda Eifu, "Seiyuki" (Record of counsel to the throne), dated 5 Nov. 1886, in Kaigo, *Motoda Eifu*, p. 187.
150. Motoda Eifu, "Rinri kyōkasho ni tsuki ikensho" (Written opinion on the ethics textbook), undated but probably 1888, in Kaigo, *Motoda Eifu*, p. 210.

had had little to do with education; that old-fashioned Confucianists were still the bane of the Japanese school system; and that *chūkun* (loyalty) and *aikoku* (patriotism) could never be instilled by words alone, but only through practice. He had agreed with Motoda's point that training of the intellect had been unduly favored at the expense of the other human faculties, but expressed his intention to reestablish the balance by means of physical, rather than moral, education.

Motoda in his memorandum reminds Mori of the emperor's long-standing concern over the decline of *chūkun* and *aikoku*, attributes this loss to the continued sway of Western-style education with its overemphasis on intellect, and expresses his fears that Mori will abandon the attempt of his recent predecessors to reverse the trend. Motoda protests that he is not a Confucianist of the literary, Sinophile school; that the worst evils of the old Confucianism—obscurantism and bookworming—long since have been rooted out by the new education; and that the Confucianism he wishes to foster is not a religious faith in the sense of Buddhism or Christianity, but a moral code calculated to promote family and national loyalties in the context of contemporary Japan. Motoda closes by questioning Mori's real intentions with regard to the school system. He recalls what his own former tutor, Yokoi Shōnan, once told him of Mori's early religious experience in the Harris community, reminds Mori that many Japanese consider him to be a believer in Christ, and raises doubts as to whether an education minister imbued with the Christian spirit can be counted on to promote the desired Confucian code.

Mori ignored Motoda's reproaches, as did his patron Itō, and the conflict here was in some respects an extension of the confrontation, in 1879, between Motoda and Itō. The ideological cleavage in 1887 was even greater, and Motoda's memorandum shows how fixed in his own mind were the images of Mori as "Christian" and of his educational policies as "American." But again, as in 1879, there was a significant degree of political agreement—this time on the desirability of *chūkun* and *aikoku*—obscured as before by the bitter quarrel over means.[151]

151. Motoda Eifu, "Mori bunsō ni taisuru kyōiku ikensho" (Written opinion on education, addressed to Education Minister Mori), 1887, in Kaigo, *Motoda Eifu,* pp. 207–209; Kaigo, *Kyōiku chokugo,* pp. 393–397; OTM, pp. 104–105; Miyahara Seiichi, *Nihon gendaishi taikei: kyōikushi* (Tokyo, 1963), p. 77. Takagi Yasaka, son of Kanda Naibu and grandson of Kanda Kōhei, told the author in 1967 that Uchimura Kanzō once remarked to him personally that Mori had been "the finest Minister of Education

The later development of *shūshin* texts was inconceivable, of course, apart from the "Kyōiku chokugo," or Imperial Rescript on Education of 30 October 1890. Because of the swiftness with which it followed upon Mori's reign at the Monbushō, the Education Rescript—even more than ultranationalistic *shūshin*—has been misunderstood as the realization, posthumously, of Mori's plans. As a matter of fact, it was at the annual prefectural governors' conference in Tokyo in February 1890, a full year after Mori's assassination, that the government for the first time took under serious consideration the call for a definitive imperial pronouncement on moral education. The initial push came from the governors themselves, who since 1888 had been importuning the ministry of education for greater attention to moral training only to find themselves blocked by what Governor Ishii Shōichiro of Iwate took to be the obstinacy of a claque of American-trained officials that had gathered around Minister Mori.[152]

Pressed for an explanation of Monbushō policy, Mori's successor (once removed), Enomoto Takeaki (March 1889–May 1890), announced to the assembled governors at the ministry on 26 February 1890 that moral education would henceforth take Confucianism as its foundation. The then minister of the interior, Yamagata Aritomo, who had just supervised the establishment in 1889 of the new local government system and had convened the governors' conference in the first instance, thought the matter sufficiently important to be taken out of the Monbushō and placed before the cabinet. The Meiji emperor, who had been attending the cabinet meetings, and who had long since come to share Motoda's views, took an immediate interest in the matter, and Enomoto was placed under instructions to compile an official statement on moral education. When Yamagata became prime minister in May 1890 he replaced Enomoto at the Monbushō with his own confidant, Yoshikawa Akimasa, during whose tenure (May 1890–June 1891) the Imperial Rescript on Education finally was prepared.[153] As a political device, Umetani Noboru has seen the rescript as the handiwork above all of Yamagata, with Inoue Kowashi, assisted by Motoda, responsible for the drafting and the general concept.

Japan ever had." Whether the Christians themselves looked upon him as one of their number or not, it is clear that they regarded him, as Niijima had regarded him, as a sympathetic friend.

152. Horimatsu, *Kyōikushi*, pp. 164–165.

153. Ibid., pp. 164–165; Umetani Noboru, "Kyōiku chokugo seiritsu no rekishiteki haikei," in Sakata Yoshio, ed., *Meiji zenpanki no nashonarizumu* (Tokyo, 1958), pp. 103–106.

Writing in 1944, Ōkubo Toshiaki suggested that "although the Rescript came after his death, we may suppose that Mori, had he been alive at the time, would have given it a sincere and reverent reading.[154] Postwar scholarship however suggests a dramatically different interpretation. Kaigo Tokiomi has viewed the rescript as an emphatic reaction to Mori's policy on moral education and *shūshin* texts, as an effort to fill the vacuum and to still the clamorous public debate which had only been exacerbated by Mori's refusal to develop a more pronounced ideological program. Kaigo raises the ironic possibility, at least, that had Mori not been quite so successful in reversing the traditionalist countertrend of the early 1880's, the rescript in its historically familiar form might never have been issued. Mori's probable attitude toward the idea of an education rescript was suggested by his highly negative reaction to Nishimura's proposals, which included the concept of a "Sacred Edict." And Kaigo goes so far as to surmise that had Mori still held the ministerial chair in 1890, the complaints of the governors probably would have gone no further than a formal protest.[155]

Hayashi Takeji, indeed, has viewed much of the Monbushō's policy after 1889 as the negation rather than the extension of Mori's ideals not only of *jitaheiritsu* but of administrative decentralization as well and has identified three important documents of 1890–1891 as the point of no return: (1) the Imperial Rescript on Education, which defined, in effect, the "national faith" or orthodoxy; (2) the Shōgakkōrei (Primary School Ordinance), also of October 1890, which was drafted by the *kokugaku* scholar Egi Kazuyuki, and which reaffirmed the importance of moral education in the primary schools; and (3) Education Minister Ōki Takato's "Gakuji setsumeisho" (Explanation of school matters) of November 1891, which specifically adopted the rescript as the basis of elementary school *shūshin* courses, and which reasserted the full control of the ministry over the purposes and methods of education, and over teaching regulations, textbooks, teachers, and students.[156]

154. OTM, p. 134.
155. Kaigo, *Kyōiku chokugo,* pp. 377, 383, 397. I am also indebted to Professor Kaigo (Emeritus, Tokyo University) for suggesting, in the course of a discussion in October 1966, that Mori's policies—even had he lived—would have depended on the protection of Itō, and that with the accession to the prime ministership of Yamagata, Mori in all probability would have lost his post, and something similar to the education rescript would have been drawn up anyway.
156. Hayashi, "Mori Arinori to nashonarizumu," p. 86; Hayashi, "Kyōshokukan no rekishiteki haikei," pt. 1, p. 3; Hayashi Takeji, "Meiji

What this meant after 1890 was the increasingly direct involvement of the central ministry, down to the lowest level, in what we have called the instructional coordinate of education. Mori's solicitude for freedom of thought precluded any crude ideological tinkering with textbooks, curricular content, or formal pedagogical theory. These he was inclined to leave well enough alone; and since what he left well enough alone was Japan's heritage of the 1870's—modern, Western-oriented subject matter and a teaching profession still largely inspired by Oswego—Motoda was less than accurate in speaking of the re-westernization of education; what Mori had accomplished rather was the defeat of the first effort at Confucianization. Mori's plans for modest decentralization, and his real motives for textbook authorization, confirm the impression that he probably would have been less than satisfied, had he lived, with the Monbushō's growing intrusion into instructional matters.

KEIZAISHUGI:
ECONOMIC RATIONALISM

If Mori's ethical individualism as exemplified by *jitaheiritsu* provides one important qualification of his statism, another was provided by his economic rationalism or *keizaishugi* (economy principle). Granted, Mori's economy-mindedness was not in itself an affirmation of individualism or democracy or any other explicitly antistatist viewpoint; but as an operational principle it often had much the same effect. *Keizaishugi,* Mori time and again explained, "has a meaning broader than the usual sense of 'economy.' "[157] He might, indeed, as easily have used the terms "efficiency" or "quality," for what he had in mind was not saving money so much as getting one's money's worth. And this he allowed to be the most important procedural principle of his educational administration: "The purpose of our school ordinances is, in one word, to produce scholars and educated persons in response to the national requirement; and the method of production must accord entirely with the economy principle. By 'economy principle' I mean that every outlay of time or labor in the educational enterprise should always be examined to determine whether the final result fully measures up to the anticipated objective; if that objective has been attained,

---

kyōiku no shuppatsu to zasetsu: Mori Arinori o chūshin to shite," *Ushio,* spring 1967 (special number), p. 103.

157. *Zenshū* I, 581, SPM : 15 Nov. 1887 : "Wakayamaken Jinjō Shihangakkō."

we may say that the economy principle has been satisfied . . . it is not necessarily a matter of greater or lesser sums of money."[158]

In terms of the normative coordinate of our paradigm, the purpose of education remains the service of the state. As noted in the previous chapter, however, the administrative and the instructional coordinates have certain independent imperatives of their own, such as operational efficiency or quality control, and it was in these two areas—respectively represented by the issues of decentralization and textbook authorization—that Mori's *keizaishugi* most clearly came into play. The finality with which Mori fixed the structural outlines of the Japanese school system has often led observers to assume that the tight centralization and heavy-handed administrative interventionism of the ministry from the 1890's onward were, like the *shūshin* texts and the imperial rescript itself, part of Mori's original intention. As a matter of fact, Mori in the last year of his life was very busy laying plans for a significant abdication to prefectural and local authorities of control over the elementary, Ordinary Middle, and Ordinary Normal Schools, that is to say, over all institutions not under the direct supervision of the ministry.

The new system of local government announced in April 1888 was scheduled to come into full effect on 1 April 1889, and in the course of a tour of northern Honshu in the fall of 1888 and again in a meeting with prefectural educational officials in Tokyo six days before his assassination, Mori announced plans to establish Educational Societies (*kyōikukai*) at the prefectural and subprefectural levels to achieve the "self-government" (*jiri*) promised by the new *shichōson* (city-town-village) system. Mori told officials in northern Honshu in October 1888: "Self-government means that all units of the nation from individual citizens up through the prefectures discharge their respective responsibilities and contribute to the gradual attainment of our nation's true independence . . . So long as individuals merely watch and criticize the actions of others while neglecting their own duties, or as long as they show concern only over national or prefectural affairs while neglecting their tasks at the town and village level, so long will it be difficult to realize fully the system of self-government."[159]

Mori then announced that he hoped to see his *kyōikukai* established at all levels from village to prefecture to serve as advisory councils to the respective local government heads. He felt that the virtually total control by governors and county or ward heads over

158. *Zenshū* I, 545, SPM : 22 June 1887 : "Fukushimaken Gijidō."
159. *Zenshū* I, 647, SPM : fall 1888 : "Ōu rokken gakuji junshi."

appointments of Ordinary Normal and Ordinary Middle School directors and staff, for instance, was a serious obstacle to "self-government in education" (*kyōiku jiri*), and suggested that the education societies be given a veto power over all appointments of school directors, and that they be permitted to review and initiate proposals in the area of school regulations and to devise means for improving rates of attendance. Property holders over twenty-five years of age, licensed teachers, and persons who had made significant contributions financially or otherwise to local education, would be eligible for election to the societies. One gathers that Mori envisioned each *kyōikukai* as having a rather broad and numerous membership, out of which a special committee of five to ten members would be selected to function as an advisory council. The societies, Mori suggested, would at first be set up under private initiative; then, as and if they proved their effectiveness, quasi-official powers gradually would be transferred to them. The ministry would publish guidelines for their establishment which, however, might be undertaken without any ministerial order.[160]

In a speech before journalists, prefectural assemblymen, and educators in Tokyo in September 1888, Mori had made a somewhat similar proposal, in which he explained that the hierarchy of administrative chiefs, from governor down to mayor, were not infallible in educational matters, and that prefectural assembly members were not experts either.[161] His scheme for a parallel tier of education societies with important advisory—and veto—powers was a close conceptual ally of his scheme of functional representation put forward in *Representative System*. Mori on occasion himself sought the advice of the Dai Nihon Kyōikukai (Japan Education Association), the privately organized national teachers' organization,[162] and that he had also given thought to an advisory council at the ministerial level was suggested by a newspaper report in 1887 to the effect that: "the government contemplates establishing an Educational Committee, the members to be elected from among senators, teachers in the University, judges . . . and teachers in private schools, with the object of discussing some important subjects in connection with educational matters."[163]

Perhaps more significant than any specific institutional device, however, was Mori's general attitude toward decentralization. He

---

160. Ibid., 648–649.
161. *Zenshū* I, 632, SPM : 25 Sept. 1888 : "Tōkyōfu Shōgakkōchō Fukaigiin."
162. Discussion with Hayashi Takeji, Sendai, August 1966.
163. JWM, 22 Jan. 1887.

was in such earnest with his expectations for "educational self-government" that on 5 February 1889 he called in to the ministry, to press home his point, the *fuken gakumukachō,* or heads of the educational affairs sections of the prefectural governments, from all over Japan. Explaining that they were more knowledgeable on local conditions than the ministry or its central inspectorate could ever hope to be, and exhorting them to work closely with city, town, and village authorities, Mori insisted: "From now on I would ask you to stop thinking, 'the Minister would like this,' or, 'the Minister would approve of that.' Hereafter I would like you to consult first of all, as much as possible, the opinion of people directly involved in local affairs. The Minister will have his say in due course, and will try to say as little as possible. In other words, you should try to accomplish your business without having to announce that, 'this is the Ministry's opinion,' or, 'this is the Ministry's policy.' "[164]

These tentative steps toward decentralization were all aborted by the firm centralizing hand of Mori's successors, particularly that of Ōki Takato with his "Gakuji setsumeisho" of 1891. One gets the impression, nevertheless, that in terms of motivations Mori's interest in decentralization stems primarily from his long-standing concern for professional expertise and efficiency, with only the most incidental overtones of political democracy. He makes much of the spirit of *jiri,* but this seems to be less an end in itself than just one more means of promoting national independence.[165] For, having just explained the educational societies to the *fuken gakumukachō,* Mori then proceeded at once to what was perhaps the most undemocratic statement of his entire career, with a typical sequence about education being for the state, and the desirability of making the state the "central idol," and ending with a warning to the effect that, "persons with a shallow concept of such a state [as ours] simply cannot be tolerated within that state."[166] Mori's remarks to the *fuken gakumukachō* regarding the *kan'ika* or Simplified Primary Course were especially revealing. Since these were to be financed wholly by local taxation, it was particularly important to secure value for money. This could be done only by

164. *Zenshū* I, 673, SPM : 5 Feb. 1889 : "Fuken gakumukachō ni taisuru enzetsu" (Speech to the heads of the Educational Affairs Sections of the prefectural governments). Delivered at the Monbushō.
165. This interpretation is most strongly suggested by Mori's language in *Zenshū* I, 629ff., SPM : 25 Sept. 1888 : "Tōkyōfu Shōgakkōchō Fukaigiin."
166. *Zenshū* I, 674, SPM : 5 Feb. 1889 : "Fuken gakumukachō ni taisuru enzetsu."

adjusting each individual *kan'ika* course to the conditions of its locality; and in evaluating those conditions the ministry would have to rely entirely on the judgment of the *fuken gakumukachō*. Mori himself, however, had in 1887 already confessed his basic motivation: "Let me say a word about philosophies of education. There are quite a variety of them around, with slogans such as 'laissez faire' or 'interventionism.' But if you ask me what my philosophy right now is, I would at once reply: 'the economy-principle [*keizaishugi*].' "[167] It was likewise the quest for efficiency, not for thought control, which led to the "Kyōkayō tosho kentei jōrei" (Educational textbook authorization ordinance) of 10 May 1887. This required the ministry's authorization (*kentei*) for textbooks used in the primary and Ordinary Middle Schools. Texts for the normal schools were to be directly prescribed. Karasawa Tomitarō, in *Kyōkasho no Rekishi* (A history of textbooks) has viewed Mori's action as a deliberate blow at the Popular Rights Movement, and as the first step toward the state prescription (*kokutei*) of all texts throughout the system from 1904 onward.[168] An entirely different interpretation, however, is possible.

One of Mori's first acts as minister, as has been mentioned, was to overhaul the compilation bureau, replace Nishimura Shigeki with his own man, Izawa Shūji, and throw out the Confucian *shūshin* primers which, in an indirect way, at least, really had been directed at the political opposition. Mori's revised regulations for textbook compilation both inside and outside the ministry show him concerned with the rapid production of high-quality, low-cost textbooks, rather than with ideological content. Mori wanted to see primary and normal school students eventually provided with texts either free for the keeping or on free loan. Appropriate manuscripts were to be prepared by the compilation bureau, or solicited from the private sector along general ministry guidelines—in the drawing up of which, however, the opinion of private scholars and writers was to be widely consulted. Since public funds were involved, cost was a major factor governing the final selection of a manuscript. Apart from that, "authorization" would depend on the following three points: impartiality, accuracy, and speed of production.[169]

Izawa's biography describes the problem which the prefectural governments (responsible for textbook selection) had with private

---

167. *Zenshū* I, 536, SPM : 21 June 1887 : "Miyagi Kenchō."
168. Karasawa, *Kyōkasho no rekishi*, pp. 148, 191–192.
169. OTM, 175; Inagaki Tadahiko in Kaigo et. al., "Mori Arinori no shisō to kyōiku seisaku," pp. 124–126.

publishers, who through their monopoly of the textbook trade were in a position to engage writers, set quality standards, and fix prices not in accordance with educational need but purely on the profit principle. The ministry estimated it could distribute its own texts, at cost, for one-third of the publishers' price.[170] Complaints against Mori's measures were indeed raised not by the political opposition but by publishers and writers, many of whom had been profiting from the production of expensive, inferior, and redundant school texts.[171] As with decentralization, however, it was Ōki Takato who shifted ministerial policy away from the direction and the spirit which Mori had given it. Plans for free textbooks were dropped, and in December 1891 fresh regulations issued for strict control by the ministry over the content of *shūshin* texts.[172]

THE HISTORICAL AND COMPARATIVE PERSPECTIVE

Taken as the totality of institutions, ideas, and personalities involved in it, education is a diffuse, pervasive, slow-moving, and on the whole thoroughly undramatic process. Even education in the narrower, more tangible, sense of a national school system lacks the clear outlines for instance of the political process, in which the confrontation of personalities and ideas, as expressed in organized parties or in the formal vote, is far more explicit and direct. Systematic thought, in the form of educational philosophy or pedagogical theory for instance, plays only a limited role in an institution the development of which is more likely to be determined by extrinsic pressures of a sociological, political, or—as we have so notably seen in the case of Mori—economic nature.

It is therefore particularly difficult to establish with any precision the influence or impact of any one man's ideas or policies on the educational picture as a whole. The history of education, indeed, reveals important discontinuities. The "great educators," as they often appear in education history textbooks—Pestalozzi, Froebel, Herbart, Dewey—made their impact almost exclusively at the level of instruction. System-builders like Napoleon or Horace Mann, on the other hand, influenced administration and structure (pretty much to the exclusion of instruction), or, like Humboldt

---

170. Ko Izawa Sensei Kinen Jigyō Kai, ed., *Rakuseki Izawa Shūji sensei* (Tokyo, 1919), pp. 99–101.
171. JWM, 31 July 1886, 19 May 1888.
172. Inagaki Tadahiko in Kaigo et. al., "Mori Arinori no shisō to kyōiku seisaku," p. 26.

with the University of Berlin, left their mark on one particular part of the structure. Still others, like Rousseau or Jefferson or Matthew Arnold or Fukuzawa—general philosophers rather than pedagogical theorists or educational bureaucrats—exercised a profound if indirect influence in the realm of educational values and purposes. Although Mori's "influence" is most safely left at those half dozen points already covered, the reactionism and the German orientation with which posterity for the most part has charged him require that his career at the Monbushō be placed both in the historical perspective of modern Japanese education and in the comparative perspective of world education in the late nineteenth century. And in so doing, we would do well to bear in mind this highly differentiated pattern of educational influences and to distinguish Mori's contribution in terms of our four analytical coordinates.

At the level of administration, Mori left virtually no lasting mark whatsoever. Japan, with the blessing of her earliest American advisers, already had opted for a highly centralized pattern for controlling education which over the years would prove impervious to any efforts at fundamental revision, whether those of Tanaka Fujimaro and his abortive school boards of 1879, or those of the American occupation and its elective local boards, which were downgraded to an appointive status under the new education law of 1956.[173] Mori's educational societies, had he lived to realize them, would have represented a serious challenge—if not in actual powers then certainly in spirit—to the prevailing practice. Even though Mori's motives in this area seem to have been those of efficiency rather than of political democracy, his scheme represented in outlook a throwback to the 1870's, when central intervention was hopefully viewed as a catalyzer for local initiative, and when educational decisions rested more in the hands of professional experts, and less in those of political authorities, than was the case after 1880. Mori's scheme would have returned to strictly educational circles some of the powers surrendered to the prefectural governors by the Kaisei kyōikurei. Not only, however, did his societies fail to get off the drafting table; with Mori's death the fact that he had ever thought of them was quickly forgotten, and his very active and well-publicized intervention in the university, Higher Normal School and Higher Middle Schools, which were all under direct ministerial control to begin with, led later observers erroneously to lump Mori together with outspoken centralizers like Kōno Togama or Ōki Takato who preceded or followed him. As a matter of fact, Mori's successor, Enomoto Takeaki

173. Matsumoto and Suzuki, *Genten*, p. 348.

(March 1889–May 1890), was greeted with hopes that the new minister would at last get around to giving elementary education the attention due it.[174] The impression of "comparative neglect" of the primary schools was no doubt chiefly created by Mori's highly unpopular reliance on *jugyōryō* as his chief financing principle. This too was short-lived, as Japan progressed toward relatively quick achievement of "free" (i.e., tax-supported), compulsory and universal primary education.

The economic necessity underlying *jugyōryō* and strapping Mori's well-recorded and longstanding interest in the promotion of popular education likewise prevented him from adding any new types of schools in women's or technical-vocational education, two areas of particular personal interest to him. It only points out the obvious to say that what Mori wanted to do and what he actually did are two different matters, but we certainly have here an excellent example of a discrepancy between educational philosophy and educational policy, and a cogent reminder to the effect that it is not necessarily safe to deduce or reconstruct the former from the latter.

As a matter of fact, Mori added very little to the existing classification of Japanese schools. The bifurcation of the primary and secondary courses, even the reorganization of the university, represented in effect a reshuffling of elements already on hand. The one new institution which may truly be described as Mori's unique and original creation was the Kōtōgakko (Mori's "Higher Middle School"), one of the most distinctive features of Japan's prewar educational system. The very epitome of Mori's elitist approach, this was also the one institution which would disappear, with symbolic appropriateness, almost without a trace in the educational reforms of the postwar period.

Mori's great impact at the structural level lay rather in redefining the scope of educational opportunity, in rearticulating the component parts of the system, in subtracting from, if anything, rather than adding to its compass. As shown by the experience of nations modernizing more recently than Japan, widespread educational opportunity beyond the elementary level is simply not to be had in the earlier stages of economic development; and the dual track, already emerging before Mori's time, was perhaps inevitable. But in this instance Mori was motivated not only by economic considerations but also by an elitist social philosophy. Mori's elite, it is true, was strictly one of talent, and this very modern and rational aspect of Japanese education was certainly one of his more impor-

174. JWM, 11 May 1889, reporting on the vernacular press.

tant and more fortunate legacies to posterity. But he defined his elite very narrowly and went very much out of his way to set up distinctions between research and applied learning, between the primary and secondary and between the lower and higher secondary levels, and finally between the government and private sectors. The result was that Japan, once she did reach a stage economically and socially at which she could have afforded and profitably utilized a more flexible system, found herself unnecessarily burdened with a tightly constricted, rigidly hierarchical, privilege-ridden educational structure. Mori's ghost still strides the Japanese campus eighty years later, in the increasingly violent struggle for university reform.

Mori's reputation as regards the instructional level, however, has been, as I have suggested, less than fair to him. His policies on textbook authorization and *shūshin*, and his connection (virtually none, as it turns out) with the education rescript, have been greatly misunderstood and confused with what came later, much of it in conscious reaction against Mori. By suspending the use of the new Confucian-oriented *shūshin* texts, Mori checked the traditionalist forces where they briefly had succeeded in establishing a beachhead, namely in the curriculum. His own conservatism lay not in traditionalism but in statism, yet even here he expected the proper attitude to be instilled by the personal example and homemade precepts, so to speak, of individual teachers, not by special courses in the curriculum or through specially prepared texts. The unusually high expectation he placed on his teachers led Mori, however, to reorganize the normal schools along an unnecessary and entirely inappropriate military model which in fact produced a type of teacher all too pliant in the hands of the forthcoming traditionalism, ultranationalism, and militarism.

Mori's anti-Confucian stance, together with his alternative formula of *jitaheiritsu,* derive basically from his long-standing concern with liberty of conscience and freedom of the mind. His militarized teacher training partakes of a moral fervor traceable in great part to his own training at Brocton and in the Gōjū, while his *keizaishugi* owes a great deal in inspiration to his own rationally-oriented, mathematically inclined mind. Nearly everything else in Mori's educational policy, however, fits more or less under the rubric of the supremacy of the state which was to dominate his very considerable impact on the basic values and specific purposes of Japanese education.

In its view of man, that is to say in its most fundamental philosophical orientation, Japanese education before Mori had been in a considerable state of flux, reflecting the general intellectual currents of the times. The preamble to the Gakusei set forth certain individualistic, egalitarian premises which held their own during the 1870's not because the preamble had the force or the intention of a definitive orthodoxy but because the utilitarianism of Mill and the laissez-faire of Spencer dominated not only professional educational circles but also the general philosophical climate of those years. The chief challenge to those premises, contained in Motoda's "Kyōgaku taishi" of 1879 and purporting to convey the sentiments of the emperor, likewise represented at the time no more than the opinion of one competing school. What Mori in effect did was to make official and rather final pronouncements of a statist nature, closing the ideological options which a less articulate minister might—unwittingly even—have left open. He managed to throw the philosophical balance of the school system from the individual to the collectivity and from a somewhat egalitarian to a specifically elitist ideal a full four years ahead of the education rescript, and even before the anti-Western reaction and the lively debate over a national religion in the late 1880's had gotten up full steam. The rescript when it did come said very little about the educational system as such, presenting rather an orthodoxy to be taught in the schools. That left Mori's statism, as expressed in his speeches and particularly in his ordinances, the chief ideological prop of the Monbushō down through World War II, much as Fukuzawa's *Gakumon no Susume* had provided a basic philosophical framework for the ministry during its first decade.

As regards the social dimension of knowledge, modern Japanese education from its very inception right down to the present day has placed a relatively higher valuation on functional information than generally has been the case in Europe or even in America. Or perhaps the real point is better made by saying that the Japanese have placed a relatively lower valuation on nonfunctional information. Even the charge of "ivory-tower" seclusion popularly directed at the state universities today has as its real target the elitist snobbery, rather than any academic escapism, in these institutions; and the Japanese since early Meiji have had nothing as remote from the living literary heritage as the Latin or Greek taught in the French *lycées,* the German *Gymnasien,* the British public schools, or some of the American private preparatory schools.[175] The Gakusei, like Fukuzawa's *Gakumon no Susume,*

---

175. The Chinese classics as taught in Japan up to 1945 were the approximate secondary-school equivalent not of the *Aeneid,* but of the King James version of the Bible: an ancient tale, couched in archaic language,

placed heavy emphasis on practical knowledge as indispensable for *risshin shusse,* or "making one's way in the world," and Mori's espousal of *ōyō gakumon* and of "practical" subjects in the middle schools simply reidentified the ultimate benefactor of all this functional information as the state rather than the individual and attempted to steer the politically ambitious away from "applied politics," so to speak, into careers that were both politically innocuous and of greater usefulness in the industrial and commercial development of the nation.

Respecting the social dimension, Mori's most tangible innovation was, rather, to reverse the priorities placed on cultivation of character and training of intellect in primary and secondary education. Pedagogy during the 1870's, under the inspiration of Pestalozzi and Oswego, had turned its attention almost exclusively to the problem of developing the young mind in the most effective manner. The almost total inattention to character-building was, as Hayashi Takeji has pointed out, a luxury afforded by the fact that the moral qualities were still represented, and conveyed, by the person of the teacher—himself educated in the pre-modern era—and therefore were largely taken for granted.[176] The intellectualistic orientation of contemporary Western pedagogy likewise rested on the assumption that moral training would be accomplished for the most part by the church or in the home. Although Mori expected character-building to be achieved chiefly through the physical and disciplinary regimen of *heishiki taisō,* his explicit downgrading of the three "R's" in favor of character-building provided—well in advance, it may again be noted—congenial soil for *shūshin* as it developed under the inspiration of the education rescript. The gradual philosophical reorientation of Japanese higher education away from Anglo-American empiricism and toward German idealism was, however, not, as we shall see, the intention of Mori, who himself remained very much the product of the former tradition.

Specific purposes, unlike basic values, in education are less beholden to the general intellectual climate and more amenable to change by energetic and articulate statesmen or educators; and it is here that Mori's hand was most evident. Although his "Gakusei yōryō"[177] mentioned the economic well-being of the individual, the foremost purpose of Mori's educational statism was to place the

---

yet somehow still familiar and part of everyday life. Classical Chinese was not nearly as foreign or "dead" a tongue as Latin and Greek have been for Western schoolchildren.

176. Hayashi, "Kyōshokukan no rekishiteki haikei," pt. 2, p. 4.
177. See note 54 above.

school system at the service of the economic growth and viability of the Japanese state. *Fukoku,* or national wealth, of course had never for a moment been absent from among the major purposes of education, but under the spirit of the Gakusei it had coexisted in an undefined and (one might have gathered) balanced relationship to the welfare of the individual. Mori's function here again was to delimit and to specify, and to place an explicit priority on *fukoku*. The creation of an elite of talent, another of Mori's specific purposes, had enormous consequences for the subsequent development of Japanese society. He did not, however, view the school system as the appropriate vehicle for the dissemination of any particular political viewpoint. However much his emphasis on the creation of emperor-centered national loyalties may in fact have played into the hands of specific political interests, his subjective model very probably remained the American, in which the public school system, while hypersensitive to any signs of party-political influence, had been deliberately used to foster the national consciousness, to turn young persons into good citizens and immigrants into good Americans. Unspoken in Mori's policy, of course, was the assumption that the nonparty or "transcendental" elements of the government, including his own ministry, could and would remain politically neutral.

It was in his opposition to the subordination of the school system to any religious or philosophical orthodoxy that Mori most appears as the heir (or revivifier, as Motoda had it) of the spirit of the 1870's, rather than as a harbinger of the 1890's. Even his statism (to the extent that it was indeed purely political and reserved to the individual a wide freedom of religious, philosophical, and moral choice in the private or nonpolitical realm), was at least as hostile to Confucian or Shintoist traditionalism as it was to Western liberalism. As mentioned in Chapter Nine, the political and cultural traditionalism of Motoda and the modernistic, rational statism of Itō had struck something of an unstable compromise in the early 1880's based on the convergence, during the heyday of the Popular Rights Movement, of their respective antipathies to the westernism of the school system and to political radicalism. It was Inoue Kowashi who in his five-point plan of 1881 had suggested to Itō the potential use of traditional studies in curbing the political opposition, and it was Inoue who with the education rescript would forge that tentative compromise into an indissoluble alliance. Perhaps Itō, with his own political preeminence securely established by mid-decade, felt himself in a position to sanction Mori's antitraditionalism, so close in spirit to what he himself had proclaimed in his "Kyōikugi" of 1879. Inoue, who had also drafted that document, was like Mori both a close confidant of Itō and a member of what posterity would call the *kaimei kanryō ha,* or "enlightened bureaucrat faction," of the Meiji government. They shared a very similar political view, even if taught by tutors as widely different as Hermann Roessler and Herbert Spencer. But Mori unlike Inoue Kowashi maintained to the end a deep suspicion of the traditionalist element and managed in effect to keep that eventual marriage of statism and traditionalism off balance during his half-decade at the Monbushō. With his death the *kaimei ha* lost the man who in cultural terms was beyond a doubt its most Western-oriented member.

Inoue, it may be recalled, had also urged upon Itō in 1881 the introduction of German studies, again with patently political motivations; and this brings us, finally, to the problem of the specific national orientation, if any, of Mori's westernism. A late-blossoming Germanism has been imputed to him not only by his biographers Kaimon Sanjin and Ōkubo Toshiaki.[178] A very recent and non-Japanese work, for instance, says of Mori's educational viewpoint: "In the early controversy over the educational system, he was usually on the side of American theory against the German . . . Eventually, however, he went over to the Germanist ideas and supported nationalistic tendencies in the developing educational system."[179] Not only were the alternatives of the educational (as opposed to the constitutional) debate seldom put so vividly in terms of national schools; not only was Japan's educational borrowing far more piecemeal and ad hoc, with ample reference to France and America and other Western European countries as well. We have, as a matter of fact, not so much as one statement (to my knowledge) from Mori as minister of education singling out German educational practice for special praise or recommending the adoption of any particular educational institution from Germany.

The one place where one might look for specific German influence in Mori's administration would be in the brief career in Japan of Hermann Techow, invited to Tokyo by Itō in place of Lorenz von Stein as advisor to the cabinet on legal, local government, and educational affairs. Tsuchiya Tadao, in the one brief account we do have of Techow, has pointed out that this Prussian educational

---

178. KSM, p. 73; OTM, pp. 95–96. Tsuchiya, *Seisakushi,* p. 292, makes the same point.
179. John Bennett, Herbert Passin, and Robert McKnight, *In Search of Identity* (Minneapolis, 1958), p. 30 and note 11, p. 324.

official (unlike David Murray) was not actually involved in the Monbushō and reported not to the minister but directly to the cabinet and to Itō.[180] The hard proof of Techow's influence on Japanese education is slim indeed, and after comparing Techow's reports with later education ordinances Tsuchiya has been able to produce only three concrete instances:[181] (1) the provision in the Shin kyōikurei of August 1885 for a half-day schedule in the primary schools exactly as in Prussia, together with the fact that Itō early in August had asked to see a translated copy of Techow's recommendations on the school system; (2) the direct adoption in Mori's regulations for primary school curriculum (Ministerial Ordinance 8, 25 May 1886, Clause 5) of Techow's suggestion for a ceiling of eighty pupils per teacher in the Ordinary Primary School and sixty in the higher division; and (3) the provision in the "Chihō gakuji tsūsoku" (General rules for local educational affairs) of 3 October 1890 for *gakkō kumiai* (school associations) at the town and village level, very similar to the Prussian *Schulvereine,* charged with providing and maintaining primary school plant and with raising funds and collecting primary school fees.[182]

This was really very little from which to deduce that "Techow was . . . a person who played a certain role in the reorientation of our educational policy toward the German style."[183] This also assumes that policy was, in fact, so reoriented. That this assumption should have achieved such wide and axiomatic acceptance stems most probably from the following circumstances. First, it was easy enough to suppose, since Mori was close to Itō, that his own political statism derived from the same German sources and that a preference for German politics further would imply a preference for German education. Second, the sudden popularity of German culture from about 1884 onward and the heavy influx of German advisors into the government and professors into the university[184] might have led a casual observer to conclude that the educational system as a whole had been reoriented, as was the political system, toward a specific foreign model. Thirdly, we have a simple lack of information: Mori at no point acknowledged his debt, if any, to foreign example; and scholarly studies of comparative education, which generally cover *in detail* only the twentieth

180. Tsuchiya, *Seisakushi,* p. 289.
181. Ibid., pp. 286, 288.
182. For the *gakkō kumiai* see *Gakusei gojūnenshi,* pp. 145–146.
183. Tsuchiya, *Seisakushi,* p. 289.
184. PRO, Japan/General Correspondence, FO-46-365, dispatch from F. R. Plunkett to Marquis of Salisbury, 29 Jan. 1887.

century, have done very little to recreate and remind us of the actual nineteenth-century context in which Mori worked.

There is much in Mori's handiwork that does not come from Germany, or from Germany alone; and much of what did can be traced to the original mediation of England or America. Conversely, some of what came from Germany was not Mori's handiwork.

Some German inspiration is most evident in the two fields in which Prussia had excelled: in primary and in university education. Techow, whose stay in Japan (December 1833–ca. June 1886)[185] corresponded to Mori's period as *goyō kakari* rather than minister, had busied himself almost exclusively with primary education.[186] Prussian primary education, however, had been held up as an ideal not only by American educators since Horace Mann, but also—and very eloquently so—by Matthew Arnold and A. J. Mundella. Both Prussian and American practice emphasized local initiative in contrast to the centralism of the French system on which the Gakusei had been patterned and to which the Kaisei kyōikurei had reverted after a very brief flirtation with Tanaka's American model. What accrued to the localities in 1890 in connection with the new local government system, however, were the fiscal and organizational responsibilities and duties of the Prussian *Schulvereine* rather than the powers and rights of the American local school board. It was to be sure a step away from centralism, away not from the American but from the French model. But Mori evidently would have gone even further, perhaps to a point equidistant between the Prussian and the American forms of local initiative. His proposed educational societies in their advisory function and in their attachment to the several levels of government bear a formal resemblance to the *Schulvorstand* and *Provinzialschulkollegium* of Prussia. But in their veto powers, and in the very energetic leadership which Mori hoped to see from them, they stand closer in spirit to the American boards. There is no reason, in any case, to believe that relations between Mori and Techow were anything but cordial and cooperative. Mori had gotten his ideal of universal, compulsory primary education from the United States; but the Americans in turn, on that score, had learned a great deal from Prussia.

That the organization of the imperial university should have followed in the main the German plan[187] was chiefly determined

---

185. Tsuchiya, *Seisakushi*, pp. 288–289.
186. Ibid., pp. 286–289; *Yūbin hōchi shinbun*, 4 Jan. 1884.
187. Ōkubo, *Nihon no daigaku*, p. 306.

by the fact that it was, in the mid-1880's, the only model available. In France, as has been pointed out, university-level faculties operated on an independent, uncoordinated basis; Oxford and Cambridge were still undergraduate seminaries; the United States had Johns Hopkins—patterned after Berlin—but Harvard still meant Harvard College. The University of Berlin, however, placed a heavy emphasis on what Mori called *junsei gakumon:* not only on scientific research but on speculative philosophy and classical studies as well. Technological application of research became a prominent feature after 1870,[188] but the Tokyo institution, with its heavy emphasis on *ōyō gakumon,* bore a greater spiritual resemblance perhaps to the citadel of French technocracy, Napoleon's Ecole Polytechnique.

Indeed, if Japanese education both before and after Mori had to be classified in terms of taxonomical affinity for one particular foreign model, the decision would have to be in favor of France. Mori's Higher Normal School, for instance, in its virtual dominance of the profession, resembled nothing in Germany nearly as much as it did the École Normale Supérieure, and the whole concept of a leadership elite based strictly on intellectual performance was *par excellence* the hallmark of France, not of Germany, which still retained some attachment—thought not as deeply as England—to the hereditary principle. The Ordinary (i.e., prefectural) Normal Schools and other structural survivals from the Gakusei represented direct importations from France, as did the massive administrative centralization of the system. Most easily forgotten of all, perhaps, is the fact that the French school system was as nationalistically oriented as the German, and that in the higher-level state-supported institutions the purposes of the state had been made explicit ever since their Napoleonic inception.

Mori's educational *étatisme,* therefore, had its model both in France and Germany, and, in Matthew Arnold, its most articulate English-language apologist. As already mentioned, *heishiki taisō* was inspired originally by the Swiss example, while with the dual track Mori simply fell in line with the practice throughout Europe. As a matter of fact, the single track would remain an American anomaly well into the twentieth century. Mori's policy as a whole, therefore, is best described not as German but as mixed-European; or, since Britain lacked both strong centralization and advanced technical education, as mixed-continental. We have no record of Mori's having inspected or studied the French system, or

---

188. Friedrich Paulsen, *German Education Past and Present,* tr. T. Lorenz (London, 1908), pp. 184–186, 192.

of his having read or met Matthew Arnold. What we do know is that he spoke, with considerable satisfaction by his own account, to Mundella and Huxley and other unidentified authorities; that forward-looking British educationists were all looking to the continent, as testified by the repeated dispatch of royal commissions to the greater and lesser states of Europe; and that there was a broad overlapping between their hopes and ambitions and the specifically German educational philosophy propounded to Itō by Stein.

Fundamentally, of course, Mori's policy is most properly described as Japanese. Here again the supposed similarity of political and educational borrowing has obscured the fact that while the constitutions or polities of the major Western powers were by the late 1880's distinct and stable entities among which one might effect a choice, education, under the pressure of industrialism, nationalism, and social change, was in a state of great flux and development, with an enormous amount of mutual interchange among the Western nations themselves as each sought for itself, or passed on to others, the latest development in any particular field. Universal elementary schooling, technical education, research-oriented universities, in short, most of what we generally associate with modern education, goes back in the West itself not much before the 1870's and 1880's. Japan, therefore, entered relatively early into the game, took what seemed best or most appropriate, and by 1900 had outstripped each of her tutors on certain counts: better technical education than Britain; popular education unburdened by the confessional quarrels of Germany or France; greater recognition of talent than America.

Subjectively, Mori's frame of reference was quite naturally Japanese. He was far less concerned with countries of origin than would be the later student of cultural borrowing. The dual track was interesting not as a problem in French social history but as a means for replacing the fast-disappearing samurai class with something very similar to it functionally, in terms of loyal service and intellectual ability; military drill could have been observed in any number of schools in Britain or the Continent, but the moral and psychological archetype of *heishiki taisō* more probably remained for Mori his own Gōjū; even his educational statism, though congenial to that of Stein and conformable to the politics of his own *Representative System,* continued to place education in a broad moral and political context in a fashion reminiscent of his letters to Yokoyama or of Shimazu Nariakira's regulations for the Zōshikan.

The most important doubts concerning Mori's alleged Germanism, however, are raised by his own philosophical viewpoint and way of life, and by the fact that we have no record of his having encouraged the "German studies" recommended by Inoue. If Mori was the least bit attracted to German idealism, or impressed for that matter with Herbartism, he most likely would have made some use of them in his ethics primer. Instead, the *Rinrisho* gives us something that is basically Spencer. Nōsei Sakae's recollection of Mori's impatience with particular philosophers and their systems makes it doubly difficult to believe that Mori in his busy Monbushō years could have become enamored of difficult thinkers with whom he had had no contact in his years of intellectual formation. Brought up on Mill and Spencer, he remained, on the basis of all evidence, a child of the English school.

The gradual penetration of the imperial university by a German philosophical viewpoint is a story which both antedates and postdates and ostensibly has little to do with Mori. Hegel had already been introduced by the American Ernest Fenellosa between 1879 and 1885, and Kant by the Englishman Charles Cooper between 1879 and 1881. The German philosophy was first taken up by a German with the arrival of Ludwig Busse in 1887, who lectured on Kant and Lotze; Schopenhauer was first introduced by Busse's replacement, Raphael von Koeber, after 1893.[189] There were German appointments to other departments which, to the British legation at least, seemed part of a deliberate Japanese effort to deepen their German ties,[190] but the science and engineering colleges of the university both remained under British dominance for the entire decade.[191] The appointment in 1888 of Emil Hausknecht to the college of literature, where he established a special department of pedagogy based on Herbartian principles, was undertaken not on the initiative of Mori but on the recommendation of Shinagawa Yajirō, then minister at Berlin, to Itō.[192]

As a matter of fact, Mori did take the initiative in introducing the study of English in the higher elementary course, and he gave it great encouragement in the middle schools. Kanda Naibu, who

189. Horimatsu, *Kyōikushi,* pp. 211–212; Gino K. Piovesana, *Recent Japanese Philosophical Thought, 1862–1962: A Survey* (Tokyo, 1963), pp. 49–51.

190. PRO, Japan/General Correspondence, FO-46-365, dispatch from F. R. Plunkett to Marquis of Salisbury, 29 Jan. 1887.

191. Robert S. Schwantes, "American Influences in the Education of Meiji Japan" (unpublished Ph.D. dissertation, Harvard University, 1950), p. 44.

192. Horimatsu, *Kyōikushi,* p. 214.

accompanied Mori to America as his youngest student in 1870 and who later became professor of English at the Tokyo University of Commerce, remembered Mori as "a champion of the cause of Anglo-Saxon civilization in Japan." Nitobe Inazō, too, characterized him as "an ardent admirer of Anglo-American spirit and institutions."[193] And perhaps the most conclusive judgment came from the Eisenach *Gymnasium* professor, Otto Schmiedel, who resided in Tokyo from 1887 to 1892 and later wrote the authoritative chronicle of the German community in Japan. Schmiedel recalled Mori as *ein ausgesprochener Engländer-freund:* a pronounced friend of the English.[194] Despite the growing diplomatic rivalry between Germany and Britain as regards Japanese affairs, Mori's Anglo-American background would not necessarily, as I have suggested, have predisposed him to a hostile view of German culture. It would most probably, however, have precluded any active or enthusiastic support for German studies.

It was Mori's misfortune that the features of his educational philosophy and policy which survived to establish his later reputation were precisely those which adapted themselves most readily to purposes, or at least to nuances, not within the scope of his original intention. Ironic as it seems for a man who had placed so much emphasis on the need to consider the native environment, Mori failed, from the standpoint of certain of his goals, to take the Japanese context sufficiently into account. Of this phenomenon, *heishiki taisō* was of course the prime example: Japan possessed neither the social structure nor the humanistic tradition on which the Arnoldian principle originally was premised; and even Kimura Kyō in a public address in 1895 could remark with satisfaction how very well Mori's military drill was proving its effectiveness and worth in the China war.[195] Mori's rather cut-and-dried, economy-oriented educational statism, too, merged very soon after his death with a moral traditionalism which he definitely had opposed and with a Germanism to which he very probably had been indifferent, while the modernistic *aikoku*-centered nationalism which he represented found itself irresistibly drawn, under the aegis of the education rescript and in the general intellectual climate of the nineties, to its traditional complement, *chūkun*. Even Mori's struc-

---

193. Kanda Memorial Committee, ed., *Memorials of Kanda Naibu* (Tokyo, 1927), p. 8; Nitobe Inazō, *The Japanese Nation: its Land, its People and its Life, with Special Consideration to its Relations with the United States* (New York, 1912), p. 182.
194. Otto Schmiedel, *Die Deutschen in Japan* (Leipzig, 1920), p. 195.
195. KKM, pp. 297–298.

tural elitism, thanks to peculiar features of Japanese social structure and psychology, eventually would find itself hobbled and rigidified by a degree of hierarchism, factionalism, and compartmentalization unknown, for instance, in France or Germany.

The most important lesson of the comparative perspective, perhaps, is how swiftly borrowed elements do change when taken out of their original context. A harsh critic could have argued rather cynically, again as of about 1900, that Japanese education had taken not the best, but the worst, from the West: Anglo-American utilitarianism without democracy, the centralism and elitism of France without its individualism or liberty, the German university without its considerable humanism. But in judging Mori's intentions, at least, it is necessary to reestablish and argue from the immediate point of borrowing, not the later development. In terms of that later development, Japan succeeded magnificently in creating the loyal, intelligent, hard-working subjects Mori had hoped for. Of course we shall never know, but there is a presumption in favor of the conclusion that Mori would have been somewhat less than satisfied with the quality of that loyalty and intelligence. Unfortunately, those elements which qualify his statism, such as his ethical individualism or plans for modest decentralization, are precisely the ones which did not take root in the educational establishment and which were promptly forgotten.

The brief year and a half between Mori's assassination and the promulgation of the education rescript reminds us how minutely we must focus our historical lenses if we are not to confuse Mori's intention with that which very soon followed. It is this historical perspective which gives us our best clue as to the multiplicity of images regarding Mori's educational administration; for if posterity in the long run would behold almost exclusively the statist element, there were Westerners and Japanese alive at the time who might have been more struck by the forceful individualism of *jitaheiritsu*. But what, then, may now be made of Mori's images in the perspective of his entire career?

Conclusion

THE IMAGE REVISED

Perhaps the most important thing that needs to be said in evaluating Mori as thinker and doer already has been said by Fukuzawa Yukichi, who wrote a few years after his younger friend's assassination:

> Mori returned to Japan at the very time that the government required many new officials . . . But this was Mori's bad luck. For, times being what they were, once he joined the government he found himself preoccupied with official business and had little leisure to spare for reflection on other matters. When Mori began his service, therefore, he was still rather young and had not yet developed his scholarly ability or his experiences to the full. He assumed high government position just as his studies were beginning to bear fruit, and his natural intelligence accordingly never attained its true maturity . . . This is not to say that Mori failed to produce any sound arguments or eminent views, but there were among his views and arguments a good many which somehow were lacking in logical coherence and consistency of pace.[1]

1. Quoted in KKM, p. 288.

A "WORLD THINKER" DEBUNKED

A short biography of Mori has recently appeared among the first seventeen volumes of a projected eighty-eight-volume *Sekai shisōka zenshū* (Collected works of world thinkers), right alongside Plato, Bacon, Nietzsche, Jaspers, Confucius, and Motoori Norinaga.[2] Strange company for a man who by no stretch of the imagination could be called a philosopher. As Hayashi Takeji has put it, Mori was "needless to say, no educationist, much less a thinker; he was through-and-through a statesman (*seijika*) who dealt with educational problems from the standpoint of a statesman."[3] Okubo Toshiaki, in a phrase which does justice to Mori as a man of culture and as an intellectual, which he certainly was, hit upon the most appropriate caption when he summed up his subject as a *bunkateki seijika no tenkei:* the model of a cultural statesman.[4] This was no doubt the characterization with which Mori himself most would have agreed: it well fitted his own self-image as proclaimed in the memorandum assigning to the education minister the chief responsibility for the cultural life of the entire nation.[5]

On the one hand, therefore, Mori was something of an anomaly within the power-holding clique—a high-ranking official, an ambassador and cabinet minister no less, who although neither a systematic philosopher nor a trained pedagogue had been directly and significantly involved in the introduction of Western thought and culture into Meiji Japan. His role, I have suggested, was properly speaking that of propagandizer, impresario, academic dean. In the world of education and of ideas, Mori was much more the amateur than the professional; he was, nevertheless, a real insider, a genuine habitué. This set him apart from statesmen such as Inoue Kaoru, for instance, who could promote ballroom dancing strictly as a diplomatic maneuver.

On the other hand, Mori consistently viewed the cultural and educational scene in a broadly conceived political context, both national and international. His government position served not only, as Fukuzawa suggested, to cut short a promising scholarly career; it also, in a more positive sense, gave Mori a statesman's grasp of the possible—in terms of Japan's international position, of economic contingencies, of the actual working of Western institu-

2. Harada Minoru, *Mori Arinori,* a volume in the unnumbered series, Maki Shoten, *Sekai shisōka zenshū* (Tokyo, 1966).
3. Hayashi Takeji, "Meiji kyōiku no shuppatsu to zasetsu: Mori Arinori o chūshin to shite," *Ushio,* spring 1967 (special number), p. 101.
4. Ōkubo Toshiaki, *Nihon no daigaku* (Tokyo, 1943), p. 303.
5. See note 24, Chapter Ten.

tions in their original Western context—insights or concerns or perspectives not fully encompassed even by first-rate thinkers like Fukuzawa who were unburdened with Mori's policy-making responsibilities, much less by the Epigoni, who approached Western culture in its purely conceptual dimension, often as not through the thick filter of literary translation. Also unlike Fukuzawa, who viewed the intellectual uplift of Japan primarily as a matter of individual effort and private initiative, Mori from the time of his supervision of Japanese students in Washington had come to think of education mainly in terms of systematic national organization under government auspices.

Fukuzawa does us a great service, nevertheless, in calling attention to Mori's shortcomings as a thinker. And if the ambiguity of Mori's educational administration is to some extent explained by the time differential (by the succession, that is, of generations who did or did not recall the qualifications of his statism), then Fukuzawa gives us an important clue in resolving such ambiguity as confronts us in Mori's thought as a whole. For what we have so often in Mori's case are neither the tensions of the cultural hybrid, nor the complex inner dialectic of the profound thinker, nor the self-contradictions of the apostate, but simply lacunae—the gaps and omissions of a man of affairs who collected his formal ideas on an ad hoc, problem-oriented basis, and who gave vent to his own thinking in a series of brief, flamboyant bursts alternating with lengthy periods of silence.

This is indeed the most exasperating aspect of the man. He was, as it were, a Kabuki actor who, after striking expressionistic poses, or *mie,* all over the stage of Meiji history fled the set in mid-act, never to return, without playing out his role or letting us know what it was all really supposed to add up to. We are bedevilled, indeed, by a double problem. For Mori's thinking not only lacked systematic and explicit articulation; it also failed to reflect on itself; and Mori was singularly remiss in acknowledging his intellectual debts. His basic philosophical affinities, I have tried to show, were overwhelmingly for the English school. This was not only a matter of his generally utilitarian, empirical (as opposed to rationalistic or idealistic) outlook. He was also specifically under obligation to Mill for some of his ideas on women (in the "Saishōron"), and to Spencer—the inventory is most impressive—for much of his thinking on topics as diverse as physical education (in "Shintai no nōryoku"), social ethics (in the *Rinrisho*), constitutionalism (in *Representative System*), and commerce (in his Social Darwinistic harping on the trade war).

We have had however to dig all this out pretty much by ourselves; and the same lack of acknowledgment applies also to intimate, decisive personal influences such as those of Laurence Oliphant or Thomas Lake Harris, and to professional contacts such as Joseph Henry or Birdsey Northrop or Thomas Huxley or A. J. Mundella. The biographies by Kaimon, Kimura, and Ōkubo all dispose of Harris, Oliphant, and the Brotherhood of the New Life in approximately one paragraph; while none of the three discusses *Representative System* or "Daigi seitairon" at all.

It would be unwise, however, to deduce any further influence upon Mori, by any particular individual, than that for which we have concrete evidence; unwise, in other words, to suppose that a reading of the complete works of Spencer, or the novels of Oliphant, or the sermons of Harris would necessarily shed any additional light on Mori's unspoken thoughts. For one thing, we do not know whether Mori ever read any of his philosophers beyond the particular point that interested, or satisfied, him. In this respect he compares most unfavorably with serious students of English thought such as Fukuzawa or Nishi Amane or their Chinese contemporary Yen Fu,[6] who not only read but also left a record, in their translations and commentaries, of what they had read. For another, we know in the case of Spencer that his private political advice to Mori contradicted his public testimony, and that as regards education and the state the views of the two men were virtually antipodal.[7] In the case of the progressive (i.e., interventionist) British educationists—Mundella, Huxley and Matthew Arnold, with respect to whom our evidence is mostly circumstantial—we have merely a strong presumption, not absolute proof, against German advice, or against the possibility that Mori first may have heard during a brief visit to Berlin what many an Englishman could have told him during his four years in London.

It would not be necessary to belabor Mori's intellectual shortcomings had he not presumed to speak out so boldly on such a variety of topics and given himself the reputation of being something of a problematical thinker. The point, of course, is not that Mori was not a thinker but that he was not primarily a thinker; that Mori's thought as we have been able to reconstruct it was neither the mainspring of his life as a whole, nor even the prime mover of its own internal development. Mori's thought itself did

---

6. See Benjamin Schwartz, *In Search of Wealth and Power: Yen Fu and the West* (Cambridge, Mass., 1964).

7. See for example Spencer's *The Man versus the State,* published in 1884, with its running attack on what Spencer called "overlegislation."

not proceed neatly from idea to corollary to further evolution of the original idea; much less did he consistently derive an action program from such a conceptual fund as he did possess.

The key to Mori lies rather in his pursuit of the very basic goals he set himself in realms which broadly may be distinguished as political, social, and personal (or existential). These goals, very deeply felt and very obvious from the record, appear nevertheless to the outside observer as more implicit than explicit and were for Mori himself on the whole intuited rather than conceptualized. There are certain phrases or concepts, such as *dokuritsu* (national independence) or *kōhei* and *jōri* (justice and reason) or the overcoming of self, which correspond very closely to these goals; but such verbalizations are more in the line of incidental clues from which we may reconstruct Mori's underlying purposes; they are not the leitmotifs of an articulate and developed scheme.

In the pursuit of these goals, Mori of course had resort to ideas; nor were these ideas embraced in a cynically instrumental fashion. But where a more reflective thinker might have shown a greater concern for intellectual consistency, Mori's thought was significantly deflected by the objective pressures of his professional position, by the subjective pressures of his somewhat unusual mental and temperamental make-up, and by the nature of his association with the West, which was not only deep and sustained but in which the most important dimension was perhaps the social rather than the intellectual, in which precept played perhaps a lesser role than example, and in which ideas themselves were largely transmitted piecemeal across a succession of individual, personal contacts.

A remarkable consistency, as a matter of fact, emerges if we attempt to see as a response to Mori's underlying purposes not only his "views and arguments," taken in isolation, but the whole unraveling skein of his ideas, attitudes, actions, and institutional creations. And the chief breaks in that continuity, such basic changes of direction as there were, will be seen to have occurred not during Mori's third sojourn in the West, as a response to a fresh political inspiration, but at least a decade earlier, primarily as a gradual shift of mode from adolescent to adult and from critical observer to responsible participant.

POLITICAL, SOCIAL, AND PERSONAL GOALS

Mori's political goal remained from start to finish the security and independence of the Japanese nation, and as means to that end he consistently embraced four points of view which, in the popular parlance of the day, would have been identified as *aikoku* (patriotism), *sonnō* (reverence for the emperor), *fukoku* (national wealth), and *kyōhei* (military power). We have pointed out later qualifications of Mori's *sonnō* (as a primarily political loyalty) and of his *kyōhei* (as a primarily defensive posture); but *aikoku* and *fukoku* retained a massive stability throughout the man's career.

Aikoku appeared first, under the impetus of Hayashi Shihei, as an anxiety over the outward defenses of the Japanese islands. From the perspective of London, in Mori's letters to Yokoyama, it shifted to a concern for the internal cohesion of the nation, a theme repeated in Mori's support of a centralized *gunken* system in the Kōgisho in 1869. From the vantage point of Washington Mori could both foresee and welcome the inevitable tide of westernization, the compatibility of which with *aikoku* was established by identifying Japanese tradition itself with the dynamic of adaptation and change: an identification not sophistical but ingenuous, based on Mori's own inner blend of the two. With *dokuritsu,* or the doctrine of national sovereignty taken from the law of nations, Mori found the conceptual handle with which he thought he best could move the Western powers toward treaty revision, making very active use of it while in London, after taking pains not to have it undercut by any heavyhanded Japanese policy toward Korea. With this background it was, finally, virtually inevitable that Mori's national orientation would dominate his policies as minister of education.

Mori's loyalist sentiments, cultivated in the home and loudly proclaimed to the Bakufu students in St. Petersburg, were presented to Americans in his introduction to *Education in Japan.* The evidences of *sonnō* among the Japanese people were simply noted in the early 1870's. By the early 1880's, however, Mori was ready to utilize the *sonnō* sentiment as an important element of his constitutional scheme; by the mid-1880's he was calling for its cultivation in the schools; and in 1888 the chief object of his verbal forays during the privy council debates was to protect this sentiment against constitutional arrangements which seemed to threaten it.

The arguments of Shimazu Nariakira and Godai Tomoatsu on behalf of *fukoku* found magnificent confirmation in the booming trade and industry of Britain, and later America. Most of the questions Mori addressed to his American educators were related to this theme, and his "Kokugo haishiron" showed how far he was prepared to go to insure the nation's commercial viability. His emphasis on *ōyō gakumon* in the university and on practical education in the middle schools was in a sense an extension of the work begun with his commercial institute. But the Social Darwinism of Spencer which eventually provided the theoretical prop for Mori's *fukoku* was so emphatically economic as to take much of the aggressive military edge off Mori's *kyōhei*. This, from the Kagoshima Kaiseijo to University College to the assiduous investigations of his London legation, remained naval and defensive in orientation. Mori in his political goal, therefore, was consistently what we would call a nationalist; and we marvel that he ever could have been considered not to be one.

National sovereignty, security, independence, defined, however, only the exterior surface, so to speak, of Japan's future; they in no way described the quality of Japanese life that was to be striven for in such areas as thought or culture or morality or interpersonal relations. Here, in what we may very broadly characterize as his social goal, Mori was with virtually the same unswerving regularity a westernizer. Reconstructing this goal (once again, more from Mori's implicit concerns and attitudes than from any explicit formula), the new civilization envisioned for Japan may be seen to partake of the three basic attributes of justice, reason, and humanity, with justice (embracing both reason and humanity) as perhaps the central element among the three.

By justice I mean something broader than mere legal equity, or even the *kōhei* or "fairness" which to Mori was the hallmark of wise legislation; what Mori had managed to grasp, chiefly by the osmosis of intimate and continuing personal contact, was rather the whole structure and spirit of social and interpersonal relations which typified the West. Under the aegis of Greek philosophy, Roman Law, and Judeo-Christian religion this Western tradition had enjoyed a lengthy historical development, of most of which Mori probably was not aware. But in late nineteenth-century Britain, and particularly America, he touched this tradition at the furthest development of that individualism, rationality, and horizontality of human relations which most set the West apart from the pattern of China and Japan. If this justice, then, may be viewed as Mori's social goal in its formal aspect, reason, or *jōri,* was for Mori the practical operating principle governing everything from the marriage partnership to interstate relations. The qualitative aspect of that goal, finally, is best described as humanity, or humaneness, for which Mori does not even give us a phrase of his own, but which inspired everything from his own small acts of charity to his sweeping distinctions between "enlightenment" and "barbarism."

The striking similarities between Yokoyama's suicide note and

Mori's own Korean policy remind us that this humaneness, at least, had its traditional springboard. Confucianism was not devoid of universalistic insights and, in a family all the members of which seem to have run to extremes, Yokoyama displayed an almost fanatical embrace of the social humanitarianism of Mencius. It was, however, the example of Victorian England, together with the running commentary of Oliphant, which first really opened Mori's eyes to the desirability of a new social dispensation based on justice and reason, and the linking up of that social vision with the eminently satisfying personal ethic of Harris gave Mori's social goal lifelong strength and permanence, in all its stark, radical Westernism.

Strength he needed; for that goal went against so much that was absolutely fundamental in the native culture. The "Haitōron," striking at the externalized morality of brute force and pride of caste, sounded Mori's initial call for a society based on justice, humanity, and reason. With the "Saishōron," which drastically questioned traditional family and marital relations, Mori in effect proclaimed the dignity of the human individual by respecting the personality of the individual woman. Meanwhile, *Religious Freedom in Japan,* by extending that respect not only to the person but to the thoughts of the individual as well, had grasped one of the most important theoretical bases, at least, of Western individualism. Mori's prosaically civilian commercial contest, his continued encouragement (if only verbal) of women's education, and his proscription of Nishimura's *shūshin* texts, all represented variations during his last few years of the themes originally proclaimed in these earlier documents.

Despite Mori's heavy brush with Anglo-American Protestant Christianity, not only at Brocton but also among many of his later Washington and London friends, and despite the deep, even determinative, mark that it left upon his own ethical attitude and personal conduct, Mori's social goal was not stated in the idiom of orthodox Christianity. At least not for long: the language of regeneration, whether Harris-style or more ordinarily Christian, may have been used by Mori at Kanda and Kagoshima during 1868–1870, but it did not long survive his posting to Washington. There of course remained, very strongly, the urge to reshape the nation morally, through the contract marriage for instance or, later, through the discipline of *heishiki taisō*. But for his articulate social ethic Mori already in the early 1870's was turning to Western secular philosophy for guidance and seems to have found Spencer's homely balancing of egoism and altruism sufficient for his purposes. With the *jitaheiritsu* of his ethics primer, however, Mori had hit upon a theoretical formula which, if ever carried out, would have entailed the restructuring of Japanese personal relations along very typically Western lines. The westernization subsumed under Mori's social goal was an end in itself. If one adds to this the westernization espoused merely as means to his political goal, such as adherence to the law of nations, or the establishment of business schools, or the encouragement of English language training, the sum total is prodigious and leaves one wondering how he ever could have been taken for anything other than a westernizer.

Mori's personal or existential goal retained the greatest stability of all, changing merely its outward guises. Best summed up as the traditional Tokugawa samurai's ethic of self-perfection, this goal as originally appropriated by the young Mori of the Gōjū and Zōshikan comprised both the overcoming of self, particularly of the impulses toward economic and sexual self-indulgence, and the self-sacrifice of loyal political service. This political service, which Mori referred to in 1865 as his "great task," came increasingly to focus on the area to which his own particular talents inclined him, namely education, and his appointment as education minister was not only a professional but also a personal fulfilment in the profoundest sense of the term. Later overtones of Mori's early economic and sexual puritanism are to be found not only in the modesty and sobriety of his personal habits, and in the new sexual ethic of the "Saishōron," but also (one suspects) in his *keizaishugi* (economy principle) and in the severe disciplinary regimen he imposed on his normal schools.

Looking at Mori strictly in his existential dimension, he remained very much, of all things, the traditionalist: commendable or reprehensible depending on how one views the self-perfecting ethic, either in principle or for its effects on his personality, pedagogy, and political thinking. It is my general conclusion that Mori's self-perfectionism on the whole had a braking effect on his own emotional emancipation, on the development of a more liberal and psychologically sounder disciplinary device than *heishiki taisō*, and on his achievement of a true appreciation of Anglo-American political habits.

The relation between Mori's own self-flagellation and his efforts to whip all Japan into patriotic and morally upright shape requires little further elaboration. The effect of Harris, in terms of Mori's personal psychology, was to reinforce the injunctions to self-perfection already inherited from a Satsuma upbringing. Harris, whom Brocton children grew up to hate and whom Japanese with a sense of humor like Yoshida Kiyonari had eventually fled in haste, was swallowed whole by Mori. Mori's literal cast of mind perhaps predisposed him to take other people at face value or at their own word; it deprived him of a certain questioning skepticism; it left him terribly square, with all the gullibility of the square; and it finally combined with his self-perfectionism (projected in the end onto the entire nation), to create expectations that moral virtue might be created through military drill. Toward the end of Mori's life, and particularly in what Erwin Baelz described as his "violent wrangle" with the university students,[8] we sense in him, as earlier in Yokoyama, a potentially self-destructive acceleration of this drive to perfection, marked by a mounting impatience with the imperfections of the world at large.

Mori, as Fukuzawa noted, remained half-baked as a thinker, and my effort here to bake him, to bring out meanings and nuances to which he himself never gave vent, may be presumptuous. The three categories of political, social, and existential goals are admittedly Procrustean, but they do manage to subsume and explain his total record, including his thought, better than does any attempt to deduce his action (and his thought in detail) from an adherence to and further development of any formal religious or philosophical scheme. The possible deficiency of this analysis lies not in seeing Mori as a man of action responding to deeply felt if somewhat inarticulate goals but in having perhaps described those goals themselves in too simple a fashion.

There is some merit, nevertheless, in having at least attempted to depict those goals as multiple, and in suggesting that Mori was pursuing several goals in several areas, rather than being driven by one single overriding purpose. Mori's contrasting images as nationalist or as westernizer derive basically from the crude supposition that he lived only for the national power or only for the spiritual and cultural regeneration of Japan. Our three goals correspond to three parameters of human thought and activity which almost any person would inhabit concurrently. The burden of proof falls rather on the view which supposes any man could exist wholly for politics, or wholly for some social crusade, or wholly for self-perfection; the images which one could conjure up as near cases—Joseph Goebbels? Carrie Nation? St. Simeon Stylites?—properly belong in the cartoonist's sketchbook.

The distinctness of these parameters, indeed their frequent disjunction from a strictly logical standpoint, are worth bearing in

8. Erwin Baelz, *Awakening Japan: The Diary of a German Doctor*, tr. Eden and Cedar Paul (New York, 1932), p. 82.

mind in catching the full complexity of any individual caught up in the swirl of modernization. It is only natural that traditional patterns should survive longest in the existential dimension. No great marvel, for instance, need attach to the messianism which links the Communist leadership of the Soviet Union (particularly the older generation) to Russian Orthodox Christianity (revile that as they may). In the realm of existential motivations, the break comes not with the Revolution but with the appearance decades later of a new generation of technocrats. On another point, Gandhi and Nehru provide a forceful reminder of how very much, beyond an identical political goal, visions of a new society and culture can still differ.

It would not be necessary so to belabor the obvious were it not for the several Mori images, with all their problematical contrasts. The notion that somehow Mori's westernism was no more than instrumental—that what I have called his social goal was not an end in itself but simply means to his political goal—is particularly tenacious. My own reading of the images argues for a wide congruence of westernism and nationalism, both as goals, held neither in dialectical succession nor in antithetical tension but rather simultaneously and in affable harmony. The most accurate evaluations of Mori, I believe, still remain those of his Western or westernizing Japanese friends like Griffis or Fukuzawa, who could appreciate and see nothing unusual in that harmonious congruence. The assumption of an antagonism between "westernism" and "nationalism" (in the shorthand of our Mori images) was first introduced by fabricators of the second image (Westernizer Reprehensible) like Motoda and Nishino, who whether rightly or wrongly abhorred westernization of the social and cultural realm, but unfairly charged Mori in effect with political treason. This supposed antagonism was further built up by Inoue Kowashi and other architects of the third—or Nationalist Commendable—image, who likewise failed to distinguish between Mori's social and political goals, who similarly assumed social and cultural westernism to be incompatible with political nationalism, and who attempted to rehabilitate Mori politically by divesting him of his westernism. The creators of the fourth, or Nationalist Reprehensible, image, such as Tokutomi Sohō, widened the dichotomy from still another direction, regretting that Mori's westernism did not extend to cover certain specific Western democratic political devices, but mistakenly concluded that this necessarily cast his social and cultural westernism in a suspicious light.

The exponents of the first image, of Mori as Westernizer Commendable, were closest to the truth because, knowing Mori personally, they appreciated and accepted his political loyalty—his nationalism—as a matter of course. Our runners-up are the exponents of the fourth image, who (as noted in the Introduction) most generally retain something also of the first image, if in rather mutilated condition; they too basically accept the genuine presence of both nationalist and westernist elements, although they do not care for the former and view the latter as seriously compromised. Neither the second image, which denied Mori's nationalism, nor the third image, which argued away his westernism, is to be taken seriously. It may be said in support of those who created the second image that their fears were well founded, although they failed to appreciate the broad secular basis of Mori's hostility to traditional Japanese religion and social relations and mistakenly took the danger to lie in Mori's alleged Christianity. Also, for the virulence of that second image Mori perhaps had no one better to thank than himself, for his belligerent, censorious, and in many ways unsympathetic personality went a long way to goad his opponents from mere disapproval into outright hatred. It is the third image, however, which has done Mori the greatest injustice; for, by reducing his social goal to no more than an instrument, or his westernism to no more than youthful folly, it eradicated the essential Mori.

My revised image, then, is that of Mori as both nationalist and westernizer in his goals, distinguishing between his political and social goals, and qualifying his westernism as something which in the realm of means, i.e., of specific institutions, did not encompass orthodox Christianity or political democracy. And this brings us to the two final and most important questions which need answering. First, Mori's assumption that one could westernize the social and cultural realm and still remain a good Japanese involved a certain conception, or definition, of Japan. Second, Mori's assumption that the omission of political democracy would not undermine the viability of social and cultural westernization involved a certain conception, or definition, of the West. Whether Mori's definitions were sound is, of course, beside the point. They provide, however, as Mori's own images of the world around him, perhaps our most important clues to the distinctive development of his life and thought.

MORI'S IMAGES OF JAPAN AND THE WEST

Mori's political and existential goals—national security and self-perfection—were firmly in place before he left Kagoshima. What first became clear to him during the three years in London and

Brocton were the outlines of his social goal. With his determination to "abandon backward ways of thought and behavior" he evinced, very soon after his arrival in Europe, a deep dissatisfaction with the traditional Japanese dispensation; a year later, at St. Petersburg, his dissatisfaction was matched only by his perplexity in hitting upon a proper corrective; two years later, upon leaving America, however, his social goal too was firmly in place. That his social goal should have defined itself in such strikingly Western terms is attributable above all to the fact that both Oliphant (who opened Mori's eyes to the workings of justice, reason, and humanity in society at large) and Harris (who provided an ethic relating these ideals to Mori personally) were not only openly sympathetic to Japan's diplomatic plight, but firm tutors in self-perfection as well. Mori's later feeling that there was nothing anomalous about a westernized Japanese derives from this early conjunction of all three goals, political and social and existential; and Mori's approach to Japan reflects therefore the nature of his first encounter with the West.

Mori's westernism from that point forward, whether in the service of his social or his political purposes, was concerned largely with the selection of specific institutions that would fulfill them; and institutions, from their very nature, were less easily adopted than the original ideal. This process went on continually, pretty much on a trial-and-error basis, with Mori sticking by some devices consistently (such as the contract marriage or international law), abandoning others quite quickly (such as the adoption of English), and coming across others (such as *heishiki taisō*) fairly late in his life. The two chief omissions in his westernism, however, were evident by the time of his second visit to the West. *Life and Resources in America* in 1871 expressed a great wariness of representative institutions; while Mori's back-page entry in "Bibō daini" (sometime between 1871 and 1873) lumped Christianity together with Buddhism and Confucianism as something less than a "reliable creed." Harris of course had been hostile to orthodox Christianity to begin with, while Mori's failure to get very far with the Broctonian idiom in either Kanda or Kyushu or Washington gradually led him to place more and more distance between himself and Harris. Mori's disappointing experience in the Kōgisho, climaxing with the unanimous rejection of the "Haitōron," likewise must have shattered such early enthusiasm as he may have had for parliamentary institutions. It was after all the experimental parliamentary model, the Kōgisho, not the autocratic Dajōkan, which had quailed at the social and moral implications of the "Haitōron."

Christianity certainly represented the spiritual root of westernism, and political democracy one of its noblest branches. But much of the late nineteenth-century West had moved beyond Christianity, while much of it had as yet to move on to political democracy, and Mori's omissions remind us how much of the West, not only in technological but in cultural, social, moral, and ethical terms as well, could still be had without the formal adoption of these two institutions. Their omission stems in the main from Mori's disappointments of 1868–1870. Instant reform was not to be had; nor would individual zeal alone turn the trick—a point on which Yokoyama's suicide must have provided a very forceful reminder. These years represented also Mori's passage from the ingenuousness and introspection of adolescence to the greater intellectual and social maturity of the adult. By Washington, Mori could be, when he wanted to, very much the man of affairs. And his selective approach to the West in later years would continue to reflect the experience—the sobering-up, so to speak—of his first homecoming to Japan.

Mori in his own personal confrontation with Western culture did not, as far as we can tell, have so much as a whiff of what might be called an "identity crisis." On the contrary, he displayed from the very outset extraordinary integrative powers together with total self-confidence. One is led to suspect, indeed, that Mori's real significance and interest, as an individual, lies less in the field of intellectual history than in that of psychology or cultural anthropology, as one of the most highly developed instances of his own particular type. Mori, emerging from what generally has been characterized as a highly "other-directed," "shame" culture, possessed to a remarkable degree what, superficially at least, looks like "guilt" and "inner-direction." This we can only mention in passing here; but it does suggests the potential value of an entirely different study of the man, based on the formal disciplinary approaches of psychology or anthropology, backed up by information on other Meiji personalities in the same category. In any case, whatever it was that gave Mori what we have called his temperamental individualism, it was this trait which, in terms of his own personal psychology, enabled him to latch on so quickly to the individualism, and to the individualists, of the West.

In his concept of the assimilative and adaptive capacity of the Japanese, that is to say in his theoretical rationale for westernization, Mori hit upon what is certainly one of the most plausible definitions of Japanese cultural development and national identity. As Mori explained to the Americans in *Education in Japan* in 1873, to the Chinese statesman Li Hung-chang in 1876, and to British readers of the *Pall Mall Gazette* in 1884, the assimilative instinct was not a weakness but rather the very genius of his countrymen, with the reception of Western culture in the nineteenth century as necessary and appropriate as had been the reception of Chinese culture centuries earlier. What Mori apparently had perceived (without saying so, however, in so many words) was that the Japanese really had no other choice. Given their geographical isolation and the comparatively low level of their original indigenous civilization, cultural progress and development remained unusually dependent on a dynamic of deliberate, repeated, and rather obvious appropriation from the outside. Japan was not China, where the basic cultural fund was so rich and so self-sufficient that its development could proceed in endogenous fashion, relying primarily on a dynamic of self-reflection with outside stimuli playing only a secondary role. Japan was not Europe either, where the dynamic of development had been provided by the manifold political, ethnic, cultural, intellectual diversity—not only within the proper confines of Western civilization but also in its myriad and continuing external contacts. Mori's implicit definition of the national identity as the sum total of these successive accretions, plus that adaptive instinct itself, strikes one as more felicitous on the whole than the purist viewpoint which would see the true Japan in Yamato culture, or the orientalist viewpoint which would encompass the Sino-Japanese heritage to the exclusion of post-Restoration westernization. By the same token, Mori's rubric further implies that the Japanese would also be the first on earth to learn from, shall we say, Martian invaders—if our hypothetical Martians indeed had something to offer—and that any definition of Japan in terms of mid-twentieth-century westernization would in turn be out of date.

    The unusual thing about Mori was the equanimity with which he faced the forthcoming round of cultural adaptation. The process of change was in fact bound, for most Japanese, to be disturbing if not painful, and in that sense Mori's formula was a bit too facile and glib. Had he been a more systematic and reflective thinker he might have shown a greater awareness of the actual complexities involved. Had he been a more careful student of his own culture he might to some extent have anticipated that his commercial combativeness, or his Arnoldian principle, or the overcompensating conservatism of his Western mentors would, in the given Japanese context, dovetail very easily with militaristic chauvinism or tend to produce the *shihan taipu* (as it came to be known) or lend its weight to the more reactionary political elements.

    Mori's subjective intentions were of course most readily apparent to his contemporaries, who could characterize him as Westernizer Commendable. The generations that have characterized Mori as

Nationalist Reprehensible, by contrast, had to live with the objective consequences of his educational policies and of his statism, his elitism, and his military drill, which seemed of a piece (although we have attempted to point out significant discontinuities) with his failure to opt for Western democratic institutions. In terms of Mori's fundamental political and social goals, political institutions as such may be viewed as means or instruments which could have been harnessed to the service of either objective. As Maruyama Masao has pointed out, the presumption is that Mori's modernization of the "civil" realm (i.e., of the area covered by his social goal) would have been more securely based had he more wisely chosen his political instrument. And one is led to ask whether that choice is explained simply by a crude subordination of his political instrument to the imperatives of national security or whether he also failed to appreciate the possible implications of his political instrument for his social goal.

That Mori's overcompensatingly conservative Western advisors themselves did not see those implications is abundantly clear. To state their conception somewhat inelegantly, they somehow expected Japan to proceed eagerly to intellectual freedom, individual rights, perhaps even to Christianity—all under the tutelage of a benign autocracy—and then emerge a couple of decades later (in Grant's mind), or a couple of centuries later (in Spencer's), as a parliamentary democracy. Mori's choice of political instrument was more than anything else influenced by the advice of his Western mentors, particularly Spencer, and his own blind spot reflects theirs, as regards the full implications of that choice. So far had Mori identified himself with their viewpoint, that it was almost as if he had taken upon himself the "white man's burden." Beyond that, his blind spot was also to some extent traceable perhaps to the braking effect, as we have called it, of his existential goal.

Mori's self-perfectionism was one of his initial points of junction with the West. But it was less an encounter in which his Kagoshima upbringing leaned forward, so to speak, toward the West, than one in which the West—in the self-perfecting gospel of Harris—reached back toward Mori's own original Satsuma-bred ethic. I have suggested that Mori's failure to find an emotionally liberating experience in Christianity, and his failure to achieve a deeper philosophical grasp of Western religion, may have deprived him of important resources in developing a fuller concept of the individual—a concept which would have demanded that he place further limitations even on his narrowly legal-political statism.

The self-perfecting ethic worked, however, not only to close certain intellectual and spiritual doors for Mori. It also served to keep alive in this man, who openly denounced the formal social and political principles of Confucianism, some typically Confucian attitudes about the nature of politics and of political behavior. The perfection of self in its political extension became the self-perfection of the ruler; and the rule of virtue, in which politics and morality were inextricably intertwined, lay at the heart of the Confucian political view. In the West, politics and morality had never enjoyed so close a union, certainly not since medieval Christendom; and in the Anglo-American political tradition politics was openly and positively viewed as an accommodation of conflicting interests, a balancing of competing egos and egoisms. The idea that politics is something other than this, that it is the fulfillment of some utopian ideal, that it should be in effect the rule of virtue, has indeed historically contributed one of the obstacles to the development of practical, workable democracy not only in Japan but in much of Europe as well.

Granted that Mori was presented with some fairly discouraging examples in Washington in the early 1870's, his discomfiture with American politics was more than purely political. There was also the moral disdain of which the Reverend Octavius Perinchief had taken worried note; and that disdain would crop up again a decade later in *Representative System*. One further suspects that moral disdain was evoked not only by the pungent rhetoric that might be heard on the hustings but by the whole process of give-and-take and the unrestrained expression of the political ego which marked the American scene. Yet this was the essence of democracy; and Mori missed it.

Mori's image of virtuous and honest bureaucrats laboring selflessly for the welfare of the masses who have humbly and gratefully entrusted their well-being to them is still strikingly Confucian in its assumptions, and much of Mori's instinctive elitism derives from it. Confucian in many respects is also his vision of a "divine army" of clerks and foremen and primary school teachers, all well scrubbed and very well behaved, fending off all dangers with abacus, lathe, and grammar book held at the ready. The willingness to sacrifice oneself for a moral purpose is noble; the willingness to legislate morally for others, however, is presumptuous; while the willingness to sacrifice others for a political purpose is execrable. These distinctions, in the Anglo-American political tradition in particular, were crystal clear, if somewhat tacitly assumed. In the Confucian world view the boundaries were not so well defined, and it was easier to slip from the first mode to the second and from the second to the third.

With his institutional ideas in the realm of politics greatly influenced by Spencer, and his view of politics as morality at least indirectly confirmed by Harris, Mori was a bit unlucky in his gurus, in the men who introduced, and largely helped him to define, the West.

In conclusion, it must be borne in mind that Mori was assassinated at the age of forty-one, and that we can only guess as to how he would have turned out at eighty-two. Age fifty would have taken him up through the China War, age sixty through the war with Russia, age seventy almost to Versailles, age eighty well into Taishō democracy and early Shōwa. It is not unreasonable to suppose that at some point Mori might have become prime minister, and there is every reason to believe that he would have brought to Japanese parliamentary politics a salutary and astringent dose of ethical probity. For if his aggressive moralism in personal relations perhaps tended a bit to prudery, it was also a quality in great scarcity in the parties and in the government leadership alike. This, however, is all speculation. So much that would prove determinative of Japan's final style of modernization came after Mori: her first two wars, her parliamentary politics, her gradually crystalizing orthodoxy beginning with the education rescript, her confrontation with a more virulent Western imperialism at the turn of the century. These all would have tested Mori's beliefs, forced him to take more explicit positions, revealed where his real sympathies and intentions lay. Mori was not, however, a man of late Meiji; he was early Meiji and some of mid-Meiji, but no more; and it is important not to read later events back into his prematurely arrested career.

A final evaluation of Mori might best proceed by attempting to establish what would have happened without him. Early Japanese-American relations in all likelihood would have been amicable enough, but the image of Japan might have remained for Americans a bit less familiar, a bit less sympathetic. Modern thought, modern journals, modern scholarly societies no doubt all would have have made their appearance by the mid-1870's; but the Meirokusha not only gripped the imagination of the public; it also provided Western-oriented scholars with a new sense of common purpose. Perhaps the Japanese in 1876 would have avoided a costly military adventure in Korea without Mori's staying hand, perhaps not.

There were other fields on which Mori commented, but where he really had little influence. One was politics, and the development of the constitution; that was entirely out of his hands. Another was education during the 1870's. There were general trends and forces in education even during his own administration over which Mori did not really have control. But it was here, with the dual track and the regimentation of the normal schools, that he left his most permanent and distinctive mark. With these, and particularly with *heishiki taisō,* one wonders if Japanese education would not better have been left alone to flounder along on its own for a few more years and allowed to find its own eventual equilibrium, which very probably would have been weighted somewhat more in favor of opportunity and informality.

More redeeming, least tangible, yet perhaps most significant of all, was Mori's symbolic function. As the most flamboyant innovator in the power-holding group, he represented in his own person in highly concentrated form that maverick genius which enabled his countrymen to place themselves early and ahead of all Asia on the road to modernization. He was an earnest both to them and to the West of what Japan intended to do. In that sense Mori was a symbol displayed in two directions, and one thing that sets him apart from so many of the early Meiji statesmen and thinkers is that he worked nearly as hard to introduce Japan to the West as the West to Japan. At the time, however, his was a symbol which managed to outrage the great majority of his countrymen—and a function, therefore, which ultimately cost him his life.

APPENDIX
BIBLIOGRAPHY
GLOSSARY
INDEX

Appendix

SUGGESTIONS AS TO
THE AUTHORSHIP OF "THE
PROPOSED NATIONAL ASSEMBLY IN
JAPAN: BY A JAPANESE"

Neither Mori's *Representative System* nor his "Daigi seitairon" are discussed in the Kaimon Sanjin, Kimura Kyō, or Ōkubo Toshiaki biographies. Ōkubo does, however, mention the latter in his bibliographic list of Mori's works (p. 156), together with the fifty-six-page anonymous English-language pamphlet, *The Proposed National Assembly in Japan: by a Japanese* (Washington, D.C.: Gibson Brothers, 1883; hereinafter *Proposed National Assembly*), which Yoshino Sakuzō attributed to Mori in *Kandan no kandan* (Tokyo, 1933; p. 179).

From the standpoint of both style and content, however, it is virtually impossible to ascribe the writing of *Proposed National Assembly* to the author of *Representative System*. Yoshino, without presenting any evidence for it, simply mentions in passing that the anonymous pamphlet is a published version of a memorandum submitted by Mori to Itō Hirobumi during the latter's visit to London in early 1883. F. V. Dickins in his *Life of Sir Harry Parkes* (co-authored with Stanley Lane-Poole, 2 vols., London, 1894, II, 315) attributes *Proposed National Assembly,* by contrast, to Yoshida Kiyonari, Japanese minister at Washington until 1882, but likewise fails to present evidence for the ascription, although the "pencil indications by Sir Harry" on Dickins' own copy possibly may have identified the author.

The sophisticated English of *Proposed National Assembly,* far more polished (if at times quite pretentious and florid) than Mori's blunt, matter-of-fact, somewhat repetitious style in *Representative System,* strongly suggests that the anonymous pamphlet was prepared by an Englishman or an American on commission from the nominal Japanese author. Arguing under the motto, *natura non operatur per saltum,* and riddled with the pseudo-erudition of the tortuous chemical-historical analogies so much in intellectual fashion at that time, *Proposed National Assembly* heaps scorn on Japan's modest experiments with deliberative assemblies to date (p. 53) and explicitly opposes (p. 51) the introduction of representative government into Japan "now, or even for a number of years to come." Mori's essay, on the contrary, is committed to the introduction of an assembly in some form by 1890 and argues for Japan's preparedness. It is indeed inconceivable that Mori, who was so concerned to emphasize Japan's progress to Westerners in support of treaty revision, would have undercut his own position with the self-deprecating assertions of Japan's backwardness which characterize the anonymous pamphlet. In terms of publication dates, *Proposed National Assembly* (1883) is earlier than *Representative System* (1884) by one year. If the documents were written by the same person, how does one then explain the odd sequence from better to poorer English, and from a more to a less conservative viewpoint?

Pending the production of incontestable evidence to the contrary, it seems most reasonable to attribute the authorship of *Proposed National Assembly* to the most prominent Japanese resident in Washington during the year of publication, namely Minister Terajima Munenori (Yoshida Kiyonari's successor), or more properly speaking to his American secretary (Charles Lanman's successor) Durham White Stevens. Terajima's attitude on representative government was recorded by Ernest Satow following an interview on 11 July 1886, as follows: "Considers that no benefit will be derived from the institution of a Parliament in 1890. It is only bringing 600 ignoramuses together to talk about what they do not understand. Has written a pamphlet in English on the subject, and will give me a copy" (Ernest Satow, *Diary,* November 1885–December 1886, PRO 30/33, 15–10, Public Record Office, London).

Terajima's remarks summarize, very crudely, the essential spirit of *Proposed National Assembly,* which well may have been the pamphlet received by Satow. That Terajima wrote his pamphlet while in Washington is suggested by a report of the *Jiji shinpō* of 19 May 1884 to the effect that: "while Mr. Terajima Munenori held the post of Minister Extraordinary and Plenipotentiary at

Washington, U.S.A., he spent all of his spare time investigating the American and other political systems, and devising schemes in connection with a national parliament and constitution, shutting himself up in his library in order to read and write . . . [much to the mystification of Washington society]."

Our most significant clues, however, are provided by Terajima himself, in his reminiscences as compiled by Yokoyama Kendō under the title "Terajima Munenori haku joden" (A narrative of Count Terajima Munenori) in *Denki* (Biography), volume 3, numbers 4-6 (April–June 1936). Page 129 of the June installment quotes Terajima (no date given) as recalling that he visited Yamagata Aritomo, shortly before his departure for Washington in 1882, to express his doubts regarding the wisdom of the proposed parliament—doubts which Yamagata shared and which led him shortly thereafter to commission a study of the subject by Nishi Amane. Terajima continues: "I promised to send the books [required] from America. The following year I sent several hundred volumes from Washington, but I have not heard whether they were used or not. In addition I prepared a pamphlet in English arguing against a parliament and sent it to Yamagata. I imagine that he had it translated so that he could read it, although I cannot say whether he was able to comprehend it . . . Stevens was originally Secretary at the American Legation in Japan . . . I attached him to my own legation staff and took him over with me. My English-language writings in America were produced by explaining my general intention to this man and having him prepare the text."

BIBLIOGRAPHICAL NOTE
ON THE MORI BIOGRAPHIES

The most adequate, balanced, general-purpose account of Mori, written in the modern idiom, may be found in Ōkubo Toshiaki, *Mori Arinori,* 1944. The basic biographical authority remains the much lengthier *Mori sensei den,* 1899, of Kimura Kyō, which quotes many important documentary sources at length but is rather short on interpretation, following as it does the traditional eulogistic mode. Kaimon Sanjin, *Mori Arinori,* 1897, is a brief study with many interesting points of an anecdotal or interpretative nature not found in the foregoing two studies. Kaimon Sanjin is a *nom de plume;* the actual author has never been identified but possibly may have been either the historian Shigeno Yasutsugu, who according to the *Japan Weekly Mail* of 23 February 1889 had been "ordered to compile a biography" of Mori, or perhaps Hiwatari Kaimon, an authority on education in Satsuma and author of *Sappan no bunkyō* (Education in Satsuma han; Tokyo, 1913). For a succinct, easy-to-read survey of Mori which incorporates some of the recent research of Hayashi Takeji, the reader with only a general interest in Mori is referred to Harada Minoru, *Mori Arinori,* 1966. Finally, attention must be called to the work, both published and forthcoming, of Professor Hayashi, to whom virtually all the new research on Mori since 1944 may be attributed.

A NOTE ON THE *ZENSHŪ*

The projected arrangement of contents for the three-volume *Mori Arinori zenshū,* edited by Ōkubo Toshiaki and scheduled for publication by the Senbundō Shoten in the near future, is as follows: *Zenshū* I: politics, diplomacy, culture, education; *Zenshū* II: diaries, personal correspondence, miscellany, reminiscences by Mori's friends; *Zenshū* III: English-language writings.

In the footnotes, page references in *Zenshū* I have been given for most items to be published in the first volume, my proof copy of which is complete except for several pages. Present locations in the readily accessible *Meiji bunka zenshū* (MBZ), however, have been retained here for important writings of Mori scheduled for *Zenshū* I. Finished proof copies of the second and third volumes were not available at the time of writing, but the reader is advised that nearly everything written by Mori (with the major exception of the diplomatic correspondence at the Public Record Office, London, and the National Archives, Washington, D.C.) will eventually appear somewhere in the *Zenshū,* together with many of the shorter biographical items written by other people about Mori. Projected publication in *Zenshū* II or *Zenshū* III has been indicated for certain items the original sources for which are particularly difficult of access.

BIBLIOGRAPHY

Araki, Tadao Johannes. *Geschichte der Entstehung und Revision der ungleichen Verträge mit Japan: 1853–1894.* Marburg, 1959.
Armytage, W. H. G. *A. J. Mundella, 1825–1897: The Liberal Background to the Labour Movement.* London, 1951.
——*Four Hundred Years of English Education.* Cambridge, England, 1965.
——*The Rise of the Technocrats: A Social History.* London, 1965.
Arnold, Matthew. "Schools and Universities on the Continent," in R. H. Super, ed., *The Complete Prose Works of Matthew Arnold.* 10 vols. Ann Arbor, Mich., 1960–1965.
Asō Yoshiteru 麻生義輝. *Kinsei Nihon tetsugaku shi* 近世日本哲学史 (History of Japanese philosophy in recent times). Tokyo, 1942.
Baba, Tatui. *Elementary Grammar of the Japanese Language: Easy Progressive Exercises.* London, 1873.
Bellah, Robert N. "Values and Social Change," in *Asian Cultural Studies*, vol. 3. Tokyo, International Christian University, October 1962.
Bird, Isabella L. *Unbeaten Tracks in Japan.* 2 vols. London, 1880.
Block, Marguerite Beck. *The New Church in the New World.* New York, 1932.
Bowle, John. *Politics and Opinion in the Nineteenth Century: An Historical Introduction.* Galaxy Book ed. New York, 1964.
Brinton, Crane. *English Political Thought in the 19th Century.* Harper Torchbook ed. New York, 1962.
"A Celestial Utopia," *The Sun* (New York), April 30, 1869.

Connell, W. F. *The Educational Thought and Influence of Matthew Arnold.* London, 1950.
Conroy, Hilary. *The Japanese Seizure of Korea, 1868–1910.* Philadelphia, 1960.
Cowper Papers. "Conversations of Thomas Lake Harris, 1867–1871." Notebook of Mr. and Mrs. William F. Cowper. Hampshire Record Office (Winchester).
——"Conversations of Mr. Harris, May 16 to June 1871." Notebook of Mr. Cowper. Hampshire Record Office (Winchester).
Cuthbert, Arthur A. *The Life and World-Work of Thomas Lake Harris.* Glasgow, 1908.
Danshaku Megata Tanetarō 男爵目賀田種太郎 (Baron Megata Tanetarō), ed. Ko Megata Danshaku Denki Hensankai (Editorial Association for the Biography of the late Baron Megata) 故目賀田男爵伝記編纂会. Tokyo, 1938.
Dictionary of American Biography, ed. American Council of Learned Societies. 22 vols. New York, 1943.
Duncan, David. *Life and Letters of Herbert Spencer.* London, 1908.
Earl, David M. *Emperor and Nation in Japan: Political Thinkers of the Tokugawa Period.* Seattle, 1964.
Fish, Hamilton. Papers. Correspondence, vol. 88. Library of Congress, Manuscripts Division.
——Papers. Diary, vol. 3. Library of Congress, Manuscripts Division.
——Papers. Miscellaneous. Library of Congress, Manuscripts Division.
Fujiwara Kiyozō 藤原喜代蔵. *Kyōiku shisō gakusetsu jinbutsu shi: Meiji zenki hen* 教育思想学説人物史：明治前期篇 (History of educational thought, theory and prominent educators: Early Meiji period). Tokyo, 1942.
Fukuzawa Yukichi 福沢諭吉. *Gakumon no susume* 学問のすすめ (On the encouragement of learning). Iwanami Shoten ed. Tokyo, 1966. Originally published 1872.
——"Tsūzoku kokkenron" 通俗国権論 (A popular account of national rights), 1878, in vol. 4 of *Fukuzawa senshū* 福沢選集 (Selected works of Fukuzawa). 8 vols.; Tokyo, 1951–52.
Granville Papers. PRO–30–29–312/313. *Further Correspondence respecting the Revision of the Treaty between Great Britain and Japan* (printed for the Foreign Office). Parts 3–7 (1879–1884). Public Record Office Manuscripts, Great Britain.
——PRO–30–29–314. *Correspondence respecting Quarantine Laws in Japan* (printed for the Foreign Office). Public Record Office Manuscripts, Great Britain.
Great Britain Foreign Office Manuscripts. Japan/General Correspondence, FO–46–61/68/74/113/262/278/365/375/379. Public Record Office.
——Ministry of Education Manuscripts. "Minutes and Reports of the Committee of the Privy Council on Education, 1839–1899," ED–17–50 through 53, reports for 1879–80, 1880–81, 1881–82, 1882–83.

Griffis, William E. *The Mikado's Empire*. 2nd ed. New York, 1877.
——"The Japanese Students in America," in *The Japanese Student: A Bimonthly for Japanese Students in America* (October 1916).
Harada Minoru 原田実. *Mori Arinori* 森有礼, an unnumbered volume in *Sekai shisōka zenshū* 世界思想家全集 (Collected works of world thinkers). Maki Shoten ed. Tokyo, 1966.
Haraguchi Torao 原口虎雄. *Bakumatsu no Satsuma* 幕末の薩摩 (Satsuma in the Bakumatsu period). Tokyo, 1966.
Hardy, Arthur S. *Life and Letters of Joseph Hardy Neesima*. Boston, 1891.
Harris, Thomas Lake. "A Prophecy of Japan." Unpublished memorandum, July 2, 1867, in Harris and Oliphant Papers. Columbia University Library, Special Collections.
——"The Book of O-I." Unpublished manuscript, 1876, in Harris and Oliphant Papers. Columbia University Library, Special Collections.
——"Annunciation of the Son of Man." Unpublished manuscript (1878?), in Harris and Oliphant Papers. Columbia University Library, Special Collections.
——"A Study of Occultism." Unpublished manuscript, 1888, in Harris and Oliphant Papers. Columbia University Library, Special Collections.
——*The Brotherhood of the New Life*. Fountain Grove, Calif., 1891.
——*The Song of Theos*. 3 vols. Glasgow, 1903.
——"The Bridal Word." Unpublished and undated manuscript in Harris and Oliphant Papers. Columbia University Library, Special Collections.
Harris, Mrs. Thomas Lake. "Letters and Diary, 1899–1906," in Harris and Oliphant Papers. Columbia University Library, Special Collections.
Harris and Oliphant Papers. Correspondence addressed by Laurence Oliphant to Mr. and Mrs. William F. Cowper. Columbia University Library, Special Collections.
Hayashi Shihei 林子平. *Kaikoku heidan* 海国兵談 (On the defense of a maritime country). Iwanami Shoten ed. Tokyo, 1930.
Hayashi Takeji 林竹二. "Kindai kyōiku kōsō to Mori Arinori" 近代教育構想と森有礼 (Mori Arinori and the conception of modern education), in *Chūō kōron* 中央公論, August, 1962.
——"Mori Arinori to Tomasu Rēku Harisu" 森有礼とトマス・レーク・ハリス (Mori Arinori and Thomas Lake Harris), in *Nichibei fōramu* 日米フォーラム, March, 1963.
——"Bakumatsu no kaigai ryūgakusei" 幕末の海外留学生 (Overseas students in the Bakumatsu period), in five parts, *Nichibei fōramu*, January, February, April, June, July-August, 1964.
——"Mori Arinori to nashonarizumu" 森有礼とナショナリズム (Mori Arinori and nationalism), in *Nihon* 日本, April, 1965.
——"Meiji kyōiku no shuppatsu to zasetsu: Mori Arinori o chūshin to shite" 明治教育の出発と挫折：森有礼を中心として (The outset and

setback of Meiji education: with focus on Mori Arinori), in *Ushio* 潮, spring 1967 (special number).

——— "Mori Arinori kenkyū: dai ichi: Mori chūbei dairikōshi no jinin" 森有礼研究：第一：森駐米代理公使の辞任 (Studies on Mori Arinori, no. 1: the resignation of Mori, Chargé d'Affaires in America), reprinted from *Tōhoku daigaku kyōiku gakubu kenkyū nenpō* 東北大学教育学部研究年報, 1967.

——— *Mori Arinori kenkyū: dai ni: Mori Arinori to kirisutokyō* 森有礼研究：第二：森有礼とキリスト教 (Studies on Mori Arinori, no. 2: Mori and Christianity). Sendai, by the author, 1968.

——— "Bakumatsu kaigai ryūgakusei no jiseki" 幕末海外留学生の事蹟 (The achievements of the overseas students in the Bakumatsu period), in *Yamagata kōkō toshokan* やまがた高校図書館, no. 3, n.d.

——— "Kyōshokukan no rekishiteki haikei" 教職観の歴史的背景 (The historical background of the professional outlook of teachers), in four parts. Unpublished mimeographed manuscript, Sendai, n.d.

——— "Mori Arinori to Arai Ōsui ni kansuru oboegaki" 森有礼と新井奥邃に関する覚え書 (A memorandum concerning Mori Arinori and Arai Ōsui). Mimeographed manuscript, Sendai, n.d.

Henderson, Philip. *The Life of Laurence Oliphant: Traveller, Diplomat and Mystic*. London, 1956.

Holloway, Mark. *Heavens on Earth: Utopian Communities in America, 1680–1880*. London, 1951.

Horimatsu Buichi 堀松武一. *Nihon kindai kyōikushi: Meiji no kokka to kyōiku* 日本近代教育史：明治の国家と教育 (History of modern Japanese education: the Meiji state and education). Tokyo, 1959.

Inada Masatsugu 稲田正次. *Meiji kenpō seiritsushi* 明治憲法成立史 (History of the framing of the Meiji Constitution). 2 vols. Tokyo, 1960–1962.

Inatomi Eijirō 稲富栄次郎. *Meiji shoki kyōiku shisō no kenkyū* 明治初期教育思想の研究 (A study of educational thought in the early Meiji period). Tokyo, 1956.

Inau Tentarō 稲生典太郎. *Nihon gaikōshisōshi ronkō: dai ichi: jōyaku kaiseiron no tenkai* 日本外交史論考：第一：条約改正論の展開 (A study of the history of Japanese diplomatic thought, no. 1: Development of the controversy over treaty revision). Tokyo, 1966.

Inoue Kiyoshi 井上清. *Jōyaku kaisei shi* 条約改正史 (History of treaty revision). Tokyo, 1956.

Inoue Mitsusada 井上光貞. *Nihonshi* 日本史 (History of Japan). 3rd rev. ed. Tokyo, 1961.

Ishii Takashi 石井孝. *Meiji ishin no kokusaiteki kankyō* 明治維新の国際的環境 (The international environment of the Meiji Restoration). Tokyo, 1957.

Itō Hirobumi den 伊藤博文伝 (Life of Itō Hirobumi), comp. Shunpō Kō Tsuishōkai 春畝公追頌会. 3 vols. Tokyo, 1940.

Japan Weekly Mail (Yokohama). Files for 1873–1890.

Japanese National Commission for UNESCO. *Development of Modern System of Education in Japan.* Tokyo, 1960.
Jones, F. C., *Extraterritoriality in Japan: and the Diplomatic Relations Resulting from its Abolition.* New Haven, Conn., 1931.
Kagoshima ken (prefecture), comp. *Kagoshima ken shi* (History of Kagoshima Prefecture), 6 vols. Kagoshima, 1939–44.
Kagoshima Shidan Kai 鹿児島史談会, comp. "Gakusha to Gōjū narabi shusshin meishi" 学舎と郷中並出身名士 (Academies and village fraternities and their famous graduates). Mimeographed brochure, Kagoshima Prefectural Library, n.d.
Kaigo Tokiomi 海後宗臣. "Nihon kyōiku saku kaidai" (Introductory note on "An educational scheme for Japan"), in *Meiji bunka zenshū*, vol. 10.
——*Motoda Eifu* 元田永孚 (Motoda Eifu), vol. 19 of Ishikawa Ken 石川謙, gen. ed., *Nihon kyōiku sentetsu sōsho* 日本教育先哲叢書 (A library of the great men of Japanese education). Tokyo, 1942.
——"Morurē" モルレー (Murray), in Tsuchiya Tadao 土屋忠雄, gen. ed., *Kindai Nihon kyōiku no kaitakusha* 近代日本教育の開拓者 (Pioneers of modern Japanese education). Tokyo, 1950.
——*Kyōiku chokugo seiritsushi no kenkyū* 教育勅語成立史の研究 (A study of the framing of the Imperial Rescript on Education). Tokyo, 1965.
——with Inagaki Tadahiko 稲垣忠彦, Yokosuka Kaoru 横須賀薫, Kishii Isao 岸井勇雄, et al. "Mori Arinori no shisō to kyōiku seisaku" 森有礼の思想と教育政策 (The thought and educational policy of Mori Arinori), in *Bulletin of the Faculty of Education, University of Tokyo*, 8: 1 (1965).
Kaimon Sanjin 海門山人. *Mori Arinori* 森有礼. Tokyo, 1897.
Kanda Memorial Committee, ed. *Memorials of Kanda Naibu.* Tokyo, 1927.
Kaneko Kentarō 金子堅太郎. "Supensā shi to no danwa" スペンサー氏との談話 (A talk with Mr. Spencer), in Itō Hirobumi 伊藤博文, ed., *Kenpō shiryō* 憲法資料 (Materials on the Constitution). 3 vols. Tokyo, 1936.
Karasawa Tomitarō 唐沢富太郎. *Kyōkasho no rekishi* 教科書の歴史 (History of textbooks). Tokyo, 1956.
——*Kyōshi no rekishi* 教師の歴史 (History of teachers). Tokyo, 1956.
——*Kindai nihon kyōikushi* 近代日本教育史 (History of modern Japanese education). Tokyo, 1968.
Keenleyside, Hugh L., and A. F. Thomas. *History of Japanese Education and Present Educational System.* Tokyo, 1937.
Kido Takayoshi 木戸孝允. *Nikki* 日記 (Diary), ed. Tsumaki Chūta 妻木忠太. 3 vols. Tokyo, 1932.
Kikuchi, Dairoku. *Japanese Education.* London, 1909.
Kimura Kyō 木村匡. *Mori sensei den* 森先生伝 (Life of Mori). Tokyo, 1899.
Kinoshita Naoe 木下尚江. *Kami, ningen, jiyū* 神・人間・自由, (God, man and freedom). Tokyo, 1934.

Kiyosawa Kiyoshi 清沢洌. *Nihon gaikōshi* 日本外交史 (Japanese diplomatic history). 2 vols. Tokyo, 1942.
Koba Sadanaga 木場貞長. "Mori Arinori shi" 森有礼氏 (Mr. Mori Arinori), in *Taiyō* 太陽, 18.9 (June 13, 1912).
───"Mori monbudaijin no kaikaku" 森文部大臣の改革 (The reforms of Education Minister Mori), in *Kyōiku gojūnenshi*.
───"Mori Arinori sensei o shinobite" 森有礼先生を偲びて (Remembrances of Mori Arinori), in Sappanshi Kenkyūkai (Society for the Study of the History of Satsuma Han), eds., *Nangoku shisō* 南国史叢 (Historical series on the South Country), no. 4 (1939), in "Mori Arinori zenshū" vol. 2.
Kōsaka, Masaaki. *Japanese Thought in the Meiji Era*, tr. David Abosch. Tokyo, 1958.
Kyōiku gojūnenshi 教育五十年史 (Fifty years of education), ed. Kokumin Kyōiku Shōreikai 国民教育奨励会. Tokyo, 1922.
Lanman, Charles. *The Japanese in America*. New York, 1872.
───*Octavius Perinchief: His Life of Trial and Supreme Faith*. Washington, D. C., 1879.
───*Recollections of Curious Characters and Pleasant Places*. Edinburgh, 1881.
───*Haphazard Personalities: Chiefly of Noted Americans*. Boston, 1886.
───*Japan: Its Leading Men*. Boston, 1886.
───*Leaders of the Meiji Restoration in America*, Hokuseido Press reprint of *The Japanese in America*. Tokyo, 1931.
Lawton, George. Interview with Nagasawa Kanaye, n.d. Columbia University Library, Special Collections.
Layard Papers. British Museum, Manuscripts Division.
London and China Telegraph (London). Files for 1865–67, 1880–84, and 1889.
Mallinson, Vernon. *An Introduction to the Study of Comparative Education*. London, 1957.
Maruyama Masao 丸山真男. *Nihon no shisō* 日本の思想 (Japanese thought). Tokyo, 1961.
Matsumoto Hikosaburō 松本彦三郎. *Gōjū kyōiku no kenkyū* 郷中教育の研究 (A study of Gōjū education). Tokyo, 1932.
Matsumoto Kenji 松本賢治 and Suzuki Hiroo 鈴木博雄. *Genten: kindai kyōikushi* 原典近代教育史 (Original documents: the history of modern education). Tokyo, 1962.
Matsumoto Sannosuke 松本三之介. *Kyōkoku o mezashite: 1889–1900* 強国をめざして: 1889–1900 (In pursuit of national power: 1889–1900), vol. 8 of Tsurumi Shunsuke 鶴見俊輔, gen. ed., *Nihon no hyakunen* 日本の百年 (A hundred years of Japan). Tokyo, 1963.
Mayo, Marlene J. "The Iwakura Embassy and the Unequal Treaties." Ph.D. dissertation, Columbia University, 1961.
Meiji bunka zenshū 明治文化全集 (Collected works of Meiji culture), ed. Yoshino Sakuzō 吉野作造. 24 vols. Tokyo, 1928. Volumes used in this study: IV: *Kenseihen* 憲政篇 (Constitutional government); VI:

Gaikōhen 外交篇 (Diplomacy); X: *Kyōikuhen* 教育篇 (Education); XI: *Shūkyōhen* 宗教篇 (Religion); XVIII: *Zasshihen* 雜誌篇 (Periodicals).

Meiji ikō kyōiku seido hattatsushi 明治以降教育制度発達史 (A history of the development of the educational system from the Meiji period onward), ed. Kyōikushi Hensankai 教育史編纂会. 10 vols. Tokyo, 1938–1939.

Meiroku zasshi 明六雜誌 (Meiji Six magazine) in *Meiji bunka zenshū*, vol. 18.

"Memorandum of the Conversation between His Majesty and General Grant, August 19th 1879 at Hama Rikiu," English-language transcript in *Guranto Shōgun to no Gotaiwa hikki* グラント将軍との御対話筆記 (Notes on the conversation with General Grant), ed. Kokumin Seishin Bunka Kenkyūjo 国民精神文化研究所. Tokyo, 1937.

Mill, John Stuart. *Considerations on Representative Government*, ed. Currin V. Shields. New York, 1958. Originally published in 1861.

———. *The Subjection of Women*. New York, 1911. Originally published in 1865.

Miyahara Seiichi 宮原誠一. *Nihon gendaishi taikei: kyōikushi* 日本現代史大系：教育史 (Outline of modern Japanese history: educational history). Tokyo, 1963.

Monbushō 文部省 (Ministry of Education). *Monbushō dai ichi nenpō* 文部省第一年報 (First annual report of the Ministry of Education). Tokyo, 1873.

———comp., *Rinrisho* 倫理書 (Ethics textbook). Prepared by Nōsei Sakae 能勢栄 under the direction of Mori Arinori 森有礼. Tokyo, 1888.

———comp., *Gakusei gojūnenshi* 学制五十年史 (Fifty years of the school system). Tokyo, 1922.

Mori Arinori 森有礼. "Mori Arinori zenshū" 森有礼全集 (Collected works of Mori Arinori), ed. Ōkubo Toshiaki. To be published in 3 vols. Tokyo, Seibundō.

———"Shi tashinamu beki jōjō" 士可嗜条々 (Points to be cultivated by the samurai). Dec. 5, 1864. In "Mori Arinori zenshū," vol. 2.

———"Kōro kikō" 航魯紀行 (Journal of a voyage to Russia). August–September 1866. In "Mori Arinori zenshū," vol. 2.

———"Sozei no gi" 租税之議 (On taxation). April or May 1869. In "Mori Arinori zenshū," vol. 1.

———"Gokokutai no gi ni tsuki mondai shijō" 御国体の儀につき問題四条 (Four questions relating to the matter of the national polity). June 1869. In "Mori Arinori zenshū," vol. 1.

———"Keibatsu wa sono isshin ni todomeru beki gi" 刑罰ハ其一身ニ可止議 (On the confining of penalties to the criminal concerned). June 1869. In "Mori Arinori zenshū," vol. 1.

———"Tsūshō o haishi jitsumei nomi o mochiuru beki koto" 通称ヲ廃シ実名ノミヲ可用事 (On disuse of the popular name, and exclusive use of the true name). June 1869. In "Mori Arinori zenshū," vol. 1.

———"Haitōron" 廃刀論 (Proposal for the abolition of sword-wearing). Popular designation for "Kanri heitai no hoka taitō o haisuru no gi" 官吏兵隊之外帯刀ヲ廃スルノ議 (On abolishing the wearing of swords by all persons other than civil officials and soldiers). July 6, 1869. In "Mori Arinori zenshū," vol. 1.

———"Yōgaku kyōiku ni kansuru jōsho" 洋学教育に関する上書 (Memorial on instruction in Western Learning). June 20, 1870. In "Mori Arinori zenshū," vol. 1.

———"Bibō daini" 備忘第二 (Notebook no. 2). Diary for October 1870–February 1871. In "Mori Arinori zenshū," vol. 2.

———*Life and Resources in America*, prepared under the direction of Arinori Mori by Charles Lanman. Originally printed in 1871. Reprinted as Part III of Charles Lanman, *The Japanese in America* (New York, 1872).

———"Letters: Japanese Legation, U.S.A.," Sept. 3, 1872–Mar. 18, 1873 (A letter copybook of correspondence addressed by Mori and his subordinates mainly to private American citizens; personal property of Mori Arimasa, Paris, France). To be published in "Mori Arinori zenshū," vol. 3.

———*Religious Freedom in Japan: A Memorial and Draft of Charter* (Washington, D. C., 1872). In *Meiji bunka zenshū*, vol. 11.

———*Education in Japan: A Series of Letters Addressed by Prominent Americans to Arinori Mori* (New York, 1873). To be reprinted in "Mori Arinori zenshū," vol. 3.

———"Gaikoku kōsai ni jōjitsu o mochiizaru beki no gi" 外国交際に情実を用いざるべきの議 (On the avoidance of sentiment in diplomatic intercourse). Early 1874. In "Mori Arinori zenshū," vol. 1.

———"Gakusha shokubun ron no hyō" 学者職分論の評 (A critique of arguments concerning the role of the scholar), *Meirokuzasshi*, no. 2 (March 1874) in "Mori Arinori zenshū," vol. 1.

———"Kaika dai ichi wa" 開化第一話 (Civilization: part one), *Meirokuzasshi*, no. 3 (April 1874) in "Mori Arinori zenshū," vol. 1.

———"Minsen giin setsuritsu kengonsho no hyō" 民撰議院設立建言書の評 (Critique of the petition for the establishment of a popular assembly), *Meirokuzasshi*, no. 3 (April 1874), in "Mori Arinori zenshū," vol. 1.

———"Dokuritsu kokken gi" 独立国権義 (The meaning of national sovereignty), *Meirokuzasshi*, no. 7 (May 1874) in "Mori Arinori zenshū," vol. 1.

———"Saishōron" 妻妾論 (Discourse on wives and mistresses), *Meirokuzasshi*, nos. 8, 11, 15, 20, 27 (May, June, August, November 1874; February 1875) in "Mori Arinori zenshū," vol. 1.

———"Shūkyō" 宗教 (Religion), *Meirokuzasshi*, no. 6 (May 1874) in "Mori Arinori zenshū," vol. 1.

———"Gaikoku kōsai o tadasu no gi" 外国交際を正すの議 (On the reform of our diplomatic intercourse). June 12, 1874. In "Mori Arinori zenshū," vol. 1.

———"Meirokusha dai-ichi nenkai yakuin kaisen ni tsuki enzetsu" 明六社第一年回役員改選に付演説 (Speech delivered on the occasion of the first annual election of officers of the Meiji Six Society), *Meirokuzasshi*, no. 30 (February 1875) in "Mori Arinori zenshū," vol. 1.

———Kyōikurei ni kansuru ikenshoan" 教育令に関する意見書案 (Draft of a written opinion on the Education Ordinance). 1879. In "Mori Arinori zenshū," vol. 1.

———"Shintai no nōryoku" 身体の能力 (On physical fitness). September 1879. In "Mori Arinori zenshū," vol. 1.

———"Kanri tōyōhō narabi ni taikyūhō seido kengon" 官吏登用法並に退休俸制度建言 (Memorial on the rules for appointing, and the system for pensioning, government officials). March 16, 1881. In "Mori Arinori zenshū," vol. 1.

———"Kyōtei gakushi kaiin shoken" 恭呈学士会院諸賢 (A letter respectfully addressed to the Honorable Members of the Academy). June 23, 1882. In "Mori Arinori zenshū," vol. 1.

———"Gakusei hengen" 学政片言 (A few words on educational administration). Sept. 12, 1882. In "Mori Arinori zenshū," vol. 1.

———"Nihon seifu daigi seitairon" 日本政府代議政体論 (On a representative polity for the government of Japan). Late 1883. In "Mori Arinori zenshū," vol. 3.

———*On a Representative System of Government for Japan* (London, By the Author, 1883). To be reprinted in "Mori Arinori zenshū," vol. 3.

———"Gakusei yōryō" 学政要領 (Essentials of the government educational administration). 1884 or 1885. In "Mori Arinori zenshū," vol. 1.

———"Shōgyō kyōiku no hitsuyōsei ni kansuru enzetsu" 商業教育の必要性に関する演説 (Speech concerning the necessity of commercial education). Delivered before the Osaka Chamber of Commerce, April 1885. In "Mori Arinori zenshū," vol. 1.

———"Kyōikurei ni tsuki iken" 教育令に付意見 (Opinion on the Education Ordinance). July 1885. In "Mori Arinori zenshū," vol. 1.

———"Saitamaken Jinjō Shihangakkō" 埼玉県尋常師範学校 (Saitama Prefectural Normal School). Speech delivered Dec. 19, 1885. In "Mori Arinori zenshū," vol. 1.

———"Heishiki taisō ni kansuru kengon" 兵式体操に関する建言 (Memorial concerning military-style physical training). Late 1885 or early 1886. In "Mori Arinori zenshū," vol. 1.

———"Kakushō daijin sekinin jūkei no shidai" 各省大臣責任重軽の次第 (An order of precedence for the respective responsibilities of the several Cabinet Ministers). From 1886–1889. In "Mori Arinori zenshū," vol. 1.

———"Seitō naikaku no hi o ronsu" 政党内閣の非を論す (The argument against party cabinets). From 1886–1889. In "Mori Arinori zenshū," vol. 1.

———"Kakugian" 閣議案 (Draft cabinet proposal). 1887. In "Mori Arinori zenshū," vol. 1.

———"Kyūshū kakuken/shōgakkō" 九州各県小学校 (All Kyushu prefectures/primary schools). In "Mori Arinori zenshū," vol. 1.
———"Miyagi Kenchō" 宮城県庁 (Miyagi Prefectural Office). Speech delivered Jan. 21, 1887. In "Mori Arinori zenshū," vol. 1.
———"Kyūshū/gunkuchō" 九州郡区長 (Kyushu / county and ward heads). Speech delivered February 1887. In "Mori Arinori zenshū," vol. 1.
———"Tozen chihō gakuji junshi" 豊前地方学事巡視 (Toyama/Ishikawa/Fukui District educational inspection tour). Speech delivered February 1887. In "Mori Arinori zenshū," vol. 1.
———"Fukushimaken Gijidō" 福島県議事堂 (Fukushima Prefectural Assembly Hall). Speech delivered June 22, 1887. In "Mori Arinori zenshū," vol. 1.
———"Daisanchihō gakuji junshi" 第三地方学事巡視 (Third District educational inspection tour). Speech delivered Fall 1887. In "Mori Arinori zenshū," vol. 1.
———"Wakayamaken Jinjō Shihangakkō" 和歌山県尋常師範学校 (Wakayama Prefectural Normal School). Speech delivered Nov. 15, 1887. In "Mori Arinori zenshū," vol. 1.
———"Tōkyōfu shōgakkōchō fukaigiin" 東京府小学校長府会議員 (Tokyo Prefecture primary school principals and prefectural assembly members). Speech delivered Sept. 25, 1888. In "Mori Arinori zenshū," vol. 1.
———"Ōu rokken gakuji junshi" 奥羽六県学事巡視 (Educational inspection tour of the six prefectures of northern Honshu). Speech delivered Fall 1888. In "Mori Arinori zenshū," vol. 1.
———"Monbushō/chokkatsu gakkōchō" 文部省直轄学校長 (Ministry of Education/heads of directly administered schools). Speech delivered Jan. 28, 1889. In "Mori Arinori zenshū," vol. 1.
———"Fuken gakumukachō ni taisuru enzetsu" 府県学務課長にたいする演説 (Speech to the heads of the Educational Affairs Sections of the prefectural governments). Delivered at the Monbushō on Feb. 5, 1889. In "Mori Arinori zenshū," vol. 1.
Mori Hiroko 森寛子, as told to Mori Arimasa 森有正, "Mori Arinori no omoide" 森有礼の思ひ出 (Recollections of Mori Arinori), in *Mikuni* みくに, 4.3 (March 1938). In "Mori Arinori zenshū," vol. 2.
———as told to Mori Arimasa, "Mori Arinori no omokage" 森有礼のおもかげ (Memories of Mori Arinori), Pts. 1 and 2, in *Mikuni*, 4.4 (April 1938) and 4.6 (June 1938). In "Mori Arinori zenshū," vol. 2.
Motoyama Yukihiko 本山幸彦, "Bunmei kaika ki ni okeru shin chishikijin no shisō: Meirokusha no hitobito o chūshin to shite" 文明開化期における新知識人の思想： 明六社の人々を中心として (The thought of the new intellectuals of the Era of Civilization and Enlightenment: with focus on the members of the Meiji Six Society), in *Jinbun gakuhō* 人文学報, 4 (February 1954).
———"Mori Arinori no kokka shugi to sono kyōiku shisō" 森有礼の国

家主義とその教育思想 (The statism and educational thought of Mori Arinori), in *Jinbun gakuhō*, 8 (1958).
Murray, David. Papers. Library of Congress, Manuscripts Division.
——"Dabitto Morurē Shinpō: Meiji rokunen" ダビット・モルレー申報：明治六年 (Report of David Murray: 1873). Submitted to the Ministry of Education; tr. anon. In *Meiji bunka zenshū*, vol. 10.
Nagai Michio. "Herbert Spencer in Early Meiji Japan," *Far Eastern Quarterly*, 14.1: 55–64 (November 1954).
——永井道雄. "Chishikijin no seisan rūto" 知識人の生産ルート (The production-line of the intellectuals), in *Chishikijin no seisei to yakuwari* 知識人の生成と役割り (Formation and role of the intellectuals), vol. 4 of *Kindai Nihon shisōshi kōza* 近代日本思想史講座 (Lectures on the intellectual history of modern Japan). Tokyo, 1959.
——"Mori Arinori: Meiji kyōiku no kensetsusha" 森有礼：明治教育の建設者 (Mori Arinori: builder of Meiji education), in vol. 1 of Asahi Jānaru 朝日ジャーナル, ed., *Nihon no shisōka* 日本の思想家 (Thinkers of Japan). 3 vols. Tokyo, 1962.
Nagashima Tadanobu 永島忠重. *Arai Ōsui sensei no omokage to sono danwa* 新井奥邃先生の面影と其の談話 (Memories and conversations of Arai Ōsui). Tokyo, 1929.
——*Ōsui goroku* 奥邃語録 (Sayings of Ōsui). Tokyo, 1931.
——*Arai Ōsui sensei* 新井奥邃先生 (Arai Ōsui). Tokyo, 1933.
Nakajima Tarō 中島太郎. *Kindai Nihon kyōiku seidoshi* 近代日本教育制度史 (A history of the educational system of modern Japan). Tokyo, 1966.
Nakamura Masanao 中村正直. "Gitaiseijin jōsho" 擬泰西人上書 (Memorial on the imitation of Westerners), in *Shinbun zasshi* 新聞雑誌, no. 56 (September 1872).
Nakane Chie 中根千枝. *Tate shakai no ningen kankei* タテ社会の人間関係 (Personal relationships in the vertically structured society). Tokyo, 1967.
Nihon kindaishi jiten 日本近代史辞典 (Dictionary of modern Japanese history), ed. Kyōto Daigaku Bungakubu Kokushi Kenkyūshitsu 京都大学文学部国史研究室. Tokyo, 1958.
Nishida Chōjū 西田長寿. "*Meiroku zasshi* kaidai" 「明六雑誌」解題 (Introductory note on the *Meiroku zasshi*), *Meiji bunka zenshū*, vol.18.
——*Meiji jidai no shinbun to zasshi* 明治時代の新聞と雑誌 (Newspapers and magazines of the Meiji period). Tokyo, 1966.
Nishimura Shigeki 西村茂樹. *Ōji roku* 往事録 (Record of the past). Tokyo, 1905.
Noguchi Entarō 野口援太郎. "Shihan kyōiku no hensen" 師範教育の変遷 (Changes in teacher training), in *Kyōiku gojūnenshi*.
Norbeck, Edward, and George A. DeVos. "Japan," in L. K. Hsu, ed., *Psychological Anthropological Approaches to Culture and Personality*. Homewood, Ill., 1961.
Nōsei Sakae 能勢栄. *Tokuiku chinteiron* 徳育鎮定論 (On the suppression of moral education). Tokyo, 1890.

Obata, Kyugorō. *An Interpretation of the Life of Viscount Shibusawa*. Tokyo, 1938.

Ōkubo Toshiaki 大久保利謙. *Nihon no daigaku* 日本の大学 (Japanese universities). Tokyo, 1943.

——— *Mori Arinori* 森有礼, vol. 18 of Ishikawa Ken 石川謙, gen. ed., *Nihon kyōiku sentetsu sōsho*. Tokyo, 1942.

——— "Meirokusha no hitobito" 明六社の人々 (The people of the Meiji Six Society), in Konishi Shirō 小西四郎, ed., *Kindai: I* 近代: I (Modern times: I), vol. 5 of *Nihon jinbutsushi taikei* 日本人物史大系 (An outline history of famous Japanese). Tokyo, 1960.

——— ed., *Meiji bunka shiryō sōsho: kyōikuhen* 明治文化資料叢書：教育篇 (A library of materials on Meiji culture: Education), vol. 8 of Meiji Bunka Shiryō Sōsho Kankōkai 刊行会 eds., *Meiji bunka shiryō sōsho*. Tokyo, 1961.

——— *Meiji keimō shisō shū* 明治啓蒙思想集 (Anthology of the thought of the Meiji enlightenment), vol. 3 of *Meiji bungaku zenshū* 明治文学全集 (Collected works of Meiji literature). Tokyo, Chikuma Shobō, 1967.

——— "Meiji jūshinen no seihen" 明治十四年の政変 (The political turnover of 1881), in Meiji Shiryō Kenkyū Renrakukai 明治史料研究連絡会, eds., *Meiji seiken no kakuritsu katei* 明治政権の確立過程 (The process of the establishment of the Meiji regime), vol. 1 of *Meijishi kenkyū sōsho* 明治史研究叢書 (A library of studies on Meiji history). Rev. ed. Tokyo, 1968.

Oliphant, Margaret W. *Memoir of the Life of Laurence Oliphant and Alice Oliphant, His Wife*. London, 1891.

Ōmura Kakichi 大村喜吉. "Mori Arinori: eigaku o sasaeta hitobito: dai-roku" 森有礼：英学を支えた人々：第六 (Mori Arinori: Promoters of the study of English: No. 6), in *Eigo seinen* 英語青年 (July 1965).

Osanai Kaoru 小山内薫. *Mori Arinori* 森有礼, a play in five acts, in Osanai Kaoru, *Gikyokushū* 戯曲集 (Anthology of plays). Tokyo, 1926.

Osatake Takeki 尾佐竹猛. *Ishin zengo ni okeru rikken shisō* 維新前後における立憲思想 (Constitutional thought before and after the Restoration). 2 vols. Tokyo, 1929.

——— *Nihon kenseishi no kenkyū* 日本憲政史の研究 (A study of the history of constitutionalism in Japan). Ichigensha ed. Tokyo, 1943.

Ōyama Azusa 大山梓. "Iwakura kaisei sōan to Terajima sōan" 岩倉改正草案と寺島草案 (The Iwakura revision draft and the Terajima draft), in *Kokusai seiji* 国際政治, no. 3 (autumn 1957).

Pall Mall Gazette (London), February 26, 1884.

Passin, Herbert. *Society and Education in Japan*. New York, 1965.

Paulsen, Friedrich. *German Education Past and Present*, tr. T. Lorenz. London, 1908.

Peterson, A. D. C. *A Hundred Years of Education: A Comparative Study of Educational Patterns in Western Europe and the United States*. Collier Books ed. New York, 1962.

Phillimore, Robert J. *Commentaries Upon International Law*, 3 vols. Philadelphia, 1854–1857.

Rakuseki Izawa Shūji sensei 楽石伊沢修二先生 (Rakuseki Izawa Shūji), ed. Ko Izawa Sensei Kinen Jigyō Kai 故伊沢先生記念事業会. Tokyo, 1919.

Renwanz, Johannes. *Matthew Arnold und Deutschland*. Greifswald, 1927.

Sakai Kunio 坂井邦夫. *Meiji ansatsushi* 明治暗殺史 (History of assassinations in the Meiji era). Tokyo, 1933.

Sansom, Sir George B. *The Western World and Japan*. New York, 1950.

Sappan kaigunshi 薩藩海軍史 (Naval history of Satsuma han), comp. Kōshaku Shimazuke Henshūjo 公爵島津家編集所. 3 vols. Kagoshima, 1928.

Sappan no bunka 薩藩の文化 (Culture of Satsuma han), comp. Kagoshima Ken Kyōiku Kai 鹿児島県教育会. Kagoshima, 1935.

Satow Papers. PRO–30–33–11–4. Correspondence for 1904–1920. Public Record Office Manuscripts, Great Britain.

———PRO–30–33–15–3/7/10. "Diaries" for 1868–1871, January 1882–March 1884, and November 1885–December 1886. Public Record Office Manuscripts, Great Britain.

Schmiedel, Otto. *Die Deutschen in Japan*. Leipzig, 1920.

Schneider, Herbert W., and George Lawton. *A Prophet and a Pilgrim*. New York, 1942.

Schwantes, Robert S. "American Influences in the Education of Meiji Japan." Ph.D. dissertation, Harvard University, 1950.

Sera Ryōichi 世良嗃一, ed., *Sappan katei kyōiku no kenkyū* 薩藩家庭教育の研究 (Studies of home education in Satsuma han). Kagoshima, 1937.

Shimada Saburō 島田三郎. "Kaisei kyōikurei no happu" 改正教育令の発布 (The promulgation of the Revised Education Ordinance), in *Kyōiku gojūnenshi*.

Shimizu Shin 清水信. *Doku-ō ni okeru Itō Hakubun no kenpō chōsa to Nihon kenpō* 独墺に於ける伊藤博文の憲法取調と日本憲法 (The constitutional researches of Itō Hirobumi in Germany and Austria and the Japanese Constitution). Tokyo, 1939.

Shimomura Fujio 下村富士男. "Iwakura shisetsu no ō-bei haken to taibei kōshō" 岩倉使節の欧米派遣と対米交渉 (The dispatch of the Iwakura mission to Europe and America and its negotiations with the United States), in Kodama Kōta 児玉幸多, ed., *Nihon shakaishi no kenkyū* 日本社会史の研究 (Studies in Japanese social history). Tokyo, 1955.

———*Meiji shonen jōyaku kaiseishi no kenkyū* 明治初年条約改正史の研究 (A study of the history of treaty revision in the early years of Meiji). Tokyo, 1962.

Shinbun shūsei Meiji hennenshi 新聞集成明治編年史 (A chronicle of Meiji compiled from newspapers), comp. Nakayama Yasumasa 中山泰昌. 15 vols. Tokyo, 1934–36.

Shōgiku Kido kō den 松菊木戸公伝 (Life of Prince Shōgiku Kido), comp. Kido Kō Denki Hensanjo 木戸公伝記編纂所. 2 vols. Tokyo, 1927.

Spencer, Herbert. *Education: Intellectual, Moral and Physical.* London, 1904. First published in 1861.
———*An Autobiography.* 2 vols. New York, 1904.
———*The Principles of Sociology.* 3 vols. 3rd ed. New York, 1921–1925.
Stein, Lorenz von. *Handbuch der Verwaltungslehre.* Stuttgart, 1870.
Suzuki Tadashi 鈴木正. "Meiji kanryō to kindai shisō: Mori Arinori o meguru kōsatsu" 明治官僚と近代思想：森有礼をめぐる考察 (The Meiji bureaucrat and modern thought: an inquiry centering on Mori Arinori), *Rekishi hyōron* 歴史評論, no. 90 (November 1957).
Tabohashi Kiyoshi 田保橋潔. *Kindai nissen kankei no kenkyū* 近代日鮮関係の研究 (A study of modern Japanese-Korean relations). 2 vols. Tokyo, 1940.
Takahashi Korekiyo 高橋是清. *Jiden* 自伝 (Autobiography). Tokyo, 1936.
Takahashi Tatsuo 高橋竜雄. "Kokugo kokubun kara mita Fukuzawa sensei" 国語国文から観た福沢先生 (Fukuzawa viewed from the standpoint of Japanese language and literature), in *Shigaku* 史学 (November 1934).
Takeda Kiyoko 武田清子. *Ningenkan no sōkoku* 人間観の相剋 (Conflict of the views of Man). Tokyo, 1959.
Tanaka Kazutoshi 田中万逸. *Kinsei ijin hyakuwa* 近世偉人百話 (Divers tales of the great men of recent times). Tokyo, 1922.
Tenterden Papers. FO–363–1. Correspondence with Granville and Kennedy, 1879–1881. Public Record Office Manuscripts, Great Britain.
Thut, I. N., and Don Adams. *Educational Patterns in Contemporary Societies.* New York, 1964.
The Times (London). Files for 1865–67 and 1880–90.
Tocqueville, Alexis de. *Democracy in America,* ed. Phillips Bradley. Vintage Paperback ed. 2 vols. New York, 1954.
Tokutomi Sohō 徳富蘇峰. "Mori Arinori kun" 森有礼君 (Mori Arinori), in *Kokumin no tomo* 国民の友, 4.42 (February 1889).
Tōyama Shigeki 遠山茂樹. *Meiji ishin* 明治維新 (The Meiji restoration). Tokyo, 1951.
Toyoda Takeshi 豊田武 and Kagoshima Ken Kyōiku Iinkai 鹿児島県教育委員会, comps. *Kagoshima ken kyōikushi* 鹿児島県教育史 (History of education in Kagoshima Prefecture). 2 vols. Kagoshima, 1960.
Trevelyan, George Macaulay. *British History in the Nineteenth Century and After (1782–1919).* Pelican Books ed. Harmondsworth, 1965.
Tsuchiya Tadao 土屋忠雄. "Mori Arinori no kyōiku seisaku" 森有礼の教育政策 (Mori Arinori's educational policy), in Ishiyama Shuhei 石山朱平 et al., *Kyōiku no shiteki tenkai* 教育の史的展開 (Historical development of education). Tokyo, 1952.
———*Meiji zenki kyōiku seisakushi no kenkyū* 明治前期教育政策史の研究 (A study of the history of educational policy in the early Meiji period). Rev. ed. Tokyo, 1968.
Tsukada Akio 塚田彰夫, comp. *Kagoshima: kyōdo no rekishi to monogatari* かごしま・郷土の歴史と物語 (Kagoshima: history and tales of our ancestral home). Kagoshima, 1964.

Umetani Noboru 梅渓昇. "Kyōiku chokugo seiritsu no rekishiteki haikei" 教育勅語の歴史的背景 (Historical background of the framing of the Imperial Rescript on Education), in Sakata Yoshio 坂田吉雄, ed., *Meiji zenpanki no nashonarizumu* 明治前半期のナショナリズム (Nationalism in the first half of the Meiji period). Tokyo, 1958.
United States Commission on Education. Letter Books. No. 12. National Archives, Washington, D.C.
United States Department of State. Despatches from United States Ministers to Japan: 1855–1906. Microfilm no. M–133, Roll no. 17 (1871). National Archives, Washington, D.C.
———Notes from the Japanese Legation: 1871–1872. National Archives, Washington, D.C.
———Japanese Embassy: Minutes of Conferences, Drafts of Treaties Submitted, etc., 1872. National Archives, Washington, D.C.
———Papers Relating to the Foreign Relations of the United States. Nos. 288 and 548. National Archives, Washington, D.C.
Vattel, Emerich de. *The Law of Nations; or, Principles of the Law of Nature Applied to the Conduct and Affairs of Nations and Sovereigns*, tr. Joseph Chitty and E. D. Ingraham. Philadelphia, 1859.
Washington Evening Star. Files for 1871–73.
Watanabe Ikujirō 渡辺幾治郎. *Nihon kenpō seiteishi kō* 日本憲法制定史講 (Lectures on the history of the establishment of the Japanese Constitution). Tokyo, 1937.
Whitney Manuscripts. Yale University Library, Historical Manuscripts.
Wilson, Robert A. *Genesis of the Meiji Government in Japan: 1868–1871*. University of California Publications in History. Berkeley, 1957.
Wong, George H. C. "Mori Arinori's Mission to China, 1876," *Chung Chi Journal* (November 1963).
Woolsey Manuscripts. Yale University Library, Historical Manuscripts.
Yamazaki Masashige 山崎正董. *Yokoi Shōnan den* 横井小楠伝 (Life of Yokoi Shōnan). 3 vols. Tokyo, 1942.
———comp. *Yokoi Shōnan ikō* 横井小楠遺稿 (Posthumous manuscripts of Yokoi Shōnan). Tokyo, 1942.
Yoshida Kumaji 吉田熊次. "Dabitto Morurē shinpō kaidai" ダビット・モルレー申報解題 (Introductory note to the "Report of David Murray"), in *Meiji bunka zenshū*, vol. 10.
———and Kaigo Tokiomi 海後宗臣. *Kyōiku chokugo kanpatsu izen ni okeru shōgakkō shūshin kyōjū no hensen* 教育勅語渙発以前に於ける小学校修身教授の変遷 (Changes in the teaching of moral education in the primary schools prior to the promulgation of the Imperial Rescript on Education). Tokyo, 1934.
Yoshino Sakuzō 吉野作造. "Nihon shūkyō jiyū ron no kaidai" 日本宗教自由論の解題 (Introductory note to the essay on Japanese religious freedom), in *Meiji bunka zenshū*, vol. 11.
———*Kandan no kandan* 閑談の閑談 (Random conversations).Tokyo,1933.
Young, G. M. *Victorian England: Portrait of an Age*. Doubleday Anchor ed. Garden City, N. Y., 1954.

GLOSSARY

aikoku 愛国
Akamatsu Tomohiro 赤松友裕
Akizuki Taneki 秋月種樹
Amamori Kenzaburō 雨森謙三郎
anshō 暗誦
Aoki Shūzō 青木周蔵
Aoyama Yoshiaki 青山良顕
Arai Ichirō 新井一郎
Arai Ōsui 新井奥邃
Arisugawa no miya (Prince) 有栖川宮
ashigaru 足軽
Ashikaga Gakkō 足利学校

Baba Tatsui 馬場辰猪
baishin 陪臣
Baka-fu 馬鹿府
Bakufu 幕府
Bakumatsu 幕末
bankoku kyōsō 万国競争
Bansho shirabedokoro 蛮書調所
benrikōshi 弁理公使
Bunbu Gakkō 文武学校
Bunbu Kōshūjo 文武講習所

bungen 分限
bunka daigaku 分科大学
bunkateki seijika no tenkei 文化的政治家の典型
bunsai 分際
bunseika 文政家
bushidō 武士道

Chichibu Tarō 秩父太郎
chigo 稚児
chigogashira 稚児頭
chigyō tori 知行取り
Chihō Gakumukyoku 地方学務局
chiji 知事
chō 町
chō-son 町村
chokkyo 勅許
chokusen 勅選
chokuyu 勅諭
chōrō 長老
Chōshū 長州
chōsonkai 町村会
Chōya shinbun 朝野新聞
Chu Hsi (Shushi) 朱熹（朱子）

chūbenmushi 中弁務使
Chūgakkō 中学校
Chūgakkōrei 中学校令
chūgaku-ku 中学区
chūkun 忠君
chūshin ni shite 中心にして

daibenmushi 大弁務使
Daigakkō 大学校
Daigaku 大学
daigakuin 大学院
Daigaku Nankō 大学南校
Daigaku shōku 大学章句
daigi 代議
daigisha 代議者
daimyō karuta 大名かるた
Dai Nihon Kyōikukai 大日本教育会
dairikōshi 代理公使
dajō 大丞
dajō daijin 太政大臣
Dajōkan 太政官
dappan 脱藩
Date Munenari 伊藤宗城
Denki 伝記
dōken 同権
dokuritsu 独立
dokuritsu kokken 独立国権
dōtō 同等
dōtoku 道徳

Edo 江戸
Edogawa Juku 江戸川塾
Egi Kazuyuki 江木千之
eiken no minamoto 栄権の源
Enatsu Sōsuke 江夏壮助
Enbukan 演武館
Enomoto Takeaki 榎本武揚
Ensei kiki jutsu 遠西奇器述

fuchimaitori 扶持米取り
fuchū 府中
fūfu betsu ari 夫婦有別
fūfu dōken 夫婦同権
fūfu o betsu ni suru 夫婦を別にする
Fujisaki Ryūsuke 藤崎竜助
fu-ken 府県

fuken gakumukachō 府県学務課長
fukoku 富国
Fukuchi Gen'ichirō 福地源一郎
fukuchiji 副知事
Fukuoka Kōtei 福岡孝弟
Fukushima Taneomi 副島種臣
fukushū zamoto 復習座元
fukusōsai 副総裁
fumoto 麓
Fukuzawa Yukichi 福沢諭吉

Gaikokukan 外国官
gaikokukan gonhanji 外国官権判事
Gaimushō 外務省
gakkan 学監
"Gakki" 学規
Gakkō 学校
gakkō kumiai 学校組合
"Gakkō kyōin hinkō kentei kisoku" 学校教員品行検定規則
Gakkōrei 学校令
Gakkō Torishirabe 学校取調
"Gakuji setsumeisho" 学事説明書
gakumon 学問
"Gakumon no taihon" 学問の大本
Gakumuiin 学務委員
Gakusei (Fundamental code of education) 学制
gakusei (government educational administration) 学政
gakusei (student) 学生
"Gakusei ni tsuki chokuyu" 学制ニ付勅諭
Gekū 外宮
genbun itchi 言文一致
genri 原理
genrōin 元老院
"Gianroku" 議案録
gichō jimu sekkō 議長事務摂行
Gijiteisai Torishirabesho 議事体裁取調所
gikan 議官
Ginkōgakukyoku 銀行学局
Giseikan 議政官
Godai Kyōta 五代競太
Godai Tomoatsu 五代友厚
Godaiin Mihashira 後醍院真柱

goichimonke 御一門家
Gōjū 郷中
gōjūbanashi 郷中放し
gokashi 御下賜
"Gokokusei kaisei no gi" 御国制改正の議
gōshi 郷士
gōshi seido 郷士制度
Gotō Shōjirō 後藤象次郎
goyō kakari 御用掛
gun 郡
gun-ken 郡県
gunkuchō 郡区長
Gunmukan 軍務官
gyōsei 行政
Gyōseikan 行政官

han 藩
Hanashiaijū 咄相中
hanji 判事
Hashima 羽島
Hatakeyama Yoshinari 畠山義成
heika hōtai shite 陛下奉戴して
heinō bunri 兵農分離
heinō itchi 兵農一致
heishiki taisō 兵式体操
henpeki 偏癖
Hensankyoku 編纂局
hiemondori 冷物取り
Higashikuze Michitomi 東久世通禧
Hijikata Hisamoto 土方久元
Hirata Atsutane 平田篤胤
Hito wa shiro, hito wa ishigaki, hito wa hori 人ハ城、人ハ石垣、人ハ堀
Hiwatari Kaimon 樋渡海門
hōgiri 方限
hōi 宝位
hōken 封建
honzon 本尊
Hori Takayuki 堀孝之
Hosokawa Junjirō 細川潤次郎
hōsoku 法則
Hozumi Yatsuka 穂積八束
Huang Hui-Lien 黄恵廉
hyōgikai 評議会

Hyōron Shinbun 評論新聞
Hyūga 日向

iaku jōsō 帷幄上奏
Ichijō Jūjirō 一条十次郎
Ichikawa Bunkichi 市川文吉
Ichiki Hirotsura 市来広貫
Ichiki Kanjūrō 市来勘十郎
ie no ko 家の子
Igakusho 医学所
igi 威儀
ijū 威重
ikki 一揆
inakabito 田舎人
Inari 稲荷
Inoue Kaoru 井上馨
Inoue Kowashi 井上毅
ippan kyōiku 一般教育
Iroha uta イロハ歌
Ise shinbun 伊勢新聞
Ishigaki Einosuke 石垣鋭之助
Ishii Shōichirō 石井省一郎
Ishikawa Kakutarō 石川確太郎
Ishūin Kaneyoshi 伊集院兼良
Iso 磯
Isonaga Hikosuke 磯永彦助
isshōmochi 一所持
isshōmochikaku 一所持格
Itagaki Taisuke 板垣退助
Itō Hirobumi 伊藤博文
Itō Miyoji 伊東巳代治
Iwakura Tomomi 岩倉具視
Iwashita Hōhei 岩下方平
Izawa Shūji 伊沢修二
Izumi Senzō 出水泉蔵

jigenryū 示現流
jiho 侍補
Jiji shinpō 時事新報
Jinjō Chūgakkō 尋常中学校
Jinjō Shihangakkō 尋常師範学校
Jinjō Shōgakkō 尋常小学校
jinmin no chichi 人民の父
jiri 自理
jiriki 自力
jishu dokuritsu 自主独立
jitaheiritsu 自他並立

jitō 地頭
jitsugaku 実学
Jitsugyō Chūgakkō 実業中学校
Jitsugyō Hoshū Gakkō 実業補習学校
jitsugyō kyōiku 実業教育
jiyū minken undō 自由民権運動
Jōdo Shinshū 浄土真宗
Jōgatani 城ヶ谷
jōi 攘夷
jōjitsu 情実
Jōkōmyōji 浄光明寺
jōri 条理
"Jōshinsho" 上申書
Jōyaku Kaitei Torishirabe Kyoku 条約改定取調局
jūgoi-ge 従五位下
jugyōryō 授業料
jūjun 従順
"Jukajō no kun'yu" 十か条の訓諭
junryō 順良
junsei gakumon 純正学問

Kabayama Hisanobu 樺山久言
kachū 家中
Kagoshima 鹿児島
Kagoshima Kaiseijo 鹿児島開成所
kaidoku 解読
"Kaika o susumeru hōhō o ronsu" 開化ヲ進ル方法ヲ論ス
kaikoku 開国
kaimeiha 開明派
kairaku 快楽
Kaiseijo 開成所
Kaisei kyōikurei 改正教育令
Kaitakushi 開拓使
Kaiyakusha 会訳社
Kajiya 加治屋
kakari 掛
kakei 家系
kakugian 閣議案
Kakumaru 鶴丸
Kakyoku 下局
kamishimo kihajime 裃着初
kan'ika 簡易科
kana 仮名
kanbun 漢文

Kanda 神田
Kanda Kōhei 神田孝平
Kanda Naibu 神田乃武
Kaneko Kentarō 金子堅太郎
K'ang-hsi 康熙
kanji 漢字
Kanmachi 上町
Kansei 寛政
kariya 仮屋
karō 家老
Kasuga 春日
katagi no tanren 気質の鍛錬
katei kyōiku 家庭教育
Katō Hiroyuki 加藤弘之
Katsu Kaishū 勝海舟
Katsura Tarō 桂太郎
Katsura Uemon 桂右衛門
Kawakami Kazen 川上嘉善
Kawamoto Miyuki 川本幸
Kawashima Jun 河島醇
kazoedoshi 数え年
Keian 桂庵
keimō undō 啓蒙運動
Keiō 慶応
keizaishugi 経済主義
ken 県
kenri gimu 権利義務
kentei 検定
kettō 血統
Kido Ichisuke 木戸市助
Kido Takayoshi 木戸孝允
kijiku 機軸
kikai 機械
kikan 機関
Kimura Kahei 木村嘉平
Kinshiroku 近思録
Kinshiroku kuzure 近思録崩れ
Kitō Takekiyo 木藤武清
kizoku 貴族
Kizokuin 貴族院
Koba Sadanaga 木場貞長
koban 小番
Kobekichō-rokuchōme 木挽町六丁目
kochigo 小稚児
"Kochigo aijū okite" 小稚児相中掟
kochō 戸長

kōdoku 講読
kōdō shugi 皇道主義
kogaku kuzure 古学崩れ
Kōgisho 公議所
"Kōgisho hōsokuan" 公議所法則案
"Kōgisho nisshi" 公議所日誌
kogumi 小組
kōhei 公平
Kōjimachi 麹町
Kōka 弘化
Kōkai shinsetsu 航海新説
kokka 国家
Kokkai 国会
kokkyō 国教
Kokkyōron 国教論
kōkoku 皇国
Kōkokuji 興国寺
kokoro 心
kokudaka 石高
kokugaku 国学
kokugaku kuzure 国学崩れ
"Kokugo haishi eigo saiyō ron" 国語廃止英語採用論
kokumin no kōfuku 国民の幸福
kokutai 国体
kokutai no kyōiku shugi 国体の教育主義
kokutei 国定
"Kokuze kōmoku" 国是綱目
Komatsu Terumori 小松壽盛
Kōno Togama 河野敏鎌
kōsei no jōri 公正の条理
koshōgumi 小姓組
koshōgumi bangashira 小姓組番頭
kōtei 皇帝
Kōten Kōkyūjo 皇典講究所
Kōtō Chūgakkō 高等中学校
Kōtōgakkō 高等学校
Kōtō jogakkō kitei" 高等女学校規定
kōtōkanshiho 高等官試補
kōtō kyōiku 高等教育
Kōtō Shihangakkō 高等師範学校
Kōtō Shōgakkō 高等小学校
kōzoku 皇族
ku 区

Kuga Katsunan 陸羯南
Kuki Ryūichi 九鬼隆一
Kumazawa Banzan 熊沢蕃山
kumi 組
kunaikyō 宮内卿
Kunaishō 宮内省
kuni no chizon naru tōshu 国ノ至尊ナル頭首
kuramaitori 蔵米取り
Kurimoto Jōun 栗本鋤雲
Kuroda Kiyotaka 黒田清隆
Kuroki Tamesada 黒木為楨
Kusunoki Masashige 楠木正茂
kutōshijo 句読師助
"Kyōgaku taishi" 教学大旨
kyōgi suru 協議する
kyōhei 強兵
kyōiku 教育
"Kyōiku chokugo" 教育勅語
kyōiku jiri 教育自理
"Kyōikugi" 教育議
"Kyōikugi fugi" 教育議附議
kyōikukai 教育会
Kyōikurei 教育令
"Kyōkayō tosho kentei jōrei" 教科用図書検定条例
"Kyōmon ron" 教門論
kyōsō 競争
kyūchū 宮中
kyūchū komonkan 宮中顧問官

Li Hung-chang 李鴻章
Lü Tsu-ch'ien (Ryo Soken) 呂祖謙

Machida Hisanari 町田久成
Machida Kiyozō 町田清蔵
Machida Shinjirō 町田申四郎
Magome Tamesuke 馬込為介
Makino Nobuaki 牧野伸顕
Matsuda Kuni 松田久二
Matsukata Masayoshi 松方正義
Matsuki Kōan 松木弘庵
Matsumura Junzō 松村淳蔵
Megata Tanetarō 目賀田種太郎
Meiji ishin 明治維新
Meirin'in 明倫院
Meirokusha 明六社

mekake 妾
mie 見得
mimaihin 見舞品
Minami Teisuke 南貞助
Minobe Tatsukichi 美濃部達吉
Mishima Michiharu 三島通陽
Mishima Michitsune 三島通庸
Mito 水戸
Mitsukuri Rinshō 箕作麟祥
Mitsukuri Shūhei 箕作秋坪
Miura Iemura 三浦家村
Miura Yasumura 三浦泰村
Miura Yoshimura 三浦義村
Miyake Setsurei 三宅雪嶺
Miyakonojō 都城
Mizuno Tadakuni 水野忠邦
monbu daijin 文部大臣
monbukyō 文部卿
Monbushō 文部省
mono 物
Mōri 毛利
Mori Akira 森明
Mori Arimasa 森有正
"Mori bunsō ni taisuru kyōiku ikensho" 森文相に対する教育意見書
Mori Genshirō 森元四郎
Mori Hide 森英
Mori Hiroko (née Iwakura) 森寛子（岩倉）
Mori Jirōsaburō Yukishige 森二郎三郎行重
Mori Jusae 森十左衛
Mori Kihachirō 森喜八郎
Mori Kinnojō Arinori (Yūrei) 森金之丞有礼
Mori Kitōta 森喜藤太
Mori Kiuemon Arinaga 森喜右衛門有長
Mori Kiuemon Yūjo 森喜右衛門有恕
Mori Kiyoshi 森清
Mori Mikuma 森三熊
Mori Osato (née Kumasaki) 森阿里（隈崎）
Mori Tsuneko (née Hirose) 森常子（広瀬）

Mori Yoshitaka Mutsu no Rokurō 森義隆陸奥六郎
moto no gakumon 本の学問
Motoda Eifu 元田永孚
Motoori Norinaga 本居宣長
muga 無我
Mukai Shinbei 向井新兵衛
mukaku 無格
mukoyōshi 婿養子
Murahashi Naoe 村橋直衛

Nabeshima Naomasa 鍋島直正
Nagai Iosuke 永井五百介
Nagasawa Kanaye 長沢鼎
"Nagasawa Kanaye den" 長沢鼎伝
Nagata-chō (Kagoshima) 長田町
Nagata-chō (Tokyo) 永田町
Nagoshi Heima 名越平馬
naijitsu 内実
Naikaku 内閣
Naikaku ni komon shi 内閣に顧問し
naimukyō 内務卿
Naimushō 内務省
Naitō Seitarō 内藤誠太郎
Nakahara Kuninosuke 中原国之助
Nakai Hiroshi 中井弘
Nakamura Masanao 中村正直
Nakamura Sōken 中村宗見
Narishima Ryūhoku 成島柳北
Nawa Michikazu 名和道一
nengō 年号
"Nihon dōtokuron" 日本道徳論
"Nihon kyōiku saku" 日本教育策
Nihon no unda seiyōjin 日本の生んだ西洋人
Niijima Jō 新島襄
Niiro Keibu 新納刑部
Niiro Tadamoto 新納忠元
ninka 認可
Nire Kagenori 仁礼景範
nise 二才
"Nise banashi kakushiki jōmoku" 二才咄格式定目
nisegashira 二才頭
Nishi Amane 西周
Nishikimachi 錦町

Nishimura Shigeki 西村茂樹
Nishino Buntarō 西野文太郎
"Nisshin shūkō jōki" 日清修好条規
nitō kyōiku 二等教育
Noda Chūbei 野田仲平
Nomura Ichisuke 野村市助
Nomura Sōshichi 野村宗七

ōban 大番
Ogata Jōjirō 緒方城次郎
Ogyū Sorai 荻生徂徠
Ōhara Shigesane 大原重実
Okakura Kakuzō 岡倉覚三
Okamoto Seien 岡本清遠
Ōki Takato 大木喬任
okon o sentaku suru 汚魂を洗濯する
Ōkubo Ichiō 大久保一翁
Ōkubo Toshimichi 大久保利通
Ōkuma Shigenobu 大隈重信
ōmetsuke 大目附
onjin 恩人
Ono Seigorō 小野正五郎
osachigo 長稚児
"Osachigo aijū okite" 長稚児相中掟
ōsei ishin 王政維新
Ōshiro Baiichirō 大城梅一郎
Ōsumi 大隅
Ōtsuki Hikogorō 大築彦五郎
Ōyama Iwao 大山巌
ōyō gakumon 応用学問
Ōyōmei (Wang Yang-ming) 王陽明
Ozawa Seijirō 小沢清次郎

Paoting 保定

rangaku 蘭学
Rangaku Kōshūjo 蘭学講習所
"Rekidai uta" 歴代歌
ri 里
Riji kōtei 理事功程
rinri 倫理
"Rinri kyōkasho ni tsuki ikensho" 倫理教科書に付意見書
rippō 立法
"Rirekisho" 履歴抄

risshin shusse 立身出世
roku 禄
Rokumeikan 鹿鳴館
ryūgaku 留学

Saigō Takamori 西郷隆盛
Saigō Tsugumichi 西郷従道
saijōkan 最上官
Sain 左院
saiyō shinai hō ga yoi 採用しない方が良い
Sakamoto Hirazaemon 坂元平左衛門
Sakatani Shiroshi 阪谷素
Samejima Naonobu 鮫島尚信
samurai 士
Sange kogoto 散華小言
sangi 参議
Sangiin 参議院
Sanjiin 参事院
Sanjō Sanetomi 三条実美
Sankokushi 三国誌
Sano Tsunetami 佐野常民
Sappan no bunkyō 薩藩の文教
Sasaki Takayuki 佐佐木高行
satori 悟り
Satsuma 薩摩
Satsunan 薩南
Sawa Nobuyoshi 沢宣嘉
Sawai Tetsuma 沢井鉄馬
Seido Torishirabesho 制度取調所
Seidoryō 制度寮
seifu no kijiku 政府の機軸
Seiin 正院
seijika 政治家
seiki 正気
"Seiron" 政論
seishin 精神
seitai 政体
Seitaisho 政体書
Seiwa Genji 清和源氏
Seiyō jijō 西洋事情
Seiyōken 精養軒
"Seiyuki" 聖喩記
Seki Kenzō 関研蔵
Sekigahara 関ヶ原
sekinin 責任

sekiten 釈奠
sengi 詮議
senkyo 薦挙
senmon gakkō 専門学校
Senmon gakkōrei 専門学校令
senmon kōtō no kyōiku 専門高等の教育
sennin 選任
sensei 先生
"Sensei no hanmen" 先生の半面
Sera Taichi 世良太一
shi (exemplar) 師
shi (samurai) 士
Shibata Masanaka 柴田剛中
Shibusawa Eiichi 渋沢栄一
shichōson 市町村
Shigeno Yasutsugu 重野安繹
Shihangakkōrei 師範学校令
shihan taipu 師範タイプ
shiketsubako 四傑箱
Shimada Saburō 島田三郎
Shimazu Hisamitsu 島津久光
Shimazu Nariakira 島津斉彬
Shimazu Narioki 島津斉興
Shimazu Shigehide 島津重豪
Shimazu Tadamasa 島津忠昌
Shimazu Tadayoshi 島津忠良
Shimazu Yoshihiro 島津義弘
Shimizu Usaburō 清水卯三郎
shin'ai 信愛
Shin kyōikurei 新教育令
Shinagawa Yajirō 品川弥二郎
shinban 新番
"Shinbunshi jōrei" 新聞紙条例
"Shinbunshi jōmoku" 新聞紙条目
shinmin 臣民
Shioda Atsunobu 塩田篤信
Shirao Kunihashira 白尾国柱
Shiroyama 城山
shishi 指示
Shizu no odamaki 倭文麻環
shō (mekake) 妾
shōbenmushi 小弁務使
"Shōgakkō kyōin kokoroe" 小学校教員心得
"Shōgakkō kyōsoku kōryō" 小学校教則綱領

"Shōgakkō o tateru no shui" 商学校ヲ建るの主意
Shōgakkōrei 小学校令
"Shōgaku jōmoku niken" 小学条目二件
Shōgaku shūshin kun 小学修身訓
shōgoi 正五位
Shōgyō Gakkō 商業学校
Shōhei Gakkō 昌平学校
Shōheikō 昌平黌
Shōhō Kōshujo 商法講習所
shosei 書生
shōyū 少輔
Shūgiin 集議院
shugodai 守護代
"Shūkai jōrei" 集会条例
Shunden 舜田
Shūseikan 集成館
shūshin 修身
"Shūshin chikoku hinitoron" 修身治国非二途論
"Shutain-shi kōgi hikki" 斯丁氏講義筆記
soba yaku 側役
sodoku 素読
Soejima Taneomi 副嶋種臣
Soga monogatari 曽我物語
somatsunagara 粗末ながら
sonnō 尊王
sonnō aikoku 尊王愛国
sonsū suru 尊崇する
sorizashi 反り差し
sōrōbun 候文
sōsai 総裁
sue no gakumon 末の学問
Sugi Kyōji 杉享二
Sugiura Kōzō 杉浦弘蔵
Sugiyama Takatoshi 杉山孝敏
Sukegorō 助五郎
Sūmitsuin 枢密院
sunawachi Jōin 即上院
sunawachi Sūmitsukaku 即枢密閣
Suzuki Tomoo 鈴木知雄

Tachibana Kōsai 橘耕斉
Taguchi Bunzō 田口文蔵
taifu 大輔

taigi meibun 大義名分
Taiheiki 太平記
taiiku 体育
Taika 大化
taishōfusegi 大将防ぎ
Taisō Denshūjo 体操伝習所
taka 高
Takagi Saburō 高木三郎
Takagi Yasaka 高木八尺
Takahashi Korekiyo 高橋是清
Takami Yaichi 高見弥一
Takasaki Goroēmon 高崎五郎右衛門
Takasaki Masakaze 高崎正風
Takashima Tokuemon 高島徳右衛門
tamashii o irekaeru 魂を入れ替える
Tanaka Fujimaro 田中不二麻呂
Tanaka Jirō 田中二郎
Tanaka Seisu 田中靖洲
Tanegashima Keisuke 種子ケ島敬輔
Tanimoto Heiuemon 谷元兵右衛門
teikoku 帝国
Teikoku daigakurei 帝国大学令
Teikoku Gakushiin 帝国学士院
tei suru 呈する
tennō 天皇
tennō shinsei 天皇新政
Tenpō 天保
tenpu jinken 天賦人権
Terajima Munenori 寺島宗則
"Terajima Munenori haku joden" 寺島宗則伯叙伝
tōbun gichō 当分議長
Tōgō Ainoshin 東郷愛之進
Tōgō Heihachirō 東郷平八郎
tojō 外城
tojō no zatsukishi 外城の座附士
tojō seido 外城制度
Tokudaiji Sanenori 徳大寺実則
Tokugakukyoku 督学局
Tokugawa 徳川
tokuiku 徳育
Tōkyō Gakushi Kaiin 東京学士会院

Tōkyō Jogakkō 東京女学校
Tōkyō Kōtō Shōgyō Gakkō 東京高等商業学校
Tōkyō nichi nichi shinbun 東京日日新聞
Tōkyō Shōgyō Gakkō 東京商業学校
Tōkyō Shōka Daigaku 東京商科大学
Tomita Tetsunosuke 富田鉄之助
Toragari monogatari 虎狩物語
torishimari 取締り
torishirabe kakari 取調掛り
Tosa 土佐
Totei Gakkō 従弟学校
Tōtōmi 遠淡海
Toyama Masakazu 外山正一
Toyotomi Hideyoshi 豊臣秀吉
tsubo 坪
Tsuboi Kōzō 坪井航三
Tsuda Masamichi 津田真道
Tsuda Umeko 津田梅子
Tsukiji 築地
tsune ni 常に
Tsungli-yamen 総理衙門
tsūshō 通称

Uchida Masao 内田正雄
Uchimura Kanzō 内村鑑三
Uemura Masahisa 植村正久
Ueno Keihan (Kagenori) 上野景範
Ueno Ryōtarō 上野良太郎
Uesugi 上杉
umamawari 馬廻り
Unjōsho 運上所
Unyō 雲揚
Uraga 浦賀

Wada Shinjirō 和田慎次郎
wakashūgumi 若衆組
Washizu Shakuma 鷲津尺魔
Watanabe Senjirō 渡辺専二郎

yakata 館
Yamada Akiyoshi 山田顕義
Yamagata Aritomo 山県有朋
Yamagawa Hiroshi 山川浩

Yamamoto Denzō 山本伝蔵
Yamamoto Gonnohyōe 山本権兵衛
Yamanote 山の手
Yamanouchi Sakuzaemon 山之内作左衛門
Yamanouchi Toyonobu 山内豊信
Yamato 大和
Yamazaki Ansai 山崎闇斉
Yano Jirō 矢野次郎
Yasui Shinpachirō 安井真八郎
Yatabe Ryōkichi 矢田部良吉
yobanashi zamoto 夜話座元
yōgaku 洋学
Yōgaku kōyō 幼学綱要
Yōgakukan 洋学館
"Yōji o motte kokugo o shosuru no ron" 洋学ヲ以テ国語ヲ書スルノ論
"Yōkō nikki" 洋行日記
Yokoi Shōnan 横井小楠
Yokoyama Kendō 横山健堂
Yokoyama Shōtarō Yasutake 横山正太郎安武
Yokoyama Son'ichirō 横山孫一郎
Yokoyama Yasukata 横山安容
yōmyō 幼名
yoriai 寄合

yoriainami 寄合並
yoriki 与力
Yoritaka Mori Kanja 頼隆森冠者
yorozuya 万屋
Yoshida Kiyonari 吉田清成
Yoshida Shōin 吉田松陰
Yoshihara Shigetoshi 吉原重俊
Yoshikawa Akimasa 芳川顕正
yoshiya 吉屋
Yūbin hōchi shinbun 郵便報知新聞
Yuchi Sadamoto 湯地定基
yūjō 友情
yūki 勇気
Yūki Yukiyasu 結城幸安
Yung-cheng 雍正
Yuri Kimimasa 由利公正

Zada Shigehide 座田重秀
zamoto 座元
"Zanbō ritsu" 讒謗律
zanshin hoshu no shugi 漸進保守の主義
zatsukishi 座附士
zazen 坐禅
zenkenkōshi 全権公使
zen o okonau 善を行う
Zōshikan 造士館
Zusho Hirosato 調所広郷

Index

Agricultural College at Amherst (later University of Massachusetts), 176, 180
Aikoku (patriotism), 428–429, 444, 465, 472
Akamatsu Tomohiro, 60
Akizuki Taneki, 132, 133, 135, 138
Alcock, Rutherford, 70
Alexander III, Tsar, 291
Amamori Kenzaburō, 141
Amaterasu (Sun Goddess), 102
America: Mori's evaluation of, 85; Mori's visits to, 105–128 (Brotherhood of the New Life), 155–187 (Washington)
Anecdote(s) (about Mori), 145–146, 236–237; of the Unserviceable Swords, 129; of the Parboiled Pachyderm, 130; of the Squandered Ballot, 135–136
Aoki Shūzō, 282
Aoyama Cemetery, 6, 10
Aoyama Yoshiaki (originally Mori Kihachirō; brother of Mori), 30
Arai Ōsui, 153, 203, 205, 207
Arisugawa, Prince, 291
Armytage, W. H. G., 381
Arnold, Matthew, 290, 376–377, 453; probable influence of, on Mori, 381–385, 462–463, 470; and Prussian primary education, 461
Arnold, Thomas, 367, 379, 433, 434
Asiatic Society of Japan, 235, 394
Assassination, of Mori, 1, 3–6
Aston, W. G., 143
Athenaeum Club (London), 236, 289–290, 316, 317, 379, 381; Mori's interview with Herbert Spencer at, 228
Audacious (flagship), 388
Australian (ship), 61
Ayrton, W. E., 379

Baba Tatsui, *Elementary Grammar of the Japanese Language*, 194
Baelz, Erwin, 476
Bagehot, Walter, 316
Bain, Prof. Alexander, 290, 345; *Mind and Body*, 340
Bakufu, Mori on the, 82
Bankoku kyōsō (the competition of nations), Mori's insistence on. 399–400, 408
Bansho Shirabedokoro (Office for the Investigation of Barbarian Books), 56
Barnard, Henry, 179
Belknap, William W., 170
Bellah, Robert N., 209

Benyowsky, Moritz von, 59
"Bibō daini" (Notebook 2), Mori's diary, 152, 206, 442, 479
Biedermann, F. K., 263
Bingham, John A., 271, 281, 286
Bird, Isabella L., 288, 294
Bismarck, Otto von, 387, 388
Blaine, James G., 8
Blüntschli, J. C., 263
Bosanquet, Bernard, 382
Boutwell, George S., 182, 183–184
Brandt, Max von, 167
Brinkley, Captain F., 8
Brocton, see Brotherhood of the New Life
Broek, J. K. van den, 57
Broglie, Albert de, 373
Brooks, Charles, 180–181, 386
Brotherhood of the New Life (Brocton, New York), 18, 95–96, 98, 206, 433–434, 470; Mori's sojourn at, 105–128 passim; proposed Japanese branch of, 152; removal of Nomura Ichisuke from, 204; decline of, at Santa Rosa, 205. See also Harris, Thomas Lake
Bunbu Gakkō (Literary and Military Academy), proposed, 59
Bunbu Kōshūjo (Literary and Military Training Center), 55
Burke, Edmund, 316
Busse, Ludwig, 464

Capron (steamer), 161, 169, 256
Capron, Horace, 158, 160, 184
Carlyle, Thomas, 381
Cecil, Robert, Third Marquess of Salisbury, 282
Chamberlain, Basil Hall, 414
Charter Oath of 1868, Mori's translation of, 214
Chichibu Tarō, 51
Chihō Gakumukyoku (Provincial Educational Affairs Bureau), 352
Chin-ssu lu, see Kinshiroku
China, Mori's appointment as ambassador to, 233, 275–278
Chinese language, Mori's desire to interdict the teaching of, 190
Chitoshi Yanaga, Japan since Perry, 14
Cholera epidemic and quarantine (1877–1879), 279, 280–281
Chōya shinbun (newspaper), 10, 16, 276
Christianity, 52; Mori's alleged, 12, 260, 478, 479–480; first appearance of, in Japan, 53; proposed allotment of land in Hokkaido for, 140, 153; religious liberty for, 195–202; influence of, on Mori's family, 394. See also Brotherhood of the New Life
Chu Hsi, 49–50, 52
Chūgakkō, see Middle schools
Chūkun (loyalty), 408; and aikoku (patriotism), 428–429, 444, 465
Civil service, Mori on, 314–316
Clarendon, Foreign Secretary, 73–74, 143
Coleridge, Samuel Taylor, 381
Commercial Institute, see Shōhō Kōshūjo
Compilation Bureau (Hensankyoku), 351, 438, 442, 451
Confucian Academy (Shōheikō), 30, 413
Confucianism, Mori's anti-, 441–444, 447, 455, 483
Conroy, F. Hilary, 275, 278
Cooper, Charles, 464
Cooper, Peter, 180, 182, 183
Court of St. James, Mori's appointment as minister at, 279
Cowper, Georgiana (Mrs. William F.), 98, 106, 116, 124, 153
Cowper, William Francis (later Baron Mount Temple), 66, 98, 106, 116; on the Brotherhood of the New Life, 108, 113–114; on sexual impurity, 121
Cuthbert, Arthur A., 103, 112

Dai Nihon Kyōikukai (Japan Education Association), 449
Daigaku (formerly the Gakkō), 176, 422
"Daigi seitairon," see "Nihon seifu daigi seitairon"
Daily Telegraph (London), 322
Dajōkan (council of state), 137, 346; decree of 4 September 1872, 332–333
Daplyn, W. J., 159
Date Munenari, 131
Davis, Andrew Jackson, 97
Davis, J. Bancroft, 156
Davis, Dr. (Professor, University of London), 69
Delong, Charles, 157
DeVos, George A., 28–29
Dewey, John, 452
Dial (journal), 235–236
Dickins, F. V., 74, 76
Dimon, Theodore W., 225–226

Index

Diplomacy, Mori's 269–278, 280–288
Disraeli, Benjamin, 316, 383
"Dokie," 107
Dokuritsu (national independence), Mori's insistence on, 399–400, 408, 471, 472
"Dokuritsu kokken gi" (The meaning of national sovereignty), 240, 272–273, 281
Draft Cabinet Proposal, *see* Kakugian
"Draft Opinion," *see* "Kyōikurei ni kansuru ikenshoan"
Duncan, David, 319
Dutch learning, 56–57, 60
Dyer, Henry, 379

Eaton, John, 180, 335, 377, 380
Eckhart, Johannes, 123
Education: Mori's policy on, 12–13; Mori's focus on, in America, 154, 174–187; coordinates (4) for the arrangement of significant material on, 324–330; phases of Meiji, 330–353; European, Mori's discovery of, 364–375; Mori's impact on Japanese, 452–566. *See also Education in Japan;* Gakkōrei (School Ordinances); Gojū; Imperial University; Middle schools; Normal schools; Primary schools; Technical and vocational schools; Women, status of; Zōshikan
Education in Japan (1873), 156, 313, 331, 337, 480; Introduction to, 169, 406, 472; contributors to, 173, 176, 180, 181–184, 186; and Mori's letter to American educators, 177, 178; on abolition of the Japanese language, 189–195 *passim;* on decline of Buddhism, Shintoism, and Confucianism, 200–201; on politics and government, 212–216; delay in publication of, 225; on "transition period," 227; passage on language in, 256; on the Japanese sovereign, 310
Education ministry, *see* Monbushō
Education Ordinances, *see* Gakusei; Kaisei kyōikurei; Kyōikurei; Shin kyōikurei. *See also* Gakkōrei (School Ordinances)
Education rescript, *see* Imperial Rescript on Education

Educational Societies (*Kyōikukai*), proposed, 448–449, 450, 453
Egi Kazuyuki, 346, 351–352, 446
Elementary education, *see* Primary schools
Eliot, Charles W., 182
Emerson, Ralph Waldo, 172, 235
Emperor, role of, in Japanese polity, 309–310, 311, 406–407, 472. *See also* Sovereignty; Throne
Enatsu Sōsuke, 106
England, Mori's visits to, *see* London
English education, 365–367, 373–375
Enlightenment Movement (keimō undō), of the 1870's, 233
Enomoto Takeaki, 203, 445, 453–454
Erigena, Johannes Scotus, 123
Erikson, Erik H., 20
Evarts, William, 272, 281
Exhortation, tenfold (Shimazu Nariakira's), 54–57

Family life, Mori's early, 20–32
Felkin, H. M., 377
Fenellosa, Ernest, 464
Ferry, Jules, 369
Fish, Hamilton: and the Iwakura mission, 155–172 *passim*, 197; on Shimonoseki Indemnity, 178–179; on Mori's "Religious Charter," 198–199; on Mori and "the crime of being young," 225–226; on Mori's view of diplomacy, 270
Foreign loan, flotation of, clash between Mori and Yoshida over, 189, 216–224
Foreign ministry, *see* Gaikokukan and Gaimushō
Forster, William E., 366, 376, 381, 388–389
Fortnightly Review, 290
Fourier, François Marie Charles, 115, 124
Fox, George, 114
Franklin, Benjamin, 356
French education, 367–370, 373–375; compared with German, 371–373; as model for Japanese education, 462
Freud, Sigmund, 20
Froebel, Friedrich, 373, 452
Fujisaki Ryūsuke, 61
Fujiwara Kiyozō, 421, 424, 431
Fukoku (national wealth), 53, 71–

Fukoku (national wealth) (*cont.*)
72, 93, 154, 458, 472–473. See
also *Kyōhei*
Fukuoka Kōtei, 132, 138, 346, 352
Fukushima Taneomi, 233
Fukuzawa Yukichi, 292, 315, 356,
396–397, 412, 453; on Mori's
assassin, 9–10; on Mori's moral
character, 236; and the
Meirokusha, 237, 238–239, 242–
244; *Seiyō jijō*, 240; and Mori's
marriage, 252; and the Shōhō
Kōshūjo, 255–258; and proposal
for popular assembly, 263; on
relationship between people and
government, 265–269; *Gakumon
no susume*, 266–267, 332–333,
456; cynicism of, 282; and the
Tokyo Academy, 336; unsuitability of political treatises of,
352; friendship with Mori, 394;
and *jugyōryō*, 420; and "temperamental individualism," 435; on
Mori as thinker and doer, 467,
468–469, 476, 477; compared
with Mori, 470

"Gaikoku kōsai ni jōjitsu o
mochiizaru beki no gi" (On the
avoidance of sentiment in diplomatic intercourse), 270–271
"Gaikoku kōsai o tadasu no gi"
(On the reform of our diplomatic intercourse), 273–274
Gaikokukan (early name for
foreign ministry), Mori's appointments to, 129, 131
Gaimushō (foreign ministry),
Mori's appointments to, 233, 279
Gakkō (forerunner of ministry of
education), 133 and n11, 148,
176
Gakkō Torishirabe (Committee for
the Investigation of the Educational System), 133
Gakkōrei (School Ordinances) of
1886, 330, 391, 396, 409, 447;
Imperial University Ordinance
Teikoku Daigakurei), 412, 414,
415; Middle School Ordinance
(Chūgakkōrei), 412, 416, 423;
Primary School Ordinance
(Shōgakkōrei), 412, 420, 421,
446; Normal School Ordinance
(Shihangakkōrei), 412, 427;
Special Schools Ordinance
(Senmon Gakkōrei), 422

Gakumon no susume, see under
Fukuzawa Yukichi
"*Gakumon no taihon*" (Cardinal
principles of learning), 54
Gakumon versus *kyōiku*, 411–412
Gakusei (Fundamental Code of
Education) of 1872, 133, 176,
333, 409, 456; establishes modern
system, 330; described, 332;
centralism of, 334, 461; compared
with Kaisei kyōikurei, 343–344;
and establishment of universities,
413; and establishment of
middle schools, 415; on
eight-year elementary course,
420; on practical knowledge,
456–457. See also Kaisei
kyōikurei; Kyōikurei; Shin
kyōikurei
"Gakusei hengen" (A few words on
educational administration),
359–362, 424
"Gakusei ni tsuki chokuyu"
(Imperial instructions regarding
the educational system), 349,
350
"Gakusei yōryō" (Essentials of the
government educational administration), 410–412, 457–458
"Gakusha shokubunron no hyō" (A
critique of arguments concerning
the role of the scholar), 240, 259,
267–269, 313, 315
Gallagher, Mrs. (member of
Brotherhood of the New Life),
107
Gandhi, Mohandas Karamchand,
477
Garfield, James A., 183
Genrōin (senate), 307, 309, 334,
345, 346
George & Emily (ship), 77
German education, 370–375
Germany, alleged influence of, on
Mori, 14, 15, 386–387, 453,
459–466
Gijiteisai Torishirabesho (Bureau
for the Investigation of a
Deliberative Assembly System),
132–133, 134, 135, 137, 145
Ginkōgakukyoku (bank training
section) within finance ministry,
255
Girls' High School Regulations
("Kōtō jogakkō kitei"), 423
Gladstone, William E., 283, 291,
376, 387

Glover, Thomas, 61, 70, 100, 101, 107
Gneist, Rudolf von, 313, 354, 403
Godai family, 46
Godai Kyōta, 32, 39
Godai Tomoatsu (alias Seki Kenzō), 39, 57, 134, 472; on learning from the West, 32, 62; at Nagasaki naval academy, 60; voyage of, to the West, 61, 66, 69–74; on weaponry, 82, 92; influence of, on Mori, 85
Godaiin Mihashira, 56
Gōjū (village fraternity): Mori's participation in, 32–46; codes of conduct of, 36–37, 43–44, 433–434; compared with the Zōshikan, 47
Goshkevitch, Iosif A., 79; and son, 79, 80
Goyō kakari (commissioner), Mori's appointment as, 390–391, 461
Grant, Ulysses S., 155, 172, 209, 222, 482; visit of, to Japan, 281; friendship with Mori, 322
Granville, Earl of, *see* Leveson-Gower, George
Great Republic (steamer), 174, 203
Greeley, Horace, 209
Green, Thomas Hill, 382
Green, Dr. (Professor, University of London), 69
Gregory, Dr. J. M., 180
Griffis, William Elliot, 9, 125, 131, 294, 477
Groote, Gerhard, 123
Grotius, Hugo, 274
Guizot, François Pierre Guillaume, 240, 369
Gunmukan (military affairs office), 133–134

"Haitōron" (Proposal for the abolition of sword-wearing), 131, 140–145, 154, 170, 474, 479
Hanashiaijū, *see* Gōjū
Harrington, James, 269
Harris, Thomas Lake, 94, 131, 171, 200, 434, 444, 482; Oliphant, the Japanese and, 95–105; at Brotherhood of the New Life (Brocton, N.Y.), 106–128 *passim;* moral influence of, on Mori, 152–153, 227, 293, 470, 474–476, 479, 484; Mori's relationship with, while in Washington, 202–208; and Mori's marital ethic, 254. *See also* Brotherhood of the New Life
Hatakeyama Yoshinari (alias Sugiura Kōzō), 67, 100, 177, 208; voyage of, to England, 67, 69, 75; at Brotherhood of the New Life, 105, 106, 125, 126; and U.S. Commission on Education, 335
"Hatori," 107
Hausknecht, Emil, 436, 464
Hawley, John Hugh, 74, 75
Hayashi Shihei, 60, 62, 93, 472; *Kaikoku heidan* (On the defense of a maritime country), 47, 57, 58–59
Hayashi Takeji, 205, 437, 446, 457; on Mori's westernism, 64–65; on Mori's religious involvement, 99–100, 197; on Mori's admiration for T. L. Harris, 105, 204; on clash between Mori and Yoshida, 221; on Mori's attempted resignation, 223, 225, 226–227; on Mori's public school policy, 434; on Mori as statesman versus educationist, 468
Haynes, Miss (English instructor), 184
Hearne, Lafcadio, 432
Hedge, Frederic, 235
Hegel, Georg Wilhelm Friedrich, 464
Heine, Heinrich, 383
Heishiki taisō ("military drill"), Mori's introduction of, into normal schools, 424–437, 457, 463, 465, 474, 475, 479, 485
"Heishiki taisō ni kansuru kengon" (A memorial concerning military-style physical training), 426, 428
Henderson, Philip, 115–116
Henry, Joseph, 200, 222–223, 235; and Charles Lanman, 159–160, 161; Mori's friendship with, 171–173, 322, 470; and the Shimonoseki Indemnity, 178, 179, 234; and *Education in Japan*, 182, 183, 184; and abolition of the Japanese language, 190, 192; on Mori's lack of aptitude for business, 256
Hensankyoku (Compilation Bureau), 351, 438, 442, 451
Herbart, Johann Friedrich, 373, 436, 452, 464
Hideyoshi (Toyotomi), 33, 35, 150, 214

Higashikuze Michitomi, 131
Hijikata Hisamoto, 439
Hikki, see Shutain-shi kōgi hikki
Hirata Atsutane, 56
Hirose Tsuneko (Mori's first wife): marriage of, 251–253; divorce of, 393
Hitotsubashi University, 232, 256, 258
Hobbes, Thomas, 404
Hokkaido, Mori's proposal for resettlement of Japanese Christians at, 140, 153
Holloway, Mark, 115
Holme, Ryle, 61, 67, 69, 70
Holmes, Oliver Wendell, 172
Hooper, Mr. (of London), 107
Hopkins, Mark, 182, 183
Hori Takayuki, 61, 67, 69, 70
Hosokawa Junjirō, 133
Hozumi Yatsuka, 443
Huang Hui-lien, 277
Hubbard, Richard B., 8
Hughes, Thomas, 377, 379
Humboldt, Wilhelm von, 374, 384, 452–453
Hunter, William, 156
Huxley, Thomas Henry, 290, 375, 378–379, 385, 463, 470

Ichijō Jūjirō, 146–147
Ichikawa Bunkichi, 78–80
Ichiki Hirotsuwa, 60
Ichiki Kanjurō, *see* Matsumura Junzō
Ieyasu (Tokugawa), 33
Igakusho (medical college), 413
Igi (dignity), Mori on, 427, 428
Ijichi Sumimasa, 136
Imperial Rescript on Education ("Kyōiku chokugo") of 1890, 347, 437, 445–446, 448, 456, 466
Imperial University at Kyoto, 413
Imperial University at Tokyo, 3–4, 6, 234, 397, 412–415; Ordinance, 412, 414, 415
Inagaki Tadahiko, 408
Inau Tentarō, 226, 272
Individual and the state, Mori on relationship of, 232–233, 258–269
Inoue Kaoru, 10, 70, 219, 468; conference proposal of, 282; on Mori as a young diplomat, 285; and the right of denunciation, 286; and Stein, 355
Inoue Kowashi, 397, 407; and the *kakugian*, 12–13, 408, 426; and "Kyōikugi," 347, 353, 459; his five-point plan, 353, 458–459; role of, in educational structure, 421; his Continuation and Apprentice Schools, 422; and the Imperial Rescript on Education, 445; and introduction of German studies, 459, 464; and Mori's image as nationalist, 477
Intermarriage, racial, 185–186, 250–251. *See also* Women, status of
Iroha uta (Alphabet poem), 40, 49
Ise, Grand Shrine of, alleged incident of Mori's sacrilege at, 5, 11–12
Ise shinbun (newspaper), 11
Ishigaki Einosuke, *see* Niiro Keibu
Ishii Shōichirō, 445
Ishikawa Kakutarō, 56, 57, 60
Iso village, 21
Isonaga Hikosuke, *see* Nagasawa Kanaye
Itagaki Taisuke, 292, 323; his petition for popular assembly, 241–242, 263–265
Itō Hirobumi, 70, 314, 367, 391, 409; on Mori as "a Westerner born of Japan," 1, 64; and Iwakura mission, 162–163, 164, 166; and appointment of Mori to ministry of education, 219, 223; John R. Young on, 222; and Mori's attempted resignation, 224, 227; meeting with Spencer, Satow, and Lang, 289; discussions with Mori in London, 291–293, 312; and "organ" theory, 311, 313; and Herbert Spencer, 319; meeting with Mori in Paris, 331, 354, 358–364; and Japanese education in the 1870's, 334; conflict with Motoda, 342–353 *passim*, 444; his "Kyōikugi," 342, 347–348, 350, 353, 362, 458–459; Gneist, Stein, and, 354–358; Mori's letter to, on Mundella and Huxley, 375; entente with Mori on educational matters, 386; Mori's recommendations of Italy and Britain to, 291; friendship with Mori, 395; and the Meiji Constitution, 402–407 *passim*, 424; and Nishimura Shigeki, 439; and Techow, 459–460; and Hausknecht, 464
Itō Miyōji, 355
Iwakura Hiroko, *see* Mori Hiroko
Iwakura Tomomi, 131, 142, 233, 353, 358; mission of, in Washing-

ton, 155–174 passim, 176, 178, 180, 183, 196–197, 198, 294; and clash between Mori and Yoshida, 216–217, 221; and Mori's attempted resignation, 226; and U.S. Commission on Education, 335; Mori's marriage to daughter of, 393
Iwashita Hōhei, 96, 100
Izawa Shūji, 438, 451
Izumi Senzō, see Terajima Munenori

Japan Education Association (Dai Nihon Kyōikukai), 449
Japan Philosophical Society, 394
Japan Weekly Mail, 8, 265, 289, 425; on Mori's "Kokugo haishiron," 194–195, 231; review of the Rinrisho, 441, 442
Japanese-American treaty, Mori's draft of a, 271–272
Japanese language, Mori's proposal to abolish and replace with English, 189–195, 231–232, 238–239
Jefferson, Thomas, 453
Jiji shinpō (newspaper), 9–10
Jitaheiritsu, Mori's concept of, 441, 442, 446, 447, 455, 466, 475
Jōdo Shinshū, 52
Jōgatani district, 20–21, 25
Johonot, J., 438
Jōjitsu, see Jōri versus jōjitsu
Jomini, Antoine Henri Baron, 74, 75
Jōri (reason), 274, 275, 282, 471, 473; versus jōjitsu (sentiment), 270–271
Jōyaku Kaitei Torishirabe Kyoku (Investigative Bureau for the Renegotiation of Treaties), 271
Jugyōryō (tuition fees), 420–421, 454
Jūjun (obedience), Mori on, 427–428

Kabayama Hisanobu, 51
Kabuki, Mori's reaction to, 237
Kagoshima city, Mori's residence in, 20, 145, 147–152
Kaigo Tokiomi, 14, 446
"Kaika daiichi wa" (Civilization: part 1), 240
Kaikoku heidan, see under Hayashi Shihei
Kaimon Sanjin, Mori Arinori, 3, 16, 18, 470; on images of, 13, 14; on parents of, 26; on influence of Yokoyama Yasukata on, 31–32; on T. L. Harris and Christianity, 96, 202–203, 204; on visit to America, 105; on the Kōgisho, 135; on proposal for abolition of sword-wearing, 143; on friendship between Charles Sumner and, 172; on Charles Brooks and, 180–181; on educational policies of, 386; on influence of Germany on, 459; identity of Kaimon, 491
Kaisei kyōikurei (Revised Education Ordinance) of 1880, 330, 334, 409, 453, 461; described, 342–346; and moral conduct of teachers, 353; on elementary education, 420, 421. See also Gakusei; Kyōikurei; Shin kyōikurei
Kaiseijo (School for Western Studies): Mori's attendance at, 46, 47, 56, 60, 62–63, 413; Mori on, 88
Kaitakushi (Development Bureau for Hokkaido), 158–159
Kaiyakusha (fellowship of Western learning scholars), 234
Kajiya district, 21
Kakugian (draft cabinet proposal), 12–13, 407–408, 426, 428–429
Kanda, Mori's residence in, 145–147
Kanda Kōhei, 130, 133, 138, 174; and plans for a deliberative assembly, 132; and the Tokyo Academy, 336; and the Kaisei kyōikurei, 345
Kanda Naibu, 174–175, 464–465
Kaneko Kentarō, 185, 251, 317–320
K'ang-hsi Emperor, 439
"Kanri tōyōhō narabi ni taikyūhō seido kengon" (Memorial on the rules for appointing, and the system for pensioning, government officials), 314–316
Kant, Immanuel, 464
Karasawa, Tomitarō, 451
Katō Hiroyuki, 133, 269, 299, 438; and the Meirokusha, 237, 241–242, 243–244; opposition of, to proposal for popular assembly, 241–242, 263; on equality of husband and wife, 249; on government and the people, 265–266; and the Tokyo Academy, 336; unsuitability of political treatises of, 352
Katsu Kaishū, 255
Kawakami (interpreter), 292

Kawakami Kazen, 50
Kawamoto Miyuki, 57
Keenleyside, Hugh L., *History of Japanese Education* ... (with A. F. Thomas), 13
Keian (Zen monk), 49, 50, 51
Keiō (school), 412, 413, 420
Keizaishugi (economy principle), 447–452, 455, 475
Kennedy, J. G., 284, 285, 286
Kenri gimu (rights and duties), 404–406
Kido Ichisuke, 106
Kido Takayoshi, 136, 162, 164–168, 176; on education, 177, 215; and clash between Mori and Yoshida, 216–217, 219, 221, 224; and Mori's attempted resignation, 226; and Korean crisis, 275; and U.S. Commission on Education, 335
Kikuchi Dairoku, 414
Kimura Kahei, 57
Kimura Kyō, *Mori sensei den* (Life of Mori), 3, 16, 18, 470; on images of, 12, 13; on genealogy of, 23; on memory of, 39; on Brotherhood of the New Life, 105, 108, 125; anecdotes on Mori by, 129–130, 135–136, 236–237, 395; Iwakura's impression of, 131; on the Gijiteisai Torishirabesho, 135; on proposal for abolition of sword-wearing, 143; on Yokoyama's suicide, 151; on the Japanese legation in Washington, 171, 172, 174, 179; on *Life and Resources in America*, 175; on Nomura Ichisuke's removal from Brocton, 204; on reading of Mill, 210; and Kurile Islands dispute, 270; and the "Daigi seitairon," 296; on military drill, 465
Kingsley, Charles, 379
Kinnojō (name for Mori), 22–23
Kinshiroku, 50, 51
Kitō Takekiyo, 51, 54
Koba Sadanaga, 11, 358–359, 391, 393
Koeber, Raphael von, 464
Kōgisho (Deliberative Assembly), Mori's activities in, 132–142 *passim*, 479
Kokkai (national assembly), 305
Kokugaku (national learning), 24, 27–28, 47, 52, 56, 57. See also *Yōgaku*

Kokugakukan (Institute of National Learning), proposed, 56
"Kokugo haishi eigo saiyōron" (Proposal for the abolition of the Japanese and adoption of the English language), 189–195, 231–232, 238–239, 289, 472
"Kokugo haishiron," see "Kokugo haishi eigo saiyōron"
Kokutai (national polity), 12–13, 397, 405, 408
Komatsu Terumori, 224
Kōno Togama, 334, 336, 345, 346, 351, 453
Korean crisis (1875–1876), Mori's role in, 233, 245, 275–277
"Kōro kikō" (Journal of a voyage to Russia), 66, 76–80, 90–92, 93–94, 253
Kōsaka Masaaki, 201
Kōten Kōkyūjo (Research Institute for Japanese Classics), 12
Kōtōgakkō, see Middle schools
Kuki Ryūichi, 391
Kumazawa Banzan, 435
Kurile Islands, dispute over, 270
Kuroda (steamer), 161, 256
Kuroda Kiyotaka, 5, 21, 60, 184, 186; and Kurile Islands dispute, 270; and Bismarck, 387; friendship with Mori, 394
Kusunoki Masashige, 213
"Kyōgaku taishi," see *under* Motoda Eifu
Kyōhei (military power), 53, 71, 93, 154, 472–473. See also *Fukoku*
Kyōiku, see *Gakumon* versus *kyōiku*
"Kyōikugi," see *under* Itō Hirobumi
Kyōikukai, see Educational Societies
Kyōikurei (Education Ordinance) of 1879, 178, 330, 346, 409; essay on, 331, 335, 336; collapse of, 332; described, 333–334; on primary education, 336; compared with Kaisei kyōikurei, 343–344; on elementary education, 420, 421. See also Gakusei; Kaisei kyōikurei; Shin kyōikurei
"Kyōikurei ikenshoan," see "Kyōikurei ni kansuru ikenshoan"
"Kyōikurei ni kansuru ikenshoan" (Draft of a written opinion on the Education Ordinance) of 1879, 331, 335 and n9, 336, 344, 410
"Kyōikurei ni tsuki iken" (Opinion

on the Education Ordinance) of 1885, 335n9, 410
"Kyōkayō tosho kentei jōrei" (Educational textbook authorization ordinance) of 1887, 451

Land Grant Act (U.S.) of 1862, 180
Lang, Andrew, 289
Lanman, Charles, 170, 175, 200, 235, 322; and Joseph Henry, 159–160, 161; on American esteem for Mori, 168; on Mori's publications, 169; and Mori's command of English, 171; as colorful figure in Mori's life, 172–173, 341; on the Japanese in America, 174, 175, 184; on Prussian education, 181; on racial intermarriage, 185–186; and *Life and Resources in America*, 202, 204, 211–212; on Yoshida Kiyonari, 221–222; on tension surrounding Mori in Washington, 222–223
Lanman, Mrs. Charles, 184
Laws, English, Mori's admiration for, 88–90, 93
Layard, Sir Austen Henry, 72
Leavey, Mr. and Mrs. (of Brocton, N.Y.), 106
Leland, Dr. George A., 339
Leveson-Gower, George, Second Earl of Granville, 282–286, 291
Li Hung-chang, 245, 260, 276–278, 338, 480
Libel Ordinance, *see* Press and Libel Ordinances
Life and Resources in America (1871), 156, 207, 240, 299, 313; and Charles Lanman, 159, 181; purpose of, 163, 175; chapter on religion in, 195–196, 202, 203–204; on Republican government, 209–212, 215; on representative institutions, 479
Lincoln, Abraham, 268, 269
Lloyd, Royal Navy Chaplain, 107
Locke, John, 269
London, Mori's years in, 65–77, 279, 282–323 *passim*
London and China Telegraph (London), 72, 321, 388; Mori's obituary in, 8
Longfellow, Henry Wadsworth, 172
Lotze, Rudolf Hermann, 464
Lowe, Robert, 383
Lowell, James Russell, 379
Lü Tsu-ch'ien, 50

Machida Hisanari (alias Ueno Ryōtarō), 66, 105, 131; voyage of, to England, 66, 70, 74
Machida Kiyozō, 67, 69
Machida Shinjirō, 67, 69, 75
Magome Tamesuke, 156
Maine, Sir Henry, 316
Makino Nobuaki, 290
Manchester Guardian, 322
Mann, Horace, 179, 180, 187, 386, 452, 461
Markham, Edwin, 104
Marriage, 232, 236; Mori's to Hirose Tsuneko, 251–253; contractual, 251–253, 258–259. *See also* "Saishōron" (Discourse on wives and mistresses); Women, status of
Martin, Rev. Dr. W. A. P., 260
Maruyama Masao, 404–405, 407, 482
Masson, Dr. David, 290
Matsui, Lieutenant, 426
Matsukata Masayoshi, 21, 28, 344
Matsuki Kōan, *see* Terajima Munenori
Matsumoto Kenji, 344
Matsumura Junzō (originally Ichiki Kanjurō), 161; "Yōkō nikki" (Diary of a voyage to the West), 67–69; voyage of, to England, 67, 69, 73, 75; voyage of, to Russia, 76–80; on Laurence Oliphant, 87, 121; on T. L. Harris and Christianity, 96, 208; and modern diplomacy, 101; at Brotherhood of the New Life, 105, 106, 125
Matsuura Akira, 133
Maurice, Frederick Denison, 98
Mayo, Marlene J., 157
McCosh, James, 182, 183
Meerdervoort, Pompe van, 57
Megata Tanetarō, 168, 171
Meiji Constitution, 1, 4, 400–406
Meiji Six Society, *see* Meirokusha
Meiroku zasshi (Meiji six magazine), 232, 233, 236, 238, 240–245, 249; Mori's contributions to, 239–240, 259, 261, 269, 272
Meirokusha (Meiji Six Society), 138, 232, 233–245, 259, 265
Mekake ("mistress"), 247
Mencius, 93, 474
Middle Schools, 397, 415–418; Ordinance, 412, 416; Chūgakkō, 417–418, 422; Kōtōgakkō, 417–418, 422, 454

Military drill, see *Heishiko taisō*
Mill, John Stuart, 171, 266, 298–299, 331, 464; *On Liberty*, 200; *Considerations on Representative Government*, 210–211, 316; *The Subjection of Women*, 253–254, 469; utilitarianism of, 456
Minami Teisuke, 107, 131
Minamoto Yoshitomo, 23
Minobe Tatsukichi, 311
"Minsen giin setsuritsu kengonsho no hyō" (A critique of the petition for the establishment of a popular assembly), 240, 259, 263–265, 297. See also Popular assembly
Mishima Michiharu, 28
Mishima Michitsune, 28
Mitsukuri Rinshō, 133, 255, 345
Mitsukuri Shūhei, 237, 238, 255, 336
Miura Iemura, 23
Mizuno Tadakuni, 22
Monbushō (ministry of education), 176, 223, 224, 234, 343, 345–346; Mori's appointment to, 129, 390. See also *Rinrisho* (Ethics textbook)
Montblanc, Count Descantons de, 71, 100
Montesquieu, Baron de, 269
Morgan, Mr. (English merchant), 78, 79
Mori, character and style of, 392–397; his political statism, 12–13, 397–408, 455, 456, 458, 463; his educational elitism, 409–424; ethical individualism of, 437–447; economic rationalism of, 447–452; as thinker and statesman, 467–471; his political, social, and personal goals, 471–478
Mori Akira (son of Mori), 393, 394
Mori Arimasa (grandson of Mori), 393
Mori Genshirō (brother of Mori), 30–31, 61. See also Yokoyama Shōtarō Yasutake
Mori Hide (son of Mori), 288–289, 393
Mori Hiroko (Mori's second wife), 6, 288, 388, 392, 393–394
Mori Jirōsaburō Yukishige, 23
Mori Jusae, 23
Mori Kihachirō (later Aoyama Yoshiaki; brother of Mori), 30
Mori Kitōta (brother of Mori), 30
Mori Kiuemon Arinaga, 23

Mori Kiuemon Yūjo (father of Mori), 22, 23, 61, 62; and Mori's early life, 24–29; poems of (quoted), 27–28; funeral of, 393
Mori Kiyoshi (son of Mori), 288–289, 393
Mori Mikuma (brother of Mori), 30
Mori Osato (née Kumasaki; mother of Mori): and Mori's early life, 22, 26–27, 28–29, 31; death of, 393
Mori Tsuneko (Mori's first wife): marriage to Mori, 251–253; divorce from Mori, 393
Mori Yoshitaka Mutsu no Rokurō, 23
Morley, John, 290
Morning Post (London), 322
Mosse, Albert, 313, 354
Motoda Eifu, 331, 360, 362, 363, 458; on Mori as Christian, 12; conflict with Itō, 342–353 *passim*, 444; "Kyōgaku taishi," 342, 347–348, 349, 438, 456; "Kyōikugi fugi," 342, 349; "Kokkyōron," 349; Yōgaku kōyō, 350; opposition of, to appointment of Mori as education minister, 391; and the Meiji Constitution, 403, 407; absolutism of, 406; on teacher's character traits, 427; conflict with Mori, 443–445, 447; on westernization, 477
Motoori Norinaga, 468
Motoyama Yukihiko, 15, 269
Mueller, Friedrich Max, 194, 291
Mukai Shinbei, 58
Mukoyōshi (adoptive son-in-law), 247–248
Mundella, Anthony John, 380, 381, 383, 463; as leading educational official in England, 375–377, 385; and Prussian primary education, 461; influence of, on Mori, 470
Murahashi Naoe, 105; voyage of, to England, 67, 69, 75
Murray, David R., 9, 224, 361, 460; appointment of, as chief overseer of Japanese affairs, 176–177; and *Education in Japan*, 181, 182, 183, 184, 187; on Mori's proposal for abolition of the Japanese language, 195; and Japanese education in the 1870's, 331–332, 334, 336

Nabeshima Naomasa, 133

Nagai Iosuke, *see* Yoshida Kiyonari
Nagai Michio, 13, 258
Nagai Shige, 184–185
Nagasawa Kanaye (originally Isonaga Hikosuke), 153; voyage of, to the West, 67, 70; meeting with Harris, 96; at Brotherhood of the New Life, 105, 106, 108, 109, 125
Nagoshi Heima, 105; voyage of, to England, 67, 69, 75
Naimushō (ministry of the interior), 343, 344, 390
Naitō Seitarō, 146–147
Nakahara Kuninosuke, 146–147
Nakajima Tarō, 424
Nakamura Masanao, 107, 199, 237, 242, 336
Nakamura Sōken, 67, 69–70, 75, 96
Napoleon I, 367–371 *passim*, 452, 462
Napoleon III, 373
Nariakira, *see* Shimazu Nariakira
Narioki, *see* Shimazu Narioki
National assembly (Kokkai), 305, 311
Nationalist Commendable and Reprehensible (images of Mori), 2, 7–16 *passim*, 473, 477–478
Natural rights, Mori's digression on, 403–406
Nature (journal), 379
Nawa Michikazu, 152, 156
Neesima, Mr., *see* Niijima Jō
Nehru, Jawaharlal, 477
New Education Movement, 432
New York *Sun*, 109, 110, 121, 123
Nicolai (Russian Orthodox priest), 153, 203
"Nihon kyōiku saku" (An educational scheme for Japan), 181
"Nihon seifu daigi seitairon" ("Daigi seitairon"; On a representative polity for the government of Japan), 295–312 *passim*, 401, 405, 406, 470
Niijima Jō, 94, 120, 176, 269; as interpreter for Iwakura mission, 167, 178; Mori's assistance to, 197–198, 293
Niiro Keibu (alias Ishigaki Einosuke), 66, 69, 70, 74
Niiro Tadamoto, 35–36, 37
Nire Kagenori, 106
Nishi Amane, 194, 269; and the Meirokusha, 237, 239, 243, 261; opposition of, to proposal for popular assembly, 241–242, 263; and the Tokyo Academy, 336; compared with Mori, 470
Nishimura Shigeki, 263, 351, 394, 442, 474; *Ōji roku*, 234; and the Meirokusha, 237; conflict with Mori, 438–440, 446; replaced by Izawa Shūji, 438, 451; *Nihon dōtokuron*, 439
Nishino Buntarō (assassin of Mori), 16, 477; assassinates Mori, 4–5; his manifesto, 5, 12; Fukuzawa Yukichi on, 9–10; burial of and eulogies for, 10–11
Nitobe Inazō, 465
Nixon, Richard M., 242
Noda Chūbei, *see* Samejima Naonobu
Noguchi Entarō, 431
Nomura Ichisuke, 106, 111, 204
Norbeck, Edward, 28–29
Normal schools, 397–398, 418–419; Saitama, Mori's address at, 399, 426–428; Ordinance, 412, 427; introduction of military drill into, 424–437, 457, 463, 465, 474, 475, 479, 485
Northrop, Birdsey G., 177, 364, 377, 470; his friendship with Mori, 179; contribution of, to *Education in Japan*, 182, 183
Norton, Lord, 377
Nōsei Sakae, 440, 441, 464

"Obah," 107
Ogata Jōjirō, 78–80
Ogyū Sorai, 50
Ōhara Shigesane, 133
Okakura Kakuzō, 391
Okamoto Seien, 4–5
Ōki Takato, 132, 138, 346, 452, 453; opposition of, to Mori's appointment to the Monbushō, 391; his "Gakuji setsumeisho," 446, 450
Ōkubo Ichiō, 252, 255
Ōkubo Toshiaki, *Mori Arinori*, 3, 16, 18, 470; on Christianity and, 12; on images of, 13, 14; on mother of, 29; on the Bakufu and, 82; on Russo-Japanese relations and, 85; on his interest in the West, 89; on admiration of, for America, 105; on departure of, from Brotherhood of the New Life, 125–126; on participation of, in the Gijiteisai Torishirabesho, 135; on proposal for abolition of

Okubo Toshiaki (*cont.*)
  sword-wearing, 142, 143; on proposal for the abolition of the Japanese language, 195; on clash between Yoshida and, 217, 221, 223; on the Meirokusha, 244; on racial intermarriage, 251; on meeting in Paris of Itō and, 359; on educational ideas of, 392; on his concept of state, 403; on Imperial Rescript on Education, 446; on influence of Germany on, 459; as cultural statesman, 468
Ōkubo Toshimichi, 21, 25, 265, 394; admiration of, for Nariakira, 57; letter from Mori to, 134–135; and Mori's proposal for abolition of sword-wearing, 142, 143–144; dispatched from America to Japan, 162; and appointment of Mori to Monbushō, 219; and Mori's attempted resignation, 223, 224
Ōkuma Shigenobu, 292, 413
Oliphant, Sir Anthony (father of Laurence), 98
Oliphant, Laurence, 70, 78, 136, 173, 203, 341; letters of, to Cowper, 66; and Terajima, 72, 73–74; influence of, on Mori's development, 85–87, 92, 93, 470, 474, 479; and Harris and the Brotherhood of the New Life, 95–128 *passim*, 293; his esteem for Mori, 153; influence of, on Mori's attitude toward diplomacy, 270
Oliphant, Lady Mary (mother of Laurence), 95, 98; letters from Laurence to, 118–119
Oliphant, Margaret W. (cousin of Laurence), 117
On a Representative System of Government for Japan (1884), 138, 401, 406, 449, 463, 469; discussed, 295–312 *passim;* influence of Spencer on, 316–323; conservatism of, 386; not discussed by Mori's biographers, 470; moral disdain of, 483
Ono Seigorō, 142
Osatake Takeki, 135, 136–138, 140
Osato, *see* Mori Osato
Ōtsuki Hikogorō, 78–80
Owen, Robert, 115, 124
Ōyama Iwao, 21
Ōyō gakumon ("applied science"), 411, 415, 457, 462, 472–473

Ozawa Seijirō, 78–80

Pall Mall Gazette, 290; interview with Mori in, 287, 295, 300–301, 303, 304, 310, 379, 406, 480
Palmerston, Prime Minister (Henry John Temple), 73, 98
Parkes, Sir Harry, 74, 143, 280, 285, 379
Party cabinets, Mori's argument against, 402–403
Pauncefote, Julian, 286
Pensions, Mori on, 314–315
Perinchief, Rev. Octavius, 184–185, 200, 222, 483; on Mori's command of English, 171; his contribution to *Education in Japan,* 173–174, 182, 184, 186; on Mori's interest in Christianity, 202; on Mori and the American political system, 211–212
Perry, Commodore Matthew, 22, 212, 273
Pestalozzi, Johann Heinrich, 331, 373, 438, 452, 457
Peterson, A. D. C., 433
Phillimore, Sir Robert J., 240, 261–262, 274
Physical fitness, Mori's essay on, 337–342
Plotinus, 123
Plunkett, F. R., 285
Political system, Mori's views on the, 209–216
Popular assembly: Mori's critique of petition for, 240, 259, 263–265, 297; Itagaki Taisuke's petition for, 241–242, 263–265
Popular Rights Movement (*jiyū minken undō*), 260, 292, 323, 333, 343, 345; Inoue Kowashi's memorial for dealing with, 353; Mori's aversion to, 364, 451; schools during, 412
Popular Rights party, 362
Press and Libel Ordinances ("Shinbunshi jōrei" and "Zanbō ritsu"), 243, 245
Primary schools, 419–421; Ordinance, 412, 420, 421
Public Assembly Ordinance (Shūkai jōrei) of 1880, 343, 346–347
Purges, at Zōshikan: "Ancient Learning Purge" (1774), 50; *Kinshiroku kuzure* (1808), 51, 52; "Takasaki Purge" (1849), 51–52

Putiatin, Admiral and Mme., 79

Rangaku Kōshūjo (Dutch Learning Institute), 56, 60
Reed, Sir Edward James, 378–379
Rekidai uta (Chronicle poem), 40
"Religious Charter," Mori's, 198–200
Religious freedom, 195–202
Religious Freedom in Japan (1872), 156, 202, 267, 437, 474; Mori's educational philosophy in, 178, 186–187, 348; "Religious Charter" appended to, 198–200; on Western religion, 201, 207; on freedom of conscience, 208, 261, 293, 405; delay in publication of, 225; on state religion, 294
Representative government, 295–305; Mori's constitutional scheme for, 305–311
Representative System, see *On a Representative System of Government for Japan*
Resignation, Mori's attempted, 223–227
Restoration, Mori's views on, 212, 213, 214
Rinrisho (Ethics textbook), 206, 440–443, 464, 469
Ripley, George, 235
Roessler, Hermann, 459
Rokumeikan, 394
Rousseau, Jean Jacques, 453
Royal Asiatic Society, 291
Royce, Josiah, 341
Russell, Lord John, 73
Russia: Mori's visit to, 65–66, 77–80; Mori's evaluation of, 84–85, 90–92. See also "Kōro kikō" (Journal of a voyage to Russia)
Ruysbroeck, Jan van, 123
Ryukyu Islands, dispute over, 270

Saigō Takamori, 21, 25, 28, 57, 394; on Mori's brother Genshirō, 30; and the Gōjū, 38; and clash between Mori and Yoshida, 219
Sain (Ministry of the Left), 265
St. Francis Xavier, 53
Saint-Simon, Claude Henri, Comte de, 370
"Saishōron" (Discourse on wives and mistresses), 232, 239–240, 245–254, 423, 469, 474, 475; relationship of the spouses, 246–247; fate of the offspring, 247–248; problem of mutual fidelity, 248–249, 250; role of the mother, 249–251; draft marriage contract, 251–252, 258–259. *See also* Women, status of
Saitama Normal School, Mori's address at, 399, 426–428
Sakatani Shiroshi, 239, 243; on equality of husband and wife, 249
"Salem-on-Erie," *see* Brotherhood of the New Life
Samejima Naonobu (alias Noda Chūbei), 60, 100, 145, 152, 153; voyage of, to England, 67, 69, 75; at Brotherhood of the New Life, 94, 95–96, 105–106, 109, 114, 117, 125–127; appointed assistant inspector, 131; and the Kōgisho, 132, 135; appointed chargé d'affaires, 151; receives promotion, 225; received coolly by British, 227; assigned to Paris to promote westernization, 282; funeral of, 292, 293
Samurai, Satsuma, social grades of, in Bakumatsu period, 24–25
Sangiin (house of councillors), 307, 309
Sanjiin (secretarial board), Mori's appointment to, 390
Sanjō Sanetomi, 131, 198, 222, 314, 353, 358, 439
Sankokushi (History of the three kingdoms), 40
Sano Tsunetami, 439
Sansom, George, 14–15, 134, 322–323, 413, 432
Sasaki Takayuki, 162, 439
Satow, Ernest, 74, 140, 288–289, 396
Sawa Nobuyoshi, 157
Sawai Tetsuma (alias of Mori's), 22
Schmiedel, Otto, 465
School Ordinances, *see* Gakkōrei
Schopenhauer, Arthur, 464
Schweitzer, Albert, 123
Scott, Marion M., 332
Secondary education, *see* Middle schools; Normal schools
Seelye, Julius H., 182, 183
Seido Torishirabesho (Bureau for the Study of Governmental Institutions), 133

Seidoryō (Bureau for the Study of Governmental Institutions), 132–133
Seitaisho structure, 131, 137
"Seitō naikaku no hi o ronsu" (The argument against party cabinets), 402–403
Seiyōken (restaurant and meeting place of Meirokusha), 237, 239
Seki Kenzō, see Godai Tomoatsu
Sera Ta'ichi, 238
Sexual purity, Mori's concern for, 44–45, 91–92, 120–121, 127–128, 475
Shibata Masanaka, 73
Shibusawa Eiichi, 219, 255
Shimada Saburō, 345
Shimazu Hisamitsu, 31, 51–58
Shimazu Tadamasa, 49
Shimazu Nariakira, 33, 47, 59, 92, 463; and Iso industries, 21; and the Gōjū, 37–38, 42, 43; and the "Takasaki Purge," 51–52; educational policies of, 53–58, 60, 62; his "Cardinal Principles" and "Exhortation" on learning, 54–57; Yokoyama's suicide at residence of, 149; on *fukoku*, 472
Shimazu Narioki, 21, 51
Shimazu Shigehide, 37, 47, 51, 53
Shimazu Tadayoshi, *Iroha uta* (Alphabet poem), 40, 49
Shimazu Yoshihiro, 36, 40
Shimizu Usaburo, 238
Shimonoseki Indemnity, 158, 172, 178–179, 190, 234
Shin kyōikurei (New Education Ordinance) of 1885, 330, 344, 390, 409, 460. See also Gakusei; Kaisei kyōikurei; Kyōikurei
Shinagawa Yajirō, 464
"Shintai no nōryoku" (On physical fitness), 337–342, 359–360, 380, 385, 424, 430, 469
Shinto, 294, 393–394
Shioda Atsunobu, 165
Shirao Kunihashira, 44
Shōgakkōrei (Primary School Ordinance), 412, 420, 421, 446. See also Gakkōrei (School Ordinances)
Shōhei Gakkō, see Gakkō
Shōheikō (Confucian Academy), 30, 413
Shōhō Kōshūjo (Commercial Institute), Mori's, 232, 252, 254–258, 330
Shūgiin (Deliberative Assembly), 134, 149, 214, 312
Shūkai jōrei (Public Assembly Ordinance) of 5 April 1880, 343, 346–347
"Shūkyō" (Religion), 240, 259, 261, 274, 294
Shunden, 49
Shūshin (moral training) texts, 437–447 *passim*, 448, 451–452, 455
Shutain-shi kōgi hikki (*Hikki;* Transcript of Mr. Stein's lectures), 355–356, 358
Sino-Japanese Friendship Protocol ("Nisshin shūkō jōki"), 276
Smith, E. Peshine, 160, 271
Soejima Taneomi, 439
Soga Monogatari (Tale of the Soga), 40
Sonnō (reverence for the emperor), 472. See also Emperor; Sovereignty; Throne
Sovereignty, national: Mori on the meaning of, 240, 272–273, 309–310; his memorandum on party cabinets, 402–403. See also Emperor; Throne
Spencer, Herbert, 331, 379, 403, 459, 470; Mori's readings of, 171, 206–207; Mori's interview with, in London, 208, 216, 228; on the reorganization of Japanese institutions, 227; his vision of global peace, 288, 400; friendship between Mori and, 289–290, 293; Itagaki's interview with, 292; traces of, in Mori's *Representative System*, 316–323, 469; *Education: Intellectual, Moral and Physical*, 337, 339, 340–341, 342; laissez-faire principles of, 345, 385, 456; slow-paced doctrine of political evolution of, 406, 482; influence of, on Mori's *Rinrisho*, 442, 464, 469; his concept of egoism and altruism, 474–475; influence of, on Mori, 483–484
Spinoza, Baruch, 404
State, relationship of individual and, *see* Individual and state
Statism, Mori's *see* Character and style of Mori
Stearns, William A., 182, 183

Stein, Lorenz von, 313, 360, 403, 463; proposed as chief educational advisor for Japan, 354–358, 459; *Handbuch der Verwaltungslehre,* 356–358; on European education, 367, 368, 370, 382, 383, 385
Stremoukhov, Petr, 79
Sugi Kyōji, 237
Sugiura Kōzō, *see* Hatakeyama Yoshinari
Sukegoro (name for Mori), 22
Sumner, Charles, 172, 200
Suzuki Tadashi, 16
Suzuki Tomoo, 146–147
Swedenborg, Emanuel, 97, 102, 121
Swedenborgianism, 95, 97–98, 110, 118, 121
Sword-wearing, *see* "Haitōron"

Tabohashi Kiyoshi, 274
Tachibana Kōsai, 79, 80
Taiheiki (Record of the great peace), 40
Taisō Denshūjo (Physical Training Institute), 339
Takagi Saburō, 156
Takahashi Korekiyo, 146–147, 390
Takami Yaichi, 105; voyage of, to England, 67, 69, 75
Takasaki Goroemon, 52
Takasaki Masakaze, 136
Takashima Tokuemon, 234
Takeda Kiyoko, 15
Tanaka Cemetery, 10
Tanaka Fujimaro, 224, 345, 351, 461; educational study commission of, 176, 177; *Riji kōtei,* 178; and Japanese education in the 1870's, 331, 333, 334, 335, 336, 338, 342,453
Tanaka Jirō, 78–80
Tanaka Seisu, voyage of, to the West, 67, 69–70, 75
Tanegashima Keisuke, 106
Tanimoto Heimon, 106, 111
Taxation, proposal submitted by Mori on, 139
Taylor, A. J. P., 259
Technical and vocational schools, 421–424
Techow, Hermann, 358, 459–461
Teikoku Daigakurei (Imperial University Ordinance), 412, 414, 415. *See also* Gakkōrei (School Ordinances)

Teikoku Gakushiin (Imperial Academy), 336
Tenkō (intellectual recantation), 7–8, 13
Tenpu jinken (natural rights), doctrine of, 260, 269
Terajima Munenori (formerly Matsuki Kōan; alias Izumi Senzō), 60, 61, 87, 127, 293; voyage of, to England, 66, 70, 72, 73–74; and foreign trade, 101; anecdote concerning Mori and, 130; receives promotion, 225; becomes foreign minister, 233; and Korean crisis, 275; Mori serves under, 280; replaced as foreign minister, 282
Thomas, A. F., *History of Japanese Education* . . . (with H. L. Keenleyside), 13
Thomas à Kempis, 123
Thornton, Edward, 179
Throne, Mori's views on, 213, 309–310. *See also* Emperor; Sovereignty
Times (London), 379
Tocqueville, Alexis de, 210, 212
Tōgō Ainoshin, 105; voyage of, to England, 67, 69, 75
Tōgō Heihachirō, 21, 28, 60
Tojō (outer castle system), 33–35
Tokuda (principal, Fukuoka Normal School), 396
Tokudaiji Sanenori, 349
Tokutomi Sohō, 13–14, 15, 136, 477
Tokyo Academy (Tōkyō Gakushi Kaiin), 336–339
Tōkyō Gakushi Kaiin, *see* Tokyo Academy
Tokyo Imperial University, *see* Imperial University at Tokyo
Tōkyō nichi nichi, 253
Tokyo School for Girls (Tōkyō Jogakkō), 254–255
Tomita Tetsunosuke, 255
Toragari monogatari (Tale of the tiger hunt), 40
Torishirabe kakari (investigation officer): appointment of, 351; functions of, 352
Toyama Masakazu, 156, 394, 414
Tōyama Shigeki, 16
Transcendental (or "Hedge") Club, 235–236
Treaty of St. Petersburg, 270
Treitschke, Heinrich von, 400
Trevelyan, G. M., 387

Tsuchiya Tadao, 16, 459–460
Tsuda Masamichi, 269; and the Meirokusha, 237, 239, 240, 243, 261; support of, for popular assembly, 242, 263; and the Tokyo Academy, 336; and the Kaisei kyōikurei, 345
Tsuda Umeko, 184–185, 246

Uchida Masao, 133
Ueda Tei, 184–185
Uemura Masahisa, 394
Ueno Kagenori (Keihan), 47, 58, 219
Ueno Ryōtarō, see Machida Hisanari
Umetani Noboru, 445
Universities, see Imperial University
Unjōsho (municipal customs bureau), 132
Unyō (Japanese surveying ship), 275

Vattel, Emerich de, 240, 261–262, 274
Viscount, Mori's elevation to, 392

Wada Shinjirō, 107
Wang Yang-ming (Ōyōmei) school, 52, 435
Waring, Miss Jane Lee, 110
Waseda (school), 413
Washington, George, 30
Washington Evening Star, 164–165, 170, 190, 215
Watanabe Senjirō, 257
Weber, Max, 124
Webster, Daniel, 173
Westernism, Mori's, 1–2, 6–16 passim, 478–485
Westernizer Commendable and Reprehensible (images of Mori), 2, 6–16 passim, 391, 477–478
Whitney, William C., 255
Whitney, Prof. William D., 182, 235; and abolition of the Japanese language, 190–194
Wilkinson, Mr. (English "delegate"), 281
Williams, General George B., 160, 219
Williamson, Prof. Alexander H., 70, 86–87
Willis, William, 148
Wilson, Henry, 172

Women, status of: education, 184, 246, 251, 421–424; intermarriage, 185–186, 250–251; marriage, 232, 236; "Saishōron" (Discourse on wives and mistresses), 232, 239–240, 245–254
Woolsey, Theodore D., 182, 183, 295, 297

Yamada Akiyoshi, 10, 355, 358, 403
Yamagata Aritomo, 424, 445
Yamagawa Hiroshi, Colonel, 426
Yamakawa Sutematsu, 184–185
Yamamoto Denzō, 50, 51
Yamamoto Gonnohyōe, Admiral, 28, 42
Yamanouchi Sakuzaemon, 78–80
Yamanouchi Toyonobu, 132, 133, 135, 138
Yano Jirō, 256, 257–258
Yasui Shinpachirō, 107
Yatabe Ryōkichi, 156, 414
Yen Fu, 470
Yōgaku (Western learning), 27, 47, 56, 57, 58; memorial on instruction in, 147–148. See also Kokugaku
Yōgakukan (Institute for Western Learning), proposed, 56
"Yōkō nikki" (Diary of a voyage to the West), see under Matsumura Junzō
Yokoi Shōnan, 109, 117, 118, 131, 136, 444
Yokoyama family, 46
Yokoyama Shōtarō Yasutake (originally Mori Genshirō), 30–31, 61, 214, 340, 476; correspondence between Mori and (quoted), 76, 80–85, 87–89, 148 (mentioned), 65–66, 99–100, 123, 147, 187, 313, 463, 472; and legal institutions, 139, 273; suicide of, 149, 150–151, 223, 480; his memorial and attachment (suicide note), 149–150, 276, 473–474; and American friendship, 163
Yokoyama Son'ichirō, 234
Yokoyama Yasukata, 30, 31–32, 39
Yoshida Kiyonari (alias Nagai Iosuke), 82, 100, 124, 153, 476; voyage of, to England, 67, 69, 71–72, 75; at Brotherhood of the New Life, 94, 95–96, 105–106, 114, 124–125, 126, 127; meeting with Harris, 96; succeeds Mori

in Washington, 173; clash between Mori and, 189, 216–224; and Japanese-American treaty, 272, 281; assigned to Washington to promote westernization, 282
Yoshida Shōin, 435
Yoshihara Shigetoshi, 106
Yoshikawa Akimasa, 445
Yoshimasa Ryō, 184–185
Yoshino Sakuzō, 198, 358
Youmans, Edward L., 290
Young, John Russell, 222
Yuchi Sadamoto, 106
Yūjo, *see* Mori Kiuemon Yūjo
Yūjō (friendship), Mori on, 427, 428
Yūki Yukiyasu, 107, 112
Yung-cheng Emperor, 439
Yūrei (name for Mori), 23
Yuri Kimimasa, 141

Zada Shigehide, 4, 5, 10
Zōshikan (han Samurai School), 26, 37, 39–40; Mori's attendance at, 46–57; Mori on, 88
Zusho Hirosato, 51

Harvard East Asian Series

1. *China's Early Industrialization: Sheng Hsuan-huai (1884–1916) and Mandarin Enterprise.* By Albert Feuerwerker.
2. *Intellectual Trends in the Ch'ing Period.* By Liang Ch'i-ch'ao. Translated by Immanuel C. Y. Hsü.
3. *Reform in Sung China: Wang An-shih (1021–1086) and His New Policies.* By James T. C. Liu.
4. *Studies on the Population of China, 1368–1953.* By Ping-ti Ho.
5. *China's Entrance into the Family of Nations: The Diplomatic Phase, 1858–1880.* By Immanuel C. Y. Hsü
6. *The May Fourth Movement: Intellectual Revolution in Modern China.* By Chow Tse-tsung.
7. *Ch'ing Administrative Terms: A Translation of the Terminology of the Six Boards with Explanatory Notes.* Translated and edited by E-tu Zen Sun.
8. *Anglo-American Steamship Rivalry in China, 1862–1874.* By Kwang-Ching Liu.
9. *Local Government in China under the Ch'ing.* By T'ung-tsu Ch'ü.
10. *Communist China, 1955–1959: Policy Documents with Analysis.* With a foreword by Robert R. Bowie and John K. Fairbank. (Prepared at Harvard University under the joint auspices of the Center for International Affairs and the East Asian Research Center.)
11. *China and Christianity: The Missionary Movement and the Growth of Chinese Antiforeignism, 1860–1870.* By Paul A. Cohen.
12. *China and the Helping Hand, 1937–1945.* By Arthur N. Young.
13. *Research Guide to the May Fourth Movement: Intellectual Revolution in Modern China, 1915–1924.* By Chow Tse-tsung.

14. *The United States and the Far Eastern Crisis of 1933–1938: From the Manchurian Incident through the Initial Stage of the Undeclared Sino-Japanese War.* By Dorothy Borg.
15. *China and the West, 1858–1861: The Origins of the Tsungli Yamen.* By Masataka Banno.
16. *In Search of Wealth and Power: Yen Fu and the West.* By Benjamin Schwartz.
17. *The Origins of Entrepreneurship in Meiji Japan.* By Johannes Hirschmeier, S.V.D.
18. *Commissioner Lin and the Opium War.* By Hsin-pao Chang.
19. *Money and Monetary Policy in China, 1845–1895.* By Frank H. H. King.
20. *China's Wartime Finance and Inflation, 1937–1945.* By Arthur N. Young.
21. *Foreign Investment and Economic Development in China, 1840–1937.* By Chi-ming Hou.
22. *After Imperialism: The Search for a New Order in the Far East, 1921–1931.* By Akira Iriye.
23. *Foundations of Constitutional Government in Modern Japan, 1868–1900.* By George Akita.
24. *Political Thought in Early Meiji Japan, 1868–1889.* By Joseph Pittau, S.J.
25. *China's Struggle for Naval Development, 1839–1895.* By John L. Rawlinson.
26. *The Practice of Buddhism in China, 1900–1950.* By Holmes Welch.
27. *Li Ta-chao and the Origins of Chinese Marxism.* By Maurice Meisner.
28. *Pa Chin and His Writings: Chinese Youth Between the Two Revolutions.* By Olga Lang.
29. *Literary Dissent in Communist China.* By Merle Goldman.
30. *Politics in the Tokugawa Bakufu, 1600–1843.* By Conrad Totman.
31. *Hara Kei in the Politics of Compromise, 1905–1915.* By Tetsuo Najita.
32. *The Chinese World Order: Traditional China's Foreign Relations.* Edited by John K. Fairbank.
33. *The Buddhist Revival in China.* By Holmes Welch.
34. *Traditional Medicine in Modern China: Science, Nationalism, and the Tensions of Cultural Change.* By Ralph C. Croizier.
35. *Party Rivalry and Political Change in Taishō Japan.* By Peter Duus.
36. *The Rhetoric of Empire: American China Policy, 1895–1901.* By Marilyn B. Young.
37. *Radical Nationalist in Japan: Kita Ikki, 1883–1937.* By George M. Wilson.
38. *While China Faced West: American Reformers in Nationalist China, 1928–1937.* By James C. Thomson Jr.
39. *The Failure of Freedom: A Portrait of Modern Japanese Intellectuals* By Tatsuo Arima.
40. *Asian Ideas of East and West: Tagore and His Critics in Japan, China, and India.* By Stephen N. Hay.
41. *Canton under Communism: Programs and Politics in a Provincial Capital, 1949–1968.* By Ezra F. Vogel.
42. *Ting Wen-chiang: Science and China's New Culture.* By Charlotte Furth.
43. *The Manchurian Frontier in Ch'ing History.* By Robert H. G. Lee.

44. *Motoori Norinaga, 1730–1801*. By Shigeru Matsumoto.
45. *The Comprador in Nineteenth Century China: Bridge between East and West*. By Yen-p'ing Hao.
46. *Hu Shih and the Chinese Renaissance: Liberalism in the Chinese Revolution, 1917–1937*. By Jerome B. Grieder.
47. *The Chinese Peasant Economy: Agricultural Development in Hopei and Shantung, 1890–1949*. By Ramon H. Myers.
48. *Japanese Tradition and Western Law: Emperor, State, and Law in the Thought of Hozumi Yatsuka*. By Richard H. Minear.
49. *Rebellion and Its Enemies in Late Imperial China: Militarization and Social Structure, 1796–1864*. By Philip A. Kuhn.
50. *Early Chinese Revolutionaries: Radical Intellectuals in Shanghai and Chekiang, 1902–1911*. By Mary Backus Rankin.
51. *Communication and Imperial Control in China: Evolution of the Palace Memorial System, 1693–1735*. By Silas H. L. Wu.
52. *Vietnam and the Chinese Model: A Comparative Study of Nguyễn and Ch'ing Civil Government in the First Half of the Nineteenth Century*. By Alexander Barton Woodside.
53. *The Modernization of the Chinese Salt Administration, 1900–1920*. By S. A. M. Adshead.
54. *Chang Chih-tung and Educational Reform in China*. By William Ayers.
55. *Kuo Mo-jo: The Early Years*. By David Tod Roy.
56. *Social Reformers in Urban China: The Chinese Y.M.C.A., 1895–1926*. By Shirley S. Garrett.
57. *Biographic Dictionary of Chinese Communism, 1921–1965*. By Donald W. Klein and Anne B. Clark.
58. *Imperialism and Chinese Nationalism: Germany in Shantung*. By John E. Shrecker.
59. *Monarchy in the Emperor's Eyes: Image and Reality in the Ch'ien-lung Reign*. By Harold L. Kahn.
60. *Yamagata Aritomo in the Rise of Modern Japan, 1838–1922*. By Roger F. Hackett.
61. *Russia and China: Their Diplomatic Relations to 1728*. By Mark Mancall.
62. *The Yenan Way in Revolutionary China*. By Mark Selden.
63. *The Mississippi Chinese: Between Black and White*. By James W. Loewen.
64. *Liang Ch'i-ch'ao and Intellectual Transition in China, 1890–1907*. By Hao Chang.
65. *A Korean Village: Between Farm and Sea*. By Vincent S. R. Brandt.
66. *Agricultural Change and the Peasant Economy of South China*. By Evelyn S. Rawski.
67. *The Peace Conspiracy: Wang Ching-wei and the China War, 1937–1941*. By Gerald Bunker.
68. *Mori Arinori*. By Ivan Hall.